The Baseball Hall of Fame *Corrected*

Eddie Daniels

Published in the United States of America

First paper edition, 2016

ISBN 978-0-9970739-4-2

Contact the author at chrisekeedei@yahoo.com.

CONTENTS

Chapter One

~ ~ Please Read This Chapter ~ ~

In a book like this, it can be tempting to skip ahead to the individual player profiles. But please read this part first so you can understand where I'm coming from. I swear, I'll try to keep it interesting.

About Me: What You're All Really Here For, Clearly

When I was a teenager, I was obsessed with the Baseball Hall of Fame. I would study each Hall-of-Famer as if I were a seminarian studying the lives of the saints. During boring classes I would try to name every member from memory by writing them in the margins of my notebooks. (Obviously, I was extremely hip and had hundreds of girlfriends.)

I felt like having that Hall of Fame designation next to a person's name put him in an entirely different class. It's like the difference between becoming a king and staying forever a lord. It says basically "This man is an immortal. This name should be etched on the side of a mountain, to grace the mouths of humanity once our civilization is but dust. I stand on Mount Olympus and sound the name 'Arky Vaughan' with a barbaric yawp!"

So it still sticks in my craw that a handful of Hall-of-Famers really don't deserve that special "Hall of Fame" patina. I should say that for the most part, the Baseball Hall of Fame does a tremendous job selecting the best players in history. But there's nothing that can't use a bit of editing. Even "Hamlet" could lose a couple of scenes. (Osric's scene should go. Does he have any purpose besides slowing the plot down and making Hamlet look like a condescending jerk? Anyway, that's neither here nor there.)

It's actually surprising that the Hall of Fame membership is as good as it is, since its election procedures were poorly planned and have undergone about a thousand temporary fixes. As Bill James details in "Whatever Happened to the Hall of Fame" (aka "The Politics of Glory"), the founders weren't terribly concerned with who was going to be elected. They concentrated mostly on the facilities and funding and all that business-y stuff.

Speaking of business-y stuff, the election procedures for the Hall of Fame have followed a pattern that might be familiar to anyone who works in the corporate world. You first set up a slapdash system with little forethought. Then you get bad results, which in the case of the Hall of Fame would be things like no one being honored for years, an unworthy player being selected, or a great player being ignored. Then you slap on a band-aid that addresses only a few glaring symptoms of a greater problem. Those band-aids then make things worse in unforeseen ways. Time for more band-aids. Repeat ad infinitum. No one ever seriously considers a complete overhaul, because that would offend too many people who have been empowered by the current, crappy system.

By now, with the benefit of hindsight, almost anyone could look at the whole of baseball history and institute a more logical, systematic approach to selecting Hall-of-Famers. Luckily for you, I qualify as "almost anyone." I'm not a professional baseball historian (not an easy job to get, by the way). I'm not a famous writer (though I've written a lot of blog posts that my sister liked!) I'm definitely not a former player, unless you count my Little League experience in seventh grade, in which I managed two hits all season. (One actually got out of the infield. My family reacted as if they were watching Kirk Gibson in the 1988 World Series.) I'm basically just someone who has studied baseball a whole lot for fun. If that doesn't make me qualified, oh well, I guess I'm going to do it anyway.

Let's Set Some Standards

There are few things more chaotic than Hall of Fame arguments. Birthday parties for four-year-olds have more structure. Each argument tends to be a wild whirlwind of numbers and ideas thrown around by people talking past each other, each of whom aims only to push his or her viewpoint by any means necessary. People seldom look to learn from other people and possibly adapt their views. Really, most arguments in life are like this.

You can cut down on the chaos by establishing well-defined standards for inclusion. If one person thinks a Hall-of-Famer must have a productive career and the other only believes in electing guys with funny names, they'll never meet in the middle on anyone (with the possible exception of Arky Vaughan). But if both can agree that hitting 500 career home runs is a good credential, they at least have some common ground.

Of course, you need much more extensive standards than that. I believe in going by the standards the Hall of Fame has already set through its hundreds of selections. As I mentioned earlier, it didn't start out with standards of any kind. But throughout its awkward stumbling over the decades, the Hall of Fame's electors have managed to assemble a group of great players (and a handful of not-so-great). By looking at these players, and all these players, you can suss out the standards that constitute a Hall-of-Famer.

This doesn't sound too controversial, I hope. But this in itself is a bold pronouncement, if you go by almost every Hall of Fame argument I see. People tend to have very firm ideas of what constitutes a Hall-of-Famer, but these ideas are almost never based on the actual, entire composition of the Hall. Often they're based on their own subjective impressions of players, impressions created not only by performance but also by hype. An underrated player always gets short shrift because he hasn't benefited from years of broadcasters telling us that he's a future Hall-of-Famer.

The larger problem is that people tend to judge Hall of Fame candidates by the 50 or so Hall-of-Famers they've heard of. These 50 are invariably the cream of the Hall's 200-plus membership, so going by these guys sets a too-high standard for new inductees. These are the people who look at Roy Halladay and say, "He's no Greg Maddux. Definitely not a Hall-of-Famer."

You know who else is not Greg Maddux? Almost all the pitchers in the Hall of Fame. Bob Feller is no Greg Maddux. Jim Palmer is no Greg Maddux. The standards for the Hall of Fame can't just be the members the average baseball fan has heard of. There are also Ted Lyons and Buck Ewing and Billy Herman and lots more. If you want to make a Hall of Fame of just Greg Maddux-level players, you'll have maybe 50 guys in there.

I suppose, in this book, I could do exactly that. I could just pick the 50 best guys and be done with it. But that's been done to death. And moreover, that's not really relevant to the actual Hall of Fame of 200-plus people. It says nothing about which new candidates are worthy of it.

I'm not just saying that regular fans judge Hall of Fame candidates this way. The people making the selections are often no different. In case you don't know, the first crack at electing Hall-of-Famers is given to the BBWAA (a.k.a. Baseball Writers' Association of America, which really should be called the BWAA since no one has spelled it "base ball" for a hundred years, but that's besides the point.) I'm always shocked at the number of BBWAA members who clearly aren't basing their decisions on the actual composition of the Hall of Fame. BBWAA members will write articles that make it clear they have never bothered to look through the full list and learn about the guys that fans don't regularly discuss.

I remember one columnist (who will remain nameless) making categories of different Hall-of-Famers, which of course included only the Hall-of-Famers that most baseball fans remember. The top tier was Babe Ruth and Willie Mays etc. That part made sense. But this guy's lowest tier encompassed Robin Yount and other players he deemed as lasting a long time but not having many big seasonal totals.

This is ludicrous. Robin Yount is by no stretch of any imagination on any lower tier of the Hall of Fame. He is well above average, as anyone who bothered to look over the actual Hall of Fame membership would learn in a few minutes.

Then there was another BBWAA member who admitted that he made up his own personal standards for inclusion. It was a lot of vague stuff about being a "impact player" and "true winner" and a "good clubhouse presence" and "was willing to talk to me when I was a cub reporter" etc.

There's nothing wrong with constructing your own standards for inclusion, and no one's set of standards will be exactly the same. But it strikes me as pretty arrogant to do it based on your own subjective feelings of what makes for a good player, instead of forming standards based on the collective wisdom of hundreds of knowledgeable, passionate voters over the 70+ years of the Hall's existence. I'm not saying they always made the best choices. But their choices should at least constitute your starting point.

This is the central point of this book, so I really want to underline it. In fact, I will literally underline it: <u>Any opinion about who should be in the Hall of Fame should be grounded in standards set by those who are already in.</u>

This means going by standards established by the Hall of Fame membership, as opposed to standards you have conjured up through limited exposure to a few guys. It also means you should probably have some familiarity with each player in the Hall. You should know about more than just Babe Ruth and Willie Mays. You should also know at least something about Burleigh Grimes and Bid McPhee and Chick Hafey.

In fact, I'd be in favor of a standardized test before you're allowed to send in a ballot. Maybe you should have to name as many Hall-of-Famers as you can off the top of your head. Or maybe you're given a list of 500 players and have to put checkmarks next to the ones who are in. I'm not saying you have to provide an essay comparing the relative contributions of Morgan Bulkeley and William Hulbert; just some basic awareness of who the Hall of Fame is actually composed of would be nice.

But Isn't The Hall of Fame Too Big?

I never understood this sentiment. There have been more than 17,000 players in major league history. And that's not counting Negro Leaguers, umpires, owners, general managers, etc. Out of a likely 20,000-plus candidates, I don't think it's unreasonable to select the 300 or so best for a special honor. That's about 1.5%. That's not excessive, is it? Keep in mind that this is a game that has been played professionally for more than 130 years in a hugely populous country. Nowadays it has expanded to take in players from around the world. You're going to collect quite a few heroes doing that.

I've never heard a rational basis for this idea that the Hall of Fame is too big. When I'm left with nothing else to go on, I have to theorize. My theory is that this is more of an emotional reaction, from people who look at the full list of Hall-of-Famers and feel a little intimidated. These are people who think they know a lot about baseball from having spent lots of time watching and talking about it. Then, all of a sudden, they're confronted with an allegedly important list of names they've never heard of. These people might not be accustomed to scouring the records of guys who have been dead for 100 years.

Then the natural human faculty of "I refuse to let it be my fault, so let's find someone else to blame" kicks in. "Being a baseball expert is central to my identity, so not knowing half these guys can't be my fault! It must therefore the Hall of Fame's fault for being too big! Geez Hall of Fame, what a jerk you are for making me feel bad!"

Obviously, I don't have a lot of sympathy for this perspective. I didn't know all the Hall-of-Famers either before I saw them on the list; no one could learn about them through pure osmosis. Just check out a few books and catch yourself up. In fact, I think that's one of the central missions of the Hall of Fame, to spark an interest in learning about the past.

But I'm Not Talking About You!

Now dear reader, know that I'm not criticizing you. How could I be? You bought my book! (Unless you borrowed it. In which case, you need to wire me a rental fee. Hey, I don't make the rules.) I recognize that you might not know all the Hall-of-Famers -- unlike the members of the BBWAA, it's not your job to. But if you want to know about them, and want to have Hall of Fame opinions that have some solid grounding in the real Hall of Fame, you've come to the right place.

In going through all the Hall-of-Famers in this book, I will try my best to use the standards that have already been established by those hundreds of voters over the past 70+ years. Then I'll evaluate each Hall-of-Famer by these standards.

Most players will be within the standards that, after all, they themselves create. But there will be some outliers who don't measure up. I'll indulge in a fantasy of kicking them out of the Hall. Also, I'll find many players who are not in the Hall but do measure up to its standards, and make arguments on their behalf. Any retired player is fair game. This gets to the "corrected" part of this book's title.

In so doing I'll provide you with at least some small introduction to each player. Even if you don't agree with the standards that I construct or how I apply them, you will hopefully finish this book with more knowledge about the players who actually make up the Hall. That alone will make you better able to make future judgments (probably better than many BBWAA voters).

The Average is Not the Standard

I'm not special. Many other people have tried to establish Hall of Fame standards based on the actual composition of the Hall. Sometimes, though, these people refuse to elect anyone who is below the average Hall-of-Famer. This includes Jay Jaffe, a great baseball writer whose work I use extensively in this book. He and others often say that any candidate below the level of an average HOFer would "lower the standards" of the Hall.

With all due respect to Jaffe, this reveals a fundamental misunderstanding of what "standards" are. Standards for inclusion in an organization are never the average of that organization. That would actually set up a double standard, in which the established members have to be great and new candidates have to be super-great.

To give some perspective, here is a team made of players who are below the Hall of Fame averages at their positions, as per Jay Jaffe's own system for judging Hall of Fame worthiness, JAWS (more about that later):

C: Gabby Hartnett

1B: Harmon Killebrew

2B: Roberto Alomar

3B: Frank "Home Run" Baker

SS: Joe Sewell

LF: Willie Stargell

CF: Kirby Puckett

RF: Dave Winfield

SP: Juan Marichal

RP: Rollie Fingers

All these guys are in the Hall of Fame, and there is little controversy about any of their selections. Any new player as good as any of these should be inducted, in my view.

That said, we definitely don't need to elect players who match up with the dregs of the Hall. As we'll see in future chapters, there are a lot of Hall-of-Famers who just don't belong. We don't want to throw in a bunch of players under the 25th percentile of Hall-of-Famers, at the point when qualifications really start to get sketchy.

But accepting only guys above the 50th percentile means that you think about half the current members don't belong, and that any future candidates should be held to a different standard than anyone else ever has. That's not raising the standards -- that's wrecking them.

The Standards Start With Stats

Man, I wish the standards could start with courage and heroism and the thrills that players give fans, etc. But that stuff is pretty darn subjective. It's really not a solid grounding -- everyone is going to have wildly different feelings, and there's no way to ever to come to an agreement. Stats are objective measures that can provide at least some level of consensus.

Besides, stats work well for baseball. Baseball is a very mathematical game, and stats reveal almost all of a player's value. In sports that occur in more of a melee, like football and basketball, stats do a less complete job of encapsulating everything a player does. It's hard to measure the value of how well a safety covers his man. But by comparison, how well a guy hits is quite straightforward: he gets on base or doesn't. He doesn't have to drive through a mess of teammates and opponents to get a hit. (Though that could be fun. Ooh, new game: Basefootball. You hit the ball and then have to run through a line of scrimmage to get to each base. Every game would be 1-0 in about 20 innings.)

Stats Don't Lie. They're Just Misunderstood

You may have heard the old canard "There are three types of lies: lies, damn lies, and statistics." It's a load of crap. Statistics don't lie -- people lie by misusing statistics. A more accurate old canard holds that people tend to use statistics the way a drunk uses a lamppost: for support, not illumination. People have preconceived notions, and then seek out numbers that will support those notions, while ignoring those that don't. This is backwards: You should have an open mind and then see what the numbers say. You don't have to rely solely on numbers, but you should at least be willing to adapt your views based on the data.

But even if you don't come into an argument with biases, you can very easily misinterpret statistics. This is especially common in Hall of Fame debates, when you're comparing players from different eras.

Within a single season, conventional numbers, everything from batting average and homers to fancier things like on-base percentage and OPS, can do well in measuring a player's contributions. This is because, for the most part, there is a similar baseline among all players -- if the league batting average that year is .260, you can be confident that a guy hitting .310 BA/.410 OBP/.510 SLG is better than a guy hitting .280/.380/.480. There may be a caveat that the .310 guy might be hitting in the great hitter's park in Colorado and the .290 guy might be doing it in the pitcher's haven of San Diego, so it might not be a perfect comparison. It's still a little messy, but not terrible.

But when you're comparing players from different eras, it gets terribly messy. Baseball has changed dramatically over the years, sometimes being dominated by hitters and sometimes being dominated by pitchers. The hitters from the big-hitting days sure look amazing, because we all naturally salivate when we see a guy with a .350+ batting average and 130 or more RBIs. From 1920-1947, that happened 32 times. In 1930 alone seven players reached those numbers. Since 1947, it's only happened nine times. Would anyone really believe that 1930 had almost as many great hitting performances as later occurred in an entire 65-year span?

Let's give a more concrete example. Compare Carl Yastrzemski to Al Simmons (whose real last name, by the way was Szymanski. If Yastrzemski had come up in the 1930s, we'd probably be calling him Carl Yazzons or something.) Yaz hit .285 in his career, while Simmons hit .334. Man, Simmons looks much better, at least in terms of career batting average.

But Yaz played in the 1960s, and Simmons in the 1930s. Yaz won the batting title in 1968 with a .301 mark, which sounds weak until you learn that the league as a whole hit .230. Yaz's number was 30% better than the league. Simmons led the American League in 1930 by hitting .381, but the league hit .288. That's 32% better than the league. They come out at about the same, in relative terms.

Yaz hit .301 in a season where hits were scarce; Simmons hit .381 when hits were plentiful. As any viewer of "Antiques Roadshow" knows, scarcity plus demand equals value. The demand for hits is always about the same, since you need them to win ballgames. So when the demand is the same, but the hits are more scarce, each hit becomes more valuable. Each hit in a 3-2 game is more valuable than each hit in a 10-9 game -- when there are fewer hits, there is a higher chance that a specific hit could win the game. That means each of Yaz's individual hits is more valuable in the context of their time than each of Simmons'.

Simmons was clearly one of the best hitters in 1930, and Yaz one of the best in 1968. But when you're comparing the best of all-time, from very different eras, conventional numbers lose their usefulness. The meaning of the numbers changes over time. A .301 average means something different in 1968 than it does in 1930. In 1968 it means you're the best in the league, while in 1930 it means you're slightly above average.

Even knowing this, it's still hard to get past the natural biases we feel when we see Yaz's .301 average and Simmons' .381. This is especially true when you go further down the rankings. The tenth-best AL batting average in 1968 was Frank Howard, at .274. The tenth-best AL batting average in 1930 belonged to Sam Rice, who hit .349. It's very easy to look at Sam Rice's numbers and say "that looks like a Hall-of-Famer." It's harder to look at Frank Howard's numbers and think that.

As baseball fans, we have deeply ingrained notions of what the conventional numbers mean. This is part of the reason that the hitters in the Hall of Fame are so lopsided, with way too many coming from the big-hitting 1920s and 1930s. Here's a chart showing the percentage of players with at least 50 ABs who are in the Hall of Fame, year by year:

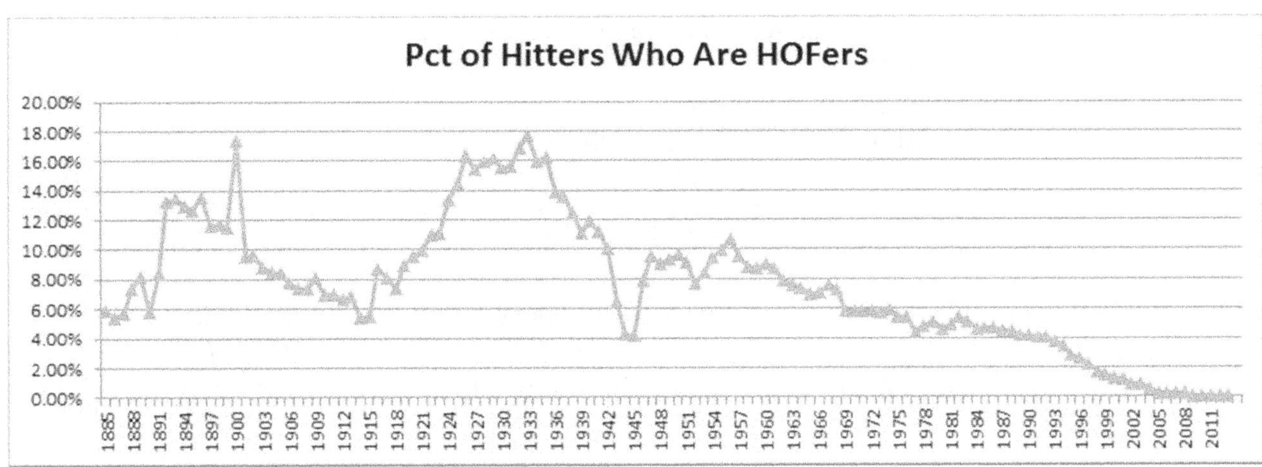

For a decade, from 1926-1935, there are more than twice as many Hall of Fame hitters, proportionally speaking, than from all the 1960s. Does anyone really believe that there were twice as many great hitters from 1926-1935 than there were in the 1960s? I know I don't. This is what using only the conventional numbers will get you.

Keep in mind that this does not include Negro League players, most of whom had their heyday in those same 1920s and 1930s. I really wanted to include them in the above, but Negro League stats are so incomplete and complex that I couldn't manage it. Adding the Hall-of-Famer Negro Leaguers would be easy; they would just go into the numerators of the above percentages. Determining which non-HOF Negro Leaguers should go in the denominators would be a lifelong project, and I'm writing this book to make a quick buck. Just debating which of the dozens of different Negro leagues count as "major" could fill a book.

Besides, as I detail more later, the Negro League selections are not the problem. They've been handled very well, and a reasonable percentage are in the Hall. I'm confident that if I did somehow corral all the Negro Leaguers into the above chart, the percentages wouldn't move much.

I should make a few more notes about this graph before I go on. First, note that the 1890s have higher percentages than the 1880s. That's largely because one of the two major leagues, the American Association, collapsed after the 1891 season. 1892 had the same number of Hall-of-Famers (the numerator) but the entire pool of major-league players (the denominator) was much smaller. It peaks further in 1900 because the only league left, the National League, contracted from 12 to 8 teams. The American League came along in 1901, enlarging the pool of all players but not the number of Hall-of-Famers by many.

1914 and 1915 have the opposite issue, in that the Federal League expanded the number of major-league jobs but not the number of Hall-of-Famers. Also, ignore the low point from 1943-45. That's when a bunch of Hall-of-Famers were off fighting in World War II.

Like the 1960s, the dead-ball era from 1901-1919 is underrepresented among Hall of Fame hitters. It was a pitching-dominated time, meaning that hitting stats look less impressive than they really are.

Let's Try Something Different Then

Back to the point: When you're looking at players from different eras in baseball history, you can easily misinterpret conventional numbers. Like Ben Kenobi said to Luke in "Star Wars," "Your eyes can deceive you. Don't trust them." (My nerdiness has several outlets.)

Luckily, people have devised a better way. Newer stats build on the old ones but cut out the biases given by particular eras. Al Simmons and Carl Yazzons can be compared on equal footing.

I'm sure some of you will get your dander up at the very suggestion of using stats you haven't heard of before. But why? Stats are nothing but tools for measurement. If someone comes up with a better way to measure something, one that gets more at the core of what you're really trying to measure, you'd be a fool not to at least try it. If a carpenter came across a hammer that could possibly hammer 20% better, I think he/she would give it a shot. If it doesn't work, fine. But don't pass up on a chance to improve.

People who heap disdain on new sabermetric numbers always seem like they're really just scared of something they don't understand. They're comfortable with the old numbers, they've memorized them and used them to make judgments since they were kids. Anything threatening that comfort gets rejected, often angrily. They're afraid they won't understand the new numbers, and that fear gets translated into rage.

If you're doing this, I should inform you that it's a sure sign of old age. Grumpy old men often get confused by new things, and then protect their egos by angrily dismissing them. It's the same thing that makes them think that no good music has been made since they were young, and in their day they had real movies without all those nasty four-letter words, etc., etc.

Maybe I'm being a bit snotty. I suppose you could argue that the people who made all the selections until now didn't use these fancy-pants numbers. If you say you respect what hundreds of Hall of Fame voters have done in the past, and want to build standards based on their selections, shouldn't you use the same numbers they used? Huh, Daniels? You think you're so smart?

OK, that's a fair point. And people have taken that approach, notably a fellow named James F. Vail in a book called "Outrageous Fortune: What's Wrong with the Hall of Fame Voting and How to Make it Statistically Sound" (MacFarland, 2001). It starts with hundreds of players, both in and out of The Hall of Fame, and groups them by position and also by era (1800s, dead-ball era, etc.) Then it takes dozens of career stats, from hits to fielding percentage, and calculates how far above or below the average each player is in each stat. It compiles all those calculations into a few numbers called Z-Scores.

It's an interesting approach, but fundamentally flawed, in my view. Almost all stats he uses are given equal weight in the formula. It gives greater weight to a few major stats, like home runs and RBIs, over less well-loved ones like walks and stolen bases. But that isn't enough adjustment. As far as actually winning ballgames, walks are much more important than stolen bases. And guys like Tony Gwynn, whose excellence is mainly tied up in one stat (in Gwynn's case, batting average), get undervalued in a system that uses so many stats. And then some of Vail's stats measure much the same thing (e.g. home runs, home run percentage, total bases, slugging percentage and "on-base plus isolated power" all reward a guy for his home runs). It all gets very messy.

You probably don't need my full book report; suffice to say that trying to use dozens of different statistics in a Hall of Fame evaluation is unwieldy and awkward. It would all be much simpler if we could put everything together into one or two numbers that represent the totality of a player's contributions. Something that wouldn't double- or triple-count contributions, and would give appropriate weight to the contributions that did the most to help the team win. We need something like a quarterback rating for baseball players.

There are many newfangled numbers that try to do this. Throughout this book I'll be referring to just a few that have gained enough acceptance and support to be relatively universal. Here's the set of stats that lead off each player entry:

Luke Appling (1930-1943, 1945-1950; career OPS+: 113)

	Career	rank	Hitting	rank	Fielding	Rank	Peak	rank	bests	JAWS	rank
WAR	74.5	8	70.6	7	19.0	29	43.8	11	0	59.2	9
WS	376.4	8	268.3	7	108.6	13	203.7	8	2	NA	11

The years after Appling's name in the above span his major-league career. If a player was out of the majors for a span in the middle of his career, I'll leave that year out, as I did for Appling's 1944. I might mention in the text why he missed that year, and I might not. I'm mysterious that way. I'm a loner, baby. A rebel.[1]

OPS+: This isn't just OPS. This is OPS *plus*. This is an exclusive statistic available only to our most valued customers (i.e., anyone who pays). Join our special OPS+ Club and you will get:

> OPS normalized so that individual seasons and careers can be compared across time periods.

What does that mean for you? It means you can compare the OPS of Al Simmons in 1930 and Carl Yastrzemski in 1968 on equal footing. OPS, as savvy baseball fans like yourself are very aware, is on-base percentage plus slugging percentage. Simmons in 1930 had an OPS of 1.130. That's amazing. Yaz in 1968 had an OPS of .922. That's great, but on the surface, less amazing.

But wait, that doesn't take into account the context of their eras. OPS+ does just that, all for you, at no extra charge! OPS+ tells how how far above or below average a player's OPS was vs. all players in the same time period. An OPS+ of 100 means that it was average. Above 100 is better than average, and below 100 is below average.

In 1930, Al Simmons' OPS+ was 175, meaning his OPS was 75% better than average for his league that year. In 1968, Carl Yazooski's OPS+ was 171, meaning his OPS was 71% better than average. As with the batting average comparison we saw above, this shows that their performances were pretty similar in context.

You can do the same for careers, so in each player profile, I provide the career OPS+ as calculated by Baseball-reference.com. Keep in mind that this number covers only the contributions already covered by OPS. So it doesn't say anything about fielding or baserunning. But I thought I should throw in at least one number that's kinda sorta (not really) conventional.

ERA+: Same deal as OPS+, except in normalizes ERA, which I assume you're familiar with. Much the way OPS+ does a pretty good back-of-the-envelope approximation of a player's hitting, ERA+ does a pretty good approximation of a pitcher's pitching. Again, I'm using Baseball-reference.com's version. There are a lot of other issues specific to pitchers that I'll explain in their section.

WAR (Wins Above Replacement): As I write this, this one is really gaining traction in the baseball world. Through a very complex formula, it distills everything a player does -- hitting, pitching, fielding, everything -- into one number. That number represents how many wins the player adds to

[1] Reference explanation: A running gag from "Pee-Wee's Big Adventure." "Reference explanation" explanation: When I make a reference to something not baseball-related, I like to explain it in a footnote. Cultural references can be fun, but they can be irritating when you don't know them, as any reader of the "Baseball Prospectus" annual knows all too well.

his team's total, beyond what would be contributed by a "replacement-level" player. A "replacement-level player" is some ordinary, easily available AAA guy who could quickly and cheaply replace any player.

To continue with the Yaz vs. Simmons example from above, Yaz's 1968, in which he had a .301 BA, .426 OBP and .495 SLG in 664 PAs, was worth 10.4 WAR, as per Baseball-reference's version of the stat. That's an astoundingly high number, one of the 50 best of all time. It means that if you replaced, say, 1995 Matt Mieske with 1968 Carl Yastrzemski, your team would gain 10 wins in the standings.

Matt Mieske, by the way, is my personal definition of a replacement-level player (apologies to Mieske and his loved ones). You probably don't remember him, but he was an outfielder for the Brewers in the 1990s, and was the most uninteresting player imaginable. He was not great at anything, not outstandingly bad at anything, just boring. He didn't even have a particularly interesting name (or a particularly boring one, which would itself be kind of interesting). At boring moments in ballgames I like to try to come up with the most boring player in baseball -- not necessarily to watch, but more in terms of their stat profile. I've never thought of a better boring player than Mieske.

Anyway, back to the point here: Al Simmons in 1930 went .381/.423/.708 in 611 PAs, putting him at 7.8 Wins Above Replacement. That is very good, often MVP-level. But it doesn't compare to Yastrzemski's 1968. In 1930 alone, Simmons's WAR was below that of Babe Ruth (.359/.493/.732), Lou Gehrig (.379/.473/.721) and Joe Cronin (.346/.422/.513 and some great defense at shortstop). No one was within a mile of Yaz in 1968. Looking just at the raw numbers, there's no way you could know that Yastrzemski's 1968 is considerably better than Simmons' 1930. You have to use numbers like WAR.

I use several different totals of WAR for each player. **Career WAR** is of course all the WAR the person compiled in his entire career. For hitters, I break it down further to **Hitting WAR** and **Fielding WAR**, which are, respectively, the wins above replacement gained from being a good clubhouse presence and the wins above replacement gained from "just knowing how to win." No! Jokes! They are, of course, the wins above replacement gained from a player's hitting and fielding, respectively.

Both Hitting and Fielding WAR have positional adjustments built in, meaning extra credit is given if you're playing a tough position like catcher or shortstop, and points are subtracted if you're playing first base or left field. This accounts for the fact that it's much harder to get good offense from defense-first positions than it is from offense-first positions. The Career WAR number therefore is not just a simple adding of the Hitting WAR and Fielding WAR, since that would double-count the positional adjustment.

If you used only these numbers, you'd get most of the great players. But there's more to greatness that just career totals. So it's important to also look at **Peak WAR**, which covers only the player's seven best seasons, from any point in his career. This is based on the assumption that to be a Hall-of-Famer, you should have a few seasons in which you're a superstar.

JAWS: Most people think it's equally important for a Hall-of-Famer to have great career totals and great peak totals. JAWS provides one number for this by averaging Career WAR and Peak WAR. It was invented by aforementioned sabermetrician Jay Jaffe and it stands for Jaffe's Awesome Wicked Stat. (He's from the South Side of Boston, and he has a rare form of dyslexia in which he transposes words used in regional slang terms.)

Rank: The problem with learning new stats is that you have no baseline for judgment, so an individual number means nothing to you. If I told you "Pebbly Jack" Glasscock had a Career WAR of

61.8, would you think that was good or bad? Or would you be so busy giggling at his name that you wouldn't even get that far? (If so, grow up. Geez.)

But if I told you that Pebbly Jack's total was 19th-best among all shortstops in history, then you get a frame of reference. So for every number I provide for a player, I also give a rank that shows how high that number is among all major leaguers at that player's position. That last part is crucial; **I'm really only comparing players against their position-mates**.

It's generally standard practice in Hall of Fame arguments to group players by their positions. Baseball-reference uses JAWS this way, comparing each player to the average of only the Hall-of-Famers who played that player's position. People assume that, at least among hitters, each position should be represented by roughly the same number of players. That doesn't mean that having 23 first basemen in the Hall automatically means there should be 23 catchers in too. But every team needs both a first baseman and a catcher, so you'd think the two positions would provide a similar number of great players from throughout 130+ years of baseball history.

And if you didn't go by comparisons of position-mates, some positions would be severely underrepresented in the Hall of Fame. Even though WAR makes adjustments that give catchers a boost, the list of the top 200 hitters in Career WAR contains 11 catchers and 33 first basemen. I don't think many people really think that there have been three times as many great first basemen as great catchers. It's more that catchers have much tougher jobs and can't be expected to stack up as many achievements as first basemen do, either per season or per career.

Some guys played multiple positions, so are difficult to place in just one group. Rod Carew, for example, spent half of his career at second base and the other half at first base. I almost always go by the position that the Hall of Fame gives the guy. I usually mention if a player is an awkward fit at the position given.

Despite being very stat-focused, I don't have strict cutoffs determining what ranking means a player is high enough for the Hall and what's below the line. In general, though, anyone above 20th is probably qualified, as there are about 20 players per position in the Hall of Fame. (Pitchers are a whole different ball of wax that I'll get into later.) Anyone significantly below 20th in several categories, especially the overall rankings in the farthest right of the chart, is in danger of being kicked out.

Win Shares: I could just go entirely by WAR. But I don't believe any one system, as well-supported as it may be, should ever be considered gospel. It's always good to get a second opinion. I do this in every aspect of my life, when dealing with doctors, mechanics, tax lawyers, hairdressers, tax auditors investigating why I've deducted so many hairdresser expenses, defense lawyers, federal judges, federal prison wardens, etc.

So I got some Win Shares numbers for all players from 1876-2008. (I couldn't find any data past 2008. It's surprisingly difficult to get Win Shares data in an electronic format.) Win Shares is another system that attempts to put a player's entire set of contributions into one number.

This one was invented by Bill James, and it comes at the issue of encapsulating all of a player's value in the opposite direction. While WAR adds up a player's achievements to arrive at one number representing wins, Win Shares takes a team's wins and then divides them up among players according to their achievements. So instead of giving bits of wins for each of 1968 Carl Yastrzemski's hits, as WAR does, Win Shares takes the win total of the 1968 Red Sox and divides them among Yaz and all of his teammates, based on their relative contributions. It then multiplies the results by three, basically just to make the numbers look nicer. That's not a terribly good reason, but what can you do?

If you're interested how Win Shares or WAR are calculated, go look somewhere else. I ain't got time. It's incredibly complicated, and I got players to judge.

I use Win Shares the same way I use WAR. I have **Career**, **Hitting**, **Fielding** and **Peak** (top 7 seasons) Win Shares numbers, each accompanied by ranks among position-mates. The big difference is that instead of giving an analog to JAWS, I use Bill James' own rankings by position in his "New Historical Baseball Abstract." Those will make up the numbers on the bottom far right of every chart -- so the below says that Bill James ranked Luke Appling the 11th-best player all-time at his position.

Luke Appling (1930-1943, 1945-1950; career OPS+: 113)

	Career	Rank	Hitting	Rank	Fielding	Rank	Peak	Rank	Bests	JAWS	Rank
WAR	74.5	8	70.6	7	19.0	29	43.8	11	0	59.2	9
WS	376.4	8	268.3	7	108.6	13	203.7	8	2	NA	11

If you haven't read "The New Historical Baseball Abstract," by the way, put this book down and go read that instead. In fact, throw this book in the fire right now. If you're reading it on an e-reader, throw the e-reader in the fire. Now get out of the house very quickly, as your house will probably start filling with toxic fumes. Since you're out of the house anyway, go buy and read Bill James' "New Historical Baseball Abstract." It's a lot like this book, except much, much better. Then buy my book again, since you foolishly burned up your last copy. Man, you are a drama queen, aren't you?

Point is, unlike the ranking next to the JAWS number, the overall Win Shares ranking at the far right of the table involves some subjectivity, namely Bill James's. He mostly used career and peak Win Shares to create his rankings, but his own knowledge and judgment also come into play.

Difference Between Win Shares and WAR

I already mentioned the way Win Shares are multiplied by three and thus always much higher than WAR, which is dopey, but that's just how it is. The ranks by position will be more meaningful to you. For the most part, WAR and Win Shares come to similar conclusions in terms of ranks.

Sometimes they differ dramatically on fielding, though. This is largely because a central part of WAR is rating any replacement-level performance at a zero. Win Shares give some value to replacement-level performance, but not much. It's easy to get negative WAR, but very, very hard to get negative Win Shares.

Why does that affect fielding more than hitting, you ask? Well, because different positions vary so widely in how much their defense can really contribute to wins. The greatest-fielding first baseman in the world has much less overall defensive value than even a mediocre-fielding shortstop. The shortstop just has a much more difficult job, handling many more tough plays that could determine the outcome of the game. But all positions must be on the same Defensive WAR scale. To account for the fundamental difference between the positions, WAR gives first basemen a major hit, putting them well into negative numbers for defense, while shortstops get a boost.

Offense doesn't have the same issue, as everyone gets up about the same number of times per game. The job of hitting isn't much different for first basemen and shortstops. (Though WAR still makes adjustments to account for the fact that's harder to find a good-hitting shortstop than a good-hitting first baseman.)

In terms of hitting, WAR's zero point doesn't make much difference, since few players are below the replacement level. But in fielding, almost all outfielders and first baseman end up in negative territory. Say you have an exceptional performance playing OF/1B that, against all odds, exceeds zero in Fielding WAR. If, the next year, you only do very well, you will get a negative number that will erase your exceptional year from your career total. It's like you did nothing at all.

There was another influential but now largely discredited system for encapsulating player value in Total Baseball, which was the Baseball Encyclopedia for 1990s Gen-Xer baseball nerds (like me!). It put its zero point at an average major-league performance, and judged performances by how far above or below average they were. This skewed the numbers in weird ways. It left a guy who had a bunch of major-league average performances -- your Lyle Overbays, your Alex Gonzalezeses -- with the same career value as Moonlight Graham, who famously played in one inning of one major-league game, and then spent the rest of his life looking dewy-eyed and dispensing nostalgia to any weird Iowa farmer who wandered onto a rather cheesy-looking Hollywood sound stage.[2]

Obviously, a player who managed average performances throughout a long major-league career is more valuable than Moonlight Graham, by every possible measure besides capacity for wistfulness. It's not that easy to find even average major-league performance: If you can play at an average level for a few years, you will contribute many wins to your team's total (and become a multimillionaire). Again, the place you put the zero on your scale can make a big difference. (And it reflects back on the silly idea that any new Hall-of-Famer has to be better than the average Hall-of-Famer. The average always makes for a terrible zero point. Take it from someone who is average in almost every way.)

By putting the zero point at replacement level, you get a similar, if less extreme, result as when you put it at the average. It distorts the numbers in weird ways, particularly for fielding. Our buddy Carl Yastrzemski's career Fielding WAR is 0.3. That puts his 24,620.1 career innings in the field (for which he won six Gold Gloves) at the exact same value as spare outfielder Mario Encarnacion's 163.1 innings from 2001-2002. There are hundreds of examples like this. You'll see a few more in the pages to follow.

How can that happen? No system is perfect, granted. But one that rates the defense of Carl Yastrzemski as equal to that of Mario Encarnacion has a serious flaw. You just can't have so many negative numbers in a system like this and expect to get sensical results. You need to have all performances on a continuous spectrum, from most valuable to least. With WAR fielding, the spectrum stops abruptly at this amorphous zero point called replacement level. Then it slides back with a vengeance, erasing previous good performances through the power of negative numbers.

Maybe the positional adjustments could be reworked so that first basemen and outfielders like Yastrzemski don't get such severe negative-number punishments for playing their positions as well as can be expected for a long time. But if you did that, they would end with huge overall WAR totals much higher than those of shortstops and catchers. Then to compensate, shortstop and catcher fielding numbers would have to jump into the stratosphere, well beyond what they're actually worth. It's a mess.

I've asked the good people at baseball-reference.com how they define replacement level at various positions, and the answers are pretty unsatisfying. They tend to apply a blanket adjustment to each position in each era. This adjustment ignores the subtleties of park effects, and is often skewed by a

[2] Reference explanation: "Field of Dreams." If you've gotten this far, you probably knew that, or maybe knew it once and just forgot.

few outlier great players. So add that to WAR's problems: Replacement level, the all-important dividing line between positive and negative, is often sloppily defined.

I'm not trying to trash the baseball-reference people; they're good folks. They're doing the best they can to prop up the outdated concept of "replacement level." Add "replacement level" to the long list of ideas that sound great in theory but don't work as well in practice.

Again, WAR seems to do well in measuring hitting. It's just that Win Shares does better in measuring fielding, because it doesn't have a replacement level messing things up with negative numbers. At defense-first positions like catcher and shortstop, the two systems tend to rank players similarly. If the guy dares to play the outfield or first base, WAR goes out of whack. Keep that in mind when perusing the numbers that follow.

PAs: I don't include PAs in the chart, but if I need to refer to the length of a hitter's career, I'll use PAs (plate appearances) instead of ABs (at-bats). At-bats is one of these outdated statistics that we probably shouldn't use any more. It leaves out walks or hit-by-pitches, because people in the past assumed they were all the doing of the pitcher, instead of the hitter. This makes as much sense as leaving out home runs from the pitcher's ERA because they should be credited only to hitters. In reality, everything that happens in the batter's box is partially due to the skill of the hitter and partially due to the skill of the pitcher. Nothing should be left out, on either side of the ledger.

If you still think walks result entirely from pitchers, you would have to conclude that they're evenly distributed among comparable hitters, no? Two players with great power should draw similar numbers of walks, since they are equally dangerous. But in fact, walks vary more dramatically among hitters than hits do. Facing roughly the same pitchers, Alfonso Soriano might walk 35 times a year, while Adam Dunn might walk 110 times a year. Why would pitchers "pitch around" Dunn but not Soriano, when both have great power?

This is not a fluke; baseball history is full of powerful hitters who didn't draw walks, and similar ones who did. Our friend Al Simmons drew 30-50 walks a year, while the similarly powerful Goose Goslin drew 50-90. The idea of walks being entirely the pitcher's fault was debunked long before "Moneyball." Thus PAs should be used instead of ABs.

But It's Not Just Stats

While stats are the main thing we can hang our collective hats on when judging a Hall of Fame candidacy, I recognize that it's not the only thing. It would be extremely boring indeed if we just lined up all players by the WAR and Win Shares numbers, picked a 20 or better positional ranking as a cutoff, and then rejected everyone below that line. There are always more factors to consider.

A player can also become a good manager. The Hall of Fame has firmly established that managerial success is Hall-of-Fame stuff; at this writing 23 people have been elected primarily because of their managing. If a player with a borderline playing career also led a team to a few championships, that tips things in his favor.

I am also sympathetic to the argument that "It's the Hall of Fame, not the Hall of Stats." Some guys end up very famous even though, upon further study, they turn out to not really be that valuable. Unless they have truly undeserving records, I'm inclined to leave those guys in.

The guys I really want to kick out are the ones who have never been true legends, in their own time or otherwise. These are the players who were elected by some poor decision-making process on the part of the Hall of Fame voters. They really don't need to be remembered, at least not among the very best who ever played the game.

In these determinations, I rely on both the numbers I explained above and the views of experts. Bill James' "New Historical Baseball Abstract" (The Free Press, 2001) and "Whatever Happened to the Hall of Fame" (a.k.a. "The Politics of Glory") (Fireside, 1995) are terrific sources, as are the SABR biographies of almost every player. Almost all of the stories I tell about players' lives are from the SABR biographies, which anyone can access through the baseball-reference.com player pages. They have the advantage of being painstakingly researched to be as accurate as possible, as opposed to the hazy memories of old guys that pass as facts in most sources.

Plus, I know stuff. That's pretty much my main point with this book. I want to show you all the stuff I know about baseball history. It's not like I have any other use for it. Heinie Manush's career batting average was shockingly absent from the SATs.

What About "The Character Clause"?

The BBWAA rules have always contained the clause "Voting shall be based on the player's record, playing ability, integrity, sportsmanship, character, and contributions to the team(s) on which the player played." The "integrity, sportsmanship, and character" bit is commonly referred to as "the character clause", even though it's just part of the clause that tries to set (vague) standards for inclusion. "The character clause" will sometimes come up when someone wants to justify excluding a great player he or she doesn't like.

I would be happy to base my choices on my impressions of players' integrity, sportsmanship, and character. The problem is that I believe in basing my choices on the standards created by actual Hall of Fame selections. And actual Hall of Fame selections have never bothered with considerations of character. Ty Cobb was considered by most to have very little integrity, sportsmanship, or character, and he was part of the inaugural class. The Hall of Fame has only cared about how well you played.

It could have gone a different way. Commissioner Kenesaw Mountain Landis invoked the character clause in promoting Eddie Grant for the Hall. Grant was a mediocre third baseman for a few years and then became one of the first ballplayers to enlist in World War I. He served heroically and was killed in battle. (A much more fun fact about Grant was that he went to Harvard, and when a pop fly came near him he insisted on saying the grammatically correct "I have it" instead of "I got it.") Grant epitomized character, and Hall voters certainly could have elected him, but they didn't. And no other player has gotten in primarily because of character.

The only times character has been a factor was to exclude gamblers like Pete Rose and Shoeless Joe Jackson. So that's the only exception I'll make. I may have a lot of arrogance in thinking I can remake the Hall of Fame. But I don't have so much arrogance that I'm going to remake it by imposing my personal standards of character. Especially when the actual Hall of Fame has almost completely ignored it as a factor.

In retrospect, it shouldn't be surprising that the character clause never caught on. It's so subjective that you'll never get a majority to agree on who possesses Hall-of-Fame character. And then weighing that against a player's record and ability? Forget it.

For instance, what would you do with Joe Cronin? He was a great player and manager, no doubt. But when he was the Red Sox G.M. from 1948-1958, he conspicuously failed to bring on any African-American players. Meanwhile, every other major league team integrated. How much should that detract from his case? Or was he just a product of his times, and it shouldn't count at all? Maybe it wasn't even his fault that he never hired a black player? Who knows what went on behind the scenes?

It's hard enough to select Hall of Famers based on playing records. Throwing in the second dimension of character would just make it even more of a chaotic jumble. I'd be all for a separate Character Hall of Fame. But that's just not what the Baseball Hall of Fame is.

Negro Leagues

I'm using the term "Negro Leagues" as a stand-in for the actual Negro Leagues plus Cuban leagues, Mexican leagues, and pre-Negro League play, from the late 1800s through 1954. It encompassed more than African-Americans, also including Latin-American players, particularly Cubans. Some light-skinned Latin players, like Dolf Luque and Mike Gonzalez, were accepted into the white majors before the color line was broken. Others, like all-time great Cristobal Torriente, weren't brought in because their hair was too kinky. If it sounds crazy, it was.

It's a challenge to judge the Hall of Fame credentials of players from the Negro Leagues. Their statistics are not nearly as complete as those of white leagues. And the Negro Leagues themselves were unstable, forming and collapsing while players moved from team to team with regularity. Plus, league play was only a small part of the picture for Negro Leaguers; much of their lives involved barnstorming against everything from semi-pro clubs to All-Star teams from the white majors.

None of this is any excuse to leave Negro Leaguers out of this book. They do have some records, and there are plenty of sources willing to rank the players.

There is some danger that cutting a Negro Leaguer from the Hall will come across as a terrible offense. But I believe it would be more offensive to patronize Negro Leaguers by failing to hold them to similar standards as those of white players of the same era. It's unlikely I'll end up cutting many, anyway. The selections from the Negro Leagues are known for being well thought-out and reasonable, the results of extensive research and painstaking procedures.

I admit, though, I was a little skeptical in 2006 when 17 additional Negro League players and executives were inducted. I wondered if some political correctness might be behind electing such a large class. So I wanted to find some objective measure to help me figure it out.

That 2006 election brought the total to 29 Negro Leaguers in the Hall primarily for their playing. From 1906-1946, which covers almost all of the Hall-of-Fame Negro Leaguers' careers, there were 96 white MLB players who made the Hall and earned at least 100 Win Shares (meaning that they had significant playing time in that span). That makes the Negro Leaguers 30% of the total Hall of Fame membership from that time.

After integration, from 1947-1987, 84 Hall-of-Famers earned at least 100 Win Shares. Of those, 28 were African-American or Latin American, and thus likely would have been banned before 1947. That's 33%. It's about the same percentage. This is admittedly not the most airtight system, but at least it suggests that 29 Negro Leaguers is a pretty solid number. It might even be a titch low.

By no means am I saying that there should be some sort of quota of Negro Leaguers. I'm just trying to get a sense of how many Negro Leaguers is reasonable. Since their stats are basically apples and oranges with those of white players, this is the best way I can think of to do so.

With that in mind, let's proceed under the assumption that an appropriate number of Negro Leaguers are in the Hall. With 29 players, you're close to an All-Star team. That means two or three per position, with about ten or so pitchers. A player is likely qualified if he's among the top four in Negro League history at his position and the top fifteen or so among pitchers.

Here's the table I have for Negro Leaguers:

John Henry "Pop" Lloyd (1907-1932; career OPS+: 159)

	Rank at Position Among Negro Leaguers	Rank Among All Negro Leaguers
Bill James	1	5
SABR	1	5
Monte Irvin	2	NA

Here are the sources of the above information:

Bill James: These are the rankings from Bill James' "New Baseball Historical Abstract": Surprised that I'm going by that book? If so, you haven't been reading this very carefully, and you are very awfully susceptible to surprises. Seriously, you probably shouldn't be knocked off your stool by someone citing a book. So anyway, as I was saying, look in that direction over there and .... BOO! Did that surprise you? Oh God, you're dead. That could have gone better.

My point is that Bill James helpfully ranks the best Negro League players by position. I'll list both where James ranks each player among position-mates and where he ranks the player overall. If a player isn't mentioned, I'll say "Unranked." James' ranks by position include ten guys each, so you can bet every Hall-of-Famer or Hall of Fame candidate will get a ranking. His overall rankings of Negro League players are interspersed among his top 100 players of all time, so that includes only 12 players. If a guy got an overall rank from James, he's a definite Hall-of-Famer. If not, he might be worthy and might not.

SABR: SABR stands for the Society for American Baseball Research, the group behind a lot of the analytical innovations in baseball. I've been to a SABR convention, by the way, and if you have ever yearned to watch a bunch of old white men argue vociferously about alleged inaccuracies in Ken Burns' "Baseball" documentary, hoo boy do I have a recommendation for you.

I kid SABR because I love it. This is where baseball nerds like myself go when their kids go to college and they're left with lots of free time. We're a sort of unusual breed: We're obsessed with sports, which is typically not a nerdy thing. Jocks are similarly obsessed. But we find a way to nerd it up, obsessing in a sitting-alone-in-front-of-a-computer sort of way that is more typical of those pure-blood geeks who pore over "Star Trek" or comic books.

Perhaps it is even more geeky to subvert the square-jawed, All-American world of sports by turning the nerd prism on it. But at least our knowledge gives us something to talk about with all those mudblood[3] non-nerds. Go try telling your co-workers that Pike was actually the best "Star Trek" captain and see where that gets you.

I've gotten off track again; the point is that SABR released their own list of the 40 Greatest Negro League Figures in 1999. This takes a slightly different angle, ranking both players and owners according to how important they were to Negro League baseball, as opposed to just how they

[3] Reference explanation: In "Harry Potter," some wizards looked down on the ordinary non-magical people, calling them "mudbloods."

produced on the field. Adding a slightly different perspective gives us a more complete picture of Hall of Fame qualifications. Again, I'll list both where SABR ranks each player among position-mates and where it ranks him among all figures.

Monte Irvin: In 2007, Hall-of-Famer Monte Irvin collaborated with writer Phil Pepe to produce an absolutely charming book, "Few and Chosen Negro Leagues: Defining Negro Leagues Greatness" (Triumph Books). In it, Irvin draws on his own experiences and knowledge to list the five best players at each position from the Negro Leagues. He includes players who had very brief experience in the Negro Leagues, like Ernie Banks and Hank Aaron. I leave those players out of his rankings. Irvin doesn't do any overall rankings, so that bottom-right square will always say "NA."

Irvin takes an unscientific approach, which is typically verboten in my world. But with Negro League records being so incomplete, it only seems fair to take the recommendations of someone who was there and made a lifetime of studying his predecessors. Irvin admits that he leaves out some distant predecessors that he doesn't know anything about, but co-writer Phil Pepe usually injects a blurb about the Hall-worthy ones.

OPS+: The Negro Leagues Database on Seamheads.com is a wonderful compilation of stats for Negro League players. They even have OPS+ and Win Shares! Unfortunately, at this writing they've only compiled numbers through 1934. So the OPS+ spot will be empty for the many players who played after 1934. And I couldn't devote a spot in the grid to Win Shares. I'll mention Win Shares in the text where I can.

Any RESPECTFUL Edits or Counterarguments?

When you write a book, you're supposed to act like you're the ultimate authority, with zero doubt about any of your facts or conclusions. I refuse to do that. I know a lot and have thought a lot about baseball, but I'm not omniscient or infallible.

This is the perspective people take in academia (or at least are supposed to): Here's what I think is true, but I'm not 100% sure. There is always some doubt about everything. Certainty is for religion, not science. If I or someone else discovers that what I'm saying is false, and presents good arguments and evidence demonstrating so, then I'll adapt my views. This is the key to scientific inquiry: Without doubt, there is no questioning, and without questioning, there is no new discovery and no progress. Applying scientific methods to baseball might seem silly, but a lot of people do it nowadays, from Bill James to Baseball Prospectus to SABR, etc., etc.

So I want anyone with conflicting information or perspectives to write me at chrisekeedei@yahoo.com. It's the email address of Chris E. Keedei, a good friend of mine. If you contribute something that makes me want to do some revising, I'll do so and then mention your help in the acknowledgements of any future versions.

Here's the crucial thing, though: your emails must be respectful. If they aren't, Chris won't even bother forwarding them to me, regardless of what points they make. If you start with phrases like "How can you ..." or "I can't believe that ...," stop, take a breath, and rewrite. Besides, if you're feeling inchoate rage building inside over something like Luis Aparicio's defensive abilities, you might not be thinking rationally enough to impart useful information.

And There's More To Say...

... but this introduction has already gone on long enough. Instead I'll go through other arguments and ideas while reviewing the players. Some concepts come up often, and I don't want to reintroduce them every time. **So I recommend you read this book in order.**

I know, I know; you're a massive Travis Jackson fan and want to skip straight to his section. But I ask you to just bite the bullet and slog through all the ho-hum hoo-ha about Johnny Bench and Stan Musial to get to that sweet, sweet Travis Jackson reward. It'll make more sense in order, I swear. If you skipped straight to Travis Jackson you'd be very confused about why his comment immediately starts with a tirade against Frankie Frisch. But if you've already read the George Kelly comment, you'll be there with me, throwing your head to the heavens, clenching your fists, and screaming "Friiiiiiisch!"

Chapter Two

~ ~ Catcher ~ ~

Catchers get relative short shrift in the Hall of Fame. They tend not to have the most eye-popping hitting statistics because the rigors of their position shorten their seasons and their careers. I don't know if you've tried squatting and rising 100-plus times a day at your job, but if you did, you might be too sore to hit a home run or create a spreadsheet or anaesthetize a dog or whatever you do for a living.

Remember that "rank" in each case means "rank among catchers." And the final rank for Win Shares is not JAWS, but the spot Bill James put the player among catchers in his 2001 "New Historical Baseball Abstract."

Johnny Bench (1967-1983; career OPS+: 126)

	Career	Rank	Hitting	Rank	Fielding	Rank	Peak	Rank	Bests	JAWS	Rank
WAR	75.0	1	65.2	3	19.3	5	47.2	2	5	61.1	1
WS	354.9	3	255.2	3	99.6	11	212.8	1	4	NA	2

When Johnny Bench joined the Reds, he was a revelation. He was only 20 years old when he won the Rookie of the Year award in 1968. In 1970, at age 22, he led all of baseball with 45 home runs and 148 RBI, playing Gold-Glove defense and winning the MVP. 1972 saw another home run title, RBI title, Gold Glove, and MVP. Imagine if Mike Piazza could win Gold Gloves and you start to get the idea.

Bench didn't sustain that level of offense forever, but he was still amazing throughout the Reds' run as the best NL team of the 1970s. The Big Red Machine won World Series titles in 1975 and 1976, reached the series in 1970 and 1972, and won their division in 1973 and 1979. It was a team known for pretty good pitching and absolutely merciless hitting. In 1975, the Reds scored 840 runs, more than 100 better than any other NL club. They were led by Hall-of-Fame manager and all-around charmer Sparky Anderson, and starred Bench, Hall-of-Famer and possibly the best second baseman of all time Joe Morgan, Hall of Fame third baseman/first baseman Tony Perez, and the biggest star of all, non-Hall-of-Famer Pete Rose.

Johnny Bench, in my view, is the best catcher in MLB history. The WAR stats show him having the top combination of excellent hitting and top-flight defense. In his final estimation, Bill James has him below Yogi Berra. But I'm unconvinced, especially since James acknowledges Bench has a big advantage on defense, while I don't see evidence that Berra's offense was tons better than Bench's.

Bench is Hall-of-Famer among Hall-of-Famers; he should be the starting catcher in the Hall of Fame's All-Star team. I'm not sure who the Hall of Fame would play against in this hypothetical All-Star Game, but you get the idea. Maybe they could play the Washington Generals, like the Harlem Globetrotters do? I'd love to see Johnny Bench throw the ball through a batter's legs and nab the runner at second.

Yogi Berra (1946-1963, 1965; career OPS+: 125)

	Career	Rank	Hitting	Rank	Fielding	Rank	Peak	Rank	Bests	JAWS	Rank
WAR	59.3	6	56.3	5	8.7	39	36.8	10	5	48.1	6
WS	372.0	1	267.6	1	104.6	7	208.7	3	7	NA	1

When I was a kid, I thought Yogi Berra's name was a take-off on Yogi Bear's name. When I asked my older sister about it, I learned that cartoons tend to be based on real people, not the other way around, and also that I was a doofus. The latter was made particularly clear.

Berra did not take the homage in good humor. He sued Yogi Bear's creators, Hanna-Barbera, for defamation. Hanna-Barbera rather implausibly claimed the names were just a coincidence, because, y'know, Yogi is such a common name. Who *wasn't* named Yogi in the 1950s? I challenge you to think of a single person who lived in the 1950s and was not named Yogi.

Hanna-Barbera's excuse apparently made Berra drop the suit, though I bet someone pulled him aside and told him he had zero chance of winning. Defamation, Yogi? Really? It's just a silly pun. Otherwise, there is no connection. It's not like Yogi Bear spent each episode staring at the camera making inflammatory accusations about Yogi Berra's personal life. Maybe Berra was worried people would think he liked to steal pick-a-nick baskets?

Yogi Bear is probably still more famous than Yogi Berra, but it could be close. Grown-ups with no interest in baseball know Berra from his quotes, which are used as opening jokes for an estimated 79.65% of all corporate speeches, making Berra the all-time leader in CSOJP (corporate speech opening joke percentage). You've heard the Yogi quotes, I bet. They are always dopey on the surface but still make some sort of sense that can be spun into some larger point. "Baseball is 90% physical - the other half is mental." "You can observe a lot just by watching." "It was impossible to get a conversation going -- everyone was talking too much." Sometimes it's hard to tell how intentional they are, whether Berra was genuinely misspeaking or whether he was joking around.

There's a great line that someone wrote about Berra, which I wish I could find but I can't. I'll paraphrase: "Yogi, you were the kid who wanted to be like everyone else. Now they all want to be like you."

I bet that as a kid, Yogi was seen as a buffoon. He has a goofy face, a stocky body, and said strange things. I picture him being the kid who strained to fit in, the one who would hang on the periphery of a group of boys and try to jump into conversations, but would always come up with something like "He must have made that before he died." Everyone would laugh, but it would be mostly at Yogi, not with him. He was the inadvertent and perhaps unwilling class clown. Later in life he embraced this image and had fun with it, but it probably wasn't easy being a young Yogi.

His way to gain respect was through baseball, and it worked. On the field, it doesn't matter what you look or sound like; all that matters is how you play. His play turned him from an unwitting clown to a universal hero. A no-doubt Hall-of-Famer.

Roger Bresnahan (1897, 1900-1915; career OPS+: 126)

	Career	Rank	Hitting	Rank	Fielding	Rank	Peak	Rank	Bests	JAWS	Rank
WAR	41.0	21	42.8	19	4.9	66	28.9	22	4	35.0	21
WS	230.6	18	165.7	17	49.6	71	157.2	18	3	NA	16

Roger Bresnahan played from 1901-1915 (not including cups of coffee in 1897 and 1900), landing him squarely in the dead-ball era. Conventional hitting stats from that era are very low, but OPS+ overcomes that. In terms of career OPS+, Bresnahan is comparable to Johnny Bench and Yogi Berra. If you want a catcher from the dead-ball era in the Hall of Fame, there's no other choice. No one comes close to Bresnahan in WAR and Win Shares numbers.

Bresnahan wasn't just a good hitter for a catcher; he was a good hitter, period. He had a lifetime .386 OBP, which ranks seventh among all hitters, at all positions, who had at least 5000 PAs from 1901-1919 (top six: Ty Cobb, Shoeless Joe Jackson, Tris Speaker, Eddie Collins, Roy Thomas, and Honus Wagner). Bresnahan was not much of a slugger, but in the context of his time, he wasn't bad. The most comparable player nowadays would probably be Joe Mauer.

The reason Bresnahan's ranks above are not very impressive when compared to Bench, Berra, etc., is that had only 5374 career plate appearances, and only twice had more than 500 in a season. This was not a reflection on his play; catchers in the dead-ball era played much less than catchers do now. There was very little protective equipment, so catchers basically just stood there and waited to get hit in the face. Teams had to spread games among several catchers, almost like a pitching rotation. Bresnahan had only two seasons of more than 120 games, only getting into that many games because he also played the outfield.

This leads to another part of Bresnahan's Hall of Fame credentials. He made significant improvements to (but did not invent) shin guards and a padded face mask, enabling him and later catchers to catch more games. This wasn't easy: Baseball, like all sports, has always been packed with a macho, "pain don't hurt"[4] attitude, in which taking any measures to lessen any discomfort will be scorned. But if taking those measures means winning more games, they will eventually be begrudgingly accepted. Bresnahan did it and was able to catch more games, thus changing baseball and making careers like Bench's and Berra's possible.

As a bonus, Bresnahan was terrific for the Giants in the 1905 World Series. In his lone postseason appearance, he hit .313/.500/.438, the only player on either the Giants or A's to have an OPS above .700. He likely wouldn't have won the World Series MVP, though, as Christy Mathewson pitched three shutouts. The Giants' team ERA in the series, by the way, was 0.00. Joe McGinnity allowed three unearned runs and lost one game, but then shut out the A's in the other. Each side only used three pitchers in the entire five-game series. The Giants needed only a handful of runs to win, and Bresnahan was the main one to provide them.

[4] Reference explanation: The 1989 film "Road House," starring Patrick Swayze and a giant monster truck for no good reason.

Bresnahan is widely viewed as one of the worst selections ever made by Hall of Fame voters. WAR and Win Shares disagree, and they're not even accounting for how catchers got less playing time in the dead-ball era. Bresnahan deserves to be in Hall of Fame.

Roy Campanella (1948-1957; career OPS+: 123)

	Career	Rank	Hitting	Rank	Fielding	Rank	Peak	Rank	Bests	JAWS	Rank
WAR	34.2	27	33.7	26	5.7	59	32.8	15	4	33.5	26
WS	205.8	27	137.6	25	68.2	29	173.4	12	4	NA	3

Much like Roger Bresnahan, Roy Campanella had a very short career for a Hall-of-Famer, with only 4815 PAs. So that keeps a lot of the above numbers down. But I'm surprised that his Peak numbers are not higher, seeing as how he won three MVP awards with some excellent conventional stats on some great 1950s Brooklyn Dodgers teams. Hmmm, I don't know about this guy ...

But wait, you might say, (you're going to be my paper tiger in this argument, sorry) Campanella was in a career-ending auto accident in 1958! You have to assume he would've had a few more good years and then compiled numbers that would make him a shoo-in!

Well, no I don't, and please don't tell me what I have to assume, you jackass. (I show no mercy to opponents that I make up.) When Campanella was injured, he was 35, an age at which few catchers can play well. And in fact, Campy had just come off of two sub-par seasons. If we're taking the "what could have been" angle, I seriously doubt he could have padded his Hall-of-Fame resume much further in his late 30s.

People often use "what could have been" arguments when making cases for the Hall of Fame. Some hold water with me, and some don't. Injuries or freak accidents don't. You get in the Hall of Fame for what you did, not what you could have done if the winds of fate hadn't turned against you. There are hundreds of players, especially pitchers, who could have been Hall-of-Famers if not for a freak injury. Life ain't fair, kid; get used to it.

The "what could have been" arguments that do hold water with me involve some systemic societal condition preventing you from playing in the major leagues. And this is definitely true of Campanella. He got his start in the Negro Leagues when he was 15 (!) years old and was not brought to the white major leagues until he was 26. His Negro Leagues record should clearly be counted in his favor. And that was interrupted by World War II, which took at least one season of baseball out of his record.

The JAWS ranking for Campanella does not account for these Negro League and war years. Bill James does, and ranks Campanella third among all catchers. That might be a bit high, but regardless, Campanella is clearly a Hall-of-Famer. (As if it were ever really in doubt. Or did I make you think I might go against him? Hee hee hee, I'm so mischievous.)

Gary Carter (1974-1992; career OPS+: 115)

	Career	Rank	Hitting	Rank	Fielding	Rank	Peak	Rank	Bests	JAWS	Rank
WAR	69.9	2	55.6	6	25.5	2	48.2	1	5	59.1	2
WS	338.2	4	214.7	9	123.9	2	201.8	4	6	NA	8

A no-doubter, one of the top five catchers of all time, in my view. Surprisingly, it took six ballots by the BBWAA to get him in the Hall. Carter is quite famous, but might be a bit underrated.

He played in a low-offense time, so his conventional numbers don't blow you away. And Carter had his last good offensive season in 1986, after which he hung on as a part-time catcher for six years. Perhaps this made his past brilliance fade a bit in people's eyes.

Plus, Carter's offense was only half the story. He was a tremendous defensive player, something that's always been hard to quantify and thus is often misjudged. The defensive numbers are less trustworthy than the offensive ones, but when both WAR and Win Shares say Carter was the second-best defensive catcher in history (behind Ivan Rodriguez in both cases), I tend to believe it.

Combine the offense and defense, and I'd put him on the Hall of Fame All-Star team, backing up Johnny Bench and cheering the team on with his characteristic kid-like enthusiasm.

Mickey Cochrane (1925-1937; career OPS+: 129)

	Career	Rank	Hitting	Rank	Fielding	Rank	Peak	Rank	Bests	JAWS	Rank
WAR	52.1	10	52.2	11	4.4	74	36.9	9	9	44.5	9
WS	275.0	11	193.5	10	81.2	19	189.1	5	6	NA	4

Mickey Cochrane's real name was not "Mickey," or "Michael," or anything of the kind. He was born Gordon Stanley Cochrane. On the ballfields Gordon was called "Mick" or "Mickey" because people thought he was Irish. He wasn't -- he was of Scottish ancestry -- but casual bigotry is not known for its allegiance to factual accuracy.

Cochrane was an excellent hitter whose conventional stats look even excellent-er because he played in the 1920s and 1930s. He was not great on defense. The differences in measuring fielding between WAR in WS are pretty evident here; Cochrane provided a lot of replacement-level defense, which is valued in WS but not in WAR.

He was forced into becoming a catcher, in a way that would never occur nowadays. While still in college at Boston University, he was playing shortstop and outfield on a Class D team, the Dover Senators, under the assumed name of "Frank King." (If you were in college, you were not supposed to play for professional teams, but many did under fake names.) The Senators needed a catcher, so they forced Cochrane/King to start catching for the first time in his life, at the age of 20. It took a lot of work, all the way to the major-league level, before Cochrane became a passable defensive catcher.

He never had any trouble hitting. Along with fellow inner-circle Hall-of-Famers Lefty Grove, Jimmie Foxx and Al Simmons, he led a Philadelphia A's dynasty that won World Series titles in 1929 and 1930. But A's owner and manager Connie Mack decided to cash out in 1933, and sold Cochrane to the Tigers.

In Detroit, Cochrane became a player-manager and had immediate success. His Tigers went to the World Series in 1934 and won it all in 1935. To a nation in the midst of the Great Depression, Cochrane became a hero. He was seen as a humble but fiercely competitive man who pulled himself up from lowly beginnings to steer the long-despairing Tigers to their first World Series appearance in 25 years. Even in far-flung Oklahoma, when the Mantles had a boy, they named him Mickey after

Cochrane. That same Mickey Mantle went on to get a good job in New York City! (As one of the best ballplayers in history.)

Unfortunately, the gentle, self-effacing Cochrane was not up for the workload he soon found himself with. In 1936 he was made general manager of the Tigers on top of both managing and playing. It proved to be too much, and he suffered a nervous breakdown. Then in 1937 Cochrane was beaned and nearly killed. His playing career was over.

In Al Stump's biography of Ty Cobb and the 1994 film "Cobb," Cochrane was portrayed as a sad simpleton who depended on handouts from Ty Cobb in his old age. This was a fabrication motivated by the book's and film's agenda of making Ty Cobb look like a sociopath with a heart of gold -- you know, like all sociopaths, right? Cochrane actually recovered just fine from both his breakdown and his beaning, happily running a ranch in Montana into his old age.

Cochrane ended up with a relatively short career of only 6207 career plate appearances. But he dominated when he did play: His 9 times leading his position in WAR ties him for seventh among all non-pitchers with Lou Gehrig, Willie Mays, Ted Williams, Eddie Collins, Billy Hamilton, and Nap Lajoie. Cochrane's great hitting, good managing and acceptable defense clearly put him in the Hall of Fame.

Bill Dickey (1928-1943, 1946; career OPS+: 127)

	Career	Rank	Hitting	Rank	Fielding	Rank	Peak	Rank	Bests	JAWS	Rank
WAR	55.8	8	53.8	8	7.6	48	34.2	13	4	45.0	8
WS	312.8	10	217.9	7	95.0	13	177.6	9	4	NA	7

Bill Dickey is pretty similar to Mickey Cochrane. Dickey also compiled tremendous batting stats in the hitting-crazy 1930s while fielding his position well enough. Both anchored some great teams filled with even bigger hitting stars.

Dickey was known as "The Man Nobody Knows" because he played alongside Babe Ruth, Lou Gehrig and later Joe DiMaggio on Yankees teams that won eight World Series titles. It was a silly nickname; being a star on the best team in the universe for nearly twenty years meant he was hardly obscure. "The Man Fewer People Know than Know Babe Ruth" would have been more apropos. But New Yorkers are not exactly known for understatement.

Because of those inflated batting stats, Dickey and Cochrane are sometimes confused as the best catchers of all-time. They aren't, but they're close. Definite Hall-of-Famer.

Buck Ewing (1880-1897; career OPS+: 129)

	Career	Rank	Hitting	Rank	Fielding	Rank	Peak	Rank	Bests	JAWS	Rank
WAR	47.7	12	42.2	20	9.4	34	30.5	17	2	39.1	16
WS	242.7	15	185.4	13	54.6	58	149.7	22	2	NA	17

Finally, an interesting case! I was getting tired of all those shoo-ins. Buck Ewing, like Roger Bresnahan, played under very different conditions than we're used to. He was of a generation before

Bresnahan, but also had few PAs per season and a low career total. Catchers just couldn't play much in his time.

Unlike Bresnahan, Ewing's conventional stats sometimes look great. In the crazy days of the 1800s, conditions would change radically from year to year as the bosses tinkered with the rules. One year seven balls would make a walk, and the next they'd switch to four. Another year they'd change the distance between the mound and home plate from 50 feet to 60. When Ewing had a .277/.327/.445 BA/OBP/SLG line in 1884, he actually had a better OPS+ than when he went .344/.394/.496 in 1893.

Compared to his league, Ewing was almost always an excellent hitter, as his 129 career OPS+ shows. Admittedly, this number can be a bit deceptive when looking at players from more than a century ago. In those days, the majors had many more truly awful hitters, making the good hitters look amazing in stats like OPS+ that compare a player to the league average.

It's like if I walked into a homeless shelter, and then compared my income to the average of the people in the room. I would have an amazing "Income+" number, maybe better than Bill Gates would at a billionaire convention. But that doesn't make me one of the richest people in the country. (This book will, though. I assume that you bought several copies, so you can read it more than once. Reading the same book twice is a strict violation of copyright law.) Sometimes averages don't tell the whole story.

Still, Ewing was undoubtedly the best catcher in his era, and that counts for something. And he was regarded by many players and managers of the time as the best player in baseball. Take it all together, and Ewing is a Hall-of-Famer.

Rick Ferrell (1929-1945, 1947; career OPS+: 95)

	Career	Rank	Hitting	Rank	Fielding	Rank	Peak	Rank	Bests	JAWS	Rank
WAR	29.8	33	30.2	31	5.5	61	19.8	59	0	24.8	45
WS	206.3	26	102.4	37	66.8	31	115.9	46	0	NA	29

Woof. Are you a little depressed by those numbers too? I need to sit down. (Normally I write while standing up, of course. In fact, I'm usually writing while running a marathon, managing a Fortune 500 company, and punching Nazis in the face. But man, sometimes even I have to sit down under a warm blanket and cry the pain away.)

In terms of career OPS+, Ferrell is comparable to A.J. Pierzynski or Ramon Hernandez; i.e. good for a catcher but below average for all major leaguers. In terms of the WAR numbers, he's in the neighborhood of Terry Steinbach and Tim McCarver. Bill James ranks him below Darren Daulton and just above Jim Sundberg. All were good catchers, but none were really close to being in the Hall of Fame.

Ferrell never had a single great season, with his top Win Shares total being 18 in 1934. That total tied him for 40th among all non-pitchers in 1934, behind fellow catchers Mickey Cochrane, Gabby Hartnett, and Bill Dickey. Not only did Ferrell never have a year in which he was the best catcher in baseball; he was never the second-best, or even the third-best. He had a few fourth-place finishes, which might be good if you were representing Liechtenstein in the triple-jump, but likely won't get you in the Olympic Hall of Fame.

OK, enough negativity. Let's all go around the room and say something nice about Rick Ferrell. He could get on base, notching a lifetime career mark of .378, fourth among Hall of Fame catchers (behind Cochrane, Bresnahan and Dickey). He played a long time, at one time holding the record for most games caught. I understand that he was a pillar of his community, volunteering at the PTA and organizing the annual bake sale, which ironically was so successful that they were able to buy a bomber.[5]

But he sure as heck ain't a Hall-of-Famer. His conventional numbers look OK only because he played in the 1930s. There's no shortage of catchers from the 1930s in the Hall. If I had my way, there would be one less. **Rick Ferrell is out.**

Carlton Fisk (1969, 1971-1993; career OPS+: 117)

	Career	Rank	Hitting	Rank	Fielding	Rank	Peak	Rank	Bests	JAWS	Rank
WAR	68.3	4	65.7	2	16.3	11	37.6	6	3	53.0	4
WS	368.2	2	254.7	4	113.3	3	184.7	7	3	NA	6

Fisk is in the upper tier of catchers, with Bench and Carter. Really, choosing between them is a bit nitpick-y. Fisk had a longer career than either of them, but had fewer great seasons. Bench was a better hitter and Carter a better defender. Whatever. It's not like any would be any easy choice over the others.

It does trouble me a bit, though, that my top three catchers are all from the 1970s and 1980s. I prefer to believe that the greats from each position are evenly spread among the years. Sometimes, though, the law of averages will land something like this, where the talent randomly concentrates at a particular time.

Is this entirely random, though? If WAR and WS are to be believed, almost all the best defensive catchers have played recently. The top ten catchers in career Defensive WAR are Ivan Rodriguez, Gary Carter, Bob Boone, Jim Sundberg, Johnny Bench, Yadier Molina, Brad Ausmus, Charlie Bennett, Tony Pena, and Rick Dempsey. Bennett is the only one who played before 1967, and he was from the 1880s.

Win Shares gives a similar list, except that it includes Carlton Fisk, Gabby Hartnett, Yogi Berra, and Lance Parrish, knocking Dempsey, Bench, Bennett, and Molina all lower (though my WS numbers are only through 2008, meaning that Molina would probably make it in if they kept updating an electronic version of the WS numbers). That leaves us with two players who played before 1967 instead of one; it's still quite a slant.

Perhaps part of the reason is that modern medicine has allowed players who play especially strenuous positions like catcher to stay on the field longer and more effectively. Should older players get more consideration because they didn't benefit from this? Is it a bit like how catchers were used less in the 1800s, never getting full seasons? I'm not sure.

---

[5] Reference explanation: Anyone remember those T-shirts and bumper stickers that said "It will be a great day when our schools get all the money they need and the air force has to hold a bake sale to buy a bomber"? Or is that a hopelessly dated reference?

Regardless, even if you chuck out defense entirely for catchers, you still get a pretty similar list of greats. The leaders in career Offensive WAR for catchers are Mike Piazza, Carlton Fisk, Johnny Bench, Joe Torre, Yogi Berra, Gary Carter, Ivan Rodriguez, Bill Dickey, Ted Simmons, and Gabby Hartnett. If you want, you could tell me that Berra was better all-around than Carter because the defensive numbers are bunk. I would probably not get too mad.

At any rate, none of this changes the fact that Fisk is clearly in.

Josh Gibson (1930-1940, 1942-1946)

	Rank at Position Among Negro Leaguers	Rank Among All Negro Leaguers
Bill James	1	2
SABR	1	5
Monte Irvin	1	NA

Forget what I said about Johnny Bench. Josh Gibson is, by popular acclaim, the best catcher in baseball history. Bill James doesn't just rank him as the best catcher in history; he ranks him as the ninth-best player ever, from any position and any league, right after Walter Johnson and ahead of Stan Musial. James also lists the best players each year of the Negro Leagues, and Gibson takes this pseudo-MVP award five times.

He was called "the black Babe Ruth," and that could be an apt comparison. Maybe he was as good as Babe Ruth. But that's the kind of huge claim that I don't feel comfortable with without more evidence. Babe Ruth was the greatest player in baseball history, bar none. If Gibson were as good a hitter as Ruth, while playing a tougher position of catcher, then Gibson would be Ruth times two. Again, it could be true, but it seems a bit much.

Monte Irvin compares Gibson to Jimmie Foxx as a hitter, which sounds a bit less hyperbolic. This is hardly an insult; it still means Gibson hit far, far better than any other catcher in history, and is the best overall catcher in history hands down.

In 1946, when he was 34 years old, Gibson suffered a stroke. He died a year later, just a few months before Jackie Robinson broke the color barrier. If he had lived, Gibson very well could have appeared in the MLB. We'll never see anyone like him. No-doubt Hall-of-Famer.

Gabby Hartnett (1922-1941; career OPS+: 126)

	Career	Rank	Hitting	Rank	Fielding	Rank	Peak	Rank	Bests	JAWS	Rank
WAR	53.4	9	52.6	10	6.6	53	30.3	19	2	41.9	12
WS	325.6	7	216.1	8	109.4	4	173.0	13	4	NA	9

Like Cochrane and Dickey, Gabby Hartnett was a great-hitting catcher from baseball's Golden Age. The true Golden Age of baseball was the 1920s and 1930s, by the way. Then baseball was at its peak of popularity, before football and television stole away eyeballs. The Golden Age is not the 1950s and 1960s, regardless of what the Hall of Fame thinks. The division of the former Veterans' Committee in charge of reviewing players from the 1950s and 1960s is called the Golden Age Committee. It's a terrible name; maybe the Baby Boomer Nostalgia Committee would be more apropos.

Baby boomers will tell you that the 1950s were the Golden Age of baseball, but they just say that because they were kids then. They think everything that happened in the 1950s represented a Golden Age. The 1950s were supposedly the Golden Age of baseball, the Golden Age of television, the Golden Age of comedy, the Golden Age of sexual repression, the Golden Age of fear of nuclear annihilation, the Golden Age of terrifying marionettes anchoring popular kids' shows,[6] etc., etc.

I suppose you could make a case that you can't have a true Golden Age when you're banning African-American players from the National and American Leagues. That's fair. But in decrying segregation, let's not minimize what the Negro Leagues were able to accomplish in the 1920s and 1930s. They had their own heroes and glories and were rich with fun and fervor. Despite working under adverse conditions, they became a large part of what made the the pre-World-War-II years a peak for organized baseball. The Negro Leagues were part of what made the age golden.

Just in terms of attendance for the National and American Leagues, there was not a huge boom in the 1950s, like there was in almost every other aspect of American life. In fact, overall attendance dropped more than 30% from 1948 to 1953. It stabilized only after teams moved to new cities that were hungry for major-league baseball.

Meanwhile, the Negro Leagues withered away. This was necessary for integration, but it still represented the losses of many great baseball institutions. And it points to an even greater decrease in overall baseball attendance than I already mentioned. The numbers in MLB parks fell dramatically despite pulling new crowds of African-Americans away from the Negro Leagues.

Plummeting major-league attendance was a well-known problem at the time. People blamed television; per usual, the new technology is the go-to scapegoat for any change that people find disturbing. It could have been a factor, but it's also possible that people outside of the Bronx got bored of the Yankees winning the World Series every year. Attendance is always low for teams that haven't won anything in ages. There were probably many reasons for the fall; regardless, it's hard to see how an industry suffering a severe drop in paying customers could be seen as going through a Golden Age.

Anyway, all of my Gen-X contrariness has nothing to do with Gabby Hartnett. He was a very good hitter for the Cubs throughout the 1920s and '30s, and a competent fielder. He didn't have Cochrane's batting averages, but he had better power. He's a clear Hall-of-Famer.

Ernie Lombardi (1931-1947; career OPS+: 126)

	Career	Rank	Hitting	Rank	Fielding	Rank	Peak	Rank	Bests	JAWS	Rank
WAR	45.9	16	48.3	13	2.9	86	27.8	25	4	36.9	18
WS	219.2	22	167.5	16	51.9	65	129.3	30	2	NA	22

[6] Reference explanation: "Howdy Doody" always scared me when I was a little kid. He was too much like a ventriloquist dummy, and those terrified me for some reason. I just could not tell whether they were alive or not.

Ernie Lombardi is a fun player. In the "New Historical Baseball Abstract," Bill James spins a long and affectionate tribute to Lombardi. Part of Lombardi's appeal is his less-than-godlike qualities. He was ridiculed for being the slowest player in baseball, the type who could stretch a double into a single. And he had a nose so big his nickname was "Schnozz."

He was also a star of a team I'm fascinated by, the 1939-1940 Reds. At a time when everyone was trying to outslug each other, Hall of Fame manager Bill McKechnie did some clever counter-programming, loading his team with defensive whizzes. Their infield called themselves "The Jungle Club," made up of Frank "Wildcat" McCormick, Lonny "Leopard" Frey, Billy "Jaguar" Myers, and Billy "Tiger" Werber. Tell me that ain't adorable.

All that aside, Lombardi is no shoo-in for the Hall of Fame. Despite having two batting titles, one of four catchers to ever get one (Buster Posey, Joe Mauer, and Bubbles Hargrave being the other three), Lombardi had very few truly great seasons. And his defense was pretty bad.

Still, I think the Hall of Fame's big enough for a catcher with a 126 OPS+ over 17 seasons. The overall rankings demonstrate he's on the low end, but he's far from an embarrassment. I say leave him in.

Biz Mackey (1920-1931, 1933-1942, 1945-1947)

	Rank at Position Among Negro Leaguers	Rank Among All Negro Leaguers
Bill James	3	unranked
SABR	2	17
Monte Irvin	2	NA

Biz Mackey was both a predecessor and a contemporary of Josh Gibson, starting his career ten years earlier than Gibson and retiring a year after Gibson died. That's 27 years for Mackey, which is downright ludicrous for a catcher. It's like combining Buck Ewing and Roger Bresnahan into one career. Granted, Mackey didn't play terribly well after 1933, when he was 36, but he was still a regular at age 42 and had his last at-bat at 49.

Mackey wasn't the home run hitter that Josh Gibson was. He was a great line-drive hitter in the Ernie Lombardi vein. But Mackey was a better overall player than Lombardi, because he could run like a normal human being and could field exceptionally well. He actually came up as a shortstop, and then in his sophomore season made the most unusual position switch possible by converting to catcher.

On top of it all, Mackey had a successful managerial career. First he led the Baltimore Elite Giants, where he mentored a very young Roy Campanella. Then he managed the Newark Eagles, one of the premier Negro League teams. There he guided Don Newcombe, Monte Irvin and Larry Doby. I have no doubt that Mackey is a Hall-of-Famer.

Mike Piazza (1992-2007; career OPS+: 143)

	Career	Rank	Hitting	Rank	Fielding	Rank	Peak	Rank	Bests	JAWS	Rank
WAR	**59.4**	**5**	**65.9**	**1**	**1.0**	**93**	**43.1**	**3**	**4**	**51.3**	**5**
WS	**326.5**	**5**	**240.6**	**6**	**52.7**	**63**	**210.7**	**2**	**6**	**NA**	**5**

(Note: Because Piazza's career was too recent to be covered adequately in "The New Historical Abstract," the Bill James overall ranking has been replaced with the ranking of the average of his career and peak Win Shares, which uses the same formula used to calculate JAWS. Let's call that "WSAWS.")

Everyone knows Piazza is one the best-hitting catchers in history, if not the best. And he was a not a great defensive catcher, but who cares? If you have a catcher who can hit like that, you can sacrifice a few opponent stolen bases. Piazza wasn't good at throwing out opposing runners, but he was acceptable at all the other more important, less flashy aspects of catching: calling pitches, blocking balls in the dirt, grabbing pop flies, etc.

Steroid-obsessives have cast aspersions on Piazza, based on some off-the-record comments. Allegedly he used steroids occasionally to recover faster from injury, but was never a chronic user. Allegedly, he had a serious case of acne on his back. Again, it's all unsubstantiated rumor, and besides, I can't imagine that his limited alleged usage turned him from a non-Hall-of-Famer to a guy with a first-ballot career. I'll get more into steroids in the Ivan Rodriguez comment; for now, Piazza belongs.

Louis Santop (1910-1924; career OPS+: 163)

	Rank at Position Among Negro Leaguers	Rank Among All Negro Leaguers
Bill James	2	unranked
SABR	3	22
Monte Irvin	3	NA

The great Negro League catchers managed to carefully organize themselves into different eras. Gibson dominated the 1930s and 1940s, Mackey was the man in the 1920s, and Louis Santop was the great one in the 1910s. The Negro Leagues were especially good at producing catchers. If I could have a "bests" column above that combined Negro League and MLB players, Negro League catchers would probably dominate until Yogi Berra came along.

Santop was a giant for his time, 6'4" and 240 pounds. He channeled that bulk into dominant power hitting, a very rare commodity in the 1910s. He was a brash showman with his home runs, often calling his shots. Before Josh Gibson, Santop was the first to be known as "the Black Babe Ruth."

Negro League records are far from complete, especially before 1920. But Seamheads.com has enough information to give Santop a .336 BA, .397 OBP, and .476 SLG in 1672 PAs. It's hard to say whether he could have hit that well in the white major leagues. Before the Negro National League was established in 1920, black and Latin baseball was extremely unstable, and probably didn't draw the best competition together very efficiently. So Santop's numbers could be inflated by playing against guys who had no business being on the same field as him.

Still, I think Santop gives Roger Bresnahan some good competition for the title of best dead-ball era catcher. He's a Hall-of-Famer.

Ray Schalk (1912-1929; career OPS+: 83)

	Career	Rank	Hitting	Rank	Fielding	Rank	Peak	Rank	Bests	JAWS	Rank
WAR	28.5	40	23.6	53	13.7	17	22.2	46	0	25.4	40
WS	192.1	32	94.4	50	97.5	12	130.8	27	1	NA	35

Ray Schalk was Captain Clean Sox. He was one of the few players on the 1919 White Sox not involved in throwing the World Series. This is honorable, but doesn't transform him into a good hitter.

And he was not a good hitter. An 83 OPS+ is pretty darn low. To give some perspective, 1980s catcher Tony Pena was at 82 for his career. It's a pretty solid comparison all around. Bill James has Pena 34th and Schalk 35th among catchers, and Pena's JAWS number is 24.6 while Schalk's is 25.4. Both Pena and Schalk rank as high as they do because they were great defensive players.

As I mentioned in the Carlton Fisk comment, the defensive numbers might be a bit skewed in favor of recent players. But even if you give Schalk 4 more defensive WAR to put him even with Tony Pena, you still don't get him anywhere near a Hall-of-Famer. I gave Roger Bresnahan some credit for playing in a time when catchers played less -- add that to the pile for Schalk and he's still not close to the top 20 catchers of all time.

One credential I haven't brought up much in these comments is postseason performance. It's not that I don't think it should count in a guy's favor. It's more that I look at it as a tiebreaker, one that could tip a close case. Making it an essential qualification for everyone is unfair to players like Ernie Banks who never had the good fortune to be surrounded by the kind of team that could make the playoffs.

As far as postseason performance, Schalk played pretty well in every game of the 1919 World Series, but as you know it was in a losing effort. Conspirators Shoeless Joe Jackson and Buck Weaver actually hit better (though they may have done a bunch of more subtle things to help throw games, but that's a topic for a different time). In the 1917 Series Schalk wasn't as good, but didn't embarrass himself.

Schalk deserves an extra few points for his World Series play. I still don't think it gets him over the hump of that career of bad hitting. The grand total isn't the worst Hall-of-Famer; Rick Ferrell's case is weaker. Schalk is close to the borderline, but still below it.

A message to be gained from Schalk is that it's very hard for defense alone to get you into the Hall of Fame. It's just not as important as hitting. Look at it this way: Winning baseball games is half scoring runs and half preventing them. For scoring runs, you have nine guys roughly dividing up the responsibility, with a caveat about pinch hitters, etc. That gives each player approximately one-ninth.

In the half of the game charged with preventing runs, there are the same nine guys, plus a pitcher. The pitcher has the lion's share of the responsibility, probably at least half. This leaves the position players with much less than one-ninth of the responsibility of preventing runs. Even a shortstop probably doesn't carry one-ninth of the burden, and I seriously doubt that catchers do.

If this sounds like gobbledygook, let's go back to the numbers. The all-time leader in offensive WAR among catchers is Mike Piazza, with 65.9. The all-time leader in defensive WAR among catchers is Ivan Rodriguez with 28.7. Ivan Rodriguez's all-time great defense added less than half as many wins to the standings as did Piazza's hitting.

Win Shares gives much more value to fielding, for reasons I covered in the introduction (which I told you to read, and if you didn't, you're not allowed to go back and read it now. Next time, follow instructions!) Rodriguez again wins the top spot in catcher defense, with 140.0 Win Shares. Yogi Berra leads in catcher offense, with 267.6. That's nearly twice as much value in Berra's hitting than Rodriguez's fielding. And keep in mind that catching is often a defense-first position. If we were talking about right fielders, you'd see hitting numbers ten times the defense numbers.

Players often make it into the Hall of Fame if they have a "hook," one trait that can look especially superlative. A few players have made it into the Hall with a hook of great defense. While it's certainly possible that a player could be so good defensively that it makes up for poor offense, I'm not seeing it with Schalk.

It's probably no shock at this point that, in my estimation, **Schalk is out**.

Who's In, Who's Out

I managed to cut out Rick Ferrell and Ray Schalk, leaving just 13 Hall of Fame catchers. That's a low total, but luckily, I have a lot of guys to replace them. I'll list them in descending order of most-deserving to most-marginal. I'm only including players retired as I write this, in 2015.

Ivan Rodriguez (1991-2011; career OPS+: 106)

	Career	Rank	Hitting	Rank	Fielding	Rank	Peak	Rank	Bests	JAWS	Rank
WAR	68.4	3	53.9	7	28.7	1	39.6	4	4	54.0	3
WS[7]	326.1	6	186.3	12	140.0	1	174.2	11	8	NA	7[8]

(Note: Win Shares numbers are through 2008, but I-Rod only had a few more bad years left, so he probably wouldn't be much higher if they kept calculating Win Shares. Bill James actually ranked Ivan Rodriguez 13th but did so in 2001, when Rodriguez had quite a few good years left. Instead I'm going with the average of Rodriguez's career and peak Win Shares (WSAWS), just like with Piazza.)

Ivan Rodriguez was the best defensive catcher of all time. That might not be Hall-of-Fame-worthy if he hit like Ray Schalk, but he definitely didn't. His career OPS+ is only as low as it is because he hung on long after the hits dried up; his defense remained so good that he kept getting work. I can't imagine anyone objecting to him as a Hall-of-Famer.

Well, actually, I can. Here steroids rear their ugly head. Not that Rodriguez has ever been an admitted user, but there are rumors. He once showed up on a list of players who had used steroids. That's not much of a case against him. But when he comes to the ballot, some people will decide to keep him out as a precaution until more evidence comes in, as they have with Jeff Bagwell.

---

[7] Win Shares numbers are through 2008, but I-Rod only had a few more bad years left, so he probably wouldn't be much higher if they kept calculating Win Shares.

[8] Bill James actually ranked Ivan Rodriguez 13th but did so in 2001, when Rodriguez had quite a few good years left. Instead I'm going with the average of Rodriguez's career and peak Win Shares, using the same formula used to calculate JAWS. Let's call that "WSAWS."

But what if it never does? Do we just lock out everyone who could have possibly maybe taken steroids at some point? Is everyone guilty until proven innocent? Moreover, what if they did use once and only once? Is it "one strike and you're out"?

I strongly suspect this extreme moral outrage over steroids, to the point where any conceivable user is tarred forever with a red "S," is one part genuine disgust and one part the guilt of the complicit, which converts itself, through the power of cognitive dissonance, into the rage of the betrayed.

I'll unpack that. We all thrilled at the home runs of the late 1990s, and breathlessly recounted how they were reviving interest in baseball from the doldrums of the 1994-1995 strike. Like an investor in mortgage bonds in 2006 or a teenager watching Hollywood sex scenes, we probably should have realized that what we were seeing was too good to be true. But we didn't want to think about it; it was too much fun to believe that this was the new reality.

Now that steroids have wrecked our fantasy party, we have to think about it. And like all human beings, we have a very deep, fundamental need to believe we are and always have been morally unimpeachable. People like us would never stand for such a thing, we think. That self-image of fundamental goodness is more important to us than the facts.

So, subconsciously, we convince ourselves that it's not us, it's them. We were just innocent victims who were duped by these evil characters. Our newfound righteous rage then gets inflicted on every player who carries a whiff of steroid-i-ness, including the catcher who had a surge of power while playing with Jose Canseco and Rafael Palmeiro.

If you want to dock Rodriguez a few points for maybe possibly having tried steroids, go ahead. But I'm pretty sure steroids didn't make him a major-league catcher at age 19 and a Gold Glove catcher at age 20. I'm pretty sure steroids were not the only reason he compiled 2427 games as a catcher, best in history by more than 200. It's possible steroids helped his hitting and recovery time from injuries. But I seriously doubt he would have been much worse without them (if he even did them, which is a big "if").

And I definitely don't think Ivan Rodriguez should spend more than one eligible year outside the Hall of Fame.

Ted Simmons (1968-1988, career OPS+: 118)

	Career	Rank	Hitting	Rank	Fielding	Rank	Peak	Rank	Bests	JAWS	Rank
WAR	50.1	11	53.0	9	4.7	69	34.7	12	0	42.4	10
WS	315.4	8	242.3	6	73.0	26	181.2	8	0	NA	10

I can see why Ted Simmons was overlooked for the Hall of Fame. Yet another catcher from the 1970s, Simmons was overshadowed by Bench, Fisk, and Carter. And playing in the 1970s meant his conventional hitting stats don't look overwhelming. Like Carter, he may have hung on too long and given people the impression that he wasn't Hall of Fame material.

But Simmons was a great hitter for a very long time. He managed to play 150 games in a season eight times, which is very rare for a catcher. He had five full seasons of OPS+ over 130, better than Fisk or Carter's totals (four each). Simmons wasn't the defensive player that Bench or Carter was, but he wasn't bad either.

Simmons was up for a recent Veterans Committee vote and didn't make it. I read one columnist arguing "no way that Simmons should be in before Mike Piazza." You get this argument a lot, that a good player should not get in before a better player does. It's a crazy idea. It's hard enough figuring who should be in and who should be out -- now we have to arrange them in the proper order for selection?

Does it really matter when players get into the Hall? Cy Young didn't get in until his second year of eligibility. Interesting factoid, but do you really care? Either way, he's in. In 1946, Jack Chesbro was selected by the Veterans Committee while Lefty Grove, who was about ten times better, got only 23% of his first final BBWAA vote. Who cares? They're both in; that's what counts.

Both WAR and Win Shares show Ted Simmons is good enough to be in the Hall of Fame, so he should be in. Simple as that.

Joe Torre (1960-1977; career OPS+: 129)

	Career	Rank	Hitting	Rank	Fielding	Rank	Peak	Rank	Bests	JAWS	Rank
WAR	57.6	7	59.4	4	-0.4	99	37.3	7	2	47.5	7
WS	313.4	9	258.2	2	55.3	55	188.2	6	3	NA	11

I don't need to put Torre here, because he is of course already in the Hall as a manager. I just wanted to highlight the fact that he may have been an even better player than manager.

The WAR rankings above put Joe Torre among catchers; in Baseball-reference.com, he is listed among the JAWS rankings for first base. I'm not sure why they did that, since Torre had more games, innings and WAR at catcher than any other position. Granted, he played a lot of first base and third base and didn't have a majority at one position. So maybe they thought it was unfair to compare the lifelong catchers with Torre.

Still, even if you list Torre among the first basemen, he's 24th in JAWS, and among third basemen, he'd be 17th. In neither case would he be a shoo-in, but he also wouldn't be out of place.

A big reason Torre moved around the diamond was that he wasn't a great defensive catcher. But he was a heck of a hitter. He was the best-hitting catcher of the 1960s by a wide margin. When he moved to third base with the Cardinals in 1971, he exploded, winning an MVP and collecting the second-best Win Shares total ever for a season by a third baseman, 41. (Number one was Al Rosen with 42 in 1953.) There were no shortage of other very good years masked as mediocre by the conventional statistics of the low-hitting 1960s and 1970s.

What the heck; let's put Joe Torre in the Hall twice.

Bill Freehan (1961, 1963-1976; career OPS+: 112)

	Career	Rank	Hitting	Rank	Fielding	Rank	Peak	Rank	Bests	JAWS	Rank
WAR	44.7	18	43.0	17	11.8	23	33.7	14	2	39.2	15
WS	264.9	12	175.1	15	89.6	14	177.6	10	3	NA	12

Freehan is yet another player whose offensive contributions look less impressive because he played in the 1960s and 1970s. Freehan had incredibly bad timing, doing his best hitting in 1967 and 1968, when offense was at its lowest point since the dead-ball era. Granted, even when normalized with OPS+, his career offensive contributions are very good but not on par with the top-tier Hall-of-Famers.

But he also was a very good defensive catcher. And the combination of very good offense and very good defense can be a very valuable thing. Take his 1968 season, which according to Win Shares was the third-best ever by a catcher. (I personally always hate it when people trot out rankings like that but don't tell me who else is in the list, so here they are are: Mike Piazza's 1997 and Johnny Bench's 1972.)

Freehan's conventional 1968 hitting stats might not look like barn-burners: .263 BA, .366 OBP, .454 SLG in 635 PAs. But this was 1968, when you could only score a run if you secretly switched Denny McLain's daily case of Pepsi with Coke.[9] Freehan's OPS+ that year was 9th in the AL. Win Shares ranks his 1968 offensive contribution as 10th of all time among catchers.

And of course, with a catcher, defense is a huge component. Freehan garnered 10.4 Fielding Win Shares in 1968. That's a very good total; only 43 catchers in history have ever reached 10 Fielding Win Shares in a season. Freehan's 1968 could be the best-ever combination of offense and defense by a catcher: only Gary Carter (in both 1982 and 1985) and Elston Howard (in 1964) also managed both 20 Batting Win Shares and 10 Fielding Win Shares in a season.

Sometimes a player doesn't need to have one big, bright, shiny characteristic to make him worthy of the Hall. He just needs to contribute in a lot of different ways. Often this type contributes more wins to the standings than the one-trick ponies. Freehan was one of those players. He won't make it on the Hall of Fame All-Star Team, but he deserves to be in.

Wally Schang (1913-1931; career OPS+: 117)

	Career	Rank	Hitting	Rank	Fielding	Rank	Peak	Rank	Bests	JAWS	Rank
WAR	45.0	17	47.4	15	3.5	78	25.2	30	3	35.1	20
WS	243.1	14	181.9	15	61.1	45	127.5	34	2	NA	20

The Hall of Fame picked the wrong 1910s and 1920s catcher with a last name starting with "Scha." Wally Schang's career spanned 1913-1931 and Ray Schalk's was from 1912-1929, but in every other way they were quite different.

Schalk was a great defensive player but a poor hitter; Schang was great offensive player but a mediocre fielder. If you read the Ray Schalk comment (as you should have), you know where my sympathies lie in the great defense vs. great offense debate.

Schang had 500 PAs in a season only once, which is largely due to the usage of catchers at the time. I gave Roger Bresnahan a bit of a boost for playing in an era when no catcher played a full season, and

[9] Reference explanation: Denny McLain went 31-4 in 1968 and had a weird addiction to Pepsi, drinking about a case per day. After his career was over he got involved in organized crime and went to jail for embezzlement. I'm no psychologist, but he has every marker of being a sociopath.

Schang should get the same boost. Schang's Peak numbers are low for the same reason, as he didn't get enough playing time each year to compile a lot of stats. It's similar to the way pitchers nowadays can't be compared directly to pitchers from the dead-ball era, who almost always pitched complete games.

I'm not saying Schang is a shoo-in by any means. But I feel comfortable with Schang taking Schalk's place in the Hall.

Gene Tenace (1969-1983; career OPS+: 136)

	Career	Rank	Hitting	Rank	Fielding	Rank	Peak	Rank	Bests	JAWS	Rank
WAR	46.8	13	47.4	14	1.6	91	34.9	11	1	40.9	14
WS	231.0	16	190.4	11	40.6	88	172.8	14	1	NA	23

I tried to resist, I really did. Despite what the above numbers say, I refused to accept that Gene Tenace could be a Hall-of-Famer. He had a short career of only 5,527 PAs. He was poor defensively and spent 40% of his career at first base. I already have a glut of catchers from the 1970s; Tenace's two best years, 1975 and 1976, also featured Johnny Bench, Gary Carter, Carlton Fisk, Bill Freehan, Ted Simmons and Joe Torre (though Torre was playing first and third at the time).

But after I looked closer at Tenace's hitting, I gave in. Only Mike Piazza has a better OPS+ among catchers with at least 3,000 career PAs. Tenace had power, but most of that OPS is from walks. And boy, the guy could walk. Fans the world over thrilled to the sight of him slowly trotting to first base. (Not really. That's the problem with walks: They're very important but very boring.) Tenace topped 100 walks six times and twice led the league. The walks brought him seven 20-Win Share seasons and one above 30. He also had three 5-WAR seasons and three others above 4.5.

OPS, and by extension, OPS+, is not perfect. A point of SLG is given equal weight to a point of OBP, even though almost all players are going to have a higher SLG. And getting on base another time is more valuable than a getting a single extra base; if you have the choice between two walks and a double, take the two walks. That gives you a chance of scoring two runs instead of one. Granted, two walks might not drive in a run, while a double almost certainly will. But that is relevant only when someone else is on base. It all gets complicated quickly, but when you work out all the odds, as many analysts have, you discover that OBP is more important than SLG.

My point is that Tenace's career 136+ OPS+ is even more impressive than it looks. He got that number by hitting .241/.388/.429. He would have had the same OPS+ if he'd hit .241/.368/.449, but would have produced fewer runs.

WAR and Win Shares do a better job weighting OBP and SLG, and they say he had the 11th or 14th best career hitting record for a catcher, despite only 5,527 PAs. In Hitting Win Shares per PA, Tenace is the all-time leader among catchers. He is also first among catchers in Hitting WAR per PA (if you leave out active players, who have an unfair advantage in stats like this because they haven't experienced the downswing of their later years). So per PA, Gene Tenace was the greatest-hitting catcher ever. That's pretty darn Hall-of-Fame-y.

Plus, he went by "Fury Gene Tenace," perhaps in preparation for a professional wrestling career that never transpired. "Fury" is not the first name I would associate with a guy whose value comes mostly from walks, but it's still fun. It's all an Anglicization of his real name, Fiore Gino Tennaci. I suppose there isn't any other reasonable Anglicization for "Fiore." "Furry Gene Tenace"? That sounds adorable, but it may not be ideal for a professional athlete.

Without Tenace, I have only 19 catchers in my corrected Hall of Fame, which would be the lowest total of any position. It's the toughest spot on the diamond, so you have to make allowances. I think such allowances allow Gene Tenace a place.

Chapter Three

~ ~ First Base ~ ~

First base, as you probably know, is the most offense-first position on the diamond. For the most part, it's where you stick guys who can hit very well but can't field. There is, of course, some skill involved in first base defense, but less than for any other position besides DH.

As such, I hesitate to even include the defensive stats in the below charts. In Defensive WAR, almost every first baseman has a negative career total. It's really hard for a first baseman to get a positive Defensive WAR in a season, for reasons I already discussed in the first chapter. The more seasons you play at first base, the more negative numbers you pile on, and the worse your career Defensive WAR total gets. You get punished for playing OK first base defense for a long time. Again, that replacement-value zero point is a problem. Pay attention to Win Shares' assessment of defense instead.

Or, as you do with real-life first basemen, you could probably just ignore the defense and concentrate on the hitting.

Cap Anson (1871-1897; career OPS+: 142)

	Career	Rank	Hitting	Rank	Fielding	Rank	Peak	Rank	Bests	JAWS	Rank
WAR	93.9	5	90.9	4	4.8	2	41.8	17	6	67.9	5
WS	379.5	9	338.1	8	40.6	8	168.7	40	3	NA	11

Cap Anson is a monumental figure in baseball history. He's important not only because of his stellar batting record, but also because of his role in popularizing the sport. He started his professional career in 1871 at age 19 (with a team called the Rockford Forest Citys -- I love these 1800s team names.) By the time Anson retired in 1897, at age 45, he had done more than anyone to make sure that professional baseball would survive.

The 1800s were a time of constant turmoil in baseball. Leagues and teams rapidly formed and folded, players frequently broke contracts and switched teams, and fundamental rules were tinkered with to make for a better viewing experience. Throughout it all, the larger-than-life, egomaniacal Anson was a fixture, working tirelessly to promote the game and win over fans.

His stats are perhaps even more impressive than all that. Anson managed 3,435 hits despite spending his 20s in leagues that played 50-80 league games per season. He could have approached 5,000 hits in a career of 162-game years. The Win Shares totals above are incomplete, as they start in 1876, after Anson already had five great years under his belt with a short-lived league called the National Association.

Anson was also a very successful manager, winning five pennants in the 1880s. His success came largely because he adopted many then-revolutionary strategies, including signals, the hit-and-run, platoons, and spring training. He was one the first to realize that maybe pitchers shouldn't pitch every day, that the team would be better served if you put them in a rotation. Very few people had a greater impact on the game of baseball.

Let's throw in a wrinkle, though. In Cap Anson's time, baseball was still struggling with whether to allow African-American players. Many were for it, and many were against it. Anson was a vocal opponent. He didn't single-handedly ban African-American players, but his voice carried a lot of weight.

It is of course a terrible injustice that African-American players were banned from the so-called "major" leagues. That's hardly an original sentiment. Here's a newer one: In helping ban African-American players, didn't Anson tip the balance of the game in his favor? Because many good players were banned, Anson, and indeed all white players, end up with better stats. Instead of facing the best white and best African-American pitchers, white hitters faced the best white and the lesser white pitchers. This "inflates" their stats compared to what they would have been if the playing field had been fair and inclusive.

Isn't this the same underlying principle that makes us angry at steroid users? Drugs pump up your achievements unnaturally, which perverts fair competition. And without fair competition, you don't have a game. The stats and achievements of those players are untrustworthy, because something besides just talent and hard work was responsible for creating them. Is Anson guilty of the same thing?

I know, taking steroids and banning black players feel very different. They're horrible in very different ways. And while those who use steroids get an unfair advantage over those who choose not to, banning black players gives an unfair advantage to all white players, regardless of their personal choices. It's not a perfect analogy, but I think it's an interesting thought.

I'm just throwing this idea out there. As repulsed as I am by Anson's racism, the Hall of Fame is not a Hall of Decent People. It's Hall of People Who Could Hit, Catch, and/or Throw Baseballs Very Well. I don't think my argument is nearly strong enough to keep Cap Anson out of the Hall of Fame.

Jake Beckley (1888-1907; career OPS+: 125)

	Career	Rank	Hitting	Rank	Fielding	Rank	Peak	Rank	Bests	JAWS	Rank
WAR	61.5	17	59.3	18	-0.4	14	29.8	47	2	45.7	26
WS	316.7	20	256.5	26	35.1	21	141.1	76	2	NA	52

Like Cap Anson, Jake Beckley had tremendous longevity in a time when players tended to have shorter careers. Unlike Anson, that's pretty much all there is to say about Beckley.

That's not entirely fair. Beckley was a good hitter; a 125 OPS+ in more than 10,000 PAs is nothing to sneeze at. He was known as a good fielder, but had such a poor arm that runners knew they could always take an extra base when he had the ball. Defensive WAR and Win Shares for first basemen are a bit messy, as I mentioned in the first part of this chapter, but both put him a respectable range.

For what it's worth, Beckley was also a popular player and a true character. His favorite word to shout at opposing pitchers was "chickazoola!", which made about as much sense then as it does now. He always sported a large, bushy mustache, even into the early 1900s, when facial hair was about as passe as a Kid 'n' Play haircut in 1996.[10] His favorite thing to do was try the hidden ball trick on every rookie he met.

The problem with Beckley as a Hall-of-Famer is that he had no truly great seasons. Look at the Peak numbers. Win Shares has Beckley's seven best seasons on par with the seven best seasons of Tino Martinez and Eric Karros. WAR is a bit more charitable, putting his peak near that of Mark Grace or Cecil Cooper. All were good players, but not Hall-of-Famers.

Of course, neither Grace nor Cooper had Beckley's longevity. If Mark Grace had collected 2,934 hits like Beckley did, would he have been a Hall-of-Famer? Some might say yes, some might say no. (I would definitely say no, but mostly out of spite. An ex-girlfriend who dumped me was in love with Mark Grace, even though she was a big Twins fan and thus never rooted for his team. Somehow Grace inspired that kind of weird devotion, despite always being a good-but-not-great kind of player.)

Beckley also reminds me of Harold Baines, who also got close to 3,000 hits but was seldom really great. But that's not entirely fair either, because Baines was mostly a DH, thus contributing nothing on defense. First base is the least valuable position defensively, but at least it's something.

Beckley was the best first baseman in baseball twice according to both WAR and Win Shares. In 1893 he led with a 4.5 WAR, good for seventh among all non-pitchers in baseball. That same year he got 17 Win Shares, leading first basemen, but ranking 25th amongst hitters. (Win Shares does not like Beckley much.) In 1900, his 4.3 WAR led first basemen, and again Win Shares agrees that he topped 1Bs, with 21. WAR has him as sixth among all non-pitchers in 1900 and Win Shares puts him 11th.

In no other year is Beckley among the top ten in WAR, and Win Shares never has him in the top ten for any season. So if you believe WAR, Beckley may have been a legitimate MVP candidate once; if you believe Win Shares, he never was. He was a guy who always contributed, but would never be the star player of a championship-quality team.

And indeed, there are no postseason heroics to add to Beckley's resume, as his teams never won a pennant. He shouldn't be downgraded for never having good enough teammates to win a championship, but he obviously doesn't get any boost.

In the end, is longevity enough? Does Jake Beckley need to be immortalized just for playing pretty well for a very long time? Do we really need to remember him? It's a tough call, but I'm thinking no. **Beckley is out.**

Jim Bottomley (1922-1937; career OPS+: 125)

	Career	Rank	Hitting	Rank	Fielding	Rank	Peak	Rank	Bests	JAWS	Rank
WAR	35.3	56	42.8	35	-15.8	86	28.7	51	0	32.0	55
WS	258.8	43	232.6	38	26.0	58	169.8	39	0	NA	36

[10] Reference explanation: Kid of Kid 'n' Play had a giant cylinder of hair on his head that looked like a pencil eraser. They were big in 1989, when hip-hop was goofy, poppy, and day-glo colored. By 1996, gangsta rap had taken over, and chart-topping rappers were being killed for being from the wrong coast of the United States. I'm guessing Kid had shaved his head around 1991 and secured himself in a safehouse throughout the decade.

That last one was a tough one. This one is easy. Jim Bottomley was a good power hitter in the 1920s, when there weren't many of those. He played for a number of great Cardinals teams. His nickname was "Sunny Jim," and everyone loves a nice guy.

He's clearly not a Hall-of-Famer. Bottomley was one of the many hitters from the 1920s and 1930s to be elected because he had a few nice-looking conventional numbers and played with Frankie Frisch (I'll explain that in the George Kelly comment -- suspense!). He ranks about even with Kent Hrbek in WAR and OPS+ numbers. Bill James has him ranked near Wally Joyner and that Hrbek fellow again. No amount of postseason success would make that sort of player a Hall-of-Famer, and Bottomley had just some, hitting well in the 1926 and 1928 World Serieses but poorly in the 1930 and 1931 ones.

Jim Bottomley is the kind of player who's good enough to make a single team's Hall of Fame, and indeed he is in the St. Louis Cardinals one. But he's not good enough to make the national one. **Bottomley is out.**

Dan Brouthers (1879-1896, 1904; career OPS+: 170)

	Career	Rank	Hitting	Rank	Fielding	Rank	Peak	Rank	Bests	JAWS	Rank
WAR	79.4	9	81.6	6	-1.8	19	47.2	9	6	63.3	9
WS	354.7	12	326.6	11	25.2	66	200.2	17	4	NA	18

Dan Brouthers was the best major-league hitter in the years before the offensive explosion of 1894. He led his league in OPS+ six straight years, from 1882-1887, and then again in 1892 and 1893. He had the best WAR among all non-pitchers four times. He's tied for seventh among all players in major league history in OPS+ (with the caveat that he played with a lot of terrible players who lowered the averages, thus boosting his number).

He is also the best hitter in the history of the initial incarnation of the Buffalo Bisons, which is kind of a redundant team name and kind of not. The animal we Americans call a buffalo is actually a bison -- no true buffalos have ever been native to the Western Hemisphere. So there's a fact you can whip out at dinner parties if you're hoping to get people to say "Hmm, that's interesting ...", leave an awkward pause, and then change the subject.

One other interesting fact, and this one is actually relevant: After his retirement from baseball, Brouthers did not move to Florida and work on a beer belly the way modern players do. You didn't make that kind of money playing baseball in his day. Instead he worked as an assistant watchman at the Polo Grounds, along with fellow ex-Giant and Hall-of-Famer Amos Rusie. John McGraw intimated that he got both of them the job because of the sympathy he felt for old ballplayers. Retirement wasn't really "retirement" in those days; it was more of an abrupt, mid-life career change. Baseball stardom did not set you for life; it left you as a middle-aged guy with little in the way of marketable skills or experience.

At any rate, if any player from the 1880s deserves to be in the Hall, it's Dan Brouthers.

Rod Carew (1967-1985; career OPS+: 132)

	Career	Rank	Hitting	Rank	Fielding	Rank	Peak	Rank	Bests	JAWS	Rank
WAR	81.0	7	80.4	7	-2.4	24	49.8	5	3	65.4	7
WS	385.5	8	331.9	10	53.5	2	201.5	16	1	NA	9

Bill James lists Carew among the second basemen, but the Hall of Fame lists him as a first baseman, perhaps because he had 50 more games there. According to WAR, he had the second-greatest season of the 1970s when he played first base in 1977. (Can you guess who had the best season of the 1970s? The answer is in the Joe Morgan comment. No spoilers!) Regardless of Carew's position, he's clearly a Hall-of-Famer, and you probably remember him, so I doubt I have to convince you.

One other note about Carew: He could have been a lifelong Minnesota Twin if owner Calvin Griffith hadn't said some very racist things. At a Lion's Club meeting in 1978, Griffith was asked why he chose to move the club from Washington to Minnesota. He said to the crowd, "I'll tell you why we came to Minnesota. It was when we found out you only had 15,000 blacks here. Black people don't go to ballgames, but they'll fill up a rassling (sic) ring and put up such a chant it'll scare you to death. It's unbelieveable. We came here because you've got good, hardworking white people here." (Source: "Griffith spares few targets in Waseca remarks," Minneapolis Star-Tribune, Nick Coleman, October 1, 1978).

More recently, Los Angeles Clippers owner Donald Sterling admonished his girlfriend to not be photographed with black people. It came after a career of discriminatory comments and behaviors. Sterling was summarily banned from basketball for life.

Griffith didn't suffer a similar punishment in 1978. He was universally despised, and tried to find ways to apologize for the rest of his life. Eventually he got to the point where he could barely admit that the Lions Club incident had even occurred. But unlike Sterling, he got to keep his team.

He didn't get to keep Carew, though. After hearing about the comments, Carew called Griffith a bigot and refused to be "another slave on his plantation." It also didn't help that Griffith consistently underpaid Carew, and in the fateful Lions Club meeting said Carew was a "damn fool" for sticking with the Twins despite the low salary. (I recommend reading the whole article about the incident; it's pretty crazy stuff.) Carew was quickly traded to the Angels for a pack of ho-hum players.

The Twins weren't very good at the time, but losing Carew definitely didn't help. It took another African-American star, Kirby Puckett, to lead them to glory in 1987. By that time Griffith had sold the team to local billionaire and budding C. Montgomery Burns[11] impersonator Carl Pohlad, so Griffith never got to own a winning team. I don't know if that's justice or not, but maybe it's close.

---

[11] C. Montgomery Burns is the name of the ancient, cruel power plant owner from "The Simpsons." He was basically Carl Pohlad. Pohlad was a miserly old plutocrat who tried several times to rip the Twins from Minnesota, presumably because the team wasn't producing enough thousand-dollar bills to paper his maid's maid's toilet. I saw him at a Twins Fest once and the resemblance to Mr. Burns was unmistakable. He even had a sycophantic Mr. Smithers who kept smiling children at a safe distance. Luckily, Pohlad's kids and heirs have turned out to be pretty cool. One of them, Bill Pohlad, is a

Orlando Cepeda (1958-1974; career OPS+: 133)

	Career	Rank	Hitting	Rank	Fielding	Rank	Peak	Rank	Bests	JAWS	Rank
WAR	50.2	31	50.2	28	-14.0	82	34.4	35	2	42.3	32
WS	310.2	23	262.8	23	25.6	62	191.2	26	2	NA	17

This is a tough one. WAR has Cepeda in the neighborhood of Carlos Delgado and Fred McGriff -- great power hitters who wouldn't be ridiculous in the Hall of Fame, but probably won't make it. Bill James likes Cepeda better, but still puts him close to Keith Hernandez and Dick Allen, far from the greatest of all time.

Cepeda's conventional numbers don't look super-impressive largely because he played in the 1960s, when you could only score a run if Sandy Koufax's arm fell off in the fourth inning. The OPS+ stat gets beyond those biases, and Cepeda has the same career OPS+ as Earl Averill, Fred Clarke, Chick Hafey, Todd Helton, Charlie Hickman, Al Simmons, Danny Tartabull and Billy Williams. Those are all Hall-of-Famers (with varying degrees of worthiness) except Hickman and Tartabull, who had short careers, and Helton, who will hopefully get in someday.

Still, it bothers me that neither system has Cepeda's Career or Peak numbers ranking above 20. He was a bad fielder, for what that's worth for a first baseman. He was also not great in postseason play, with a .202/.242/.368 line in 91 PAs.

I'm tempted to kick Cepeda out. But Bill James' ranking of 17th overall keeps reining me back in. I don't think I would have voted to elect Cepeda to the Hall. But that doesn't necessarily mean I want to cut him. I'm trying to pretend-remove the guys who are well below the line, not at or near it. Cepeda is perhaps as borderline as borderline cases get. But in such cases, the tie goes to the status quo. Cepeda stays in.

Frank Chance (1898-1914; career OPS+: 135)

	Career	Rank	Hitting	Rank	Fielding	Rank	Peak	Rank	Bests	JAWS	Rank
WAR	45.6	36	40.1	40	2.8	4	35.7	31	4	40.7	34
WS	236.2	54	213.8	48	22.2	83	176.9	34	4	NA	25

Frank Chance was known as the "Peerless Leader" of the 1906-10 Chicago Cubs, when they were the dominant team in baseball, reaching four World Serieseseses and winning two. Included in that stretch was a 1906 season in which the Cubs went 116-36, the best record in baseball history.

Chance was the star hitter and manager of the club. In those days managers also served as general managers, scouts, coaches, mascots, peanut vendors, ticket takers, obnoxious fans, umpires, and

---

Hollywood producer responsible for "Brokeback Mountain," "12 Years a Slave," "Into the Wild," and several other great films.

Morgannas the Kissing Bandits.[12] More than anyone besides previous manager Frank Selee, Frank Chance deserves credit for the Cubs' last dynasty.

Chance's WAR numbers are not high, but that's largely because he managed only 5103 plate appearances. He had a long list of injuries from many life-threatening beanings. These were the days before batting helmets, and Frank Chance always defiantly crowded the plate. He kept doing it even after the plunkings resulted in hearing loss, blood clots in his brain that required surgery, and, for some reason, a weird, high-pitched voice.

This voice must have seemed especially odd coming from a very hard-nosed guy like Chance, who was known for starting brawls and working as an amateur boxer in the offseason. Once, when Brooklyn fans were throwing beer bottles at him, he threw one back into the crowd. It was a very different time.

When Chance did manage to stay on the field, he was superb. He only had six full seasons, but in four of those he registers as the best first baseman in baseball according to both WAR and Win Shares. He had 31 Win Shares in 1903, behind only Honus Wagner and Jimmy Sheckard among major-league non-pitchers, and 35 in 1906, behind only Wagner, George Stone and Art Devlin.

Chance hit well in the World Series, especially in 1908 and 1910. His career World Series numbers are 82 PAs of .300/.402/.371. That's a plus in his favor.

Sigh ... if only he stayed healthy ... but I don't give Chance any special allowances for time missed because of injuries, especially when he's sticking his darn fool blood-clot-filled head in front of pitches. If he didn't also manage the Cubs I'd probably kick him out. But he did, to the tune of a .664 winning percentage. He led the greatest team in Cubs history, and probably the greatest team in National League history. Chance stays.

Roger Connor (1880-1897; career OPS+: 153)

	Career	Rank	Hitting	Rank	Fielding	Rank	Peak	Rank	Bests	JAWS	Rank
WAR	84.1	6	78.8	8	6.3	1	47.0	10	7	65.6	6
WS	362.5	11	310.7	14	37.7	13	195.8	22	3	NA	22

If you're trying to memorize the Baseball Hall of Fame (and you should quit your job immediately and devote your life to doing so), pair Dan Brouthers and Roger Connor in your mind. Both were dominant hitters in the 1800s, both peaking before the cuckoo-ball 1894 offensive explosion. They were teammates on the 1880 Troy Trojans. Connor was the one who stuck with the team.

Troy, in case you're wondering, is a city in upstate New York, near Albany, that has never had more than around 77,000 people. In the early 1870s, teams were formed when a few rich guys decided to hire ten ballplayers (one for each position plus one utility man) and see what happened. In the National Association, the predecessor to the National League, you just needed a $10 entry fee and a gleam in your eye, and your team could go on tour to compete against Cap Anson's Philadelphia Athletics.

[12] Reference explanation: Morganna the Kissing Bandit was a fan who would run onto baseball fields and kiss players on the cheek during the 1970s and 1980s.

This was not a good system. Most such teams, like the Fort Wayne Kekiongas and the Elizabeth Resolutes, collapsed after a few dozen games and left little mark. They'd lose so much money that they'd refuse to play out the rest of the season, and no one could force them to. The first Troy team, the Haymakers, were like that: Their history consists of 54 games over two seasons from 1871-1872. If remembered for anything, it would be for their big slugger, Jewish-American Lipman Pike.

The Troy Trojans were different. In 1879, they joined the National League, which had stricter controls about finishing up seasons. Apart from Connor, the Trojans fielded Hall-of-Famers Buck Ewing, Tim Keefe, and Mickey Welch.

Despite their star power, the Trojans were mediocre. In 1883, the team was disbanded and replaced by a team in a slightly bigger market, New York City. The New York Gothams' name was soon changed to the New York Giants, the same Giants we know and love today. I've never been to Troy, but I'd hope they're proud of their town's contributions to baseball.

The "Giants" name may have been a reference to their star first baseman Roger Connor, who at 6'3" and 220 pounds was positively massive for his time. Connor would have been a bit abashed that the team chose its name to honor him. He was a quiet, dignified man, never starring in the many crazy stories that come out of the rough and lawless days of 1800s baseball.

As such, he was largely forgotten until Hank Aaron broke Babe Ruth's career home run mark in 1974. People started to wonder who had the record before Ruth, and it turned out to be Roger Connor. Connor's batting record was rediscovered and he was rushed into the Hall of Fame, where he clearly belongs.

Jimmie Foxx (1925-1942, 1944-1945; career OPS+: 163)

	Career	Rank	Hitting	Rank	Fielding	Rank	Peak	Rank	Bests	JAWS	Rank
WAR	96.4	4	94.3	3	-5.5	41	59.5	4	4	78.0	4
WS	434.4	3	381.9	4	45.4	4	244.5	4	4	NA	2

Many first baseman and outfielders from the 1930s got into the Hall of Fame because they have a few inflated numbers. I'll be savagely chopping out many of these guys in the pages to come.

Jimmie Foxx, though, won't be going anywhere. Even if you deflate his numbers a bit to account for the era, they're still spectacular. He's considered the second-best first baseman of all time, unless you count Stan Musial as a first baseman, as I do in the above. WAR ranks Albert Pujols higher, but barely.

On top of it all, Foxx earned 2.1 Win Shares as a pitcher. In 1945, when he was 37 years old, he pitched 22.2 great innings, with a 1.59 ERA. Granted, it was a war year, and many of the good hitters were off showing Tojo what a little American moxie can do. Still, a 37-year-old first baseman suddenly logging 22 terrific relief innings -- you gotta love that. Jimmie Foxx is an inner-circle Hall-of-Famer.

Lou Gehrig (1923-1939; career OPS+: 179)

	Career	Rank	Hitting	Rank	Fielding	Rank	Peak	Rank	Bests	JAWS	Rank
WAR	112.4	2	112.1	2	-8.9	61	67.8	1	9	90.1	2
WS	489.6	2	456.7	2	32.8	32	278.7	2	9	NA	1

I mentioned that Jimmie Foxx is considered the second-best first baseman ever if you don't count Stan Musial as a first baseman (as all the above stats do, except Bill James' overall ranking). By that same measure, Lou Gehrig is clearly the best. For all Gehrig's second-place finishes above, Musial is first, largely because Musial had a longer career. Gehrig is fourth all-time among all players in career OPS+, behind Babe Ruth, Ted Williams, and Barry Bonds. I don't think even Albert Pujols has a chance to overtake Gehrig.

I'm one of those jaded, ironic Generation-X types who never saw anything that he couldn't roll his eyes at. Of course, I'd heard parodies of the Lou Gehrig "luckiest man on the face of the Earth" speech a hundred times. But when I saw the whole speech as part of Ken Burns' "Baseball" documentary, I cried like a baby. It still gives me chills just thinking about it. Of course, I then gather myself and tell everyone that I meant those chills ironically, but down deep I know the truth.

One other note about Gehrig: He had more nicknames than Ol' Dirty Bastard.[13] You probably know he was "The Iron Horse" because of his 2131-game playing streak. You may have also heard that he was known as "Larrupin' Lou," presumably because he "larruped" frequently and with alacrity. (I looked it up: "Larrup" means to "flog soundly.")

One nickname you may not have heard was "Ol' Biscuit Pants." This referred to the fact that Gehrig had baggy trousers covering thick legs and a rather, ahem, generous posterior. Even Lou Gehrig wasn't so respected that he couldn't endure a little good-natured razzing. Gehrig is a central member of the Hall of Fame.

Hank Greenberg (1930, 1933-1941, 1945-1947; career OPS+: 158)

	Career	Rank	Hitting	Rank	Fielding	Rank	Peak	Rank	Bests	JAWS	Rank
WAR	57.5	22	55.9	20	-4.3	34	47.7	8	2	52.6	16
WS	266.7	36	240.5	32	26.2	58	216.9	9	1	NA	8

Hank Greenberg was a Lou Gehrig/Jimmie Foxx type with a shorter career because of three years of service in World War II, when he was 31-33 years old. After single-handedly winning the Battle of Wake Island by beating Hitler's head in with a bat (I'm not as good with military history as I am with baseball history), he returned to lead the league in home runs and RBIs in 1946. Clearly he should be

[13] Reference explanation: "Ol' Dirty Bastard" was the most common nom de rap for Russell Jones, but he had loads of others ("Ranking All of Ol' Dirty Bastard's 28 Nicknames," Uproxx.com, Josh Karp, November 15, 2012). He was also Osirus, Ason Unique, Dirt Dog, Peanut the Kidnapper, Joe Bananas, The Man of All Rainbows, Dirt McGirt, Big Baby Jesus, and about 20 more.

given credit for those years. Greenberg's peak rankings should be given more credence than his career ones.

Side note of interest: Greenberg was the first Jewish-American baseball superstar. At 6'4", with broad shoulders and towering home runs, he defied the prevailing stereotypes of Jewish men being small and unathletic. Anti-semitism raged in Europe, of course, but was rampant in the United States as well. Greenberg was barraged with racial epithets by opposing teams, perhaps the worst offenders being the Gas House Gang Cardinals during the 1934 World Series. He pushed on through this treatment, but it stuck with him. When Jackie Robinson was a rookie in 1947, Greenberg befriended him and helped him deal with the abuse.

Greenberg's experience isn't a legitimate parallel to Robinson's, in that Greenberg didn't break down a strict barrier. Fellow Jewish-Americans Moe Berg and George Stone had preceded him in the majors, and, if you recall, a nice Jewish boy named Lipman Pike was a star with the Troy Haymakers in 1871. But as a Jewish-American star playing in the 1930s, Greenberg did change a lot of people's minds. I'd add this to his qualifications for the Hall of Fame.

Even if you don't agree with that, Greenberg makes it on his batting record alone. A definite Hall-of-Famer.

George Kelly (1915-1917, 1919-1930, 1932; career OPS+: 109)

	Career	Rank	Hitting	Rank	Fielding	Rank	Peak	Rank	Bests	JAWS	Rank
WAR	25.2	90	20.8	97	-1.2	18	23.9	77	0	24.6	85
WS	193.3	81	155.3	82	30.1	42	145.0	66	1	NA	65

George "Highpockets" Kelly is yet another player from baseball's golden age of the 1920s and 1930s. Like Foxx, Gehrig and Greenberg, he played first base. Also similar to these greats, Kelly had two arms, two eyes, and countless fingers (actually, ten very countable fingers). The comparisons end there.

Even if you only look at the conventional numbers, Kelly is unimpressive. He had good power for his time, but still managed only a .297/.342/.452 BA/OBP/SLG line. That puts him in the range of Wally Joyner, John Mayberry and Mike Hargrove. But even that's too generous for Kelly, as he had 95% of his at-bats in the high-offense 1920s. In terms of OPS+, he's closer to Tino Martinez and Chris Chambliss. His company in JAWS consists of Carlos Pena and Ryan Klesko. Bill James has him near Bill Buckner and Chambliss.

Kelly's Giants won the pennant every year from 1921-1924. But he never played very well in the Series. During each of those seasons he was never the best player on his team, always behind Frankie Frisch and Ross Youngs and usually behind Dave Bancroft.

George Kelly even has the most boring possible name for the Hall. Other members include King Kelly, Joe Kelley and George Kell. George Kelly might as well be John Doe.

You get the idea: George Kelly is as worthy of the Hall of Fame as I am. As Method Man might say, if he were passionate about first basemen's qualifications for the Hall of Fame, "What the blood clot?" (There's another reference for me and the world's other two baseball history/hip-hop fans. Don't ask what it means,)

Sometimes, you understand a little bit why the unworthy HOFers got in. Jim Bottomley was part of some great teams, had a fun personality, and put up some impressive-looking seasons. Jake Beckley had so many hits that it just seems, at first blush, like he should be above the cut-off. George Kelly, though, is baffling.

In "Whatever Happened to the Hall of Fame," Bill James provides some explanation. From 1967-1973, The Veterans Committee was dominated by Frankie Frisch. Like most old ballplayers, he was certain that the fellows he played with were the best players ever, in ways that don't show up in the numbers, much better than those goshdarn players nowadays who are only interested in money and what's wrong with these kids and their hully-gully dancing, etc.

Frisch didn't do it by himself, of course. His partners in crime on the Veterans Committee were former Giants teammate Bill Terry and sportswriters Fred Lieb and Dan Daniel, who covered the Giants, and sportswriter J. Roy Stockton, who covered Frisch's Cardinals teams. When Frisch died in 1973, Terry, Lieb, and Daniel carried the torch and threw in a couple more undeserving players.

The point is, George Kelly played with Frankie Frisch on some good Giants teams in the 1920s, and that pretty much got him in. Not in my America. **Kelly is out.**

Harmon Killebrew (1954-1975; career OPS+: 143)

	Career	Rank	Hitting	Rank	Fielding	Rank	Peak	Rank	Bests	JAWS	Rank
WAR	60.3	18	71.2	12	-18.8	95	38.1	27	0	49.2	21
WS	372.0	10	337.1	9	34.8	22	210.6	14	1	NA	7

I'm downright shocked that Charmin' Harmon fares so poorly in the WAR numbers. Not Harmon! He's the most adorable power hitter in history! He's the hero of my hometown team, the Twins! He was very friendly to every young player he met, and had a weird obsession with convincing them to make their autographs readable! (Seriously, at a ceremony honoring him after he died, every active player came to the podium with the same story about Harmon insisting that that their autographs be legible. I felt bad for them; it was like watching teenage girls come to prom to discover they're all wearing the same dress.)

More relevantly, Killebrew had 9833 PAs of a 143 OPS+, the latter of which ties him with Alex Rodriguez, Mike Piazza and Eddie Mathews. Could his defense have been so bad that it knocked him to the margins of Hall of Fame?

Well, Bill James likes him better. And even by WAR, Killebrew is still qualified, if barely. I'm saying he's a Hall-of-Famer.

Buck Leonard (1934-1948)

	Rank at Position Among Negro Leaguers	Rank Among All Negro Leaguers
Bill James	1	8
SABR	1	1
Monte Irvin	1	NA

Negro League teams were almost always on the edge of bankruptcy. They had to provide entertainment, by any means necessary, to keep people coming back. First basemen were expected to be the clowns of the field, in a sort of Harlem Globetrotters sort of way. Nothing against that approach (and maybe baseball could use a bit of it nowadays), but Buck Leonard just couldn't do it. It just wasn't in him; he was a serious, dignified, all-business kind of guy. He was a Rakim in a world of Biz Markies.[14] Leonard got away with bucking (pun!) the trend because he hit so well.

Leonard played for the Homestead Grays for all of his 15-year career, an extreme rarity in Negro League baseball. Players regularly jumped from team to team, as better offers came their way. Leonard was paid five times the average Negro League salary so he would stick around.

I mention this not as an indictment of Leonard or Negro League players, by the way. Salaries were very low overall, so when some starry-eyed businessman decides he wants to give you twice as much money to play on a championship-level team, you take it. I'm betting you've made similar moves in your career.

In fact, in the 1800s, white baseball worked much the same way. Players switched teams and broke contracts regularly, without consequences. Eventually National League founder William Hulbert established the reserve clause, which bound a player to his team forever. It was draconian -- imagine if you could never quit your company to work somewhere else -- but it did make things much more stable.

Anyway, Leonard and Josh Gibson made for a Ruth-Gehrig combo with the Homestead Grays. The Grays started in Pittsburgh, but the city also had the Pittsburgh Crawfords, and never had a large enough black population to support two teams. So in 1937, Homestead moved to Washington D.C., a.k.a. "Chocolate City," according to George Clinton. There they won nine straight Negro National League titles.

The Grays sometimes played in Griffith Stadium, home of the American League's Washington Senators. Monte Irvin tells a story about Clark Griffith, the owner of the Senators, sitting in his office watching Gibson and Leonard blast home runs. Allegedly Griffith was close to bringing Gibson and Leonard to the Senators, about ten years before Jackie Robinson's debut. But Griffith was just too afraid to pull the trigger. (Ironically, Clark was the adoptive father of Calvin Griffith, the man who moved the Senators to Minnesota because it had fewer African-Americans.)

On the one hand, cheers to Griffith for seriously considering breaking the color line in a big, dramatic way. Jeers for chickening out. But then, Washington D.C. in 1937 was not Brooklyn in 1946. I'll bet Griffith was nervous about his potential players' safety playing so close to a then-very segregated South. In comparison, 1946 Brooklyn was a melting pot, with no Jim Crow laws in effect for hundreds of miles. And in 1946, the case for civil rights was strengthened by the contributions of black soldiers in World War II.

But man, what if? If Griffith had brought on Gibson and Leonard, maybe he could have tipped Washington into contention. Maybe the Senators could have become a legendary team, and could have stayed in Washington to this day, rather than moving to that lame old icebox Minnesota in 1961.

---

[14] Again with the hip-hop references. This one is actually relevant though. In the mid-'80s, rap was dominated by jokey songs, the best of which were made by Biz Markie. Then Rakim burst on to the scene with a very serious style in songs like "I Ain't No Joke." Rakim is still considered one of the most brilliant rappers in history, while most of the jokey rappers have faded from memory.

More importantly, maybe both Gibson and Leonard could have had Jackie Robinson-esque bursts into the national spotlight. Imagine two players supporting each other through the brutal gauntlets of firmly entrenched racism and the world's best (white) competition. Both, together, could have proven not only that African-Americans can compete with white players, but also beat them soundly. It would have radically changed baseball, of course, but it also could have changed the civil rights struggle in dramatic ways.

These kinds of dreams are besides the point. Buck Leonard was one of the best Negro League players in history, and thus one of the best baseball players in history. He's in.

Willie McCovey (1959-1980; career OPS+: 147)

	Career	Rank	Hitting	Rank	Fielding	Rank	Peak	Rank	Bests	JAWS	Rank
WAR	64.4	14	71.7	11	-21.8	98	44.8	14	3	54.6	13
WS	406.6	5	376.4	5	26.3	57	223.4	7	4	NA	9

I always put Harmon Killebrew and Willie McCovey together in my mind: Both are power-hitting 1960s first basemen who made it into the 500-HR club (which I can recite in order for you right now. OK, here goes ... where are you going?) WAR indicates that McCovey was a bit better, and Bill James ranks Killebrew a bit higher in his final assessment. WAR says McCovey was the worst-fielding first baseman with 3000 or more PAs in history, (the third-worst being Killebrew), which is of course his punishment for playing a long time. However you slice it, both he and Killebrew are Hall-of-Famers.

Johnny Mize (1936-1942, 1946-1953; career OPS+: 158)

	Career	Rank	Hitting	Rank	Fielding	Rank	Peak	Rank	Bests	JAWS	Rank
WAR	71.0	12	69.2	14	-6.5	50	48.8	6	5	59.9	10
WS	336.6	18	299.3	16	25.2	67	222.2	8	5	NA	6

Mize is yet another in the Gehrig/Foxx/Greenberg mold, a big-hitting first baseman from the big-hitting years. Mize actually started his career a bit later than those guys, when offense was starting to cool down a bit. That makes his stats look even better in context.

If you looked at Mize's body in any context, you'd have a good idea what kind of hitter he was. He was a big lumbering guy, so of course he was very slow and hit lots of home runs. He played first base because the DH hadn't been invented yet.

A smile seldom left his face. Born and raised in Georgia, Mize was easygoing and kind in a good ol' relaxed Southern way. He sat on the bench in a white linen suit drinking mint juleps, fannin' himself with a floppy hat and sayin' "y'all come back now, y'hear?" over and over until his teammates shouted "We get it, you're Southern!" (That last sentence is an unsubstantiated rumor that I just made up.)

You might not look at Mize and predict his strikeout rate, which was quite low. Strikeouts were much rarer across baseball in those days, but Mize took it to an extreme. In 1947, he hit 50 home runs but had fewer than 50 strikeouts. He is still the only player to manage that odd combination of stats.

Mize was a scientific hitter in a way that power hitters are not known for being. He had dozens of different bats, one for each situation. For harder-throwing pitchers, for example, he would bring out a lighter bat. His bat collection got so massive that his Cardinals had to take two bat trunks on the road, one for Mize and one for the rest of the team.

World War II pulled Mize into service during his age-30 to age-32 seasons. He could have ranked among the top 5 first basemen of all time if someone would finally follow through on the idea to use a time machine to go back and kill Hitler. No-doubt Hall-of-Famer (Mize, not Hitler).

Eddie Murray (1977-1997; career OPS+: 129)

	Career	Rank	Hitting	Rank	Fielding	Rank	Peak	Rank	Bests	JAWS	Rank
WAR	68.3	13	61.2	17	-12.8	79	38.9	23	2	53.6	15
WS	434.3	4	391.4	3	37.0	17	205.4	15	3	NA	5

If you told a computer to spit out a batting record for a Hall of Fame first baseman, it would give you something like Eddie Murray's. Good power, good on-base ability, hitting at or close to .300. Seldom leading the league in major categories, but always in the top five. Starts strong, peaks in his late 20s, and then slowly regresses until retirement around age 40. There is one little blip up in 1990, when Murray had one of his best seasons at the age of 34. But for the most part, it's a smooth, predictable progression. He comfortably landed just above 500 career home runs and coasted into the Hall of Fame. Smooth and easy.

But this wouldn't be a very carefully crafted computer program, because it would leave out the tendency of major league players to have injuries. Durability is perhaps Murray's most exceptional trait, one shared by longtime teammate Cal Ripken. Murray managed 600+ plate appearances almost every year for 17 years, from 1977 through 1993 (excepting the strike year of 1981 and a 576-PA season in 1986). He amassed an incredible 12,817 career PAs, good for seventh all-time. (Top six: Pete Rose, Carl Yastrzemski, Hank Aaron, Rickey Henderson, Ty Cobb and that Cal Ripken guy.)

Here's a fun fact for you: Eddie Murray holds the all-time career record for sacrifice flies. (Number 2? Cal Ripken.) So I guess he stands out there. Except that he never led the league in the category, and not one of his season totals are among the 200 highest of all time. He would just notch a workmanlike eight or so sac flies every year for a very long time. How very Eddie Murray. Hall-of-Famer, easy. Smooth and easy.

Stan Musial (1941-1944, 1946-1963; career OPS+: 159)

	Career	Rank	Hitting	Rank	Fielding	Rank	Peak	Rank	Bests	JAWS	Rank
WAR	128.1	1	124.6	1	-9.3	62	64.2	2	13	96.2	1
WS	605.6	1	538.8	1	66.8	1	283.1	1	13	NA	2

The Hall of Fame lists Musial as a first baseman, so I put him among the first basemen for the totals above. Baseball-Reference puts him among the JAWS charts for right field, and Bill James' overall ranking has him with the left fielders. If you count outfield as one position, he was clearly an outfielder. But if you count the outfield as three separate positions, as I and the Hall of Fame do, then Musial had more PAs at first than anywhere else. Whatever. No matter where you put him, Stan Musial is among the very best.

There's always something wonderful about a truly great player. There's something especially wonderful about a truly great player who spends his entire career with one team. And then, when that player is an exceptionally kind, charming and gregarious guy, you get something that happens a handful of times in history.

Few players have ever had the kind of relationship with a city like Stan Musial did with St. Louis. For decades after his playing days were over, Musial would often show up in Busch Stadium wearing a red sportcoat, wave joyfully to fans, and then play a quick harmonica solo. He would do this into his 90s, and it was heartwarming every time. I never saw him play, but when he died, I lost one of my favorite players.

Tony Perez (1964-1986; career OPS+: 122)

	Career	Rank	Hitting	Rank	Fielding	Rank	Peak	Rank	Bests	JAWS	Rank
WAR	53.9	26	50.6	26	-6.9	52	36.5	28	0	45.2	28
WS	346.5	14	299.2	17	47.4	3	191.1	27	1	NA	13

You know how most people base their Hall of Fame arguments on whether a guy "felt" like a Hall-of-Famer? As if Hall-of-Fame-ness is something that arises from the pit of your soul, like when Darth Vader "feels" Ben Kenobi's presence on the Death Star? That "feeling," I think, usually comes from the more concrete actions of actually "hearing" broadcasters and "reading" sportswriters directly "stating" that a guy is a future Hall-of-Famer. Those fans might not explicitly remember hearing and reading these things. But the statements create a Hall-of-Fame glow around a guy which remains stuck to him long afterwards.

Most often, these feelings are right, but sometimes they aren't. There's more to being a Hall-of-Famer than getting hyped as one.

That said, I'm not impervious to those feelings. When Tony Perez was elected to the Hall of Fame in 2000, I felt they had made a mistake. Perez was certainly good, but he had never led the league in anything besides GIDPs (grounded into double plays), which is very unusual for a Hall-of-Fame first baseman. He had more than 10,000 PAs but not terribly impressive career totals. He seemed more like an Al Oliver or a Rusty Staub, a very good player who played a long time but isn't Hall-of-Fame worthy.

But the WAR numbers show Perez as being significantly better than Al Oliver (49th-best JAWS among CFs) and Rusty Staub (35th best among RFs). JAWS still has Perez a little below the borderline of the Hall of Fame.

Win Shares puts him in a better position, in part because it's better at judging defense. Perez spent five years as a third baseman, which boosts his Win Shares Fielding number. In WAR, Perez's work at third is erased by all the negative numbers that punish him for his many years playing first.

At first, Perez might seem similar to Jake Beckley. But Perez had some truly exceptional seasons: 7.2 WAR and 33 Win Shares in 1970, 6 WAR and 31 Win Shares in 1969, and a few other great ones. Beckley never had more than 4.5 WAR or 23 Win Shares in a season. Perez may not have led the league in anything of consequence, but he was at least a solid MVP candidate a few times.

I still don't see a good reason to include Perez in the Hall of Fame. But I don't see a good reason to kick him out either. He's very borderline, but as with Cepeda, the tie goes to the status quo. Perez stays.

George Sisler (1915-1922, 1924-1930; career OPS+: 125)

	Career	Rank	Hitting	Rank	Fielding	Rank	Peak	Rank	Bests	JAWS	Rank
WAR	54.5	24	53.7	24	-7.6	53	47.0	11	7	50.8	19
WS	293.4	28	246.9	30	23.1	79	188.8	29	4	NA	24

From 1916 to 1922, George Sisler was unquestionably the best first baseman in baseball. In each of those years he led the league in WAR among first basemen. He was the best hitter in all of baseball in 1918, and then caught the first wave of the hitting explosion of Baseball's Golden Age. Sisler compiled conventional numbers in 1920 and 1922 that are truly eye-popping.

Then Sisler's eyes popped. He contracted a severe sinus infection in 1923 that weakened the muscles around his eyes and gave him double vision and migraines. He returned to baseball in 1924 but wasn't nearly as good, registering eight more seasons that hovered around league-average. The injury basically turned Sisler from Albert Pujols into Shea Hillenbrand.

The injury not only took down Sisler; arguably, it took down an entire major-league franchise. I'm surprised I've never heard anyone talk about the Curse of George Sisler's Eyes. In 1922, when Sisler had his last great season, the Browns were a terrific team. They finished 93-61, one game behind the Yankees. They had plenty of talent beyond Sisler: a star outfield of Ken Williams (163 OPS+, 39 HR, 155 RBIs, 37 SB), Baby Doll Jacobson (115 OPS+), and Jack Tobin (120 OPS+), along with an ace pitcher in Urban Shocker (which would be a great rap name). That year the Browns had better attendance than the other St. Louis major-league club, the Cardinals, as they had had for 12 of their 21 years of existence.

In 1923 the Browns were a .500 team while Sisler convalesced. Then for a few years they wavered between mediocre and bad while Sisler himself wavered between mediocre and bad. The Cardinals were bad too, though, so the Browns outdrew them every year until 1926. That 1922 season had created quite a few Browns fans.

In 1926, everything changed. All of Branch Rickey's work in the Cardinals front office started paying off, and they squeaked into a pennant with a 89-65 mark. Then they shocked the world (well, at least the small part of the world paying attention to American baseball) by beating the mighty Yankees in the World Series, thanks in part to Babe Ruth's moronic failed attempt to steal second with two outs in the bottom of the ninth of the deciding game. (Kids, don't be like Babe Ruth.) The Cardinals then outdrew the Browns every year from 1926 until the Browns left for Baltimore in 1954, except the fluke year of 1944 when the two teams met in the World Series.

The city of St. Louis was never big enough to support two major-league teams. It supported two bad teams badly from 1901 until 1926, when that surprise championship turned St. Louis into a Cardinals town. The Browns devolved into a sad, unloved Quadruple-A team, selling whatever good players they stumbled upon to the Yankees just so they could keep the lights on. If George Sisler hadn't busted his peepers in 1923, maybe St. Louis would be a Browns town to this day. C'est la vie.

To this day, Sisler is overrated. Baseball-reference.com has a crowd-sourced ranking of all players' all-time rank -- look up most any player you'll see it right above the year-by-year record. It tends to be a surprisingly good ranking, as Baseball-reference users tend to be smart folks. But Sisler is ranked at #44 among all hitters as I write this, right above Mike Piazza and Willie McCovey. This is way too high for a guy who looks like a low-end Hall-of-Famer by the above numbers.

You can understand why people would think that, though. Sisler was truly spectacular in a time when "truly spectacular" meant .400 batting averages. He then suffered a freak injury that hurt his play but still allowed him to hang around long enough to compile respectable career totals.

As I've mentioned, you have to judge players on what they did, not what they could have done (with a few caveats -- see Roy Campanella). What Sisler did at his peak was good enough to be in the Hall of Fame. But judging his career on the whole, he's on the low end. I'm leaving him in, but with a bit of reservation.

Mule Suttles (1921, 1923-1944)

	Rank at Position Among Negro Leaguers	Rank Among All Negro Leaguers
Bill James	2?	6
SABR	2	13
Monte Irvin	3	NA

The "2?" above is because Bill James rates Suttles as second among left fielders, behind Turkey Stearnes. He mentions that Suttles played a lot of first base and would rate about even with Buck Leonard there. Every other source lists him as a first baseman.

Regardless of where you put him in the field, Suttles' natural position was in the batter's box. His nickname ("Mule" is not his Christian name) came from his tremendous strength and his 6'6", 250-pound frame. He was legendary for massive home runs produced by a 50-ounce bat that is about a third heavier than any bat you've seen in the past 80 years.

As part of the 1933 World's Fair in Chicago, the white major leagues had their first All-Star Game. In response, Pittsburgh Crawfords owner Gus Greenlee arranged a similar contest, the Negro Leagues East-West Game. Mule Suttles became a hero of this first game when he hit a huge home run. The East-West Game quickly became a vital part of Negro League life, more important than the All-Star Game ever was to the MLB. Over the years, leagues came and went, but the East-West Game remained the moment when all of black baseball came together for a grand showcase and celebration.

Suttles reminds me of Harmon Killebrew and Jim Thome. They're the kind of guys who hit a baseball so hard that you live with their strikeouts and find a place to play them. But then, Suttles had high batting averages, more reminiscent of Lou Gehrig or Stan Musial than Killebrew or Thome. Either way, he is a no-doubt Hall-of-Famer.

Ben Taylor (1909-1929; career OPS+: 160)

	Rank at Position Among Negro Leaguers	Rank Among All Negro Leaguers
Bill James	3	unranked
SABR	4	33
Monte Irvin	unranked	NA

Ben Taylor starred in dead-ball-era Negro Leagues with his brothers, Charles Isam (known as "C.I. "), "Candy" Jim, "Steel Arm" Johnny, Harpo, Zeppo, Ringo, Moe, Curly, Meschach, Shadrach, Happy, Doc, Chablis, Chardonnay, and Captain O.G. Readmore.[15] The first three of those were even real people! And you thought the Molinas had a big baseball family! (And you were right about that, incidentally. The Molinas do indeed have a big baseball family. But the Taylors had one more brother in the game than the Molinas, so they were bigger by one. That's my point, which I think I have made in an admirably succinct fashion.)

Monte Irvin didn't include Ben Taylor his rankings. But his co-writer, Phil Pepe, added a piece about Taylor and his brothers, noting that Ben escaped Irvin's focus because Taylor played so long before his time.

As evidenced by the 160+ OPS above, Seamheads.com's stats rank Ben Taylor quite highly. He finished with a .338/.397/.466 career line in 3255 PAs. Taylor earned 148.5 Win Shares, topping all first basemen by a large margin, with the caveat that the Seamheads database only goes through 1934 as of this writing. So it doesn't include the careers of Buck Leonard, Mule Suttles, etc.

Among all hitters in the database, Taylor's 148.5 Win Shares is fifth-best, behind outfielders Oscar Charleston, Cristobal Torriente, and Pete Hill, and shortstop Pop Lloyd. Ben Taylor certainly looks like one the best hitters in the early years of the Negro Leagues. As with Louis Santop, I can imagine Taylor being a star in the MLB. Maybe not a Lou Gehrig-level star. But Eddie Murray-level stardom doesn't seem farfetched.

Taylor also managed and served as a mentor to Buck Leonard. Total it all up, and he is a Hall-of-Famer.

---

[15] Reference explanations: Harpo and Zeppo were two of the Marx brothers; you might have known those. I certainly hope you know who Ringo is. Ditto for Moe and Curly. Shadrach and Meshach, along with Abednego, were brothers who refused to bow to Nebuchadnezzar in a Bible story. Happy and Doc are also gimmes. Chablis and Chardonnay were the painfully pretentious names of some dogs that Kathy Lee Gifford had in the 1980s. Captain O.G. Readmore was a cartoon cat who would pop up during 1980s Saturday morning cartoons and tell kids to read books, which is a bit like waking up a heroin addict and shouting "Hey, you know what you should try instead? Tea!"

Bill Terry (1923-1936; career OPS+: 136)

	Career	Rank	Hitting	Rank	Fielding	Rank	Peak	Rank	Bests	JAWS	Rank
WAR	54.2	25	47.3	31	-0.3	13	41.3	19	0	47.8	23
WS	278.1	34	245.6	31	32.1	35	197.2	20	0	NA	26

Bill Terry is a lot like George Sisler, except that he didn't have a wonky optic nerve. Terry was also a very good hitter who remains overrated because he hit .400 and had a crazy number of hits one year (254 in 1930). Even in that year, though, Terry was not the best first baseman in baseball -- Lou Gehrig was, by a pretty substantial margin.

You can hardly fault a guy for not being as good as Lou Gehrig.[16] Terry was a great hitter, and as an added bonus, a successful manager, leading the Giants to three pennants and one championship from 1932 to 1941. If not for the managerial career, he might be borderline. But with it he's a clear Hall-of-Famer.

Who's In, Who's Out

We managed to kick out three players: Jake Beckley, agonizingly, and Jim Bottomley and George Kelly, joyfully. It's no coincidence that all of them were elected by the Veterans Committee in the 1970s. You gotta understand, the '70s were a crazy time. Wild experimentation within every aspect of society had proved so much fun in the 1960s that people kept doing it in the 1970s. But they found diminishing returns. The 1960s had already broken all the clearly stupid rules, leaving the 1970s to break the rules that should probably remain in place. The 1960s gave us premarital sex, while the 1970s gave us key parties. The 1960s provided low-grade marijuana and the 1970s provided brain-destroying cocaine. The 1960s had "Bonnie and Clyde," while the 1970s had "I Spit on Your Grave." The 1960s were "Sgt. Pepper's Lonely Heart Club Band," and the 1970s were Lou Reed's "Metal Machine Music."

What was I talking about … oh yeah, the Veterans Committee in the 1970s. Frankie Frisch and Lou Reed would spend all day watching "I Spit on Your Grave" and … anyway, here are some better candidates for the Hall of Fame:

Jeff Bagwell (1991-2005; career OPS+: 156)

	Career	Rank	Hitting	Rank	Fielding	Rank	Peak	Rank	Bests	JAWS	Rank
WAR	79.6	8	74.0	10	-7.9	57	48.2	7	4	63.9	8
WS	387.6	7	355.4	7	32.1	34	225.8	6	3	NA	10

See my rant about Ivan Rodriguez if you want my view on the "guilty until proven innocent" attitude that's keeping Jeff Bagwell out of the Hall. But wait, I feel another argument coming on … here it comes ...

[16] Made you look! Ha ha, that never gets old. For me, anyway.

Let's say that after electing Bagwell or Rodriguez, we found that they had tried some steroids a few times, but were never chronic users. I think the many moral absolutists over steroid use would throw up a hue and cry, demanding that both players should be summarily excommunicated, tortured into a full confession, declared guilty of heresy, and burnt at the stake.

I'm being a bit glib. But there seems to be a Puritanical bent among the people who insist that any player who ever takes any performance-enhancing drug should be banned from the Hall, period. Hey, I understand that it can be very emotionally satisfying to make such bold moral pronouncements. It can make you feel superior. It can also permit you to stop having to deliberate issues more carefully. It makes the crazy, complex world we live in feel more simple and manageable.

Those of us who insist on living in the real world, though, know that nothing is ever that cut-and-dried. Athletes have been using performance-enhancing drugs since the beginning of time. In the 1970s, each major league clubhouse had a basket of "greenies," illegal amphetamines that players would pop to keep themselves focused. Mike Schmidt freely admitted using them, and most likely saw his performance enhanced as a result. (Source: "Schmidt an Open Book on Greenies," The New York Times, Murray Chass, February 28, 2006) Should Schmidt be kicked out of the Hall?

Paul Waner drank a half-pint of whiskey before every at-bat, and swore he couldn't hit without it. He said the pitch came in looking like a basketball after he'd had a few shots, and like an aspirin tablet if he hadn't. One time his manager, Pie Traynor, made him switch to beer, and Waner hit terribly for a month. (Source: Waner's SABR biography, by Joseph Wancho.) It certainly looks like alcohol was a performance-enhancing drug for Paul Waner. Does that make him unworthy of the Hall?

Well, that's different, you might say. Steroids are much more powerful than greenies or alcohol. That's true, and actually brings me to my point: that we're talking about a difference of degree, not kind. Many substances can enhance performance. But steroids, as far as we can tell, are much better at doing so than anything we've ever seen. It's not that they're the only performance-enhancing drugs ever. It's that, by all appearances, they enhance performance so incredibly well. They do it so well that they apparently can turn baseball into a home run derby and make 35-year-old players explode into the best seasons anyone's ever seen.

Another reason steroids are so terrifying are their negative side effects. I agree that those side effects are extremely revolting. But amphetamines and alcohol also can do some pretty nasty things to your body -- not as disturbing, perhaps, but still very bad. Again, it's a difference of degree, not kind. I understand that steroids elicit a more visceral disgust than greenies or alcohol. But disgust is feeling, not an argument. People often feel disgust and then construct arguments to rationalize that feeling. But that's not a good way to approach anything.

So if drugs are distinguished by a difference of degree, the effect of drugs on Hall of Fame cases should be a matter of degree as well. If a player was helped to a large degree by steroids, to the point where a non-Hall-of-Famer achieves Hall-of-Fame stats, then leave him out. If steroids only made a Hall-of-Famer into a super-duper-ba-looper Hall-of-Famer, then he should go in.

And by the way, I don't think being elected to the Hall of Fame should be an irrevocable honor. Nothing in life should be; even Supreme Court justices can be impeached under extreme circumstances. Heck, this book is largely about kicking out players who did nothing more offensive than playing less spectacularly than a majority of Hall-of-Famers. I believe that if later, we discover that Jeff Bagwell's famous hand protectors contained IV bags that mainlined HGH into his veins, we should be able to kick him out.

That's not going to be allowed any time soon, so we can't proceed assuming it's possible. As it stands now, though, the whole process of electing Hall-of-Famers is being screwed up by barring guys like Bagwell on the basis of nothing but rumor and moral absolutism. He should be in.

Jim Thome (1991-2012, career OPS+: 147)

	Career	Rank	Hitting	Rank	Fielding	Rank	Peak	Rank	Bests	JAWS	Rank
WAR	72.9	10	77.1	9	-17.2	90	41.6	18	3	57.3	11
WS	349.2	13	321.7	12	27.8	49	200.1	18	0	NA	11[17]

When good ol' Peoria-born farmboy Jim Thome hit his 600th home run with the Twins in 2011, it was barely mentioned in the national press. A few months earlier, when Derek Jeter got his 3000th hit, holy cow, it was as if Jesus had come back to Earth, made peace in the Middle East, cured cancer, achieved cold fusion, and finally resolved the eternal Kirk vs. Picard debate. (The answer: Picard. Kirk is better only in terms of kitsch value.)

Never mind that Thome was only the 8th player in history to achieve 600 home runs, and Jeter was the 29th to get to 3000 hits. Jeter had spent decades being heavily marketed as Everything That's Right With Baseball, the team player who is unselfish and honest and humble and brave and noble and true in every imaginable way. (I'm not saying Jeter isn't a great player and stand-up guy. I'm just saying the hype surrounding him can get a bit exhausting.)

Jim Thome, meanwhile, did nothing but play extremely well, unselfishly, honestly, humbly, bravely, nobly, but, because of his incredibly poor judgement, never playing for the Yankees, and never making flashy postseason plays that got Joe Buck's wig all a-twitter.

I sound bitter, but I'm really not too upset. I'm from the Midwest, so I'm used to the things I love being underhyped and snootily dismissed, sight unseen, by the people on the coasts. You guys go ahead and compete over who can fulminate most effusively over Derek Jeter's incredible wonderful wonderfulness. I'm happy to just sit back and quietly appreciate a job well done, like the job Jim Thome did for 22 years.

Thome was a tremendous natural power hitter, reminiscent of Harmon Killebrew: someone who can't hit for average but was seemingly bred in some baseball player farm to draw walks and hit home runs. I certainly hope he has no trouble entering the Hall of Fame.

Dick Allen (1963-1977; career OPS+: 156)

	Career	Rank	Hitting	Rank	Fielding	Rank	Peak	Rank	Bests	JAWS	Rank
WAR	58.7	20	69.9	13	-16.5	88	46.0	13	1	52.4	17
WS	341.9	17	312.5	13	29.7	44	239.7	5	4	NA	15

I really didn't want to advocate for Dick Allen. I've heard many stories about how immature and destructive he was to his teams. I've heard how he picked fights and divided clubhouses, to the point

[17] The ranking of the average of Thome's career and peak Win Shares, just like with Piazza and I-Rod.

where his personality allegedly caused more losses than his bat could make up for. In "Whatever Happened to the Hall of Fame?", Bill James says "[Allen] did more to keep his teams from winning than anyone else who ever played major league baseball. And if that's a Hall of Famer, I'm a lug nut." (p. 325)

But after seeing the above rankings, I had to reconsider Allen. Could someone who played that well really have kept his team from winning that much? I'm generally skeptical that one player's personality can really be a huge factor in a major-league team winning or losing. Maybe in your beer league one jerk could make everyone lose motivation. But these are major league baseball players we're talking about. They are the cream of the cream of the cream of the crop. To even get to this level, they have to endure years of playing meaningless games in tiny towns for almost no pay. These are people with incredible internal motivation to excel on a baseball field, and a singular, proven ability to do so. I seriously doubt that such battle-tested warriors can be rendered impotent because there's this one mean guy on the bench who is making them feel sad.

Many baseball players will tell you that clubhouse chemistry is vital for a winning team. They should know what they're talking about; after all, they've played and I haven't. But they often seem to be confusing causes and effects. Winning brings clubhouse chemistry much more than chemistry brings wins. When you win, everyone smiles and high-fives and you feel close bonds even with the guys who annoy you off the field. But after a loss, you're not allowed to be happy. If you don't have a hangdog expression, someone will pull you aside and tell you to get one, pronto. After the team piles up enough losses, recriminations and job insecurity are sure to follow. Morale will collapse.

You then search for reasons why things are going badly. You know that you're trying your best, so effort can't be the problem. You can't let yourself think you might not have the talent (even if it's true), because without confidence you have no chance. Your mind then goes to the thing that's already bugging you, that one guy who acts like such a jerk. Maybe if we got rid of him, we'd all become better at throwing and hitting baseballs! Yeah, that's it!

I'm not saying that clubhouse chemistry can't be a small factor. Maybe Dick Allen's disruptions could knock him down about five places in the above overall rankings. Even then, he'd still be in Hall-of-Fame range. He was that good of a hitter. His excellence was masked by his era; if he had played in the 1990s, he'd have Frank Thomas numbers.

Plus, it's hard not to feel for the guy, at least on some level. Allen grew up in a small Pennsylvania town which was relatively well integrated racially. In 1963, he was thrown onto the AAA Little Rock team and became the first African-American to ever play non-Negro-League baseball in the city. Just a few years before, Little Rock became a flashpoint in the civil rights struggle when Arkansas governor Orval Faubus refused a federal order to integrate a grade school. It was a tough city for an African-American. The Phillies organization did not prepare Allen for the brutality he would experience from the stands or for the notes left on his car that contained death threats. After a policeman harassed him on the street, he was afraid to go outdoors.

When Allen was brought up to the Phillies, they insisted on calling him "Richie," even though he hated the name and wanted to be called "Dick." More importantly for his performance, he was put at third base, a position he had never played. Of course, he committed loads of errors, 41 to be exact. And of course, Phillies fans booed him mercilessly.

Never mind that he had perhaps the all-time greatest rookie season, ending with an 8.8 WAR and 41 Win Shares. The WAR total was third in 1964 behind Willie Mays and Ron Santo. The 41 Win Shares led all of baseball by substantial margin. And that's not the half of it; only 22 hitters in history have had more than 41 Win Shares in a single season. The list of other players who topped out at 41 is pretty impressive: Hank Aaron, Joe DiMaggio, Jimmie Foxx, Albert Pujols, Frank Robinson, and a few others.

That was only the beginning of great hitting and terrible treatment from Phillies fans. Things got worse in 1965. Before one game, Allen and teammate Johnny Callison were razzing Frank Thomas (the 1950s version) about his recent failed bunt attempts. Thomas responded by shouting at Allen "What are you trying to be, another Muhammad Clay, always running your mouth off?" Allen ran over to Thomas and punched him in the jaw. Thomas hit Allen with a bat. Soon after, Thomas was released.

Allen thought Thomas was being racist, but I'm not so sure. "Muhammad Clay"? If you were trying to be racist, you'd just say "Cassius Clay." That was the name that Muhammad Ali went by before 1964, when he joined the Nation of Islam. Converts to the Nation of Islam rejected their birth names as being remnants of slavery. They took on the last name "X," as in "Malcolm X," or traditional Muslim names like "Muhammad Ali." Racists at the time refused to respect Ali's name change and kept calling him "Cassius Clay." Saying "Muhammad Clay," though, is just weird. When Thomas said it, only a year had passed since Ali's conversion. Thomas probably misspoke.

Regardless, there's no justification for violence. Allen was clearly at fault. But the hometown fans went nuts, way out of proportion for Allen's behavior. They turned on Allen big-time and made Thomas into a beloved martyr. Thomas was old and ineffective, but Philadelphians brought signs to the park that declared they'd rather have him than Allen. They regularly threw things at him, and Allen started wearing a helmet on the field to protect himself.

I can perceive a lot more racial motivation in Phillies fans' reactions to the incident than in Thomas' weird taunt. The level of hatred they spewed was excessive. Other players have gotten into fights in their clubhouses and have been derided for them, but never to that degree. It took on the character of a mob mentality, one that gave fans the opportunity to release their anxiety over watching a black man succeed in a traditionally white world. Granted, that's my impression 50 years after the fact; I wasn't there.

The point is that all this was a lot for a player to handle. And Allen didn't handle it well. Jackie Robinson he was not. Robinson demonstrated how to ignore the abuse and let his bat do the talking. Allen trashed the fans in the papers, saying "I'd like to get out of Philadelphia. I don't care for the people or their attitude, although they don't bother me or my play. But maybe the Phillies can get a couple of broken bats and shower shoes for me." (Source: Allen's SABR biography, by Rich D'Ambrosio.) During games, Allen wrote the word "BOO" with his foot in the dirt near third base. When the Phillies told him to stop it, he wrote "NO" and "WHY" in the dirt instead.

The bad attitude is clear. But there is also a note of sadness in Allen's dirt doodles and his "couple of broken bats and shower shoes" assessment of his worth. As the years wore on, Allen's determination to keep up the fight wore away. He showed up late to several games, which in baseball is a very serious offense. He seemed more interested in going to the horse tracks than in playing baseball. There, I imagine, he could experience the thrill of sports without having to spend every moment locked in combat with the world.

The Phillies eventually traded Allen, and then he ran through several other teams, wearing out his welcome with each. He would refuse to follow orders, create his own cliques, and make dubious accusations of management. But he also kept hitting extremely well. He had another all-time great season with the White Sox in 1972, getting 40 Win Shares, 8.6 WAR and an MVP award. The White Sox sure weren't destroyed by Allen's personality; they surged from the doldrums into contention.

In the end, I think Dick Allen's play put lots more runs on the board than his behavior took off. And I also think that the conditions he played under should be taken into consideration. He may have been immature, but he was not a monster. He was thrown into the pressure cooker of 1960s pseudo-integration and navigated it poorly. I think he hit enough in the process to qualify as a Hall-of-Famer. And Bill James, apparently, is a lug nut.

Buck O'Neil (1937-1943, 1946-1949)

	Rank at Position Among Negro Leaguers	Rank Among All Negro Leaguers
Bill James	4	unranked
SABR	3	26
Monte Irvin	3 (as manager)	NA

If you've seen Ken Burns' "Baseball" documentary, you've fallen in love with Buck O'Neil. In it, O'Neil was asked to sing "Take Me Out to the Ballgame" and sheepishly responded "I'm not such a good singer." Then he sang beautifully, radiating warmth from his every pore. His other charming appearances in the documentary made him a national star.

Many talk show appearances followed, and he never failed to come across as almost preternaturally good-hearted and affectionate. He even found a way to be magnanimous about being barred from the white major leagues; his love for his Negro League days inspired him to write a book called "I Was Right on Time."

O'Neil may have not been the greatest player. Bill James describes him as a Mark Grace/Mickey Vernon type, a high-batting-average hitter who was low on power but terrific defensively. He also managed the Kansas City Monarchs to four straight league championships, starting in 1948. Many of his players had great success in the MLB, including Ernie Banks and Elston Howard.

After integration, O'Neil worked as a scout, signing Lou Brock and many others. In 1962, he became a coach for the Cubs, the first African-American to serve as a major-league regular-season coach.

SABR rates him highly not only because of his play and managing, but also because of his importance as a national figure. O'Neil led the effort to create the Negro Leagues Baseball Museum in Kansas City, and served as its honorary chair for the rest of his life. I can't think of anyone in the last 50 years who has brought more attention to Negro League baseball. He was a true ambassador of the game, in a way that few have been before or since.

I'm not moved by sentiment when it comes to Hall-of-Fame selections. My choice of Buck O'Neil is not based on sentiment, but on the above rankings and a careful review of his entire career in baseball. Like Frank Chance, his playing record alone may have been a step below Hall-of-Fame level. But when you add it to his managing and other contributions, he finishes a step above. You can put him among the first basemen or the managers or the pioneers and executives; regardless, you should put him in the Hall of Fame.

Keith Hernandez (1974-1990; career OPS+: 128)

	Career	Rank	Hitting	Rank	Fielding	Rank	Peak	Rank	Bests	JAWS	Rank
WAR	60.1	20	45.6	32	0.7	9	41.0	21	2	50.6	21
WS	312.3	22	256.2	27	33.2	31	194.5	23	3	NA	16

There was a time when you didn't have to hit home runs to be considered a great first baseman. George Sisler didn't. Bill Terry didn't. In fact, both are pretty good comps for Hernandez. Both had much higher career batting averages than Hernandez, though, so they're seen as legends while Hernandez is seen just as a pretty good player.

Of course, that's a factor of their times. Hernandez's lifetime .296 batting average ranks 23rd among all players playing during his career span (minimum 3000 PAs). During Terry's career span, the 23rd-best batting average belonged to Pie Traynor, at .324. And even if you ignore context, Hernandez had a higher lifetime on-base percentage than Sisler, and was just ten percentage points below Terry's. In context, Hernandez was a better on-base threat than either.

Also, Hernandez was a tremendous defensive first baseman, winning 11 Gold Gloves. First base is the least important defensive position, so there's not a huge difference between a great and a mediocre defensive first baseman. Still, that adds points to his case. I'd put him in to accompany Bill Terry and George Sisler on the low, but still deserving, end of the Hall.

Todd Helton (1997-2013, career OPS+: 133)

	Career	Rank	Hitting	Rank	Fielding	Rank	Peak	Rank	Bests	JAWS	Rank
WAR	61.5	16	54.0	23	-5.9	46	46.5	12	2	54.0	14
WS	264.6	39	232.9	37	31.9	36	196.7	21	1	NA	31[18]

Win Shares, Win Shares, Win Shares. You don't go past 2008, and Todd Helton had good years in 2009 and 2011. What am I to do with you?

I suppose I can make an estimate. In terms of WAR, Todd Helton collected about 10% of his career total from 2009-2013. Add another 10% to his career Win Shares total and you get 291, good for 27th all-time among first basemen. I'm assuming none of those late years would land among his peak Win Shares numbers, since none cracked his peak in WAR. Still, that puts Helton's overall WSAWS ranking to 243.6, 27th all-time. That's still a bit low, but it makes his WAR ranking seem more reasonable.

Todd Helton was the first genuine superstar in Colorado Rockies history. They had a few pretend superstars, players whose numbers looked amazing because they played in that goofball crazyball pinball machine called Coors Field. WAR, Win Shares, and OPS+ know how to weed these guys out.

For example, Vinny Castilla hit 30 home runs five years in a row for the Rockies, including three years with 40 homers. That looks awfully good for a third baseman. But his WARs during those years

[18] The average of Helton's Career and Peak Win Shares, but Win Shares only goes through 2008. Helton was much too recent to be mentioned in Bill James' "Historical Baseball Abstract."

were 2.7, 2.7, 2.9, 5.0 and 0.5. His Win Shares were 13, 23, 21, 21, and 11. His OPS+s were 113, 112, 115, 127, and 84. It's good, but not really great. Dante Bichette's numbers look worse in context, but I thought I should foresake exploration of such sordid figures out of propriety, for fear that ladies might be present.

Todd Helton is in a different class. He had the power you'd expect from a Rockie. But he also got on base incredibly well, twice leading the league in OBP. Walks are not as park-dependent as home runs are. And he was a great defender, for what that's worth from a first baseman.

Helton got a bit of a late start for a Hall-of-Famer and declined rather early, so he didn't end up in the top of the class at his position. But at least his record doesn't scream of steroid use, unlike ...

Intentionally Overlooked

These players I am not recommending for the Hall of Fame. But I thought I should at least say why I'm not.

Mark McGwire (1986-2001, career OPS+: 163)

	Career	Rank	Hitting	Rank	Fielding	Rank	Peak	Rank	Bests	JAWS	Rank
WAR	62.0	15	64.8	16	-12.8	78	41.9	16	1	52.0	18
WS	342.7	16	299.9	15	18.1	113	213.9	12	1	NA	3

In the Ivan Rodriguez and Jeff Bagwell comments, I laid out my feelings on steroids. If there's nothing but rumor you may have tried steroids at some point, and if you would have been a HOFer either way, you should be in.

But if your steroid use is well-established, and likely turned you into a Hall-of-Famer, then no dice. I suspect, but can't say for sure, that this is the case with McGwire. He came up with an amazing power stroke, winning the 1987 AL Rookie of the Year with a then-incredible 49 home runs. He was skinny as a rail, and I doubt he was juicing.

After a few years he fell into regular injuries. Then, all of a sudden, he became a lot healthier and bulked up to a remarkable degree, both symptoms typical of steroid use. More relevantly, in 2010 he admitted that he juiced. After years of evasion, he was finally honest. It was late in coming, but commendable considering he still had a shot at the Hall.

It's important to note that even if McGwire hadn't been a user, his record wouldn't necessarily make him a slam-dunk Hall-of-Famer. He's 18th among first basemen in JAWS, between Dick Allen and George Sisler. Bill James ranked him 3rd among first basemen, but it seems like an odd rating considering McGwire is 17th among career Win Shares and 12th in Peak Win Shares. Even Bill James got a little overexcited in the height of the Steroid Era.

It's my gut feeling that the steroids boosted McGwire from 25th or thereabouts to Hall-of-Fame-area rankings. Without the juice he probably would have been a Frank Howard or Ryan Howard (hey, that's a weird coincidence): massive sluggers who ended below Hall-of-Fame level.

I don't like going by gut feelings, though. None of this constitutes the kind of objective evidence I prefer. In my ideal world, I'd be able to tease out a percentage of McGwire's home runs that can be credited to steroids.

I can't be that scientific. But I can approach this like it's a legal argument. And to borrow from legal terminology, there seems to be "probable cause" to believe that steroids could have given Mark McGwire Hall-of-Fame stats. There's not enough evidence for a conviction. I think he should be kept out as more evidence is collected. With Jeff Bagwell, there was no such probable cause. With McGwire, there is.

Rafael Palmeiro (1986-2005, career OPS+: 132)

	Career	Rank	Hitting	Rank	Fielding	Rank	Peak	Rank	Bests	JAWS	Rank
WAR	71.6	11	66.7	15	-11.7	73	38.8	25	3	55.2	12
WS	396.4	6	357.0	6	39.6	10	191.0	28	1	NA	19

I'm not sure why McGwire has managed to stay on the BBWAA ballot while Rafael Palmeiro has dropped off. Maybe it was because McGwire's mea culpa came earlier, or maybe it was because he had more dramatic seasons, like the 70-HR performance in 1998.

Palmeiro's case is similar, but even murkier. He failed a test, but kept emphatically denying any wrongdoing, often in a rather implausible way. After dropping off the ballot for good in 2014, he sort of took responsibility for his mistakes. Sort of. He still insisted that a tainted B-12 supplement led to the failed drug test. And he snuck in the bitter, petty statement "I should have trusted no one." (Source: "Rafael Palmeiro says falling off Hall of Fame ballot is 'disheartening,'" CBSSports.com, Mike Axisa, January 9, 2014.) Yeah, that was the problem, Raffy. You were just too pure of a soul to live in a world where everyone who ever lived was conspiring against you.

I have more respect for how McGwire handled his situation than how Palmeiro did, but that's not terribly relevant. More important how is much Palmeiro took and how much it affected his performance.

On the face of it, Palmeiro's record is stronger than McGwire's. He comes in at 12th in JAWS, between Jim Thome and Willie McCovey. James ranked him 19th in 2001, before Palmeiro logged a few more good seasons. He is 6th in career Win Shares and 28th in Peak Win Shares; if you average the two together, the same way the calculation for JAWS is made (which I'm calling WSAWS), Palmeiro ranks 7th.

Could steroids really be so powerful that they changed Rafael Palmeiro from a non-Hall-of-Famer into the 11th- or maybe 7th-greatest first-baseman of all time? It seems implausible. But we did see what steroids probably did to Barry Bonds and Roger Clemens, turning what should have been their twilight years into the best of their careers.

I don't have a good answer here. As with McGwire, there appears to be probable cause to suspect that steroids had too large of an effect on Palmeiro's career. But I don't have enough evidence to convict. Such is the ambiguity that steroids cause. Kids, don't do steroids. Nobody likes ambiguity.

Gil Hodges (1943-1963; career OPS+: 120)

	Career	Rank	Hitting	Rank	Fielding	Rank	Peak	Rank	Bests	JAWS	Rank
WAR	44.9	37	41.6	37	-5.4	40	34.2	37	2	39.6	35
WS	263.8	40	229.2	40	34.2	28	172.0	37	0	NA	30

Gil Hodges, as we all know, injected metabolic steroids straight into his eyeball before, after, and during every game he played. No! Kidding! Gil Hodges was a star during the so-called/inaccurately-called Golden Age of Baseball, when baby boomers were babies booming with excitement for the New York-based team of their choice.

I'm including Hodges here because there is still a strong contingent trying to get him elected to the Hall. They argue that he was a good hitter for a good amount of time who deserves extra consideration for his managerial experience.

As the above shows, he was a indeed good hitter for a good amount of time. But so were Fred McGriff, Norm Cash, Dolph Camilli, Carlos Delgado, Ed Konetchy, Mark Grace, and a bunch of other guys surrounding Hodges in the JAWS list and Bill James' list. They're all a step below the Hall of Fame.

But none of them served as a manager. So Hodges is another Frank Chance, right? Well, hold on. Chance piloted four pennant-winners and two world champions. Another of his teams went 104-49, and two others won 90 games. His lifetime winning percentage as a manager was .664, with 768 wins and 389 losses.

Meanwhile, Gil Hodges managed one good team, the Miracle Mets of 1969. They surprised everyone by winning 100 games and the World Series. It was a genuinely terrific year. After that, they had two straight 83-win seasons. Then Hodges died, at only 47 years old of age.

It is of course tragic that Hodges died so young. We'll never know what else he could have accomplished. But, I'm sad to say, an early death does not qualify as a societal constraint for which we can give extra Hall-of-Fame consideration. It's not like war or segregation. Baseball is full of stories of "what could have been" if not for death or injury; we can't elect everyone based on what could have been if not for health problems.

And let's be honest: Hodges had a long way to go to become a legendary manager like Frank Chance. Before the Miracle Mets, Hodges had six unsuccessful seasons. He finished with a career managerial record of 321-444, for a .420 winning percentage. Hodges had one great year and eight others that ranged from mediocre to terrible.

You could argue that a manager is only as good as his players, and there is some truth to that. But it doesn't change the fact that Gil Hodges didn't manage for very long, and led only one good team. That one team can only add so many points to his credentials. I can't see those points being enough to get him into Hall-of-Fame range.

Don Mattingly (1982-1995; career OPS+: 127)

	Career	Rank	Hitting	Rank	Fielding	Rank	Peak	Rank	Bests	JAWS	Rank
WAR	42.2	41	39.0	42	-6.8	51	35.7	32	2	39.0	37
WS	263.4	41	233.0	36	30.4	40	191.7	25	2	NA	12

When I was a kid in the mid-1980s, Don Mattingly was the biggest baseball star on the planet. I was a huge baseball card freak, and his rookie card was the Holy Grail, valued at the then-unfathomable sum of $30.

Mattingly wasn't actually the best ballplayer on the planet; he just had the best Triple-Crown stats for a few years. Rickey Henderson and Wade Boggs both had significantly better WAR and Win Shares totals. Still, Mattingly was unquestionably great from 1984-1989, scoring 5+ WAR and 24+ Win Shares each year.

But it didn't last. After 1989, when he was just 28, back problems turned Mattingly into a mediocre hitter. Thereafter he peaked at 2.7 WAR and 20 Win Shares, always scoring at average or below average among starting first basemen. He finished with just 7722 PAs. Even those Triple-Crown stats he was known for didn't turn out amazing: .307 BA, 222 HR, 1099 RBI. In an OK era for hitters, those aren't great numbers for a first baseman.

In putting Mattingly 12th all-time among first basemen, Bill James only says "100% ballplayer. 0% bull****." ("New Historical Baseball Abstract," p. 437.) Yes, Mattingly was admirably non-nonsense. But so were a lot of guys who are not in the Hall of Fame. Bill got a bit overwhelmed by sentimentality here. In WSAWS (averaging Career and Peak Win Shares), Mattingly ranks 34th, among Boog Powell, Mickey Vernon, and Steve Garvey. All were good first basemen, but not Hall-of-Famers.

Here's to hoping that Mattingly's managerial career gets him over the hump for the Hall, a la Frank Chance. As of now, he's just not there.

Chapter Four

~ ~ Second Base ~ ~

Second base is kind of an odd position, if you think about it (and I do). It's more defense-first than hitting-first, but not as much as shortstop or catcher are. While defense is important, you better hit too if you want to be in the Hall of Fame. It's a lot like third base and center field that way. Let's see if the Hall has been good at choosing the second basemen who contribute on both sides.

Roberto Alomar (1988-2004; career OPS: 116)

	Career	Rank	Hitting	Rank	Fielding	Rank	Peak	Rank	Bests	JAWS	Rank
WAR	66.8	10	70.0	7	2.4	77	42.8	13	1	54.8	12
WS	375.8	7	280.6	7	95.3	8	215.3	8	4	NA	10

Roberto Alomar was not retired yet when Bill James ranked him as the 10th-best second baseman of all-time in 2000. But Alomar only had one great season left (2001) and then went to the Mets and started playing worse, like you're supposed to when you join the Mets. So Alomar probably wouldn't have gotten much higher.

Remember when Alomar spat on an umpire in 1996? Occasionally people would say that the incident could affect his Hall of Fame chances. This is a silly idea. It's blowing one moment of poor judgment way out of proportion. Alomar apologized for the incident. He made a mistake that he regrets, like we all have and all do. But because it was a big story, it colored people's views of Alomar for years.

There is a psychological principle underneath this called the "fundamental attribution error." When we see someone do something terrible, we assume that the person is a genuinely terrible person, through and through. We erroneously attribute the action as being something fundamental to the person, hence the name "fundamental attribution error."

In reality, though, everyone does dumb things in moments of weakness, and it doesn't mean anything. I'm generally a nice guy, but I've had moments of screaming insanely at other drivers on the highway. I regret doing so, of course. But those people I screamed at probably think I'm a psychopath, and will always think so, even if I play second base at a very high level for 15 years (which is admittedly unlikely at this point).

Roberto Alomar was a wonderful player who once did something stupid that grabbed headlines. He's a definite Hall-of-Famer.

Craig Biggio (1988-2007; career OPS+: 117)

	Career	Rank	Hitting	Rank	Fielding	Rank	Peak	Rank	Bests	JAWS	Rank
WAR	65.1	12	75.1	6	-3.9	95	41.6	14	3	53.4	13
WS	432.6	5	332.1	5	100.9	6	223.5	5	5	NA	5

In the "New Historical Baseball Abstract," Bill James rated Craig Biggio as the fifth-best second baseman of all time. And this was a good six years before Biggio's retirement. James also argued, pretty cogently, that Biggio was a better player than Ken Griffey Jr. Griffey hit more homers, but Biggio beat Griffey in everything else, including little things like hit-by-pitches and grounded-into-double-plays that can make differences in the margins.

He goes as far as rating Biggio as the 35th-best player of all time, between Eddie Mathews and Warren Spahn. Later James said he may have been a bit overenthusiastic about Biggio. But still, there's no question he's a Hall-of-Famer.

It's crazy that it took three years to get Biggio elected. No one seriously thinks little ol' Pigpen was juicing, do they? More likely, it's because he wasn't a big power hitter, and there is a bias towards power hitters. It's the old Biggio vs. Griffey thing again; I bet Griffey won't have to wait a day.

Also, the BBWAA ballot is currently so overstuffed with valid candidates nowadays that voters can't find room for them all. Before the the class of 2015 was announced, Jayson Stark had a great column ("Explaining my Hall of Fame ballot," ESPN.com, January 5, 2015) decrying the rule that restricts him to voting for only ten players. The intent of this rule is probably to prevent too many players from getting in at once. But it ends up preventing conscientious voters like Stark, who understand the Hall's true dimensions, from doing their jobs.

Stark knew that more than ten players deserved induction. He couldn't vote for them all, so he had to pick the ten best. He was forced to leave out Alan Trammell and other guys who may not be first-ballot types but are clearly solid mid-range HOFers. The class of mid-range HOFers includes guys like Gabby Hartnett and Bert Blyleven. Hartnett, Blyleven and many like them slowly gained momentum over years of voting, as more and more people became convinced of their credentials.

This long, labored process is necessary only because most Hall of Fame voters have no clue about the true size of the Hall, as I mentioned in the first chapter. They base their standards on the 50 or so guys they've heard of, or on whatever other arbitrary feeling they've conjured up. It then takes years to get these voters on board. Stark's fellow ESPN writer David Schoenfield revealed himself to be one of these when he said Biggio was a "borderline" Hall-of-Famer ("Winners and losers on Hall election day," ESPN.com, January 6, 2015).

But because Stark and his fellow right-minded voters are restricted to ten players, these mid-range HOFers can't gain momentum. Instead their percentages drop each year as writers must prioritize the brand-new shoo-ins. If players don't make it in their first few years on the ballot, they might as well give up.

This begs the question: Why is the BBWAA ballot so full nowadays? Good question! Well begged! (And congratulations again on asking a good question! They say that there are no stupid questions, but that's a lie. People who say that are just being nice so that you will feel comfortable asking any question, stupid or smart. Those people are usually teachers who are desperate for people to ask questions.)

I should probably answer your great question. Here's why the BBWAA ballot is so full. There are almost twice as many major-league teams now than there were before expansion. If we stay true to the standards that the Hall has established, choosing the same 1.5% of all players, then we need to elect almost twice as many Hall of Famers per year. That's hard to do when you have artificial, arbitrary restraints like the ten-only rule. It serves as a completely pointless bottleneck.

Thankfully, the 2014 and 2015 BBWAA elections were nice and big: Greg Maddux, Tom Glavine, Frank Thomas, Randy Johnson, Pedro Martinez, John Smoltz, and our buddy Biggio all made the club.

Those selections helped rectify the damage made by the 2013 BBWAA vote, which was an absolute disgrace. No one got in despite a load of deserving candidates, including Biggio, Mike Piazza, Tim Raines, Jeff Bagwell, and of course Barry Bonds and Roger Clemens.

It was the height of anti-steroid self-righteousness, and many voters sent in blank ballots as some sort of childish, melodramatic protest. Yeah, good job, that really showed them, guys. Craig Biggio definitely needed to be punished for never being involved with steroids in any way. And, mind you, he avoided steroids when temptations to do so were rampant. He epitomized the values you were supposedly fighting for. By the way, I think you guys would be great for this protest I'm planning: We're speaking out against genetically modified crops by destroying all the food in the world.

Let's hope the last few elections suggest that writers may have learned from that mistake. Let's hope reason continues to reign, and no more Craig Biggios have to wait longer than they should.

Eddie Collins (1906-1930; career OPS+: 142)

	Career	Rank	Hitting	Rank	Fielding	Rank	Peak	Rank	Bests	JAWS	Rank
WAR	123.9	2	119.6	2	8.2	39	64.2	2	9	94.1	2
WS	572.3	1	463.3	1	108.6	3	277.9	2	10	NA	2

Eddie Collins is one of those inner-circle Hall-of-Famers that casual fans don't know about. I like to do quizzes on this Web site called Sporcle (name check, Sporcle! Give me free stuff like ... um ... your quizzes, which are already free ... man, I'm a terrible pitchman). One of my favorite quizzes, perhaps not surprisingly, involves naming all the Baseball Hall-of-Famers in 20 minutes. At the end they show you how many previous quiz-takers successfully named each name.

It's a convenient, if unscientific way to find out how famous a player is amongst people who think they know a lot about the Hall of Fame. Among more than 200,000 plays by these dyed-in-the-wool baseball nerds, Eddie Collins was named by only 55%. He is in the middle of the pack, below guys like Johnny Evers and Bill Mazeroski who couldn't hold Collins' glove if it were made of duct tape.

(Pop quiz: Which Hall-of-Famer do you think the most quiz-takers successfully named? Which got named the least? Answers at the end of this comment.)

I suppose I can understand why Collins isn't better known. He played a very long time ago and doesn't have ultra-flashy stats like Rogers Hornsby's .400 batting averages. Fans of not tanking World Series games might know Eddie Collins as one of the Clean Sox in 1919. But they still might not realize how good he really was.

Well, now you know. Eddie Collins was a superstar, a good candidate for the best second baseman of all-time. He's obviously in.

(Answers: The player the most people guessed correctly in the Sporcle quiz was Babe Ruth. Zero points if you guessed that, because it's pretty easy. Negative a million points if you guessed anyone else. The player people named the least was Jake Beckley. A million points if you guessed Beckley, because there are a lot of competitors for the most obscure Hall-of-Famer. But, as you know if you read the Beckley comment, Beckley is an apt choice for most obscure, since his record was unremarkable to say the least. So give me those million points back. You get zero points.)

Bobby Doerr (1937-1944, 1946-1951; career OPS+: 115)

	Career	Rank	Hitting	Rank	Fielding	Rank	Peak	Rank	Bests	JAWS	Rank
WAR	51.2	20	46.1	22	13.4	18	36.4	19	0	43.8	19
WS	282.0	18	196.4	19	85.6	16	176.6	17	1	NA	18

Doerr was a good hitter and fine fielder whose hitting stats were inflated by playing for the Red Sox in a time when Fenway Park was like Coors Field. In his career, Doerr hit .315/.396/.533 at home and .261/.327/.389 on the road. But a run scored in Fenway was still a run.

Doerr spent 1945, his age-27 season, as an infantryman in Portland, Oregon. He was waiting to do two things: kick some fascists and drink some beer (only to discover, perhaps ironically considering he was in Portland, that he had almost run out of beer.[19]) The war ended before he got the chance, so instead he helped the Red Sox to the 1946 A.L. pennant. Doerr hit .409/.458/.509 in the World Series. But because one guy in Worcester wasn't wearing his lucky hat while listening to the games, the curse of the Bambino held firm and the Red Sox lost to the Cardinals.

At age 33, Doerr bent down for a grounder and felt something snap in his back. Serious back pain became chronic, taking him out of the lineup for long stretches. Rather than risk a more serious injury, he retired.

Doerr could have tried to tough it out a few more years. But realistically, the most likely outcome of that approach would have been poor performances and long stretches of inaction. It would have gotten him some "guttiness" points among the more macho-minded, but would have only hurt his team. Doerr was a reasonable, down-to-earth guy, so he accepted that his time was up.

The back injury gives us a what-could-have-been story with Doerr. But it doesn't change his credentials, which aren't spectacular. The war service and World Series performance bump him up a bit. Doerr is a pretty solid low-end Hall-of-Famer.

Johnny Evers (1902-1917, 1922, 1929; career OPS+: 106)

	Career	Rank	Hitting	Rank	Fielding	Rank	Peak	Rank	Bests	JAWS	Rank
WAR	47.7	24	33.1	42	15.4	14	33.4	28	0	40.6	26
WS	267.0	21	194.2	20	66.8	25	170.4	21	0	NA	25

Johnny Evers, Joe Tinker and Frank Chance were all elected together, by the now-maligned 1946 Old Timers Committee. Ten players and one executive were chosen, and the three Cub infielders are only a few of the questionable ones.

[19] Reference explanation: In the 1994 film "Dazed and Confused," a tough guy notes "I only came here to do two things: kick some ass and drink some beer. Looks like we're almost out of beer."

People now assume that the trio got in because the "Tinker to Evers to Chance" poem, which is actually called "Baseball's Sad Lexicon." It also contains the phrase "pricking our gonfalon bubble," which means "ruining our hopes for a pennant." I've tried to get this phrase back into circulation by calling "Boomer and The Mad Dog" on KFAN every day and asking whether the Red Sox will prick the Yanks' gonfalon bubble. But I always just get a goofy sound effect in response.

I'm not so convinced the poem really had that much influence on Tinker, Evers, and Chance being elected. In 1946, there was a different focus for the Hall of Fame. Voters were much less interested in career stats and much more interested in electing people who were integral to legendary teams, like the juggernaut Cubs of 1906-1910. The Committee's choices were widely applauded at the time. It's worth noting that in the BBWAA nominating vote the same year, Frank Chance and Johnny Evers finished first and second, respectively. Both were ahead of many players with much better numbers, including Lefty Grove, Frankie Frisch, Mickey Cochrane, and Carl Hubbell. None got over the 75% threshold for the BBWAA, though. (Why, you may ask, were the BBWAA and Old Timers' Committee voting on the same players? It's complicated. Bill James' "Whatever Happened to the Hall of Fame" has the details, if you're interested.)

Since those days, the Hall's elections have put more emphasis on career numbers. Plenty of integral players to great teams, from Roger Maris to Gil Hodges, have failed to make the Hall largely because their career stats were not at the level of other Hall-of-Famers. I'm not saying this is necessarily a better or worse way of determining a Hall-of-Famer. But the career-numbers focus has been dominant for a very long time, shaping almost the entire membership. I believe in going by what the Hall has already established. So that means I take career numbers seriously.

That prevailing career-numbers focus is a big reason why people jump on selections like Evers'. Lifetime he hit .270/.356/.334, which is just a touch lower than Luis Castillo's line. Yikes.

Of course, you and I know that Johnny Evers and Luis Castillo played in very different times. Evers was squarely in the dead-ball era (his last year of more than one game was 1917), when a single was a reason for a parade, and no one hit homers. Castillo played in the 2000s, when a single was a reason to sigh and say "Really? Not a homer?"

Granted, being better than Luis Castillo does not make you a Hall-of-Famer, not by a long shot. Among recent players, a better comparison for Evers is Chuck Knoblauch. Both had a few terrific years, a few good ones, and some subpar ones in a not-very-long career. Knoblauch was probably a better hitter, even when context is taken into account. But Evers was a better fielder, in part because he didn't contract the yips late in his career.

So does Chuck Knoblauch belong in the Hall of Fame? Most fans would say no. Does Johnny Evers deserve to get kicked out? Ehhhh ... the issue of being integral to the 1906-10 Cubs holds some weight with me, but not a ton. The talents of your teammates, in my book, should not be a huge factor in deciding awards like Hall of Fame inclusion. Hall of Fame membership is an award for an individual, not a team. They have team awards already, called championships, and they're at least supposed to be the main goal of the game.

But what if I told you that Evers was part of another great team, and showed clear leadership in making them great? I should start by saying that Evers was a high-strung fellow, to say the least. He was known as "The Crab" for his fiery, argumentative personality. He was so acerbic that he and his otherwise agreeable double-play partner Joe Tinker refused to speak to each other for years.

Evers had a brilliant, fervent mind but couldn't sit still, existing as a tight bundle of jagged edges and sharp movements. Nowadays he might be diagnosed with ADHD or an anxiety disorder and given some good medications. He might learn how to channel all that mental acuity and nervous energy into a successful career in academia or business. But in those days, a person like Evers had no choice but to do something that involved moving his body constantly. So he played baseball every day until he exhausted himself enough to get to sleep.

Even here are two paths for a personality like Evers'. The typical one is to spew your volcanic emotions on other people. During the 1910 World Series Evers was injured and on crutches, but remained in the dugout so he could hurl his customary torrent of abuse at his opponents. Even teammates who couldn't stand him felt some appreciation for his devotion to the team.

But then, in 1911, when some of his investments failed, Evers suffered a nervous breakdown and had to sit out most of the season. Sometimes all that fury can direct inwards and wreak havoc.

He finally got on the Cubs' last nerve in 1913. Through a complicated, acrimonious series of public arguments and negotiations between Evers, Cubs owner Charles Murphy, and the brand-new Federal League, Evers ended up on the pathetic Boston Braves, who hadn't finished above .500 in more than a decade.

Braves manager George Stallings immediately made Evers the team captain. Nowadays, team captain is an honor almost no player ever gets, and when one does, his responsibilities run from "smile for the cameras" to "uhhh ... I don't know -- we're just trying to say that we like you." But in Evers' days, when there were few if any coaches, being team captain was like being the manager's right hand man.

Evers took his new role as captain of the 1914 Braves very seriously, pushing his fellow players hard and leading by example. The fervor with which he approached everything had found a constructive outlet. The team won a surprise world championship and became known as the "Miracle Braves." Evers hit pretty well that season, and the combination of performance and leadership earned him the Chalmers Award, the MVP of the time.

Add that to the mix, and Evers does not have a bad case for the Hall of Fame. But the numbers in the table above still give me pause. Part of me wants to dump Evers, but I just can't. Evers is standing on a trap door, and I have my hand on the lever, but .... most everyone above Evers on the charts is in the Hall of Fame or should be. No one below him really should be, but still ... I give Evers a D- in his Hall of Fame qualifications, which still passes my class. He's going to stay.

Nellie Fox (1947-1965; career OPS+: 93)

	Career	Rank	Hitting	Rank	Fielding	Rank	Peak	Rank	Bests	JAWS	Rank
WAR	49.0	23	36.7	34	21.0	5	36.8	18	2	42.9	20
WS	304.8	15	193.1	21	111.8	2	178.8	16	4	NA	15

I was a bit shocked to discover that Nellie Fox's OPS+ was that low. He got lots of hits, leading the league four times, but I suppose he didn't have any power or walk much.

But he was a great defensive player, a close second to Bill Mazeroski in Fielding Win Shares. In career Defensive WAR, he scores fifth, again not far behind the leader, Mazeroski. (I am physically unable to not tell you who the other three were: Joe Gordon, Frankie Frisch, and Frank White).

I mentioned in the Ray Schalk comment that it's very hard for great defense alone to make you worthy of the Hall of Fame. But Schalk hit like Tony Pena. Fox hit like Mark Ellis or Luis Castillo (there he is again). That's a significant difference, the difference between an 8th-place hitter and a leadoff guy. For Fox, his qualifications are mostly great defense, but all those hits help too. Like Doerr and Evers, he squeaks in.

Frankie Frisch (1919-1937; career OPS+: 110)

	Career	Rank	Hitting	Rank	Fielding	Rank	Peak	Rank	Bests	JAWS	Rank
WAR	70.4	8	56.8	12	21.6	3	44.3	11	4	57.4	7
WS	364.8	8	257.9	9	106.7	4	194.9	10	2	NA	11

I'm kicking Frankie Frisch out of the Hall because of his role in the Veterans Committee of the 1970s, which made a whole bunch of terrible selections. Done. Next. Charlie Gehringer was also involved in the Veterans Committee in the 1970s, so he's out automatically. Next.

OK, I can't do that. Frisch is clearly worthy, with stats registering about average among HOF second basemen. He hit for average, slapped doubles, stole lots of bases, and played superior defense. He also managed the 1934 "Gas House Gang" Cardinals to a championship, and led several other successful teams. He's in for sure.

Charlie Gehringer (1924-1942; career OPS+: 124)

	Career	Rank	Hitting	Rank	Fielding	Rank	Peak	Rank	Bests	JAWS	Rank
WAR	80.6	5	77.5	5	10.7	26	50.5	6	6	65.6	5
WS	382.5	6	295.4	6	87.0	15	216.0	7	6	NA	8

Charlie Gehringer was nicknamed "The Mechanical Man" because he was a cyborg sent back from the year 2029 to kill John Connor.[20] There was a glitch in his programming, though, and his naked body was accidentally transported to the Detroit Tigers clubhouse in 1924. Manager Ty Cobb immediately slapped a uniform on him and told him to get out on the field, pronto, you goshdarn ne'er-do-well (or words to that effect that are not fit for this publication.)

Another more factual reason for Gehringer's nickname was that he could be relied on, year after year, to produce the same combination of great offense and good defense. Both Win Shares and WAR show a remarkable level of sustained excellence. A score of 30 Win Shares in a season is considered MVP-level, and Gehringer got at least 30 every year from 1934 to 1937. A comparable WAR is around 7, and Gehringer accomplished that every season from 1933-1937. And he had plenty of other great years before and after his peak.

The "Mechanical Man" nickname also fit his personality: quiet and efficient, with never any wasted words or motions. In fact, it would be an affront to Gehringer's legacy to use up any more words or motions describing him. A no-doubter.

---

[20] Reference explanation: "The Terminator." You should really know that one.

Joe Gordon (1938-1943, 1946-1950; career OPS+: 120)

	Career	Rank	Hitting	Rank	Fielding	Rank	Peak	Rank	Bests	JAWS	Rank
WAR	57.1	15	41.4	29	22.4	2	45.8	10	6	51.5	14
WS	242.7	27	172.8	34	69.8	19	183.9	14	4	NA	16

It took a while for Joe Gordon to make the Hall, probably in part because his career was short and in part because people were thinking "Really? Do we need another Yankee? We get it, they're good. Enough already."

But Gordon wasn't just another Yankee -- he also played for Cleveland! And on each team he was clearly the best second baseman in baseball, leading 2Bs in WAR in 1939, 1941, 1942, 1943, 1947 and 1948. He might have led in 1944 and 1945 too if he wasn't busy giving Tojo the what-for in World War II.

WAR might be a bit over-enthused about Gordon's defense, though. It has his career number just 1.5 WAR below Bill Mazeroski's, despite playing in 27% fewer games. Win Shares are less giddy about Gordon defensively, but still gives him the title of best second baseman in baseball four times out of his scant 11 major-league seasons.

Gordon was also a class act and a great leader. When Larry Doby became the second African-American to join an MLB team, he got the cold shoulder from most of his new Cleveland teammates. In the warm-ups before Doby's first game, no one tried to play catch with him. Gordon saw what was happening and yelled "Hey, kid. Come on. Throw with me." (Source: Gordon's SABR biography, by Joseph Wancho.) Gordon ended up taking Doby under his wing, as he did with many other young players.

A few more good years and Gordon might have been on par with Frankie Frisch. Either way, he's a Hall-of-Famer.

Frank Grant (1886-1907)

	Rank at Position Among Negro Leaguers	Rank Among All Negro Leaguers
Bill James	6	unranked
SABR	unranked	unranked
Monte Irvin	unranked	NA

Frank Grant is an interesting player. He played for several years in the minor leagues of the 1880s before the color line pushed him out.

These leagues were nothing like the minor leagues of today. There was much less formal structure in the 1800s, with no strict hierarchy. Teams in "higher" leagues didn't own teams in "lower" leagues and couldn't call up players whenever they wanted. Instead there were dozens of independent leagues, displaying varying levels of skill, constantly forming and folding. The major leagues were only "major" because their teams were in the biggest cities, had the highest attendance figures, and could afford to buy players from minor league teams. Maybe it's a bit like college football today, if college players routinely transferred schools.

Grant was never brought to the major leagues despite his excellent play. Even before the color line was firmly established, African-American players had a hell of a time getting work. Fans were not the problem; Frank Grant was a huge fan favorite. The problem was other players.

Pitchers aimed for Grant's head. Reportedly, the feet-first slide with the intention of spiking the second baseman was invented to hurt him. He had to invent wooden shin guards to keep his legs intact. His teammates were no better.

But Grant's teams did well, so they resisted competitors' calls to establish a color line. Different leagues, minor and major, banned African-Americans at different times. Usually teams with black players would get hounded by league-mates until they gave in and released their players. Eventually Grant's teams gave in under the pressure.

This was how the color line was established: by unofficial, off-the-books "gentleman's agreements" among baseball owners. It never took the form of a straight-up "rule" because such a rule could have been challenged in the courts. Owners knew they might not get away with formal league-wide bans based solely on race.

Not until 1896, in the infamous Plessy vs. Ferguson decision, did the Supreme Court make so-called "separate but equal" Jim Crow laws explicitly legal. And even then, Jim Crow laws were much more prevalent in the South. Most professional baseball teams were in the North and Midwest, and would have encountered resistance if they tried to institute clearly defined bans. In the days before anti-discrimination laws, it was much easier just to decline to employ people for your own, unofficial (but universally understood) reason.

When he could no longer play for white teams, Grant moved to black teams like the Cuban Giants, which barnstormed exclusively. The Cuban Giants deserve a digression here. Despite the name, the Cuban Giants played on the East Coast exclusively, never in Cuba. And the team was not made of Cubans. The first Cuban Giants were African-American waiters from Babylon, Long Island who pretended to be Cuban so they could be accepted by white patrons. At the time, white people held dark-skinned Cubans in much higher esteem than they did African-Americans. The team even spoke gibberish on the field that was meant to sound like Spanish. In 1885, the Giants were able to give up their jobs as waiters and become full-time barnstorming ballplayers. The same way the 1869 Cincinnati Reds are remembered as the first fully professional white team, the 1885 Cuban Giants should be remembered as the first fully professional black team.

To be clear, Grant did not play on that pioneering Cuban Giants team. He played for them later, and for other black-only teams. But Seamheads.com has only 74 PAs for him on such teams. In the aforementioned white minor leagues, Grant's 1185 PAs show some good numbers: .336 career batting average, .486 slugging. (There is no on-base percentage because walks were not tallied.)

Unfortunately, there's not much I can do with those numbers. Grant looks to be among the best players in several high minor leagues in the 1880s, but how do you translate those results to something comparable to other Negro League players or MLB players? Not to sound like an ogre, but there are dozens of players who did as well in the minors but are not in the Hall of Fame.

Of course, I'm mostly influenced by the results in the chart above. Bill James has Grant as the sixth best second baseman in Negro League history, below the threshold for the Hall. SABR doesn't have him among their top 40 most influential figures. Monte Irvin and his co-writer Phil Pepe make no mention of him at all. These are the sources I'm trusting to provide me with the judgments I can't get from just numbers, and they're not telling me Grant was a Hall-of-Famer.

There are plenty of anecdotes saying that Grant was the best black player of the 1800s. But others say it may have been George Stovey, Robert Higgins, or Bud Fowler. And then there's Moses Fleetwood Walker, who made the major-league American Association in 1884 and played relatively well under extreme harassment. They all might have a claim. I don't really know who to believe, and I don't feel comfortable relying just on hearsay.

And moreover, even if Grant were the best African-American player in the 1800s, does that necessarily mean he had Hall-of-Fame ability? Louis Sockalexis may have been the best Native American player of the 1800s -- does that necessarily mean he had Hall-of-Fame ability?

Now I'm really starting to sound like an ogre, or worse. But the unfortunate fact is that African-American baseball was in a very, very early stage of development in the 1800s. There were just a handful of professional African-American players, and once they were banned from white ball, it took decades to build separate, stable teams and leagues. The color line meant Grant suffered from systemic societal conditions and should get credit for that, just like Roy Campanella did. But Campanella clearly demonstrated that he had major-league-level talent. I just don't see solid evidence of that with Grant.

Racism was clearly the major reason there was little organized Negro League baseball in the 1800s. But demographics played a role too. At the time, professional baseball was the province of Northern cities that had very small African-American populations. Grant was born in Massachusetts, which was 1% African-American from 1880-1890. The National League teams in 1885 were in Chicago (1% African-American in both the 1880 and 1890 censuses), New York (2%), Philadelphia (4%), Providence (2%), Boston (2%), Detroit (2% in 1880, 1% in 1890), Buffalo (less than 1%) and St. Louis (6%). Rural areas in the North had barely any African-Americans at all. Combine all these cities' African-American populations and you get around 100,000 men, women and children. That's not a large number of people to draw players from, or, for that matter, to draw fans from. (Data source: Minnesota Population Center. National Historical Geographic Information System: Version 2.0. Minneapolis, MN: University of Minnesota 2011)

Things changed after the first Great Migration of 1910-1930 brought millions of African-Americans from the rural South to the industrial North. A much larger pool of potential players and fans came to baseball cities. But even during the heyday of the Negro Leagues from 1920-1945, most players came from the South to play in the North. There were likely tremendous African-American athletes in the South in the 1800s, but they wouldn't make the move north unless they knew they could find work.

My point is that there's not much reason to assume that a Hall-of-Fame talent necessarily had to exist in the tiny African-American baseball-playing community of the North before 1900. Even if Frank Grant was the best of this small community, which is a big "if," it's hard to know if he could have hacked it in the majors.

Maybe Grant should be in the "Pioneers and Executives" category? Other early players who were important but don't have full playing records are taken out of the Hall of Fame gen pop and considered a "pioneer." For example, Sol White is in the "Pioneers and Executives" wing. He was another African-American player from the 1800s who later established and ran teams and leagues. Frank Grant doesn't have qualifications like these; he played well, but otherwise did not contribute to the development of the Negro Leagues.

Another possible reason Frank Grant got the nod was to give the Hall of Fame a second baseman from the Negro Leagues. My sources obviously don't think Grant was the best choice on that count. Bill James and Monte Irvin pick Bingo DeMoss as the best second baseman in Negro League history. The SABR list goes with Newt Allen, but DeMoss is not far behind. Neither is in the Hall, and neither is considered by any source to be among the top 30 players of Negro League history. Second base is just not a strong position among Negro Leaguers.

I should say that the people who selected Negro Leaguers for the Hall of Fame were very good at what they did, much more knowledgeable and qualified than the BBWAA or Veterans' Committee has ever been. They might know more than I do; in fact I know they do. Shouldn't I just trust their judgment?

I contacted Leslie Heaphy, a member of the committee that chose Grant for the Hall. She argued that the lists I'm using for my rankings don't cover many 1800s players because of lack of information. Grant excelled for 15 years on black teams, she said, and the minor-league teams on which he starred were just a step below the major leagues. She also sent over a quote from Sol White:

"Frank Grant ... in those days, was the baseball marvel. His playing was a revelation to his fellow teammates, as well as the spectators. In hitting he ranked with the best and his fielding bordered on the impossible. Grant was a born ballplayer." (Source: Grant's SABR biography, by Brian McKenna.)

These are good arguments, and I'm tempted to give Grant a pass. But in her correspondence with me Ms. Heaphy also said "Using the rankings you do certainly adds consistency but was not the criteria used to judge any of those inducted in 2006." That gets to the whole point of this book. I'm trying to set up standards that provide consistency that real selection processes have never had. That is so essential to this book that I don't see how I can contravene it for a single player.

The standards in the above chart are saying Frank Grant is not a Hall-of-Famer. Maybe the 2006 committee knew something that SABR, Bill James, Monte Irvin and Phil Pepe did not. But when push comes to shove, I have go with the outside resources over the Hall-of-Fame selection committees, even committees as good as the 2006 Negro Leagues one. Otherwise I'm just rubber-stamping Hall-of-Fame selections according to my own whims.

And I certainly do not have the standing or reputation to do that. I'm not a writer who people know and respect enough to trust with those sorts of predominantly subjective judgements. I can only act as the caretaker and interpreter of the standards I've established. I allow myself to inject just a bit of personal opinion in the final assessment, but not nearly enough to overcome Grant's low rankings.

The "It's the Hall of Fame, not Hall of Stats" argument doesn't apply here either, as Grant was never very famous. I'm unsure about this, but as it stands now, **Frank Grant is out**. I'm very willing to hear new evidence that might reopen his case. (Again, the email is chrisekeedei@yahoo.com. Any disrespectful emails will be deleted and I will never see them.) For now, his case is closed.

Billy Herman (1931-1943, 1946-1947; career OPS+: 112)

	Career	Rank	Hitting	Rank	Fielding	Rank	Peak	Rank	Bests	JAWS	Rank
WAR	54.7	17	49.3	16	12.4	23	35.5	24	0	45.1	18
WS	258.6	20	188.7	23	70.1	18	184.3	13	0	NA	14

Ugh, that last one was brutal. Centuries of horrific systemic racism sure make it hard to judge Hall-of-Famers. That's it; I've decided I don't like racism any more. (Joke, joke. I still love racism. (JOKE JOKE JOKE.))

Here's a less difficult one. Playing at the same time as Charlie Gehringer and Joe Gordon, Billy Herman was never the best second baseman in baseball. But since those guys played in the AL, Herman was often the best in the NL. And he spent 1944 and 1945 giving those fascist schnitzel-eaters a little American apple pie through the barrel of a howitzer (I'll start running out of weird ways to say "he fought in World War II" soon, don't worry). He was good before and after his time overseas.

If Herman had retired yesterday, those people who think they know the Hall of Fame but have never actually familiarized themselves with all its members (i.e., most everybody) would scoff at the idea that he's worthy. It's similar to the way Lou Whitaker dropped off the ballot in his first year of eligibility. Whitaker never had an MVP-type season, being mentioned in MVP voting only once. But he spent a long time being very good.

You might not think it should be this way, but the Hall of Fame has already firmly established that "a long time being very good" is worthy of induction, particularly for catchers and middle infielders. Herman joins Johnny Evers, Bobby Doerr and Nellie Fox at the bottom rung of the Hall.

Rogers Hornsby (1915-1937; career OPS+: 175)

	Career	Rank	Hitting	Rank	Fielding	Rank	Peak	Rank	Bests	JAWS	Rank
WAR	127.0	1	121.6	1	13.9	17	73.5	1	11	100.3	1
WS	502.6	3	439.4	2	59.2	39	283.6	1	9	NA	3

Rogers Hornsby played through some of the dead-ball era and then, with Babe Ruth, made the 1920s the crazy time they were. Together they danced the Charleston, sat on flagpoles, wrote "The Great Gatsby," and monopolized the Atlantic City whiskey trade under the pseudonyms "Nucky Thompson" and "that self-conscious murderer with half his face blown off."[21]

WAR goes crazy for the Rajah, giving him the number one spot among second basemen across the board and reworking its acronym to mean "We Adore Rogers." According to WAR, Hornsby was not only the best second baseman, he was the best NL non-pitcher every single year from 1917 to 1929, except 1923, when he missed 40 games with an injury, and 1926, when he just had an off year.

Bill James is less complimentary, noting that Hornsby was a bad fielder, which he was. Second base was more of an offense-first position at the time, so leaving Hornsby at second was a little like trying Miguel Cabrera at third base again. Win Shares' assessment of his defense seems a bit more realistic.

In terms of whether Hornsby really is the best second baseman of all time, I don't know if I would go with WAR or James. And please don't make me choose between my baseball-analysis-world mommy and daddy. Regardless, I use my judicious judgment to judge that Hornsby is a HOFer.

---

[21] Reference explanation: Watch "Boardwalk Empire." It's great.

Nap Lajoie (1896-1916; career OPS+: 150)

	Career	Rank	Hitting	Rank	Fielding	Rank	Peak	Rank	Bests	JAWS	Rank
WAR	107.4	3	97.8	4	10.1	27	60.2	3	9	83.8	3
WS	495.2	4	381.4	4	91.8	12	258.0	4	10	NA	6

You have a favorite player, right? Derek Jeter? Derek Holland? Derek Lilliquist, if you're a member of his family? Derek Bell, if you love players who go into "Operation Shutdown" if they aren't given starting jobs they don't deserve?[22]

Let me ask you this: Has a team ever considered renaming themselves after your favorite player? The American League Cleveland team did, changing their name in 1903 from the Bronchos (huh?[23]) to the Naps. They stayed the Naps until 1915, when they sold the actual Nap to the Philadelphia A's. Because it felt a bit weird to have a team named after a competing player, they changed their name again, to the Indians.

You may have heard that they chose the name to honor Louis Sockalexis, a Native American who played for the Cleveland Spiders from 1897-1899. This always seemed an odd choice to me, since Sockalexis was hardly a star; he hit pretty well but had only 395 career PAs.

The truth is that the 1914 "Miracle" Boston Braves were so popular nationwide that Cleveland thought they could make a splash by choosing a similar nickname. The Sockalexis myth is often trotted out to make the name seem less offensive.

I don't know how you feel about the Cleveland team being called the "Indians," and I don't care, because I don't know you, and therefore I don't like you. (Joke.) Being a writer, I care only about what I think, and about forcing others to think the same. (Joke again, though with some truth in it.) And I think that if actual real-life Native Americans find a sports team name offensive, what does it matter if I, a non-Native-American, am accustomed to that name? How does it hurt me to start calling the team by a new name? Does my slight inconvenience outweigh the genuine pain that people are feeling? What stake do I have in this?

People often rebut arguments like that by saying "It's tradition!" or something along those lines. But what does that really mean? "It's tradition" means "I am used to it, enjoy it, and will have to adjust to it going away." Well, that can be said for just about anything that has ever existed. For everything there is always someone who is used to it, enjoys it, and will have to adjust to it going away. That says nothing about whether it actually *should* exist, especially if it insults millions of people.

---

[22] Reference explanation: That tells most of the story, but here are the details. During spring training in 2002, outfielder Derek Bell was shocked to discover from a reporter that he was in competition for a starting spot. He had played poorly the year before, and was always overrated. But he had clearly been signed by the Pirates to be a regular. The team should have let him know. But Bell didn't handle this news well, and declared that he would go into "Operation Shutdown" if he had to win a job. This only made the Pirates' decision easy. They released him before opening day despite still owing him $4.5 million.

[23] "Bronchos" are nachos for bros. Taco Bell has helpfully suggested that people "slam" said "bronchos" when "bangin'" out a ballgame with their best "brohams," "dude" (exclamation point). In addition, bronchos are a type of horse.

It was once tradition for white singers like Al Jolson to dress up in blackface and do an insulting pantomime of black performers. People were used to it, enjoyed it, and had to adjust to it going away. They probably had no idea how painful it was for African-Americans. That doesn't make them bad people; they just didn't know. They would only be morally questionable if they were doing it nowadays, after it's been firmly established that it's offensive.

As a kid, it didn't occur to me that the Cleveland Indians' name would be offensive. I didn't think about it one way or the other. But then I heard actual Native Americans talk about it. They talked about the depths of despair they felt when entire stadiums of people indulged in gross stereotypes of Native Americans as one-dimensional warrior savages.

Then there's that logo, with its big cartoonish grin, ridiculously red skin, and single feather sticking out from its head. It's hard to think of something more demeaning. The National Conference on American Indians put this in context, depicting similar hats for imaginary teams called the New York Jews and the San Francisco Chinamen.

What if a sports team were called the Cleveland Honkeys? What if their logo was a cartoon version of me, with a big dumb grin and a ridiculously large nose? Wouldn't that seem unnecessarily cruel? Maybe it just doesn't work to name a sports team after a human ethnic group. Maybe we should stick to animals and more recently, vaguely positive conceptual nouns (the Magic, the Heat, the Wild, etc.)

But the Cleveland Honkeys doesn't really come close to capturing how the Native American team nicknames make people feel. We white folks did not experience what Native Americans did. About 99% of the people many call "Indians," (even though they have never had anything to do with India) were obliterated in the few centuries after white people arrived. Many died in wars, but most died from diseases for which they had no natural immunities. Some settlers discovered this and intentionally gave natives blankets infected with smallpox.

You and I didn't hand out any smallpox blankets personally; I get that. We were just born into this world; we didn't make it. But we can still adapt the tiniest bit. We can at the very least show at a small gesture of contrition for the actions of our ancestors by changing the name of a sports franchise. That feels like a very, very small gesture. In real terms, does that cost me anything? I don't see how it could.

So after hearing the perspectives of Native Americans, I thought about what it would be like to be in their shoes. And I had to say "Well, you make a good point. I hadn't thought of that. Now that I know that, I don't see any reason why it should continue." You learn, and you adapt to new knowledge.

At this point, I'm hoping some readers will have a similar moment of reflection and adaptation. I don't want anyone to feel any shame or guilt for calling the Cleveland team the Indians. Maybe it never entered your mind to think that anyone would take offense. That's OK. You didn't know. How could you, until someone told you?

It happens. Maybe you once inadvertently used an offensive term for an ethnic group. Maybe you said "Negro" or "colored" long after those terms were deemed acceptable. Maybe you're still saying "gypsy" or "midget." ("Roma" and "little person" are the preferred terms.) I understand. You're not a bad person. But I'm here to tell you, as a friend, that you shouldn't do that again. Now you know. You learn, and you adapt to new knowledge. It's OK.

I'm belaboring this because I strongly believe that this sort of gentle, constructive, educational approach should be used more in these sort of arguments. Every day, my Facebook feed is filled with the outrage du jour, in which someone says or does something that offends a whole group of people. It usually takes a political cast: Liberals respond with rage and then conservatives respond with counter-rage. They bark back and forth for a few hours. Then when they're both exhausted, they return to their corners. The next day, there's a new outrage. Repeat ad nauseam. Nothing is learned, and no one changes. It becomes a pointless exercise.

There has to be a better way. When people are offended, they should definitely make their feelings known, no doubt. But they should not make the mistake of immediately responding with fury. "What's wrong with you?" "How could you think that's acceptable?" "Who wouldn't know not to do that?" Taking this aggressive tack might vent some frustration and thus be more emotionally satisfying. But it is not going to convince anyone or bring about any positive change. It's just going to spark defensive responses.

When people are confronted with those sort of accusations, they feel backed into a corner. Then they lash out with whatever justifications they can muster. Pushed to a point of desperation, the logic of their arguments hardly matter. Their real motive is to demonstrate that they're not bad people, by any means necessary, regardless of whether any of it makes sense.

This is a very typical human tendency. We all need to think we're good people, and we'll do most anything to maintain that belief. Making logical sense becomes less important than protecting our self-image. That's why the "What's wrong with you?" approach doesn't work. It makes it about more than just one issue; it makes it about the person's core belief in their own worth. And people don't tend to give that up easily.

I'm trying to avoid all that mess here. I could go through more of the typical arguments in defense of offensive team nicknames, and rebut them all, no holds barred. If you're not convinced by the above, and really need to read that, see Appendix 1. But let's try to avoid that. I'd rather tell you that regardless of what you think about the Indians, you're not a terrible person. Not by a long shot. I'm just here to gently inform you that calling a team "Indians" is needless offense to an ethnic group that has already experienced genocide.

So that's my speech. And I already have a candidate for a new name for the Cleveland team: the Naps. Why not honor the team's best all-time player right in the team's name? And there is a history of this particular team name, much the way there was when the latest Washington team chose the "Nationals."

Anyway, Nap Lajoie was a real good player and Hall-of-Famer. The end.

(Postscript: I just realized that calling a team the "Naps" gives rivals some very easy punchlines: your players take naps on the field, people take naps when watching the Naps, etc. Rats. Well, it's too late now, because I already typed the above, and I don't know how to use the delete key.)

Tony Lazzeri (1926-1939; career OPS+: 121)

	Career	Rank	Hitting	Rank	Fielding	Rank	Peak	Rank	Bests	JAWS	Rank
WAR	49.9	22	50.3	15	5.2	59	35.1	25	1	42.5	21
WS	252.6	25	196.9	18	51.5	68	164.7	23	1	NA	19

Another Golden Age second baseman who's on the borderline of the Hall of Fame, Tony Lazzeri was a worse fielder than Doerr or Herman, but a better hitter. Lazzeri was known as an RBI man, but you would be too if you hit behind Babe Ruth and Lou Gehrig.

More interesting was the fact that Lazzeri suffered from epilepsy. He had to hide his condition as much as possible because many people at the time thought epileptic seizures were signs of demonic possession. He could have collapsed into a seizure on the field at any time. But he never did.

I'm reminded of a touching tribute to Jim Eisenreich in a Baseball Prospectus annual. The author of Eisenreich's blurb knew a boy who suffered from Tourette's syndrome. People tend to think Tourette's syndrome is tremendously hilarious because it involves shouting obscenities uncontrollably at random times.

But if you actually suffer from it, it's not so funny. It's completely debilitating. You can't trust yourself to be in public, because you're terrified that you'll suddenly, involuntarily make an embarrassing scene. You conclude that you'll never be able to have anything close to a normal life, that you'll be forever consigned to agonizing loneliness.

This boy suffering from Tourette's was absolutely floored to discover that Jim Eisenreich also suffered from the syndrome. You and I might be inspired by a player who came from our home town or was of the same ethnic group. Imagine if you had a brutal chronic condition, one that strictly defines and limits your life. And then you found out that someone who has the same condition made it all the way to the major leagues.

I hope epileptics look at Tony Lazzeri the way that boy looked at Jim Eisenreich. It takes great courage to play major league baseball at all. It takes something more than great courage to play major league baseball for 14 years while having a condition that can strike from nowhere and make you so vulnerable that you collapse, fall into unconsciousness, and approach death.

Epilepsy may not have stopped Lazzeri from playing baseball, but it did take his life. In 1946, he suffered a seizure and fell down a flight of steps. The coroner's report said it was heart failure, but that was unlikely. Lazzeri was only 42 years old and very fit. The medical establishment didn't know much about epilepsy at the time, and probably just put down "heart failure" for most sudden collapses. And I'm sure his family didn't proffer information about his epilepsy, considering it was still stigmatized.

All that aside, Lazzeri does not look out of place in the Hall of Fame.

Bill Mazeroski (1956-1972; career OPS+: 84)

	Career	Rank	Hitting	Rank	Fielding	Rank	Peak	Rank	Bests	JAWS	Rank
WAR	36.2	45	19.1	89	23.9	1	25.6	57	1	30.9	48
WS	217.5	36	105.5	73	112.5	1	132.6	53	0	NA	29

Is being the best defensive second baseman of all time enough to put you in the Hall of Fame? The JAWS rank says no, although WAR supports the conclusion that Mazeroski is the best defensively all-time at second base. Bill James' overall ranking of 29th says "maybe," and in "Whatever Happened to the Hall of Fame," he says "yes."

Here we have a similar situation as we did with Ray Schalk, who was a great defensive player but a poor hitter. Schalk was a good comp for 1980s catcher Tony Pena. For Mazeroski, I'd pick Frank White. White had a career 85 OPS+ and 21.4 Defensive WAR, very close to Maz on both counts. JAWS has White ranked 57th among second basemen, and James has him 31st, each again both close to Maz. Neither players have Hall-of-Fame-worthy overall rankings. It's not looking good for Mazeroski.

While both systems rate Mazeroski as the best-fielding defensive second baseman of all time, neither considers him the most valuable defensive player ever at any position, as many people claim. WAR has Ozzie Smith comfortably ahead of Maz, 43.4 to 25.6. Win Shares shows about a dozen shortstops as having more valuable defensive contributions than Maz. It doesn't look like any second baseman should get into the Hall of Fame on glovework alone.

Should I invoke the "It's the Hall of Fame, not the Hall of Stats" here? It would certainly help Mazeroski's case. Take my unofficial, unscientific "Hall-of-Famer Q score" that I mentioned in the Eddie Collins comment. Mazeroski was named by 60.7% of the 200,000 baseball nerds trying to recite all of the Hall-of-Famers, just above Lefty Grove and Juan Marichal (and well above Eddie Collins). Schalk was named by 33.2% of quizzers, and most of those probably entered his name ironically. Mazeroski is clearly quite famous.

It also helps that Maz hit a dramatic home run to win the 1960 World Series. He had a great Series overall, though, oddly, Yankee Bobby Richardson won the World Series MVP. Richardson had similar numbers but no Series-winning homer, and was obviously not on the winning team.

So those factors give him a boost ... but man, that hitting is really poor ... I can't do it. The Hall is about the sum of your accomplishments. Mazeroski's great fielding, his fame, and his single great World Series just don't add up to enough to overcome his bad hitting. **Mazeroski is out.**

Bid McPhee (1882-1899; career OPS+: 107)

	Career	Rank	Hitting	Rank	Fielding	Rank	Peak	Rank	Bests	JAWS	Rank
WAR	52.4	18	39.8	30	16.3	11	29.5	43	3	41.0	25
WS	305.4	14	206.9	15	98.7	7	149.3	44	1	NA	30

McPhee was very unusual for a player in the 1800s, in that he played for the same team, Cincinnati, for 18 years. He was also unusual in that he didn't get blinding drunk and fight all the time. Baseball in the 1800s would make a good HBO show, I'm telling you. It was crazy.

McPhee was a very good fielder and pretty good hitter who has low Peak rankings. He's reminding me of Jake Beckley. And if you're reading this in order like I told you to, you know where I ended up with Beckley. McPhee is on thin ice.

Like Beckley, McPhee was the best at his position a few times. But neither was ever a dominant force. McPhee had four seasons above 4 WAR but peaked at 5.2. Win Shares gives basically the same result: five totals above 20 but none exceeding 27. McPhee was the kind of player who would have gotten a few votes for third or fourth in the MVP voting, but probably never any first-place votes.

I bet McPhee was inducted in part because people realized the Hall didn't have a second baseman from the 1800s. The first to pop up is Nap Lajoie in 1898, unless you count John "Monte" Ward, a Hall-of-Fame shortstop who played second from 1892-1894.

Sometimes there just isn't a great player at a position for a couple of years. It is unprecedented for one position to have no Hall-of-Famer for a 20-year period. But then, by all evidence, the Negro Leagues never had a Hall-of-Fame second baseman. Maybe it's just the law of averages at work: Occasionally you're bound to get a strange result.

There were definitely better-hitting second basemen in the 1800s. Among all second basemen from 1871-1899 with 3000+ PAs, McPhee ranks 5th in OPS+, well behind Fred Dunlap and Cupid Childs, and a bit behind Hub Collins and Tom Daly. But they all had careers half as long as McPhee's, except Childs, who had 6,766 career PAs to McPhee's 9,429. Childs was in fact a much better hitter, with a 119 career OPS+. But because he was washed up by age 31, he ended up with a career Offensive WAR only a bit above McPhee's (42.7 to McPhee's 40.1) and a Batting Win Shares total significantly below (179.7 to McPhee's 206.9).

And McPhee's defense was much better than Childs', or indeed better than anyone of his generation. This was a time when no one wore gloves, because wearing gloves was regarded as about as manly as running away from the ball, collapsing into the fetal position, and crying your eyes out. (Brings me back to my Little League years.) It might not be entirely rational, but some part of me feels like fielding 2129 games at second base as well as McPhee did, sans glove, is pretty darn Hall-of-Fame-y. It is about 25% more than anyone else managed in the 1800s.

McPhee's longevity was truly outstanding for his time. Only Cap Anson played more games than McPhee did from 1871 to 1899. And Anson was playing the relatively cushy position of first base. Even today, second basemen are known to crap out early, probably earlier than any other position. There's something about that double-play pivot and those spikes to the knees that tends to make even the best ones fall apart around 35 years old.

I'm not a big fan of longevity being a primary Hall of Fame credential. If you're sticking around for years past your prime, padding out your numbers when your organization could easily find a better replacement, then those extra years should count against you, not for you. But this was not McPhee. His last three years had WARs of 1.8, 1.5, and 1.6 and Win Shares totals of 11, 15, and 12: not great, but still useful.

I don't like the fact that McPhee had no MVP-type seasons. But in the context of the 1800s, his defense and longevity were pretty special. Combine those with above-average offense, and I'll let him stay.

Joe Morgan (1963-1984; career OPS+: 132)

	Career	Rank	Hitting	Rank	Fielding	Rank	Peak	Rank	Bests	JAWS	Rank
WAR	100.3	4	103.7	3	3.3	74	59.3	4	8	79.8	4
WS	514.8	2	423.8	3	91.1	13	258.4	3	10	NA	1

Joe Morgan was absolutely astounding, in a way that might be hard to understand for those of us who grew up thinking that a player's accomplishments can be summed up by his Triple Crown numbers. He was not a huge home run hitter, and didn't win batting titles. But Morgan did everything else that a ballplayer can do extremely well. He drew walks like no other. He stole lots of bases and almost never got caught. He played great defense. His 1975 campaign was the best season by a non-pitcher in the 1970s, according to both WAR and Win Shares. Both WAR and Win Shares also agree that he was the best player of the 1970s period. Joe Morgan has a good case for being the best second baseman of all time, a case that Bill James espouses.

Too bad he's such a jackass. Morgan was a play-by-play man for many years and clearly had plenty of raw intelligence. But he seemed to direct his intelligence towards remaining ignorant. He had set-in-stone notions that he desperately did not want questioned, so he refused to ever even consider new concepts or come up with new insights. As was well-documented in the greatest sports blog of all time, "Fire Joe Morgan," Morgan would rail against "Moneyball," which he had never read and even thought was written by Billy Beane. Ironically, it's sabermetrics and Moneyball-type thinking that point towards Morgan being better than Hornsby or Collins. Not that Morgan himself would listen long enough to find out.

Morgan is one of these people who angrily dismiss any new idea as if it were some kind of mortal threat that will magically make them dumb. Because of this irrational defensiveness, Morgan always came across as incredibly arrogant, humorless, and self-important.

That's all besides the point, but I had to get my digs in. The Hall of Fame is not for guys who channel their intelligence into worthwhile pursuits; it's for great baseball players. Joe Morgan is unquestionably an inner-circle Hall-of-Famer.

Jackie Robinson (1947-1956; career OPS+: 132)

	Career	Rank	Hitting	Rank	Fielding	Rank	Peak	Rank	Bests	JAWS	Rank
WAR	61.5	13	54.2	13	10.0	28	52.0	5	3	56.8	9
WS	256.8	24	201.7	17	55.1	50	208.4	9	3	NA	4

I tend to be a bit of a contrarian. When I see everyone in the world standing in line to bend over backwards to kiss someone's butt, I get annoyed. I know that some of them are just blindly following the leader and then considering themselves part of the in-group for doing so. This is when I search for a way to poke holes in the logic, or lack thereof, of the mob mentality.

Jackie Robinson worship is off the charts, to the point where it naturally triggers the contrarian in me. It's at the point where no one can even wear the number 42, except the one day each spring when everyone wears it. For me that smacks of opportunism, of an attempt to manufacture a "moment" that will get broadcasters fulminating and get players dispensing sound bites at a conveniently PR-friendly time every year.

But, you know what, I have to concede that in this case, it's all deserved. Even I can't find any fault in Jackie Robinson. He really was that good, both as a player and as a human being. And it wasn't easy for him. He was by no means an easygoing guy who naturally let all the brutality slide off his back. Instead of responding in kind, he sublimated his rage into a performance that is legitimately among the best of all time. Keep in mind that the above totals were accomplished in only ten years, starting at age 28. Imagine what he could have done with just five more prime MLB seasons.

Believe the hype: Jackie Robinson really did change the world like no one else in baseball history. And he really was as good as anyone has ever been at the game. If the Hall of Fame could contain only one person, my nominee would be Jackie Robinson.

Ryne Sandberg (1981-1994, 1996-1997; career OPS+: 114)

	Career	Rank	Hitting	Rank	Fielding	Rank	Peak	Rank	Bests	JAWS	Rank
WAR	67.5	9	59.5	10	12.8	22	46.9	8	7	57.2	8
WS	343.3	11	249.6	11	93.7	10	219.1	6	3	NA	7

I grew up in the 1980s, so I'm biased. But I feel like the 1980s featured the most enjoyable brand of baseball in history. Among hitters, there was a diversity of talents. You had plenty of power hitters, but not so many that home runs became a cheapened commodity, like in the late 1990s. It was a heyday for stolen bases, which are fun to watch (even though they may often be of negligible benefit). Players were not yet especially enamored with working the count and drawing walks, which is a very wise strategy but, let's be honest, doesn't exactly make for riveting viewing.

And, perhaps most importantly, you had very few batters leaving the batter's box after each pitch to adjust their gloves, screw on their helmets, take a few practice swings, look around at the crowds, discover their true loves, marry them in beautiful ceremonies on the Amalfi Coast, celebrate the births of several children, grow apart from their wives as their careers consume most of their energies, launch into bitter divorces in which child custody is a primary source of rancor, grow old stewing in a mix of regret and wistful remembrance, and then finally return to the batter's box to take the next pitch.

My point is that if I ruled the world, my first edict would be that if you leave the batter's box in between pitches, you better have a gnat in your eye or something. And the same goes for pitchers: Stay on the f%^%&^ mound and pitch. The delaying tactics on both sides might be good strategy, disrupting timing and all that, but it quickly turns into an arms race of tedium. He steps out so I will step off. He delays, so I will delay. It makes for boring entertainment, and don't ever forget that, in the end, baseball is a form of entertainment.

Did you know that during the 1920s, games always averaged 2 hours or less? And that was a time when runs were being scored by the bucketload. A game longer than three and a half hours caused sportswriters to marvel that anyone had the patience to stay in the stands.

Nowadays, three and half hours would be a breezy Red Sox-Yankees game. The average nine-inning game exceeded three hours for the first time in 2014, despite the fact that runs were scarcer than they've been since the 1960s. Modern attention spans have supposedly declined, but we're somehow willing to watch the same amount of baseball take 50% longer to complete.

Thank goodness that when Rob Manfred was installed as commissioner in 2014, the first thing he did was enact a list of measures to speed up games. I could have kissed him when I saw that hitters would no longer be allowed to step out of the box between pitches unless they made contact with the ball. I'm nominating him for the Hall of Fame right now.

What was this supposed to be about? Oh yeah, Ryne Sandberg. He seems to encapsulate 1980s baseball better than any other player, because he was a great base stealer almost as an afterthought, like "of course, what else would I do?" More importantly, he got on base, had power, played great defense, and was the best second baseman of his generation. I can't imagine anyone objecting to him being a Hall-of-Famer.

Red Schoendienst (1945-1963; career OPS+: 94)

	Career	Rank	Hitting	Rank	Fielding	Rank	Peak	Rank	Bests	JAWS	Rank
WAR	42.1	32	35.6	37	15.2	15	31.9	33	1	37.0	32
WS	261.3	22	137.0	47	83.4	17	155.0	34	1	NA	28

"Schoendienst" is German for "beautiful servant." It's actually a shortened version of his full German surname, which is "Schoendienstgesundheitschadenfreudeblitzkriegdoppelganger." That translates as "beautiful servant plus all the German words I know." Perhaps it's no surprise that Schoendienst was born in Germantown, IL and spent his off-hours listening to Kraftwerk and eating pig intestines boiled in gravy. (At least the first part of that is true.)

Schoendienst was a Nellie Fox-type hitter: good batting averages but not much in the way of power, speed, or walks. Red didn't have Fox's terrific defense, instead showing up as very good. Fox is at the margins of the Hall of Fame, so being a bit less than Fox puts you in the Hall of Very Good But Not Good Enough for The Hall of Fame (which I would genuinely like to establish some day. I'm fascinated by the guys who were close but not quite there, guys like Norm Cash, Robin Ventura, etc.).

But wait, Schoendienst was also a successful manager, leading the Cardinals to a World Series championship in 1967 and a pennant in 1968. He spent 12 years as the Cardinals manager, a tenure surpassed only by Tony La Russa. After hanging up his manager's uniform he worked as a coach for the Athletics and then coached for the Redbirds, where he stayed for-freakin'-ever. At this writing he still holds the position of Special Assistant Coach at the age of 92. I'm not sure what the job description is for Special Assistant Coach, but I suspect the chief duties are "coming in occasionally" and "spinning nostalgic stories." Regardless, it's well-deserved.

Schoendienst's managerial success should be counted in his favor. I'm not as sure about his coaching experience, which might not contribute that many wins to the standings. Or maybe I just say that because no coach has ever been elected to the Hall, so I'm not sure what to do with them. That's a separate but interesting question: What do you do with a guy like Leo Mazzone or Dave Duncan, who clearly had a large impact, but one that's very hard to quantify?

That's all besides the point, or as Schoendienst might say, it's a "Schleckendiefierschliechen," which translates as "a bunch of German-sounding nonsense syllables." I have to use my powers of subjectivity here, but I semi-arbitrarily judge that Schoendienst's success as a manager and a coach tips him above the line for the Hall of Fame.

Who's In, Who's Out

I managed to kick two second basemen out of the Hall, Frank Grant and Bill Mazeroski, and I didn't feel good about either one. The Hall of Fame has probably done its best job with second basemen. It may have helped that Frankie Frisch was himself a second baseman, and couldn't plausibly push his backups into the Hall.

That doesn't mean I'm restricted in the number of second basemen I can plausibly push in myself. Unlike Frisch, I don't even have to convince a bunch of other old, sentimental ballplayers; I just have to convince myself, and hopefully, you. Here are a few guys I'm convinced deserve the Hall:

Bobby Grich (1970-1986; career OPS+: 125)

	Career	Rank	Hitting	Rank	Fielding	Rank	Peak	Rank	Bests	JAWS	Rank
WAR	70.9	7	62.1	9	16.2	12	46.3	9	3	58.6	6
WS	330.5	12	236.6	12	94.2	9	192.7	12	2	NA	12

Look at those numbers. Now consider that Bobby Grich was only on the Hall of Fame ballot once, gaining only 2.6% of the vote and then dropping off for good. The question is not why Grich should be in the Hall of Fame, but why isn't he already?

Well, he played in a low-offense time. From 1970 to 1986, only a handful of players per year hit the nice, neat, round statistical benchmarks that people really perk their ears at: your .300 BA, your 30 HRs, your 100 RBIs. Grich managed each of those numbers once. And in terms of career benchmarks, Grich also doesn't blow you away, since he amassed only 6890 at-bats and 1833 hits.

Look deeper and you'll see Grich excelled at everything a baseball player could possibly excel at, in a Joe Morgan-Lite sort of way. Grich was a great defender, winning four Gold Gloves. He got on base very well, drawing tons of walks and ending with a .371 career OBP. And he had good power for a second baseman, on par with Morgan or Ryne Sandberg.

Grich is no Joe Morgan, granted. But he seems like a Sandberg in just about every respect except stolen bases, which are exciting but never a huge factor in pushing a team to a pennant. Sandberg managed to put it all together in one great year, 1984, when his team managed a surprise playoff appearance. Grich had several seasons in which he was the best player on a playoff team (1973 Orioles, 1974 Orioles, 1979 Angels), but never it did with the same flair as Sandberg did.

Ultimately, the reason Bobby Grich is not in the Hall of Fame is one of flair. He didn't have many of the flair-acious qualities that get columnists and broadcasters all hot and bothered into Hall of Fame talk. Instead, Grich just went about his business putting together a Hall of Fame career through every imaginable means. After Ron Santo was finally selected, Grich became probably the most deserving player not on any BBWAA or Veterans Committee ballots.

Lou Whitaker (1977-1995; career OPS+: 117)

	Career	Rank	Hitting	Rank	Fielding	Rank	Peak	Rank	Bests	JAWS	Rank
WAR	74.9	6	67.1	8	15.4	13	37.8	17	2	56.4	10
WS	352.8	9	265.8	8	87.2	14	171.5	20	1	NA	13

Lou Whitaker is similar to Bobby Grich. Both were good at everything, from power to on-base ability to defense. Neither had one big "hook" that made them stand out, like Bill Mazeroski's defense or Tony Lazzeri's RBIs or my beautiful feet (seriously, you should see them sometime. Gorgeous.) Like Grich, Whitaker fell off the BBWAA ballot in the first year, getting only 2.9% of the vote.

Again, it was a low-offense time, so Whitaker's numbers don't jump out at you. It's worth noting that Whitaker's OPS+ is better than half of the second basemen in the Hall, including not just Mazeroski, Red Schoendienst and Nellie Fox but also Ryne Sandberg, Roberto Alomar, Bobby Doerr and Frankie Frisch. And, his fielding was good enough to win three Gold Gloves. Gold Glove voting has always been problematic, but both WAR and Win Shares give positive marks to his defense.

Whitaker is one of those guys who in the past would be overlooked by the BBWAA but would eventually be elected by the Veterans Committee. Unfortunately, at this writing, he's not on any Hall-of-Fame ballots. He should be, and he should be elected.

Jeff Kent (1992-2008; career OPS+: 123)

	Career	Rank	Hitting	Rank	Fielding	Rank	Peak	Rank	Bests	JAWS	Rank
WAR	55.2	16	59.3	11	-0.7	88	35.6	23	2	45.4	17
WS	323.9	12	254.6	10	69.0	22	194.4	11	2	NA	11[24]

---

[24] WSAWS, not Bill James' ranking. Tell you what: From now on, I'll just put an asterisk next to the overall Win Shares rankings that are WSAWS instead of Bill James' rankings. If you read this book in

Let's compare Jeff Kent and Bobby Grich. Grich was a much better fielder. Their Career OPS+s are pretty similar, with Kent contributing more power and Grich being considerably better at getting on base. If you think Kent "just looks like a Hall-of-Famer" and Grich doesn't, you're being tricked by context and then further bamboozled by the power of those dastardly, infernal Triple Crown stats.

Seriously, we all need to ban the use of batting average, home runs and RBIs as a way to sum up a player's season. We do need a quick-and-dirty summation of a player's contributions. But could anyone have picked a worse trio than those? I suppose triples, GIDPs and sac flies would be worse, but not by a ton.

Batting average is an out-of-date stat, based on the premise that walks are all the pitcher's fault, and thus should be removed from the batter's contributions. I covered this with the Adam Dunn vs. Alfonso Soriano example in the first chapter (which you read), so I don't need to rehash it here.

But home runs and RBIs are not great measures either, because they're all about cleanup hitters. Leadoff hitters seldom have either homers or RBIs, but they're still very valuable. It's just as important to score a run as it is to drive one in. The problem is that homers and RBIs are dramatic, so we overvalue them. No one ever begins an end-game wrap-up with "Here's the play of the night: Tim Raines walked, stole a base and then scored the game-winner when someone drove him in." It's always more like "Andre Dawson singled in the game-winning run, which was scored by some nobody who did nothing important."

That's why I prefer the so-called "slash line" of BA/OBP/SLG. Really, you could chuck out batting average, since it only covers part of the player's hitting, leaving out those sweet, sweet walks. Since OBP does include those walks, along with the hits, OBP is basically BA corrected. But I don't want to get too wacky with y'all. Baby steps.

Anyway, Jeff Kent is one of the better second basemen in history as far as conventional Triple Crown stats; only Rogers Hornsby looks better on those. That alone doesn't make him a HOFer, but the above rankings do.

Willie Randolph (1975-1992; career OPS+: 104)

	Career	Rank	Hitting	Rank	Fielding	Rank	Peak	Rank	Bests	JAWS	Rank
WAR	65.5	11	53.6	14	19.4	6	36.1	20	3	50.8	15
WS	310.4	13	206.6	16	92.7	11	162.4	25	1	NA	17

In my first draft of this book, I forgot all about Willie Randolph. He's easy to pass over. He never had flashy numbers except in walks. (Can walks ever be considered "flashy"?) He never won a Gold Glove. His personality was quiet and modest. On Yankees teams that featured first Reggie Jackson and then Don Mattingly, Randolph was never the focus.

Secretly, Randolph was adding tremendous value to his clubs. He was exceptional in the field, and would have won Gold Gloves if he didn't play in the same league as Frank White and Lou Whitaker.

---

order, like you're supposed to, you'll understand what the asterisks mean. If you don't, and then you cause a hue and cry over asterisks that you think don't lead to anything, then I'll know you did not follow instructions, and I will murder you. Or, failing that, I will be slightly disappointed in you.

Randolph didn't have the power of White or Whitaker, but got on base better than either. In 1980, Randolph led the league with 119 walks and finished second in OBP with a .427 mark. He finished with a .373 career OBP over 9461 PAs.

If you want to contribute lots of runs without anyone realizing it, draw lots of walks. Let's say you were an international spy and your cover was playing major-league baseball (perhaps not the best cover, admittedly). Just learn the strike zone really well and no one will ever connect the dots. I'm convinced that if a player somehow retired with a .250/.500/.250 line over 10,000 plate appearances, he'd be dropped from the Hall of Fame ballot in the first year of eligibility. People like Harold Reynolds would say moronic things like "he clogged up the bases." Yeah, Harold, he clogged the bases *with baserunners*. That's what you're supposed to do. When bases are unclogged, it's really hard to score runs. It's like saying that a subway can move more people around when it doesn't clog up its trains with so many darn people.

To be a bit more fair, I think Harold is looking at this as if the hitter is choosing to draw a walk rather than hit a single. It is true that a single is better than a walk. But that's not really the choice here. When a pitch is outside the strike zone, your choice is basically between taking the ball, fouling it off for a strike, or hitting yourself into an out. The chance that you'll turn that outside pitch into a hit is very, very low (unless you're Vladimir Guerrero -- more on him later).

After he was done drawing all those walks like some big selfish jerk, Randolph had a strong ambition to manage in the major leagues. He got his wish in 2005 and took over his boyhood favorite, the Mets. He had considerable success, with a .544 winning percentage and one division title in three and a half years. His name often comes up for other managerial jobs. But at this writing he's still waiting for another chance. Here's to hoping he gets it, and that he has enough good years to give someone the idea that he deserves the Hall of Fame.

Chapter Five

~ ~ Shortstop ~ ~

Shortstop is a position that is overrated for being underrated. A lot of baseball fans think the little guys who make the plays in the infield are neglected by people who don't know the real game, those philistines who glom onto the big sluggers at first base and the outfield. In reality, everyone is wowed by the plays that shortstops make, and people know that less offense is expected from them.

Maybe that's why there are so many shortstops in the Hall of Fame. There are 24 to be exact, more than first basemen and many more than third basemen. Looks like it's time to cull the herd, heh heh heh...

Luis Aparicio (1956-1973; career OPS+: 83)

	Career	Rank	Hitting	Rank	Fielding	Rank	Peak	Rank	Bests	JAWS	Rank
WAR	55.8	19	41.9	29	31.6	5	32.7	35	0	44.3	22
WS	293.3	19	170.7	26	122.9	7	140.4	55	0	NA	13

That's a pretty big difference between Luis Aparicio's career rankings and his peak rankings. Aparicio never had more than 22 Win Shares or 5.5 WAR in a season. You can be a star with those numbers but not an MVP candidate. Neither system has him as the best shortstop in any baseball any year; each shows him as second-best once, in 1958. That year he trailed Ernie Banks by a huge margin.

Instead of excellent individual seasons, Aparicio had longevity. He had a 11,230 plate appearances, good for 33rd-most all-time. I kicked Jake Beckley out of the Hall (in my imaginary universe, anyway) for having longevity and little else. Should I do the same with Aparicio?

Beckley and Aparicio could hardly be more different: a good-hitting first baseman and a speedy, slick-fielding middle infielder, respectively. Beckley was never on a playoff team, but Aparicio was integral to two pennant-winners, the 1959 White Sox and the 1966 Orioles.

In terms of raw fame, it's no contest. That could be partially because Aparicio is more recent. But I bet even in 50 years Aparicio will be relatively well-known among baseball fans. He's just one of those guys that has a clear persona, that of the speedy, light-hitting, great-fielding shortstop.

Bill Mazeroski might be a better comp. Both were famous, great fielders, and bad hitters. Maz hit about the same (84 career OPS+) but had about 2000 fewer plate appearances. Luis was one of the speediest players in history, leading the league in stolen bases nine straight years and rarely getting caught. That adds to his hitting Win Shares and WAR but not to his OPS+.

Speed tends to be overrated -- getting on base is much more important than stealing bases. But in cases like Aparicio's, it's no small thing. On Baseball-reference, they have stat called "Runs from Baserunning," which compiles all the speed-based stats. Aparicio ranks fourth all-time in this stat, with 91.7 (top three: Rickey Henderson, Willie Wilson and Tim Raines). Mazeroski's career Baserunning Runs are -6. This makes Aparicio a better offensive weapon than Mazeroski.

In the postseason, Maz has a bit of an advantage, being the hero, if not the MVP, of the 1960 Series. Aparicio was pretty good in the White Sox' loss to the Dodgers in 1959 but less good in the Orioles' win over the Dodgers in 1966.

And Maz was the best defensive second baseman of all time, while Aparicio is merely in the top ten of shortstops. Ah, but a great defensive shortstop is more valuable than a great defensive second baseman. Shortstop is the most defense-first position on the diamond, except possibly catcher. Second base is up there, but it's not like shortstop. Aparicio's Fielding Win Shares and Fielding WAR reflect this: Despite not being the best ever for a shortstop, both numbers are comfortably above Mazeroski's totals.

In the Mazeroski and Ray Schalk comments I found that their great gloves weren't deserving of the Hall alone. Is Aparicio doing it here?

I came in thinking that I'd be kicking out Luis Aparicio, who I knew was a poor hitter. But longevity, speed and great defense are keeping him in the Hall.

Luke Appling (1930-1943, 1945-1950; career OPS+: 113)

	Career	Rank	Hitting	Rank	Fielding	Rank	Peak	Rank	Bests	JAWS	Rank
WAR	74.5	8	70.6	7	19.0	29	43.8	11	0	59.2	9
WS	376.4	8	268.3	7	108.6	13	203.7	8	2	NA	11

Luis Aparicio and Luke Appling have a few similarities. Both made their bones with the White Sox. Both are Hall-of-Fame shortstops who lasted a very long time. Both were known in the Hollywood gossip pages as "Lu-Ap." (Not true, though both did briefly date Taylor Swift.)

Unlike Aparicio, Appling was a great hitter but not a great fielder. He was called "Old Aches and Pains" for his constant complaints about small maladies. But he missed very few games because of them. In his career, he only had one major injury, a fractured ankle in 1938, and is one of 11 shortstops with more than 10,000 PAs.

In 1936, Appling won the batting title with a .388 average, still a record for shortstops since 1901. He was promised a $5,000 bonus, about $83,000 in 2013 dollars -- strip-club money for modern players, but a sizeable chunk of change for a 1930s player. But then White Sox GM Harry Grabiner refused to give it to him. No excuse -- just refused. Appling tore up his 1937 contract in frustration. Eventually he had to cave and sign for $2,500 less than he wanted.

The days before free agency are full of these kinds of stories. Players had no choice but to stay with the clubs that owned them, and their clubs could just pay them whatever they felt like paying each year. Players' only options were to sign the contracts or hold out for the year, meaning they couldn't play for any team in organized baseball and couldn't earn any money for their families.

Imagine if you had to work under those kinds of conditions. Say you're a zookeeper (which I assume you are). You're under contract with the St. Louis Zoo, and you have a banner year keeping the zoo. The zoo is so unbelievably kept that it set a new record for zookeepingness. You grace the cover of Zoo Beat magazine under the headline "Zootastic! Everyone's WILD About [Your Name Here]. Pics Inside!"

But in the off-season, the general manager of the St. Louis Zoo, Jack Saintlouiszoo, decides to cut your salary. If you don't like it, too bad. You can't quit and go work somewhere else. Other zoos might want you, but they aren't allowed to hire you. You could refuse to zookeep at all. St. Louis will miss your contributions, but they can easily bring up a fresh, eager young zookeeper from their Louisville affiliate. Eventually your choice becomes to either go become a dog walker (which for a zookeeper, is like a five-star chef working at McDonald's) or just give in and sign the contract.

I would think about this sort of thing (Appling's story, not zookeeping) whenever people whined about ballplayers making so much money. People are used to it now, but in the 1980s, people seemed to talk about little besides players' rapidly increasing salaries. It was and is an obscene amount of money, no doubt. And of course it is unsettling that teachers are paid so much less.

But keep in mind that before free agency, baseball players were abused in a way that no other worker in any capitalist system would be. They were prevented from earning what they were worth in the open market by a system of permanent indentured servitude. These are people with very special skills, for which there is huge demand and very little supply. Defying the market forces behind ballplayer salaries was little besides institutionalized socialism.

Anyway, that's all beside the specific point of Luke Appling's Hall-of-Fame worthiness. He's clearly in.

Dave Bancroft (1915-1930; career OPS+: 98)

	Career	Rank	Hitting	Rank	Fielding	Rank	Peak	Rank	Bests	JAWS	Rank
WAR	48.5	24	39.0	35	23.5	15	37.2	24	3	42.9	25
WS	242.0	31	148.7	34	93.3	30	168.0	26	3	NA	28

You get one guess about how Dave Bancroft got the the Hall of Fame. I'll give you a hint: He was selected by the 1971 Veterans Committee, which was dominated by ex-teammates Frankie Frisch and Bill Terry. (That may have been a bit of a giveaway.)

To be fair, Bancroft is no George Kelly. He was known as a great fielder and a good hitter for a shortstop. He was the best shortstop in baseball three times according to both WAR and Win Shares. While George Kelly was about as valuable as Chris Chambliss, who no one would ever think was a Hall-of-Famer, Bancroft is in the neighborhood of players like Tony Fernandez and Miguel Tejada. You might not think of either of those guys as HOFers, but really, they're not far off.

Bancroft had some very good seasons on pennant-winning teams. A 30 Win Share season and 8.0 WAR season are both loosely defined as deserving of an MVP, though in practice a 7.0 WAR is more comparable to 30 Win Shares. Meanwhile, 20 Win Shares and 4.0 WAR are very good, meaning you're a likely All-Star. Bancroft earned 21 Win Shares and 4.2 WAR on the 1915 NL Champion Phillies, 31 Win Shares and 7.3 WAR on the 1921 Giants (leading the team in both stats), 27 Win Shares and 6.0 WAR on the 1922 Giants (again leading the team in both), and 21 Win Shares and 3.7 WAR on the 1923 Giants. In World Series play, though, Bancroft was good only in 1915, hitting poorly in each Giants postseason.

I dunno, maybe I'm becoming an old softie, but I'm inclined to let Bancroft stay. All right Frisch, you can have this one. But you're on notice. At least restrain yourself from throwing in any more of your shortstop teammates.

Ernie Banks (1953-1971; career OPS+: 122)

	Career	Rank	Hitting	Rank	Fielding	Rank	Peak	Rank	Bests	JAWS	Rank
WAR	67.5	14	61.9	13	4.9	87	51.9	4	6	59.7	7
WS	331.8	13	265.0	8	67.0	71	193.1	12	5	NA	5

The Hall of Fame lists Ernie Banks as a first baseman, but I say nuts to that. (Apologies for the strong language.) He did have about 130 more PAs at first base, but a huge majority of his career value was at shortstop. Of his 331.8 career win shares, 211 came from 1953-1961, when he was at short. WAR is even more dramatic, giving 54.9 of his 67.5 career WAR to his shortstop span.

It wasn't just that Banks went from a tough defensive position to an easy one, thus losing a lot of defensive value. He also hit much worse as a first baseman because of a chronic knee problem. His OPS+s as a shortstop, from 1955 to 1961, were 144, 136, 149, 155, 156, 146, 123. That's pretty amazing stuff, comparable to Alex Rodriguez in his shortstop years.

Now imagine if instead of moving to third base and getting even better, Alex Rodriguez moved to first base and became Lyle Overbay. After switching to first base in 1962, Banks' OPS+s were 110, 94, 107, 116, 105, 112, 118, and 92. That's Overbaysian territory if I ever saw it. Positively Overbaysterrific.

Cubs manager Leo Durocher knew that he could find a better first baseman. But he also knew that fans would revolt if he tried. So he stuck with Banks, even though his team also included Ron Santo and Fergie Jenkins and thus had legitimate chances to contend.

It goes to show that sometimes what the fans want is actually bad for their team. Sentimentality doesn't win ballgames. Keep that in mind next time you get mad at a team for not showing "loyalty" to an aging or injured star.

Could dumping Banks have brought the Cubs a single division title? This is a good task for Win Shares, since it takes a team's wins and divides them among players. What if Banks were replaced and no other changes were made? How good would his replacement have to be to get the Cubs enough Win Shares, and thus enough wins, to hypothetically finish first?

Let's look at Banks' Win Shares each year and what additional Win Shares would have been necessary for the Cubs to finish first:

Year	Banks' WS	Cubs games out	Extra WS needed	1B WS needed
1967	17	14	42	59
1968	18	13	39	57
1969	14	8	24	38

So maybe just replacing Banks wouldn't have have brought championships to the Cubs in the late 1960s. No first baseman in history has ever had 57 or 59 Win Shares, or anything close. Tops is 44, and only a select few ever reached 38. In 1969, Willie McCovey actually had 39 Win Shares, his best year by far. But imagine what the Cubs would have had to give up to get him. They probably would have had to subtract lots of Win Shares at other positions.

Banks was replaced in 1970 by Jim Hickman, who had an incredible year (.315/.419/.582, 155 OPS+). But the Cubs still ended up 5 games out of first. They remained good for a few years but never got any closer than that to a pennant. It demonstrates that, in baseball, one upgrade is very seldom enough to launch a good team into greatness.

At any rate, Banks' string of 1950s excellence greatly outweighs his Overbudlian second half, and he is a no-doubt Hall-of-Famer.

Lou Boudreau (1938-1952; career OPS+: 120)

	Career	Rank	Hitting	Rank	Fielding	Rank	Peak	Rank	Bests	JAWS	Rank
WAR	63.0	18	50.3	18	23.3	16	48.7	6	4	55.8	15
WS	276.8	23	187.4	18	89.4	36	199.0	9	2	NA	12

In 1948, Lou Boudreau had the fourth-best season ever by a shortstop, at least according to WAR. (Top three real quick: Cal Ripken 1991, Honus Wagner 1908, Robin Yount 1982). Boudreau also managed the Cleveland You-Know-Whats all the way to a World Series championship. Later it became especially legendary because it broke the post-war Yankee hegemony; it was one of three years from 1947-1964 in which a team besides the Yankees won the A.L. pennant.

Luckily, Boudreau was more than a one-year-wonder. A great hitter and good fielder, he was also known as Handsome Lou, and you can see why: (see http://www.baseball-reference.com/players/b/boudrlo01.shtml).

Yowza yow yow. If I were a heterosexual woman or a gay man, I'd be all over that. More relevantly, Boudreau's numbers look lovely among the shortstops in the Hall of Fame. He's no one's idea of an inner-circle, first-ballot type, but he's well within the established standards.

Joe Cronin (1926-1945; career OPS+: 119)

	Career	Rank	Hitting	Rank	Fielding	Rank	Peak	Rank	Bests	JAWS	Rank
WAR	66.4	15	63.6	10	14.2	46	43.9	10	4	55.2	16
WS	333.1	12	235.4	12	97.6	21	209.9	6	4	NA	8

Much the same way the St. Louis Browns were actually good before George Sisler's eyes broke, the Washington Senators were not always a laughingstock. They won at least 90 games each year from 1930 to 1933 and won the pennant in 1933. Joe Cronin was their best hitter each year and started managing the club in 1932, at age 26. Player-managers were common in those days, but 26-year-old ones were unheard of. The pressure on Cronin was intense, and he delivered.

After a disappointing season in 1934, Cronin was traded to the Red Sox for shortstop Lyn Lary and $250,000. Cronin himself made less than a tenth of that, $22,000 a year, and he was one of the better-paid players in the league. $250,000 was a crazy amount of money during the Great Depression, about $4.4 million in today's dollars. It was the kind of money that made Red Sox fans think their team had just bought a pennant. And of course, we all know how patient and measured

Red Sox fans are. I believe the motto of Red Sox Nation is still "Hey, maybe we'll win, maybe not. C'est la vie."

Actually, it was a very different Red Sox Nation then. It was more of a village at best. It's hard to imagine now, but the 1920s Red Sox were a comic underachiever of the post-war Senators/Browns vein. From 1919 to 1933, the Red Sox finished fifth twice, sixth twice, seventh twice, and dead last a whopping nine times. Harry Frazee, the villain who sold Babe Ruth to the Yankees, sold off every other good player as well, dooming the franchise for 15 years. It's not a new thing for owners to put money ahead of winning.

A big reason that owner Tom Yawkey is in the Hall of Fame was because he bought the Red Sox in 1933 and immediately threw money at the problem. This is also a time-honored strategy; the only difference nowadays was that then, the money went to the teams that own the players, not the players themselves. First Yawkey bought star pitchers Lefty Grove from the Athletics and Wes Ferrell from Cleveland. Then he bought Cronin to both play shortstop and manage.

It worked, to some extent. The Red Sox became a .500 team and after a few years turned into a contender, or as much as any team can be playing in the same league as the Gehrig/DiMaggio Yankees. By the time of the War of Hitlerian Aggression, Cronin was pretty much done as a player and stepped aside in favor of Johnny Pesky. But he kept managing and led the Sox to a World Series in 1946.

Then Cronin became the general manager of the Red Sox. Here he finally found a job he couldn't do well. Throughout his tenure, the Sox farm system was poor, and they couldn't take advantage of Ted Williams' all-time great seasons to win any pennants. A big problem was that during the post-Jackie Robinson years, Cronin refused to hire any African-American players. A few months after Cronin resigned as GM, the Red Sox debuted their first African-American player, Pumpsie Green. They were the last major league team to do so.

Cronin was then bumped up further, to league president. The leagues were more independent then than they are now, so it was a very important job. He hired the first African-American umpire in 1966, Emmett Ashford, several years before the National League integrated. So maybe he had learned from his past mistakes. (Source for all the above: Cronin's SABR biography, by Mark Armour.)

In one respect, Joe Cronin ended on the wrong side of history, but his playing and managing put him well within Hall range.

George Davis (1890-1909; career OPS+: 121)

	Career	Rank	Hitting	Rank	Fielding	Rank	Peak	Rank	Bests	JAWS	Rank
WAR	84.7	4	70.2	8	24.0	14	44.4	9	3	64.6	4
WS	396.9	6	296.8	4	100.2	18	190.8	13	3	NA	14

Bill James's overall rating puts George Davis a little low for my tastes. Bill (we're on a first name basis, of course) tends to rate players from the 1800s lower than Win Shares alone would suggest. He argues that the level of play then was quite poor, and major leagues did not assemble the nation's greatest talent efficiently.

At least he acknowledges that 1800s players exist. Most baseball writers ignore the century entirely. I imagine it feels very foreign. There was no American League, and the rules were changing dramatically year to year. Baseball was a popular diversion but not the huge professional pastime it became later. And it's easy psychologically to just push years starting with "18" to the side; that entire century seems like very distant history.

All that may be true, but in my way of thinking, it's irrelevant. Professional baseball was played in the 1800s. It had heroes who helped their teams win games. The Hall of Fame exists to honor the heroes who best helped their teams win games, regardless of the conditions surrounding their play.

Negro League play was also very different than the white majors in the 1900s. In fact, it was a lot like 1890s baseball, with teams in constant flux and an inefficient assembly of talent. Does that make its heroes lesser as well? I doubt many would say so.

As to the specific argument that 1800s play was relatively poor, well of course it was. The level of play always advances, as players get better trained, strategy gets smarter, and systems for promoting great players improve. Maybe there was a big jump from 1899 to 1900, but so what? There was likely a much bigger jump from 1929 to 1979. I don't see Bill James making a similar adjustment for that advance. I don't see him knocking Babe Ruth down in the rankings because Ruth wouldn't have a chance against an average 1970s pitcher.

That last part might sound crazy, but I'm now convinced it's true. In the past I always assumed that if Babe Ruth were plucked out of the 1920s and dropped at any point in history, he would hit 50 homers. But one day on the MLB channel, Rob Neyer said Babe Ruth probably would struggle in AA if he played now. He'd have to go through lots of extra training to catch up to modern fastballs.

The more I thought about it, the more it made sense. The game has advanced an incredible amount over the years on both the hitting and pitching sides. In sports like track and field or swimming it's easy to see athletic performance constantly advancing, since record times are broken every year. In baseball it's harder to tell because there is a "zero-sum" aspect to its numbers. Both hitting and pitching improve at similar rates, cancelling each other's progress out in the stats. Sometimes pitching advances faster than hitting, and you get a pitcher's era. Sometimes hitting advances faster than pitching, and you get a hitter's era. When things get too crazy in one direction or the other, the powers that be intervene to reassert balance. Throughout, both pitching and hitting are continually progressing.

As you know, I believe firmly in going by the standards that the Hall of Fame sets through its selections (even though it doesn't always follow them itself, which means I have to make corrections). And the Hall's choices have been context-first, choosing the best from each era. As it should. If it really only contained the most skilled ballplayers in history, a huge majority would come from the last few decades. That would be lame. We want the heroes, not just the most technically skilled. To pick the heroes, we pick the best players in context, whether that context was the 1890s or the 1990s.

Judging George Davis within his context, he was a top-ten-all-time shortstop. He was an all-around player, excelling in both hitting and defense, at the most crucial fielding spot on the diamond, and doing it all for a very long time. Davis didn't have the durability of Cal Ripken (as if anyone ever has) but in every other way they're pretty comparable. No-doubt Hall-of-Famer.

Travis Jackson (1922-1936; career OPS+: 102)

	Career	Rank	Hitting	Rank	Fielding	Rank	Peak	Rank	Bests	JAWS	Rank
WAR	44.0	33	30.6	54	22.9	17	35.1	28	3	39.6	29
WS	211.3	47	137.1	43	74.0	59	146.2	49	2	NA	40

Frisch, are you kidding me? Travis Jackson? The other shortstop you played with on the Giants, after Dave Bancroft? OK, maybe that's not entirely fair, since Jackson was selected by the Veterans Committee in 1982, and Frankie Frisch had been dead for ten years. We can't pin this on former Giants teammate Bill Terry either, since he left the committee in 1976. Well, consarnit, I got my blamin' finger on, and it's itchin' to do some blamin'. Who was on the committee in 1982 … let's see, Stan Musial was. OK, that means Stan Musial stinks. Done.

Actually, this indicates that my villainization of Frankie Frisch might be a little misplaced. The problem was the entire Veterans Committee before 2001. Before that year it was just 15 former players making the decisions on their own. It took a long time and many bad selections before the Hall made the committee less reliant on the biases of a handful of old ballplayers. It makes you wonder if we might have too much reverence for people who can hit or throw baseballs well.

That might sound ironic in a book about the Hall of Fame, which is devoted to little else. But think about it: The BBWAA may be far from perfect, but it's dozens of people who write about baseball all day each submitting votes by a secret ballot. This group is entrusted with the easy part, choosing the obvious Hall-of-Famers. Then, until recently, the tough cases got sent to … a committee of baseball historians who were vetted through a careful process, and then deliberated over months over all players' relative merits? No, the tough cases got sent to a dozen nostalgic old farts in a room.

Perhaps that's a bit rude. Hall of Fame ballplayers obviously know a lot about playing baseball. But there's no reason to assume they know a ton about baseball history, or that they own the analytical skills necessary to make the borderline calls. It reminds me of a bit by the late, great comedian Mitch Hedberg. I'll quote it in full so that I do it the most justice possible:

"As a comedian, I always get into situations where I'm auditioning for movies and sitcoms, you know? As a comedian, they want you to do other things besides comedy. They say "all right you're a comedian, can you write? Write us a script. Act in this sitcom." They want me to do [stuff] that's related to comedy, but it's not comedy, man. It's not fair, you know? It's as though if I was a cook, and I worked my ass off to become a really good cook, and they said "alright you're a cook... can you farm?"("A Complete Ranking of (Almost) Every Single Mitch Hedberg Quote," Buzzfeed.com, Logan Rhodes, March 29, 2014)

As with stand-up and acting, or cooking and farming, playing baseball and choosing Hall-of-Famers are semi-related skills that certainly could exist in the same person. But there's no reason to think that one necessarily leads to another. We only assume they do because we're used to thinking great baseball players are superhuman beings who would excel at anything that could possibly have to do with baseball.

This blind reverence used to extend to choosing managers. The best players were always tapped to be managers, including Rogers Hornsby and Ty Cobb. Those two were the Barry Bonds and Alex Rodriguez of their time: terrific ballplayers who completely lacked people skills. Rogers Hornsby insisted that his players all sleep 11 to 12 hours a night and eat lots of steak, because it worked for him, so therefore he thought it must work for everybody. Ty Cobb knew more about baseball than anyone, but his teaching method was basically "scream at them until they become as smart as me." They both became managers not because they had any managerial skills but because they could hit balls well.

Nowadays, we understand that it's more important for managers to have strategic and leadership abilities; a good playing career is irrelevant. Similarly, in the 2000s the Hall of Fame finally involved more people in the Veterans Committee who have demonstrated an ability to analyze baseball. They didn't kick retired Hall of Fame players out of the process entirely; that would be a trifle impolitic. But now a Historical Committee formulates the ballot for the old farts to vote on, and they don't put anyone on the ballot who would be really out of place in the Hall of Fame. The new process has unfortunately swung too far in the other direction, making it too difficult for players to get in. But at least they've recognized that old ballplayers are not necessarily analytical whizzes.

I guess I should try to see if there's anything Hall-of-Fame-y about Travis Jackson. Bill James ranks him near Garry Templeton, clearly outside the Hall of Fame. WAR is more charitable, ranking him near Dave Bancroft, who I let stay in the Hall, and Miguel Tejada and Tony Fernandez, who I mentioned are not crazy as Hall-of-Famers. That puts Jackson within striking distance.

He was the best shortstop in baseball a few times. In 1927 he led shortstops with 24 Win Shares and in 1929 led them with 23. He had plenty of other seasons just a few notches below those. WAR likes him better, giving him four seasons of 5 or more WAR, leading shortstops in 1927 and 1929 and tying with Joe Sewell in 1928. That's not bad. There are 33 Hall-of-Famers who have fewer than three 5-WAR seasons. Most don't deserve to be in the Hall, so we can't go by those, but some borderline cases, like Bid McPhee and Luis Aparicio, fall into this category.

So Jackson was probably the best shortstop in the MLB for a three-year run, from 1927-1929, and had plenty of other good years. Yet, his Peak numbers are pretty poor, in part because he never got much above 5 WAR or 20 Win Shares. He never had an MVP-type season.

The postseason doesn't help Jackson. He got there four times with some great Giants teams, but each time hit terribly. In 74 career World Series plate appearances, Jackson turned in a positively Bill Bergen-ian .149/.183/.164. (If you don't know who Bill Bergen was, look him up and marvel at his offensive futility.)

If I were just going by WAR, I might give Travis Jackson a pass. WAR likes his defense, but I take WAR's defensive stats with a grain of salt. Accounts of the time don't credit Jackson as being that special defensively, a view shared by Win Shares. Jackson looks like a Dave Bancroft with worse defense, and anything below Bancroft is not a Hall-of-Famer. **Travis Jackson is out.**

Hugh Jennings (1891-1903, 1907, 1909-1910, 1912, 1918; career OPS+: 118)

	Career	Rank	Hitting	Rank	Fielding	Rank	Peak	Rank	Bests	JAWS	Rank
WAR	42.3	37	37.8	37	9.0	71	39.2	21	5	40.8	28
WS	214.8	45	139.3	42	64.4	80	176.2	21	4	NA	18

If the Peak number above included the player's best four years instead of his best seven, Hughie Jennings would rank ninth among all shortstops in Win Shares and eighth in WAR. If you restricted it to four consecutive years, Hughie would move up a few notches more. From 1895 to 1898 he had WARs of 7.5, 8.3, 7.3, and 7.5 and Win Shares of 29, 36, 29, and 32. Each of those is an MVP-level number. WAR has him as the best non-pitcher in baseball every single one of those years. Win Shares gives him the number-one spot once and puts him in the top 5 each year. He played on a legendary team, the National League Baltimore Orioles (now defunct), which finished first each year from 1894-1896 and second in 1897 and 1898, out of 12 teams.

A big reason I love Jennings' run of excellence is that he accomplished it in large part through hit-by-pitches. Usually the league leader in HBPs will have 15-25. Every once in a while you get a huge total: Craig Biggio had 34 in 1997, Don Baylor had 35 in 1986, and Ron Hunt had a crazy 50 in 1971. Hughie Jennings' totals in that 1895-1898 heyday were 32, 51, 46, and 46. He and Ron Hunt are the only players in history to have more than 40 HBPs in a season, with Hunt doing it once and Jennings doing it in three consecutive years. Despite having only 5860 career PAs, Jennings holds the all-time record for career HBPs. (If you're wondering, Craig Biggio is second, with two fewer HBPs in more than twice as many PAs. No wonder it took Biggio so long to make the Hall. He's clearly no Hugh Jennings.)

Remember, these were the days before batting helmets. In 1897, Jennings was hit in the head by an Amos Rusie throw, which fractured his skull and left him unconscious for four days. Jennings came back the next season and logged another 46 HBPs. The kind of guys who do Ultimate Fighting nowadays were playing baseball in the 1800s.

Here's the problem with Jennings' Hall of Fame candidacy: He had only 5860 career PAs. Apart from those four terrific years, he had one other good year, a few good half-seasons, and the rest is pretty poor. He blew out his arm in 1899, at age 30, and had to move to first base, where he was no good at all. Don't be fooled by all those extra years above the stats chart; his last year of more than 10 PAs was 1903. He got occasional at-bats in later years because he was a manager, and would put himself in as a pinch-hitter every so often just for Shasta and giggles.

Maybe this should be revived. Imagine Joe Maddon getting the last-at-bat of a meaningless end-of-season game. It would at least justify him wearing a uniform, which I think is dumb, by the way. Why do we force paunchy 60-year-old men to wear tight-fitting uniforms in the dugout, as if they need to be ready to jump on the field at a moment's notice? Can't it be more like basketball, where the head coach gets to wear a nice, dignified suit? Anyway, this is besides the point.

We passed by another one of Jennings' Hall of Fame qualifications; did you catch it? No, not the part about pinch-hits after his playing days were over. No, not "Shasta and giggles," though I am pretty proud of that euphemism. Jennings was a manager, and a good one, leading the Tigers from 1907 to 1920 and having a few short stints later. The Tigers won the pennant in Jennings' first three years but lost in the World Series to the Cubs, the Cubs again and then the Pirates. (It was a very different time.)

In the spring training of Jennings' first year as manager, 1907, a 20-year-old outfielder named Ty Cobb was getting into fights with anyone and anything that moved. The previous year, he had not taken the normal rookie hazing in stride, and a huge, violent rivalry developed between him and the Tiger veterans. The dissension had already sunk the previous manager. Many wanted Jennings to trade Cobb, but instead he put him in the lineup full-time and the Tigers won their first of three straight pennants.

Jennings was an endlessly cheerful, chatty, enthusiastic guy, yelling "Ee-yah!" every time the Tigers did something good. He was also a big fan of dirty tricks, which was a trademark of the 1890s Orioles. The rival A's had a dominant pitcher named Rube Waddell who was what nowadays we'd call "developmentally disabled." Waddell went crazy for dogs, so one day Jennings brought a dog into the third-base box while Waddell was pitching, in an effort to distract him. It didn't work, but it certainly could have. (There are lots of Rube Waddell stories like this; just wait til we get to him in the pitchers section.) (Source: Jennings' SABR biography, by C. Paul Rogers III.)

Anyway, it takes some real skill to manage a team that includes Ty Cobb and other human beings. Add that to Jennings' few amazing seasons and handful of other contributions, and I think he's a Hall-of-Famer.

Barry Larkin (1986-2004; career OPS+: 116)

	Career	Rank	Hitting	Rank	Fielding	Rank	Peak	Rank	Bests	JAWS	Rank
WAR	70.2	13	67.5	9	13.8	52	43.1	12	2	56.7	13
WS	347.5	10	247.9	11	99.7	19	197.4	11	3	NA	6

Once Ozzie Smith's skills started to wane, the title of best shortstop in the National League was very clearly passed to Barry Larkin. In fact, I've never seen such a peaceful transfer of status; usually there are several candidates or none. This was like George VI giving way to Elizabeth II, while most of the time it's much more like the War of the Roses, with a similar level of ceremoniousness and ultimate meaninglessness.

Actually, let's test that. Taking only the National League, here are the best shortstops each year of Smith and Larkin's careers, as per WAR and Win Shares.

NL SS	WAR	WS
1978	Larry Bowa	Dave Concepcion
1979	Dave Concepcion	Garry Templeton
1980	Ozzie Smith	Garry Templeton
1981	Dave Concepcion	Dave Concepcion
1982	Dickie Thon	Dickie Thon
1983	Dickie Thon	Dickie Thon
1984	Ozzie Smith	Ozzie Smith
1985	Ozzie Smith	Ozzie Smith
1986	Ozzie Smith	Ozzie Smith
1987	Ozzie Smith	Ozzie Smith
1988	Barry Larkin	Barry Larkin
1989	Ozzie Smith	Ozzie Smith
1990	Barry Larkin	Barry Larkin

1991	Barry Larkin	Barry Larkin
1992	Barry Larkin	Barry Larkin
1993	Jay Bell	Jeff Blauser
1994	Barry Larkin	Jay Bell
1995	Barry Larkin	Barry Larkin
1996	Barry Larkin	Barry Larkin
1997	Jeff Blauser	Jeff Blauser
1998	Barry Larkin	Barry Larkin
1999	Barry Larkin	Barry Larkin
2000	Rafael Furcal	Rich Aurilia
2001	Rich Aurilia	Rich Aurilia
2002	Jose Hernandez	Edgar Renteria
2003	Edgar Renteria	Rafael Furcal
2004	Jack Wilson	Jimmy Rollins

The passing of the torch was clear between 1988 and 1990. After Larkin got too old, look at the chaos that laid blight upon the land. It was a regular Year of Three Monarchs, with Rich Aurilia playing the part of Lady Jane Grey, the unprepared ruler shoved awkwardly and briefly into prominence, and Edgar Renteria as Bloody Mary I, forcing himself into power but seldom having unquestioned hegemony. I always wondered why Renteria tried to execute so many Protestants.

Anyway, few things are more certain in this sceptred isle, this earth of majesty, this seat of Mars,[25] than that Barry Larkin was the best NL shortstop of the 1990s and a clear Hall-of-Famer.

John Henry "Pop" Lloyd (1907-1932; career OPS+: 159)

	Rank at Position Among Negro Leaguers	Rank Among All Negro Leaguers
Bill James	1	5
SABR	1	5
Monte Irvin	2	NA

[25] Reference explanation: "Richard II," by William Shakespeare. I do know about a few things besides baseball history and 1980s rap music.

Pop Lloyd was known as the "Black Honus Wagner." It was a huge compliment at the time, but is the kind of thing that now sounds a bit racist. In that kind of nickname, "black" is the "other" -- the white person is the "regular" person that creates the frame of reference, and then there's the "black" version. No one ever said Honus Wagner was the "White Pop Lloyd."

And nowadays you'd never hear C.C. Sabathia referred to as the "Black Roger Clemens." The fact that that sounds preposterous is one of the hidden benefits of integration. You may notice that C.C. Sabathia is African-American, and people might remark on him being an inspiration to black youths. But he's never referred to as a "black" version of anyone else.

Honus Wagner was apparently quite a good comp for Lloyd. Wagner himself said "It's an honor to be compared to him." Babe Ruth said that Lloyd was the best baseball player ever. Bill James floats the idea that Lloyd may have been the best shortstop in history, ahead of Wagner, who he gives the number one spot running away among MLB shortstops (after-the-fact spoiler alert). Connie Mack claimed that if you picked randomly between Lloyd and Wagner, you couldn't go wrong either way.

League play was strictly segregated in those days, but black and white players still played exhibition games against each other. In 1909, Lloyd played in five exhibition games against Ty Cobb and the Tigers. Cobb hit .369 but didn't get a steal, instead being tagged out three times by Lloyd. Cobb, ever the gracious sportsman, stomped off the field and vowed never again to play African-Americans (not the term he used, of course). Lloyd hit .500 in the series.

Lloyd was the opposite of Cobb in terms of personality: a kind, humble gentleman whose expletive of choice was "Gosh bob it!" But he was not so gentlemanly that he was willing to play for peanuts. He played for 10 different teams, always going to the highest bidder for his services.

Seamheads has Lloyd down for 4027 PAs, a .343 BA, .392 OBP, and .449 SLG. He's the best shortstop in their database by a mile, and his 194.5 Win Shares is better than all but three other pre-1934 Negro League players, outfielders Oscar Charleston, Cristobal Torriente, and Pete Hill. Clearly, Pop Lloyd is a Hall-of-Famer.

Rabbit Maranville (1912-1933, 1935; career OPS+: 82)

	Career	Rank	Hitting	Rank	Fielding	Rank	Peak	Rank	Bests	JAWS	Rank
WAR	42.8	36	29.5	60	30.7	6	30.4	46	0	36.6	37
WS	301.8	18	158.9	30	142.7	2	156.6	38	2	NA	38

If you get annoyed by Yasiel Puig's bat flips or Carlos Gomez's slow home run trot, just be glad you never saw Rabbit Maranville play. He was an entertainer of a kind you've never seen on a baseball diamond. Here are just a few things he did that would get him excommunicated from the self-serious world of present-day baseball:

- He would make fun of the second-base umpire by standing behind him and imitating his gestures, swatting at flies, scratching his nose, etc.
- When he tagged out a runner sliding into second, he would sit on the poor guy for a moment, beaming from ear to ear.
- If the game started to drag, he would do a big, exaggerated, pretend yawn, checking an imaginary watch. Sometimes he would lean against an imaginary wall and then flop onto the base.

- His signature play was to catch pop flies by letting them hit his chest and roll into his mitt, just for show.

This kind of thing wasn't totally unusual in the dead-ball era. After his arm blew out, a pitcher named Nick Altrock became a first base coach. His main responsibility was to do silly pantomimes during games, pretending to knock himself out, wrestle himself to the ground, spike his own shoe, etc. He had free reign as long as his antics didn't interfere with play. The team mascots of today are descendents of Altrock and Maranville.

I may be of a minority here, but some of this stuff doesn't sound too bad. There's a presumption nowadays that baseball players have to be like Puritans at church: just frown your way through the slow dirges as if your eternal soul depended on it. But maybe baseball could use a little jolt of rafter-rattling gospel music now and again. It is a game after all. This is supposed to be entertainment. You're not negotiating peace treaties here, guys; you're throwing a ball around. Get over yourselves.

There are limits of course. You can't slow down the game or otherwise influence fair competition with your shenanigans. But if you show some swagger that doesn't actually affect the play of the game, who cares? The only breach of etiquette should come if your opponent retaliates with violence. Trotting slowly around the bases doesn't hurt anyone. Retaliating by intentionally throwing a 90-mile-per-hour pitch at another human being does. Calm down, drama queen. If you want to get revenge for "showing you up," then get the game-winning hit.

Granted, Rabbit Maranville might not be the best role model. He also abused umpires, and his off-the-field antics often resulted in arrests. He served briefly as a manager (of course -- who better to take charge of a bunch of young men than a bizarre, possibly sociopathic man-child?), and his favorite activity was to run with his players through train cars pouring buckets of cold water on strangers. "The New Historical Baseball Abstract" comment for Maranville is my source for all these anecdotes, in which Bill James notes "there are as many Rabbit Maranville stories as there are Babe Ruth stories."

OK, fine, he was a crazy man, but what about his play? As you can see above, he was a Ray Schalk/Luis Aparicio type hitter: that is to say, bad. He was the equal or better of Aparicio on defense, a big reason why he compiled 11,256 PAs, 31st-most of all-time. Rabbit stole some bases but not like Aparicio did, which might partially explain why Maranville fares worse in the overall numbers than Aparicio does.

If Aparicio was on the borderline, Maranville looks to be on the wrong side of it. Maranville's numbers in the above say "no." It's not a George Kelly-style "no," which is more of a "NOOOOOO!!!!" Maranville's numbers are a Travis Jackson-esque polite-but-firm "No thank you, and please take me off your list."

Postseason? Maranville played pretty well in both the 1914 and 1928 World Series. Both were sweeps, and Rabbit hit exactly .308 (4 for 13) with one walk in each. It helps his case a bit, but I don't know that it can knock him ten spots up the rankings.

What about "It's the Hall of Fame, not the Hall of Stats?" Well, Maranville was certainly well-regarded in his time. We can measure this to some extent in MVP voting. The MVP award we now know and love was started in 1931, when Maranville was 39 years old. But there was an odd sort of MVP called the Chalmers Award from 1911-1914. Maranville's first full year was 1913, and he finished third in the Chalmers voting with an 83 OPS+, 17 Win Shares and 1.8 WAR. These are not numbers befitting a third-place MVP finisher. Maran-mania was already outstripping his actual performance.

In 1914 Maranville led the "Miracle Braves" to a surprise pennant despite an 85 OPS+. This time his defense was so good that he led all MLB shortstops with 24 Win Shares, good for eighth-best among all NL non-pitchers. WAR doesn't put him as the best shortstop in all of baseball, but actually ranks him higher among NL non-pitchers, an impressive third with 5.1 WAR. Maranville finished second in the Chalmers voting, which is far from unreasonable. Worse seasons have won MVPs.

Ten years passed before another MVP award was handed out. The League Awards hit the NL in 1924, and Maranville got seventh place with an 86 OPS+, 3.5 WAR and 15 Win Shares. He doesn't look like the seventh-best player in the league, but by then he was well-established as the kind of guy everyone felt was more valuable than his stats. For almost every other year that he played a full season, he got down-ballot MVP support, even when he scored a 59 OPS+, a -0.3 WAR, and 1 Win Share in 1932. His final full year, 1933, was much the same: 60 OPS+, -0.9 WAR, 6 Win Shares, and 12th in the MVP voting. Even when the numbers show him as below replacement level, people just could not stop thinking Maranville was valuable.

So, Maranville definitely did not lack for fame. Am I invoking "It's the Hall of Fame, not the Hall of Stats"? I think I am. I didn't do it for Bill Mazeroski, but I'm doing it for Rabbit Maranville. If you don't like it, call your congressperson. Maranville stays.

Pee Wee Reese (1940-1942, 1946-1958; career OPS+: 99)

	Career	Rank	Hitting	Rank	Fielding	Rank	Peak	Rank	Bests	JAWS	Rank
WAR	66.3	16	55.6	15	25.6	11	40.8	19	2	53.6	17
WS	315.0	17	203.7	14	111.2	12	183.4	20	1	NA	10

Thank goodness that Pee Wee Reese is a much easier case than Rabbit Maranville. Reese was one of history's best leadoff hitters, drawing walks, stealing bases and scoring runs for the great post-war Dodgers teams. He was also terrific on defense. Plus, he spent the early heart of his career, ages 24-26, demonstrating to Hitler, Tojo, and Mussolini that Americans have specific skills that are advantageous in the pursuit of military goals (not my best way of saying "he fought in World War II," but at this point I'm a bit out of practice). Reese is a Hall-of-Famer.

One other note about Reese. He was a soft-spoken, dignified, mild-mannered fellow, the type who earns respect without demanding it. His leadership qualities made him the captain of a Brooklyn team that won six pennants after World War II.

He was also a Southern boy from Louisville, Kentucky who grew up with Jim Crow laws. Other Southern boys were, shall we say, not terribly welcoming to Jackie Robinson. At first, Reese was shocked to hear of Robinson's signing, but his sense of fair play quickly overtook him. He became Robinson's mentor and close friend. When people saw the universally respected Reese accepting Robinson, they followed his example.

Before a game in Cincinnati, which was close to Reese's birthplace, the crowd was hurling slurs and insults at Robinson. The Reds players joined in, and it got uglier and uglier. Reese walked over to Jackie and threw his arm around him. The crowd and the Reds quieted down. Reese may not have intended to make some big important point. But to the world it spoke volumes. There is a statue commemorating the moment outside MCU Park in Brooklyn.

The story might be a bit apocryphal, as there are many different versions occurring in different times in different parks. But it relates how important Pee Wee Reese was to Robinson's success. Reese would be a Hall-of-Famer anyway, but helping make integration a reality adds to his case.

Cal Ripken (1981-2001; career OPS+: 112)

	Career	Rank	Hitting	Rank	Fielding	Rank	Peak	Rank	Bests	JAWS	Rank
WAR	95.5	3	77.2	5	34.6	3	56.1	3	5	75.8	3
WS	427.1	2	290.6	5	136.5	5	209.8	7	6	NA	3

This guy's a bit obscure, so I'll provide some background for you. Cal Ripken was a shortstop of some renown from the bygone era of the 1980s and 1990s. He played in 2,632 consecutive games, a number unfathomable today because all modern players are weak, overpaid whiners, unlike the Real Men of yesteryear. (In my grumpy-old-man mind, all players from my childhood are exactly like the few superstars I remember fondly.)

I was always more impressed with Ripken's consecutive innings streak of 8,243, which stretched from 1982 through 1987. Imagine not having to roster a backup shortstop for more than five years. The second-best streak is believed to be by George Pinckney, who played in 5,152 straight innings from 1885 to 1890. If you want to get all math-y up in here, which I do, that means Ripken had 60% more consecutive innings played than the all-time second-best. Meanwhile, he beat Lou Gehrig's consecutive games streak by a measly 20%. Ho-hum. Hardly a record at all, really. He shouldn't have bothered.

Some of you might be shocked that Cal isn't considered the number one shortstop by either WAR or Win Shares. If you're wondering who could have beat him, well, I'm not going to tell you. You gotta keep reading. Suspense! This book is officially now a "page-turner." I gotta remind Stephen King to put that in his blurb for the cover.

My favorite memory of Cal Ripken is hearing about his "rib game." Brady Anderson explained it like this: Cal punches you in the ribs as hard as he can. Then you punch Cal as hard as you can. Whoever gives up first is the loser. According to Brady, Cal would win and then pull up his shirt to show that he didn't have a single bruise. (Source: "Weaver got Ripken started," TheJournalTimes.com, Susan Shemanske, September 6, 1995) The man was a freak of nature, like the cheerleader in "Heroes,"[26] and baseball is better for it. Obvious Hall-of-Famer.

---

[26] Reference explanation: "Heroes" ran from 2006 to 2010 and involved a cheerleader, played by Hayden Panettiere, who instantly healed from any injury. It was a pretty entertaining show for a few years, until the chief villain became a guy with a lame soul patch who could move dirt around with his brain. You don't want to know.

Phil Rizzuto (1941-1942, 1946-1956; career OPS+: 93)

	Career	Rank	Hitting	Rank	Fielding	Rank	Peak	Rank	Bests	JAWS	Rank
WAR	40.6	39	28.1	67	22.9	18	33.7	29	2	37.2	34
WS	230.1	38	132.9	45	97.3	24	172.9	23	1	NA	16

Hm. Phil Rizzuto had a short career of 6,718 PAs, but he did spend 1943-1945 in some sort of conflict doing something or other. This was the part of his career, ages 25-27, when most players achieve their peak performance.

In past comments I've said that we have to give extra credit to those who spent years in World War II. In all other cases, the players passed the test even without the extra credit. Rizzuto might not.

So let's try to quantify what those three years could have done for Rizzuto's numbers. These kind of what-if games are always dangerous; you can't know if he would have spent those years injured or ineffective or caught in a love triangle with Betty Grable and Lucky Luciano and subsequently forced to play sans kneecaps. But just for the sake of argument, let's give it a shot.

Here are Rizzuto's WAR and Win Shares by year:

Age	Year	WAR	WS
23	1941	4.5	21
24	1942	5.7	25
25	1943	WWII	WWII
26	1944	WWII	WWII
27	1945	WWII	WWII
28	1946	1.8	12
29	1947	4.1	26
30	1948	1.5	15
31	1949	2.9	22
32	1950	6.7	35
33	1951	3.5	23
34	1952	5.3	21
35	1953	3.9	18

36	1954	0	6
37	1955	0.7	6
38	1956	-0.1	1

Rizzuto doesn't exhibit a smooth Eddie-Murray-style career progression. He started quite well, but after the war he alternated good and not-so-good years, with his MVP campaign in 1950 standing out. The average scores from his age 23-35 years are 4.0 WAR and 22 Win Shares.

Let's be conservative and give Rizzuto three more of those 4.0 WAR, 22 Win Shares seasons. This is not a huge gift to Rizzuto, mind you, especially considering players at age 25-27 usually have their best years, not their average ones. In modern times, 4.0 WAR was achieved by 2010 Stephen Drew with 633 PAs, .278 BA, .352 OBP, .458 SLG, and much less impressive defense than Rizzuto. A recent shortstop with 22 Win Shares was Stephen Drew again, but a different year: 2008, when he had 668 PAs, a .291 BA, .333 OBP, .502 SLG, and again defense well below Rizzuto's level. You get the idea: I'm adding Stephen Drew seasons, not Derek Jeter seasons.

Here's what the above stats become with those 4.0 WAR, 22 Win Shares seasons replacing the WWII years of 1943-1945:

	Career	rank	Hitting	rank	Fielding	rank	Peak	rank	bests	JAWS	rank
WAR	52.6	23	?	?	?	?	34.3	29	?	43.5	25
WS	296.1	19	?	?	?	?	174.9	23	?	NA	16

Adding those three average seasons doesn't affect the Peak numbers, because he has five actual years better than the pretend seasons and two that are almost as good. But his career numbers jump into lower-level Hall of Fame territory, the domain of Dave Bancroft and Bobby Doerr etc. As a result, his JAWS rank improves from 34th to 25th.

I think Bill James accounted for Rizzuto's military service in ranking him 16th, so I left that in there. But let's calculate WSAWS, which, as you remember, averages Career Win Shares and Peak Win Shares. James uses more than that in his rankings, but WSAWS can at least provide an approximation. After adding the new seasons, Rizzuto climbs from 34th in WSAWS to 19th.

If I were a better person, I'd go through this exercise for every World War II player and then see how Rizzuto ranks with those guys. Since I'm a horrible human being, I'll just leave it at that. I'm satisfied that if you account for Phil Rizzuto's war years, he tips into Hall of Fame territory.

Joe Sewell (1920-1933; career OPS+: 108)

	Career	Rank	Hitting	Rank	Fielding	Rank	Peak	Rank	Bests	JAWS	Rank
WAR	53.7	20	53.8	16	9.1	68	37.3	23	6	45.5	19
WS	277.8	22	188.2	17	90.0	35	175.1	22	5	NA	23

If Joe Sewell is famous for anything, it's for never striking out. As a dissolute young ne'er-do-well, he dared strike out 12-20 times a year. But from 1925-1933 he behaved like a responsible adult, logging strikeout totals in the single digits every season.

As with walks, the view of strikeouts has evolved over time. Until recently, they were seen as abject failure, the worst thing you can do in a batter's box besides throwing your bat in the crowd and hitting a nun. I understand the sentiment: Strikeouts are certainly frustrating to watch. One of my favorite players as a kid, Cardinals outfielder Ray Lankford, was always strikeout-prone. But in 2001 it was getting to be once every three at-bats. Cardinal fans, usually a loving and forgiving bunch, turned against him, and he was traded to San Diego. I was sad, especially since he was still hitting well (114 OPS+).

Nowadays, strikeouts are increasingly shrugged off, and there is some strategic thinking behind that. Sometimes strikeouts are just an unfortunate by-product of working the count. On balance, that kind of patience tends to also result in more walks and fewer groundouts. After all, a strikeout is not the worst thing you can do at bat. Grounding into a double play is much worse, bringing you two outs instead of one.

This newer perspective makes Joe Sewell seem less like a true exemplar of How the Game Should Be Played and something more like "Hey Joe, what if you took a close pitch on 3-2 now and again? You might risk a strikeout, but you might also get a walk. Over a season, that might prove more productive than slapping at a borderline pitch. You tend to get a lot of groundouts when you routinely swing at close pitches on full counts. The pitcher knows you'll swing, and will throw just outside the zone."

Maybe we shouldn't second-guess Joe Sewell, because he made it work pretty well, to the tune of .312/.391/.413 in 8333 PAs. His stats are live-ball-inflated, big-time, though: other players who had a 108 career OPS+ include dead-ball-era outfielder Bob Bescher (.258/.353/.351) and 1950s/1960s shortstop/outfielder Harvey Kuenn (.303/.357/.408).

Still, a shortstop who hits significantly better than average, fields well enough, and lasts a pretty long time is good enough for the Hall of Fame. Sewell stays.

Ozzie Smith (1978-1996; career OPS+: 87)

	Career	Rank	Hitting	Rank	Fielding	Rank	Peak	Rank	Bests	JAWS	Rank
WAR	76.5	6	47.8	21	43.4	1	42.3	14	2	59.4	8
WS	327.0	14	187.1	19	139.8	4	169.7	25	0	NA	7

I grew up in St. Louis in the 1980s, when Ozzie Smith was a god. In 1987, I caught a serious dose of Cardinal fever. Inspired by Ozzie, I would make diving catches in our family rec room by throwing a tennis ball in the air and catching it while flopping onto a giant floor pillow. Technically, I wasn't pretending to be Ozzie; I was pretending to be a defensive whiz nicknamed "The Taxman." The Beatles song "Taxman" would play in my mind as I envisioned a highlight reel of diving catches. In retrospect, I should have practiced something besides diving catches of tennis balls lofted gently in the air. But I was less interested in actually playing baseball than in being in highlight reels.

WAR says Smith and his diving stops made for the best defensive shortstop in history. Win Shares has him below Bill Dahlen, Rabbit Maranville, and Honus Wagner, but it's very close; Dahlen leads

Smith by only 3.5 Win Shares. As with Luis Aparicio, Smith shows that shortstops can get over the Hall of Fame line with great defense and below-average offense in a way that second basemen can't.

Ozzie wasn't a complete zero at the plate, though. He started out as one, looking like the new Mark Belanger. Belanger was the Orioles' shortstop in the late 1960s and the 1970s. He is second place in Defensive WAR among shortstops, and 15th in career Defensive Win Shares, despite playing in about 75% as many career games as Ozzie, Maranville, Honus Wagner, etc. But Belanger hit so badly, with a 68 career OPS+, that he's no one's idea of a Hall-of-Famer.

Smith's OPS+ numbers in his first four years were 82, 48, 71, and 62. That 48 OPS+ score in 1979 was one of the 50 worst among all seasons long enough to qualify for the batting title. He earned 0.1 Offensive Win Shares that year, which is about as bad as you can get, and that incorporates Smith's 28 SBs with only 7 CSs. Belanger was no doubt getting nervous.

Then in 1982 Ozzie was traded from the Padres to the Cardinals for shortstop Garry Templeton, and Smith's offense gradually got better and better. It peaked with a .303 BA/.392 OBP/.383 SLG line in 1987, which happened to be the Greatest Season in Baseball History. (I may be a bit biased in that assessment.) Smith earned 33 Win Shares that year, just one behind the leader, Tim Raines, and a good 13 above 1987 MVP Andre Dawson. WAR has Ozzie 6th in the NL that year, well behind Tony Gwynn but still far above Dawson.

In a way it's unfair to judge Smith's offense by OPS+ and BA/OBP/SLG. None of those stats includes stolen bases, and Ozzie's 580 career stolen bases mean he kinda sorta turned 580 singles into doubles. Of course, the 148 caught stealings mean 148 fewer singles, sort of ... this is a bit of a fudge, because some of those caught stealings erased doubles, and a single and a stolen base is not technically as good a double, since it can't often drive in a guy on first. But let's just see how Smith's BA/OBP/SLG line looks if we add his stolen bases and caught stealings into the mix.

Without SBs and CSs (i.e., the normal way): .262/.337/.328, OPS: .665, OPS+: 87

With SBs and CSs (the slightly fudge-y way): .246/.323/.374, OPS: .697, OPS+: 91

OK, that's not a huge difference, but it's something. It gets Ozzie's career OPS+ in the range of Nellie Fox and Red Schoendienst and farther from Ray Schalk and Bill Mazeroski. Regardless, Ozzie's defense puts both his Win Shares and WAR numbers in the realm of a clear Hall-of-Famer.

Joe Tinker (1902-1916; career OPS+: 96)

	Career	Rank	Hitting	Rank	Fielding	Rank	Peak	Rank	Bests	JAWS	Rank
WAR	53.2	21	32.5	44	34.3	4	33.1	32	0	43.2	24
WS	258.3	31	144.9	38	113.5	10	159.3	34	0	NA	33

And now we reach the third installment of the Tinker to Evers to Chance series of films. The third one looks to be the worst, as with the "Star Wars" trilogy. (I'm not talking about the prequels, which are not canon as far as I'm concerned. I lump them in with the Extended Universe stuff that explores C-3PO's awkward teenage years and Chewbacca's cousin's heroic battles to get his chest waxes recognized as a business expense for tax purposes, etc., etc.). Tinker's overall ranks of 24th in WAR and 33rd according to Bill James are not inspiring.

What went wrong here? In fielding, Tinker shows up quite strong. His career OPS+ is low but better than that of Luis Aparicio, Rabbit Maranville, and Ozzie Smith, and not far from Dave Bancroft (98) and Pee Wee Reese (99).

The problem is that Tinker had a short career, 12 full seasons plus one that was nearly full. His Peak numbers are not Hall-of-Fame worthy; he had one MVP-level year in 1908 (32 Win Shares, 7.9 WAR) and a handful of other years that that might get you a backup spot on the All-Star team but also might not. In 1908 and 1911, both WAR and Win Shares say Tinker was the second-best shortstop in baseball, behind Honus Wagner each time. It's hard to fault Tinker for never being first, since Honus Wagner was the best shortstop in history by a mile (too-late spoiler alert/suspense-killer.) But Tinker was never third-best according to either system, usually scoring in the middle of the pack.

Tinker hit well in the 1910 World Series, OK in the 1908 one, and poorly in the 1907 and 1906 ones. His 235/.307/.309 in 82 World Series PAs doesn't help his case much.

The grand total looks like something a little less than Dave Bancroft, which is something a little less than a Hall-of-Famer. Do I dare keep two of the famous double-play combo and reject the third?

That poem does keep Tinker relatively famous now. In the Sporcle Hall of Fame quiz I mentioned earlier, Tinker was named about as often as Eddie Collins, around the middle of the pack. I don't think that's terribly relevant though.

More relevant for the "It's the Hall of Fame, not the Hall of Stats" get-out-of-jail-free card is whether he was famous and well-regarded in his time, like Maranville was. Tinker did relatively well in the aforementioned Chalmers Award, scoring 10th in 1911 (when he had the NL's 6th-best WAR and 11th best Win Shares among non-pitchers) and 4th in 1912 (12th in WAR, 15th in Win Shares). That's good, but not much of a sample.

How about Hall of Fame voting? Hall of Fame voting is largely what I'm trying to override with this book, but it still might give us some insight. In the first-ever Hall of Fame vote in 1936, Tinker wasn't even on the ballot. Chance and Evers were on it, getting 6 votes each. In 1937, Chance got 49 votes, Evers 44, and Tinker 15. 1938 saw Chance at 133, Evers at 91, and Tinker at 16. You get the pattern.

It keeps going like this until the infamous 1946 Old Timers' Committee vote that threw in all three players. As I mentioned in the Evers comment, all three were considered by both the Old Timers' Committee and the BBWAA that year. Chance and Evers finished first and second in the BBWAA vote, but neither got the 75% necessary for admission. Tinker was 14th that year.

This discrepancy was probably because Chance and Evers both had leadership cred to their name. Chance was the manager of perhaps the greatest National League dynasty of all time, the 1906-1910 Cubs. Evers was team captain of the 1914 Miracle Braves and was so well-regarded in that role that he won the 1914 Chalmers Award. Tinker had success as a manager in the Federal League, but not in the National or American League, so he didn't gain much leadership luster.

There was apparently a general sense in the 1930s and '40s that Chance and Evers were more worthy of the Hall of Fame than Tinker. That's my sense too. **Tinker is out.**

Arky Vaughan (1932-1943, 1947-1948; career OPS+: 136)

	Career	Rank	Hitting	Rank	Fielding	Rank	Peak	Rank	Bests	JAWS	Rank
WAR	72.9	9	70.9	6	12.0	60	50.6	5	7	61.8	6
WS	355.9	9	275.6	6	80.4	48	236.9	4	6	NA	2

And here's the best baseball player in history that you may have never heard of. Vaughan gets lost in the noise of amazing-looking hitting stats in the 1930s, and he spent most of his career with mediocre Pirates teams. His 7722 career PAs mean he doesn't end up with high career hitting totals. It all makes him underrated, so underrated that he had to be inducted by the Veterans Committee.

He didn't play from 1943-1946, his age 32-34 seasons, but for once it wasn't Hitler's fault. Vaughan refused to play for manager Leo Durocher and, because of the reserve clause, had no other option but to sit out of baseball.

At this time, Vaughan was playing for the Dodgers. He was the dignified, universally respected elder statesman of a very talented club. Like most people, he didn't get along well with the fiery Durocher. It came to a head one morning when Vaughan learned that Durocher had criticized Dodgers pitcher Bobo Newsom in the press. Vaughan quietly took in the information, but was fuming inside.

Later that day, at the ballpark, Vaughan confronted Durocher about his comments. Durocher said he meant everything he said. Vaughan went to his locker, gathered up his uniform, brought it back to the manager's office, and threw it in Durocher's face. "Take this uniform and shove it right up your ass," he said. "If you would lie about Bobo, you would lie about me and everyone else."

Vaughan and Newsom started to watch that day's game from the stands, and many other players were tempted to join them. Dodgers general manager Branch Rickey intervened, and convinced Vaughan to suit up. But after the year was over, Vaughan had had enough, and retired to his cattle ranch.

In 1947, Durocher was suspended the whole year, and Rickey convinced Vaughan to come back to the Dodgers. It was also Jackie Robinson's first year. Vaughan went out of his way to be welcoming to Robinson, and his veteran presence was a calming influence in the clubhouse. (Source: SABR biography of Vaughan, by Ralph Moses)

I don't give Vaughan any extra consideration for those lost years, but he doesn't need it. Bill James was surprised to find Vaughan coming up as his second-best shortstop of all time, but the numbers were clear. If the "New Historical Baseball Abstract" had been written today, Vaughan may have been bumped down by Alex Rodriguez, who takes the number two spot in WAR. Obviously, no matter where you rank Vaughan, you can't exclude him from the Hall of Fame.

Honus Wagner (1897-1917; career OPS+: 151)

	Career	Rank	Hitting	Rank	Fielding	Rank	Peak	Rank	Bests	JAWS	Rank
WAR	131.0	1	123.0	1	21.3	23	65.3	1	11	98.2	1
WS	656.2	1	513.9	1	141.7	3	317.2	1	14	NA	1

There's Honus Wagner, and then there's everyone else. In the "New Historical Baseball Abstract," Bill James says "The distance between the number one shortstop (Wagner) and the number two shortstop (whoever it is) is about the same as the difference between the number two shortstop and the number 30 shortstop."

That was 2001, but the Win Shares totals still tell much the same story. In WSAWS, which averages Career Win Shares and Peak Win Shares, Wagner scores a 486.7. Second place is Alex Rodriguez, at 329.8. And you can put several asterisks next to A-Rod's total, because he spent time at the less demanding position of third base, his alleged steroid use, and the fact that everyone has decided he's a big dumb poophead (which seems to be a major motivating factor in many A-Rod arguments, but anyway, let's not get into that now).

Point is, Wagner's WSAWS is 48% better than Alex Rodriguez's. Think about that. As good as Rodriguez has been for the last 20 years, Honus Wagner was nearly 50% better. It's about the same difference between Alex Rodriguez and Vern Stephens (221.2 WSAWS), a great-hitting shortstop who crapped out in his 30s due to injuries and alcoholism.

WAR is not as lopsided for Wagner. Rodriguez is at second place with 90.1 JAWS, just 9% less than Wagner. Why the difference between the two systems? A key difference is that WAR assigns bits of wins based on performance, while Win Shares goes the opposite direction, dividing a team's wins among its players. Wagner's teams won a lot. They had other good players, but Wagner was clearly doing most of the work. With so many wins to divide up, he ended with a lot of shares. Maybe the Win Shares system is capturing something that WAR can't. People talk about all the "intangibles" that go into winning and aren't captured by numbers; maybe Win Shares is able to get at those by starting with actual team wins and working from there.

Regardless, no one should ever say that anyone beside Honus Wagner is the best shortstop in history. If any man dare do so in your presence, be sure to remove your glove and slap him across the face. Protocol then requires he take off his glove and slap you back. Then commences the glove fight. No wool gloves allowed; they're too scratchy.

You better stock up on gloves now, though, because casual fans don't know much about Wagner. Many know about his famously rare and valuable T206 tobacco card, one of which sold for more than $2 million. But that's about it, apparently. In 1999, Major League Baseball had fans vote on an All-Century Team. Honus Wagner finished fourth in the vote among shortstops, behind Cal Ripken, Ernie Banks, and Ozzie Smith. Only the top two at each position made it on to the team in the fan vote. Thankfully, a special panel then added Honus and four others.

Why isn't Honus Wagner better known? If you guessed "less impressive conventional stats because he played in the dead-ball era," then you've been paying attention. In 1908, Wagner played great defense at baseball's most defense-first position while hitting .354/.415/.542. Those numbers will always get some eyebrows a-poppin' (I just invented a new phrase!), but it's not as wowie-zowie-kapowie (OK, that one didn't work as well) as, say, George Sisler going .420/.467/.594 in 1922.

But, you guessed it, here comes the context. The National League in 1908 hit .239/.299/.306. Mind you, that's an *average* hitter; if your shortstop had that line in 1908, you'd be pretty happy. Wagner was so much better than that that he scored 59 Win Shares, which is a cuckoo-ball number, the best of any non-pitcher in history. A 30 means you're an MVP candidate; a 59 means you're two MVP candidates at once. (WAR is less excited but still gives 1908 Wagner 11.5 WAR, good for 11th of any non-pitcher in history.)

And as you probably assumed, my straw man, 1922 George Sisler, was not as impressive in context. His American League hit .285/.348/.398. Sisler got 29 Win Shares and 8.7 WAR that season; still MVP-level, but not quite eyebrow-poppin' wowie-zowie-kapowie stuff. (Sorry.)

Anyway, I think Honus Wagner is one of the five best players in history. Bill James rates him as second-best, behind Babe Ruth. WAR doesn't really rate all players together, but Wagner's JAWS number is 10th all-time, ahead of Ted Williams and Stan Musial. It's a tough call, but I think Honus Wagner deserves to be in the Hall of Fame.

Bobby Wallace (1894-1918; career OPS+: 105)

	Career	Rank	Hitting	Rank	Fielding	Rank	Peak	Rank	Bests	JAWS	Rank
WAR	70.2	12	56.3	14	28.7	7	41.6	16	2	55.9	14
WS	345.9	11	201.5	15	114.1	9	166.2	29	1	NA	36

Bobby Wallace was an exact contemporary of Honus Wagner and, obviously, did not hit as well. But Wallace hit quite well for a shortstop; his 105 career OPS+ is a tick higher than Johnny Damon's. If you had a Johnny Damon-level hitter playing shortstop for 9612 PAs, you'd win a few championships.

More importantly, he was a terrific defender for a very long time. WAR and Win Shares both agree on that count. Bill James is downright rude in rating Wallace 36th overall, seeing as how all of his other Win Shares rankings are much higher. In WSAWS, Wallace is 14th among shortstops. Dropping him from 14th to 36th is a pretty big downgrade, Bill. I know you turn up your nose at people who dared to play major-league baseball in a year beginning with "18", but geez.

Sometimes this sort of discrepancy between James' rankings and WSAWS occurs because Bill James defines a Peak as being a guy's best five seasons, while I'm going with best seven. That means a player who has seven dynamite seasons instead of five will look better in the Peak Win Shares ranking above than in Bill James' final assessments. This is not the case with Bobby Wallace, who had 12 20-Win-Share seasons and none above 26.

Wallace's consistent good play made him perhaps the greatest St. Louis Brown in history (though most people would choose George Sisler). But in a fair world, he would have been a lifelong Cleveland Spider. He started his career with the Spiders, a good team in the 1890s. Behind Hall of Famers Cy Young and Jesse Burkett, they finished above .500 each year from 1892 to 1898. They never won the National League pennant, but three times they finished 2nd among 12 teams.

Then a few days before the 1899 season began, Wallace, Young, Burkett, and other good players were suddenly transferred to the St. Louis Perfectos, also of the National League. Not traded, mind you, and not sold -- just sent over for nothing in return. The owners of the Spiders had also bought the Perfectos, and decided that concentrating every good player in St. Louis would bring better profits.

It was an example of "syndicate ownership," which was a fancy-sounding name for "plutocrats screwing entire cities of baseball fans for a few extra bucks." There was nothing stopping one person from simultaneously owning two NL teams and destroying one in favor of the other.

This was a big problem in the National League in the 1890s. It was the kind of stupid crap that owners shouldn't have been allowed to get away with. It created a need for a competitor league that wouldn't do such things, one that realized the survival of the game depended on owners playing by some rules too. The American League came in to save baseball from itself in 1901.

In 1899, stripped of every major-league quality player, the Spiders finished 20-134. Clevelanders knew what was happening from day one and refused to show up. The team's attendance for the entire year was 6,088 over only 42 home games, fewer than 200 per.

The Spiders still played a full 154 games, though. As the season progressed, Cleveland home games brought in so few fans that opponents refused to even come to town. They knew their portion of the gate receipts would be too low to even cover travel expenses. So the Spiders spent the rest of their season on the road, logging 112 road games in total. The job of their poor bedraggled players was to go to a new city, get shellacked, and then move on to the next. Only one Spiders pitcher ended the season with a positive WAR, and he pitched only 3.2 innings.

A great comedy film is in there, I think. The climax could be the game on September 18 when they squeaked by the Washington Senators 5-4, after 24 straight losses (and before 15 straight more).

Meanwhile, the life of Bobby Wallace would make a pretty bad movie. You might get a few good scenes exploring his innovations in shortstop play, such as being one of the first to grab a grounder and throw to first all in one motion. But there were few inspiring plot lines on a St. Louis Browns team that was always terrible. And Wallace was a pretty quiet, undemonstrative guy, so it's hard to imagine much off-the-field drama.

Luckily, the Academy of Motion Picture Arts and Sciences doesn't pick Baseball Hall-of-Famers. I do (in my pretend world), and I'm ignoring Bill James' low overall ranking. To me, Bobby Wallace is a Hall-of-Famer.

John "Monte" Ward (1878-1894; career OPS+: 92; career ERA+: 119)

	Career	Rank	Hitting	Rank	Fielding	Rank	Peak	Rank	Bests	JAWS	Rank
WAR	64.2	17	30.7	54	10.4	66	37.5	22	2	50.9	19
WS	409.9	4	158.8	31	77.2	51	240.5	3	4	NA	35

Observant readers will notice something odd about the above. John Ward started out as a pitcher and then switched to shortstop. The Career and Peak numbers include both, which is why they're so much better than the hitting and fielding numbers.

It might be a bit unfair to combine his pitching with his hitting, since no one else does. On Baseball-reference.com, Ward's JAWS is 38th because they leave out his pitching. James' above ranking of Ward at 35th is also based on his contributions as a non-pitcher. I didn't think it was fair to leave out the pitching half of Ward's career, even if it does create an apples-plus-oranges situation even more extreme than guys like Rod Carew and Ernie Banks who split their careers among two very different non-pitcher positions.

And then there's the argument made by some that pitching before 1884, as Ward did, shouldn't count at all for the Hall. Before that year, pitchers had to throw underhanded at a spot requested by the batter. It was as if the pitcher were some kid's dad in a softball league for 8-year-olds.

I make fun, but actually, it made some sense. In those days, the point of the game was to create a contest between the batter and fielders, not between the batter and the pitcher. The pitcher was not really a central member of the defense. It made for a more fast-paced, exciting game, as everyone was up there to swing, and walks and strikeouts were rare (and hitters stayed in the damn batter's box through the whole at-bat, grumble grumble grumble). Nowadays, hitters are so good that a game like that would turn into a home run derby. But I gotta say, 1880s baseball sounds pretty fun.

And even though pitchers had to throw at certain spots underhanded, there was still some difference in skill involved. If you pitch faster or curvier to the requested spots, you're going to help your team win games. 1880s pitching might be less valuable, but it's still important. Ward had a 119 career ERA+, meaning that whatever Ward did, he got results that were 19% better than the rest of the pitchers.

When pitchers started having to pitch overhanded, Ward couldn't hack it. So he turned into a good but not great shortstop, of an Edgar Renteria level. Edgar finished at 94 OPS+ and 28.7 JAWS, close to the 92 and 30.2 Ward got as a shortstop. If you downgrade Ward's pitching numbers, add it to Edgar Renteria, is that a Hall-of-Famer?

But wait, Monte Ward wasn't just a pitcher and a shortstop. In the off-seasons he got his law degree at Columbia, you know, like your typical ballplayer. As an attorney he fought hard against the reserve clause, the rule that bound a player to his club indefinitely in the pre-free-agency days.

The reserve clause was really just the tip of the proverbial iceberg as far as anti-capitalist actions by owners. In 1886, owners colluded to hold salaries at a maximum of $2,000 a year. They also agreed to charge players rent for their uniforms and for the expenses of road trips. Instead of competing amongst themselves to offer the best incentives for the best talent, like business owners are supposed to under capitalism, the owners fixed the market to their own benefit, like some Soviet apparatchiks. Perhaps even the most conservative among you can understand why Ward felt the need to organize baseball's first union. It was a bold move, as it was very early in the history of the American labor movement.

When negotiations with owners of the National League and American Association (then a major league) went nowhere, Ward threatened to form his own league and take many of the great players with him. The owners thought Ward was bluffing. He wasn't. If you think baseball labor struggles were tough in the 1990s, it was much crazier in the 1880s. Donald Fehr never created his own league.

Ward's many connections among businessmen helped him form the Player's League in 1890. The new league had no reserve clause and shared profits among players. Hall-of-Famers Roger Connor, Hugh Duffy, Jake Beckley, Dan Brouthers, Buck Ewing, Old Hoss Radbourn and Pud Galvin all defected to the new league. Ward managed and played for the Brooklyn Ward's Wonders, one of the seven teams in the league that competed in the same cities as National League and American Association teams.

The Players' League did pretty well at attracting fans. But several cities now had three major league teams, which was too many. Many teams started losing money. One of the leagues was destined to die off.

It ended up being the Player's League. Its owners started to notice how little of the profits came into their pockets, instead going to the players in profit sharing. So they started secretly selling off their teams to the National League. The Players' League collapsed after just one year. It was a huge blow to players, solidifying the reserve clause and thus owners' control over their livelihoods. Sigh. I would have loved to see what could have come out of a system that wasn't so lopsided in favor of owners.

After the dissolution of the Player's League, Ward returned to the National League for a few years. He retired at age 34 to devote himself to his law practice, often representing players in their battles with owners. Later he became a team president and part owner of the Boston Braves. When another major league was formed in 1914, the Federal League, you may not be surprised to learn that Ward was involved. He served as business manager for the Brooklyn team. (Source: Ward's SABR biography, by Bill Lamb.)

But wait, there's more! Along with being a pitcher, shortstop, lawyer, team president, owner, league official and labor organizer, Monte Ward was also an expert surveyor, a champion zeppelin racer, a Nobel Prize winner in molecular phrenology, and inventor of the phrase "Hellzapoppin'!" None of those are true, but even just the real ones, when summed up, make Monte Ward a clear Hall-of-Famer in my eyes.

Willie "Devil" Wells (1924-1948)

	Rank at Position Among Negro Leaguers	Rank Among All Negro Leaguers
Bill James	2	11
SABR	2	8
Monte Irvin	1	NA

As with catchers, Hall-of-Fame Negro League shortstops neatly arrange themselves by era. As soon as Pop Lloyd started to decline, Willie Wells was ready to become the best shortstop.

While Lloyd had stiff competition in Honus Wagner, it's unlikely that any shortstop in the world was better than Wells in the late 1920s. In the MLB, the best-shortstop-by-year title alternated between Joe Sewell and Travis Jackson. But as we've seen, one is a marginally deserving and the other is a marginally undeserving Hall-of-Famer. Meanwhile, Wells is the eighth-best shortstop in history, according to Bill James; among his top 100 players, the only shortstops ahead of Wells are Honus Wagner, Pop Lloyd, Arky Vaughan, Cal Ripken, Robin Yount and Ernie Banks.

Wells was known as "Devil," well, originally "El Diablo," for his intense style of play in the Mexican leagues. He was often hit by pitches and once got a serious concussion. The story goes that he then came to the plate wearing a construction helmet, thus inventing the batting helmet out of whole cloth.

Actually, many players had experimented with batting helmets before Wells, including Roger Bresnahan and Frank Chance. You could argue that Wells' use of a construction helmet was a huge jump forward in the development of batting helmets, since Bresnahan and Chance were using the kind of leather helmets that old-timey football players wore. But that doesn't make for as good of a story. No one likes stories of gradual evolution; we want tales of inventors and their sudden sparks of inspiration, preferably encapsulated in three sentences or less. If only the truth were more snappy, people might know more of it. Dumb truth.

Regardless of what he did or didn't invent, Willie Wells is obviously a Hall-of-Famer.

Robin Yount (1974-1993; career OPS+: 115)

	Career	Rank	Hitting	Rank	Fielding	Rank	Peak	Rank	Bests	JAWS	Rank
WAR	77.0	5	82.2	4	5.8	83	47.3	7	4	62.2	5
WS	420.3	3	317.5	3	103.2	16	214.3	5	3	NA	4

Robin Yount, Robin Yount
Brewer king by all account
His career was but a fount
Of hits, too many e'er to count

(Editor's note: Actually, Yount's hits are pretty well counted: 3142.)

Well, that was a rude interruption. Ahem.

Poetic license, poetic license
Apparently some editors it frightens.
Poetry is art that e'er lightens
Life, as long as dumb editors don't get in the way.

(Editor's note: That's it -- write about Robin Yount or you're fired.)

So Robin Yount had an interesting career. He got his start extremely early, at age 18 in 1974. He didn't do anything special throughout the rest of the 1970s, always in the middle of the pack among MLB shortstops. His best season in the Me Decade was 1978, after which he demanded more money from the Brewers. If he didn't get it, he said, he'd go start a professional golf career. I have tried that line with my boss after making a really nice-looking spreadsheet, but it has been less than entirely successful.

Yount stayed in baseball and got into weight training, which sent his career to a new level. In 1980 he was the best shortstop in baseball, and in 1982 he was the best anyone had seen in more than 35 years. That year he had 39 Win Shares, the ninth-best shortstop season in history, behind six Honus Wagner years, Luke Appling's 1943 and Arky Vaughan's 1935. WAR is even bigger on Yount's 1982, giving it third place among shortstops behind Cal Ripken's 1991 and Honus Wagner's 1908. Yount won one of the easiest MVP decisions ever and led the Brewers to the World Series.

Unfortunately, at this writing, the Brewers haven't been back to the Series. They endured the longest stretch between playoff appearances of any major sports team of the time until they finally reached the division series in 2008.

People talk about Cardinals fans being the greatest fans in baseball, or maybe Cubs fans or Red Sox fans. I think Brewers fans deserve at least an honorable mention. They endured a historic stretch of mediocrity and kept coming to the park. When the Brewers finally made it to the NLCS in 2011, they were fourth in the NL in attendance, with 3,071,373 and 37,918 per game.

That wouldn't be notable if Milwaukee were a large market, but it's the smallest market in baseball. Milwaukee is the 33rd-largest metro area in the United States, just behind Cincinnati, and farther behind non-baseball metros Portland, Orlando, Sacramento, Charlotte, Salt Lake City, Columbus, Indianapolis, Las Vegas and San Antonio. The fact the 3,000,000 fans came from such a relatively small population is downright outstanding.

The Packers may rule Wisconsin, but it happens to be a great place for baseball too. And Robin Yount is the king of Wisconsin baseball. In fact, I'm so inspired I might just write a poem … ahem …

(Editor's note: Eddie Daniels has been relieved of his position effective immediately. The remainder of this book will be written by anyone else we can find.)

Who's In, Who's Out

I managed to cut Travis Jackson and Joe Tinker from the Hall of Fame, and showed admirable restraint by keeping Luis Aparicio, Dave Bancroft and Rabbit Maranville, if I do say so myself. As I mentioned in the beginning of this chapter, there are lots of shortstops in the Hall, so it's not like they need many more. I do have a few that deserve consideration:

Derek Jeter (1995-2014; OPS+: 116)

	Career	Rank	Hitting	Rank	Fielding	Rank	Peak	Rank	Bests	JAWS	Rank
WAR	71.8	10	95.5	3	-9.7	99	42.3	15	1	57.1	12
WS	319.3	15	252.6	9	66.8	72	198.1	10	2	NA	13*

Well obviously. Derek Jeter not only belongs in the Hall of Fame; the Hall of Fame should be renamed in his honor. And each player in the Hall of Fame should also be renamed "Derek Jeter." And the sportswriter or announcer who sings his praises the most fulsomely should also be immediately elected, so he may sit on the right hand of Derek Jeter at all times and ensure that any and all who approach the One shall pay deference in the manner he deserves. Then all words in the English language should be replaced with "Derek Jeter." Derek Jeter Derek Jeter Derek Jeter, Derek Jeter Derek Jeter. Derek Jeter? Derek Jeter.

OK, I'll drop the sarcasm. Look, there's no doubt that Derek Jeter is a wonderful player, well deserving of the Hall of Fame. But the hero worship for him has gotten so over the top that it's downright frustrating to watch. In 2014, Jeter's last year, it was as if MLB had set aside the year solely for Derek Jeter love. No plate appearance could go by without hitting the same themes over and over: Jeter is a great leader, unselfish, very professional, classy, terrific player. Yeah, yeah, yeah, we get it already.

I was watching a Twins-Yankees game in 2014. When Jeter came to bat, they provided a little scouting report on him, as they do for every opposing hitter. The scouting report actually said "Wonderful leader. Consummate pro." How is that a scouting report? How does that prepare the Twins to beat him? Which is, by the way, what they're supposed to do, lest we forget. Are the Twins supposed to say "Hm, apparently he's a wonderful guy. I had never heard that before! That obviously means I should throw him sliders."

By my reckoning, Yankees GM Brian Cashman is the current leader in the "Who Loves Derek Jeter the Most?" competition that everyone in the baseball world seems to be playing. Before the 2015 season, he said he'd like to retire the entire practice of having a captain, in honor of Jeter. (Source: "Cashman: retire captaincy with Jeter," ESPN.com, Wallace Matthews, March 6, 2015.) So he's saying that the Yankees should close the door on ever having another player with strong leadership qualities. Clearly, Cashman is too distraught to think straight. He is like a 14-year-old girl whose boyfriend just dumped her: The love of his life is gone, and now his life is over and he could never possibly love anyone again.

Speaking as a Twins fan, I'm all for the Yankees retiring the concept of having a captain. I also think the Yankees should retire the concept of having a shortstop. Permitting a lesser mortal to tread upon the ground hallowed by Jeter's presence would be insufficiently respectful to the Captain to End Them All.

I'm being snarky not because I dislike Jeter; I really don't. He really was a great player. I just never understand when hero worship gets to this pitch. Maybe most people need to have someone whom everyone agrees is a perfect human being. They feel some comfort and kinship when everyone recites how great this person is over and over. Anyone who dares speak otherwise is met with unbounded fury. It all starts to take the character of a religion.

Well, just call me an agnostic when it comes to Jeterism. I believe he was a wonderful player and human being, but not infallible. For starters, he was bad on defense. Both systems above agree with me, as does every other objective system I've seen.

Jeter is definitely the worst defensive player in history to win five Gold Gloves. He got it every year from 2004-2006, and then in 2009 and 2010. Here's where he ranks according to Defensive WAR and Defensive Wins Shares among A.L. shortstops (minimum 100 games at SS) in those years:

Year	D-WAR rank among A.L. SSs	D-WS rank among A.L.SSs
2004	9th of 11	3rd of 11
2005	9th of 10	6th of 10
2006	10th of 10	8th of 10
2009	6th of 11	no data
2010	9th of 10	no data

Win Shares is more charitable, and Win Shares generally seems to do better at evaluating defense. Still, it's pretty clear Jeter won those Gold Gloves with his bat. Man, I'm so glad that they changed the balloting procedures for the Gold Glove in 2013. Now it's based in large part on sophisticated statistical evaluations instead of the vague impressions of fellow players.

Granted, it was easy to be fooled by watching Jeter field. He was very good at a few eye-catching plays, like the one where he grabs a ground ball backhand and then swivels to throw to first. He tended to do those at crucial moments in games. But at the routine plays he was always subpar.

As to his being a leader, unselfish, professional, etc., I have no reason to doubt that he is. But while I've heard this characterization approximately ten billion times, I've never heard examples. I've never heard stories that exhibited these qualities. I'm sure there are some, but the media never bothers to tell them. His perfection is supposed to be taken as an article of faith, as if any proof would diminish the glory.

No doubt some of you are filled with fury upon reading someone dare question the Gospel of Jeter. But before you launch a crusade to destroy my homeland, I politely ask that you stop to analyze your emotions. Why do you feel this way? Where does this rage come from? I'm genuinely curious about why every baseball fan seems so emotionally invested in Derek Jeter being a god of perfection.

To be clear, I believe Jeter was very good for a very long time. In terms of hitting alone, he could be the second-best shortstop ever, after Honus Wagner (if you ignore Alex Rodriguez, which most people would prefer to do). The Win Shares rankings above undersell him, as they're only through 2008. I used WSAWS instead of Bill James' overall ranking, for obvious reasons, but it's still a bit low.

Still, in any unbiased rank among Hall-of-Fame shortstops, he'd remain in the middle of the pack with Pee Wee Reese and Lou Boudreau. Jeter was a much better hitter than those guys, but a much worse fielder. (And all were great leaders, by the way.) Maybe Luke Appling is the best comparison, as he was also a great hitter who lasted a long time. That clearly qualifies Jeter as a Hall-of-Famer, if not as the greatest living thing to ever walk the earth.

Alan Trammell (1977-1996; OPS+: 110)

	Career	Rank	Hitting	Rank	Fielding	Rank	Peak	Rank	Bests	JAWS	Rank
WAR	70.4	11	62.4	11	22.0	21	44.6	8	1	57.5	11
WS	317.9	16	224.9	13	92.7	32	188.0	14	2	NA	9

Alan Trammell is like Bobby Grich or Bill Freehan. Or better, he's like his double-play partner Lou Whitaker. He was good at everything, without having one trait that jumps out at you. Unlike Lou, Trammell had one MVP-style season, 1987, which, if you remember, is also the Greatest Season in Baseball History (because it's when I became a fan). You know I don't like using conventional stats, but I'll make an exception for a line that weirdly fascinated me as a kid:

G	AB	R	H	HR	RBI	SB	CS	BA	OBP	SLG
151	597	109	205	28	105	21	2	.343	.402	.551

Hello, Alan Trammell's 1987. Good to see you again. It's been a while, buddy. Trammell was my favorite player in those days, even though I didn't live near Detroit and seldom saw him play. Part of it was that my cousin said he was great, and I wanted to be like my cousin. But mostly I just had a nerdy, Asperger's-syndrome-ish fascination with those numbers. My favorite number to this day is 343, Trammell's batting average that year.

Conventional baseball stats are like my first car: I love them and had some great times with them, and of course I feel nostalgic. But now they're old and broken-down, and something new will get me places much better.

So let's jump in the new car: Trammell had the highest Win Shares total in all of baseball in 1987, 35 to Tim Raines' 34. WAR has him tied for second with Wade Boggs at 8.2, a bit below Tony Gwynn's 8.5. It was almost a 1982-Robin-Yount or 1948-Lou-Boudreau kind of year that should have snagged him an MVP. But everyone was all agog over all the home runs hit that year, in a way that looks downright quaint in this post-Steroid-Era world. George Bell won the MVP by collecting 47 home runs and a league-leading 134 RBIs. He was maybe the tenth-best player in the AL, with 26 Win Shares and 6.0 WAR.

Trammell was more than a one-year wonder, of course. He had five other great seasons and several other good ones. In a world without Cal Ripken, Trammell would have been considered the hands-down best AL shortstop of his time. The way things are going, he might never make it into the Hall. But he deserves it.

Bill Dahlen (1891-1911; OPS+: 110)

	Career	Rank	Hitting	Rank	Fielding	Rank	Peak	Rank	Bests	JAWS	Rank
WAR	75.2	7	62.0	12	28.4	8	40.2	20	1	57.7	10
WS	392.2	7	248.9	10	143.3	1	185.5	16	2	NA	21

Bill Dahlen was an Alan Trammell from a century ago. He was good at everything but didn't have one trait that stood out. He had several great years and several good ones in a long career of 10,405 PAs. Like Trammell, he was often overshadowed by other shortstops in his time, first by Hughie Jennings and then by Honus Wagner. Both Dahlen and Trammell were known for their intelligence; I'm sure that if Dahlen played today he would be a broadcaster's darling for "heads-up play" and "doing all the little things."

Broadcasters would probably be less enamored with Dahlen's tendency to intentionally get himself thrown out of games so he could go to the horse track. The 1890s were a very different time; baseball was not taken as seriously as it is now (for better and for worse). I'm betting he would not pull that kind of thing today.

The half of Dahlen's career spent in the dead-ball era brings his conventional career numbers to uninspiring totals. Even taking context into account, he was only a league-average hitter after 1900. He led the league in RBIs in 1904, with 80(!), but his OPS+ was 101. It's his excellent performances in the 1890s, in both conventional and adjusted numbers, that put him solidly in the Hall-of-Fame area according to both WAR and Win Shares.

Dahlen was an exact contemporary of George Davis, so he also gets short shrift in Bill James' overall rating. The same argument for George Davis applies to Dahlen: Maybe the level of play was lower then, but the Hall of Fame has established that it exists to honor the best 1.5% or so from each era. Bill Dahlen qualifies and should be in.

Intentionally Overlooked

Again, these are the guys who have proponents, but don't measure up to Hall standards.

Omar Vizquel (1989-2012; OPS+: 82)

	Career	Rank	Hitting	Rank	Fielding	Rank	Peak	Rank	Bests	JAWS	Rank
WAR	45.3	29	32.3	47	28.4	9	26.7	61	0	36.0	42
WS	261.1	29	148.4	35	112.2	11	133.8	63	0	NA	35*

Omar Vizquel had 2877 career hits. That's a heck of a lot; the only non-HOFers ahead of him on the career hits list are Pete Rose, Derek Jeter, Rafael Palmeiro, Alex Rodriguez, and Barry Bonds.

It's a nice factoid, but it's not a Hall of Fame case. A single conventional stat never is. There are some people who want to see some guy named Doc Cramer get in because he had 2703 career hits, which is more than a majority of Hall-of-Famers. Cramer also had an 87 career OPS+ as a center fielder and never had a season of more than 2.4 WAR or 19 Win Shares. In JAWS among center fielders, he ranks 233rd. It's a laughable case.

Omar Vizquel's case is not nearly that bad, of course. He was a shortstop, so his career OPS+ isn't entirely unseemly. He was clearly not a good hitter, but neither were Rabbit Maranville or Ozzie Smith for most of their careers.

Maranville and Ozzie made the Hall because of their defense. Vizquel's advocates will tell you that he was similar to Ozzie as a defender, but they're ignoring the fact that he definitely wasn't. Vizquel was very good, but not that good. His defensive rankings also don't compare to Maranville's. I left Maranville in my Hall mainly because of "It's the Hall of Fame, not the Hall of Stats," but Vizquel was never that famous.

Most importantly, look at those Peak rankings above. Vizquel had exactly one year that could conceivably be called great, 1999, when he scored 6.0 WAR and 22 Win Shares. In no other year did he get more than 4.0 WAR, and he had just two more 20-Win Share years, 21 in 2002 and 20 in 2005. His 2009-2012 seasons are not included in the Win Shares totals, but those years wouldn't help his case, as he spent them as a mediocre-to-poor bench player.

Omar Vizquel had a Rick Ferrell/Jake Beckley kind of career, lasting an extremely long time by being good but not great. He made for a valuable supporting piece. But if Omar Vizquel were your team's best player, you would not make the playoffs. I think Vizquel is a fine fellow and was a very good baseball player, but not deserving of the Hall.

Maury Wills (1959-1972; OPS+: 88)

	Career	Rank	Hitting	Rank	Fielding	Rank	Peak	Rank	Bests	JAWS	Rank
WAR	39.5	42	38.2	36	12.0	61	29.6	51	1	34.6	48
WS	251.2	33	155.7	32	76.5	53	166.4	27	1	NA	19

In 1962, Maury Wills had 104 stolen bases. It was a crazy number, the first time anyone had surpassed 100 since 1894. Because of that season, Wills is often credited with reviving the stolen base as a valid strategy.

That's bogus. In the American League, Luis Aparicio had been stealing more than 50 bases a year for several years. And before Wills, Willie Mays was leading the NL every season with totals in the 30s and 40s. Wills just gets credit because he put up the big, exciting three-digit number that made even casual baseball fans sit up and take notice. You could argue that Wills made the stolen base more prominent, but he didn't single-handedly bring it back from the doldrums.

More importantly, in 1962, Wills also had 130 runs, 208 hits, 32 Win Shares, 6.1 WAR, and won the MVP. It was a truly great year. He never had another season like it, but he had a few other good ones and ended with 8306 career PAs.

If Wills were a great defender, he'd deserve the Hall. But he was not a great defender. I don't want to slander him by saying he was as bad as Derek Jeter, but both systems agree he was not among the 50 best-fielding shortstops in history. He was about equal with Arky Vaughan on the field and about half of Vaughan on offense.

Wills did have some experience as a manager. But, if anything, it should count against his Hall-of-Fame credentials. Despite never managing a day in the minors, he insisted that he should be given a multi-year managerial contract. He even wrote a book that did little besides lay out his case. The lowly Mariners took him up on it in 1980, and, according to "Rob Neyer's Big Book of Baseball

Blunders," (Simon and Schuster, 2006) Wills "might have been the very worst manager ever." (p. 202-207)

Wills brought what he called his "maximum of self-confidence" to the job. That was his problem. He was so self-confident that he never bothered to prepare or even think ahead. One time he signaled for a reliever, but he hadn't told any to warm up. Another time he held up the game for ten minutes while he searched for a pinch hitter. He didn't even know his roster: Twice he talked to reporters about his plans to give more playing time to players who had recently been traded.

His comical level of managerial incompetence aside, Maury Wills does not clear the bar.

Chapter Six

~ ~ Third Base ~ ~

Third base is the Hall of Fame's biggest mess. Not only does it have the fewest inductees of any position, with 15 (not including Paul Molitor, whom the Hall of Fame lists at third but I'm putting at DH because he played the most games there). But the Hall also has several third basemen with weak qualifications. What's the dilly, yo?

The expectations for third basemen have changed more than with any other position besides pitcher. In the early days of the game, third base was a defense-first position, where any offense was a bonus. Third basemen hitting home runs were as common as second basemen hitting home runs (i.e., almost never) until after World War II. Only then did third base's hitting profile evolve into the sort of "first base lite" that it is today.

Third basemen also don't get the same kind of pass that second basemen do for having less-than-entirely-flashy hitting stats. There are quite a few that have never been seriously considered for the Hall despite being good candidates for the Billy Herman/Bobby Doerr types at the lower end. And there are a few guys who got in despite not deserving it, likely because electors were like "Holy cow, we need some more third basemen!"

So let's get to some correcting.

Frank Baker (1908-1914, 1916-1919, 1921-1922; career OPS+: 135)

	Career	Rank	Hitting	Rank	Fielding	Rank	Peak	Rank	Bests	JAWS	Rank
WAR	62.8	12	59.2	9	9.6	26	46.8	6	7	54.8	11
WS	300.3	12	234.9	10	65.2	25	222.3	4	5	NA	5

Frank "Home Run" Baker was a superstar from 1909-1914. If you're a big baseball fan you might know that he led the league in home runs every year from 1911-1914 despite never totaling more than 12. You might also know that he was actually called "Home Run" for his dramatic homers in World Series play. Perhaps you don't know why he left the MLB at his peak in 1915.

From 1910-1914, Baker's Philadelphia A's made the World Series four times, winning three of them. After their one Series loss in 1914, to Rabbit Maranville's Miracle Braves, owner Connie Mack tore the team down. Salaries were getting too high, he said, especially with the brand-new Federal League competing for players, and gate receipts were too low.

I would say that it was like the 1997 Marlins, who won the World Series and then dumped all their expensive stars. But it was more crazy than that; the 1910-1914 A's were a dynasty, not just a one-year wonder.

Imagine if the Yankees, after winning the World Series every year from 1998-2000 and then losing to the Diamondbacks in 2001, traded away Derek Jeter, Mike Mussina, etc. The A's version of Derek Jeter was 1914 AL MVP Eddie Collins, then only 27 years old. He was sold to the White Sox. Hall of Fame pitchers Eddie Plank and Charlie "Chief" Bender jumped to the Federal League teams St. Louis Terriers and Baltimore Terrapins, respectively.

Frank Baker was in the midst of a three-year contract and felt he deserved a raise for being super-awesome for four straight years. Mack did not agree. So Baker sat out of professional baseball for a year, playing for some small-town teams near his Maryland farm. He was 29 years old, in prime ball-playing shape. Instead of his Hall-of-Fame talent being used against the likes of Rube Foster and Ray Fisher, it was used against farmers and smiths and wainwrights (i.e. wagon makers) and coopers (barrel makers) and fletchers (bow and arrow makers) and turners (people who turn wood into spindles) and other old-timey professions that are also baseball player last names.

Having lost all their good players, the A's finished last in 1915 and continued to finish last every year for seven straight years. Again, imagine the Yankees doing this (for some of you, it may be a very pleasant fantasy indeed).

American League president Ban Johnson intervened to convince Connie Mack to sell Baker off to the Yankees in 1916. There Baker was good, if not as great, and petered out by his mid-30s. He ended up with only 6666 career PAs. It's not hard to imagine that if he had played in 1915, after a string of gangbuster seasons, he would have been great again and would have been in better shape during later years.

What Baker did was not like spending prime years serving in World War II, so you can't exactly give similar extra credit for Baker's lost year. But to a lesser extent there were unusual conditions of the time that prevented Frank Baker from having the career he deserved. His totals were affected by the injustice of the reserve clause, in which great players had no choice but to obey the whims of the owners who quite literally owned their livelihoods

Luckily for us, Frank Baker was so good in his peak that he doesn't need any extra consideration to be a Hall-of-Famer. He was probably the best third baseman before World War II.

Wade Boggs (1982-1999; career OPS+: 131)

	Career	Rank	Hitting	Rank	Fielding	Rank	Peak	Rank	Bests	JAWS	Rank
WAR	91.1	3	80.6	5	12.9	14	56.0	2	7	73.6	3
WS	393.9	4	319.3	4	74.0	12	222.7	3	4	NA	4

Wade Boggs was a superstar in the 1980s, perhaps the best player of his time. From his first full season in 1983 to his last 200-hit season in 1989, he tops all major-league players in both Win Shares and WAR. Granted, those kind of facts always suffer a selection bias: That time span makes up the heart of Boggs' career, while his contemporaries peaked earlier or later. It still says something about how great Boggs was in the mid-to-late-1980s.

There was a controversy in the 1986 AL MVP, which went to Roger Clemens. People said a pitcher shouldn't win it and that it should have gone to Don Mattingly. But it was a dumb argument, since Wade Boggs was the best player in both the AL and all of baseball that year, according to both WAR and Win Shares. If you prefer to pick your MVPs from winning teams, Boggs qualifies there too, as his Red Sox won the pennant and then clinched the World Series on an expertly fielded routine grounder in Game 6 by Bill Buckner (alternate reality version). Boggs finished seventh in the AL MVP voting, with no first-place votes.

Before and even after he became a star, Boggs's skills were underappreciated. I think it's largely because he didn't hit homers. You can accuse me of being obsessed with stats, and I sort of am. But, at least I'm obsessed with the right stats, the ones that get at core value. The average fan tends to obsess over conventional stats, like home runs, that only tell part of the story.

Home runs are usually important to being a superstar, granted. But Boggs proved that there is more than one way to skin the superstar cat. When you hit .350 and get on base at a .450 clip in the pre-Steroid Era, you contribute a lot more runs to the board than any slugger does.

More recently, Joe Mauer experienced the same bias. People always expected Mauer to someday "turn the corner" and start hitting home runs -- as if it wasn't enough already that he was an excellent defensive catcher hitting .320/.400/.450 year after year. Rod Carew didn't hit home runs. Neither did Ty Cobb, if you want to really go back a ways. Again, there is more than one way to skin the superstar cat.

Boggs was 25 in his first full season, which is awfully late for a player of his skills. He was kept in the minors for six years to work on his defense at third base, repeating both AA and AAA. Personally, if I had a bat like Boggs' in the minors, I'd say "Screw it, just bring him up and move him to first base." In 1982, the Red Sox trotted Dave Stapleton and his 87 OPS+ out to first, so it's hard to say that Boggs was blocked at the major league level. I'm betting Boggs' lack of home run power made him not "feel" like a proper first baseman.

Regardless, Boggs did develop into a good defensive third baseman. So maybe, in the end, he was more valuable sticking with the tougher position. Regardless of which alternate reality you go with, Wade Boggs is an inner-circle Hall-of-Famer.

George Brett (1973-1993; career OPS+: 135)

	Career	Rank	Hitting	Rank	Fielding	Rank	Peak	Rank	Bests	JAWS	Rank
WAR	88.4	4	84.1	4	1.2	71	53.2	5	2	70.8	4
WS	433.3	3	371.6	3	61.5	31	221.1	5	2	NA	2

I'm a Minnesotan, but I didn't grow up here. When people ask me where I'm from originally, I say "New York," because that's where I spent my adolescence. This answer usually intrigues people, so they say something along the lines of "Wow, New York?" Then I have to disappoint them by saying "Well, on Long Island, about two hours from the city." If they press further I admit that I made it into New York City maybe a dozen times in six years. Usually they give up at that point.

When I lived in boring ol' suburban Long Island, we wouldn't see limousines often. When we did see one, I always said that Billy Joel must be in it. It was partially a joke, but part of my 12-year-old brain couldn't really fathom anyone else living in boring ol' suburban Long Island who would possibly need to ride around in a limo.

Later, after I grew older and wiser, I was taking road trips with my friend Joe to ballparks around the country. When we were in Kansas City, we saw a limo drive by, and I told Joe "Hey, it must be George Brett." He had no idea what I was talking about, so he immediately beat me within an inch of my life. Joe's got a mean streak, man. (Only half of that is true. I leave it to you to figure out which half.)

This time, the weird limo thing was more out of respect. I love it when a place besides Los Angeles and New York City gets to have a nationwide celebrity. Nothing against those two places, but they kinda hog the glitterati. I love the fact that Prince and Garrison Keillor live in my home state of Minnesota. I love that rappers stay true to their hometowns: Nelly is all about St. Louis, and Outkast is Atlanta too strong. (Break![27]) Other cities besides New York and Los Angeles have their own unique cultural flavors, and it's nice when they get their own nationwide claims to fame.

In my mind at least, George Brett is Kansas City, through and through. He was the unquestioned superstar of the Royals when they were a dominant force, from the late 1970s until the World Series-winning year of 1985.

Their quest for a championship took on a perfect narrative progression. They were division champions from 1976-1978, each time knocked out of the playoffs by the overdog culture-hog New York Yankees. That's the first act of the story. Then in the second act, in 1980, the Royals finally beat the Yankees, only to fall to the Phillies in the World Series. OK, tough loss, but hey, this was the Phillies' first championship in their 97 years of existence. They too had won their division from 1976-1978, only to lose in the championship series each time. They too had a dominant third baseman in Mike Schmidt. It must have been hard not to empathize on some level.

Then in 1985, the Royals returned to the Series, this time battling the cross-state Cardinals. The Cardinals evoked no empathy, I'm betting. They were no underdog; they were a dominant team of the time and throughout much of baseball history. They didn't even have a Hall-of-Fame third baseman! The Royals beat them in seven games. Music swells. Slow-motion shots of players going crazy and jumping into a dogpile. Fade out to credits and cue blandly inspirational Adult Contemporary hit.

Those ten years of great drama produced some of the best baseball minds of our time: Bill James, Rob Neyer and Rany Jazayerli all were raised on the Royals' glory years. A small-market Midwest team having a run of dominance culminating in a championship. I don't know who couldn't love that.

This multi-year narrative had a clear main character: George Brett, the intense warrior, a lifelong Royal and one of the best players ever. He is the personification of Royals baseball, like Cal Ripken in Baltimore or Tony Gwynn in San Diego. Brett is obviously a Hall-of-Famer.

Jimmy Collins (1895-1908; career OPS+: 113)

	Career	Rank	Hitting	Rank	Fielding	Rank	Peak	Rank	Bests	JAWS	Rank
WAR	53.2	19	42.1	29	16.8	9	38.4	19	2	45.8	18
WS	271.7	21	164.2	31	81.7	5	187.4	13	5	NA	17

Jimmy Collins was the best defensive third baseman at a time when it was a defense-first position. He was more than just good in the field; he's credited with inventing third-base defense as we know it today. For example, before Collins, the shortstop always covered bunts to the left side. Collins learned how to position himself so that he could take them instead.

Collins was the player-manager of the first-ever World Series champions, the 1903 Boston Americans (now Red Sox). He basically built the team himself, encouraging Cy Young and others to ditch their National League teams and join him in the brand-new American League. Collins had been frustrated by National League owners who, in his view, conspired to hold down salaries. After being hired by the Americans in 1901, Collins was quoted as saying "I would not go back now [to his former team, the

[27] Reference explanation: Somewhere in the Outkast album "Stankonia," Andre 3000 says "Atlanta too strong. Break!"

National League Boston Beaneaters] if they offered me the whole outfit." (Source: Jimmy Collins' Wikipedia entry.)

Collins' Boston Americans won the pennant again 1904, but there was no World Series that year. The Giants were the National League champions, but both manager John McGraw and owner John T. Brush hated American League founder/president/dictator-for-life Ban Johnson so much that they refused to play any World Series. Nowadays the National League and American League are really just divisions of the same league, but in the early days they were bitter, bitter rivals. After all, the National League was accustomed to having a comfortable, profitable monopoly, complete with the ability to abuse and underpay their workers. Then in 1901 the American League came along and turned over the apple cart.

Collins was elected to the Hall of Fame in 1945, a year before Tinker, Evers and Chance were selected. If you remember, the idea of what constitutes a Hall-of-Famer was different then. Collins was selected in large part because he was integral to a great team. Luckily, the above numbers show that he also had a Hall-of-Fame-worthy playing career, if a short one. He qualifies in every way.

Ray Dandridge (1933-1953)

	Rank at Position Among Negro Leaguers	Rank Among All Negro Leaguers
Bill James	1	not ranked
SABR	1	11
Monte Irvin	1	NA

Like Jimmy Collins, Ray Dandridge was famous for his fielding. He could have played shortstop, but his first team, the Newark Eagles, already had Willie "Devil" Wells at short. Dandridge's hitting was probably better than Jimmie Collins', approaching a Rod Carew level of high batting averages with little power. He was a small (5'7"), bowlegged man who didn't have quite the heft to hit home runs, but could slap singles with the best of them.

The Newark Eagles of the 1930s were an amazing team, featuring not only Dandridge and Wells but also Hall-of-Famers Mule Suttles, he of the Killebrew-ian power stroke, Monte Irvin, he of the rankings and great hitting, and pitcher Leon Day, he whom we haven't met yet. Their owner, Effa Manley, is the only woman in the Hall. But in 1939, Dandridge decided to stop being woefully underpaid by Manley and moved to the Mexican League.

Dandridge was perfectly capable of playing in the major leagues after integration. From 1949-1952, when Dandridge was ages 35 to 38, he played extremely well for the Minneapolis Millers, who were then at the highest level of minor league play. But Jackie Robinson's success didn't bring a flood of African-American stars; it brought a trickle. Owners were frightened to bring in too many African-American players too quickly. An older player like Dandridge was easy to pass over in favor of younger players like Monte Irvin and Willie Mays.

Dandridge's minor-league time should therefore count in his favor, but he hardly needs it. He's unanimously considered the best third baseman in Negro League history and is obviously a Hall-of-Famer.

Judy Johnson (1918-1936; career OPS+: 111)

	Rank at Position Among Negro Leaguers	Rank Among All Negro Leaguers
Bill James	2	not ranked
SABR	2	15
Monte Irvin	2	NA

Once again, Negro League superstars at a particular position carefully arrange themselves by era. As Ray Dandridge began to dominate third base, Judy Johnson was winding down his career. If I were the suspicious type, I'd conclude that the CIA conspired with Fidel Castro to control the Negro Leagues, all just to ... ummm ... make electing Hall-of-Famers easier, I guess? Why not? Can't there be a massive international conspiracy to do something nice for a change? Just once, couldn't the FBI and MI-6 covertly plan a huge surprise birthday party?

At any rate, Judy Johnson was the undisputed king of Negro League third basemen in the 1920s and early 1930s. His SABR biography describes him as a Charlie Gehringer type in both character and ability: Quiet, smart, and efficient, Johnson slapped hits all over the field but rarely hit home runs. Third basemen in the Negro Leagues tended to be defensive whizzes without much meat on their bones, and Johnson certainly was that: Despite being 5'11" he never weighed more than 150 pounds.

Johnson's incredible baseball knowledge and calmly authoritative nature made him a great candidate to manage, which he did successfully starting at age 29. He also had a terrific eye for talent. In one game, his regular catcher hurt his hand. Johnson put in his place a spectator whom he'd seen playing sandlot baseball. That was the beginning of the career of Josh Gibson and of Johnson being his lifelong mentor. After each game, Gibson would seek out Johnson's take on his performance, and Johnson would calmly, respectfully tell him how he could improve.

Johnson went on to become a successful scout and then the MLB's first African-American spring training coach, with the Phillies in 1954. In 1975, he was an easy choice to be on the committee to pick Hall-of-Famers from the Negro Leagues. When he became one of the candidates for the Hall himself, he politely withdrew from the committee, so as to not sway their decisions. He was elected by the same committee. At his Hall of Fame acceptance speech, his typical dignified composure broke down; overcome with emotion, he was unable to continue. Johnson is definitely a Hall-of-Famer.

George Kell (1943-1957; career OPS+: 112)

	Career	Rank	Hitting	Rank	Fielding	Rank	Peak	Rank	Bests	JAWS	Rank
WAR	**37.6**	**38**	**35.4**	**42**	**1.6**	**68**	**27.8**	**53**	**0**	**32.7**	**44**
WS	**230.3**	**34**	**133.1**	**63**	**42.1**	**68**	**152.8**	**41**	**1**	**NA**	**30**

I'm betting George Kell made it to the Hall of Fame based on two things: The Veterans Committee realized they didn't have enough third basemen, and Kell had good batting averages. Kell could also draw walks fairy well and hit some doubles. He was not a great fielder, but not bad. He did all this for a while. The total is a pretty inoffensive package, the kind of guy who few people get upset about being in the Hall.

But I'm not "few people." I'm just one person, and I'm mad as HELL that George Kell is in the Hall of Fame!!! Not really, but I don't think he belongs. He reminds me of Bill Madlock or Carney Lansford, both of whom also had high batting averages, some doubles, and acceptable fielding. George Kell's .306 career batting average and one batting title are usually cited as his main Hall of Fame qualifications, but Madlock hit .305 in his career and had four batting titles, while Lansford hit .290 with one batting title.

As it happens, both are near Kell in JAWS. Bill James puts Lansford 39th and Madlock 48th. But in WSAWS, my makeshift Win Shares version of JAWS, Kell ranks 33rd, immediately behind Madlock (31st) and Lansford (32nd).

I already know my answer, but I feel compelled to look at Kell season by season. His one season leading all third basemen in Win Shares was 1949, when he won the batting title. It was a good season, with 24 Win Shares, but not astounding. He had four other 20-Win Shares seasons, with none in the 30s. That total of five 20s and no 30s ties him with Travis Jackson and George Kelly, so you see the range he's in.

Kell does very well in MVP voting: too well, in my opinion. There was a time when batting averages reigned supreme as the ultimate measure of hitting ability. George Kell benefited from that in both MVP and Hall of Fame voting. Those days are done, and **Kell is out.**

Freddie Lindstrom (1924-1936; career OPS+: 110)

	Career	Rank	Hitting	Rank	Fielding	Rank	Peak	Rank	Bests	JAWS	Rank
WAR	28.3	68	26.6	73	2.6	56	26.3	57	2	27.3	66
WS	189.6	56	143.1	52	46.9	59	151.4	43	1	NA	43

I remember having a conversation with some friends who were big baseball fans but didn't know a ton about baseball history. I was talking about the Hall-of-Famers who didn't deserve to be in, and they asked for an example. I said Fred Lindstrom. They looked up his numbers and said "I don't know, he looks pretty good." I didn't have the courage to go into a whole tirade about the relative nature of baseball statistics, etc.

So, instead I wrote this book. It might have been easier just to do the tirade, in retrospect. Lindstrom had two years of being the best third baseman in baseball, 1928 and 1930. And these were indeed good seasons. In each year he had exactly 231 hits, a batting average above .350, and good power. If you had to pick two years to excel, those would be good choices. In 1930, the major league OPS was .790, second all-time behind 1894, and 1928's overall OPS was 30th all-time. Those conditions will inflate everyone's stats. Players in their primes, like Lindstrom, will look like all-time greats.

Regardless, if Lindstrom had kept it up, he would likely be a worthy Hall-of-Famer. In 1930 Lindstrom was only 24 years old. He had compiled 20.8 WAR, which is 40th all-time among hitters in their age-18 to age-24 seasons.

But he didn't keep it up, due to injuries. Lindstrom had one more good season, a bunch of subpar ones, and was gone by age 30. His career total of 6108 PAs is low for a Hall-of-Famer. If he hit like Roy Campanella, maybe he'd get a pass, but he was not that good. There are lots of guys who have half of a Hall of Fame career, but not many who had the luck to play with Frankie Frisch and Bill Terry and thus get thrown into the Hall of Fame by the crazy Frisch-Terry 1970s Veterans Committee. **Lindstrom is out.**

Eddie Mathews (1952-1968; career OPS+: 143)

	Career	Rank	Hitting	Rank	Fielding	Rank	Peak	Rank	Bests	JAWS	Rank
WAR	96.4	2	93.8	1	5.5	41	54.2	3	7	75.3	2
WS	446.3	2	375.3	2	57.4	36	244.9	2	8	NA	3

What a shock Eddie Mathews must have been in 1953. That year he was 21 years old and hit 47 home runs, destroying the record for home runs in a season by a third baseman. The previous record was 37, set by Al Rosen only three years before.

Next up for Mathews was the record for career home runs by a third baseman, 178, owned by Harlond Clift. Mathews surpassed that number by age 24. It's all so very 1950s America, isn't it: A sudden, big, confident, youthful burst of achievement, an exponential growth that no one could have foreseen, blowing the dark and dismal past from memory.

Mathews wasn't the only third baseman who was shocking the (baseball-loving) world. Al Rosen hit those 37 homers as a 26-year-old rookie for Cleveland in 1950. He was clearly ready for the majors years before, but was blocked at third by the very good Ken Keltner. Rosen's 1953 was even better. In fact it was the best season ever by a third baseman, to the tune of 41 Win Shares and 10.1 WAR. But after 1954, Rosen tailed off and retired early because of chronic injuries. With only 4374 career PAs, he's not a realistic Hall of Fame candidate.

Neither Rosen or Mathews were just about home runs. Both drew walks and hit for good averages. Not since Frank Baker 40 years earlier had anyone seen such dominant offensive seasons from a third baseman. Really, Baker was an anomaly; Mathews and Rosen were the beginning of a new breed, third basemen who hit like first basemen.

WAR paints an even more extreme picture: It says Mathews and Rosen were the first third basemen who could reasonably deserve MVP awards since Baker. Baseball-reference defines an MVP-type season as 8 WAR. Most years have two to five 8-WAR performances; some have none.

There have been 33 such seasons from third basemen in major-league history. Between Baker's 9.2 WAR in 1912 and the 1953 season that saw Mathews' 8.3 and Rosen's 10.1, there was only one 8.0 WAR season from a third baseman. It was a weird one, too: Mel Ott, normally an outfielder, played 113 games at third base in 1938. It was his only season primarily at third, so I don't know if it even really counts. The only other pre-WWII member of the 3B 8.0 club was John McGraw in 1899. So that's just three MVP 3B seasons in the in the 71 years from 1876-1946. And then from 1947-2014, a 68-season stretch, there were 33 8.0-WAR 3B seasons, exactly ten times as many.

Meanwhile, a 30-Win Share season is defined as MVP-worthy. But they're about three times as common as an 8-WAR season, so that's not a good comparison. If you raise the bar to 35 Win Shares, you get nearly three hundred seasons for all position players in history, about the same as the number of 8-WAR seasons.

Third basemen have had 32 seasons of 35 or more Win Shares since 1876: 7 of them before or during World War II and 25 after. And there may be more since 2008 that I don't have Win Share numbers for. Those pre-WWII seven consisted of Frank Baker four times, Heinie Groh in 1917, Art Devlin in 1908, and Ott's odd 1938 season again.

No other position sees this kind of slant. As I mentioned in the beginning of this chapter, third base used to be more of a defense-first position. In the deadball era, batters bunted all the time, so if you didn't have a third baseman who could come in and get those bunts, you'd give up lots of hits.

Even with all those bunts, third basemen got fewer chances than shortstops or second basemen, just as they do today. That limits the good they can do with their gloves, which limits the number of points their defense can add to the Win Shares or WAR column. It's like how Bill Mazeroski's value at second base was lower than Luis Aparicio's at shortstop, despite the fact that Mazeroski was the all-time best at second and Aparicio was maybe 12th-best at short. The ceiling for achievement is lower at a position that doesn't get as much action.

Eddie Mathews wasn't a great defensive player. Maybe if he came up in the 1920s he would have been moved to first. But man, could he hit. He starred for the duration of the Braves' tenure in Milwaukee, from 1953-1965, with only one season with the Boston Braves in 1952 and one season with the Atlanta Braves in 1966.

In 1953, the Braves became the first major-league team to move to a new city in 50 years. It was a massive success. Before the move, in 1952, the Boston Braves drew only 281,278 fans all year, an average of 3,653 per game. In their first season in Milwaukee, the Braves drew more than eight times as many fans, 1,826,397, which is 23,119 per game. It was the first of six straight years in which the lil' ol' flyover-country city of Milwaukee had the best attendance in the league.

Relocation mania then spread through the majors. The St. Louis Browns moved to Baltimore in 1954. The Philadelphia A's moved to Kansas City in 1955. Then I think there were some New York-based teams who moved somewhere in California or whatever.

With any franchise move, the fun only lasts if the team is good. The Milwaukee Braves were very good. Armed with Mathews and fellow inner-circle Hall-of-Famers Hank Aaron and Warren Spahn, they were a consistent contender, and won the World Series in 1957. It was the only World Series won by a non-New York team in a ten-year stretch, from 1949-1958. The Braves always seemed like they should have won more titles, much like the 1990s Braves. But hey, at least they got one.

Eddie Mathews was at the center of what must have been an uproariously fun time to be a baseball fan in Beer City and is unquestionably a Hall-of-Famer.

Brooks Robinson (1955-1977; career OPS+: 104)

	Career	Rank	Hitting	Rank	Fielding	Rank	Peak	Rank	Bests	JAWS	Rank
WAR	78.3	6	47.4	22	38.8	1	45.7	10	2	62.0	8
WS	354.4	6	248.2	9	106.4	1	180.9	16	1	NA	7

I like being a contrarian. But I also like it when conventional wisdom lines up with the numbers. Brooks Robinson is widely known as the best-fielding third baseman of all time, and both WAR and Win Shares agree heartily with that assessment. In fact, WAR says he was the third-best greatest defensive player of all time at any position, behind Ozzie Smith and Mark Belanger. Win Shares has Robinson's defensive contributions well below a bunch of shortstops, catchers, etc., but still puts him more than 10 Defensive Win Shares higher than any other 3B.

Like Ivan Rodriguez, Robinson paired his all-time great fielding with some good hitting over a very long career. Both were good enough defensively to make them valuable in years when their hitting was not great.

Plus, Brooks Robinson famously dominated in the Orioles' 1970 World Series win over the Reds, making spectacular plays and hitting .429/.429/.810. He would have been a Hall-of-Famer either way, but that certainly adds to the pile.

Ron Santo (1960-1974; career OPS+: 125)

	Career	Rank	Hitting	Rank	Fielding	Rank	Peak	Rank	Bests	JAWS	Rank
WAR	70.4	8	66.2	7	8.6	29	53.8	4	4	62.1	7
WS	324.2	8	255.6	7	68.7	18	214.6	6	2	NA	6

Isn't it amazing how long Ron Santo stayed out of the Hall of Fame? He was finally elected soon after his death in 2010, following decades of near-misses. As you can see from the above, his overall credentials just beat out Brooks Robinson's (if you ignore that post-season glory factor). What went wrong?

For one thing, there was the 1960s. Santo's numbers are terrific for the 1960s, but people have never been great at making adjustments for the standards of different eras, as I've discussed ad nauseam. Also, Santo got a lot of his value from walks, which is always an underrated skill. Santo had a pretty long career, 15 years and 9397 PAs, but it wasn't long enough to log the nice, pretty round numbers that make people feel nice, like 500 home runs or 3000 hits.

Moreover, I think people started assuming all third basemen should be hitting like first basemen. They got used to the Eddie Mathews standard pretty quickly. If Santo were a shortstop or catcher, his numbers would have put him in on the first ballot. But third base is in that weird middle area of being not entirely defense-first and not entirely offense-first.

Regardless, justice was eventually served, soon after Santo died. He hoped his entire life to see himself enshrined, but never got to see it. Let's try not to make this kind of mistake again.

Mike Schmidt (1972-1989; career OPS+: 147)

	Career	Rank	Hitting	Rank	Fielding	Rank	Peak	Rank	Bests	JAWS	Rank
WAR	106.5	1	90.9	2	17.6	7	58.6	1	6	82.6	1
WS	466.4	1	378.3	1	88.0	4	249.3	1	7	NA	1

The 1980s were the glory years of third basemen, much the way the 1990s were for shortstops (Jeter, A-Rod, Larkin, Nomar Garciaparra, Miguel Tejada) and the 1930s were for first basemen (Gehrig, Foxx, Mize, Greenberg, George Kelly -- just kidding on that last one). Lording over even the titans Wade Boggs and George Brett was the all-time greatest third baseman, Mike Schmidt.

Mike Schmidt. The very name shivers pitchers' souls. Two sharp syllables that slice through fastballs and make curveballs turn around mid-pitch and return, quaking, to the fools who had the audacity to hurl them. You dare challenge Mike Schmidt's glove with a sharp grounder?!? Mere hareling, Mike

Schmidt shall snatch that ball from its hustings and spit it to first, bellowing all the while with the golden throat of Zeus himself!

Mike Schmidt shall not be bested! Mike Schmidt shall rank first in both career numbers and peak numbers for both WAR and Win Shares! Eddie Mathews doth manage to beat Mike Schmidt for career Hitting WAR, but no matter! Mike Schmidt was a much better defender!

Mike Schmidt maketh even the Phillies good! Ere the coming of Mike Schmidt, the Phillies had two World Series appearances in 93 years, both losses! Under the glorious reign of Mike Schmidt (and Steve Carlton, and some other guys), said Phillies made the playoffs six times, reaching the World Series twice and winning it in 1980!

Mike Schmidt now rests. His glory shineth on, in this hallowed sepulchre, this Hall of Fame. Return, pilgrims, and revel in Mike Schmidt.

Pie Traynor (1920-1935, 1937; career OPS+: 107)

	Career	Rank	Hitting	Rank	Fielding	Rank	Peak	Rank	Bests	JAWS	Rank
WAR	36.2	43	39.9	33	2.0	64	25.6	62	1	30.9	55
WS	272.0	20	192.5	23	79.5	10	166.6	28	4	NA	15

Whoa. Something's wrong here. WAR really, really, doesn't like Pie Traynor. Win Shares isn't thrilled either, giving him a barely qualified career number and a rather unqualified peak. Bill James generously puts him at 15th overall, though his WSAWS (averaging career and peak Win Shares numbers) is 22nd. And my version of Win Shares Peak is actually nicer to Traynor than Bill James' version: defining Peak as the best five seasons, as James does, puts Traynor 36th instead of 28th.

The two systems aren't that far apart on hitting; once again, they disagree sharply on fielding. At this point, I'm putting a lot more stock in Win Shares' version of fielding, for reasons I discussed in the introduction.

The real surprise here arises from the fact that a lot of people think Pie Traynor is in the upper reaches of the Hall of Fame. In 1975, The Sporting News chose an All-Time Team and Topps made a card for each player. It had Lou Gehrig at first, Babe Ruth, Ty Cobb, and Ted Williams in the outfield -- basically all the guys you'd expect. And Pie Traynor was their best-ever third baseman. This was after Eddie Mathews retired.

I've seen plenty of other lists choosing Traynor as the best third baseman before World War II. It was a weak position before then, granted, but it's hard to imagine the 54th-best third baseman according to JAWS being the best third baseman throughout the first half of baseball history.

Actually, few of his contemporaries thought he was the best third baseman of all time. In 1937, Connie Mack picked Jimmy Collins for his all-time team. Others picked Frank Baker. The people choosing Traynor were mostly people in the 1970s and 1980s who were relying heavily on the conventional career numbers. And Pie Traynor has a big ol' sexy .320 career BA (through the heart of the live-ball era). Add to that his seven years of 100 RBIs and he sort of wins by default. Lazy writers who don't bother to read up on Jimmy Collins' defense or consider the hitting environment of Frank Baker's career just picked the guy who had numbers they understood.

As you may have guessed from that 107 career OPS+, Traynor hit an empty .320, low on walks or extra-base hits. Traynor was more of a George Kell; in fact, Kell's career OPS+ beats Traynor's, 112 to

107. Traynor had about 700 more PAs, though, so Traynor beats Kell in the WAR and Win Shares hitting numbers.

What about the postseason? Traynor was terrific in the 1925 World Series, when his Pirates beat the Senators. If a World Series MVP existed then, it would have been a tough choice between him and fellow Hall-of-Famer Max Carey. He was not nearly as good in the 1927 World Series, against the juggernaut Yankees. Regardless, his 1925 performance adds to his credentials.

He also had some moderate success as a manager. In five and a half seasons, he logged a .530 winning percentage, but no pennants. I'm not sure that can really add much to his case.

So Pie Traynor was a good, but not great, hitter for a long time, whose conventional numbers look great because of when he played. WAR says he wasn't good defensively, while Win Shares says he was. When push comes to shove, as it has here against these two systems, I'm siding with Win Shares. Add a dash of "It's the Hall of Fame, not the Hall of Stats" to the well-known Traynor, and I'll begrudgingly let him stay.

Deacon White (1871-1890; career OPS+: 127)

	Career	Rank	Hitting	Rank	Fielding	Rank	Peak	Rank	Bests	JAWS	Rank
WAR	45.5	29	48.7	20	1.6	67	26.1	58	7	35.8	33
WS	190.1	55	148.8	41	40.5	75	114.4	97	2	NA	76

Deacon White, huh? Wow, OK ... and you're sure there's no one else you could have chosen for the Hall in 2013? Bobby Grich, maybe? Alan Trammell? What about Bill Dahlen, since you are the Pre-Integration Era Committee (i.e., that was the branch of the Hall that chose White)?

That concludes my dramatic reading of my real-time reaction to hearing that Deacon White was selected for the Hall of Fame. Yes, he clearly had a mustache that current hipsters would kill for (see below). Apart from that, his numbers look bad, both in WAR and Win Shares.

But those numbers aren't fair to White. First of all, Win Shares numbers only go back to 1876, the first year of the National League. White's career began in 1871 with the first professional league, the National Association. So you can just ignore the Win Shares. I hesitate to even include them in the above.

And White was a dominant player throughout the 1870s, leading the league in batting average twice, RBIs three times, slugging percentage once, hits once, and triples once. Most of his time was spent at catcher, when catchers often didn't even have mitts, much less face masks and pads. And I believe the balls were covered in spikes dipped in acid. If you lost a finger while catching one and dared cry out in pain, the game was immediately forfeited on account of insufficient manliness.

It is of course a historical rarity for a catcher to hit that well. Because catchers never tended to catch more than half their teams' games in those days, White played the outfield often to keep his bat in the lineup. Eventually his defense at catcher regressed to the point where he moved to third. He finished out his 30s and early 40s in the 1880s as a good, but seldom great, third baseman.

Fun fact about Deacon White: He and several other players of the time were called "Deacon" because they were church-going folk who didn't smoke or drink. But White was more than your typical humble, religious fellow. He also believed wholeheartedly that the earth was flat, and often tried to convince teammates of this view. His reasoning came from the Bible, using many of the same arguments that are propounded by the modern-day Flat Earth Society.

Back to the point. In the Cap Anson comment, I noted how much time Anson spent in the 1870s, when seasons were much shorter. I made a wild guess as to how many hits Anson would have had in a career of full seasons, giving him around 5,000. With Deacon White, a much more marginal case, it's important to actually do the math. Here I go!

(Doing the math. While I'm doing the math, here's a picture of Deacon White: (see http://www.baseball-reference.com/players/w/whitede01.shtml). Hipsters, just give up. You'll never be Deacon White, so stop trying.)

OK, I'm back from doing the math. Man, did that math get done. And that done math done told me that if you project each of White's seasons out to 154 games, his career hits go from 2,067 to 3,958 and his career PAs go from 6,973 to 12,904.

Granted, that's a bit of a fudge. White played in 89% of his teams' games throughout his career, which he might not have done in full 154- or 162-game seasons. In the 1870s, White played in 99.6% of the league games, mostly as a catcher, no less. In those days, you would play a league game once or twice a week and spend the rest of your time on exhibition games. We don't have record of the exhibition games, but it's safe to assume that White took some of those off.

Still, I don't think it's an exaggeration to say that in leagues that played full, modern-length seasons, White could have approached or maybe exceeded 3,000 hits. His Career WAR and Win Shares numbers would have been much better than they are now. And his Peak ones would have been too -- his best years were in those 1870s leagues with 60-80 game seasons. You simply can't approach 8.0 WAR or 30 Win Shares in seasons that short.

Maybe it makes more sense to compare him to his contemporaries. If you isolate just 1871-1889, Deacon White scores 43.6 WAR, seventh among all hitters in baseball. Four of the six ahead of him are Hall-of-Famers: Cap Anson, Roger Connor, Dan Brouthers, and Jim O'Rourke. And the other two are not bad candidates: Jack Glasscock and Paul Hines. Hall-of-Famer King Kelly is just below White. If you isolate just the 1870s, White scores third behind Hall-of-Famer George Wright and freak-ball hitter Ross Barnes.[28]

And remember how Roger Bresnahan gets credit for improving upon the designs of catcher shin guards and padded face masks? Deacon White did the same for the face mask and chest protector. Catchers were getting injured left and right, and White wanted to stay on the field. When he wore the equipment, he was ridiculed mercilessly by fans, called a sissy and worse. But he rarely missed a game, and, most remarkably for his time, played into his 40s.

Well, I'm convinced. Deacon White was one of the first great stars of baseball, and deserves to be in the Hall of Fame.

---

[28] In Ross Barnes' time, the ball was considered fair if it landed in fair territory and bounced out, even if it did so right in front of home plate. There was no rule about having to stay in fair territory past first or third base. Ross Barnes was a master at the so-called "fair-foul" hit, spinning the ball so that it bounced in and then immediately got lost in foul territory. He hit .400 several times under these rules and led the league in everything imaginable. When the rules were changed to the current system, Barnes' performance declined dramatically.

Jud Wilson (1922-1945)

	Rank at Position Among Negro Leaguers	Rank Among All Negro Leaguers
Bill James	4	not ranked
SABR	3	26
Monte Irvin	4	NA

Jud Wilson might not be the most qualified player for the Hall of Fame. Bill James and Monte Irvin both rank non-HOFer Oliver Marcelle above Wilson among Negro League third basemen. James says Wilson was short and powerful, like Kirby Puckett, but not a deft fielder, playing everything off his chest. Irvin agrees, saying that as a third baseman, he was "just mediocre."

"But boy, what a hitter!" says Irvin. The stats seem to agree. Seamheads.com doesn't have most of his career, but baseball-reference.com has him down for .339/.388/.479 in 2994 PAs. Irvin's book has different numbers, saying he hit .345 in his career; c'est la Negro League stats. Irvin also claims that Josh Gibson cited Wilson as the best hitter in the league, and that Satchel Paige put him in the top two (presumably Gibson was the other). He was the opposite of Ray Dandridge and Judy Johnson-- an Eddie Mathews-style power hitter to their Charlie Gehringer types.

Both James and Irvin make mention of Wilson's brutal temper. He frequently assaulted umpires. When runners slapped the ball out of his glove, Wilson would chase after them instead of the ball. Off the field, it was much the same thing. One time, he got in a fight with a good friend and dangled him out of a window several stories off the ground.

This kind of thing wasn't uncommon in baseball before World War II. The most violent environment was probably the National League of the 1890s. Then, on-field violence got to the point where baseball games were dangerous events not suitable for families.

After the turn of the century, American League founder/autocrat Ban Johnson spearheaded a campaign against what was then called "rowdyism." His new league had severe punishments for fights and other transgressions. Rowdyism extended into the dead-ball era, especially on John McGraw's National League clubs. But it was on the wane in the MLB. In the Negro Leagues, less so.

If I may digress a bit … one fun thing about reading baseball history is that you get a sense of how regular people lived. Most history books tell you lots about rich and powerful people. But it's often hard to identify with them. Baseball players might eventually become rich and famous, but they almost always start as regular, working-class schmoes like you and me.

And the picture you get about working-class America before World War II is that it was very violent, much more violent than today. The weapon of choice was seldom guns, which perhaps kept fatalities down. But almost everyone got into fistfights to resolve disputes. In one famous incident, Hall of Fame umpire Billy Evans had a bloody fistfight with Ty Cobb beneath the stands of Tiger Stadium. It was not some spontaneous scuffle; it was a scheduled by Evans and Cobb, and other players came to watch and cheer. (Most of Cobb's teammates rooted for Evans, who won.) Everyone resolved not to report this particular bit of rowdyism to Ban Johnson, but of course word got out. After hearing about it, Johnson, that paragon of non-violent baseball, just chuckled and said he was "only sorry he missed it." (Source: "Deadball Stars of the American League," edited by David Jones, p. 398, Potomac Books, 2006)

Violence was not only the solution of choice for interpersonal problems. In those days, perhaps even more than now, private pain very commonly resulted in suicides. Ernie Lombardi attempted suicide, and Willard Hershberger and Chick Stahl successfully killed themselves while still active players. In the 1900s section of "The New Historical Baseball Abstract," Bill James lists 27 people associated with baseball who committed or attempted suicide from 1900 to 1925.

We tend to think of ourselves as living in a violent age, and the news is, of course, filled with war and shocking crimes. But the more you read about the average person's day-to-day existence a hundred years ago, the more you realize that life was much more violent then than it is now.

Even when I was a kid in the 1980s, popular culture was infused with casual violence. In our puritanical household, one of the few TV shows we were allowed to watch was "Little House on the Prairie," probably because it was based (very loosely) on wholesome books. The show had plenty of praying and sweet moments, no doubt. But an episode never passed without beloved, magnanimous patriarch Pa Ingalls punching somebody in the face.

Here's perhaps a better example. I recently watched the 1945 Christmas film "The Bells of St. Mary's." It stars Bing Crosby and Ingrid Bergman as a priest and a nun trying to keep a beloved old church from being bulldozed. In one subplot, a boy was being beaten up regularly by another boy at the parish school. Did Ingrid and Bing try stop the kids from pounding on each other? No, of course not. Instead the audience got an allegedly adorable sequence in which Ingrid boned up on boxing techniques so she could teach an eight-year-old kid the finer points of physically abusing other eight-year-old kids. The point is that when you're met with violence, kids, counteract it with greater violence. It's cute!

There is no shortage of violence in entertainment nowadays, granted. But it's more segregated in action movies and video games; you don't see many fistfights in family entertainment anymore. It's just not seen as something normal people do. I think this is one of those gradual improvements in human existence that people seldom notice, because they're gradual, and because they're improvements. Sudden collapses make the news; incremental progress does not. Fear sells more papers than hope. Such is human nature, unfortunately.

I get this feeling through more than anecdotal evidence, though. If you're interested in a more thoroughly researched argument, read "The Better Angels of Our Nature," by renowned social scientist Steven Pinker. It makes a convincing case that the 21st century is the least violent one in history.

Anyway, back to Jud Wilson. By mentioning his temper, I don't mean to portray him as some sort of homicidal lunatic. He was usually a kind, reasonable person. But when he got angry, he got violent. Not to excuse his behavior, but that was a more typical response at the time. Nowadays, we channel inchoate rage into furious comments underneath YouTube videos of Justin Bieber. Then, it went into fistfights. Sometimes it might not feel like an improvement, but it is.

So after all that, I don't see Wilson's temper really mattering much in his Hall of Fame credentials. More importantly, he was a very good hitter and mediocre fielder who is on the low end of Negro Leaguers. Ranking 26th on the SABR Negro League list means that everyone ahead of him is in the Hall but most below him aren't. That's good enough to stay.

Who's In, Who's Out

George Kell and Fred Lindstrom are thoroughly banished from the Hall of Fame, and Pie Traynor probably should have gone too, but I went soft on him. Now there are only 13 Hall of Fame third basemen! Whatever shall we do?

Never fear! I have lots of new inductees:

Chipper Jones (1993, 1995-2012, career OPS+: 141)

	Career	Rank	Hitting	Rank	Fielding	Rank	Peak	Rank	Bests	JAWS	Rank
WAR	85.0	5	87.4	3	-1.6	80	46.6	7	3	65.8	5
WS	353.3	7	316.3	5	37.0	81	200.2	8	2	NA	5

This one perhaps goes without saying. So I won't say it. Rats! I already did. Sigh ... I guess I gotta talk about how great Chipper Jones is.

He was an absolutely dominant hitter. His career OPS+ is better than all Hall of Fame third basemen except Mike Schmidt and Eddie Mathews. Jones was never a good fielder, but he was usually capable enough to pass.

He had a career packed with great seasons. In 1999, Jones won the MVP and deserved it, scoring 32 Win Shares and 6.9 WAR as his Braves made it to the World Series. WAR likes even better his 2007 and 2008 seasons, giving him scores of 7.6 and 7.3 respectively. In 2007 he led the league in OPS and OPS+, and 2008 he won a BA title (.364) and OBP title (.470). Win Shares prefers his 2001, when he was a left fielder, awarding him 31 Win Shares for 160+ OPS in 677 PAs.

Anyway, the verdict is clear. Chipper Jones was one of the best third basemen in history, and it would be a weird Hall of Fame without him.

Scott Rolen (1996-2012, career OPS+: 122)

	Career	Rank	Hitting	Rank	Fielding	Rank	Peak	Rank	Bests	JAWS	Rank
WAR	70.0	9	52.1	16	20.6	6	43.5	13	2	56.8	9
WS	264.3	20	207.2	17	56.9	38	201.3	7	4	NA	13*

The new Ron Santo, I think, is Scott Rolen. Rolen also has a terrific hitting record for a third baseman, but not one that would knock your socks off if he were a first baseman. Both Rolen and Santo had pretty long careers, but not long enough to achieve many fun big round numbers. Both were defensive whizzes, which is often underrated (unless it makes up your whole game, as with Bill Mazeroski and Ray Schalk).

Santo never made it to the playoffs, because he played for the Cubs, and that's just not the Cubs Way. Rolen, meanwhile, was in the thick of some tremendous Cardinals teams, which, from 2002-2007, won four division titles, two pennants and one World Series championship. In 2004, when the Cardinals lost the Series to the destiny-drenched Red Sox, Rolen, Jim Edmonds and Albert Pujols made for one of the best trios in baseball history:

Player	WAR	Win Shares
Scott Rolen	9.1	38
Albert Pujols	8.4	40
Jim Edmonds	7.1	36

Those are all MVP-worthy years, but the award went to Barry Bonds, who admittedly did pretty well, logging 10.6 WAR and 53 Win Shares by hitting .362/.609/.812 in 617 PAs. Still, have any three hitters on the same team all had MVP-level performances like this? I don't know, but now I'm determined to find out! Hold on while I find out.

OK, it turns out that there have been better trios in history. I bet you can guess which team had the best. If you guessed "1962 Mets," well, c'mon, this isn't a time for lame jokes. This is serious stuff. I can't think of a more pressing issue facing our country.

If you guessed "1927 Yankees," you would be right. Both systems agree on this one. WAR gives Babe Ruth 12.4 WAR that year, Lou Gehrig 11.8, and Earle Combs 6.9. Win Shares awards 45 to Ruth, 44 to Gehrig, and 32 to Combs. But the 2004 Cardinals aren't far off: Win Shares puts them as the fourth-best trio of hitters of all time, after the 1908 Pirates (highlighted by Honus Wagner's 59 Win Shares, but also featuring greats Fred Clarke and Tommy Leach) and the 1928 Yankees (same guys as in 1927).

WAR slots the REP boys (that's Rolen, Edmonds, Pujols -- think it will catch on?) seventh, after those same 1927 Yanks, the 1906 Cleveland Naps (Nap Lajoie, Terry Turner, and Elmer Flick), the 1961 Tigers (Norm Cash, Al Kaline, and Rocky Colavito), the 1996 Mariners (Ken Griffey Jr., Alex Rodriguez, and Edgar Martinez), the 1930 Yankees (same trio as before -- yawn), and the 1931 Yankees (same again except uber-racist Ben Chapman[29] takes the place of Earle Combs). So my point is, the Yankees are great. No wait, that wasn't my point. My point is that Rolen, Edmonds and Pujols made up a core in 2004 of a quality you rarely see.

Ditto for Scott Rolen himself. You rarely see a player of his caliber, one who could contribute so much in both defense and offense. Speaking as someone who watched Rolen play a lot and marveled almost every game at one of his great plays, I certainly hope he doesn't have to wait as long as Santo did to make the Hall.

Ken Boyer (1955-1969, career OPS+: 116)

	Career	Rank	Hitting	Rank	Fielding	Rank	Peak	Rank	Bests	JAWS	Rank
WAR	62.8	13	55.6	12	10.6	21	46.4	9	2	54.6	12
WS	280.8	16	197.0	22	66.9	21	181.5	15	1	NA	12

[29] If you saw "42," you may remember Ben Chapman as the Phillies manager who brutally taunted Jackie Robinson from the bench. When he was playing for the Yankees, Chapman would respond to Jewish fans of his own team with Nazi salutes and slurs. He was not a great guy.

Ken Boyer was the Scott Rolen of his time. (Therefore, by the logical principle of syllogism, he is also Ron Santo.) Boyer did everything well, hitting for power and average and playing Gold-Glove defense. He even led the Cardinals to a World Series championship in 1964 and won a well-deserved MVP.

Why is Boyer not in the Hall? His career wasn't terrifically long, totalling only 8272 PAs. But he spent his age-22 and age-23 seasons, 1952 and 1953, in military service in Korea. Granted, he may not have been 100% ready for the majors at that point, since he spent 1954 in the minors before debuting for the Cardinals in 1955. Still, his service may have delayed his development a bit. He might have been able to squeeze out one more major-league season if not for the war.

The major factor behind Boyer's non-inclusion is the ol' third baseman's conundrum. People look at his career totals, .287 BA, 282 HR, and 1141 RBI, and say "meh." If he had that record as a second baseman, they would likely say "Yeh!" But we have unrealistic expectations for third-base offense, as I've discussed.

The above numbers compare Ken Boyer to his peers at third, and he comes out as a Hall-of-Famer. That's where he belongs.

Darrell Evans (1969-1989, career OPS+: 119)

	Career	Rank	Hitting	Rank	Fielding	Rank	Peak	Rank	Bests	JAWS	Rank
WAR	58.5	16	53.5	13	-0.5	77	37.1	20	1	47.8	16
WS	362.0	5	287.5	6	65.3	24	190.7	10	0	NA	10

In the "New Historical Baseball Abstract," Bill James says Darrell Evans is the most underrated player in baseball history. He cites a number of reasons: Evans played for several teams and at several positions throughout his career, making it harder for people to mentally categorize him. He had low batting averages but did everything else well, including a great skill at drawing walks. There were other reasons too, but if I reference that book any more than I already have, I might get into a copyright dispute. I'll let you look up the other reasons.

I'd add to the list the third baseman conundrum I've already discussed several times. Evans' career numbers are not that impressive if he were just a first baseman. But he spent 12,223 innings at third and just 6,743 at first. He logged 228 Win Shares during seasons in which he was primarily a third baseman, and 99 when he was mostly at first.

In 1973, Evans played 145 games at third and earned 9.0 WAR, the second-best total in the major leagues, and 31 Win Shares, good for 10th in all of baseball. In the NL alone, he had the second-best WAR (behind Joe Morgan) and the sixth-best Win Shares total (behind Joe Morgan, Willie Stargell, Pete Rose, Tony Perez, and Bobby Bonds). Of course, he finished a distant 18th in the NL MVP voting.

WAR gives Evans another great season, 7.2 in 1974, but never another above 5. Win Shares likes him better, giving him nine more seasons of 20 or more win Shares, most above 25, and most when he played third base. This disparity is largely due to the fact that WAR puts him below replacement level for defense in his career, which is cuckoo. Evans was no defensive whiz, but he was adequate, which puts him well within the bounds of a mid-range Hall-of-Famer.

Let's throw some fun facts in here, even though they're not relevant to Evans' Hall of Fame credentials. Evans was known as "Howdy Doody" because he looked like the famous puppet of the same name. One day Braves owner Ted Turner wanted players to put their nicknames on their backs instead of their last names, and Evans happily played as "Howdy." His other nickname was "UFO," because he said he had an experience with one and was a lifelong believer in extraterrestrials.

OK, sorry, just felt the need for something a bit more fun there. My general point is that Darrell Evans may not "feel" like a Hall-of-Famer to you, but that's because he spent a long career being underrated. He's not a first-ballot type, but he would not be out of place among the current membership of the Hall.

Graig Nettles (1967-1988, career OPS+: 110)

	Career	Rank	Hitting	Rank	Fielding	Rank	Peak	Rank	Bests	JAWS	Rank
WAR	68.0	10	52.3	15	20.9	5	42.2	14	2	55.1	10
WS	321.1	9	228.8	13	91.9	3	168.8	25	0	NA	13

Another 1970s/1980s third baseman ... hey, if I wanted to, I could make pretty good cases for Buddy Bell and Ron Cey. Just be thankful that I can't accept that that many from one position and one era could really be Hall-of-Fame-worthy.

And, Graig Nettles is a step above those guys. He'll never make the real-life Hall because he finished with a .248 batting average, the same as Darrell Evans'. But so what? It was a low-offense era. And more relevantly, he hit homers, drew walks, and played great defense for a very long time. Longevity is a big factor for Nettles: his career 10,228 PAs is sixth among third basemen. That's why he gets good Career rankings but not as good Peak rankings.

But then, doesn't that make Nettles a Jake Beckley, a guy who lasted a long time but never had a truly great season? Thank you for asking, but no, you're wrong. And frankly, I'm offended you would ask. You've already been reading this book how long and you don't trust me?

Sorry, that's not the right attitude. Nettles scored 7.5 WAR in 1971 and 7.9 WAR in 1976, both numbers that led the entire American League. That's two WAR MVPs. Win Shares doesn't give him its pseudo-MVP either year, but still awards him 27 Win Shares in 1971 (9th in the AL) and 28 in 1976 (4th in the AL). And, he had plenty of other 5-WAR and 20-Win Shares seasons.

A good long career with plenty of dominance mixed in -- to me, that's a Hall-of-Famer.

Stan Hack (1932-1947, career OPS+: 119)

	Career	Rank	Hitting	Rank	Fielding	Rank	Peak	Rank	Bests	JAWS	Rank
WAR	52.5	20	52.7	14	1.4	70	35.2	25	5	43.9	21
WS	316.1	10	250.6	8	65.7	23	195.0	9	4	NA	9

Pity the poor leadoff hitters. They always get looked over in favor of the power guys. Stan Hack was an excellent leadoff hitter throughout the 1930s and 1940s, finishing with a .394 career OBP and leading the league in stolen bases twice (with 16 and 17 -- the 1930s were not a big time for stolen bases).

As I mentioned in the Gene Tenace comment, OPS+ is not a perfect stat. It doesn't really do guys like Hack justice, since OPS treats a point of OBP and a point of SLG as if they're equivalent. They're not; OBP is more valuable. And people's slugging percentages are almost always higher than the on-base percentages, giving slugging percentage more weight in the calculation. A contemporary of Hack's with a similar OPS+ is first baseman Frank McCormick (118 OPS+). But I'll take Hack's .301/.394/.397 any day over McCormick's .299/.348/.434.

Hack's raw numbers benefit a bit from playing in the 1930s, but not as much as you might think. His best years were from 1938-1942, when offensive levels were slowly settling down. Hack led the league in hits in 1940 and 1941 with 191 and 186, respectively. Leading the league with fewer than 200 hits is a sure sign of a league without a ton of offense; it has happened about 30% of the time, mostly in the dead-ball era and the 1960s-1970s. The National League as a whole hit .264 in 1940 and .258 in 1941, pretty average numbers historically.

Hack even had World Series heroics, despite playing his entire career with the Cubs. The Cubs were actually quite good in Hack's day, winning the NL pennant in 1932, 1935, 1938 and 1945. Hack was a backup in 1932 and wasn't great in the 1935 Series, but excelled in both 1938 and 1945. He ended his postseason career with a.348/.408/.449 line in 76 PAs. That helps his case.

What about the fact that Hack stayed in baseball during the war years of 1942-1945? Well, it means he's a yellow-bellied draft dodger who clearly doesn't love his country (or, more accurately, that he was too old). His performance during the war years may have been boosted a bit by playing against weaker pitchers. But it's not like Hack went wacky good from 1942-1944; he was pretty much his same old self, maybe a little less so. And when most of the best pitchers came back in 1946, Hack still hit .285/.431/.350 in 409 PAs.

Fame in his time? Oh, you betcha. Hack was known as "Smilin' Stan" and was beloved by young and old throughout Chicagoland. In 1935, 21-year-old Cubs employee Bill Veeck, now himself a Hall-of-Famer, had a great idea for a promotion that capitalized on Hack's fame. Fans were given mirrors with Hack's face and the caption "Smile with Stan" on the other side. Perhaps predictably, the fans used the mirrors to shine sunlight into the eyes of the opposing batters. The umpire had to threaten a forfeit to get them to stop. It would not be the last of Bill Veeck's questionable promotions. (Source: "The Top 100 Cubs of All Time: #12 Stan Hack," BleedCubbieBlue.com, Al Yellon, February 7, 2007.)

Bill James ranks Stan Hack ninth among all third basemen in history; that's pretty darn good. Stan Hack's career was not long (8508 PAs) but it was full of greatness (three seasons of more than 30 Win Shares). I think he's a Hall-of-Famer.

Sal Bando (1966-1981, career OPS+: 119)

	Career	Rank	Hitting	Rank	Fielding	Rank	Peak	Rank	Bests	JAWS	Rank
WAR	61.4	14	58.0	11	8.1	31	44.4	12	2	52.9	14
WS	282.6	15	230.0	11	52.3	45	188.8	12	3	NA	11

I really wasn't going to put in another 1970s third baseman, I swear. But I looked at Bando, and, well, I just couldn't resist. Those beautiful overall rankings, those fetching "bests" numbers, that come-hither OPS+ ... hey, I'm only human!

I'd always lumped Bando in with Buddy Bell (13th in JAWS, 19th according to Bill James), and Ron Cey (19th in JAWS, 16th according to Bill James) as products of a golden age of third basemen that is already well-represented in the Hall. But Bando isn't Cey or Bell. Neither Cey nor Bell was ever the best third baseman in baseball in any season, according to either WAR or Win Shares. Neither had a seasonal WAR total above 7.0 or a Win Shares total above 30. They are both more about longevity than excellence.

Meanwhile Bando had an MVP-level season in 1969, scoring 8.3 WAR and 36 Win Shares. He played in every game, led the league in PAs, hit 31 home runs and logged a .400 OBP in a low-offense year. For the next four years or so Sal Bando was the best third baseman in baseball, hands down. Granted, it was a good time to do so: Ron Santo and Brooks Robinson were slowly winding down their careers, Darrell Evans and Graig Nettles were slowly ramping up, and Mike Schmidt and George Brett were but two gleams in the Hall of Fame's eye. Still, both WAR and Win Shares put Bando well above any other third baseman from 1969-1972, or, for that matter, 1968-1972, or 1969-1973.

In fact, WAR says that Bando was the best non-pitcher in all of baseball from 1969-1973, a full 1.7 better than Reggie Jackson or Joe Morgan. Win Shares ranks him eighth in that period -- still, that's pretty Hall-of-Fame-y.

In the latter part of that span Bando helped the A's become a dominant force in baseball. 1971 saw their first playoff appearance since the last Connie Mack dynasty of 1929-1931. Then they won the World Series three straight years, from 1972-1974. It was a fun team that exemplified America in the 1970s: they were a motley collection of egomaniacs (Reggie Jackson), creative facial hair enthusiasts (Rollie Fingers) and weird, reckless experimenters (owner Charlie Finley, who used a live mule as a mascot and experimented with orange baseballs). Bando was the captain of the team, the stable rock around which the rest swirled.

Just like Connie Mack had in 1914, Charlie Finley started to tear down his team in 1975, after they had the effrontery to only make the playoffs and not win the World Series. Bando got a pay cut in 1976 and then signed with the Brewers for three times more money in 1977. He was already 33, though, and his Brewers years were mostly undistinguished. His career totals end up rather Ken Boyer-esque: 8287 PAs, 242 HR, 1039 RBI, .254/.352/.408. That might not look like much, but remember that it spanned the most low-offense period in history besides the dead-ball era.

After reviewing Bando more thoroughly, I now put him with Boyer and Rolen as players who hit well for third basemen, fielded well, and had relatively short careers featuring plenty of great seasons. I think he's over the line for the Hall of Fame.

Heinie Groh (1912-1927, career OPS+: 118)

	Career	Rank	Hitting	Rank	Fielding	Rank	Peak	Rank	Bests	JAWS	Rank
WAR	48.2	24	44.9	27	8.5	30	35.7	23	5	42.0	25
WS	270.8	22	191.9	24	66.0	22	190.3	11	6	NA	21

Heinie Groh? (I imagine you are thinking)? Heinie Groh?!?!? (I imagine you are thinking with increased and frankly excessive levels of emphasis)?!?!?! What? Who? Why? When? Where? How? Whence? Wherefore? Whatzit? Howzabout? Whenzabout? Whiffle? Wharton? Warburton? WAR?

I admire your journalistic thoroughness, so I'll answer each of those questions in no particular order. As far as "where" and "when," Heinie Groh was a star with Cincinnati during the deadest days of the dead-ball era. In 1918, a season shortened by World War I, Groh led the National League with 86 runs, 28 doubles, and a .395 on-base percentage. In 1919 he led the league with an .823 OPS. In 2000, that

OPS would have ranked him 36th in the National League, tied with Todd Zeile and a bit below J.T. Snow. In 1919, it was 19 points better than anyone else.

Like Stan Hack, Groh was a leadoff-type guy, as was almost everyone in the dead-ball era. Again, the 118 career OPS+ doesn't do him justice. His .292/.373/.384 lifetime slash line is much more valuable than that of say, outfielder Tillie Walker, who, during Groh's career span, had the same OPS+ but a .281/.341/.434 line. Groh's numbers mean a great leadoff hitter, while Walker's mean an OK fifth-slot guy.

But enough with the conventional numbers already. Let's get to the stats that really show us how great Groh was. In 1917, Groh earned 37 Win Shares and 7.0 WAR. In 1919, he got 30 Win Shares and 5.4 WAR. 1918 would have seen another 30 Win Shares, 5 WAR season if World War I hadn't shortened the Reds' season to 128 games; as it was Groh scored 28 Win Shares and 4.8 WAR. He had three other Win Shares scores in the 20s and two other WAR scores in the 5s.

Each system says he was the best third baseman in baseball at least five times. The only third basemen to have more firsts in WAR are Deacon White, Eddie Mathews, Wade Boggs and Mike Schmidt. Win Shares gives only Mathews and Schmidt more firsts. From 1915-1919, Groh was not only the best third baseman in baseball by a large margin, he was the fourth-best non-pitcher period according to both WAR and Win Shares (top three in both systems: Ty Cobb, Tris Speaker, and Eddie Collins).

WAR is generally a little less excited about Groh, and I bet you can guess why: It starts with "d" and ends in "fense" and is spelled "defense." Win Shares, again, looks more reliable in judging Groh's work on the field. Third base was especially crucial to the defenses of the dead-ball era, because every other player was trying to bunt. Groh was a converted second baseman, and if contemporary accounts are to be believed, was one of the best defenders of the era, if not the best. Conventional fielding stats have a mess of problems even worse than conventional batting stats, but for what it's worth, Groh often led the league in putouts and double plays and finished with a then-all-time-record .967 fielding percentage. Fielding percentage records usually get broken very quickly, but that remained the NL record until the 1970s.

Groh's World Series play alternated between "meh" and great. He didn't play well in 1919 against the White Sox, but the Reds won anyway, thanks to the Sox's ... shall we say ... unorthodox approach to ballplaying in that series. In 1922, Groh was traded to the Giants, who were in the midst of a big pennant streak. Groh probably would have won World Series MVP if it had existed that year. He hit .474/.524/.579 to help the Giants beat the cross-town Yankees. Groh was so proud of that series that for the rest of his life, his license plate was 474.

OK, all that looks fine, you might say, but still, the numbers in the chart above are low for a Hall-of-Famer. He shows up worse in both overall numbers than Buddy Bell and Ron Cey. Both of those guys may have had fewer top-flight seasons, but longevity is valuable too, and each lasted much longer than Groh's measly 7034 career PA.

I admit that I am partially motivated by getting more dead-ball hitters in the Hall. But Groh really gets over the edge because of his "bottle bat," which changed baseball forever.

In the dead-ball era, bats were often just thick dowels. They would taper a bit towards the handles, but nothing like bats nowadays. Here is a picture (see http://memory.loc.gov/service/pnp/cph/3b40000/3b43000/3b43900/3b43970r.jpg) of Ty Cobb lovingly admiring the nearly cylindrical bats of Shoeless Joe Jackson (who is, suspiciously, wearing shoes).

Heinie Groh was a small man, 5'6" on a good day. The first time he came to bat, as a rookie with the Giants in 1912, someone in the opposing dugout made the standard joke that the manager had sent the batboy to the plate. But umpire Bill Klem was suspicious that it might be true, with good reason. Klem and Giants manager John McGraw had a longstanding feud, and McGraw probably would try a stunt like that just to show Klem up. Klem gruffly asked Groh if he was actually under contract with the Giants. Groh swore he was, and then smacked out a single. Many fans left thinking that Klem had actually let the batboy get a hit. (Source: Groh's SABR biography, by John Lehman.)

Groh didn't have much success as a rookie, but John McGraw had a solution. Looking at Groh's tiny hands, McGraw suggested Groh get a bat with a thin handle. Groh took the idea and ran rather far with it. He helped Louisville Slugger design something that looked more like a cricket bat: (see http://img.bleacherreport.net/img/slides/photos/002/395/158/groh.sabr.org_original_crop_north.jpg?w=240&h=249&q=75).

After the Giants threw Groh into a trade with the Reds, lil' Heinie and his big bat became stars. Other players started emulating Heinie, looking for bats with thin handles and large barrels. It turns out that this kind of bat works well for people of all hand sizes, since it concentrates more weight and area in the sweet spot. The gradual change in bat dimensions was one small factor in turning the dead-ball era into the lively ball era.

Maybe this new bat gave Groh an unfair advantage? Only if you think Ernie Banks had an unfair advantage when he did much the same thing, using a bat with an even thinner handle to crank out home runs in the 1950s.

As with Roger Bresnahan and his improved face mask and shin guards, Heinie Groh didn't invent a thin-handled bat. True "inventions" are rare in any walk of life: most of what we call "inventions" are just significant, marketable improvements of existing designs. But Groh definitely made a significant, marketable improvement in the design of bats, reaped great rewards from it, and changed the game. To my way of thinking, that tips him over the edge and into the Hall of Fame.

The Damage

Wow, I added so many third basemen that now I have to pause and take stock. Here's your new lineup of Hall of Fame hot cornermen:

- **Frank Baker**
- **Sal Bando**
- **Wade Boggs**
- **Ken Boyer**
- **George Brett**
- **Jimmy Collins**
- **Ray Dandridge**
- **Darrell Evans**
- **Heinie Groh**
- **Stan Hack**
- **Judy Johnson**
- **Chipper Jones**
- **Eddie Mathews**
- **Graig Nettles**
- **Brooks Robinson**
- **Scott Rolen**
- **Ron Santo**

- **Mike Schmidt**
- **Pie Traynor**
- **Deacon White**
- **Jud Wilson**

That gets us to 21, which is a fair few. But it's not an excessive number. And it includes Jones and Rolen, who are not yet eligible at this writing. By the time those two get in, most positions will have more than 21 Hall-of-Famers. I think it's a valid improvement.

Chapter Seven

~ ~ Left Field ~ ~

Left field is the field on the left. Let's just get to it.

Lou Brock (1961-1979, career OPS+: 109)

	Career	Rank	Hitting	Rank	Fielding	Rank	Peak	Rank	Bests	JAWS	Rank
WAR	45.2	32	48.5	24	-17.1	92	32.0	40	1	38.6	35
WS	349.5	17	278.2	17	45.4	18	189.5	28	0	NA	15

Lou Brock is one of the most famous baseball players in history. Before Rickey Henderson, he held the all-time records for stolen bases in a career and a single season. He's in the 3,000-hit club. His nickname was "The Franchise," for Pete's sake.

So it is with a bit of shock that I look at Brock's rankings above. WAR does not give him Hall-of-Fame status. Bill James ranks him 15th, rather charitably considering that neither of Brock's Career or Peak rankings are that high. James has a soft spot for Hall-of-Famers who don't fare as well in the numbers as you would expect them to (see also: Orlando Cepeda, George Kell, and Pie Traynor).

Brock definitely had longevity, and that's not nothing: 11,240 career PAs don't grow on trees. (Imagine if they did?) But both systems are unimpressed with his peak. WAR gives Brock three seasons above 5 and none higher than 6. Win Shares gives him three seasons in the low 30s, which isn't bad but not stellar for a left fielder.

Defense? Yeah, once again, defense means the difference between the two systems. WAR thinks that if you threw a dead cat into left field for 21,492.1 innings, it would win 17.1 more games than Brock would. (That is not the textbook definition of replacement level, granted.) I don't buy it. Brock had a bad arm, but had great range. That big negative number in his fielding skews the rest of his WAR numbers.

The larger issue is that Brock excelled in an area of the game, stolen bases, that is more exciting than it is useful. It's certainly not a bad thing to steal bases, especially if you don't get caught often. But, in terms of adding runs to the board, it's not nearly as effective as the relatively boring activity of drawing walks.

Stolen bases get overvalued because they're fun to watch. That moment of excitement we feel from watching a stolen base burns the memory of it in our brains. Later, we're left with the pleasure of that memory, and it helps form our conception of the base stealer's value. "That was a great thing that guy did to help the team," we think subconsciously. "Therefore that guy is valuable in proportion to that excitement."

It sounds silly to put it in those terms, but it's really how our brains process most everything. Emotion plays a much larger role in assigning value than rationality does. Our brains are not perfect value-processing machines. Just ask any used car dealer.

Numbers don't carry these sort of emotional biases. They are just about what works and what doesn't, in the most stark and mathematical terms. I'm not saying numbers are always better than human perception; they never capture everything. But I am saying that numbers are better at a few things. This makes them a vital complement -- not replacement, but complement -- to simply watching games.

This is why digging through the numbers is important if you want to gain an edge over the competition. Many people observe lots of games and come to emotionally based conclusions. Most of the time, those conclusions are right. Sometimes, though, emotion-dominated reasoning will lead to ideas, like overvaluing stolen bases, that just don't work well when you get down to the bottom line.

If you can bear to alter your ideas based on the numbers, and your competitors can't, you can gain a big edge. This is the real principle behind the book "Moneyball," by the way. It's not just "walks = good." It's really about finding an advantage over your competition by looking a bit deeper into the stats.

As I write this, every major league team has adopted this way of thinking. They all realize that while scouting and the expertise of men who played and watched the game for decades will always be vital, computer nerds also have a place in making teams win. The world of science realized long ago that just thinking and feeling about why the sun rises and sets isn't enough; you have to also look at cold, objective data. Almost every other industry has also recognized that you need both first-hand experience and number crunchers. Baseball was late to the party, but then, it usually is.

Wow, that was a long digression. Back to Lou Brock and his stolen bases. His 109 career OPS+ is downright dreadful for a Hall of Fame left fielder. OPS has a well-documented bias against leadoff guys, but Brock isn't a Stan Hack or Heinie Groh type with a high OBP and low SLG. Brock's career line is .293/.343/.410. Even in the context of the 1960s and 1970s, a .343 career OBP is not at a Hall-of-Fame level. During Brock's career span, 50 players managed a better OBP in 5000 PAs or more. Brock just never drew walks very well.

What if I do the trick I used for Ozzie Smith and give Brock credit for total bases for each of his stolen bases while subtracting his caught stealings from his hits? That switches Brock's .343 OBP and .410 SLG to a .316 OBP and .471 SLG. Now he's close to George Bell's career marks, which is hardly a ringing endorsement. It does move Brock up to a 114 OPS+, but that's still not in the realm of a Hall-of-Fame left fielder.

But there is that longevity. As a great man once said, that's not nothing: 11,240 career PAs don't grow on trees. (Imagine if they did?) Brock is 32nd all time in career PAs, and everyone ahead of him is either in the Hall of Fame, probably will be someday, is barred because of gambling or steroids, or is Omar Vizquel.

Plus, Brock was awesome in the postseason. The 1964 World Series was his least successful, hitting .300 with no walks in the Cardinals' win over the Yankees. In 1967, Brock hit .414/.452/.655 with 7 stolen bases and led the Cardinals over the Red Sox. In a losing effort in 1968, Brock had his best World Series yet, going .464/.516/.857 and stealing another 7 bases.

In the end, Lou Brock doesn't look too bad. Bill James says he belongs. WAR doesn't, but WAR's numbers are skewed by its flawed evaluation of defense. And "It's the Hall of Fame, not the Hall of Stats" certainly applies. Brock steals his way (get it?) into the Hall. He may be the worst player ever to make it on his first ballot. But who cares? He's in, and should be.

Jesse Burkett (1890-1905, career OPS+: 140)

	Career	Rank	Hitting	Rank	Fielding	Rank	Peak	Rank	Bests	JAWS	Rank
WAR	62.9	13	64.1	10	-12.2	86	37.1	21	2	50.0	14
WS	388.5	7	335.2	9	52.9	10	210.5	13	2	NA	14

We move from the famous-but-overrated Lou Brock to the virtually-unknown-but-terrific Jesse Burkett. It's a terrible injustice ... well, it would be if any of this mattered in the grand scheme of things. I'm not saying I don't care; I'm just saying that a worldwide recognition of Jesse Burkett's superiority over Lou Brock will probably not advance the Middle East peace process.

My point is, if you needed a mediator between Israel and Palestine, Jesse Burkett would be a bad choice. (Yeah, that's clearly where I was going with that.) Burkett was known as "Crab" because of his singular commitment to being unpleasant. Newspapers would try to print his tirades against fans and umpires, but they would have to substitute "blank" for all the expletives. One actual quote went like this: "Why you blank, blankety blank, do you know what I think of you? I think you are the blankest blank blank that ever came out of the blank blankest town in the blank blank land. You ought to be put in a museum." (Source: Burkett's SABR biography, written by David Jones).

In my mind, I'm trying to substitute actual bad words for each "blank" but I'm finding it hard to come up with a sentence that makes sense. I get close, but then "You ought to be put in a museum" throws me. I don't know what that could mean. That you're old, I guess? That your timeless beauty bespeaks a transcendent truth that deserves to be admired in perpetuity? That was probably it. The ol' Crab was flirting!

One of the upsides of having no friends is that you don't care whether people like you. In the evenings, Burkett was assigned to babysit players whose alcoholism was so severe that they couldn't be trusted to get enough sleep before games. It's not easy to follow an alcoholic around all night being a killjoy, unless you don't mind being despised.

Another benefit of having no friends is that you end up with a lot of free time. (I speak from experience.) Burkett used his friendless free time to become a great hitter. He came to the majors as a pitcher, but was pretty dreadful at it. He got a second chance as an outfielder with the lowly Cleveland Spiders and gradually turned himself into an expert in the art of hitting. In 1896 he led the National League, then the only major league, in runs, hits, and batting average. It was one of his three career batting titles.

He ended up similar to Tony Gwynn as a hitter: lots of singles, some doubles and triples, not many homers, but good number of walks and stolen bases. Burkett was a pretty a bad fielder, though, making his Win Shares fielding total look a bit suspect.

With Burkett, Cy Young, and later Bobby Wallace, the Spiders became a good team. But that was cut short by the switcheroo played on the city of Cleveland that I mentioned in the Wallace comment. Jesse Burkett played out the rest of his days on the Browns, slapping singles and being crabby. Burkett clearly compiled a Hall-of-Fame career.

Fred Clarke (1894-1911, 1913-1915, career OPS+: 133)

	Career	Rank	Hitting	Rank	Fielding	Rank	Peak	Rank	Bests	JAWS	Rank
WAR	67.8	10	58.4	15	-2.7	21	36.0	28	2	51.9	13
WS	399.7	6	335.6	8	64.1	4	200.2	18	2	NA	22

There's nothing too terribly glamorous about Fred Clarke. He was a very good player for a very long time, first with the National League's Louisville Colonels and then with the Pittsburgh Pirates when the two teams were merged.

It wasn't quite as bad as the Cleveland Spiders situation, but it was close. After the 1899 season, the National League decided to contract the Spiders out of existence, which was probably the most humane option available. But, they also got rid of the Louisville Colonels, Washington Senators, and Baltimore Orioles. As with the Spiders, the Colonels and Orioles were victims of "syndicate ownership," in which one owner was allowed to have two teams and move all the good players to one of them.

In 1899, Louisville Colonels owner Barney Dreyfuss gained control of the Pittsburgh Pirates and moved Clarke to his new team, along with Honus Wagner and a host of other stars. The only difference between it and the St. Louis Maroons/Cleveland Spiders situation was that the Spiders were left in the league for a year to slowly, painfully bleed out. The Louisville Colonels got euthanasia.

The mass contraction bit the the N.L. in the butt just a few years later, as it created some openings for the upstart American League to exploit. In 1900, Baltimore was the 6th-largest city in the nation, Cleveland was 7th, and Washington was 15th. These were definitely markets that could support major-league baseball teams. The two leagues shared Chicago (2nd), Philadelphia (3rd), St. Louis (4th), and Boston (5th). And the A.L. savvily snapped up Detroit, which was 13th-largest in 1900 but 4th by 1920. Who knows if the A.L. would have survived more than a year if they hadn't been handed monopolies of several prime markets?

You'd think Baltimore would have been the shining jewel in the A.L.'s crown. Baltimore had 508,957 people in 1900, not far from the 560,892 that Boston was splitting among the N.L. Braves and the A.L. Red Sox. And Baltimore had a great baseball tradition; the recently contracted N.L. team won the pennant every year from 1894-1896 behind Hall-of-Famers Hughie Jennings, John McGraw, Joe Kelley, Willie Keeler, Wilbert Robinson, and manager Ned Hanlon. It remains the most famous team of the era, full of vibrant, violent character and brilliant, morally shaky strategy (see the Joe Kelley comment for more about them).

But the new A.L. Baltimore team was eliminated after a few years. They were replaced by the New York Yankees, which of course became the real crown jewel of the American League. The move had nothing to do with Baltimore's viability as a market. The A.L. just wanted a team in New York, and in 1903 the N.L. allowed them to establish one as a gesture of peace between the leagues. So Baltimore, a large city full of baseball fans still reveling in recent glories, had to sacrifice their only team so that New Yorkers could have three instead of two (including Brooklyn). Thus the Yankees were birthed within a bald-faced, overweening sense of entitlement that in no way characterized the franchise in decades to come. (Yankees fans, that was not sarcasm. Non-Yankee fans, that was definitely sarcasm.)

But then, poor Louisville (18th-largest American city in 1900) proved the greatest casualty of the 1899 contraction. Baltimore got yet another team when the St. Louis Browns moved there in 1954. Louisville never did.

At least Louisville's major-league-baseball martyrdom contributed to the glory to the city of Pittsburgh. The new-look Pirates became a major force in the next decade, topping the National League every year from 1901-1903 and winning the World Series in 1909. Throughout, Clarke was a star left fielder and also the manager. He managed for 19 years and attained a .576 career winning percentage.

Like Joe Torre, Fred Clarke could make the Hall of Fame as either a player or manager. Either way, he's in.

Ed Delahanty (1888-1903, career OPS+: 152)

	Career	Rank	Hitting	Rank	Fielding	Rank	Peak	Rank	Bests	JAWS	Rank
WAR	69.5	6	68.7	7	-5.4	44	48.6	6	6	59.1	6
WS	353.5	15	311.1	13	42.6	26	226.8	5	5	NA	12

Ed Delahanty was the Joe DiMaggio of the 1890s. He was great in every facet of the game, hitting for average and power while drawing a good number of walks. DiMaggio was a better fielder, and Delahanty a better base stealer, so maybe it's not a perfect analogy.

I went for it, though, because like Dimaggio, Delahanty had lots of brothers who reached the majors. The DiMaggio family had Dom and Vince living in Joe's shadow, while the Delahantys had Frank, Jim, Joe and Tom living in Ed's. Without having checked for sure and thus having no real idea, I'm going to definitively declare that the Delahantys have a record number of brothers that made the big leagues. You may remember that Negro Leaguer Ben Taylor had three ballplaying brothers, so they come in second. The DiMaggios, Alous and Molinas tie for third. Tied for fourth are the Bretts, Niekros, Perrys, Forsches, Uptons, and a whole bunch more. Tied for fifth is a few thousand families. Tied for sixth is my family and several billion others.

Unlike Joe DiMaggio, Ed Delahanty did not go on to marry Marilyn Monroe. Instead, he died. Delahanty was a destructive alcoholic who blew all of his money on gambling and booze. By 1903, when he was 35 years old, he was mired in debt. He kept trying to jump to new teams to get more money, but was stopped at every turn. As the debts mounted, Delahanty drank more.

While playing with the Senators in 1903, he started giving away his possessions and threatening to kill himself. One night, riding a train to New York, Delahanty got very drunk and caused such a commotion that he was kicked off the train. He stumbled near a bridge over the Niagara River in Buffalo. A night watchman saw him and the two got into a scuffle. Then Delahanty fell into the river and drowned. No one knows if he fell by accident or on purpose. (Source: Delahanty's SABR biography, by John Saccoman.)

Delahanty was still playing very well up to his death. He probably could have reached 3,000 hits if he'd been able to find a way through his troubles. Regardless, he's a no-doubt Hall-of-Famer.

Goose Goslin (1921-1938, career OPS+: 128)

	Career	Rank	Hitting	Rank	Fielding	Rank	Peak	Rank	Bests	JAWS	Rank
WAR	66.1	11	61.3	13	-4.7	36	43.2	10	3	54.7	10
WS	353.9	14	283.6	16	45.3	19	195.9	21	2	NA	16

Now we travel from a trio of turn-of-the-century titans to the magnificently modern era of the 1920s. Automated vehicular carriages transport humans across hill and vale sans horse or oxen! Grand moving picture houses feature special-effects extravaganzas, including a spectacular spool of celluloid in which a man speaks and then is heard![30] The right to vote is extended to actual female womanish ladies of the complementary gender, uteruses and all!

Within this national cauldron of tumult and hullabaloo lies a capital city, Washington D.C. It is firmly devoted like never before or since to not doing much of anything. After all, what is there to do? Alcohol is illegal, so of course people will not try to drink it. Enforcing those laws would just be gauche. The stock market is rising exponentially, and if there is anything on this blue-green marble that a chap can set his gold-plated pocket watch to, it is that stock markets always rise exponentially until every man Jack inhabits a fleet of mansions.

No, the nation's capital was more enthralled by its ballfield nine, the Senators. Walter Johnson patrolled the midfield dirt blob, firing pellets of zip and vinegar at boomstruck baton bearers. Second baseman Bucky Harris flipped, hustled and scrappy-ed red-stitched orbs hither and yon (but mostly hither. Some yon. Maybe 60/40 hither/yon). Right fielder Sam Rice surreptitiously slapped singles so superbly, Sue Simons sent Saul Stephens some sacks stinking softly, sandily, splendid, splarg. Sping.

But not a solitary sphere circulator showcased more stardust than Leon Allen "Goose" Goslin, slugger non pareil and left fielder after a fashion. For each fly ball that bounced comically out of his reach or off his head or down his throat, twenty were launched from his bat into the recesses of cavernous Griffith Stadium. Oh, Elysium, whence cometh this benevolent behemoth? From which lump of loam on baseball's sacred birthing ground was formed this Golem, this Goliath, this ... Goose?

You get the point: I like thesauruses. Also, the Senators were a legitimately exciting, star-studded team in the 1920s, and Goose Goslin was a central piece. In his first great season, 1924, he led the league in RBI and the Senators won their first World Series title. For the humble farmboy Goslin, the resulting accolades were quite a to-do. After a crowd awaited his return to his tiny hometown and cheered him all the way to his house, he didn't know what to say besides "Gosh, this is the life."

Goose was more than just a big, simple fella - he was also kinda dumb. But in a fun way. During his rookie season, he smashed a triple off of Hall-of-Famer Red Faber to win a game. Back on the bench, Senators first baseman Joe Judge said, "I never thought we'd beat Red Faber today." Goslin said, "That was Faber?" (Source for these stories: Goslin's SABR biography, by Cort Vitty.)

---

[30] Reference explanation: The first "talkie" was 1927's "The Jazz Singer." I wouldn't recommend it. There is one good moment in which star Al Jolson utters the first words ever heard in a major movie, "You ain't heard nothin' yet!" The rest is leaden melodrama and wince-inducing blackface.

Goose's misadventures in the field were also a major source of amusement. His nickname was not just a play on his last name; he also looked like a silly goose when he chased fly balls, running around in a panic and flapping his arms. It also helped that he had a long neck and large beak-like nose.

He made up for his poor fielding with his dominating hitting. Goslin would have logged some large home run totals if he didn't play half his games in Griffith Stadium, where no part of the outfield fence was less than 400 feet from home plate (not a joke). From 1921 until Goslin was traded to the St. Louis Browns in 1930, Goslin hit 27 homers at home and 88 on the road. As soon as he joined the Browns mid-season, he hit 30 home runs in only 396 at-bats.

But a few years of playing for the 1930s Browns will make anyone lose a few steps. Goslin spent his 30s being a good but not great player, going back to the Senators for a year and then on to the Tigers. He wrapped it up at age 37, settling on 2735 hits in 9829 at-bats. He certainly deserves to be in the Hall of Fame.

Chick Hafey (1924-1935, 1937; career OPS+: 133)

	Career	Rank	Hitting	Rank	Fielding	Rank	Peak	Rank	Bests	JAWS	Rank
WAR	30.1	61	31.3	61	-5.6	45	27.2	53	0	28.7	56
WS	184.8	72	161.3	65	23.6	102	152.5	56	0	NA	59

If you've been reading this in order like I very politely asked you to, I bet you can look at the ranks above and the years spanning Hafey's career and hazard a guess about the identity of at least one of his teammates and the year when he was elected to the Hall. Honestly, did nobody in the country give a crap about who was selected during Frankie Frisch's reign over the Veteran's Committee from 1967-73?

Granted, I give too much crap about these things. I give several metric tons of crap about the membership of the Hall of Fame, and I think the average baseball fan gives maybe 20 pounds of crap about it, maximum. But still, were there no annoying baseball nerds like me in the late 1960s and early 1970s? Or were they all too busy either taking LSD or voting for Richard Nixon (both of which can severely damage your conception of reality)?

Grumble grumble ... well, I suppose I should at least try to discover some reason that the election of Chick Hafey in 1971 didn't cause the drug/Nixon-addled people of America to drop their marijuana/Marlboros onto their bellbottoms/Sears slacks and scream foul. Hafey of course played in a high-offense time, so he got a .317 career batting average, which looks quite nice on the surface. Even the modern metric of a 133 OPS+ is pretty solid for a Hall of Fame left fielder.

But he simply did not play enough for the Hall. Hafey had 5115 career PAs and only five seasons of more than 500. He had a few legitimate All-Star seasons, but so did Kevin Mitchell, in a career at a similar level (4696 PAs, 142 OPS+, 63rd in JAWS, 51st according to Bill James). If Will Clark ends up on the Veteran's Committee in a few decades and sneaks Mitchell past us all, then it's fool me twice, shame on me. No matter what, **Hafey is out with a vengeance**.

Rickey Henderson (1979-2003; career OPS+: 127)

	Career	Rank	Hitting	Rank	Fielding	Rank	Peak	Rank	Bests	JAWS	Rank
WAR	110.8	3	104.2	3	-3.5	25	57.3	3	7	84.1	3
WS	534.9	4	407.3	5	49.6	13	227.0	4	6	NA	4

Bill James was once asked if Rickey Henderson was a Hall-of-Famer. James said that if you split Henderson in two, he'd be two Hall-of-Famers. Let's try it.

Half of Rickey Henderson (Half of career totals, every other great season for peak; career OPS+: 127)

	Career	Rank	Hitting	Rank	Fielding	Rank	Peak	Rank	Bests	JAWS	Rank
WAR	55.3	19	52.0	21	-1.7	16	48.8	6	3.5	52.1	13
WS	267.5	33	203.7	44	24.8	91	207.6	15	3.5	NA	27

WAR actually thinks Half Rickey is qualified. James' own system, Win Shares, is not so sure. James has clearly been hoisted on his own petard. Bill James, you are peddling a pack of lies. J'accuse! (Oh, and I love your work. Please love me!)

So we all know Rickey Henderson is overqualified for the Hall of Fame. More interesting are the silly stories about Rickey Henderson, of which there are many. Some are true and some are false but ring true. All of them depict an eccentric with zero self-awareness whose all-encompassing egomania was an essential tool for guiding him through the incredibly stressful life of a major-league superstar.

I'll show you what I mean. In one game, Rickey struck out. As he walked back to the bench, a teammate overheard him saying to himself "Don't worry Rickey, you're still the best." It's goofy, of course, and egomaniacal. But it also sounds like a self-soothing behavior, of the kind used to tamp down a burst of anxiety. Apparently, a simple strikeout made him doubt his ability. He then had to reassure himself of his worthiness, like many of us do after a failure. The difference is that Rickey did it out loud and referred to himself in the third person.

Before every game, Rickey would stand naked in front of a full-length mirror and say "Rickey's the best" over and over for several minutes. Again, it sounds at first like just silly egomania. But I can't think of a better demonstration of egomania serving as a coping mechanism, one that pushes away doubt and insecurity. This was something he *had* to do to get ready for a game. Most players might need to "psych" themselves up, but not to this extreme. Apparently Rickey had some severe self-doubt that needed to be pushed away.

Many other stories involve Rickey not knowing the names of his teammates or generally being unaware of their presence. One probably apocryphal story involved John Olerud. While both were playing with the Mariners, Rickey asked Olerud why he wore a batting helmet on the field. Olerud said he had a brain aneurysm at age nine and had to wear the helmet for protection. Rickey said "Yeah, I used to play with a guy that had the same thing." Olerud said "That was me, Rickey." The two had previously been teammates on both the Blue Jays and the Mets. (Source for these stories: "It's Rickey Henderson's 55th birthday: here are 25 stories that may or may not be true," The Province," December 25, 2013.)

That one likely never happened. But this story stuck to Rickey, becoming one of his most famous. That says something about him. This and similar stories depict a person with such an elevated level of self-involvement that he hardly took in any information about the people around him. It was as if simply navigating his own mind was so all-consuming that everyone else became shadows.

At the same time, Henderson was incredibly good at taking in information on the ballfield. His ability to steal bases, the greatest of all-time, came not because he was the fastest person to play baseball; he wasn't. Instead he was the best at reading every twitch and tic of every pitcher and then picking the exact right millisecond to break for second base. He made base stealing into a science of a degree of sophistication that only he could fully understand.

It all smacks a bit of the people in the more high-functioning end of the Autism Spectrum Disorder, people who used to be diagnosed with Asperger's syndrome. Such people can focus to a remarkable extent on one esoteric passion, to the point where they can achieve things that no one else thought possible. They also tend to be unusually deficient in other human functions, like social skills, that most people take for granted. High-functioning autism can actually be of huge benefit in professions like science or IT that require incredible attention to detail and little direct interaction with other people. Your stereotypical nerd, with the glasses, pocket protector, and social awkwardness, is often of this type.

It's strange to think of Rickey Henderson, the all-time great athlete, as an autism-y nerd, and suggesting as much is certainly an armchair diagnosis on my part. But I have some training in psychology and I don't think it's totally farfetched. Regardless of why Rickey was so very Rickey, he belongs in the Hall of Fame's upper reaches.

Pete Hill (1904-1924; OPS+: 178)

	Rank at Position Among Negro Leaguers	Rank Among All Negro Leaguers
Bill James	2 (basically)	not ranked
SABR	not ranked	not ranked
Monte Irvin	not ranked	NA

Pete Hill was the greatest outfielder of the early days of the Negro Leagues. Like Louis Santop, Pop Lloyd, and Ben Taylor, he was a star before the Negro National League brought greater organization and prominence to black baseball in the 1920s.

SABR completely ignores Hill. In Monte Irvin's book he isn't ranked but does get a blurb, written by Irvin's co-writer Phil Pepe. Pepe says Hill was a tremendous line-drive hitter with high batting averages and great range in the outfield. He notes that Hill was the right-hand man for Hall-of-Fame manager Rube Foster, one of the most important figures in Negro League history (tied for 5th on SABR's list). Hill served as Foster's team captain and later became a successful manager in his own right. Pepe even goes as far as to suggest that the greatest dead-ball-era outfield would consist of Ty Cobb, Tris Speaker, and Pete Hill. You get the impression than Pepe definitely thinks Hill should have been in the top 5, but that Irvin just didn't know anything about him.

Why the "(basically)" for James' ranking in the above? James puts Turkey Stearnes and Mule Suttles in left field and ranks both above Monte Irvin and Pete Hill. The Hall of Fame lists Stearnes in right field and Suttles at first, and so does the Monte Irvin book. So that's where I put those guys, leaving Irvin at number one and Hill at number two.

That might sound a little shady, but it's often difficult to know what position to assign to Negro Leaguers. The records are incomplete, of course. And the great Negro League players would routinely play all over the diamond. Rosters were small, because payrolls were small. If one starter had to sit out, everyone else moved around. Outfielders in particular were not wedded to one position.

Regardless, the rankings above are not great for Pete Hill. The fact that SABR left him out entirely is troubling. But SABR's ranking is of the "Greatest Negro League Figures," not necessarily the most talented. Pete Hill might not be on the list because he isn't well-known, because he peaked well before black ball became a big business. Maybe he's a Roger Connor who did extremely well very quietly, before people were paying much attention.

The stats sure seem to say so. Seamheads gives Hill the third-highest total Win Shares of anyone in their pre-1935 data base, behind only Oscar Charleston and Cristobal Torriente. It shows 3977 PAs with a .323/.408/.458 line and a 178 OPS+. That slugging percentage is quite good for the dead-ball era; you can't expect Hill to hit many home runs when no one could. Phil Pepe suggests that he could have hit a bunch of homers in any other era, saying he was a 1950s-1960s player stuck in the 1910s.

Is Hill like Frank Grant, the 1800s Negro Leaguer who got nothing but low or non-rankings from my sources? Grant didn't have Bill James or Phil Pepe on his side. Grant also didn't have much of a statistical record. He didn't have several good seasons of managing, like Hill did. He very well could have had Hall-of-Fame-level playing ability, but it was very difficult to tell.

With Hill, it's much easier to tell. The numbers convince me that Pete Hill did have Hall-of-Fame playing ability and deserves his spot.

Monte Irvin (1938-1956; career MLB OPS+: 125)

	Rank at Position Among Negro Leaguers	Rank Among All Negro Leaguers
Bill James	1 (basically)	not ranked
SABR	1	19
Monte Irvin	1 (basically)	NA

In the Pete Hill comment I said why Bill James "(basically)" has Monte Irvin first among Negro League left fielders: He has Mule Suttles and Turkey Stearnes in left, but no one else does. The other (basically) above is for Monte Irvin's ranking of Monte Irvin. Irvin actually does not include himself at all in his rankings. But his co-writer, Phil Pepe, interjects with another blurb saying that Irvin did so out of his natural modesty. He says Irvin was clearly the best left fielder in Negro League history. SABR agrees.

I generally don't like meeting celebrities. I've come across a few minor ones, but I've always been very nervous and ended up saying something dumb. If people ask me who I'd want to spend a day with if I could choose anyone, I say "my wife and kids." That makes them go "Awwww!" and then leave me alone. It has the benefit of also being true, because if I spent the day with some famous person, I'd just make a fool of myself and then spend a lifetime regretting it. (Bill James, keep your distance.)

But I would have made an exception for Monte Irvin, if given the chance. His book communicates the kind of man he was. He seems genuinely humble, as if it were a central part of his character, which is a very rare trait for a superstar in any field. He was also full of baseball stories and insights. I feel like I could have picked his brain for hours. Sadly, he died in 2016.

Irvin's numbers are very similar in both the Negro Leagues and in the majors. And in the majors he was terrific. I included his MLB OPS+ above (I don't have the Negro League one); keep in mind that he did that from age 30-37, when most players are on the downswing. Among Hall of Fame left fielders from age 30-37, a 125 OPS+ is about average; Goose Goslin, Al Simmons and Joe Medwick are lower, while Jesse Burkett, Fred Clarke, and Ed Delahanty are higher. I have no doubt that Monte Irvin is a deserving Hall-of-Famer.

Joe Kelley (1891-1906, 1908; career OPS+: 134)

	Career	Rank	Hitting	Rank	Fielding	Rank	Peak	Rank	Bests	JAWS	Rank
WAR	50.6	23	50.2	23	-7.3	62	36.3	25	1	43.5	22
WS	303.4	24	234.4	30	48.1	15	187.1	31	1	NA	28

Those are not overwhelming final rankings, to say the least. Kelley was yet another turn-of-the-century left fielder who could hit very well. He had some great seasons, with three above 30 Win Shares and three above 5.0 WAR. He didn't have a long career, but it wasn't too short, totaling 8139 PAs. The grand total ends up a bit low according to Career numbers, Peak numbers, and overall ranks.

Of course, Kelley wasn't elected because of his Career and Peak WAR totals. He got the call in the 1971 Veterans Committee vote, even though he never played with Frankie Frisch. This class was possibly the worst ever, also enshrining Jake Beckley, Chick Hafey, Rube Marquard, Harry Hooper, George Weiss, and Dave Bancroft. Beckley and Hafey I already kicked out. Marquard and Hooper we haven't met yet (but they should be interesting). Bancroft I let stay, perhaps unwisely. Weiss was an executive, and thus outside the scope of this book.

Kelley reminds me a bit of Bancroft. They had similar rankings: on the borderline of the Hall, if not a bit under it. Both were good contributors to great teams, Kelley on the 1890s Baltimore Orioles, and Bancroft on the 1920s Giants.

Kelley's team trumps Bancroft's, though. The 1890s Baltimore Orioles were a monumental team in baseball history. They were the Bad News Bears all grown up and committing misdemeanors. Manager Ned Hanlon taught Kelley and fellow HOFers John McGraw, Willie Keeler, Wilbert Robinson, and Hughie Jennings how to:

- Scream at umpires with strings of curses that no other team could match
- Yank the belts of opposing baserunners to slow them down
- Plant balls in the high grass of the outfield so they could pick them up after a hit and throw them to the infield

Perhaps the worst offender was the Orioles' groundskeeper, Tom Murphy. Murphy put a hard, concrete-like substance in front of home plate of the Baltimore park, so that Oriole hitters could slap the ball down and watch it bounce high and long enough for them to scamper to first. This became known as the "Baltimore chop."

Murphy also sprinkled bits of soap in the dirt behind the pitchers' mound. Opposing pitchers would grab at the dirt, hoping to dry their hands, only to find them instead greased up by the soap. It's hard to imagine that these sort of strategies weren't dictated or at least condoned by Hanlon and the rest of the Orioles' brain trust. (Source for these stories: "Level Playing Fields: How the Groundskeeping Murphy Brothers Shaped Baseball," by Peter Morris, pages 34-46, University of Nebraska Press, 2013)

Even if you hate the poor sportsmanship, you have to love the ingenuity. And not everything Hanlon espoused was beyond the pale. He also taught his players the hit-and-run and the importance of cut-off men, which were brand-new strategies in the 1890s. In a time when most hitters slapped away at whatever they saw, Orioles hitters found other ways to win. Shortstop Hughie Jennings, as we know, was an all-time hit-by-pitch machine. Third baseman John McGraw, before his managerial career, was one of the best ever at drawing walks. By using every trick in the book and inventing new ones, the Orioles won the pennant every year from 1894-1896. Joe Kelley was great during all those seasons.

Kelley was the Paul McCartney of the bunch, the cute, amiable one whom the girls loved. A section of the left field bleachers in Baltimore was named "Kelleyville" because it was always filled with admiring female fans. Kelley enjoyed the attention and kept a mirror and comb in his back pocket during games.

Like many from the Orioles, Kelley went on to manage and spread the Oriole Way throughout baseball. He had some success, but not nearly as much as McGraw, Robinson, and Jennings did. Kelley also served as team captain of the Orioles, which was no small role in those days.

I look at the sum total of Joe Kelley and I gotta say, it looks OK. Maybe he's a Ron Cey, the least of a bumper crop at his position and era. But if Ron Cey were in, I'd probably give him a pass. I might not have campaigned to include Joe Kelley in the Hall of Fame, but I'm also not going to campaign to kick him out. He can stay.

Ralph Kiner (1946-1955; career OPS+: 149)

	Career	Rank	Hitting	Rank	Fielding	Rank	Peak	Rank	Bests	JAWS	Rank
WAR	49.3	26	54.2	19	-10.8	84	43.8	9	0	46.6	19
WS	241.9	44	196.1	45	22.9	111	196.9	20	0	NA	18

When Ralph Kiner was elected to the Hall of Fame, people were scandalized. His career was short, only 10 years and 6,256 PAs. He was a bad fielder. His teams were always terrible, first the Pirates and then the Cubs.

But man, the guy could hit. He topped the National League in home runs every year from 1946-1952, twice exceeding 50. He had six straight years of more than 100 walks, leading the league twice. In 1947, 1949, and 1951 he led the N.L. in both OPS and OPS+. He ended with four years above 30 Win Shares and three years above 8.0 WAR.

Part of Kiner's P.R. problem came because his ability and character were thoroughly denigrated by his own general manager, Branch Rickey. Rickey, of course, was a genius, the founder of the modern farm system and the man who brought Jackie Robinson to the majors. He was smart enough to know that having Kiner on a terrible team like the 1940s Pirates was like putting foie gras on a Big Mac; it's just a waste of great stuff. You're better off trying to swap your foie gras for some young, unproven geese and then force-feeding the Big Mac to them (I think my metaphor broke down).

The age-old "foie gras/Big Mac strategy," as it's commonly known, is always a tricky one, because you still have fans to please. You want them coming to the park for something. If all you're offering is Big Macs every day, they're going to say, "well, to heck with you jive turkeys -- I'll just stay home and make my own Big Macs with my Big Mac machine." Or, to put it in a way that makes sense, the Pirates upper management didn't want to see how the fans would react if the only exciting player on the team were traded for a bunch of dumb ol' prospects that they had never heard of.

So Branch Rickey's brainstorm was to convince everyone that Kiner wasn't so great. Then, he thought, people would be OK with trading him. It was a strange strategy, but eventually he got his wish. In 1953 he sent Kiner and a bunch of guys to the Cubs for a bunch of other guys and cash. Unfortunately, it didn't work, as the Pirates' haul amounted to a stack of dirty pickle slices at best. The Pirates got even worse throughout the 1950s.

One of Rickey's criticisms, sincere or no, was that Kiner was a one-dimensional player. A lot of people felt this way. In the "five-tool" system, Kiner scores high on one, power, and medium on another, for logging pretty good batting averages. But the "five-tool" system should really be changed to the "six-tool" system, which adds plate discipline. When someone scores an A+ in two tools, as Kiner did, he can deserve the Hall.

Heinie Manush (1923-1939; career OPS+: 121)

	Career	Rank	Hitting	Rank	Fielding	Rank	Peak	Rank	Bests	JAWS	Rank
WAR	45.8	31	45.9	27	-7.7	65	34.6	32	0	40.2	31
WS	284.6	31	225.8	33	34.9	43	182.6	35	2	NA	30

Ugh, Heinie Manush. How did I get myself in a position where I have to delve into the trivial details of obscure dead baseball players, i.e., Manush-iae? Get it? "Manush-iae" and "minutiae"? HA HA HA HA ... hey, if you liked that one, pick up my next book, called "Puns Involving Obscure Baseball Players and Synonyms for 'Trivial Details.'" It's a pretty quick read.

Heinie Manush is another Chick Hafey, except with a longer career. Both picked a very good time to be very good, but not truly great, left fielders. Manush ended with a .330 lifetime batting average over 8419 PAs, but had little power and didn't walk much. His career .379 OBP and .479 SLG was good for a 121 OPS+, which, in context, is comparable to Jose Cruz Sr. (.284/.354/.420, 120 OPS+) and Rusty Staub (.279/.362/.431, 124 OPS+). In WAR among left fielders, Manush is just above Brian Downing. Bill James ranks him just below Jose Cruz. These are certainly good players, but not Hall-of-Famers.

Manush's example demonstrates that not everyone hated Ty Cobb. As manager of the Tigers, Cobb taught Manush to hit the way Cobb did (and thus, of course, the Right Way for Everyone, in Cobb's mind). For Manush, it worked, and the two became quite close. With Cobb managing him, Manush flourished; under other managers, he floundered.

They also had similar personalities, i.e., mean. Unlike Cobb, who found very creative ways to be a horrible human being, Manush was more of a boilerplate one. He would scream wildly at umpires and loved to spike opposing players. Yawn. Par for the course.

While it does warm at least one cockle of my heart that even Ty Cobb can have a friend, that doesn't make Heinie Manush a Hall-of-Famer. **He is out.**

Joe Medwick (1932-1948; career OPS+: 134)

	Career	Rank	Hitting	Rank	Fielding	Rank	Peak	Rank	Bests	JAWS	Rank
WAR	55.5	18	51.1	22	-4.9	39	39.7	16	4	47.6	17
WS	310.2	22	239.9	29	37.1	34	202.6	15	3	NA	13

Do not, I repeat DO NOT call Joe Medwick "Ducky." It was his main nickname, but he hated it. A female fan once looked at him and swoonily said "Ooh, isn't he the Ducky Wucky?" For whatever reason, the name stuck.

I hesitate to register a dissent on a subject in which I am far from an expert, but I've seen pictures of Medwick, and I would be hard pressed to call him even *a* Ducky Wucky, much less *the* Ducky Wucky. I suppose I'm more of a Lou Boudreau guy.

Apart from that one fan, Ducky Wucky was not well-likedy. In fact, he was downright hatedy watedy. He was very aggressive, both on the field and off. Playing for the Gas House Gang Cardinals in the 1934 World Series, he slid so hard into Tigers third baseman Marv Owen that Detroit fans started pelting garbage at him. It got so ugly that the commissioner, Kenesaw Mountain Landis, ordered that both Medwick and Owen be pulled from the game.

As a hitter he was a bit like Vladimir Guerrero. Medwick would swing at everything he saw and almost always made some kind of contact. When the contact was square, it was powerful, resulting in home runs and high batting averages. I'll mention that he won the Triple Crown in 1937, even though I think the Triple Crown is based on a pretty arbitrary selection of stats. More importantly, Medwick had 40 Win Shares and 8.5 WAR that year.

Ducky Wucky Shmoopie Poo had several other great seasons with the 1930s Cardinals and then alternated between good and poor years with a bunch of clubs. The grand total is Hall-of-Fame level.

Jim O'Rourke (1872-1893, 1904; career OPS+: 134)

	Career	Rank	Hitting	Rank	Fielding	Rank	Peak	Rank	Bests	JAWS	Rank
WAR	51.3	22	56.5	17	-10.1	80	24.2	70	5	37.8	38
WS	305.1	23	258.8	21	45.1	22	146.1	63	4	NA	37

Remember Deacon White? He was the third baseman who looked bad at first, but if you take the context of the 1870s into account, turns out to be a deserving member of the Hall. Same deal with O'Rourke, except more so. O'Rourke even ranks OK in the career numbers, despite spending his 20s in leagues that played 80 games or fewer per year. If his leagues played full seasons before his 33rd birthday, his Peak numbers would be much higher.

Plus, if you love your Hall-of-Famers coming from good teams, O'Rourke is your man. Granted, his first team, the 1872 Middletown Mansfields, was not good, going 5-19 the entire season. (Despite housing the lovely Wesleyan University, it turns out that Middletown, Connecticut may not be a prime spot for a major-league baseball team.) But in 1873 he joined the Boston Red Stockings, a team that went 43-19. In 1874 they improved further, finishing 52-18. And in 1875, they left those shameful years of double-digit losses behind, sporting a ripe 71-8 record.

O'Rourke didn't create these win-loss records alone. The team included almost everyone worth knowing from the 1870s, including Hall-of-Famers Deacon White, George Wright, Harry Wright, and Al Spalding. Their success sparked a baseball mania across the country that was partially responsible for making professional baseball a viable enterprise. Without the 1870s Boston Red Stockings, it's hard to say what baseball would be like today.

Jim O'Rourke was the team's oddball, in a loveable way. His nickname was "Orator Jim" because of his love of flowery speeches. He would regularly recite Shakespearean soliloquies for his teammates before games.

O'Rourke's love of language extended to the written word. Once, he read a popular news story about a woman who protected her cows against a lion that had escaped from the zoo. This inspired O'Rourke to write the woman a letter which began:

"The unparalleled bravery shown by you, and the unwavering fidelity extended by you to your calf during your precarious environment in the cowshed, when a ferocious, carnivorous beast threatened your total destruction, has suddenly exalted your fair name to an altitude much higher than the Egyptian pyramids, where hieroglyphics and other undecipherable mementos of the past are now lying in a state of innocuous desuetude, with no enlightened modern scholar able to exemplify their disentangled pronunciation." ("The New Bill James Historical Baseball Abstract," p. 677)

Wait, Jim, why are we now talking about hieroglyphics, exactly? So you can show off some stuff you just read about Egypt? Or did you make a bet with someone that you could work the word "desuetude" into the first sentence?

That's a modern bias talking, of course. In those days, listening to and reading over-the-top grandiloquence were major sources of entertainment. Have you ever seen the video of DeWolf Hopper reciting "Casey at the Bat"? It made him a big vaudeville star. But at the end of watching it I was surprised that there was unchewed scenery left in the country.

Anyway, later in life, O'Rourke became a great leader, both a stern taskmaster and an expansive father figure for his players. He defied the often virulent stereotypes of the day by being an Irishman who didn't smoke or drink. But he was far from a stick-in-the-mud; his massive mustache often quivered with large, robust laughter.

O'Rourke was brilliant and full of energy. Like his friend John Montgomery Ward, O'Rourke got his law degree in the off seasons, at Yale. And like Ward, he fought hard against owners' attempts to impose the reserve clause and set caps for ballplayer salaries. Both men also managed and ran teams and then ran leagues. In 1896, O'Rourke established a minor league in his home state of Connecticut, serving as both league president and starting catcher for its Bridgeport squad. He played his last game in 1912, at the age of 62.

Bill James' overall ranking of O'Rourke is low, but then he ranks everyone from the 1800s low. I don't know just how many players from the 1870s need to be in the Hall of Fame, but Jim O'Rourke definitely should be.

Jim Rice (1974-1989; career OPS+: 128)

	Career	Rank	Hitting	Rank	Fielding	Rank	Peak	Rank	Bests	JAWS	Rank
WAR	47.4	28	45.0	29	-8.6	73	36.1	27	4	41.8	27
WS	279.8	34	243.9	27	35.5	39	183	34	1	NA	27

The selection of Jim Rice for the Hall of Fame in 2009 was a controversial one. Detractors noted that he was always overrated, scoring well in flashy numbers like RBI and batting average while lacking in a lot of other less-celebrated ways. Boosters said he "was the most feared hitter of his time." They said that a lot.

Whenever you hear a vague, unprovable assertion like "the most feared hitter of his time," be skeptical. I interpret that phrase as meaning "He feels like a Hall-of-Famer to me, so here's some made-up reason to justify that feeling." What exactly does it mean that Rice was the most-feared hitter of his time? Are you sure he really was the most feared? And even if he were, is that really a reason to elect him to the Hall?

If Rice really were so fearsome, it was presumably because he could do things to beat you and win games. If fear-inducing-ness does not translate to results on the field, then it's irrelevant to any Hall of Fame consideration. It would be like inducting someone to the Hall for being the most handsome player. The point of baseball is to win games, not to make pitchers or ladies swoon.

And the results on the field can be measured by stats. Let's try to turn "most feared hitter of his time" into something provable, something that we can put some stats behind. Barry Bonds, for example, was so feared at the end of his career that he was intentionally walked an incredible number of times. Jim Rice got a respectable number of international walks, but never led the league, and only three times finished in the top ten in the AL. But then, he was usually followed by another great hitter, so maybe that's not fair.

Maybe "most-feared" has something to do with power. It has to be about power, right? Granted, if I were a pitcher, I'd be very afraid of Rickey Henderson or Tim Raines. But speed and on-base ability are not conventionally thought of as fear-inducing the way power is.

And I'm going to take "of his time" as meaning the heart of Rice's career, from 1975-1986. In that time period, Rice was third in the MLB in home runs, far behind Mike Schmidt and a bit behind Dave Kingman. That means Rice was pretty powerful.

But the fact that Dave Kingman beats him in this measure means that it's not a good one for Hall-of-Fame consideration. That is, Dave Kingman might have gotten some pitchers a-quakin' in their boots, but he wasn't a Hall-of-Famer to anyone besides his momma. The next three on the home run list in that period are Reggie Jackson (certain HOFer), George Foster (not bad, but no thank you) and Don Baylor (what's the nicest way to put this ...) Let's try something else.

What about slugging percentage as a measure of "most feared" instead? From 1975-1986, Rice was second in slugging percentage (among players with at least 3000 PAs), behind only Schmidt. Now we're talking. Next on the list is George Brett (yes please, and can I have some more?), Pedro Guerrero (amazing hitter who just didn't have the longevity for the Hall … and perhaps not the brains, if his lawyer is to be believed[31]) and Bob Horner (definitely not a Hall-of-Famer).

---

[31] Pedro Guerrero: great hitter, one of the best of the 1980s, but perhaps not the sharpest knife in the stack of pancakes. In 1999, Guerrero somehow got involved in bankrolling a 15-kilogram cocaine deal. It turned out to be a sting operation, and Guerrero was arrested and put on trial. He got a top-notch defense lawyer, whose main argument was that Guerrero's IQ was so low that he couldn't have known what was going on. It worked, and Guerrero was acquitted. It's debatable that Guerrero was really that dumb, but let's just say that that argument wouldn't have worked if Neil deGrasse Tyson were on the stand.

That's still not a wild endorsement; usually you like to see a guy surrounded by Hall of Famers in these sorts of charts. But we've established that Rice was a very good slugger in what I like to call the "Star Wars" era, i.e. the late 1970s and early 1980s. (It could also be the Muppet era, or the punk/new wave era, if you prefer.) So that's something.

But still, is that a real qualification for the Hall of Fame? If you move forward a decade and isolate 1985-1996, the top three players in slugging percentage are Frank Thomas, Albert Belle and Juan Gonzalez. Thomas is a clear HOFer, while Belle and Gonzalez were good sluggers a few notches below Hall-of-Fame level. If you'd rather go by total home runs in that period, you get Joe Carter at number one. Again, a good slugger, but not a Hall-of-Famer.

I've run through a lot of guys who were good at hitting home runs. But many, especially Dave Kingman, couldn't do much else. A fear-inducing slugger can certainly be Hall-worthy if he does other things besides hitting home runs. He needs to draw walks, play defense, exhibit speed ... but Rice was not great at any of those.

Sometimes Rice's batting averages were high, and in those years he got on base a respectable amount. But when his BA dipped below .300, his OBPs got pretty poor. His defense was always lacking, leading to lots of games at DH.

Early in his career, Rice would hit tons of triples, even leading the league during his MVP season of 1978. But he was also prolific at grounding into double plays (GIDPs), which might seem like a junk stat but sometimes isn't. GIDPs are terrible rally-killers, not only causing two outs but also erasing a baserunner. The only worse thing you can do in a batter's box is to hit into a triple play while tripping over your own feet and causing a small earthquake that snaps the rotator cuff of every pitcher in your team's dugout.

Most players don't ground into double plays often enough to really make a difference in their overall value. But Rice definitely did. He has the two highest seasonal totals in history: 36 in 1984 and 35 in 1985. His 31 GIDPs in 1983 is tied for 8th-highest all time. As Hughie Jennings was to HBPs, Jim Rice was to GIDPs. That's not good.

Like Bobby Doerr, Rice was very much a creature of Fenway Park. At home, Rice hit .320/.374/.546, while in away games he was at .277/.330/.459. A run at home is still a run, as I said in the Doerr comment, but I should qualify that by saying that in a high-scoring environment, a run is worth slightly less than a run in a regular environment. All this stuff is baked into both WAR and Win Shares, and the overall rankings of each show Rice at the wrong side of 25.

Speaking of WAR and Win Shares, what do they say about Rice's seasonal totals? Both agree he really was great in his 1978 MVP season, with 7.6 WAR and 36 Win Shares. He got four other WARs above 5 and six other Win Shares totals above 20. It's not a total that compares well to other Hall-of-Famers, but it could be a lot worse.

What about "It's the Hall of Fame, not the Hall of Stats"? Well, Rice got in the Hall largely on his stats, specifically, the Triple-Crown ones that people overvalue. Still, fame does count for something, and Rice was quite famous.

Post-season? Rice was great in the 1986 World Series but poor in the 1986 and 1988 ALCSs. On balance, his playoff record doesn't add or detract a lot from his qualifications.

I would never vote for Rice to enter the Hall. But as with Tony Perez and Orlando Cepeda (both of whom were super-duper-feared, I bet), I don't know if Rice is enough of a disgrace to the Hall of Fame to warrant being kicked out. With "It's the Hall of Fame, not the Hall of Stats" giving Rice the tiniest boost up, I'll begrudgingly, hesitantly, uncomfortably, and perhaps regrettably let him stay.

Al Simmons (1924-1941, 1943-1944; career OPS+: 133)

	Career	Rank	Hitting	Rank	Fielding	Rank	Peak	Rank	Bests	JAWS	Rank
WAR	68.7	9	62.3	12	-1.4	15	45.7	7	5	57.2	8
WS	374.0	12	297.8	14	67.0	3	215.0	8	4	NA	7

In the first chapter, I mentioned that Aloys Szymanski was a little less effective than Carl Yastrzemski despite having much better-looking conventional numbers. But if you're a little less than Yaz, you can still be one of the best hitters in baseball history.

Siz, as I call him (only his close personal friends get to call him that), was a dominant hitter of the 1920s and 1930s. He starred on one of the greatest teams ever, the 1929-1931 Philadelphia A's, which also featured Jimmie Foxx, Mickey Cochrane and Lefty Grove. The A's reached the World Series each of those years, winning twice. From 1920-1964, there's really no other true AL dynasty, besides of course the Yankees about a zillion times. If you're loose with your definition of "dynasty," you could include the 1924-1925 Senators, or maybe the 1934-1935 Tigers. Otherwise, it's just a 45-year period of Yankees, Yankees, Yankees with one interlude of A's.

Like Jesse Burkett, Heinie Manush, and Joe Medwick, Al Simmons was a jerk. He always played as if he were motivated by some insane rage and was condescending to anyone not at his level of achievement, i.e. almost everybody. What is it with left fielders? Jim Rice was not known for a sunny disposition. Rickey was misunderstood, but still hard to get along with. Kiner was never popular among his colleagues. Brock and Irvin were nice, but they were exceptions. The point is, if your kid can hit and is also a complete jackass, teach him left field.

Fun fact: I mentioned in the Goose Goslin comment that the Senators' home park, Griffith Stadium, was an absurdly difficult place to hit a home run. It was built in 1911 with home run alleys more than 400 feet from home plate, and it wasn't until 1954 when a secondary fence was built to shorten the distances. In that 45-year period, only two Senators hit 20 home runs in a season: Al Simmons and Zeke Bonura. They both did it in 1938, both in very brief tenures with the Senators. Both barely passed the mark: Simmons hit 21 and Bonura hit 22. Good ol' Zeke somehow managed to hit 11 at home, which was an all-time record at Griffith. No one else ever managed more than seven homers in a season there.

Imagine if your team tried playing in a stadium like this in the Steroid Era of the 1990s and 2000s. Maybe you'd have a great advantage in a "counterprogramming" sort of way. You could stockpile line drive hitters and speedy outfielders, a la the 1980s Cardinals. You could also get a lot of mileage out of extreme fly-ball pitchers. These players would not be in high demand among all the other slug-happy teams, so maybe you could get them for cheap. And all the pull hitters playing for your opponents would launch lots of harmless long outs in your 400-foot power alleys.

But then, strategies exploiting park effects are usually double-edged swords. Your team of slap-happy speedsters and homer-prone pitchers would do horribly in all the bandboxes on the road. The history of the Rockies demonstrates the problem with having a home park out of whack with the rest of the league. Colorado has always done well at home but badly in road games, worse than you would expect. Maybe it's hard for players to adjust to such drastically different conditions throughout the year.

Also, as the general manager of the 1990s-2000s Washington Senators at Griffith Stadium, you would be hamstrung by needing a very specific type of player. You want to draft the best player available, like any other GM. But instead you'd have to go for the best hitter who doesn't hit home runs, or pitcher who gives up lots of fly balls. Plus, opposing general managers would quickly realize your limitations, and demand too much for any speedster/fly-ball pitcher you'd want to obtain. Not to mention that no home run hitter or ground ball-pitcher would ever want to sign with your club as a free agent. In the end, the disadvantages might outweigh the advantages.

So that discussion somehow proves that Al Simmons is a Hall-of-Famer. Next.

Willie Stargell (1962-1982; career OPS+: 147)

	Career	Rank	Hitting	Rank	Fielding	Rank	Peak	Rank	Bests	JAWS	Rank
WAR	57.5	17	63.8	11	-19.8	96	37.8	19	1	47.7	16
WS	374.0	12	339.1	7	31.4	54	200.7	17	4	NA	9

A 147 OPS+ -- wow. That's so some top-notch stuff. Top-notch, top-shelf, top-drawer, top-dog. Stargell has a career OPS+ that is bested by only four left fielders in history (minimum 5000 PAs): Ted Williams, Barry Bonds, Ed Delahanty and Ralph Kiner. Yes, OPS+ is biased toward power hitters and thus gives players like Rickey Henderson short shrift. Still, Stargell's is higher than I expected.

Stargell hit loads of home runs in the 1960s and 1970s, a very difficult time for hitters. Plus, his early years were spent in the sluggers' graveyard of Forbes Field. After Three Rivers Stadium was built in 1970, Stargell started smashing home runs like no one else in baseball.

Stargell's SABR biography is pretty fascinating; I recommend you read it by visiting his page on baseball-reference.com and then clicking "View Player Bio." It depicts a complex man, one who endured a difficult, underprivileged childhood to have a rocky but ultimately fulfilling major-league career. In his early days, his weight would fluctuate, and he would always sit out for a dozen or so games per year with minor injuries. He displayed incredible talent but had a few major holes in his game, such as poor defense and an inability to hit left-handers.

Throughout the 1970s, he got better and better. When players become superstars, they are expected to be leaders, even if they don't actually have leadership qualities. Stargell, to some people's surprise, proved to have those qualities in spades. In 1973, Pirate ace pitcher Steve Blass came down with what is now called "Steve Blass disease," a psychological block that caused him to throw wildly. Stargell would stand in against him in batting practice with no batting helmet or other protection of any kind. Through his actions, Stargell was telling Blass "Hit me in the arm, the head, whatever. I don't care. I believe you can do it." It meant the world to Blass (though sadly, it did not push him past his psychological impediment).

In the Pirates' World-Series-winning season of 1979, Stargell was 39 years old and was a father figure to his teammates like few players have ever been, before or since. He would give gold stars to players who made particularly good plays. They would display those gold stars on their uniforms with incredible pride. This was the main reason he won the MVP that year (tied with Keith Hernandez). In my estimation, it's one of the few times that those amorphous "intangibles" actually made someone more valuable than their stats would suggest.

Stargell didn't live long past his retirement, dying of a stroke at age 61 in 2001. He is certainly a Hall-of-Famer.

Zach Wheat (1909-1927; career OPS+: 129)

	Career	Rank	Hitting	Rank	Fielding	Rank	Peak	Rank	Bests	JAWS	Rank
WAR	60.2	15	54.6	18	-7.0	60	34.7	31	1	47.5	18
WS	380.2	10	322.0	12	58.0	7	199.1	19	1	NA	23

Zach Wheat is the Fred Clarke of the Dodgers: You may not have heard of him, but he was a terrific dead-ball left fielder for one N.L. team for a very long time. Neither Wheat nor Clarke had super-flashy stats, but were always well above average, finishing among the league leaders many times in many categories.

Wheat actually came an entire generation after Clarke, who had his last full season in 1911. Instead of indulging in the batters' party of the naughty 1890s, Wheat got to dance the Charleston and drink bootleg gin through the hitters' hootenanny of the 1920s. He took full advantage of the lively ball, having all three of his 200-hit seasons and his only two 100-RBI seasons after his 33rd birthday. Even when you account for context, Wheat was terrific as an oldster. In 1924, at the age of 36, he logged 35 Win Shares and 6.7 WAR.

The overall rankings are too low for Wheat, in my view. Per usual, Bill James ranks the old-timer well below where he would be just based on Career and Peak rankings: Wheat's WSAWS is 11th. And it's not a case of Bill James' definition of peak (five years) yielding different rankings than my and WAR's (seven years): Wheat didn't have five great seasons that stood out from the rest.

WAR is off the mark on defense, per usual. Zach Wheat was always considered a terrific defender, an assessment that Win Shares agrees with.

Time for some fun facts. Wheat had a Cherokee mother and a father who was a direct descendant of Puritans who settled in Massachusetts in 1635. The Cherokee part was more interesting to the baseball world than the Puritan part. In the deadball era, Native Americans were seen as athletically superior by nature. The casual racism also extended to nicknames; every player with Native American ancestry was known as "Chief." There were Chief Wilson, Chief Meyers, Chief Bender, etc.

This was also the time of Jim Thorpe, possibly the greatest athlete of the 20th century. Thorpe grew up in the Sac and Fox Nation and went on to win gold medals in the 1912 Olympics for pentathlon and decathlon. He then played professional football, basketball, and baseball, logging some league-average performances with the New York Giants.

In fact, John McGraw once tried to employ an African-American player by passing him off as a Native American. Charlie Grant (no relation to Hall-of-Fame second baseman Frank Grant) was a solid second baseman who played with Hall-of-Famers Pop Lloyd, Rube Foster and Sol White. Since Grant was relatively well-known, it didn't take the newspapers long to figure out the ruse. So Grant never got to play in the majors. It's the kind of thing that makes you love John McGraw. One great thing about being obsessed with winning by every possible means, like McGraw was, is that you tend to not care about irrelevant things like a person's skin color.

Anyway, this is about Zack Wheat. He was a mild-mannered, generous fellow, defying the stereotype (that I made up) of jerkface left fielders. For fun and profit, he raised livestock in the off-seasons. Because he made a good living on his farm, he could hold out for more money before every season and not worry about feeding his family. It worked year after year because he was so good and so beloved by Brooklyn fans that the team couldn't consider letting him go. Definite Hall-of-Famer.

Billy Williams (1959-1976; career OPS+: 133)

	Career	Rank	Hitting	Rank	Fielding	Rank	Peak	Rank	Bests	JAWS	Rank
WAR	63.5	12	66.2	9	-18.2	94	41.5	12	2	52.5	12
WS	374.2	11	329.1	11	45.1	21	208.3	14	1	NA	11

Billy Williams was yet another left fielder in the Zack Wheat/Fred Clarke mold, playing very well for a long time but seldom looking like an MVP candidate. Williams actually finished second in the MVP race twice, in 1970 and 1972. Each season Williams had more than 120 RBIs, which tends to flip a little switch in the minds of baseball writers that activates the "MVP candidate" circuits of their programming. Williams wasn't the second-best player in the league either year, according to either Win Shares or WAR, but whatever. He wasn't far off either time, and in both years the Cubs finished above .500.

In fact, the Cubs had a pretty good little run in the late 1960s and early 1970s. They had Williams, Ron Santo, and Fergie Jenkins, and finished second in 1969, 1970, and 1972. In 1969, they won 92 games, and you have to wonder if they could have closed the gap if they hadn't left the desiccated remains of Ernie Banks at first base all year (92 OPS+, -0.7 WAR, 14 Win Shares). But hey, he was a nice guy, and had a cute catchphrase, so that's what's important.

Unlike Banks, Billy Williams had a very ungainly nickname, "Sweet Swingin' Billy from Whistler." At least that's what Baseball-reference.com says; I doubt anyone ever called him that in real life. "Hey Sweet Swinging Billy from Whistler, you want to take a few hacks?" It doesn't exactly roll off the tongue.

It's not really that kind of nickname, of course. It's one of those nicknames that sportswriters make up so they can wax eloquent. Those can be fun; my favorite is probably Bob "Death to Flying Things" Ferguson. For a while every great player had one of these. Mickey Mantle was "The Commerce Comet," because he was from Commerce, Oklahoma and ran fast. Ted Williams was "The Splendid Splinter" because he very good and was thin. (As a kid I thought he was known as the Splendid Splinter*er*, meaning that he would splinter bats when he made contact. My point is that I was a stupid kid.)

But I don't think those kind of names should be called nicknames. Nicknames are quick, familiar things you can call someone to their face. They can run two syllables, maybe three maximum. Old Hoss, Cool Papa, Fat Elvis, Pig-Pen, Dutch, Lefty, Tiny -- those are nicknames. Those long, labored birthplace-heavy names are strictly for the written word, to be used only by sportswriters so tired of writing the same thing over and over that out of pure desperation they search for something new. "Let's see … where is the guy from … Whistler? What else starts with 'W' … 'Whammer'? 'The Whistler Whammer?' That sounds like a toy by Wham-O. 'Whistler's Father'? That doesn't really make sense. Winger? Wanderer? Wuuuuh … screw it! 'Billy Williams Who is From Whistler'! Wait ... 'Sweet Swingin' Billy From Whistler'? Good enough; I'm tired."

Hey, I empathize; I've written enough of these profiles that now I'm left to yakkin' about nicknames. On that note, Billy "Sweet Swingin' Billy Williams Who Was Born In Whistler, Alabama" Williams is a Hall-of-Famer.

Ted Williams (1939-1942, 1946-1960; career OPS+: 190)

	Career	Rank	Hitting	Rank	Fielding	Rank	Peak	Rank	Bests	JAWS	Rank
WAR	123.1	2	126.3	2	-13.4	90	69.3	2	9	96.2	2
WS	556.6	2	512.3	2	44.0	25	298.9	2	9	NA	1

Ted Williams is a baseball god. He used his incredible intelligence to devise and implement a scientific hitting approach far beyond that of any other player. He knew the intricacies of every pitcher's approach, and often criticized pitchers for not being as analytical as he was. His extreme sensitivity to every detail extended to bat weights: When presented with four bats, one of which was 33 ½ ounces and three of which were 34 ounces, Williams could identify the lighter one every time.

Modern perspectives only make Williams look better, because he was the hands-down all-time greatest at getting on base. He holds the all-time career record for OBP, with .482. That includes three full seasons with OBPs above .500 and five others above .490, and he did not play during an especially high-offense era. He got plenty of criticism for his patience at the plate, but he ignored it, knowing that on balance, his approach won more games.

Williams was so good at drawing walks that he brought about a change in the rules about batting titles. In 1954, he hit .345 while Bobby Avila hit .341. The rules at the time stated that you needed 400 at-bats to qualify for a batting title. Williams didn't manage 400 at-bats, but he did draw 136 walks, leading to 526 PAs. Now you need 502 PAs to qualify for the batting title.

In the midst of all this, Williams spent a remarkable amount of his prime playing years in the military. He could have opted out of service in World War II entirely, because he was the sole financial support for his mother. Instead, he enlisted. He could have fulfilled the same role as many ballplayers did during the war, playing ballgames to boost morale. Instead, he signed up to become a Navy pilot. He got so good that he was given the job of instructing other pilots throughout the war. From 1942-1945, he spent prime ball-playing ages 24 through 26 serving his country in one of the most challenging ways available to him.

In 1952, the Korean War began. Ballplayers were not expected to enlist, but Williams was the exception. Along with other experienced pilots, Williams was recalled and put into active duty. He was far from pleased to leave baseball, but he complied with orders and flew 39 combat missions. On his third mission, his jet was hit and he crash-landed. He was rescued and flew again at 8:08 the next morning.

While it's true that Ted Williams was a great American hero and a mind-bogglingly great baseball player, it's also true that when Williams was playing, he was kind of a jerk. He came up to the majors full of cockiness, which tends to alienate people quickly. Even if you're not naturally humble, you kinda have to pretend you are. Williams didn't have the sense or the patience to engage in the pretense necessary to play nice on a public stage, and the Boston press and fans got on his case right away.

Then, when he demonstrated that he was the greatest hitter who ever lived, the press and fans tried to warm to him. But Williams would not let those early slights go. Throughout his career, he refused to ever talk to any member of the media, often spitting at any newsman who dared come near him. And he refused to ever tip his hat to fans, no matter how much they cheered.

Williams would later regret his tendency to nurse grudges indefinitely. He mellowed in retirement and devoted himself to worthy pursuits. He became an ace sports fisherman and raised millions for cancer care and research. In 1966 he was inducted in the Hall of Fame and used his speech to advocate Negro League players being admitted to the Hall. The powerful public statement jump-started a movement that culminated in Satchel Paige becoming the first Negro Leaguer selected, in 1971.

Before the 1999 All-Star Game in Boston, Williams was brought out in a golf cart and received a massive ovation. He tipped his cap to the fans, like he had never done before. It proved especially touching when the All-Star players spontaneously crowded around Williams. Unusually for the All-Star Game, it was genuine moment, instead of a preordained "Moment" carefully orchestrated by the MLB. Ted made sure to get in a good, fatherly chat with Tony Gwynn, the player who most embodied his scientific hitting approach. The old grudges were wiped from everyone's memory. Williams was the living king of baseball. If he weren't in the Hall of Fame, they would have to shut the place down.

Carl Yastrzemski (1961-1983; career OPS+: 130)

	Career	Rank	Hitting	Rank	Fielding	Rank	Peak	Rank	Bests	JAWS	Rank
WAR	96.1	4	77.7	6	0.3	10	55.4	4	6	75.8	4
WS	487.5	45	426.0	4	61.7	5	220.0	7	3	NA	5

When I was a kid, I remember reading a criticism of Yastrzemski that said he seldom hit .300 and often had unimpressive-looking seasonal stats. I looked at his record, and by gum, they were right! He never even had 200 hits in a season! Despite having 3419 career hits, his lifetime BA was .285! Meh! Feh! Other vaguely derisive words!

I was young then, so of course I was stupid. That kind of goes without saying. People are always stupid when they're young. It's not their fault -- they just haven't been around long enough to learn stuff.

Old people can be stupid too, especially when they think that the new crop of young people are stupider than they were. Yeah, those kids are stupid, but so were you at that age. You just don't remember, because your memory has a built-in sugar-coater.

Anyway, now that I'm a wizened elder statesman, I can recognize that Yastrzemski was incredible, and that his numbers only look modest because of the context. He was a top hitter of the Modern Dead-Ball Era, which spanned roughly 1963-1976. In that period, Yaz had the best WAR among non-pitchers, his 80.4 beating Hank Aaron's total by more than two wins. Win Shares comes close to concurring, putting Yaz just below Pete Rose and Hank Aaron. Yaz achieved this with good power, great defense, and the 2nd best OBP from 1963-1976, behind Joe Morgan (minimum 3000 PAs).

In the introduction, which you read and memorized and recite every night in a dramatic soliloquy like I asked you to, I talked about Yaz's amazing 1968 season, one of the top 50 all time among non-pitchers according to WAR. Win Shares scores it a 39, superb but just barely in the top 100 of all time.

Both systems prefer Yaz's 1967 season. That year he earned 42 Win Shares and 12.4 WAR, which is fourth all-time, behind three Babe Ruth seasons. He hit .326/.418/.622 in a league that averaged .236/.303/.351. He also led the Red Sox to a then-rare league championship. They lost the World

Series, of course, but it was still a magical year for desperate, devoted Red Sox fans. As with fellow Red Soxer Ted Williams, the Hall of Fame wouldn't be worth its charter without Carl Yastrzemski.

Who's In, Who's Out

Predictably, we found a few 1920s/1930s players who don't hold up to modern scrutiny. Chick Hafey and Heinie Manush proved unqualified. Joe Kelley and Jim Rice stayed in just because I'm a nice guy. The rest were no-doubters.

That doesn't leave us a ton of room for more left fielders. Are there any that have made a recent splash ... let's see here ...

Barry Bonds (1986-2007; career OPS+: 182)

	Career	Rank	Hitting	Rank	Fielding	Rank	Peak	Rank	Bests	JAWS	Rank
WAR	162.4	1	142.6	1	6.7	2	72.8	1	12	117.6	1
WS	712.6	1	657.2	1	55.37	8	321.5	1	11	NA	1[32]

Oh, Barry. Barry, Barry, Barry. Barry, my laddie boy, why did you have to do it? You were already so good! You were already a Hall-of-Famer, no doubt! Was it really that important to break those home run records? Was it really worth it?

While I'm reluctant to serve as judge, jury and executioner for the likes of Ivan Rodriguez and Mike Piazza, I admit that the preponderance of evidence shows that Barry Bonds used steroids after about 1998. Allegedly, he was frustrated at all the accolades accorded to Sammy Sosa, Mark McGwire, etc., and decided to dive in.

Steroids apparently turned an all-time great player into a bonkers/cuckoo-ball/bad-video-game great player. In every year from 2001-2004, Bonds had an OBP above .500 and a SLG above .700. In 2004, he drew 120 intentional walks. The previous record holder was a fellow named Barry Bonds, with 68 in 2002. The previous non-Barry Bonds record holder was Willie McCovey, with 45 in 1969. So that means Barry had almost three times as many intentional walks in a season as anyone else has. And he did this at age 39. We're through the looking glass here, people.

I gotta say, it was fun to watch. When Barry came to the plate, it was like nothing I'd ever seen. He seemed to never swing and miss. It was always either a hard hit or a walk. It must have been like watching Babe Ruth, except with a little bit of a dirty feeling because you knew something wasn't right.

So should we punish Barry for his alleged indulgence in steroids by keeping him out of the Hall? And let's not mistake it: Depriving Barry Bonds of the Hall of Fame is definitely a punishment. Some argue that election is an honor, and you can't view a refusal to give an honor as a punishment. That's just silly semantics. The standards are well established for receiving this particular honor. Barry Bonds well exceeds the established standards on every possible measure, at least on the surface. The only reason to deprive him of the honor is to punish him for this steroid use.

---

[32] WSAWS, not Bill James' ranking. James ranked Bonds third behind Ted Williams and Stan Musial, who I'm counting as a first baseman. James made this ranking after 2000, before Bonds' really bonkeroo seasons.

And I'm not against such punishments, if the person in question only became a Hall of Fame player because of steroids. As I mentioned before, it's downright impossible to tease out what is natural ability and what is steroids within a particular season. Should we chop his post-1998 totals down by 20%? 30%? Should we dock only his homers? Who knows?

Screw it - let's just lop off everything after 1998. Even 1999, which actually seems like a normal season by his standards, is gone. None of his Ruthian post-millennial seasons are included. He has to settle for his many Yastrzemskian 1990s seasons. He is left with only 13 seasons instead of 22, ending his career at 33 instead of 42. His career PAs go from 12,606 to 8,100. He drops from 762 career home runs to 411.

The point is, this is a pretty severe cut, perhaps even a bit unfairly so. This is what that looks like in terms of the Hall of Fame standards:

Barry Bonds Redux (1986-1998; career OPS+: 164)

	Career	Rank	Hitting	Rank	Fielding	Rank	Peak	Rank	Bests	JAWS	Rank
WAR	99.5	4	78.3	6	12.9	1	62.4	3	8	81.0	4
WS	418.0	5	377.6	5	38.8	30	272.2	2	7	NA	6*

So even if you cut off every clearly (allegedly) steroidal season, Bonds still shows up one of the top ten left fielders of all time. He's still well within Hall-of-Fame range. You can't say that about Mark McGwire. You might be able to say that about Rafael Palmeiro, but it's really hard to tell, because his performance didn't suddenly explode unnaturally late in career. Bonds has a relatively clear cutoff point, and when you cut it off, he is still a first-ballot Hall-of-Famer.

Maybe you don't care if he was Hall-of-Fame worthy before he started using (allegedly. But c'mon).

Maybe you think he should be punished anyway. Well, OK, but let's let the punishment fit the crime. He is already thoroughly despised, his records thrown into doubt, etc. And what was the crime? He did not try to throw a World Series. He did not try to throw a single game. Quite the opposite; he tried only to get better, by taking foreign substances (allegedly, but c'mon), and taking these substances was not really punished by baseball at the time.

That's a wrinkle that people often forget, by the way. Organized baseball, and the player's union in particular, is partially to blame for not enforcing rules against using steroids. They knew it was going on, and preferred to cover their players' ashes rather than do the right thing. There was an established tradition of looking the other way while players enhanced their performances by using illegal drugs, like the amphetamine "greenies" that Mike Schmidt freely and bravely admits to having used regularly. Steroids feel much more disturbing than greenies, since they are an injection (ick!) of terrible stuff that makes some parts of your body shrink (ick! ick!). But they are only different in degree, not kind. Anyway, I've said this before.

My point is that Bonds has already been punished in a way that fits the crime. He never tried to lose a game intentionally, which would mean an automatic disbarring. He just tried to be even better. He used extremely revolting and dangerous means to do so, which earns a punishment. But not a life sentence.

In my view, depriving Barry Bonds of the Hall of Fame is a life sentence for a player of his level of achievement. In my Hall, Bonds has a place. It might not be the most vaulted place of honor, and it might come with some asterisks. But it's still a place.

Pete Rose (1963-1986; career OPS+: 118)

	Career	Rank	Hitting	Rank	Fielding	Rank	Peak	Rank	Bests	JAWS	Rank
WAR	79.1	5	82.2	4	-14.0	91	44.8	8	2	62.0	5
WS	547.2	3	454.8	3	84.5	2	223.9	6	2	NA	5[33]

On to major Hall of Fame controversy number two. Again, the playing record is one of a no-doubt Hall-of-Famer. That's not the issue. The issue is again one of the punishment fitting the crime.

This is an important concept that tends to get lost in Hall of Fame discussions. In real life, we don't sentence people to life in prison for grand larceny. It's a serious crime, and it should mean doing some serious time. Some societies would kill a person for grand larceny, including almost all societies before the last few hundred years. But we've moved beyond that sort of thing.

Pete Rose, by all accounts, bet on his own team. He did not bet against his own team. This is the crucial distinction.

Betting on your own team is the equivalent of a felony, no doubt. It deserves a serious punishment. But it doesn't deserve a life sentence. At this point Rose has been banned from the game he loves and the Hall of Fame for more than 20 years. That's a serious enough punishment.

If he had bet *against* his own team, even for one meaningless late-season game, I'd say ban him forever. You can't discourage that kind of thing strongly enough. Before the infamous 1919 World Series, many players threw games for gamblers, and it nearly destroyed the game. It took the extreme nature of the Black Sox scandal to finally close the door on that kind of behavior. Only then could baseball thrive and grow into a true national pastime.

I don't advocate Shoeless Joe Jackson being in the Hall of Fame. Jackson participated in a conspiracy to throw a World Series. Some point to Jackson's stats in the 1919 World Series and say that he wasn't really trying to throw games. Others point to a few plays he failed to make and say that he was throwing games in a more subtle way.

Whatever. Jackson took money from gamblers to throw a World Series. In sports, that's a "life in prison" kind of crime. Morals are a little different in professional sports. It might sound bizarre to hear that morals can ever be different under any circumstance, but it's often true. It's wrong to kill people, unless you're in the military. Then it can be unquestionably be the most moral thing to do. Morals are different in different situations. That's life. It's complicated. I hope I'm not the first person to tell you this.

---

[33] James ranked Rose fifth among right fielders. Baseball-reference has him in left. He actually spent the most games at first base, but that was mostly at the end of his career when he was logging very little value. You could put him at second, or third, or team mascot, or designated hustler, or whatever -- who cares, because he clearly had a Hall-of-Fame career by the standards of any position.

In the weird and wonderful world of professional baseball, you can do all sorts of terrible things and still be "moral" enough for the Hall of Fame. You can be a racist, like Cap Anson and many others. You can be violent, like Jud Wilson. The Hall of Fame only cares about how well you made your team circle the bases more than the other team. The morality of the game arises entirely from that.

This illustrates how real life is about ten thousand times more complicated than sports. In real life, there is lots of ambiguity. There are millions of different things you have to do: You have to earn money, you have to maintain friendships, you have to make a mark in the world, you have to tip your waiter, etc. etc. And even if you do that, will you be happy? Are you doing right? Are your goals really the right ones? Who knows?

Sports are a lot simpler: All you have to do is win. This is the main reason we like sports, deep down: because they're reduced and simplified to one universally accepted goal. All you have to do is get this trophy. That's it. Incredible complexity arises from that one simple goal, but at least the goal is simple. Get that trophy, that arbitrarily chosen object. It doesn't really matter what that trophy is. It could be a rock, or a slice of ham, or a Vanilla Ice CD. The important thing is that everyone agrees that that's what you need to get, and that everyone is trying extremely hard to get it. If you end up with that trophy, it means that you were better than all the rest.

Because sports reduce everything to one simple goal, they operate in a different sort of morality. The most important thing you can do is try to make your team win. Almost all good and bad, in the context of a game, springs from that. When we talk about a "good player" or "bad player," no one thinks about whether the guy is kind to children or kicks dogs. We think about whether he hits, fields, or pitches well.

The Hall of Fame has established, through its selections, that it is about honoring the people who were best at hitting, fielding and pitching. Its morality arises from baseball's morality. As I said in the introduction, the "character clause" has never had any influence on Hall-of-Fame membership.

If this seems wrong, don't blame me, and don't blame the Hall of Fame. This is how it goes in the weird, wacky world of sports. If you're going to set up a reduced and simplified world in which everything is done just to get this arbitrarily chosen object called a "trophy," you're going to end up with these sorts of perverse separations from normal human existence and morality.

The only cardinal sin in this weird and wonderful world is trying *not* to get that trophy. That is, if one side is trying to lose, everything collapses. Suddenly you don't have a game at all. You just have a hoax. And when people discover the hoax, all the fun disappears. It would be like a movie with no conflict. It would be like a play with no actors. It would be like rain on your wedding day. It would be like a free ride when you've already paid. Isn't it ironic? Don't you think?

Rose is not guilty of undermining the score of a single game for monetary gain. He came as close to doing so as possible and has served a serious sentence for it. As with a real jail sentence, a dark cloud will remain over him the rest of his life. But at this point, he has served his time. It's time to reintegrate him into society.

If you're worried about what kind of "message" reintegrating Pete Rose will send, stop worrying. The deterrent has been clearly established. Do you really think anyone is going to look at the Pete Rose story and think "Wow, it's OK to bet on your own team! After all, Rose did it … and then went through massive public humiliation and an open-ended ban on all baseball activity including a Hall of Fame berth that he clearly deserved … hey, small price to pay to win a few bucks on the side!"

Pete Rose is not an innocent man. But he is also not game-thrower. It's time to accept his application for parole and elect him to the Hall.

Tim Raines (1979-1999, 2001-2002; career OPS+: 123)

	Career	Rank	Hitting	Rank	Fielding	Rank	Peak	Rank	Bests	JAWS	Rank
WAR	69.1	8	68.4	8	-9.4	76	42.2	11	2	55.7	9
WS	388.2	8	332.8	10	52.6	11	214.5	10	3	NA	8

Pity the poor leadoff hitter. Leaving Stan Hack and Heinie Groh out of the Hall is one thing; leaving Tim Raines out is entirely another. Raines was absolutely superb at everything except hitting home runs and throwing out baserunners. He got lots of hits, drew walks, had good range, and stole bases by the truckloads while rarely getting caught. His 84.7% stolen base success rate leads all players in history who had at least 400 attempts, and Raines had 954. He should not be outside the Hall for another second.

Tim Raines' underratedness (Underration? Underrationality?) is a chronic condition. In 2006, fans got ballots for "Hometown Heroes" along with their All-Star ballots. These Hometown Heroes ballots gave five candidates for each team's best all-time player. For instance, the nominees for best Yankee ever were Babe Ruth, Lou Gehrig, Yogi Berra, Mickey Mantle, and Joe DiMaggio. That's a very good selection of candidates; as of 2006, those were the top five Yankees in career WAR. (Derek Jeter has since overtaken Berra.)

I was as much of a pedantic baseball nerd then as I am now; perhaps more so. I took the ballot and researched the actual best five players in each team's history, according to whatever advanced metrics were available to me at the time. I then corrected each set of candidates on the ballot itself. I still have the ballot; here it is (see http://edsseriousblog.blogspot.com/2015/05/hometown-heroes-ballot.html) if you'd like to see it. It looks a lot like the crazed ravings of a lunatic before he shoots himself. Except in a cute way.

No set of candidates was more bizarre than that of the Expos. Their candidates were Gary Carter, Livan Hernandez, Rusty Staub, Jose Vidro and Brian Freaking Schneider. Brian Freaking Goldarn Motherloving Crotchstuffing Schneider. Brian F.G.M.C. Schneider, at the time, was 29th in career WAR among Expos, well behind Tim Raines (#2 in career Expos WAR), Andre Dawson (#3), Steve Rogers (#4), Tim Wallach (#5), and Vladimir Guerrero (#6). All of these famous, beloved players were passed over in favor of Brian Forkspinning Markerflipping Carpsmashing Biscuitsnorting WhothehellwasBrianSchneider Schneider.

The "Hometown Heroes" candidates were submitted by the teams themselves, and at the time, the Expos were not really a major-league baseball team. They were owned by MLB, who only took ownership because a long, weird series of events left the Expos a shell of their former selves. The Expos' previous owners had essentially "busted them out" the way Tony Soprano busted out David Scatino's sporting good store.[34] The MLB took pity on the Expos, gave them room and board, and nursed them back to health. In 2005, the Expos were ready to move beyond their abusive past and

[34] See "The Sopranos" episode "Bust Out," season 2, episode 10. Robert Patrick of "Terminator 2" fame played David Scatino, an old friend of Tony's who was a gambling addict. Tony saw an opportunity and invited David to a high-stakes poker game. When David inevitably lost and fell into major debt, Soprano's clan milked David's sporting goods store for every penny, running up its credit and forcing it into bankruptcy.

enter witness protection under the new identity of the Washington Nationals. Thank goodness that in mid-2006, the Nationals found legitimate owners who gave them the resources to become great again.

And make no mistake: In the early '80s, the Expos were great. They were consistent contenders, peaking with an appearance in the 1981 NLCS. They also drew good crowds, finishing third or fourth in N.L. attendance every year from 1979-1983. Lest you think Montreal is a tiny market, know that its metro area is larger than that of Minneapolis-St. Paul, Cleveland, Seattle, Denver, San Diego, and plenty of other functional baseball towns.

Even in 2004, the nadir of their history, there was a lot of fun to be had at Montreal Expos games. I went to a game with my friend Joe on our annual baseball trip. We were in a crowd of 8,386 people, all of whom were sitting in a tight group behind home plate. It was like being at intimate, small-theater concert instead of the typical massive, impersonal arena shows that constitute most baseball games. All 8,386 of us fans shared one of the best games I've ever seen, a pitching duel between Randy Johnson and Livan Hernandez that clocked in at 2:10. As a little bonus, Expos first baseman Nick Johnson had the coolest walk-up music I've ever heard, Radiohead's "Just".

The only discomfiting moments of the game occurred between innings, when there was nothing happening on the JumboTron or loudspeaker or anywhere else. No Kiss Cam, no trivia questions, no highlight reels, no dumb ads -- just eerie silence. I never realized before how much I need all the cheesy mid-inning schmaltz.

Anyway, as I write this, Tim Raines is probably the biggest Hall of Fame cause celebre among the sabermetric types. Sabermetrically inclined articles often scramble for reasons why Raines has been passed over. A popular reason is that he played in the same era as the all-time greatest leadoff hitter, Rickey Henderson, so in comparison Raines looks less exciting.

I'm sure there is some truth to this, but man! That is one crazy high standard. Not only do you have to be as good as Rickey Henderson to get in the Hall. But also, you can only have one great leadoff hitter per era? Does any other group of ballplayers ever suffer a similar bias? Does Trevor Hoffman seem un-Hall-worthy because he played at the same time as Mariano Rivera? Is Mickey Mantle ho-hum because he was a contemporary of Willie Mays? I tell you, if leadoff hitters were an ethnic group, they'd have solid grounds to file some discrimination lawsuits.

As I mentioned before, we put more value in the person driving in the run than the one scoring the run, even though both are equally important. When Andre Dawson hits a single to drive Tim Raines in from second, we feel a moment of excitement. In that moment, our eyes are trained on Dawson. Thus it feels more like Dawson is the hero. The driving-in part seems more important than the scoring part, even though they're both equally vital.

The numbers above are clear. Tim Raines deserves to be in the Hall of Fame.

Minnie Minoso (1949, 1951-1964, 1976, 1980; career OPS+: 130)

	Career	Rank	Hitting	Rank	Fielding	Rank	Peak	Rank	Bests	JAWS	Rank
WAR	50.1	24	47.6	25	-5.8	47	39.9	14	3	45.0	21
WS	281.9	33	218.0	39	38.9	30	191.9	24	3	NA	10

The above totals aren't entirely fair to Minnie Minoso. He spent 1946-1948, ages 20 to 22, in the Negro Leagues. In 1948, the year after Jackie Robinson's debut, he hit .403 for the New York Cubans.[35] He could have done well in the MLB if integration weren't so slow. Monte Irvin rated Minoso as the second-best left fielder in the history of the Negro Leagues.

Even after being brought to the MLB system, Minoso's climb up the ladder was suspiciously delayed. He got a cup of a coffee with Cleveland in 1949 but didn't find a permanent spot because the Cleveland brass didn't want an all-black outfield: The team already had Larry Doby and another outfielder of African descent in the wings. This was still the early years of integration, when teams were afraid of a backlash if they fielded more than a couple of black players at a time. So instead, they let Minoso spend two years destroying AAA pitchers. In the PCL in 1950 he hit .339/.405/.539 with 130 runs, 40 doubles, 10 triples, 20 home runs, 115 RBIs, and 30 SBs. But he did not get a call-up.

In 1951, Minoso was finally in the majors for good. He was traded mid-season to the White Sox, where he instantly became one of the most exciting players in baseball. At age 25, he led the American League in triples, HBPs, and stolen bases; hit .326/.422/.500; and scored 25 Win Shares (fifth in the AL) and 5.5 WAR (fourth). It was clear that he was ready for the majors years earlier.

Minoso's last real year was 1964, but then he got into a few games in 1976 and 1980 just for Shasta and giggles. Minoso was such a cheerful, charming fellow that White Sox fans couldn't get enough of him. Always up for a bit of fun, he even appeared in games with the independent league St. Paul Saints in 1993 and again in 2003, at the ripe old age of 77.

Minoso ended with 7712 major-league PAs, a bit low for a Hall-of-Famer, but nuts to that. You have to give Minoso credit for the additional seasons that he would have had in the major leagues if not for institutional racism. Doing so pushes his career totals comfortably above the line for the Hall of Fame.

Bill James accounts for all this in ranking Minoso tenth among all left fielders in history. In fact, Minoso is the only player in James' overall top 100 who is not in the Hall of Fame, apart from the betting men (Pete Rose and Shoeless Joe Jackson) and the guys who still have a chance through the BBWAA (Tim Raines, Barry Bonds, Roger Clemens, Mark McGwire, Jeff Bagwell, Mike Piazza, and Ken Griffey Jr.) Like Monte Irvin, Minnie Minoso deserves a spot.

Sherry Magee (1904-1919; career OPS+: 137)

	Career	Rank	Hitting	Rank	Fielding	Rank	Peak	Rank	Bests	JAWS	Rank
WAR	59.0	16	56.6	16	-8.3	70	38.5	18	4	48.8	15
WS	353.2	16	293.2	15	44.9	24	213.3	11	2	NA	21

There are a few dead-ball era hitters who have stats that any schmuck can look at and see are Hall-of-Fame level. Ty Cobb hit .366 for his career and had 12 batting titles. Honus Wagner hit .328 with

[35] If you're wondering, the name "Cubans" was a signal that it was an all-black team. Minoso was Cuban, but few of his teammates were. Before Fidel Castro came along and changed everything, Cuba was seen as a grand, sophisticated place. In the minds of white Americans, Cubans of African descent had a higher status than African-Americans. Thus, a lot of black teams were called the Cubans.

eight batting titles and five RBI titles. Eddie Collins and Nap Lajoie each had well over 3,000 hits. It was a time when the superstars were just leagues ahead of everyone else.

There's a second tier of dead-ballers whom you have to look at with a more precise lens. Because these guys didn't manage 3,000 career hits, their stats look modest. Hall of Fame voters get flummoxed in these sorts of situations, and their picks become more scattershot. We already went through a bunch of these picks: I judged Roger Bresnahan and Johnny Evers to be over the line when context is taken into account, but Ray Schalk and Joe Tinker to be under it.

Sherry Magee has a stronger case than any of those players. He was a six-tool Ed Delahanty/Joe DiMaggio type who could run, hit, hit for power, field, throw, and draw walks. He led the league in RBI four times, the only non-HOFer to have so many RBI titles, and it wasn't easy to lead the league in anything when it also included Honus Wagner. Magee managed to push past Honus once in batting average, in 1910, when Magee also lead the league in OBP, SLG, runs, RBIs, Win Shares (36), and WAR (6.7). He had two other 30-Win Share seasons and four others above 25. WAR gives him three other seasons above 5.

Another deadball outfielder, Elmer Flick, made it into the Hall with much weaker credentials. He had a .313 lifetime batting average, but a short career. Magee landed at .291, still a tremendous lifetime batting average for the deadball era. But we all do have a fetish for that ".300" number, don't we.

Another problem for Magee is that he was never an integral part of a pennant-winning team. It's not his fault -- he did play most of his career for the Phillies, after all. Late in his career he pushed hard to get on a winner and spent his final season as a backup outfielder for the 1919 Reds, but he got only two pinch at-bats in the series win against the Black Sox.

His Hall-of-Fame candidacy might not have been helped by the fact that Magee was a jerk. (Actually, since he was a left fielder, it should add to his qualifications). In those less-PC days, his ancestry was credited for his personality: John J. Ward in "Baseball Magazine" wrote of Magee "The Irish traits of quick-wittedness, a hot temper and an aggressive love of fighting are his by birthright." (Source: "Deadball Stars of the National League," edited by Tom Simon, p. 193, Brassey's Inc., 2004)

Umpire-baiting was commonplace in the dead-ball era, but violence against umpires was not. In a game in 1911, umpire Bill Finneran called Magee out on a close strike. Magee flipped his bat in frustration, and Finneran threw him out of the game. Magee spun around, grabbed Finneran, and clocked him in the jaw. Blood spurted from Finneran's face and he fell to the ground, unconscious. Finneran quickly came to and had no lasting injury, but Magee was suspended for the rest of the season.

Magee did mature over time, though, especially when he was named captain of the Phillies in 1914. This finally got him on the good side of Philadelphia fans, who until then had made a sport of booing Magee. Why do fans do this, by the way? When a team does poorly, the best player always gets the abuse. It makes no sense. You should be booing the bad players; they're the ones making your team lose. The good player is trying his best, but he can't do it alone.

Typical of many deadball players, Magee didn't last long into his 30s. But he started his major-league career at age 19, going straight from the sandlots to the Phillies without a single plate appearance in the minors. He still managed 8542 PAs, a respectable Hall-of-Fame total. I think that when you apply all the contextual adjustments, Magee deserves to be in.

Intentionally Overlooked

Manny Ramirez (1993-2011; career OPS+: 154)

	Career	Rank	Hitting	Rank	Fielding	Rank	Peak	Rank	Bests	JAWS	Rank
WAR	69.2	7	81.2	5	-22.2	98	39.8	15	3	54.5	11
WS	385.3	9	348.3	6	37.2	33	214.5	9	2	NA	8*

Oh, Manny. Manny, Manny, Manny. Manny, my laddie boy, why did you have to … well, actually, I don't know that anyone was surprised. Manny was always such a dope that it was inevitable that he would be caught using steroids. And that he would be caught doing it such a dumb, obvious way. He got caught using a women's fertility drug to restart the normal testosterone production after a steroid cycle. After another steroid violation, he was handed a 100-day suspension. Rather than serve it, he retired. It was all bush-league behavior, but that was Manny Ramirez.

His career was full of these sorts of lapses from normal, acceptable human behavior. He was always unhappy with whatever exorbitant salary he was earning and often brought his beef onto the field. During one Yankees series, he sat out with pharyngitis but was then caught drinking at a bar. Despite his terrific hitting, the Red Sox often tried to get rid of him, but his contract made that impossible.

Manny got into fights with teammates, but often it was hard to tell if he was really at fault. One fight probably should have landed him in jail, though. Right before a game in Houston, he went to the Red Sox traveling secretary Jack McCormick with an unreasonable request for 16 tickets. McCormick, being unable to perform magic, tried to explain that that may not be possible. Manny pushed him to the ground and yelled "Just do your job!" McCormick was 64 years old. Manny apologized to the media, but not to McCormick for years. (Source for these stories: Manny Ramirez' Wikipedia entry.)

Often, these sorts of things were brushed off with the phrase "It's just Manny being Manny." Well, I say, Manny should have tried to be someone else. When being Manny means being such a bullying thug that you push down a 64-year-old man for not meeting your ridiculous demands, you need to change.

I wish I could exclude Manny Ramirez for being a egregious egomaniac. But so are many ballplayers, and it doesn't affect how they help their teams win. Was Ramirez's personality so disruptive that it hurt his team in the standings? Few players were that bad; Dick Allen is the only Hall-of-Fame level talent who has lost points because of that. Considering the success of Ramirez's teams, I doubt his personality affected team play much, if at all.

No, I'm excluding him because of steroids. I'm lumping him in with Rafael Palmeiro as a player whose record looks Hall-level, but it's hard to tell how much of it was steroid-enhanced. As such, Manny is in purgatory, not non-Hall hell. If someday I'm able to chop off the steroidal numbers, as I did with Bonds, and Manny remains above the line, then he'll be in.

Shoeless Joe Jackson (1908-1920; career OPS+: 170)

	Career	Rank	Hitting	Rank	Fielding	Rank	Peak	Rank	Bests	JAWS	Rank
WAR	62.3	14	61.2	14	-6.0	50	52.8	5	5	57.6	7
WS	293.1	27	247.0	25	28.1	62	244.8	3	5	NA	6

Meanwhile, nothing but a time machine and some key assassinations will turn Joe Jackson into a Hall-of-Famer. Again, the record is obviously not the issue. As I mentioned in the Pete Rose comment, the issue is that he participated in throwing a World Series, which in baseball is a life-in-prison crime.

He is not the most guilty of the bunch, not by far. First baseman Chick Gandil brought the fix to the players. Lefty Williams lost three games by pitching terribly. The rest made obvious misplays during the Series, while Jackson hit and fielded well. Some say he avoided making plays that he could have, while other deny this. Reportedly, Jackson was not at any of the meetings of the conspirators and was coerced into joining the group. The gamblers wouldn't agree to the deal unless the team's star hitter was involved.

But Jackson did confess his role in court. He took the money, and he knew about the fix but didn't tell anyone. His defenders try to explain away even these three facts. They say he was plied with whiskey to he sign the confessions, and that, being illiterate, he didn't know what he was signing. They also say he refused the money several times, until finally Lefty Williams dropped the money in his hotel room. As for not informing anyone about the fix, they say he tried to warn owner Charlie Comiskey but was turned away before he could.

This is the point at which the apologists sound like they're straining to come up with excuses. Jackson was not the brightest fellow in the world, but anyone who can tie his shoes can know when he's confessing in court. And even if the money was forced into his hotel room, I don't think it's possible to be forced to pick up and then spend the money. I also don't see how being ignored by Charlie Comiskey once means you can't warn someone lower on the pecking order or maybe go to the press.

I have plenty of sympathy for Jackson. Even if I don't think he was innocent, I do think he was very conflicted about it all. He was not a bad man, not in the least. Circumstances put him in the wrong place at the wrong time. He was thrown into a very sticky, complex situation and didn't navigate it perfectly. I can't say I would have done better in his shoes.

His story is tragic, especially as he spent the rest of his life under a cloud. Long after his baseball days, Jackson owned a liquor store. Ty Cobb entered the store and Jackson silently attended to his purchase. Before leaving, Cobb said, "Don't you know me, Joe?" Jackson said "Sure, I know you Ty, but I wasn't sure you wanted to know me. A lot of them don't." (Source: Jackson's Wikipedia entry.)

But regardless of what was in Joe Jackson's soul, we know what he did. He participated in throwing a World Series. That means he can't be in the Hall of Fame. Case closed.

Chapter Eight

~ ~ Center Field ~ ~

Center field is a bit like third base. Fielding is important, but you better hit too. In the past, third base was more defense-first than center, but nowadays it's the opposite. Regardless, center fielders should definitely make the Hall with lower offensive contributions than those of right fielders, left fielders, or first basemen.

Richie Ashburn (1948-1962; career OPS+: 111)

	Career	Rank	Hitting	Rank	Fielding	Rank	Peak	Rank	Bests	JAWS	Rank
WAR	63.4	10	57.4	12	5.4	25	44.2	9	1	53.8	11
WS	329.8	11	256.0	10	74.0	9	192.2	17	0	NA	16

Richie Ashburn is exhibit number ten zillion in the class action discrimination lawsuit I'm launching on behalf of leadoff hitters. He did make it into the Hall, finally, in 1995, a good 33 years after his retirement. It should have been much earlier.

In her book "Bossypants," Tina Fey talks about her dad, who was apparently the coolest dude in the Philadelphia area. Mr. Fey groused a lot about Ashburn not making the Hall. This might be the first known instance of a hometown partisan having a valid argument about his favorite player from childhood not making the Hall of Fame. Usually it's some well-meaning old codger who grew up loving Roger Maris or someone like that. This guy will always refuse to accept that the standards of the Hall, as they have been established by current inductees, just don't allow Maris a spot. Maris was a wonderful guy and very good player, but he can be honored in other ways, such as his own museum in Fargo (go check it out sometime -- it's small but a total charmer. It's in a shopping mall, because Maris reasoned that that's where people would be anyway. Smart man.)

Man, why am I talking about Roger Maris? Where did that come from? Back to Richie Ashburn. Ashburn did everything exceptionally well except hit home runs. He was a stellar fielder, got lots of hits (three times leading the league, with two batting titles), had speed (twice leading the league in triples, once in stolen bases), and was exceptional at getting on base (four times leading the NL in walks, four times leading in OBP, lifetime .396 OBP).

Ashburn also had great durability, a skill that I haven't brought up much. Getting injured is usually seen as a fluke event. But it's not entirely; some people are just born with the ability to not hurt themselves often. It's not a perfect analogy, but in much the same way that some people are born with athletic ability and some aren't, some people are born with durability and some aren't. On the spectrum of this ability, Cal Ripken is one end, Richie Ashburn is close behind, and someone like me would be at the bottom, seeing as how I once sprained an ankle by standing up too fast.

Durability is also a skill that you can hone through practice, as you can with throwing or hitting. You can work on gaining the strength and flexibility that allows you to avoid injuries and to heal quickly when you do get a bit banged up.

The point is, Richie Ashburn managed 150+ games per year every year from 1949-1960, except 1955, and in those days, the season was only 154 games long. In his fifteen major-league seasons, Ashburn logged more than 700 PAs eight times. It gives your team a great advantage when you almost never have to be replaced by a greatly inferior backup.

Ashburn did get a bit lost in the exceptional center fielders of the 1950s. Mickey Mantle, Willie Mays, and Duke Snider were all better players than Ashburn, because they got on base well and also had power. And those three played in New York, and you know what that means. If you haven't heard your fill of New York baseball in the 1950s, then you have probably never seen Ken Burns' baseball documentary, or heard Billy Crystal speak for more than a few minutes, or been alive in the United States.

As I've mentioned, you don't have to be Mickey Mantle or Willie Mays or Duke Snider to deserve a Hall of Fame berth. Ashburn is in for sure.

Earl Averill (1929-1941; career OPS+: 133)

	Career	Rank	Hitting	Rank	Fielding	Rank	Peak	Rank	Bests	JAWS	Rank
WAR	48.0	28	51.0	22	-5.3	77	37.4	23	4	42.7	26
WS	279.2	30	215.9	31	52.0	42	197.5	14	3	NA	14

Earl Averill, you are on notice. I don't care if Bill James ranks you 14th among all center fielders; your career numbers don't stack up well.

Earl Averill: But I got my start in the majors at age 27! I still managed 7221 PAs by playing almost every game through age 35! C'mon, don't be a playa hater!

Me: I admire your use of modern slang; pretty impressive for someone who has been dead for 30 years. But you didn't get a late start because of war service or racism or something like that. You were just busy playing semi-pro ball and then boppin' along in the Pacific Coast League for three years.

Earl Averill: Dude, it was a very different time. There wasn't the strict structure to the minor leagues like you have now, where all minor-league teams are owned by major-league ones, and any player who performs well gets moved up tout de suite. The Pacific Coast League was a separate, independent league, and quite proud of it, thank you very much. It paid good salaries, got good attendance, and was not eager to lose its best players to those snobby so-called "major" leaguers out East. I was freakin' awesome for three years in a very competitive independent league. Doesn't that count for something?

Me: I don't know. Wouldn't that mean that every player's AAA stats should count toward their Hall of Fame credentials? I think you have to stick with the major-league stuff.

Earl Averill: Did you ever think that maybe we're a little too obsessed with what happens in a so-called "major" league? Granted, since the 1950s, professional baseball has been organized such that all the best talent reliably concentrates in the NL and AL. Those were clearly the major leagues from that point forward, and all players since full racial integration should be judged solely by their MLB numbers. But before that, the status of a "major" league was less well-defined. There were other leagues where the nation's best players played. There were the Negro Leagues, of course. And to a lesser extent, there were independent leagues like the PCL. The PCL voted to become a major league in 1945. In 1952, it won an "Open" classification, meaning that it was a step above AAA, and that the

MLB had limited ability to draft players from it. It was on its way to becoming a full major league until those dumb New York teams moved to San Francisco and Los Angeles.

Me: OK, OK, I'll give you a few extra points for your PCL work. But still, your career major-league numbers are only superficially great. You played in 1930s, when a basket of cross-eyed puppies could hit .300.

Earl Averill: Man, your arguments are gettin' weak! If you don't like the conventional numbers, don't use them! C'mon, I've been reading your sorry excuse for a book, and I know how you do this. I was the best center fielder in all of baseball four times according to WAR and three times according to Win Shares. I had 6+ WAR three times and 30+ Win Shares three times. In Win Shares, which you are on record as saying you trust more, I get more than 20 every year for ten straight years! That's Hall of Fame stuff! Word! Boo-yaa! Totally fab! That's how I roll! Bling, bling! YOLO! You down with OPP? I'm outtie 5000!

Me: OK, no more slang terms for you. But yeah, you're right, your major-league career may have been short, but it was clearly excellent. Bill James ranks you 14th, and WAR doesn't put you firmly outside consideration. Fine, you're in. Now leave me alone.

Earl Averill: Funky cold medina!

Cool Papa Bell (1922-1946)

	Rank at Position Among Negro Leaguers	Rank Among All Negro Leaguers
Bill James	3	10
SABR	1	3
Monte Irvin	2	NA

Books about the Negro Leagues overflow with Cool Papa Bell stories. He was a fun, vibrant player known for incredible speed. One story has it that he slapped a ball off the pitcher's mound and then was struck by the ball as he slid into second. Another said he could score from first on a bunt. Satchel Paige said he could flip off the light switch and get under the covers before the lights went out. (Paige left out that there was a delay in that particular light switch because of faulty wiring. It sounds better without that detail.)

From these kinds of stories, I always got the impression that Bell was the one doing the bragging, that he was a boastful life-of-the-party type. But he was actually a pretty modest, abstemious guy, never smoking, drinking or even saying bad words. He was definitely too sensitive a soul to play for Dominican dictator Rafael Trujillo.

I don't think that last sentence needs any further explanation. OK, maybe a short one. In 1937, Pittsburgh Crawfords owner Gus Greenlee defaulted on his players' salaries. Many of them, including Bell and Satchel Paige, left the Crawfords and took an offer in the Dominican Republic. Rafael Trujillo was assembling a baseball league, because a dictator of a country of millions apparently doesn't have better things to do. Within this league, he had his own team, which was intentionally stocked with the best players, including Bell and Paige.

Bell, Paige, and the rest were under constant armed guard. They were told in no uncertain terms that they were to win the championship, or else. After one particularly nasty threat by an army officer, Bell wept openly, desperately pleading to leave the Dominican. Bell's team eventually won the championship. But they didn't win overwhelmingly enough for Trujillo, so he disbanded the entire league. No organized baseball was played in the Dominican for the next 12 years.

Bell went on to the fully integrated Mexican League and then back to the Negro Leagues. He then managed teams for several years and later worked as a part-time scout for the Browns. Bill Veeck offered him a contract to play for the Browns in 1951, when Bell was 48 years old. Even Cool Papa Bell was a bit slow at that age, and he probably knew it would amount to little more than one of Veeck's publicity stunts. He politely declined.

SABR is very high on Bell, ranking him above Oscar Charleston. As we'll cover below, that's a bit crazy. But the SABR list is more about fame than straight playing ability. Bell wasn't better than Charleston, but he was still one of the best players in baseball history, and a definite Hall-of-Famer.

Max Carey (1910-1929; career OPS+: 108)

	Career	Rank	Hitting	Rank	Fielding	Rank	Peak	Rank	Bests	JAWS	Rank
WAR	54.2	18	45.6	31	0	45	33	32	0	43.6	24
WS	349.8	8	251.9	12	90.9	3	180.5	30	0	NA	23

Max Carey was the Lou Brock of the teens and '20s. He was the king of stolen bases in the N.L., leading the league ten times. He logged more than 10,000 PAs over 20 years. Both he and Brock were terrific in World Series play; Carey could have won the World Series MVP in 1925, if it had existed, for leading the Pirates to a championship with a .458/.552/.625 line.

Carey's rankings above don't look great, but they're actually better than Brock's in a lot of ways. Carey was a better fielder in a more defense-first position. Carey also was better at getting on base, leading the league in walks twice.

Yeah, yeah, yeah, you're saying -- but was Carey born with a different last name that means "handler of meat" in Latin? Why yes, he was! Max Carey's real name was Maximillian Carnarius. His father, August Carnarius, was a former soldier who had emigrated from Germany after the Franco-Prussian War of 1870-1871.[36] August had very definitive plans that his son would become a Lutheran minister. Starting at age 13, young Maxie completed a tough six-year pre-ministerial program.

He then moved on to Concordia Seminary in St. Louis. There, baseball's siren song pulled Maximillian away from God's service. He played for a minor-league team, but had to do so under a pseudonym to preserve his amateur status. This was such a common practice that no one had bothered to pick out a pseudonym before Max's first game. When the manager presented his lineup to the umpire, he said

[36] Want to know about the Franco-Prussian War? Of course you do! It was basically a trumped-up conflict engineered by Prussian chancellor Otto von Bismarck. Prussia is now part of northern Germany, but before Bismarck came along it had been a separate country for centuries. Bismarck wanted to unify it and the other northern German states with what is now southern Germany: Bavaria, Baden, etc. So Bismarck figured if he could provoke a war, he could force an alliance between the north and the south. It worked: The newly unified country of Germany beat France soundly. Germany was now large and powerful, which was A-OK with the rest of Europe, and there were never any more problems, the end.

that his new player was called "Carney or Carey or something like that." The umpire went with "Max Carey," and a name was born. (Source: Max Carey's SABR biography, by John Bennett.)

Though Carey is at the 20s in both overall rankings, and his Peak numbers in particular are low, I don't have much hesitation in leaving him the Hall of Fame. I think he was better than Lou Brock, but that's not a good argument. It's never valid to make a Hall of Fame case by just showing that your guy is better than a marginal Hall-of-Famer. If we did that, then everyone better than George Kelly would have a case.

More to the point, Carey had plenty of great seasons, with 11 above 20 Win Shares and two 29s. His low OPS+ is irrelevant because he was a leadoff hitter who had a high OBP. He was a great fielder. Carey might not be a charter member of the Hall, but he is over the bar.

Oscar Charleston (1915-1941)

	Rank at Position Among Negro Leaguers	Rank Among All Negro Leaguers
Bill James	1	1
SABR	2	4
Monte Irvin	1	NA

SABR has Cool Papa Bell above Oscar Charleston, which is a bit crazy. See above. Also, see below, as I try to explain how good Oscar Charleston was.

Bell had his speed and Josh Gibson had his power. Charleston didn't have one hook that sticks out in people's minds. He was just amazing at everything. He had all the tools and then some. He was fast, aggressive, and would do anything to win, a la Ty Cobb. But he also had incredible power and fielding range, a la Willie Mays. And Charleston's arm was so good that between games of double-headers he would wow fans by throwing perfect strikes from center field to home plate.

Bill James not only ranks Charleston as the best Negro League player ever, he also ranks him fourth among all players who ever lived, topped only by Babe Ruth, Honus Wagner, and Mays. John McGraw, like James, was not someone easily swayed by hype, and he said Charleston was the best player he had ever seen.

At this writing, Seamheads.com has Charleston's stats through 1935, which is pretty close to complete. It gives him a career OPS+ of 189, from a .350/.425/.566 line. Only Cristobal Torriente tops Charleston in Win Shares in their database, but Charleston beats Torriente in career WAR. The Negro League stats in baseball-reference.com disagree heartily, saying that Charleston was more of a Paul Zuvella/Bob Uecker type. No, of course not. They give him a .339/.401/.545 line in 4492 league PAs.

If you're still not convinced of Charleston's greatness, let me throw in that he was also a very effective manager. He was a player-manager from 1922 through his retirement from playing in 1941. Then he kept on managing until 1954, when he died. He was a lot like John McGraw: Despite being a tough, aggressive player always ready for a fight, he also had the patience to guide young players into stardom. Through it all, his incredible intelligence and knowledge about baseball were key to his success. The only more effective manager in the Negro Leagues was probably Hall-of-Famer Rube Foster.

So combine Willie Mays with John McGraw and sprinkle on a bit of Ty Cobb and you get Oscar Charleston. Saying he deserves the Hall of Fame is so obvious that it's almost an insult.

Ty Cobb (1905-1928; career OPS+: 168)

	Career	Rank	Hitting	Rank	Fielding	Rank	Peak	Rank	Bests	JAWS	Rank
WAR	151.0	2	150.9	1	-10.8	101	69.1	2	11	110.1	2
WS	722.6	1	639.7	1	82.7	5	311.6	1	9	NA	2

In the first edition of this book, I had a grand old time excoriating Ty Cobb for his racism and capacity for violence. It is not hard to find Ty Cobb stories that support such a perspective. Almost every source makes Cobb sound like a monster.

The exception is Charles Leehrsen's book "Ty Cobb: A Terrible Beauty." As a book, it's not a perfect, even aside from the lame subtitle (which made my wife laugh out loud). It sometimes reads as if Leehrsen is acting as Cobb's defense attorney. Anyone who dislikes Cobb is swept aside using the classic rationalization of the insufferably smug alpha male: "They're probably just jealous."

But these are small faults compared to the book's huge benefit: Leehrsen's book is actually well-researched. Before it, everyone, including myself, relied on the biased, ginned-up Ty Cobb stories propagated by Al Stump. Stump was a pathetic hack who wrote several Cobb biographies, huge portions of which were complete fiction. But they were compelling enough fictions to inspire a 1994 film, "Cobb," and infest the public image of Cobb ever since.

Ty Cobb was far from an angel. He was born hyperactive with a hair-trigger temper, much like Johnny Evers. He was violent, getting into many fistfights for stupid reasons, much like Jud Wilson. He had the sort of racial attitudes you might expect from someone who grew up in rural Georgia 100 years ago. But he was also a functional human being who could maintain friendships and even be occasionally charming. He was not the cartoonish monster that Al Stump invented.

I'll show you how the two different takes on Cobb manifest themselves. Here's the Al Stump version of an incident in 1907, just a few years after Cobb's major-league debut: There was an African-American groundskeeper named Bungy whom Cobb had known for years. One day, Bungy either tried to shake Cobb's hand or pat him on the back -- no one knows for sure. Either way, Cobb found this normal human gesture to be "overly familiar" and attacked Bungy. Bungy's wife tried to intervene, so Cobb started choking her. Cobb was only stopped when teammate Boss Schmidt knocked him out.

Here's how Charles Leehrsen tells the story. Bungy was an amiable drunk who was pretty tipsy that day. He ambled up to Cobb and draped his arm around him. Cobb gruffly shrugged his arm off. Boss Schmidt took the opportunity to knock Cobb on to the ground, and then made up the part about Cobb choking Bungy's wife. Schmidt was one of a group of Tiger veterans who had an ongoing beef with Cobb after the young star had reacted very badly to the normal rookie hazing.

You can believe either version; I believe the Leehrsen version because I know that he went by evidence instead of folklore. Still, note that it doesn't show Cobb to be blameless. He was very wedded to strict social hierarchy, one in which a black man was not supposed to be so familiar with a white man. And Cobb was immersed in a pointless feud with Schmidt and the rest of the Tigers' veterans because he couldn't take rookie hazing in good humor.

Most of Cobb's dumb fights came early in his career, when he was reeling from his father's death. A few weeks before his major league debut, Ty's father crept along the side of his own house, surprising his mother. She allegedly thought he was an intruder and shot him dead. Ty didn't blame his mother, refusing to believe the rumors of infidelity within the marriage. In modern terms, he didn't "process" the death of his beloved father, instead letting the pain fuel his war against the world.

But when he got older, he moved on. He mellowed and learned how to let things slide. Later in life he was a great mentor to young ballplayers, including Ted Williams and Joe DiMaggio. When baseball integrated, Cobb made many statements celebrating the change. He never stopped being hyperactive and grouchy, but he learned how to sometimes be gracious and charming.

Regardless of how he really behaved, Ty Cobb is one of the ten greatest players ever, and it wouldn't be a Hall of Fame at all without him.

Earle Combs (1924-1935, career OPS+: 125)

	Career	Rank	Hitting	Rank	Fielding	Rank	Peak	Rank	Bests	JAWS	Rank
WAR	42.5	41	41.8	41	-2.7	64	34.4	30	2	38.5	34
WS	226.0	54	195.0	42	31.1	114	171.9	37	2	NA	34

Earle Combs was a sort of anti-Cobb, at least in terms of personality. He was a kind, modest and deeply religious person. In his Hall of Fame induction speech, he said "I thought the Hall of Fame was for superstars, not just average players like me." (Source: Combs' SABR biography, by Ralph Berger.)

He had a point. Not that he was an average player; he was often superb. Combs was a great leadoff hitter for the Yankees' Murderers' Row, leading the league in triples three times, getting on base a ton, and scoring lots of runs. In 1927 he earned 31 Win Shares and 6.9 WAR. It could have been an MVP year if teammate Babe Ruth hadn't collected 45 Win Shares and 12.4 WAR, and other teammate Lou Gehrig hadn't turned in a 44 Win Shares/11.8 WAR season. (In the Scott Rolen comment, I found that this was the best trio of position players on any team in history.) Combs had several other hitting performances almost as good, and I'm talking Rickey-Henderson good.

The problem with Earle Combs is that he had just half of Rickey Henderson's career, or less. Combs got his first full season at 26 and managed just 6513 PAs before retiring at age 36. Also, Combs was also mediocre at best in the field, owning a weak arm that would have landed him elsewhere on any team that didn't already have Babe Ruth in right and power hitter Bob Meusel in left.

Who would be a good modern comp for Earle Combs? Lenny Dykstra? Dykstra had some absolutely superb seasons: 8.9 WAR and 35 Win Shares in 1990, 6.5 WAR and 32 Win Shares in 1993. There were some other good years, but he had an even shorter career than Combs', just 5282 PAs. Willie Wilson is a little closer to Combs in terms of JAWS and WSAWS (which is 50th for Combs; again Bill James gives the HOFer a bit of a boost). But Wilson had more longevity and fewer great seasons. Brett Butler was significantly better than Combs by every measure.

Earle Combs is hardly a disgraceful choice for the Hall. He was far from an average player. But he was no superstar. **Combs is out.**

Joe DiMaggio (1936-1942, 1946-1951; career OPS+: 155)

	Career	Rank	Hitting	Rank	Fielding	Rank	Peak	Rank	Bests	JAWS	Rank
WAR	78.2	6	73.4	6	3.2	29	51.2	6	8	64.7	6
WS	386.2	6	325.8	6	60.6	23	240.9	5	8	NA	5

In the midst of Dimaggi-mania, many people would quietly grumble that the Yankee Clipper was "cold" and "aloof." Get my soapbox ready. Here we go.

Words like "cold" and "aloof" are trigger words for introverts like me. We are often not good at small talk with people we don't know, and don't feel comfortable doing it. We usually don't want to make new friends. It's not because we think we're better than other people, and it's not because we're jerks. It is just not our thing.

The world is 75% extroverts, and they tend to have more dominant personalities anyway. So they've created societal norms that dictate everyone should be like them, that presume everyone wants to chat whenever there's a moment of silence among strangers. They force conversation on us introverts in elevators, on planes, in company lunchrooms, etc. We then have to expend loads of precious emotional energy trying to search for things to say. Or we just refuse to engage and commit to looking like weirdos. I always wish I could give chatty people a note that says "Please understand it's not because I don't like you. Please don't take offense. I just don't like small talk."

Some introverts do fine with small talk. The more universal trait of introverts is that when they need to unwind, they must be either alone or with someone they love. I'm sure that, to unwind from the incredible stress of being a major-league superstar in New York City, Joe DiMaggio needed quiet time. That meant subtly pushing away the millions of adoring people who constantly wanted to bask in his glow. Spurned, the fawning acolytes would then conclude that he was "cold" and "aloof."

DiMaggio managed to gamely sally forth through all the interviews and flashbulbs while maintaining the adulation of millions. Other ballplayers were not so good at this. Barry Bonds and Albert Belle were two introverts who made a lot of dumb mistakes, reacting to pushy extroverts with anger and condescension. They were then vilified well beyond any sense or reason.

You know about Bonds. The hatred spewed on him far, far exceeded the hatred spewed on Rafael Palmeiro, Mark McGwire, Jason Giambi or any of the other steroid stars. That's partially because Bonds broke the sacred records, and did so in the mid-Aughts when people were more upset about steroids. But I think it's also because he wasn't a very nice person. And that's not a good reason. He's a ballplayer, not a presidential candidate. He shouldn't have to shake hands and kiss babies to gain respect.

Albert Belle gives a more concrete example. In 1995, Mo Vaughn won the AL MVP. That year, Albert Belle beat Vaughn in every significant statistic except RBIs, where they tied for the league lead. Belle led the league in runs, doubles, home runs and slugging percentage. In a strike-shortened season of 144 games, he was the first player in history to log both 50 doubles and 50 home runs in a season. Meanwhile, Vaughn had a pretty conventional very good first-baseman performance, the kind that a few guys manage every year. Both were on playoff teams, so that's not a factor.

Belle most likely lost the MVP because of his personality. He had a pretty bad one, granted. He wasn't very nice to reporters. But his personality never affected the results on the field. Knocking him down in MVP rankings because he's not interested in talking to you is petty and childish, and the reporters who voted for Vaughn over Belle should be ashamed of themselves.

Why do we assume that everyone who is talented at playing baseball must also be a gadfly, willing to recite cliches to reporters before and after every game? Are we really that needy? If they're introverts, can't we just admire their play, applaud their triumphs, and then respectfully leave them alone? They're not P.R. reps; they're players. Let them play.

As I mentioned in the Pete Rose comment, we love sports because they're simplified worlds, where your only goal is to get these arbitrary objects we call "trophies." Adding "fun to be with" to the job description is nothing more than moving the goalposts after the game has started. A person who is very good at getting his team to trophies should be respected and honored for it, regardless of how much he smiles. Yes, it's much more fun when they're Tony Gwynn or Derek Jeter and we can love them for their charm as well as their playing. But that's a bonus, not a requirement.

Anyway, I'm launching into all my introversion rants because there's not much to say about Joe DiMaggio's Hall worthiness. He is as low as 5th or 6th among center fielders only because the position is loaded with super-duper-stars and because DiMaggio played only 13 seasons. He spent 1943-1945, ages 28-30, in the military, and it's fun to think where he could have ended up with three more prime years. But it doesn't matter, because DiMaggio is in the Hall-of-Fame's inner circle.

Larry Doby (1947-1959; career OPS+: 136)

	Career	Rank	Hitting	Rank	Fielding	Rank	Peak	Rank	Bests	JAWS	Rank
WAR	49.5	25	47.8	24	-0.2	46	39.4	18	1	44.5	20
WS	267.6	33	221.3	30	45.4	58	198.3	13	2	NA	11

Like Monte Irvin and Roy Campanella, Larry Doby straddled the Negro Leagues and the MLB. He started in the Negro League Newark Eagles at age 18. At 23 he became the first African-American in the American League when he debuted for the Cleveland Dignified Native American Peoples Who Do Not Deserve To Be Mascots.

Much the same way Jackie Robinson's debut didn't bring in a flood of African-American players, his success didn't single-handedly cure racism on the ballfield. Larry Doby also had to sustain abuse from teammates, opponents, and spectators who made the incredibly difficult task of playing major-league ball even harder. Like Robinson, Doby had to maintain an impeccably dignified composure through it all because he was being perceived as an exemplar for an entire ethnic group.

Later, Doby said, "It was 11 weeks between the time Jackie Robinson and I came into the majors. I can't see how things were any different for me than they were for him." (Source: Doby's SABR biography, by John MacMurray.) Doby didn't get the publicity that Robinson got because reporters weren't interested in telling essentially the same story twice. Also, Cleveland is not exactly the American media hub that New York is. But the struggle was the same, and the effect Doby had on baseball was almost as important.

Also like Jackie Robinson, Doby wasn't a naturally easy-going type. He was introspective and hard on himself. In the Negro Leagues, his quiet, reserved nature had always made many teammates think he was aloof (grrrr...). In the MLB, he had the opposite problem, wanting to make friends while many refused to acknowledge his existence.

Doby had support from the most important places. Cleveland owner Bill Veeck had long been chomping at the bit to bring in African-American players. On Doby's first day, manager Lou Boudreau introduced him personally to every new teammate. Some shook Doby's hand, and some refused. The one teammate who took Doby under his wing, as I mentioned before, was Hall-of-Famer Joe Gordon.

Doby was actually a second baseman in the Negro Leagues, and a good one. But with Gordon blocking him at second, he had to learn center field. So add that to Doby's plate: being the first African-American in the American League, being a rookie, learning a new position ... it's a wonder anyone could succeed under those pressures.

Doby's historical importance adds to his Hall-of-Fame credentials; Jackie Robinson is much more famous, but he didn't change the world alone. As with Robinson's, Doby's career stands on its own. Doby's rankings above aren't as overwhelmingly qualified as Robinson's, but they're in the Hall-of-Fame range. Furthermore, the above rankings don't include his Negro League play, nor do they account for Doby's war service in 1944 and 1945. Definite Hall-of-Famer.

Hugh Duffy (1888-1906; career OPS+: 123)

	Career	Rank	Hitting	Rank	Fielding	Rank	Peak	Rank	Bests	JAWS	Rank
WAR	43.0	39	37.8	49	-2.5	62	30.7	47	0	36.9	42
WS	293.8	23	234.6	19	59.2	26	192.7	16	4	NA	20

There's a big split here between Win Shares and WAR on Hugh Duffy. Win Shares says he can come into the Hall if he keeps his head down, but man, if WAR finds out you're here, there will be hell to pay. And it's not just the same old story about WAR judging defense differently. Win Shares likes his hitting much better too.

Duffy was selected by the 1945 Old Timer's Committee, a year before they picked Tinker, Evers and Chance en masse. You may remember that this committee had a different focus for the Hall, filling it with key players on great teams instead of players with big career stats. Duffy and Tommy McCarthy were chosen because they were the famed "Wonder Twins" of the 1890s Boston Beaneaters.

It might have been fun if the Hall had stuck with this stars-of-great-teams focus. The most exciting moments in baseball come from great teams, not from guys who collect a lot of numbers on bad teams. But as I've mentioned, that moment passed a long time ago. Now it's largely about your career. By the 1970s, the Hall was making errors on the other extreme, selecting Jake Beckley because he had a bunch of hits on a series of crappy clubs.

Still, the most we can give Duffy is a little boost for being a key player for a terrific team and playing gangbusters in an 1892 postseason series (.462/.481/.846 in a win over the Cleveland Spiders). That series was considered more of an exhibition than a true championship contest, as it pitted the first-place team against the second-place team, but it's something.

Of course, no one remembers Hugh Duffy for the 1892 series. It's not even mentioned on his Hall of Fame plaque. Instead, it talks about the one number Duffy is known for, .440.[37] That's what he hit in 1894 and is the highest single-season mark in history.

The problem is that it's a pretty meaningless stat, since 1894 was the most out-of-whack, over-the-top, offense-heavy season ever. At the beginning of the 1893 season, the pitcher's mound was 50 feet from home plate. But a pitcher named Amos Rusie was throwing so fast that people started to get nervous. From a distance of 50 feet, there just wasn't time to get your head out of the way of an Amos Rusie fastball. They could have worn helmets, of course, but in those days it made more sense to turn the game upside down than to wear commonsensical protective equipment.

During the 1893 season, the National League, the only major league at the time, radically altered the balance between pitching and hitting by moving the mound back to 60 feet, 6 inches. Pitchers were suddenly hopeless. A curveball that used to break right in front of home plate now bounced ten feet in front it. The batter got a few more crucial milliseconds to consider each pitch.

Offense went through the roof through the end of 1893 and stayed that way throughout 1894. The National League as a whole hit .309 in 1894. Of the 77 players with enough PAs to qualify for the batting title (under current rules), 57 hit .300 or better. Four players hit .400: Duffy and the entire Phillies outfield of Sam Thompson, Ed Delahanty, and Billy Hamilton.

Let's talk economic theory. To compare prices over different eras, economists use "real" dollars. For real dollars, inflation has been removed from the equation, so prices can be compared on a level playing field. This is useful because despite what your grandpa says, it's pretty meaningless to say that in the 1950s you could buy a gallon of milk for 82 cents. It's true, but what does that really mean? The real value of that 82 cents has changed because of inflation. If you translate those 82 cents into 2014 dollars, you get $7.23. Nowadays, only the fancy-pants organic RGBH-free cruelty-free insult-free fully-self-actualized milk gets past $7.00 a gallon. In real terms, milk has actually gotten much cheaper since the 1950s.

This is basically what we're doing with the OPS+ stat: You're putting everything in "real" OPS so you can compare different numbers in different eras on a level playing field. Let's do the same for batting averages. For this, I'm using one of my favorite sites, whatifsports.com. If this were a TV show from the 1950s or a podcast from nowadays, this is when I'd step away from the show and talk about how much I love whatifsports.com. It allows you to draft players from almost any season in baseball history and then pit them against each other in simulated games. It's fun for the whole family![38] Pick one up today!

In whatifsports, they have an AVG+ stat that puts every batting average into context, showing just how above or below it was from an average performance from the year in question. The all-time batting average champ by this metric was Tip O'Neill, who hit .435 in 1887. It was still a pretty high-offense year, with the league average at .273. But clearly O'Neill beat the league average by a greater margin that Duffy did in 1894 (.440 compared to .309).

---

[37] Technically, it talks about .438. That's what people thought Duffy's average was, before recent historians did some research and discovered it was actually .440.

[38] Applies only if your whole family is as nerdy for baseball history as I am, which has probably never happened. Unless Bill James and Rob Neyer finally tied the knot... (And if they did, my invitation MUST have been lost in the mail … AHEM ...)

If you insist on your stats being post-1901, Nap Lajoie is the champion of BA+, for hitting .384 in a 1910 American League that hit .243. Next in the list you have a Ty Cobb season and a Tris Speaker season and Ty Cobb again ... man, those dead-ball superstars really stood out from their leagues. The first post-WWII guy you get in this list is Ted Williams, who hit .388 in 1957 (league average: .255). And so on and so on until you get to Duffy's 1894, tied for 50th by this measure. In "real" BA, Duffy's average was amazing, but not as exceptional as it looks. It gets the same AVG+ as Tony Gwynn's .370 in 1987 and Rico Carty's .366 in 1970.

All this would be irrelevant if Duffy had an unambiguously great career. The above says he didn't. But then again, Duffy played when seasons were shorter. It wasn't quite like Deacon White and Jim O'Rourke, whose peaks were during 80-game seasons. But most of Duffy's seasons maxed out around 135 games. If they were each 154 games, Duffy's career would have contained at least 150 more games longer. Duffy was looking a little below the standards, but with the shorter seasons in mind, he goes just a little above. He belongs with Orlando Cepeda, Tony Perez and Earl Averill as guys I wouldn't vote in but won't vote out. Duffy barely stays.

Ken Griffey Jr. (1989-2010; career OPS+: 136)

	Career	Rank	Hitting	Rank	Fielding	Rank	Peak	Rank	Bests	JAWS	Rank
WAR	83.6	5	83.8	5	1.5	37	53.9	5	4	68.8	5
WS	407.7	5	342.1	5	65.6	17	208.3	9	4	NA	6*

When I was a friendless, clinically depressed teenager, I would temporarily push away the sadness by making up games involving baseball players. One was to find players whose names could be combined. For example, you can take Steve Carlton and Carlton Fisk and make Steve Carlton Fisk. I was especially proud of combining Mike Scott, Scott Terry, and Terry Harper to make Mike Scott Terry Harper. If you allow authors of seminal American novels you can add Harper Lee. If you allow inscrutably famous 1980s auto executives you can add Lee Iacocca. If you allow imaginary people with silly names you can add Iacocca McDinglewink. And so forth.[39]

My best one involving only ballplayers started with Ken Griffey Jr. Add Junior Felix, Felix Jose, and Jose Canseco, and you get Ken Griffey Junior Felix Jose Canseco. And I bet you wasted your teens achieving key developmental milestones and fostering lifelong friendships! That stuff never got you four ballplayers' names combined!

Sigh ... anyway, Griffey's many injuries late in his career seemed to squander much of his potential, at least in a lot of people's minds. He did have 630 homers and 11,304 PAs over 22 years, which is pretty darn exceptional. But when he hit 398 home runs before the age of 30, everyone was hoping he would be the son of a very good '70s outfielder to beat Aaron's lifetime record instead of that other one.[40]

---

[39] Holy cow, I just thought of a better one. Mike Scott Terry Lee Thomas Howard Johnson. Wooo! That's six! Or another direction: Chris George Brett Cecil Travis Lee Thomas Howard Johnson. That's eight!

[40] Barry Bonds, in case you didn't know, was the son of Bobby Bonds, a very unusual player. Bobby was one of only seven members of the 30 HR/30 SB club before 1987. He did it five times while no one else did it more than twice. He also held the record for strikeouts in a season from 1970 until

If only Griffey had used steroids! Not really, of course. But the Barry Bonds example seems to indicate that steroids can do wonders for an aging body and could have kept Griffey in the lineup a lot more. It actually adds more luster to Griffey's legend that he didn't give in to that temptation (as far as we know, that is. The "guilty until proven innocent" perspective that many take with steroids makes it impossible to view anyone without suspicion).

But you know, one nice thing about getting into advanced metrics like WAR and Win Shares is that you tend to care less about the all-time rankings of the traditional stats. So Barry Bonds holds the all-time records for home runs -- who cares? He still doesn't beat Babe Ruth in the more significant stats of Career WAR and Career Win Shares.

But Bonds would likely beat Griffey in Career WAR and Win Shares either way, as Bonds was always a bit better. Griffey was a tad overrated because he was so fun to watch. Compared even to pre-steroidal Bonds, Griffey wasn't tremendous at getting on base. Griffey did play a more crucial position, but didn't play it as well as everyone thought. Meanwhile Bonds was probably the all-time greatest in left field.

I have just one more "what-could-have-been" for Griffey (who was only one of the greatest players ever and a sure-fire Hall-of-Famer). Before a game in Griffey's rookie year, he was asked by a reporter if he'd be in the lineup that day against Frank Tanana. Griffey hadn't hit lefties well in the minors, and Tanana was a grizzled veteran lefty starter with more than 15 years under his belt. Griffey said "Why wouldn't I play? Who's Tanana? Some rookie?"

"I don't know who's pitching tonight," he went on. "I don't even know the schedule. How am I supposed to know who's pitching? I couldn't care less."

"He's not a student of the game," his father Ken Griffey Sr. said around the same time. "He plays on instinct and ability, and sometimes little else. Once he matures a bit -- and his mother isn't sure that day will ever come -- he'll be a very, very difficult opponent on a baseball field." (Quotes from "Ken Griffey: Superstar Centerfielder," by John Rolfe, et al., Rosen Pub Group, 2002.)

Griffey was very immature, but in a charming way. He would play silly jokes and chat with teammates about his favorite bands instead of about baseball. His nickname, "Kid," was a term of endearment. It's certainly astounding that he became a major-league star without trying terribly hard. But I wonder, if he'd prepared more, could he have been Mike Trout, i.e. the best player in baseball from day one?[41]

Blah blah blah. Ken Griffey Jr. is one of the 50 greatest baseball players ever, and is of course a Hall of Famer.

2004. Several players came very close to breaking the record before 2004, but sat out the last few games of the season so they wouldn't, like a bunch of pansies. Adam Dunn finally showed the courage to break the record in 2004, and it's been broken several times since.

[41] In case you're skeptical that Mike Trout is better than Ken Griffey Jr. at the same age, I have some numbers for you. Ken Griffey had 3.2 WAR in his first full season as a 19-year-old, 5.2 WAR at 20, and 7.1 WAR at 21. When he was 20, Mike Trout had 10.9 WAR, more that Griffey ever managed in any season. In fact it was the 22nd-best total of all time for non-pitchers, tied with Ted Williams' *best season.* At age 21, Trout had 8.9 WAR, again leading all of baseball. Trout's first two seasons easily beat Griffey's first three combined.

Billy Hamilton (1888-1901; career OPS+: 141)

	Career	Rank	Hitting	Rank	Fielding	Rank	Peak	Rank	Bests	JAWS	Rank
WAR	63.3	11	61.4	10	-5.4	78	42.5	14	9	52.9	12
WS	336.6	10	287.4	8	49.0	47	210.9	8	5	NA	9

Since we're talking about 1894, here's some more 1894 craziness. Billy Hamilton hit only .403 that year -- clearly he's no Hugh Duffy. But he did lead the National League with a .521 OBP, 100 stolen bases, 128 walks, 198 runs, and 702 PAs, all in just 132 games. He led non-pitchers with 8.2 WAR and was third in Win Shares with 29 (top two: our old friends Hugh Duffy and Joe Kelley).

As I write this, the Reds have a player called Billy Hamilton, whose main tool is blazing speed. Billy Hamilton the Elder was known as "Slidin' Billy" for much the same reason. In just 14 years and 7608 PAs, he compiled 914 stolen bases, leading the league five times and topping 100 four times.

But stolen bases were very different beasts in the 1890s. You were credited with a stolen base if you advanced a base on someone else's hit. So just making it to third on a single was a stolen base. On the other side of the equation, a pitcher could fake a throw to first without completing it, which would today be a clear balk. It was all so different that pre-1900 stolen bases really should be called something else, like "base advances" or something like that. Whatever it was, Hamilton was the best at it, by far.

More relevant for Billy Hamilton, Sr.'s Hall of Fame candidacy are his walks, hits and runs. Hamilton led the league in walks five times, OBP five times, runs four times, and batting average twice. He was one of the best leadoff hitters in history, and deserves a Hall of Fame berth.

Mickey Mantle (1951-1968; career OPS+: 172)

	Career	Rank	Hitting	Rank	Fielding	Rank	Peak	Rank	Bests	JAWS	Rank
WAR	109.7	4	116.0	4	-10	97	64.8	3	4	87.3	4
WS	565.2	4	507.0	4	58.0	30	300.1	2	5	NA	3

Did you know that Mickey Mantle's name is an anagram for "Minty acme elk"? It's eerily appropriate, isn't it? After all, Mantle was at the acme of his profession, he was fast as an elk, and he probably did magazine ads for a minty toothpaste at some point.

Sorry, it's hard to come up with something about Mickey Mantle that you probably don't already know. Remember the quiz I mentioned way back in the Eddie Collins comment that showed which Hall-of-Famers were named by 200,000+ baseball nerds? In that, Mantle was third-most popular answer, behind only Babe Ruth and Ty Cobb.

Mantle was a good combination of Ruth and Cobb, with both tremendous power and speed. "My, catlike men!" fans would often say anagramatically, while watching Mantle and fellow speedster Ken MacTimely race around the bases. The fact that Ken MacTimely is a person I just made up whose name is an anagram of "Mickey Mantle" did not quell the ardor of Yankee boosters one whit.

"Calm, mine tyke," parents would say to their children, who, eager for a tape-measure Mantle blast, instead watched him take ball four. Mantle had a Ted Williams-like ability to draw walks, leading the

American League five times and clearing more than 100 in a season 10 times. His defense in center wasn't one of the best ever, but it was good.

The total package was enough to lead the entire American League in WAR each year from 1955-1959, and then again in 1961. Win Shares sees that total and raises it, giving Mantle the AL Win Shares MVP every year from 1954-1958 and 1960-1962, plus 1964. That's nine Win Shares MVPs in eleven years. It's a streak interrupted only by Nellie Fox in 1959 and Tom Tresh in 1963, when Mantle was injured for most of the year. Mantle won three real-life MVPs, but clearly deserved many more.

And Mantle could have won several more WAR and Win Shares MVPs if not for a long list of injuries. During his first World Series in 1951, he snapped the ligaments in his knees. The knees bothered him the rest of his life. "It clammy knee!" he often shouted, because he spoke only in anagrams of his own name. He also suffered from osteomyelitis, a bone disease that causes pain and fever. "My lancet, Mike," doctors would often say to him, in an anagram he'd understand, to introduce him to one of the instruments of their trade.

"Enact me, Milky!" That's what Mantle said to every barkeep he met. Bartenders would then approach him to find out what the hell he was talking about. "Tacky lime, men?" Mantle would say. This they understood; a "tacky lime" was a popular 1960s cocktail, a mixture of vodka, lime, Easy Cheese, Spam, Twinkies, shag carpeting, aqua linoleum, lounge music, Astro Turf and Liberace's hair.

It's perhaps especially tacky to make absurd jokes while alluding to Mickey Mantle's years of excessive drinking, so I'll stop now. Mantle was a sensitive soul who took every disappointment hard. In his rookie season, at age 19, he was touted as the best thing since sliced bread with bacon, caramelized onions, and bleu cheese in between. The Yankees assigned him uniform number 6, to symbolize that he was to be next great star after Babe Ruth (number 3), Lou Gehrig (number 4), and Joe DiMaggio (number 5).[42] The pressure was on.

Mantle started out well that year but then slumped, and was sent down to the AAA Kansas City Blues. Manager Casey Stengel carefully assured Mantle that he just needed a little seasoning and would be back up to the majors soon. But after a handful of poor games with the Blues, Mantle grew despondent. He thought his career was over and decided to quit. Looking for support, he called his father, Mutt Mantle. Mutt drove all the way from Oklahoma to Kansas City to give him a good old-fashioned scream-fest. "Now you shut up! I don't wanna hear your whining! I thought I raised a man, not a coward!," shouted Mutt. Mickey broke down crying and resolved to keep playing. (Source: Mantle's SABR biography, by James Lincoln Ray.)

Add to Mantle's sensitive personality his chronic pain and the tremendous stress of being a major-league star in the pressure cooker of New York City, and you get a prescription for alcoholism. Many mornings he woke up with several forms of pain, self-inflicted and otherwise, but he kept pushing himself to show up at the park. Through it all, he ended up with 9907 PAs over 18 years.

Life after baseball was a struggle for Mantle, with more heavy drinking and several failed business ventures. His finances picked up in the mid-1980s when people started paying crazy amounts for autographs, especially Mantle's. The drinking continued, though, until he checked into the Betty Ford

[42] Both baseball and "Seinfeld" fans know that Mantle eventually ended up with the number 7. Mantle was not happy that even before his first plate appearance, his new club anointed him as the next Ruth/Gehrig/DiMaggio. They surely meant it as a compliment and an honor, but it really is a pretty terrible thing to do. There's enough pressure on rookies already without having immortality assigned to their backs.

Clinic in 1993. It proved to be too little too late, and he died of liver cancer in 1995, only 63 years old.

I make lots of dumb jokes, and many tickle me, but I genuinely lament Mickey. He was a great ballplayer, a great man, and a pillar of the Hall of Fame.[43]

Willie Mays (1951-1952, 1954-1973; career OPS+: 156)

	Career	Rank	Hitting	Rank	Fielding	Rank	Peak	Rank	Bests	JAWS	Rank
WAR	156.2	1	136.4	2	17.9	3	73.6	1	9	114.9	1
WS	641.9	2	527.6	2	102.6	2	279.5	4	9	NA	1

We've seen lots of superstars on this stage tonight. But I want you all to know one thing: This is Willie Mays' house.[44] Oscar Charleston, Ty Cobb, and Mickey Mantle would likely be the best ever at their positions if any had decided to play first base, second base, third base, or catcher.[45] But they chose center field, and there is one king at that position: Willie Mays.

As you may know, Willie Mays did everything that you can possibly do on a ballfield extremely well. He had speed, power, on-base ability, range, a powerful arm, etc., etc. He also had great durability, playing in more than 150 games each year for 13 straight seasons, most of which maxed out at 154 games. He ended with 12,946 plate appearances, 12th-most all-time. And he spent 1953 and most of 1952 in military service.

As with Mickey Mantle, voters only gave Mays the MVP if it was really, really hard to give it to anyone else. Baseball writers' jobs are to discover (or at least glom onto) exciting new stories, not to rehash what everyone already knows. So they like to give the MVP to the guy who represents an exciting new story, not the well-known guy who's actually a lot better. Mays deserved the MVP, according to WAR, every year from 1954-1959 (including a tie with Duke Snider in 1956), 1960, and 1962-1966. That's 10 or 11 WAR MVPs, depending on which way you go in 1956. It's a streak interrupted only by Ernie Banks in 1959 and Hank Aaron in 1961.

Win Shares is a bit more stingy, giving Mays only six of its MVPs: 1954, 1955, 1958, 1962, 1965, and 1966. In each year it gives Mays 40 or more Win Shares, except 1966, when he scored 37.

Just to give you some perspective on what it means to get 40 Win Shares: it means you're hella good. There, done and done. (I am now clapping my hands together up and down in the "I'm dusting off my hands" motion that people do after accomplishing something decisively.)

To add just a bit more perspective, position players have had 89 40-Win-Share seasons in history. It's so rare that you can go many years without one; in the entire decade of the 1980s, the only player to achieve 40 Win Shares was Will Clark in 1989. Babe Ruth did it nine times out of his 16 years as a

---

[43] Find the two anagrams of "Mickey Mantle" in that paragraph and win $0.45! Mail your answer with a self-addressed stamped envelope to Clank Yet Mime, 1313 Mockingbird Lane, Funkytown, AL, 12345.

[44] Reference explanation: "Run's House," by Run DMC.

[45] None would beat out Babe Ruth in right field or Honus Wagner at shortstop, in my view. It's debatable whether any could top Ted Williams in left field, or Barry Bonds, depending on your opinion of his career.

non-pitcher. Ty Cobb got there eight times, Honus Wagner six times, and Willie Mays, Mickey Mantle, Barry Bonds and Ted Williams achieved the total five times each.

Getting 10 WAR is comparable to achieving 40 Win Shares, except that it's even harder. There have been only 55 10-WAR seasons among position players at this writing. Babe Ruth did it nine times. Willie Mays and Rogers Hornsby did it six times each, Mickey Mantle, Barry Bonds, Ty Cobb and Ted Williams three times each. Mays is clearly in rarified air.

If the Hall of Fame decided to erect a Mount Rushmore outside its gates, Willie Mays should be on it.

Kirby Puckett (1984-1995; career OPS+: 124)

	Career	Rank	Hitting	Rank	Fielding	Rank	Peak	Rank	Bests	JAWS	Rank
WAR	50.9	21	52.4	21	-1.2	51	37.4	22	2	44.2	21
WS	282.3	28	223.8	26	58.4	29	188.8	21	1	NA	8

Kirby Puckett broke my heart more than any other ballplayer. When he was playing, he was the epitome of adorableness. Short, squat, and full of smiles, he smashed hits and scooted around bases with boundless energy and genuine joy.

He even had a rags-to-riches story, coming out of a tough neighborhood on the south side of Chicago. Despite his talent, he was ignored by scouts. The Twins only discovered him because their assistant scouting director, Jim Rantz, went to see his son play in a Central Illinois Collegiate League game that also happened to feature Puckett.

Kirby tended to say very charming things. When he was moved to the third spot in the batting order, he asked manager Ray Miller, disbelievingly, "Isn't that the spot for the team's best hitter?" "You're my best hitter," Miller informed him. (Source: Puckett's SABR biography, by Stew Thornley.)

In an interview, Puckett once said he wished he had a body like Glenn Braggs'. The reason you may not remember Glenn Braggs is because, as Bill James notes, he was a tenth the player of Puckett. This quote also got to the heart of the fun of watching Puckett play. In a game that was increasingly filled with statuesque gymrats, Puckett's 5'8", 175-lb body made him look less like a professional athlete and more like your goofy buddy who played in a beer league mainly for the beer.

Except that this goofy beer-league buddy could play major-league baseball alarmingly well. Puckett got hits by the dozens, four times leading the league. He started out as a speedster, but quickly developed good power. In his rookie year, Puckett had zero home runs and lots of bunt hits in 583 PAs. In his third year, after working with Twins legend Tony Oliva, he hit 31 homers. On top of it all, he was a very good fielder, often seeming to leap twice his height to turn a home-run ball into an out.

It was of course heartbreaking when Puckett came down with an eye problem that put his career to a screeching halt in 1996. He was 34 years old in 1995, but still hit .314/.379/.515. He likely could have lasted much longer. But that's not the "heartbreaking" part I was referring to at the beginning of this comment.

My heart broke when I heard about Puckett's history of alleged violence against women. In 2002, his wife Tonya Puckett sought a divorce, citing years of abuse. The breaking point, she said, came when they had an argument about his affairs with other women, and he threatened to kill her. She also said Kirby had once choked her with an electric cord. Another time, she said, he put a gun to her head while she held her daughter. Kirby also had a mistress, who sought a protective order to keep him away.

Later, Kirby was indicted for false imprisonment and gross sexual misconduct for allegedly dragging another woman into a restaurant bathroom and groping her. In 2003 he was acquitted, so it's hard to know exactly what happened. After the acquittal, Puckett was fired from his position in the Twins front office. He moved to Arizona and ballooned to 300 pounds. In 2006 he died from a stroke, only 46 years old.

Not all accusations are true. I don't know exactly what happened in any of the alleged incidents. But there comes a point when it becomes unavoidable to conclude that, in a general sense, Kirby Puckett was abusive to women. It's exceedingly unlikely that three different women would invent stories just to smear or extort him. That almost never happens once, much less three times to the same person. I've read enough to become convinced that Kirby Puckett was threatening, and probably violent, to women.

Many fans were in denial over these incidents, and spit venom on the accusers, dismissing them as "scorned women" and worse. This is a childish, immature reaction. To borrow a metaphor from Al Franken, these people looked at Puckett the way a four-year-old looks at his mommy: "My mommy is always right. Anyone who says otherwise is wrong and evil." ("Lies and the Lying Liars Who Tell Them," p. 24)

Of course, we all heard these terrible things about Puckett and wanted to believe they weren't true. But grown-ups have a responsibility to get past their immediate, painful emotional reactions and consider the facts more rationally. Sometimes our heroes turn out to be not so heroic after all. Adults have to know how to accept these kinds of disappointments and move on with their lives.

Kirby Puckett is no longer a hero of mine. But he was a wonderful ballplayer. That means he is a Hall-of-Famer.

Edd (sic) Roush (1913-1929, 1931; career OPS+: 126)

	Career	Rank	Hitting	Rank	Fielding	Rank	Peak	Rank	Bests	JAWS	Rank
WAR	45.2	33	46.1	28	-5.9	85	31.7	42	0	38.5	35
WS	313.9	15	247.9	16	56.2	32	190.3	19	1	NA	15

Why, Edd? Why? Why would you make life harder for yourself and for everyone around you by spelling "Ed" with two "d"s? What's the point?

I would almost understand if Edd were a kid born in the 2000s. Nowadays parents have this odd impulse to come up with unique names for their kids. But there are only so many unique names to go around that don't sound completely crazy. So often they just take a normal name and spell it weirdly. They probably think they're imparting a spirit of individuality in their children, but they're really just confining them to lifetimes of frustrating phone calls with service providers. "No, my name is

'Mytzch,' with a 'y' instead of an 'i.' And there's a silent 'z.' M-Y-T-Z-C-H, yeah. No, 'z,' as in "zebra." No, the 'z" is before the 'c'. Listen, can I email it to you?"[46]

That's not the only weird thing about Roush's name. His middle name is J -- just "J". It was a compromise middle name that honored both of Roush's grandfathers, Jerry and Joseph. This was a common practice of Scots-Irish people of the time; Harry S Truman's parents did the same thing. If you ever see a period on the end of the "S" in Truman's name, bask in the smug satisfaction of knowing that it's wrong. I know I do!

Oh, and Edd had a twin brother. Guess what his name was? Fred. Edd and Fred. Sigh. So Mr. and Mrs. Roush saddled their kids with a lame running gag that they will have to endure their entire lives. I really don't like Edd Roush's parents.

Besides having to live with a dumb name, Edd Roush also played baseball. He was a master of place hitting, slapping the ball all over the field to collect high batting averages. He used a 48-ounce bat, which is monstrously huge, about 30% heavier than any bat you'd see nowadays. It wasn't for creating power; quite the opposite. Roush would always take a half swing, which he called "glorified bunting," and let the weight of the bat push the ball past the infielders. Swinging slowly gave him more control, which meant he could send the ball exactly where he wanted it to go.

Roush joined fellow freaky bat enthusiast Heinie Groh in making the 1919 Reds a breakthrough team. Both started out with the Giants but floundered and got traded to the Reds. Both were terrific with the Reds in the late 1910s and early 1920s. Both were reacquired by the Giants later in their careers, but were pretty much done by then.

In terms of personality, they were quite different. Groh was quiet and polite, while Roush was what people like to diplomatically call "feisty." Every year he refused to go to spring training, insisting that working on his farm in the off-season kept him in shape. Every year he held out for more money, which coincided well with his hatred of spring training. In 1922 he held out until July.

Another thing Roush hated was the beanball. Oh, man, he hated it. I can sympathize, as I think it's barbaric and borderline sociopathic to intentionally throw a small white rock 90 miles an hour at another human being's brain (and I don't give a crap what Don Drysdale and Bob Gibson said about it, so don't bother telling me). But Roush would counter this sociopathic behavior with more sociopathic behavior. If a pitcher threw at his head and he ended up on base, he would intentionally spike the shins of every infielder he came across. It supposedly worked, as, at least according to anecdotes, infielders would press pitchers to never throw near Roush's head.

Roush eventually made the Hall of Fame on the strength of his .323 lifetime batting average and two batting titles. Meanwhile Heinie Groh isn't even on anyone's radar. Groh had two OBP titles and higher lifetime OBP than Roush, but ended with a .292 BA. Roush also got more seasons in the hitting-inflated 1920s. To be fair, Roush had about 1000 more PAs. Both were good fielders, but Groh was better at what was then a tougher position.

Anyway, I shouldn't be re-litigating the Heinie Groh case. This is Edddddddd Roush's case, and in it we are again separated by denominational differences: WAR says "nay" and Win Shares says "yay!!!!"

This is a tough one. I could just say that I trust Win Shares more, which is true. But that's not enough. Is it possible that WAR is picking up something that Win Shares is not?

---

[46] Maybe I'm just bitter. "Eddie Daniels" is my nom de plume; my real name is much more bizarre and annoying.

I don't think so. I think it's that old problematic "replacement level" concept again. In the dead-ball era, there were a few players -- Ty Cobb, Tris Speaker, Honus Wagner, Eddie Collins, Nap Lajoie, a few others -- who were so crazy good that that they threw off the averages. That then set the replacement level too high. This then downgraded the WARs of non-super-duperstars too much.

Imagine if you were in a class where your teacher graded on the curve. And imagine that a handful of kids in the class somehow got 130% by doing a lot of extra credit. Everyone else got scores in the 70-90% range. But with those lame nerds throwing off the curve, a 70% suddenly wasn't good enough to pass.

The line separating pass and fail is the replacement level. Edd Roush was not a 70% kind of player, by any means. But he was a 90% player. With those nerdy 130% outliers messing up the curve, Roush ends up closer to replacement level than he should be. I could get into the statistical concept of standard deviation, and maybe throw in something about my suspicions of an unwarranted assumption of a normal bell curve distribution within replacement-level calculations, but I'll spare you all that.

The point is that the replacement level bar really shouldn't be overly influenced by the super-good outliers. It is unrealistic to assume that a manager in the dead-ball era could easily find a replacement as good as the so-called "replacement level" set in part by Ty Cobb and those other overachieving nerds.

And as I've said before, replacement level is an unreasonably punishing boundary. If you always do better than replacement level, then you're a super-duper-star and you're golden. But if you dare dip below it, even for one season, you get negative numbers. Those negative numbers then turn back with a vengeance and erase your past good performances. If the replacement level is set just a bit too high, then it gets even more unfair. Then a lot of great-but-not-super-great players get cut below where they should be.

Edd Roush may not deserve to be in the Hall of Reasonable First Names, but I think he is just barely good enough to make the Hall of Fame.

Duke Snider (1947-1964; career OPS+: 140)

	Career	Rank	Hitting	Rank	Fielding	Rank	Peak	Rank	Bests	JAWS	Rank
WAR	66.5	9	70.6	7	-5.9	84	50	7	1	58.3	7
WS	351.6	7	296.9	7	54.9	35	224.2	6	1	NA	6

Duke Snider is Jose Carreras. Among the Three Tenors who patrolled center field for New York teams in the 1950s, Willie Mays is Luciano Pavarotti, Mickey Mantle is Placido Domingo, and Duke Snider is "the other guy."[47] Duke Snider was a wonderful player, one of the best ever, but was overshadowed by the two colleagues so famous that even non-baseball fans knew about them.

Lots of ink has been spilt bemoaning the Brooklyn Dodgers' move to L.A. in 1958. I feel like I've heard a dozen stories about salt-of-the-earth working-class Brooklyn dads who trudged to their families' formica breakfast tables each morning to ask their eager coonskin-cap-wearing kids what Jackie Robinson did last night, while Sinatra crooned in the background and the whole scene was

[47] Reference explanation: The "Seinfeld" episode "The Doll."

captured in soft-focus sepia tone. So I've always been tempted to take the other side. After all, there are a lot of people in Los Angeles who benefitted greatly from this particular move. And the Dodgers were hardly the only team to relocate in the 1950s.

But I concede that the Dodgers situation is different in a lot of ways. Unlike the Boston Braves and St. Louis Browns, the Dodgers were a very good team before the move. They won the pennant in 1952, 1953, and 1956, and won the World Series in 1955. And they drew good crowds, finishing first or second in the N.L. in attendance every one of those years.

Plus, the Dodgers weren't just the "other team" in major cities the way the Braves and Browns were. For centuries, Brooklyn was a separate city from New York, with a separate identity. It was founded by Dutch settlers in the mid-1600s and wasn't incorporated into New York City until 1898. In the 1860, 1870 and 1880 censuses, Brooklyn was the third-most populous city in the country. It was known as a "twin city" with New York, and the two were connected only by boat until the Brooklyn Bridge was built in 1883.

As I've mentioned, I live in St. Paul, Minnesota. Of Minnesota's twin cities, Minneapolis is definitely the more hip, famous and glamorous (if that word can really be applied to anything in Minnesota). St. Paul is the more mellow, family-oriented one, the Jon Cryer to Minneapolis's Charlie Sheen.[48] If St. Paul were subsumed into Minneapolis, it would hardly be a travesty, and the odd-couple pairing would surely amuse millions every Monday night at 7 p.m., 8 p.m. Eastern.[49] But I would find it a bit depressing, and I would become nostalgic for the old days when Jon Cryer/St. Paul were best known for "Pretty in Pink"/being a separate city.

Duke Snider was a bit depressed to leave Brooklyn in 1958, despite being a native of the L.A. area. His knees and home-run bat became especially nostalgic for the old days. He was 31 in the Dodgers' first season in SoCal, and it was the first of seven straight years in which injuries kept him below 450 PAs. He was still productive when he did play, but the the homers were not quite as prolific. In Brooklyn's Ebbetts Field, the right-field fence was only 297 feet from home plate. In the 90,000 seat Los Angeles Coliseum that hosted the Dodgers until 1961, the dimensions were considerably larger. Duke was the only hitter to clear the right-center-field fence in all of 1958.

Before the big move, Snider wasn't far from matching Mays and Mantle. He hit 40 or more home runs every year for five straight years, from 1953-1957. Combine his power with good on-base ability and good defense, and you get 30+ Win Shares and 7.5+ WAR each year from 1953-1956. If only he had been able to keep this level of achievement going through his 30s, he may have ... well, maybe not caught Mantle, but at least come closer. Regardless, he's clearly a Hall of Famer.

Tris Speaker (1907-1928; career OPS+: 157)

	Career	Rank	Hitting	Rank	Fielding	Rank	Peak	Rank	Bests	JAWS	Rank
WAR	133.7	3	123.6	3	2.3	33	62.2	4	8	98.0	3
WS	629.6	3	511.9	3	118.0	1	285.8	3	10	NA	4

48 Reference explanation: "Two and Half Men." I'm not proud of it, but I couldn't think of a better metaphor. Let me know if you do. Again, the email is chrisekeedei@yahoo.com. Anything disrespectful will be ignored.
49 I always put the Central Time Zone first, because it's better.

Tris Speaker is better than Joe DiMaggio. Speaker may be better than Mickey Mantle. Willie Mays is pretty untouchable, but you could make an argument that Speaker is as good as Ty Cobb if you take defense into account. WSAWS has Speaker second, after Cobb, but Bill James put Mays and Mantle above both in his final rankings.

Like Mays and Mantle, Speaker was a six-tool player, excelling in everything that a human being can do on a baseball diamond apart from umpiring and mascotting. He had only 117 career home runs, but his peak was in the dead-ball era, and power was a different thing then. Power was doubles and triples, and Speaker holds the all-time record with 792 doubles, while his 222 triples are sixth all-time.

Like Eddie Collins, Speaker isn't as well-known as he should be today. He did better in the Hall of Fame quiz than Collins did, being named by 64.4% of the 200,000+ baseball nerds. But that's not enough. We clearly need to spread brand awareness of Tris Speaker with an aggressive marketing campaign utilizing social channels to leverage incentivization through thought leaders operating within relevant demographic deciles.[50]

Few people suggest that Speaker may be better than Cobb, because Cobb's hitting numbers are so overwhelming. Comparisons are inevitable, because they were almost exact contemporaries playing the same position in the same league. Cobb hit .366 over 13,084 PAs, while Speaker hit a measly .345 over just 11,992 PAs. Cobb had 12 batting titles in a 13-year span, 1907-1919, while Speaker won it the only year Cobb didn't, 1916. (1910 saw a disputed title when Nap Lajoie ended with a higher average only because, in the last game of the season, he was allowed to get eight bunt hits down the third-base line. It's widely acknowledged that Cobb was the real winner.)

Cobb was indeed a better hitter, but not by as much as it might seem. Cobb's slight advantage was enough to lead the league in all sorts of categories, while Speaker almost always came in second, third, or fourth. Cobb's hitting record jumps out at you with a sea of black ink denoting league leads, while Speaker's does not. This gives the illusion that Cobb was miles better than Speaker, but really, he was a few yards at most.

Note that Speaker gets loads of yearly "bests" over Cobb and all other center fielders in the table above. According to WAR, Speaker was the best center fielder in baseball 8 times, while Cobb was the best 11 times, all within the same time span. Win Shares says Speaker was the best 10 times, while Cobb was the best 9 times. For 15 years, from 1910 to 1924, the title of yearly best for center field was always traded back and forth between Speaker and Cobb except 1919, when Win Shares liked Edd Roush best (WAR went with Cobb).

Cobb may have an edge in hitting, but Speaker makes up some of the difference in the field. Win Shares says Speaker was the best-fielding center fielder of all time, a common assessment. WAR says he was 33rd, behind the likes of Denard Span and Corey Patterson. (Sigh. Honestly, WAR, why am I even listening to you any more?) Cobb still gets 5th place among defensive center fielders according to Win Shares, but logged more than 35 fewer Defensive Win Shares than Speaker did. (And I'm not even dignifying WAR's defensive rankings with any further mention.)

Center field occupies a similar offense/defense balance that third base does; defense is important, but not as important as with shortstops or catchers. It would be almost impossible to make the Hall

---

[50] My real job is in marketing, so that sentence actually makes sense to me. Now you see why I'd much rather be a writer.

on center field defense alone. But you can't be too bad defensively and stick in center. If you were, you'll be moved to first base or left field or DH where you can't do too much damage.

If the defensive gap between Speaker and Cobb were small, Cobb would be clearly better overall. But the gap is large enough that Speaker has a case. All in all, Cobb probably stills has the edge. But it's close. Both, of course, are Hall of Fame royalty.

Turkey Stearnes (1920-1940)

	Rank at Position Among Negro Leaguers	Rank Among All Negro Leaguers
Bill James	1 in left	4
SABR	3	8
Monte Irvin	3	NA

As with the MLB, center field is stacked with Negro League superstars. If Bill James ranked Stearnes in center field, he would have had him above Cool Papa Bell but below Oscar Charleston. Regardless, all three are among the ten greatest Negro Leaguers ever. In his top 100 players of all time from all leagues, Stearnes ranks 25th, between Frank Robinson and Rickey Henderson. That should you give you an idea of where Stearnes belongs.

Norman Thomas Stearnes was called "Turkey" because when he ran, he flapped his arms like a bird. He was otherwise not full of personality. In private moments, he would talk to his bats, but in public he was pretty businesslike.

Stearnes isn't featured in many stories, which are crucial to being a famous Negro Leaguer, to an inordinate degree. When you don't have reliable stats, later generations can't go on much besides stories. It was the same with white players from the 1800s; remember that the quiet Roger Connor was only elected to the Hall when people in the 1970s went back and discovered his batting record.

Stearnes didn't get the call for the Hall until 2000. He should have made it much earlier. Seamheads only has 1424 of Stearnes' career PAs, but those are incredible: .353/.409/.640, for a 190 OPS+. Baseball-reference has 3697 PAs over 20 years, with a .344/.396/.618 line. According to some sources, Stearnes is the all-time leader in home runs among Negro Leaguers, topping his league in the category seven times. Other sources say Mule Suttles had more career homers. Regardless, someone with a nickname taken from a farm animal is the all-time Negro League home run leader.

Which has me thinking ... what would be the all-time animal-name team? Here's one stab at it:

C: Buck Ewing
1B: Mule Suttles
2B: Nellie Fox
SS: Rabbit Maranville
3B: Koala Kangarooface
LF: Goose Goslin
CF: Turkey Stearnes
RF: Ducky Wucky Medwick
SP: Old Hoss Radbourn, Catfish Hunter
RP: Goose Gossage
Golfing buddy: Tiger Woods

Clubhouse entertainment: Snoop Lion
Not bad! They're all Hall of Famers except Koala Kangarooface, and the only reason he isn't is because I made him up. Ducky Wucky Schmoopie Poo is a little out of position, but he'll just have to deal with that.

Anyway, Turkey Stearnes deserves better than this silliness. He is a no-doubt Hall of Famer.

Cristobal Torriente (1912-1932; OPS+: 190)

	Rank at Position Among Negro Leaguers	Rank Among All Negro Leaguers
Bill James	2	9
SABR	4	20
Monte Irvin	1 (among RF)	NA

And then there's Cristobal Torriente! The Negro Leagues keep giving and giving with great center fielders. Monte Irvin lists Torriente among right fielders, because, he says, Torriente played everywhere, and was known as "the Cuban Babe Ruth," and Babe Ruth was a right fielder, so there you go.

That's kinda silly. While it's true that Torriente played everywhere, including 300+ OK innings as a pitcher, he was a center fielder through and through. Torriente was so good in center that when he played alongside Oscar Charleston, Charleston was the one who moved to right. Seamheads says that Torriente played more than 75% of his games in center. So there, Monte Irvin. How dare you make such an ultimately meaningless mistake!

Regardless of where he played, Torriente was one of the best. He was a six-tool player, including the ability to draw walks. He might even qualify for seven tools if his pitching were a bit better. Seamheads says that Torriente hit .351/.434/.521 over 20 years and 3930 PAs. It also gives him the highest Win Shares total of any Negro League player (at least at this writing -- there are more stats from other players to be compiled). Baseball-reference cites 3381 PAs and a .331/.401/.491 line.

As I mentioned in the introduction, Torriente was a light-skinned Cuban, and a few other light-skinned Cubans played in the white major leagues before the color line was broken. In 1923, Cuban pitcher Dolf Luque had one of the all-time greatest seasons for the Reds (322 innings, 1.93 ERA, 10.6 WAR, 39 Win Shares). Mike Gonzalez was a Havana-born catcher who played in the majors from 1912-1930. Torriente was a contemporary of both and much better than either, but he never got a chance in the MLB because his hair was deemed too kinky to pass. Craziness.

You have to wonder what could have been if Torriente had become an MLB superstar. Would there have been a rush to bring in more Cubans? Would the color line have gradually changed to accept darker and darker-skinned Cubans? Would segregation have ended earlier? Probably not, but a guy can dream.

Regardless, the Negro National League was big-time too, and Torriente was an early superstar. In the league's first three years, 1920-1922, Torriente hit .411/.479/.606 (236 OPS+), .352/.429/.596 (216 OPS+), and .289/.384/.474 (160 OPS+), respectively. Each year his Chicago American Giants won the pennant.

Torriente didn't stop hitting, but eventually his drinking and carousing got him traded to the Kansas City Monarchs. He didn't last long there either, because of various fights with management. In 1926, when a diamond ring of his was stolen, he demanded that Monarchs owner Rube Foster reimburse him for it. Foster refused, and Torriente walked off the team in a huff.

While Turkey Stearnes was not at all colorful, Cristobal Torriente was perhaps a little too colorful for his own good. Torriente loved the ladies and the night life. After retiring from baseball in 1932, his alcoholism only got worse. He was alone and destitute when he died of tuberculosis in 1938, only 44 years old.

Before that, Torriente had enough great seasons to clearly deserve the Hall.

Lloyd Waner (1927-1942, 1944-1945; career OPS+: 99)

	Career	Rank	Hitting	Rank	Fielding	Rank	Peak	Rank	Bests	JAWS	Rank
WAR	24.1	100	22.9	95	-2.1	56	20.3	105	0	22.2	106
WS	244.6	47	169.9	57	67.2	16	163.2	47	0	NA	50

Wow. I was thinking that George Kelly was the most unqualified member of the Hall of Fame. But Kelly didn't get an overall rank higher than 100. Here is a list of recent center fielders that JAWS puts above Lloyd Waner, arranged by their rankings:

86. Lloyd Moseby
90. Randy Winn
97. Stan Javier
99. Al Bumbry

Win Shares is not so cruel, putting Waner in the neighborhood of Ray Lankford and Willie Wilson. That seems more appropriate. Like Wilson, Waner was a good leadoff hitter who collected a few flashy seasonal numbers over a long-enough career. Waner led the league in runs in his rookie year and ran off a string of three straight seasons of 220+ hits. But he didn't draw walks or show much power.

After those first three years, which were themselves boosted by the hitting explosion of the time, Waner managed just a few good seasons interspersed with injury-shortened ones. His last full season was in 1938, at age 32, and then he kinda farted around until 1945. He ended up with a respectable 8,334 career PAs, an empty .313 batting average and not much else. If you weren't really thinking much about it, the batting average might make him look good enough to pass.

It isn't, obviously. But it did pass. You might guess that Waner was selected by the Frankie Frisch-led Veterans Committee, and you would be right, sort of. In 1967, Waner did get into the Hall of Fame through the Veterans of the 1920s-1930s Who Had a Few Nice-Looking Numbers Committee, which did contain Frisch. But it was only Frisch's first year on the committee, so it's hard to imagine he was already dominating. In those days the Veterans Committee had a tradition of being much more staid. Their only other inductee that year was Branch Rickey, who was, of course, worthy. The previous year they had selected only Casey Stengel. But the year after Waner's selection, 1968, they chose more 1920s-1930s players of mixed worthiness, and Frisch's reign of aggressive mediocrity officially began.

It also helped that Lloyd was half of the famous Waner brothers, who made for lots of stories. They had the adorable nicknames "Little Poison" and "Big Poison." They got the names from Brooklyn fans, who were trying to say "little person" and "big person," but were physically unable to pronounce the King's English properly. "Little (ahem) Person" Lloyd was 5'9", but "Big Person" Paul was an inch shorter. The terms had more to do with their batting, as Lloyd got the little hits and Paul got the big ones.

Anyway, **Lloyd Waner is out.**

Hack Wilson (1923-1934; career OPS+: 144)

	Career	Rank	Hitting	Rank	Fielding	Rank	Peak	Rank	Bests	JAWS	Rank
WAR	38.8	52	42.5	38	-7.2	91	35.8	25	3	37.3	39
WS	223.8	59	190.4	44	27.3	133	189.1	20	3	NA	19

Like Lloyd Waner, Hack Wilson had a few great-looking stats during the hitting explosion in the 1920s and 1930s. But Wilson's stats were much more great-looking.

Wilson led the National League in home runs in 1926, 1927, 1928 and 1930. He led in RBI in 1929 and 1930. In 1930 he led in not only home runs and RBIs, but also slugging percentage, walks, and OPS. This 1930 season is what Hack Wilson is known for: a .356/.454/.723 line, 56 homers, 104 walks, and 191 RBI. That last number is still a record for a single season.

It sure looks like one of the all-time best hitting performances. But it's actually not. Astute readers will remember that 1930 was a crazy year, the best ever for hitters besides 1894. The entire National League hit .303/.360/.448 in 1930. Wilson had a great year, no doubt, but in context it wasn't too terribly outstanding. He gets 35 Win Shares, leading the National League by three over Babe Herman and Bill Terry. But WAR actually says Terry had the better year, giving him 7.6 to Wilson's 7.4. If there had been an MVP award at the time, I bet Bill Terry would have won it, since he hit .401 and people were more agog for batting averages than RBIs in those days. The point is that Hack Wilson's 1930 season was great stuff, but not among the 200 greatest hitters' seasons ever.

I'm reminded of Hugh Duffy. Duffy also picked a very good time to have a very good year (1894), and set a record in a very glamorous stat (a .440 BA). Duffy's performance also was great but not as great as it looks at first glance. Duffy also had a number of other good seasons but not a very long career.

But Wilson's career was even shorter than Duffy's. Hack managed only six full seasons and six partial ones, for a total of 5,556 PAs. This was in large part because of his alcoholism, which also afflicted both his mother and father. Hack had a strange body, 5'6" and 190 pounds with tiny size 5 1/2 feet and a neck as thick as his huge, flat-faced head. He was beloved for it, but it was probably a result of fetal alcohol syndrome.

Life after baseball for Wilson took a path you're familiar with from reading about other alcoholic players: failed business ventures, a gradual decline into poverty, and death before his 50th birthday. This sort of thing still happens, of course, but it seems to be rarer nowadays. For every Ken Caminiti, may he rest in peace, there are a dozen Jeff Reardons who hit rock bottom but bounce back and survive.

If you've got a moment, let's talk history. (And if you don't, skip down to the paragraph that starts with "At any rate." As you may have noticed by now, "At any rate" and "Anyway" are my favorite ways to get back on track.) There are many reasons that people don't drink themselves to death as much as they used to, ranging from better treatment options to the wide range of other drugs you can overdose on instead. One interesting reason, to me at least, is that the way people drink has changed since before Prohibition.

Prohibition is widely seen as a failure, and it was, in many respects. It sure didn't end drinking. And making alcohol illegal had the unintended consequence of giving organized crime a lot to do.

But before Prohibition, the United States was the hardest-drinking nation on earth. The local bar was the social center of town, the way it now is in Ireland; some men literally received their mail there. Most men lived like the guys in "Cheers," or at least like the guys in "The Iceman Cometh." The latter was probably more common, which motivated the prohibition movement. Prohibition destroyed that culture, turning bars into places for wild singles and devoted alcoholics.

Prohibition may not have stopping drinking, but it did cut it down dramatically. Alcohol consumption dropped about 70% during Prohibition. In the decades after the repeal of Prohibition in 1933, consumption climbed back up and then fell again. But the culture had changed in a fundamental way, according to "Last Call" by Daniel Okrent (page 373). Before and during the Prohibition years, if you were in a bar, the social pressure was to drink hard alcohol quickly. Pretty much everyone drank like college kids on dollar shot night. After Prohibition, there was more of a stigma attached to getting too drunk. Moderation became more normal. I think this different approach to drinking helped make cases like Hack Wilson's less common.

At any rate, not to be harsh, but Wilson's struggles with alcohol don't change his case at all. If you look at addiction as a disease, then it's no different from suffering from any other sort of disease or injury that shortens your career. If Kirby Puckett had contracted his eye problems after only 5,000 PAs, he likely wouldn't have a Hall-of-Fame career.

And I don't think Wilson does. Bill James is awfully generous putting Wilson 19th; WSAWS agrees with WAR and puts Wilson 44th. As I've mentioned, sometimes there are discrepancies between Bill James' rankings and WSAWS because James used a five-year peak instead of a seven-year peak. Hack Wilson really only had five or six good years, so he benefits from James' version of a peak. But even if you change the ratings to the best five years, Wilson only goes from 20th to 16th in Win Shares Peak. It's still not enough to make up for his 59th-best Career Win Shares total.

Maybe if only Peak WAR and Win Shares mattered, Wilson would squeak by. But that's not how it is, so **Hack Wilson is out.**

Who's In, Who's Out

Earle Combs, Lloyd Waner and Hack Wilson are all gone. All logged nice-looking numbers in the 1920s and 1930s, numbers that look less nice when you consider the context. Here are a few to take their places:

Jim Edmonds (1993-2008, 2010; career OPS+: 132)

	Career	Rank	Hitting	Rank	Fielding	Rank	Peak	Rank	Bests	JAWS	Rank
WAR	60.3	14	56.7	15	5.7	21	42.5	13	3	51.4	13
WS	302.3	19	239.5	17	63.0	21	198.9	12	1	NA	15*

I never had to bring out something akin to the "third baseman conundrum" with center fielders. That is, third base requires both defense and offense, and Hall-of-Fame voters aren't great at electing players who don't stick out on one end or the other. The same is true of center field, to a lesser extent.

Jim Edmonds was a very good hitter, with loads of power and good on-base ability. But if he were a first baseman, he wouldn't have rankings as good as the above. Luckily for him, he was a center fielder, and an excellent one. He's a bit like longtime teammate Scott Rolen, with great defense and great offense combining to make a solid Hall of Fame case that will, realistically, probably never come to fruition.

Nowadays, it's much harder to make the Hall of Fame. In one way, that's a good thing. We certainly don't want to go back to the wet 'n' wild Frankie Frisch days of the late '60s and early '70s. But I think the pendulum may have swung too far in the other direction.

Someone like Jim Edmonds will probably have to wait for the Veterans Committee, since he's in the second tier with guys like Richie Ashburn and Earl Averill. But the Veterans Committee is especially stingy nowadays when it comes to players who have already been through the BBWAA ballot.

Well, technically, there is no single Veterans Committee any more. There are three different committees reviewing different eras, and each committee meets in a different year ... ahh, it's so complicated that it's like trying to explain parliamentary procedures in Congress, and no one wants that. Suffice to say, it's tough.

Again like Congress, this new system seems to be set up so that nothing can get through. The terrible selections of the Hall of Fame have gotten more attention lately, and perhaps that has made the Hall more gunshy. Meanwhile, the pool of deserving candidates has grown.

Let's hope the pendulum swings in the other direction soon and second-tier guys from the modern era join the Ernie Lombardis and Bobby Doerrs from the old days. Granted, the Hall of Fame hasn't been perfect at distinguishing the second tier from the undeserving third or fourth tiers (George Kelly, Lloyd Waner, etc.). But that's why I'm here!

Hey, crazy idea, Hall of Fame, and tell me if I'm crazy here: Here's how we fix all this. Abolish all the various veterans committees and subcommittees and advisory groups and team meetings and club powwows and informal coffee klatches and college-buddy bull sessions and whatever else is going in your labyrinthine current system, and just put me in charge. I will do it pro bono, provided that I also get lots of cash.

Jim Wynn (1963-1977; career OPS+: 129)

	Career	Rank	Hitting	Rank	Fielding	Rank	Peak	Rank	Bests	JAWS	Rank
WAR	55.6	16	57.5	11	-6.7	88	43.3	11	3	49.5	15
WS	304.3	17	260.2	9	44.1	60	214.7	7	5	NA	10

Jim Wynn is another guy who, realistically, will probably never make it to the Hall of Fame. Wynn's chances are especially slim because a lot of his value is in walks instead of batting average. And his other numbers often don't look spectacular because he played in a very low-offense time. Plus, his home games for most of his career were in the Astrodome, an extreme pitcher's park. On top of that, his career was not very long. And, if you needed more reasons, Wynn got in the postseason only once, with the Dodgers in 1974. He probably has as much chance as yo momma of getting in the Hall of Fame. (Snap! Yo momma is so undeserving of the Hall of Fame that she makes Lloyd Waner look like Honus Wagner! Ooo! You know, perhaps that is because yo momma never played major-league baseball. Hmm. Something to ponder.)

But man, Wynn had some great years. He got more than 7 WAR three times and more than 5 another three times. Win Shares gives him four scores above 30 and three more above 25. In 1969, when the league hit .250/.319/.369, Wynn was at .269/.436/.507 with 33 home runs and 148 walks.

The above rankings show Wynn as being solidly in the second tier of Hall of Fame center fielders. You know, I talk about the different tiers of Hall of Famers a lot. Maybe I should actually try to define them more clearly.

Let's see if JAWS and Win Share numbers really do reveal distinct tiers. Time for a graph! The below plots JAWS vs. WSAWS for every center fielder with more than 34 JAWS and 193 WSAWS (arbitrary numbers I chose because I had to cut it off somewhere):

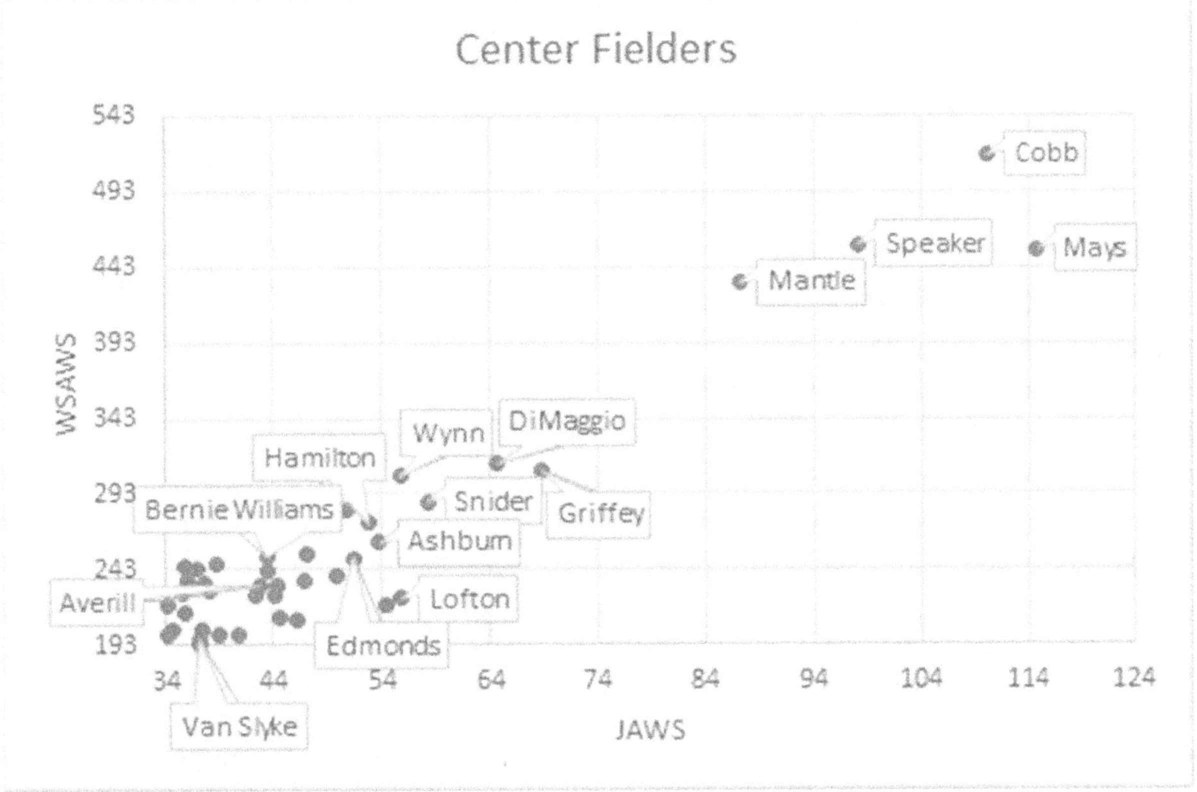

In strict terms, the first tier begins and ends with Ty Cobb, Tris Speaker, Willie Mays and Mickey Mantle. If the Hall of Fame really were as small as most people think it is (see first chapter), then it should probably just include those four.

But that's no fun. There are loads of more legends who deserve to be enshrined. You could maybe draw a diagonal line dividing Griffey, DiMaggio and Snider from the rest, but that group would have to include Jimmy Wynn. And that's still only eight players.

So maybe the line should be drawn a little lower, after Hamilton, Ashburn, and Kirby Puckett (I didn't have room to give him a label, but he's that little bashful dot peeking out between Bernie Williams' and Billy Hamilton's big, obtrusive name tags.) Jim Edmonds is so close to that line though. So is Kenny Lofton, who I'm not recommending for the Hall but isn't an unreasonable candidate.

And besides, that line would only allow in 11 guys; as you know, 20 or so is the current Hall-of-Fame standard for each position. You could just lower the line a bit more, which would take in Edmonds and Lofton, as well as the unlabeled Willie Davis, Andruw Jones, and Vada Pinson.

But then that leaves out Earl Averill, who I let stay in the Hall thanks to his stirring oratory. He's in a cluster with Bernie Williams, who isn't a terrible candidate but I'm not recommending. Averill belongs in that Tony Perez-Orlando Cepeda-Jim Rice range of "I wouldn't elect him but I wouldn't kick him out." At least Averill belongs above the cluster that includes Andy Van Slyke. That's definitely the third or fourth tier.

Earle Combs and Lloyd Waner don't even make the above chart, by the way. I have full justification to be upset about them, as they were clear mistakes. Hack Wilson is in that Van Slyke cluster (which sounds like an astronomical name). He may be more qualified than Combs and Waner, but is well below the top 20. My ejections from the Hall are almost all more clear-cut than my replacements.

My general point is that it's pretty much impossible to draw a distinct line between the second tier and the third. The first tier for any position is easy, and the BBWAA always gets those right, usually on the first ballot. The second tier is very difficult, involving lots of close judgement calls. If Bernie Williams makes it in some day and Jim Edmonds does not, I guess I can't get too upset.

Even if there is no mathematically precise line separating Hall-of-Famers from non-Hall-of-Famers, there is a sort of fuzzy line. This fuzzy line divides a range of mostly qualified candidates from mostly unqualified ones. Jim Wynn is solidly in the former.

Vada Pinson (1958-1975; career OPS+: 111)

	Career	Rank	Hitting	Rank	Fielding	Rank	Peak	Rank	Bests	JAWS	Rank
WAR	54.1	19	54.7	17	-5.7	81	40.1	17	0	47.1	16
WS	320.5	13	251.4	14	69.3	13	185.7	25	0	NA	18

Like Jim Wynn, Vada Pinson was a solid second-tier guy who is underrated because he played in a low-offense time. Otherwise, they were quite different. While Wynn had a short career of low batting averages and lots of walks, Vada had a long career of good batting averages but few walks. Pinson was a much better defensive player than Wynn.

Pinson came on strong at a young age, collecting loads of hits and runs at ages 20-26. He slowly declined from then on. I suppose he's a bit like Lloyd Waner in that respect. But Pinson was several notches better than Waner in every way. He had a longer career, better individual seasons (in context), and some real power, exceeding 20 homers in a season seven times. He also had speed, with 305 career stolen bases. Pinson got two 30-Win Share seasons and seven others in the 20s, along with one 7+ WAR season and four other 5+ ones.

Pinson belongs in the Alan Trammell/Bill Dahlen/Bill Freehan camp of players who didn't have one standout trait, instead doing everything very well. Pinson did lead the league in hits twice, doubles twice, and triples twice, so he was often prolific. Perhaps his most exceptional trait was durability. Pinson played in 154 or more games nine straight years, the first three of which were seasons that maxed out at 154 games.

Man, we need something lighter about now. It's been nothing but numbers and graphs for a while. The Jims Wynn and Edmonds didn't get a single amusing anecdote or half-baked assessment of their personalities! Let's do that for Pinson.

In Pinson's rookie year, he was a very quiet 19-year-old. He was so quiet that one of the Reds' coaches, Jimmy Dykes, thought he was a Latino who didn't speak English. After Dykes waved large gestures and over-enunciated broken English at Pinson, Vada said, "Mr. Dykes, if there is something you want me to do with my stance, please tell me." (Source: Pinson's SABR biography, by Ralph Moses.)

Pinson became fast friends with fellow Red Frank Robinson. They had grown up together in Oakland, California and went to the same high school. Robinson said it was the first close friend he had in baseball. (Robinson was not the friendliest of fellows.) They were accused of creating a clique of African-American players, but really, they were just two introverts who enjoyed each other's company, and they really were not that closed off. When Pete Rose came up as a rookie in 1963, he turned everyone off with his arrogance. Robinson and Pinson were the ones who stepped in to show him the ropes.

At any rate (back on track!), Vada Pinson looks to me like a solid second-tier Hall of Famer.

Chapter Nine

~ ~ Right Field ~ ~

Right field is a place for hitters. Sure, it helps to have a strong arm that can get a ball to third base every so often. But no one makes the Hall of Fame because of their defense in right field. The following players will be judged almost entirely on their offensive contributions.

Hank Aaron (1954-1976; career OPS+: 155)

	Career	Rank	Hitting	Rank	Fielding	Rank	Peak	Rank	Bests	JAWS	Rank
WAR	142.4	2	131.5	2	-5.0	68	60.0	2	8	101.2	2
WS	640.5	2	573.4	2	67.2	1	255.2	2	9	NA	2

David Aardsma never should have been allowed in the MLB. When he debuted with the Giants, he overtook Hank Aaron as the first player alphabetically in the list of major-leaguers. At least Aardsma was a pitcher. That means Aaron would still be listed first in the Macmillan Baseball Encyclopedia, which always put hitting records before pitching records. (I'm pretending that the Baseball Encyclopedia isn't an anachronism in this age of Baseball-reference.com. I still have a copy of the Baseball Encyclopedia, but mainly out of nostalgia for my teenage days.)

I suppose Aaron is number two in most things nowadays. In career home runs he has been surpassed, as you may have heard. In all of the above rankings except defense, Aaron is second to Babe Ruth.

Aaron still holds the career RBI record. Remarkably, he never had one of the top 150 single-season RBI totals. His high was 132 in 1957, the year the Braves won the World Series and Aaron won the MVP. Luminaries who had more than 132 RBIs in a season include Preston Wilson (141 in 2003), Zeke Bonura (138 in 1936), and Moose Solters (134 in 1936). Those three played in high-offense times, of course. Aaron played in an OK hitting environment (the 1950s) and a downright bad one (the 1960s and early 1970s). This makes his career records all the more exceptional.

Same deal with Aaron's home-run total. He never hit 50 in a season; his career-best 47 in 1971 ties for the 74th-best all-time. But he hit at least 30 home runs in a season 15 times, a record.

Win Shares tells the same story of consistent excellence without a single crazy-huge season. Aaron had 14 30-Win-Share seasons, second only to Babe Ruth's 15. Aaron's seasonal best was 41 in 1963, which is an awesome number but only the 55th-best ever for position players.

A 7-WAR season is roughly equivalent to 30 Win Shares. Aaron exceeded 7 WAR 13 times, second only to Barry Bonds' 14. Aaron had two seasons above 9 WAR, and none in the top 50 of all time. No one in history can match Aaron in performing at a very high level for a very long time.

He was like a kid who scored a 95% on every test for his entire school career, through college and two Ph.D.s. Others might get 100% on a test occasionally, or maybe 110% if they were Barry Bonds, cheating on the test, or if they were Hack Wilson, taking advantage of grade inflation. But none of them graduated with more honors than Hank Aaron.

In part because he was so reliably great without ever hitting the single-season heights of Mickey Mantle or Willie Mays, Hank Aaron was known as the quiet superstar. It helped that he was reserved and soft-spoken and didn't play on the East Coast. He never seemed like the type to do something as flashy as breaking Babe Ruth's career home run record. But he kept on working until he did, and I'm far from the first to say I wish he still had it. Whatever; he's a central member of the Hall of Fame.

Willard Brown (1935-1954)

	Rank at Position Among Negro Leaguers	Rank Among All Negro Leaguers
Bill James	1 (basically)	not ranked
SABR	not ranked	not ranked
Monte Irvin	4 (in left field)	NA

Hmm. This is a problem. Bill James says Willard "Home Run" Brown was the best right fielder in Negro League history. (Well, he actually says Martin DiHigo was, but the Hall of Fame has him as a pitcher, so that's where I put him.) But SABR doesn't even include Brown among the top 40 Negro League figures. Monte Irvin splits the difference in putting Brown fourth, though even that gets complicated because he ranks Brown in left field and doesn't include himself in the left-field rankings. And Irvin is widely regarded as the best left fielder in Negro League history.

Biographies of Willard Brown always mention untapped potential. He was a massive slugger who swung at everything, including pitches so far outside that catchers couldn't handle them. But Brown connected often enough to pile up some big home run totals and batting averages. Bill James says he was the best position player in all of Negro League baseball in 1937 and 1946.

Brown was an easygoing guy, so people often thought he wasn't hustling. If a game got boring while he stood in the outfield, he would pull a Reader's Digest from his back pocket and digest some reading. He was called stubborn because he refused to change the way he behaved or played. They all saw his wild swings and low-key style and thought "Yes, he's great, but if he just acted like the other guys, man…"

But you know, he got great results. Yes, Willard Brown would've been better if he could've drawn walks. The above rankings would have rated him higher. But maybe he was just one of those people who can't do it the normal way. Maybe if he tried to work the strike zone, he would have struck out looking every time. It takes all kinds. Once you start applying a few hard-and-fast rules to everyone, you start ruining careers. At some point you have to accept that he is who he is, and who he is still has plenty of value.

I'm reminded of David Ortiz's unhappy early years with my hometown Twins. The Twins had an organizational philosophy of doing the little things, the so-called "fundamentals," like hitting the other way in certain situations, trying hard to make contact, learning to bunt, etc. These things are done well by the "scrappy" hard-chargin' guys that old guys tend to go nuts for: your David Ecksteins, your Darin Erstads, etc. It's a philosophy that stands in strong opposition to the behavior of these goshdarn flashy youngsters who come waltzing in here like they own the place! Kids today! They just don't know the meaning of (insert relevant virtue here). Oh, and get off my lawn.

David Ortiz was a very goshdarn flashy youngster. He could not learn the little things well, and was scornful of the Twins' attempts to teach them. Later, he said "Something in my swing was not right in Minnesota. I could never hit for power. Whenever I took a big swing, they'd say to me, 'Hey, hey, what are you doing?' So I said, 'You want me to hit like a little b****, then I will.'" (Source: "The Quotable David Ortiz," SBNation.com, Steven Goldman, May 10, 2013.) After six years of trying to make David Ortiz something he wasn't, the Twins released him. He signed with Red Sox, who let him swing away and become a star.

Look, it's great to have a philosophy. But when your vision of "the RIGHT way" is so inflexible that you screw up David Ortiz, you're getting too dogmatic for your own good. Of course most players need to learn the fundamentals, but there are exceptions to every rule. David Ortiz, and I suspect, Willard Brown, represent the rare cases who didn't need to learn the little things. They were already so good at the big things, like hitting home runs, that the little things just got in the way.

There is more to the whole "untapped potential" rep that saddles Willard Brown. In "Few and Chosen" Monte Irvin notes that he joined the American League in 1947 but says he didn't pan out. Brown was 32 in 1947, and was coming off some huge seasons with the Negro Leagues juggernaut Kansas City Monarchs. Brown and young African-American infielder Hank Thompson joined the St. Louis Browns just a few months after Jackie Robinson set the baseball world on fire. Brown was much more of an established star than Jackie was, so expectations were high. He hit .179 with no walks and one home run in 67 PAs and was released.

It's unfair to blame Brown for his failure to stick in the American League. He got zero time in the minors, unlike Jackie Robinson, Roy Campanella, and every successful Negro Leaguer turned MLBer. Negro League and MLB baseball were different games, and even the greatest players needed to make adjustments from one style of play to the other. No one could do it while being thrown into the fire for just 67 major-league PAs. Hank Thompson got the same treatment from the Browns: He got no minor-league experience, logged a 76 OPS+ in 89 PAs, and was released at the same time as Brown was.

More importantly, no one in the St. Louis Browns organization seemed to want Brown and Thompson to succeed. On Brown and Thompson's first day, Browns owner Dick Muckerman (I am not making that name up) could have used the opportunity to say a few words about the monumental acquisitions. He could have at least been at the game. Instead, he skipped town.

The job of addressing the media fell to Browns manager Muddy Ruel. While managers Lou Boudreau and Leo Durocher actively supported Larry Doby and Jackie Robinson, respectively, Ruel acted as if the word "begrudging" was invented for him. He kept referring to the acquisitions as a "club decision," sidestepping any personal responsibility. He said "The club believes that something had to be done to strengthen [itself]. It happens that there is no acceptable player in our farm system at this time." (Source: "The Prospectus Q&A: Chris Wertz," by David Laurila, July 14, 2010.) Yeah, thanks, skip. I guess since no one acceptable was available, those jerks in the front office had to settle for ol' unacceptable me instead.

The St. Louis papers were also racist in a subtle way. Sportswriter Dent McSkimming (I did not make that name up either; I only wish I were that creative) didn't express hope that the two new players would make the Browns better, as writers always do when reviewing new players. Instead he published a column bemoaning that two white players would be demoted in favor of Brown and Thompson. He described at length how some guy named Jerry Witte was terribly depressed to be sent down. Oh, boo-freakin'-hoo for Jerry Witte. What about your team nabbing the legendary Willard "Home Run" Brown?

And then there were the players. It is hard to succeed without your teammates on your side; it has to be doubly so when you're breaking a color line. A well-respected veteran can set an example for others, as Pee-Wee Reese did with Jackie Robinson and Joe Gordon did with Larry Doby. A few

Browns players, including star Jeff Heath, made nice noises to the papers about the acquisitions of Brown and Thompson. But they didn't follow through.

One story captures how Brown and Thompson were treated by every level of the Browns organization, including their teammates. Before he reported to the team, Willard Brown was told that the Browns would provide bats to his liking. He had a very specific liking for big, 40-ounce bats. But the Browns didn't end up giving him any. He had to just use whatever bats he could find, and none of them worked for him. Finally he found a heavy one with a broken knob that had been discarded by Jeff Heath. Brown used it to hit his one home run. When he got back to the bench, Heath took the bat and shattered it against the wall. (Source: Brown's SABR biography, by Rory Costello.)

Why would the Browns bother to sign Brown and Thompson if they, by all appearances, had no intention of allowing them to succeed? Perhaps it was a publicity stunt that wasn't carefully thought out. Or perhaps someone in the Browns front office had genuine intentions. If so, he apparently didn't get buy-in from anyone else on the club. Regardless, you get a feeling for what a dysfunctional organization the St. Louis Browns were. Thank goodness they started over in Baltimore.

Only a few weeks after Willard Brown's lone home run, he and Thompson were released. Manager Muddy Ruel said they were released because they didn't have the talent. Thompson got another shot at the MLB, this time a legitimate one, with the Giants in 1949. He sure proved he had the talent, to the tune of .267/.372/.453 (118 OPS+) in 3579 career PAs, mostly as a third baseman. But Brown never appeared in another MLB game.

Instead Brown went back to the Negro Leagues and Puerto Rican Leagues and kept smashing home runs. Career stats are hard to come by for him; Seamheads hasn't updated past 1935 at this writing, and Baseball-reference has just 933 PAs. Those 933 PAs give some indications of Brown's talent, though: .337/.359/.539. The man wouldn't take a walk if one were offered to him dipped in Belgian chocolate, but he sure could hit.

Comparisons for Willard Brown tend to center on guys like Juan Gonzalez and Andre Dawson. The Gonzalez example doesn't make me wild about his Hall-of-Fame case. Even the Dawson one isn't a ringing endorsement, as you'll see later. Brown probably had more power than Dawson, but was a worse fielder. Vladimir Guerrero might be a better comp, as he also had approximately negative five unintentional walks a year, but hit for high averages and great power. Like Dawson, Guerrero is not an inner-circle Hall-of-Fame type, but might make it eventually.

As I mentioned in the introduction, the selection of Negro Leaguers for the Hall of the Fame was a painstaking procedure spanning years of careful research and deliberation. It had none of the "old farts in a room voting for their buddies" flaws of the old Veterans Committee. I'm inclined to trust them and Bill James and let Brown stay.

Roberto Clemente (1955-1972; career OPS+: 130)

	Career	Rank	Hitting	Rank	Fielding	Rank	Peak	Rank	Bests	JAWS	Rank
WAR	94.3	5	70.8	13	11.9	1	54.1	3	4	74.2	5
WS	375.8	12	316.5	13	59.4	3	199.8	17	1	NA	8

When Roberto Clemente came up in 1955, writers called him "Bob" or "Bobby." He hated it. He was a proud man who wanted to be called by his real name. He knew that the nickname was not just an innocent shortening; it was pushed on him because many Americans felt uncomfortable with the "foreignness" of "Roberto."

It had been only a few years since Jackie Robinson's breakthrough. Latinos were still rare in the MLB, and dark-skinned Latinos like Clemente were especially rare. In the newspapers, he was called things like a "dusky flyer" and a "chocolate-covered islander." English was a second language to Clemente, and his grammatically incorrect statements were widely mocked by sportswriters. (Reference: Clemente's entry in Encyclopedia.com, by Kelly Winters, 2004.)

Some Latino players, like Rico "Beeg Boy" Carty, embraced the goofy, broken-English-speaking image thrust on them. They weren't wrong to do so; that was their choice. But that was definitely not Roberto Clemente's choice. He was the embodiment of the word "dignified." In almost every picture you'll see of him, he wears a steely, stern gaze, as if he's willing you to challenge him. On the rare occasions when he sports a smile, it's usually an awkward one, as if the photographer demanded it. Clemente wanted to be taken seriously, and spent every game fighting for respect on his terms. And he succeeded. By the end of his career, everyone called him Roberto.

If you don't mind a quick digression, (and if you do, how did you get this far?), stories like this make me think of the role sports can play in breaking down cultural barriers. It's probably a familiar topic to many of you; we all know that Jackie Robinson's breakthrough in 1947 occurred well before the integration of many other American institutions, and helped stimulate the Civil Rights movement of the 1950s and 1960s.

But I'm thinking less about history and more about day-to-day cultural tensions. While overt racism is less common nowadays, many people still feel tense around people of other ethnic groups. A great remedy to this sort of tension is simply having more exposure to such people. This is a psychological principle called the "mere-exposure effect," in which people develop affection for people that they become familiar with. The more you're around people of a different culture, the more you realize there's nothing to be afraid of, and the more you begin to appreciate them.

But sometimes mere exposure isn't enough. Sometimes it takes working together with people from different cultures on a common goal. Sports does this well. By putting white, black, Latino, and Asian people together on teams, it creates bonds among them and moves them beyond prejudices. This can work well in the classroom too, by the way: back in the 1970s, a psychologist named Eliot Aronson found that assigning students to ethnically diverse study groups helped break down racial conflict. (Read more in the Wikipedia entry for the Jigsaw teaching technique.)

Playing alongside Roberto Clemente would teach anyone that Latinos are human beings deserving of respect. To a lesser extent, watching him would do the same. Clemente is one of the most well-respected members of the Hall of Fame, and he deserves it.

Sam Crawford (1899-1917; career OPS+: 144)

	Career	Rank	Hitting	Rank	Fielding	Rank	Peak	Rank	Bests	JAWS	Rank
WAR	75.1	7	79.8	7	-18.1	123	39.6	19	4	57.4	11
WS	447.5	5	398.8	6	48.6	12	227.3	5	3	NA	10

Like Tris Speaker, Sam Crawford was powerful before power meant home runs. He did lead the league in homers twice, but his game was triples. He led the league in triples six times, five times finishing with more than 20, and holds the career record with 309.

Guess who's number two in career triples? I'll give you a hint: He and Crawford did not get along. That's right, Ty Cobb! After Crawford's 309 triples is Cobb's 295, and then there's a big drop; no one else has ever had more than Honus Wagner's 252. The only players since World War II who had even half as many career triples as Crawford were Stan Musial (177) and Roberto Clemente (166). It looks like Crawford's mark will never be beaten.

I don't like to say "never" about baseball records, since many that everyone said were unbreakable have been broken. The game is always changing in unpredictable ways. But it's hard to imagine what could possibly bring back enough triples to challenge Crawford's career mark. Better outfield defenses and smaller stadiums mean most would-be triples become either doubles or home runs.

And don't underestimate the benefit of always playing with a solid baseball. Dead-ball teams would go through only a couple of balls per game, and pitchers were allowed to spit on them, scuff them, knife them, saw them in half, emotionally abuse them, etc. It was very hard to drive the dark, mushy globs that counted as balls in the dead-ball era.

But doesn't some part of you kind of wish baseball was still packed with triples? They're called the most exciting play in baseball for a reason. (Although to me, they're a close second to an outfielder throwing a runner out at home. Gets me every time.) You often see hits that are clear doubles. I've never seen one that was a clear triple; that's always an exciting bonus during the play. It's always like, "OK, that got by the outfielder, so that's a double; Oh wait, he's going for a triple, and … safe! Woo!"

Home runs are great and all. They're obviously the best way to score runs. But in terms of entertainment value, meh. After the ball lands in the seats, they're a bit anti-climactic. David Ortiz smashes it out, and then we get his slow, dull, obligatory, self-congratulatory trot around the bases. Again, I say, meh.

In Sam Crawford's day, you had to be able to run some to be a slugger, even for home runs. In 1901, when Crawford led the league with 16 home runs, 12 of them were inside the park. And if you think triples are fun to watch, you should see inside-the-park home runs. I've only seen one while attending a game, and it was in the playoffs against my beloved Twins. I still loved it.

Granted, part of the fun of triples nowadays is watching a speedster zoom to third. And triples were not the province of speedsters in the dead-ball era. Sam Crawford could run OK, but mostly he just hit the ball hard. Much like David Ortiz, he was not interested in doing the little things. In the dead-ball days, there was a very strict ethos of "inside baseball" and "scientific" hitting, in which you bunt and strategically slap the ball around, a la Edd Roush. Crawford and a handful of others publicly eschewed this philosophy. They got away with it because they produced runs. But there was a lot of grumbling that these fellows were not playing the "right way."

I wonder if the current hitting approach, in which working the count is paramount, might become dogma like the approaches of the old days. Are there a bunch of Willard Browns in the minors whose careers are being ruined because they're forced to watch too many pitches go by?

I doubt it; there is no shortage of Chris Carter types nowadays who swing hard and often. Now teams are packed with brain trusts looking for every edge over the competition, whether it involves more patience or less. In an environment in which change is embraced, it's less likely one philosophy will become calcified and outdated.

Anyway, Sam Crawford's triples were really just his special way of producing lots of runs. He produced so many that he's a definite Hall of Famer.

Kiki Cuyler (1921-1938; career OPS+: 125)

	Career	Rank	Hitting	Rank	Fielding	Rank	Peak	Rank	Bests	JAWS	Rank
WAR	46.7	30	45.8	34	-5.6	72	34.9	31	0	40.8	31
WS	291.6	32	235.5	32	45.2	17	187.6	28	1	NA	39

Don't pronounce Kiki Cuyler's first name "key-key." It's supposed to be "kigh-kigh." Cuyler had a terrible stutter, so when he pronounced his last name, it came out as "Kigh-kigh-Cuyler." Really, if his tormentors wanted their high-larious joke at the expense of a man with a painful, involuntary condition to be understood by future generations, they should have gone with "Cuycuy" or "Kaikai" or "Hespeaksdifferentlysoheislesser" or something like that.

No offense to the stutterers of the world, but Kiki is not looking like a Hall-of-Famer. He isn't better than 25th in any of the above rankings except Win Shares defense. Cuyler had a legitimately great year in 1925, when he got 34 Win Shares and 6.7 WAR, led the league with 144 runs, 26 triples, 14 HBPs, and 701 PAs, and hit .357/.423/.598. He had some other good seasons, and led the league in stolen bases several times. He was one of many players who were quite good, but not quite good enough for the Hall of Fame.

I mentioned way back in the Red Schoendienst comment that I'm intrigued by the players who were very good but not quite good enough for the Hall. Two of the Hall of Very Good's charter members, Tony Oliva and Rocky Colavito, are close to Cuyler in both JAWS and WSAWS. All were very good hitters but just didn't last long enough to cross the Hall-of-Fame bar. Cuyler didn't end his career early the way Oliva and Colavito did, but he started a bit late, missed a little too much time during seasons, and just wasn't quite excellent enough when he did play.

At least one hole in Cuyler's record was due to a rather bizarre set of circumstances in 1927. Before the year, Cuyler held out for more money from the Pirates. Nothing too unusual about that. It caused tension, though, which was heightened further when he refused to follow manager Donie Bush's order to bat second. He had been batting third, and wanted to stay there. The bad blood supposedly came to a head when Cuyler ran standing up into second base when he was supposed to slide. After that, Cuyler was benched the rest of the year, even during the World Series. (Source: "The Top Cubs of All Time - #21 Kiki Cuyler," Al Yellon, January 29, 2007.)

At first, this seems like a very extreme punishment, not to mention a self-defeating one for the Pirates. Cuyler was a very good hitter, coming off of two straight years leading the National League in runs. He's the kind of guy you should keep in your lineup. When I first heard this story, I thought Donie Bush was being an overly punitive drama queen. More importantly, I thought Cuyler might deserve some extra credit in his Hall of Fame case to make up for the lost time.

But the more I think about it, the more I think Cuyler was at fault. As the National League's best base stealer and not much of a home run threat, he was a good fit for the number two spot. Plus, the Pirates debuted Paul Waner in 1926, and Paul made it clear right away that he was a middle-of-the-order guy. He had one of the best rookie seasons in history, going .336/.413/.528 for a 148 OPS+. Meanwhile Kiki slipped a bit from his 1924-1925 peak, hitting .321/.380/.459, 121 OPS+. In 1927, while Kiki was having his snit fit, he hit .309/.394/.435, 115 OPS+ while Paul Waner hit .380/.437/.549, 154 OPS+. Which of those two would you bat third?

And benching Cuyler was not as self-defeating as you might think. The Pirates were loaded with great hitters. While Cuyler sat, he was replaced by Clyde Barnhart, who hit almost exactly the same as Cuyler (.319/.384/.431).

Moreover, it seems like a pretty dumb thing for Cuyler to take such a dramatic stand over. Your spot in the batting order is really not that important. Some people argue that batting orders don't matter much at all. Batting orders are always set up to make the most out of the first inning, with the OBP guys getting on base for the power guys to drive them in. Often this arrangement comes at the expense of the second inning, when your slow sluggers are usually leading off. After that, each inning's arrangement quickly becomes random, with sometimes your seventh-place guy leading off, sometimes your third, etc.

That's debatable and not a debate I really want to get into right now. One thing that's not debatable is that the leadoff spot always gets the most plate appearances per year, followed by your second spot, then your third, etc. This is a mathematically inevitable consequence of having a linear order (1 through 9 and then back to 1) rather than a boustrophedonic[51] one (1 through 9 and then 9 through 1, etc.) It's especially important to have great hitters in those first two spots, since they get the most PAs each year. Cuyler should have been flattered by the move.

All that aside, this isn't something that Cuyler should have thought he had any say in. The manager gets to choose batting orders. End of story. As a player, it's simply not your decision. Imagine the chaos that would ensue every game if players got to choose where they hit. Every game would result in a fistfight for the third or fourth spot.

Cuyler's account of the story, well after the fact, was that he only gently suggested he might not be the ideal second-place hitter. He also had a very good reason for not sliding. I suspect he might be trying to rewrite history, or at least trying to revise it. Then again, Cuyler was known as a gentlemanly, even-tempered fellow. There may be more to the story.

Regardless, all that yakety yak was probably moot; even if we added another half year and a World Series appearance, Cuyler probably wouldn't get into Hall-of-Fame range. **Kiki Cuyler is out.**

Andre Dawson (1976-1996; career OPS+: 119)

	Career	Rank	Hitting	Rank	Fielding	Rank	Peak	Rank	Bests	JAWS	Rank
WAR	64.4	14	54.5	20	0.8	15	42.4	12	3	53.4	13
WS	341.3	16	279.0	19	62.2	2	174.6	38	1	NA	19

Was Andre Dawson's 1987 MVP the worst-ever selection? That was the year everyone was so besotted with all the home runs suddenly being hit that they forgot anything else mattered. Andre Dawson had 49 homers and played good defense for the last-place Cubs, but didn't do a ton else. He scored

[51] I got my favorite word in the book! "Boustrophedonic" is from the Greek "bous-" meaning "ox," and "strephein," to turn. It refers to how you plow a field; you plow one row, then turn 180 degrees and plow the next, then turn 180 degrees again and plow the next, etc. Some ancient writing was boustrophedonic, rather than going always left to right, like English, or always right to left, like Hebrew. Next time your fantasy league has a so-called "snake" draft, snort derisively and say that it really should be called a "boustrophedonic" draft. It will make everyone love you!

20 Win Shares, which ranked 24th in the N.L., well behind Tim Raines' 34. Dawson's WAR was 4.0, less than half of Tony Gwynn's 8.5.

It wasn't the worst MVP selection ever, but it sure wasn't good. One worse one was the choice of Dennis Eckersley in 1992. He had a tremendous relief season that year, but there is a limit to how tremendous you can be in only 80 innings. (More on that in the pitchers section.) Eckersley had 18 Win Shares and 2.9 WAR in 1992. Both totals are far from Roberto Alomar's 34 Win Shares or Roger Clemens' 8.8 WAR that same year.

These examples highlight something I've mentioned before, how novelty usually trumps actual value in MVP awards. Writers are programmed to love a big story, and "Willie Mays is awesome again" is not a story. But when Andre Dawson hits 49 home runs, the most since George Foster ten years earlier, that's a story. Tony Gwynn hit .370 in 1987, but Wade Boggs had been hitting in the .360s for several years. Tim Raines led the league in runs despite being locked out of baseball for a month by the owners' evil conspiracy to hold down salaries, a.k.a. collusion ... but hey, look at all those home runs! Woo! Home runs are fun! Who had the most? Dawson? OK, MVP!

This then gets me to a larger point: Having only beat writers vote on MVP awards, and for the matter, the Hall of Fame, is a silly anachronism. Sure, at one time writers were the only people who had enough baseball knowledge to make such decisions. But times have changed, in a big way. Now we have an entire society, SABR, devoted to nothing but baseball history and analysis. That sure sounds like a group that would be qualified to vote on some awards.

Sharing the voting with such baseball nerds has already made the Gold Gloves leagues better; instead of going to the guy with the good rep and great bat, they're going to the Andrelton Simmonses who aren't well-known but actually are the best defensive players. It will probably take a few more terrible selections by the writers before there's sufficient motivation to make a change. It happened to the Veterans Committee after all.

Anyway, Dawson was about more than that one season. In his peak from 1980-1983, he was a true star, scoring 6.8 WAR or better and 25 or more Win Shares each year. He was hitting home runs and finishing at almost exactly a .300 BA each year. He was not walking, which kept his value down throughout his career. But the rest was quite good.

Perhaps most crucially, Dawson was a center fielder and a good one for half of his career. He played just a wee bit more in right, which is why he's in this list. His hitting record looks significantly more Hall-worthy when you think of him as a center fielder. He stays.

Elmer Flick (1898-1910; career OPS+: 149)

	Career	Rank	Hitting	Rank	Fielding	Rank	Peak	Rank	Bests	JAWS	Rank
WAR	53.1	26	50.4	27	-5.5	71	41.3	15	4	47.2	23
WS	290.5	33	243.3	30	30.3	65	215.0	9	4	NA	23

I was all primed to kick out Elmer Flick. I had my campaign signs ready: "Kick Out the Flick!" "The Hall Has Flick? That's Sick!" "Is It a Trick that Flick Is in with Mick?" "Hey Chick, Light a Wick, Throw a Brick, Grab a Bic, Give it a Click, Write Ford Frick, Francis Crick, Jiminy Glick, Slick Rick, Tricky Dick Nick-(Son), Each New York Knick And Every Hick in Kennewick and OUST ELMER FLICK!"[52]

Luckily, I ran out of posterboard at that point, and thank goodness I didn't have enough stationery for all those letters to dead and imaginary people. Cuz upon further review, Elmer Flick doesn't look too bad. His main problem is that his career was short, just 6414 PAs. In 1907, when he was just 31, he came down with an intestinal condition that caused him chronic pain. He struggled through the next three seasons, collecting just 376 PAs before leaving the majors for good.

As you can probably predict, the unfortunate nature of his early retirement doesn't move me a bit. Plenty of people start Hall-of-Fame careers only to be derailed by injuries or illness. It's about what you did, not what you could have done. But Flick was so good when he did play that his overall ranks remain right at the Hall-of-Fame borderline.

At first it might look like inches separate the Hall-of-Fame cases of Elmer Flick and Kiki Cuyler. In the raw numbers, Cuyler looks better, .321/.386/.474 in 8100 PAs compared to Flick's .313/.389/.445 in 6414 PAs. But of course, Cuyler played when your blind grandmother could hit .300 with one arm tied behind her back. Flick played when your fully sighted grandfather using both arms whose name is Babe Ruth would be lucky to hit .280.

In reality, Flick had significantly better seasons than Cuyler did. Flick had 30+ Win Shares five times, 25+ three times, and another in the low 20s. Cuyler had just one 30-Win Share season, four 25-29 ones, and three in the 20-25 range. In WAR, Flick gets three seasons above 6 and three more above 5, while Cuyler has just one above 6 and two above 5.

Flick could do it all, in a dead-ball-era sort of way. He was a Sam Crawford-style power hitter, with loads of triples and a respectable number of homers for his time. He hit for high averages, winning one batting title, and stole bases, twice leading the league. He even drew walks well. He was not a great defender, but was quite successful at throwing out baserunners.

And while Cuyler's little biographical aside involved him getting pouty for having to bat slightly earlier than he was accustomed to, Flick's story is actually kind of cute. He was from Bedford, Ohio. Adorable, right? I love that story.

No? Not cute enough? See, Bedford, Ohio was a small town, and small towns, by definition, are cute. Still not cute enough? OK, but geez, you guys must have hearts of stone or something.

So Flick was playing baseball at the Bedford high school in 1891, when he was 15 years old. One day he joined a large crowd at the train station to see the Bedford semi-pro team off on their big road trip. There the manager of the Bedford Whatever-the-Hells realized he only had eight players. Without a full nine, he would have to forfeit all their games. He scoured the crowd for a ballplayer, and landed on lil' Elmer Flick. Flick didn't have a uniform, or even any shoes, but he was on the team. He hit so well on the road trip that his professional career began. (Source: Surprise, it's Flick's SABR biography, by Angelo Louisa.)

---

[52] Reference explanation: Ford Frick was the commissioner of baseball from 1951 to 1965 and is a member of the Hall of Fame. Francis Crick was half of the famous duo Watson and Crick, who discovered the double helix structure of DNA (along with Rosalind Franklin, who was as important as Crick and Watson but didn't get as much acclaim because her own DNA did not contain a Y chromosome). Jiminy Glick was a character played by Martin Short who would interview celebrities very poorly. Slick Rick is a rap godfather famous for a "Children's Story," "The Show," and "La-Di-Da-Di."

That story might be a bit apocryphal. But I still love to think a world existed where any of that was plausible, from the train-station farewell of local boosters to the shoeless kid being hired on the spot. Cute stories aside, Elmer Flick squeaks above the line for Hall.

Tony Gwynn (1982-2001; career OPS+: 132)

	Career	Rank	Hitting	Rank	Fielding	Rank	Peak	Rank	Bests	JAWS	Rank
WAR	68.9	12	66.4	14	-8.2	89	41.1	17	3	55.0	12
WS	398.5	11	353.7	9	45.0	18	208.3	10	3	NA	6

I mentioned before that old guys tend to love players who are "scrappy" and hard-working, guys who hustle and know the fundamentals and give 110% and never give up and go out there ready to play every day and put their pants on one leg at a time and know when to hold them and when to fold them and so forth. Old guys identify with these kinds of players. Old guys have passionately adopted the very American notion that anyone can become a superstar if he/she works hard enough. Over the decades, they've been sufficiently humbled by life to know that they never had much natural ability, and that greatness was only possible through hard work. At this point in their lives, they probably won't work hard enough to become great, because they're old and tired and there's too much good baseball to watch. (I'm describing myself at this point.) But they can sure work hard at admiring hard work! Vicarious success still counts as success, sort of.

Several of your more waggish baseball writers from the likes of Deadspin and Fire Joe Morgan noted that the lovers of "scrappiness" tend to be old white guys, and the objects d'scrappy tend to be young white guys. David Eckstein and Darin Erstad received the most scrappy-love when the Fire Joe Morgan guys wrote blog posts instead of wasting their time making wonderful award-winning television shows.[53]

Tony Gwynn was never considered scrappy, to my knowledge. But he fit the type. That is, he worked extremely hard to elevate his play beyond the level of his natural ability. One of his nicknames was "Captain Video," because he was among the earliest to study video of his own plate appearances to help fine-tune his swing. Mind you, he started doing this in 1983, when teams did not provide video or anything of the kind. Gwynn's wife taped all his plate appearances from the stands, following him on road trips with a Betamax recorder the size of a suitcase.

Gwynn gained an edge by being on the vanguard, by being more scientific and analytical than his competitors. No wonder Ted Williams felt that Tony Gwynn was the hitter most like himself. If Williams had played in the age of video, he would have jumped on it without a moment's hesitation.

Beyond his hard work and resourcefulness, Gwynn was relatable to the average Joe in every other conceivable way. In his first few years he may have looked like a natural athlete, but before long he

[53] Reference explanation: The chief bloggers of Fire Joe Morgan are all very successful TV writers and producers. Ken Tremendous was Michael Schur, writer and executive producer of "The Office," "Parks and Recreation," and "Brooklyn Nine-Nine." He also played Dwight Schrute's Abe-Lincoln-beard-sporting brother Mose on "The Office." Junior was Alan Yang, producer of "Parks and Recreation." Dak was David King, writer for "Parks and Recreation" and "Workaholics." At the end of every "Parks and Recreation" episode, you can catch a title card for "Fremulon," which was the name of the fake insurance company that all the Fire Joe Morgan guys said they worked at.

resembled a taller Kirby Puckett. His personality was unassuming and genuinely down-to-earth, as if it could never occur to him to be any other way. Even his voice, with its high-pitched twang, was uniquely adorable.

Gwynn always did his own thing, and his own thing always ended up being both unexpected and charming. When he retired from a Hall-of-Fame career, he could have become a hitting coach just about anywhere in the MLB. Instead he chose to coach baseball at his alma mater, San Diego State University. He loved San Diego, and wanted to stay there.

As for his winters, he could have spent them in Tampa, or for that matter, the Caribbean, the South of France, Bali, or probably the moon if he wanted. Instead he chose Indianapolis. In the months when San Diego was still basking in gorgeous weather, you could catch Gwynn at an Indianapolis mall buying his kids Christmas presents. (Source: "Tony Gwynn's Second Base: Indianapolis," Indianapolis Monthly, Bruce Hetrick, June 18, 2014.) Gwynn grew up in the Los Angeles area, so it's not like Indianapolis represented a homecoming for him. He just liked it there and didn't feel a huge need to go anywhere else.

Gwynn seemed totally unchanged by fame. He lived more like your beloved uncle who worked at the factory for 40 years than a baseball Hall-of-Famer. He was a man without an ounce of pretense or artifice. He was who he was, and who he was was a truly unique treasure. His other nickname, "Mr. Padre," was given to him because he was unquestionably the most beloved baseball hero San Diego has ever seen.

It was a tragedy when cancer took him on June 16, 2014. It's hard to imagine another like him. Definitely deserving of the Hall.

Harry Heilmann (1914, 1916-1930, 1932; career OPS+: 148)

	Career	Rank	Hitting	Rank	Fielding	Rank	Peak	Rank	Bests	JAWS	Rank
WAR	72.2	11	76.8	10	-14.0	115	47.2	7	3	59.7	8
WS	356.1	14	325.1	12	30.9	60	206.3	13	2	NA	16

Is Harry Heilmann a sort of old-school Tony Gwynn? Both had very high batting averages and lots of batting titles, Gwynn winning eight and Heilmann winning four. Both came up in relatively low-offense times but experienced the meat of their careers in good eras for hitters. Both were hard-working, classy gentlemen who grew up on the West Coast. Both went on to broadcasting after their careers were over. Both died from cancer in their 50s.

Heilmann had more power while Gwynn had more speed and was a better fielder. They end up with similar overall rankings, in the middle of the pack among right fielders. WAR likes Heilmann better, while Bill James likes Tony Gwynn better. You could hardly go wrong with either.

Remember how I said Ty Cobb mellowed with age? Cobb was Heilmann's longtime teammate and manager with the Tigers. When Heilmann was on his deathbed in 1951, Cobb visited him and told him he had been elected to the Hall of Fame. It was a lie, but it gave Heilmann tremendous joy just before he died.

Heilmann was elected the very next year and clearly deserved it.

Harry Hooper (1909-1925; career OPS+: 114)

	Career	Rank	Hitting	Rank	Fielding	Rank	Peak	Rank	Bests	JAWS	Rank
WAR	53.5	25	45.2	36	-4.5	60	30.2	55	1	41.9	29
WS	321.7	23	268.5	24	53.1	7	162.3	54	1	NA	43

Harry Hooper is one of the more baffling Hall-of-Fame selections. His batting record does not look at all Hall-of-Fame-y, either to the naked eye or when adjusted for context. He was a great fielder, but you don't get into the Hall of Fame for right-field defense. He did a lot of things well for a good amount of time, and did well, but not spectacularly well, in World Series play (.293/.371/.435 in 108 PAs, plus several great plays in the outfield). It's not a terrible case for the Hall, but not a good one either.

Hooper got the call from the 1971 Veterans Committee, so now I have to bring up Frankie Frisch again. Hooper was of a generation earlier than Frisch and never played for the Giants or Cardinals, so this is not another case of Frisch electing his cronies.

More likely the Frisch contingent was persuaded by Hooper's part in the "The Glory of the Times," a hugely influential book published in 1966. "The Glory of Their Times" was catnip for nostalgic old guys. Author Lawrence Ritter interviewed old ballplayers and compiled their wistful stories, almost all of which served to validate old guys' feelings that anything that happened when they were young was objectively superior to anything that happened when they were old.

Also, Hooper has the "major contributor to a great team" thing that helped get Tinker, Evers, and Chance in the Hall. Hooper was part of the "Million-Dollar Outfield" of the 1910-1915 Red Sox, which also featured Tris Speaker in center field and Duffy Lewis in left. During Hooper's entire tenure with the Sox, 1909-1920, they won four World Series titles.

As you read in the first chapter, the Hall of Fame has decided, through its selections, that career numbers are a central criterion. But, I'm not entirely unsympathetic to the idea that being a great contributor to a great team gets a guy some extra points. Remember Dave Bancroft? He was a shortstop with the 1920s Giants who got into the Hall with a strong assist from Frankie Frisch. Bancroft didn't have the strongest career record, but was the best player on several pennant-winning teams. That counts for something.

So how integral was Harry Hooper to those great Red Sox teams? Let's call in the numbers.

The Sox' first Hooper-era world championship was in 1912. That year Hooper finished tenth on the team in Win Shares, with 15. The leader was Tris Speaker, who had an incredible 51. In terms of WAR, it's even more lopsided: Hooper's 0.8 puts him well below just about everyone, especially Speaker's 10.1. At best, Hooper was a placeholder on this team. But it was Hooper's worst year (83 OPS+), so let's give him a mulligan on this one.

In 1915, the Red Sox grabbed another title, and Hooper had another unimpressive year at the plate (103 OPS+). His defense was good enough to get him 19 Win Shares, which ranked him seventh on the team. WAR also puts him at seventh with 3.1, behind Speaker's 8.3, Duffy Lewis' 3.2 and a bunch of starting pitchers. So Hooper was an important element, but hardly a star. Both championships we've covered so far were basically the Tris Speaker Show.

On to 1916. Tris Speaker had been traded in the offseason, so the 1916 Red Sox championship was truly a team effort. Hooper finally had a good year, collecting 26 Win Shares, which trailed only third baseman Larry Gardner (27) and pitcher/good-hitter-for-a-pitcher Babe Ruth (37). Hooper got 4.0 WAR, behind Gardner, Ruth, and pitchers Dutch Leonard and Ernie Shore. So Hooper may not have been the team MVP, but he was at least among the top five most important players on the team.

In 1918, the Red Sox went back to being a one-man team, this time the one man being Babe Ruth. Ruth pitched 166 innings with a 2.22 ERA (122 ERA+) while also collecting 382 PAs and leading the league in home runs and slugging percentage. Combine his pitching and hitting and you get 40 Win Shares and 7.5 WAR. But Hooper was definitely the second-best player, with 29 Win Shares and 5.0 WAR.

In the end, it doesn't look like Hooper has the kind of leadership-of-a-pennant-winner qualifications that Bancroft had. Hooper was very good in 1918, pretty good in 1916, but a supporting piece or worse during the other championships.

And Hooper didn't have any better seasons in the non-championship years. Those 1916 and 1918 seasons were the only times he exceeded 25 Win Shares. His only 5+ WAR season was in 1918. In the end, he had longevity, a few solid performances, the fortune to play alongside great players, and not much else.

In the "Historical Baseball Abstract," Bill James says that Hooper is in the Hall because of Tris Speaker and "The Glory of Their Times." In the same way, he said, Joe Tinker is in because of Johnny Evers and that silly poem about the gonfalon bubble. Tinker is probably the best comparison for Hooper: A very good player on a very good team, but below Hall level. **Hooper is out.**

Reggie Jackson (1967-1987; career OPS+: 139)

	Career	Rank	Hitting	Rank	Fielding	Rank	Peak	Rank	Bests	JAWS	Rank
WAR	74.0	8	76.8	9	-17.2	121	46.8	8	5	60.4	7
WS	444.0	6	403.8	5	40.6	25	219.8	8	3	NA	7

Reggie! Reggie. Reggie? Reggie, Reggie; Reggie: No matter what punctuation mark you use, they all apply to Reggie Jackson. He was baseball's biggest star in the 1970s. He would make headlines by telling everyone he was the greatest player in the world, and then would hit home runs to prove it.

I'm reminded of comedian Greg Giraldo's bit about Muhammad Ali. Giraldo said that when Ali came on the scene, his wildly self-aggrandizing persona was a shock to the entire culture. Most Americans had never heard anyone say the kind of things he said, things like "There's not a man alive who can whup me. I'm too fast. I'm too smart. I'm too pretty. I should be a postage stamp. That's the only way I'll ever get licked." If you were in the public eye, you weren't supposed to say you were good, much less say you were the greatest ever. And to do so in a funny way -- that was another level. Nowadays, said Giraldo, every pimple-faced dork has a MySpace page (this was 2006) with a picture of himself shirtless, flexing, and acting as if he's the hottest guy who ever lived.

Those kids didn't learn it from Muhammad Ali, at least not directly. They learned it from hip-hop, which mostly consists of boasting in clever ways. One time, a friend of mine who knew I loved hip-hop asked me why rappers are so full of themselves. It was meant rhetorically, as an attack on my music of choice, so she wasn't entirely happy that I had an answer. I told her about journalist Nelson George's article about Ladysmith Black Mambazo, the African vocal group made famous by Paul

Simon's "Graceland" album. George asked Ladysmith Black Mambazo what their lyrics meant, and they said, "basically, how great we are." George connected this to hip-hop and concluded that there is just something in the African spirit that revels in a good over-the-top boast.

That spirit survived through slavery and Jim Crow, institutions predicated on making African-Americans feel as low as humanly possible. Many so-called "race records" from the early 1900s were full of braggadocio, particularly in coded references to sexual prowess. Blues showed the other side, depicting the despair of being made into second-class citizens, but jazz and R&B provided the just-as-necessary outlets for feelings of confidence and power.

Reggie Jackson was part of this tradition. He shoved the unabashed self-confidence of Muhammad Ali into the stodgy world of baseball. The same way it's not as easy to rap as it looks, it's not as easy to pound your chest in a public forum as you might think it is. If you can't sell it, through your every inflection and motion, you'll get booed off the stage in a second. And then if you don't back up your words with action, you're setting yourself up for a big fall. When you say you're the greatest and then show that you're not, you will get no sympathy. People will line up to take you down.

Admittedly, I'm probably the type who would relish taking someone like that down. I can't boast. I don't feel comfortable talking about myself at all except in a self-deprecating way; even in job interviews I have to fight an impulse to downplay my accomplishments. (Am I now sounding like I'm boasting about being unboastful? If so, I apologize.)

But, I can also appreciate the appeal of someone who says he's the best and then shows that he really is. I get it; it's like how kings were in the old days, when a central part of their job description was to act like they were better than everyone else. There isn't a monarch in human history who didn't put on a big show to assert dominance.

In Europe, royal peacockery eventually took on an odd form. Instead of being communicated directly, it was demonstrated by ostentatious displays of wealth. When I went to Versailles, the insanely opulent palace of King Louis XIV, I felt like I was in the middle of one of those videos where rappers flash their rings and gold chains for the camera and go "Look what I got! Bling bling!" Versailles certainly looked better than a set of gold teeth with diamonds in them, but the message was the same.

The British think of themselves as paragons of humility, supreme champions of understatement and self-restraint. But then they go bonkers for the royal family, who have no real function beyond looking impressive. Brits probably wouldn't line up in the streets and cheer if Prince William and Kate Middleton lived in a humble flat on the East End. Queen Elizabeth would never explicitly say that she's the king of rock, there is none higher, and that sucka MCs should call her sire.[54] But she doesn't have to. It's said by all the castles and jewels and servants and ceremonies.

People who don't have that kind of money have to be more direct. Because of slavery and racism, African-American communities have not historically had much wealth. So when you don't have jewels to flash, you learn how to show off with words. The rappers in those videos showed off with words until they could show off with jewels. They didn't get the chance to inherit obscene wealth and the attendant false modesty about its trappings.

The point is that flamboyant peacocks exist in every culture. It's in all our DNA to revel in them. Different cultures just peacock and revel in different ways.

---

[54] Reference explanation: Run-DMC, "King of Rock."

Reggie Jackson put it all on the line with his big words, and he followed through on them with his big bat. Even if he had come up a bit short in the rankings above, I'd probably invoke "It's the of Hall of Fame, not the Hall of Stats" and let him stay. Reggie! puts the "fame" in the Hall of Fame.

Al Kaline (1953-1974; career OPS+: 134)

	Career	Rank	Hitting	Rank	Fielding	Rank	Peak	Rank	Bests	JAWS	Rank
WAR	92.7	6	78.0	8	2.4	9	48.9	6	2	70.8	6
WS	441.6	7	382.9	7	58.5	5	199.5	18	1	NA	11

Like Hank Aaron, Al Kaline was consistently great throughout the 1950s and 1960s. Kaline is not a poor man's anything, but if Hank Aaron is Bill Gates' version of a right fielder, Kaline is Warren Buffett's version. Both Aaron and Kaline hit for good averages, drew walks, and played great defense for a very long time. Aaron had a clear edge in power and speed, but Kaline wasn't bad at either.

Again like Aaron, Kaline performed at a high level without ever breaking through into crazy-good territory. Kaline had 12 seasons of 20+ Win Shares, but never had more than 31. WAR gives him ten seasons above 5 with a top score of 8.4 in 1961. Kaline's best season was probably 1955, when he was only 20 years old. That year he hit .340/.421/.546 in 681 PAs, winning the batting title and scoring 31 Win Shares and 8.3 WAR. He would not have been a bad choice for MVP, though of course Mickey Mantle was the best player in the league.

Instead, the 1955 AL MVP went to to Yogi Berra. Berra got 24 Win Shares, sixth in the league, and 4.5 WAR, 14th best. If you could play catcher and hit in the 1950s, you could win lots of MVPs; both Yogi and Roy Campanella won a few more than they deserved. Also, Berra's Yankees won the pennant, while Kaline's Tigers were mediocre.

Since it came up, and I don't have anything else terribly interesting to say about Al Kaline, let's get into the idea that MVPs should come from pennant-winning teams. I completely disagree. As I've mentioned, baseball is a team sport like no other. In melee sports like basketball or football, one player can make a huge difference, since he can be involved in almost every play. In baseball, even Babe Ruth only gets to hit four or five times a game. In his best season, 1923, he had 14.1 WAR, meaning that he would turn a 60-win team to a 74-win one. There's only so much he can do by himself.

Some argue that a player can't have the most value if his team doesn't win. That makes no sense to me. Of course you can have the most value if your team doesn't win. All that means is that you're surrounded by guys who have less value. In a team sport, winning is a team activity, not an individual one.

Can I get pretentious for a moment? I'll give you some time to respond. (Time passes.) I will take your silence as an assent. This reminds me of the difference between psychology and sociology. Psychology is the study of individual people. Sociology is the study of groups of people. The two realms are sufficiently different to constitute two very separate disciplines. Individual human beings have lots of issues worthy of study. But, when you put a bunch of those individuals together, it creates an entirely different set of issues. There is a distinct separation between the two.

In the same way, individual accomplishments on a baseball diamond are very different from team accomplishments. Individual accomplishments include hits and home runs and diving catches and all the other things you can do to contribute to wins. But an individual can only *contribute to* wins, not win games by himself. Team accomplishments include the actual wins. Awards for individual accomplishments, like MVPs, should be based only on the things an individual can control. The things he can't control, like his team's wins, should not be considered.

Anyway, at any rate (double back on track!), this is more relevant to pitchers, if I ever get to them. Al Kaline did an incredible number of things to help his team win and is certainly a deserving Hall-of-Famer.

Willie Keeler (1892-1910; career OPS+: 127)

	Career	Rank	Hitting	Rank	Fielding	Rank	Peak	Rank	Bests	JAWS	Rank
WAR	54.1	24	52.4	24	-10.1	101	36.1	28	1	45.1	24
WS	332.8	17	281.6	17	48.3	13	181.0	32	4	NA	35

"Wee Willie" Keeler definitely was wee. He was 5'4" and 140 pounds, bigger than only a few dozen players in baseball history. Modern star Jose Altuve, known for his wee-ness, is a full two inches taller and 35 pounds heavier than Keeler's listed stats. No other ballplayer ever accomplished more with less mass than Keeler.

Keeler got loads of hits, including eight straight seasons of more than 200. His hitting strategy was famously encapsulated by the phrase "Hit 'em where they ain't." Unlike fellow place-hitting enthusiast Edd Roush, Keeler used a tiny bat, only 30 inches long, and choked up on it until it begged for mercy. If the infielders moved back, he'd lay down a bunt. If they were guarding against the bunt, he'd loft it over their heads.

Yeah, yeah, yeah, but was he really a Hall-of-Famer? Keeler was a bit one-dimensional. That's not a term you tend to hear in reference to guys with high batting averages; you hear it more about the Steve Balboni/Pete Incaviglia types who don't do anything besides hit home runs, a type of player I love, by the way. For a long time I had a fantasy league called the Sultans of Sweat, meant to honor the big, fat, unwieldy guys who would be a laughingstock in any sport but baseball. "The Sultan of Sweat" was a nickname for pitcher Terry Forster, but it could apply to any of the beer-league types.

OK, Keeler also had speed and was a good fielder, so it's not just one dimension, but that lack of power really hurts. Powerlessness can play in center field, as it did for Max Carey. But right field is a power position. A full 86% of Keeler's hits were singles, more than any of the 125 right fielders in my sample.

Max Carey might be the best comp for Keeler. Carey was also relatively low in the overall rankings, but hit well enough for long enough to stay. Keeler's WSAWS is 20th, which is solid. Keeler is overrated because had some big batting averages in the 1890s, when everyone had big batting averages. But he's an acceptable low-end Hall of Famer.

King Kelly (1878-1893; career OPS+: 139)

	Career	Rank	Hitting	Rank	Fielding	Rank	Peak	Rank	Bests	JAWS	Rank
WAR	44.2	34	49.5	29	-4.5	59	31.1	51	5	37.7	42
WS	278.3	35	215.4	40	46.1	16	171.1	41	3	NA	32

Oh no! King Kelly got 42nd and 32nd in the overall rankings? Say it ain't so, Flo! Kelly was a tremendously exciting star in the early days of professional baseball. His SABR biography, by Peter M. Gordon, asserts that "his fame helped change professional baseball from a pleasant diversion into America's most popular sport." It also notes that he was among the first ballplayers to become a successful actor on the vaudeville circuit. If you like your societal contributions a little more relevant to modern times, know that a song about Kelly, "Slide, Kelly, Slide," was the first hit musical recording in history. Or how about the fact that his signature on a piece of paper was so coveted that it popularized the practice of collecting autographs? Kelly was the life of the party, a friend to everyone, colorful, handsome, impeccably dressed, and a little too fond of the drink. Before there was Babe Ruth, there was King Kelly.

He was also a great innovator. Kelly was always experimenting with different slides and is credited with inventing the hook slide. He pioneered the practice of running inside baselines and skipping bases entirely when the game's lone umpire was distracted. When he took over as catcher for the Chicago White Stockings in 1883, he replaced Silver Flint, who did not use any protective equipment of any kind. Kelly adopted the newfangled catcher's mitt, chest protector, and face mask to stay in more games.

A sure sign of a great baseball mind is to invent plays that necessitate rule changes. In one game, Kelly was on third base while teammate Ned Williamson was on second. Kelly faked an injury, and when Williamson came over to see what the matter was, Kelly told him he was going to make a break for home on the next pitch and that Williamson should follow him. When he did so, with Williamson close behind, the opposing team was so shocked that they were late to react. When their catcher had the ball and was about to tag Kelly, Kelly spread his legs so that Williamson could sneak his leg in to the plate. After this bizarre play, the rule was changed such that a baserunner is automatically out if he passes another baserunner.

Yeah, yeah, yeah, but was he really a Hall-of-Famer?[55] Well, Kelly has the same issue as that of Deacon White and Jim O'Rourke: During his peak, teams played half or less as many league games as they do now. If you translate Kelly's shortened 1880s seasons to 154-game schedules, you get a Career Win Shares of 402.4, good for 9th among right fielders, and a Peak Win Shares of 226.3, which ranks 6th. In terms of WAR, he goes to 67.3 in his career (13th among right fielders) and 49.4 for his peak (7th).

That doesn't necessarily mean Kelly is really the 6th- or 13th-best right fielder in history. He still didn't actually collect those numbers. But it does show that in the context of those shorter seasons, Kelly was great. Note the robust number of "best" seasons above.

Kelly managed these numbers despite an early end to his career. He was never interested in training or taking care of himself, preferring to carouse all night with the boys. By age 34, his skills had eroded below replacement level. By 36, he was dead from pneumonia. Kelly's death is less easily attributable to alcoholism than that of Cristobal Torriente or Hack Wilson. But it's clear he could have had a better career if not for the infernal scourge of the serpent drink.

Regardless, when you make allowances for context and add a dash of "It's the Hall of Fame, not the Hall of Stats," King Kelly stays in the Hall.

---

[55] Reference explanation: The Willie Keeler comment, just one before this one. You have been reading these in order, right? I haven't asked for a while because I was starting to annoy even myself with that question.

Chuck Klein (1928-1944; career OPS+: 137)

	Career	Rank	Hitting	Rank	Fielding	Rank	Peak	Rank	Bests	JAWS	Rank
WAR	43.5	36	47.9	31	-11.8	107	36.6	27	1	40.1	32
WS	238.4	46	183.8	55	26.3	88	176.0	37	0	NA	40

Chuck Klein was another Hack Wilson. Both had big years during the hitting explosion of the late 1920s and early 1930s that are not as good as they look. In 1930, when Wilson had 56 home runs and 191 RBIs, Klein hit 40 homers with 170 RBIs. Klein also scored a league-leading 158 runs, still a National League record (since 1901). For fans of meaningless stats, that's the fourth-largest combination of runs and RBIs in a season, behind Babe Ruth in 1921, Lou Gehrig in 1931 and good ol' Hack Wilson's 1930 again.

In terms of WAR and Win Shares, though, it's less impressive. Klein's WAR in 1930 was 6.5, considerably lower than Wilson's 7.4, as well as Bill Terry's 7.6. Klein had 28 Win Shares while Wilson led the league with 35. Great, but a lot less great in context.

Klein had other great seasons, but not many. Both WAR and Win Shares like his 1932 (6.6 WAR, 31 Win Shares) and 1933 (7.5 WAR, 30 Win Shares) better than his 1930. In both years he led the league in home runs, hits and slugging percentage.

It's all good stuff, but there isn't much more. Klein got started a little late for a Hall-of-Famer, with his first full season when he was 24 years old. And it ended early, his last full season coming at 31.

Don't tell me Klein was another to succumb to the bewitchment of the demon rum that has felled so many of our baseballing titans? Nah, it was injuries. After the 1933 season, the Phillies traded Klein to the Cubs, because the Phillies were terrible and couldn't support his salary. The Cubs were quite good at the time, winning lots of games with catcher Gabby Hartnett, second baseman Billy Herman, and young third baseman Stan Hack. Klein looked like the final piece of the puzzle. But after two months, he hurt his leg. He struggled to stay in the lineup the rest of his career. No doubt the injury occurred because there was once a goat in Wrigley Field or whatever.[56]

Klein still had some pretty good years with the Cubs, but nothing like his Phillies days. Even without his accursed leg, he likely wouldn't have produced in Chicago like he did in Philadelphia. The Phillies played in the Baker Bowl, which had a right-field fence only 280 feet from home plate and right-center power alley only 300 feet away. When he was a Phillie, Klein hit .420 with 131 home runs in home games but .296 with 60 homers on the road. The Phillies then were like the Rockies in the 1990s; their numbers don't even feel like they should be compared to everyone else's.

Klein was no Dante Bichette, thank goodness. But he may have been an Ellis Burks or Juan Gonzalez, a very good hitter who often looked super-great because of a high-offense era and a high-offense

---

[56] What was the curse that is keeping the Cubs from winning a World Series? Some guy got kicked out of a game for bringing his goat in the stands once or something? I could very easily look it up, but it is such a boring curse that I'd probably fall asleep in mid-click. C'mon Chicago, work harder. The White Sox had the curse of the Black Sox scandal, the Red Sox had the Curse of the Bambino. Now those are curses. A curse should be based on some huge mistake by the team, not just the expulsion of an extremely unintimidating animal.

home park. In JAWS, Klein is close to Rocky Colavito and Darryl Strawberry, two good sluggers who collapsed in their early 30s and limped to inadequate career totals for the Hall. That describes Klein as well. **Chuck Klein is out.**

Tommy McCarthy (1884-1896; career OPS+: 102)

	Career	Rank	Hitting	Rank	Fielding	Rank	Peak	Rank	Bests	JAWS	Rank
WAR	16.2	127	13.3	126	-3.0	38	19.0	113	0	17.6	126
WS	170.5	91	131.7	91	37.7	35	148.8	66	0	NA	88

Holy cow. What the nut? What the what? Who the when? How the cow? Who the what to the where to the which? I'm throwing out nonsensical questions because I'm so flabbergasted that the above numbers apply to a member of the Baseball Hall of Fame. In JAWS, Tommy McCarthy is surrounded by Claudell Washington, Ruben Sierra, Bernie Carbo, Ellis Valentine and Jeff Burroughs. In Bill James' rankings he is below Tom Brunansky and Terry Puhl and just above Tony Armas and Dante Bichette. How the Winger to the Whipple to the Westheimer[57] did this guy get into the Hall of Fame?

Remember Hugh Duffy? He hit .440 in 1894 and led the Boston Beaneaters to three straight pennants from 1891-1893. McCarthy was also on the 1892 and 1893 Beaneaters teams, and the pair were known as "The Wonder Twins." McCarthy's fame was based on speed and defense more than hitting. He did hit well in 1893, but it was one of only two seasons in which he had great numbers. The other was 1890, in which the pool of major leaguers was diluted by a third league, John "Monte" Ward's Player's League.

Maybe McCarthy could have had other good performances if he'd hung around for more than eight full seasons. His career wasn't shortened by alcoholism or injuries; he just got fat. In 1893 he bought a saloon with Hugh Duffy, and became more interested in running the saloon than in staying in shape. By 1895, when he was only 30 years old, he was slow, ineffective, and grouchy, publicly criticizing his manager and getting into fights with his teammates. He was out of baseball by 32. So yeah, this guy is in the Baseball Hall of Fame and Tim Raines is not.

McCarthy was selected in the 1946 Old-Timers Committee vote that also inducted Tinker, Evers and Chance. As I've mentioned several times (and if you're reading this in order like you're supposed to, you're probably tired of hearing this. You clearly shouldn't have listened to me. What, do you do everything people tell you to do?), the 1946 Old-Timers Committee was more interested in important players on great teams than in career stats. The committee may not have even had access to the numbers.

McCarthy was quite well-known after his playing career was over, becoming a skilled hobnobber with powerful friends. The book "The Heavenly Twins of Boston Baseball" (Donald Hubbard, McFarland, 2008) notes that McCarthy was beloved by Connie Mack, one of the members of the 1946 Veteran's Committee. McCarthy died in 1922, but Hugh Duffy carried his torch, spending the second half of his

[57] Reference explanations: Winger was a band from the 1980s that tried to combine heavy metal with glam rock and prog rock. Mr. Whipple was this strange person who got upset when people squeezed Charmin in grocery stores. Dr. Ruth Westheimer was a TV sex therapist who was hilarious because she had a German accent. These were the kinds of things that qualified as cultural touchstones in the 1980s.

life telling everyone within earshot that McCarthy was the true star of the 1892-1893 Boston Beaneaters. Duffy helped McCarthy gain the reputation of a player who only sophisticated baseball connoisseurs can appreciate, the type who's much more valuable than his stats suggest. That is, McCarthy became overrated for being underrated.

People trying to justify McCarthy's selection point to his innovations in the outfield, including his invention of the trap play, in which a ball bounces but you pretend you caught it. There is good evidence that he invented the hit-and-run, a case that Bill James espouses. These are not insignificant factors. If Tommy McCarthy had something closer to a Hall-of-Fame playing record, I might give him extra credit. But his numbers weren't in the ballpark, or for that matter, they weren't in the metro area of the city of the neighborhood of the ballpark of HOF standards. So far, he is the most unqualified player we've covered. So obviously, **Tommy McCarthy is out.**

Mel Ott (1926-1947; career OPS+: 155)

	Career	Rank	Hitting	Rank	Fielding	Rank	Peak	Rank	Bests	JAWS	Rank
WAR	107.9	3	103.6	4	-5.9	74	52.9	4	6	80.4	3
WS	525.4	3	474.1	3	51.6	10	244.0	3	6	NA	4

When Leo Durocher said "Nice guys finish last," he was referring to Mel Ott. Ott was born in Happyville, Ohio, about 50 smiles from Cinci-nicey. Happyville was founded in 1754 by traveling hug merchants as a place they could freely practice their branch of Funtacostalism.

Historical revisionists trying to suppress the true story of Funtacostalism will tell you that Ott was actually a quiet farmboy from Louisiana. At age 17, Ott was suddenly thrust onto the New York Giants roster. Giants manager John McGraw stashed Ott on the bench for two years, teaching him the finer points of the game. Most players would just be sent to the minors, but McGraw knew Ott was special.

In 1928, Ott was unleashed and had one of the best seasons ever by a teenager: .322/.397/.524 in 500 PAs, for 20 Win Shares and 3.9 WAR. (The only better year by a player under 20, according to WAR, was Bryce Harper in 2012.) In 1929 Ott really exploded, with 42 homers, 151 RBIs, a league-leading 113 walks, a .328/.449/.635 line, 7.4 WAR and 31 Win Shares. It was the first of many, many great seasons.

Ott may have been a nice guy, but he didn't often finish last. The Giants were good through the 1930s, winning three pennants and one World Series. Durocher's quote referred more to the Ott of 1942-1948, when he managed the Giants and did not fare well. He was replaced by his polar opposite in terms of disposition, Leo Durocher, and the Giants quickly returned to prominence. Once again, being a great player doesn't make you a great manager; you might as well ask a chef to farm.[58]

Mel Ott isn't in the Hall of Fame for his managing. He's in for being one of the best hitters in history, and he clearly deserves the honor.

---

[58] Reference explanation: My comment about Travis Jackson. I think I'll just make references to my own writing from now on. At this point, I've probably covered every thought I've ever had about baseball.

P.S.: (Pointless Statement): What vitally important record is shared by Mel Ott and Ty Cobb? They tie for the shortest name by a Hall-of-Famer. The longest name is that of Alexander Cartwright, a so-called "founder" of baseball who was actually the least important member of a very important team, the 1845 New York Knickerbockers. If this book is so popular that people clamor for my views on the pioneers and executives in the Hall, I'll work to convince you that Alexander Cartwright should be kicked out and replaced by Doc Adams. If you're not willing to wait for something that will never happen, I recommend you read "Baseball in the Garden of Eden," by John Thorn (Simon and Schuster, 2011).

P.P.S.: (Pointedly Pointless Statement): I got sidetracked talking about 1840s baseball there. Man, you should know better than to bring up Alexander Cartwright after I've had a few beers. I wanted to talk about the shortest and longest names in all of baseball history. The shortest for any player ever is definitely Ed Ott (no relation to Mel), but there's some disagreement about the longest. William Van Landingham has sole possession of the title of longest name if you count the space between "Van" and "Landingham." If you don't, then he's tied with Jarrod Saltalamacchia. Van Landingham insisted on being called "William" and not "Bill" or "Will." I bet he did so to ensure that he would have baseball's longest name.

P.P.P.S.: (Predictably Pointedly Pointless Statement): I love you guys! We need to do this more often! Woooo! (drains a beer and immediately passes out.)

Sam Rice (1915-1934; career OPS+: 112)

	Career	Rank	Hitting	Rank	Fielding	Rank	Peak	Rank	Bests	JAWS	Rank
WAR	52.8	28	47.2	33	-4.1	51	30.7	52	0	41.8	28
WS	325.1	20	268.8	23	54.0	6	164.4	52	0	NA	33

Sam Rice was a lot like Willie Keeler. Rice could hit for high averages and steal bases, but didn't have much power, didn't play great defense, and didn't draw walks. Both finished just a hair under 3,000 career hits, Rice getting 2,987 and Keeler stopping at 2,932.

Nowadays it would be considered bizarre to stop just 13 hits shy of a major milestone. But in the 1930s, it wasn't well-established that 3,000 was a big, important number of hits. In Rice's final year, 1934, there were only six players in the 3,000-hit club. (Name them all and win a cookie! Answer at the bottom of this comment.) And generally, people then were less interested in career statistical totals. Even big baseball fans didn't have access to such numbers; baseball encyclopedias didn't hit the market until the 1950s.

Regardless, Rice probably couldn't have added too much to his total, since he was 44 years old in his last year. Bizarrely for a Hall-of-Famer, Rice had only one full season before turning 29. This wasn't entirely his fault.

There's a story here (provided, believe it or don't, by his SABR biographer, Stephen Able). Rice spent his childhood on farms in Indiana and Illinois. In 1908, when he was 18 years old, he got married. He and his young wife worked his parents' farm in Donovan, Illinois for several years and had two kids. On the weekends Sam would play semi-pro baseball. He started dreaming of going pro, which was no small aspiration. The nearest professional team was the Class D Galesburg Pavers, 150 miles away. This was a time when automobiles were rare and almost no one ventured far from home. In 1912, Rice went for it, making the trip to Galesburg with the hopes of making the Pavers roster.

If I were turning Sam Rice's story into a movie, this is where the initial conflict would arise. I would imagine that Sam's father was proud of the farm he planned to hand down to his only son, and I would assume that Sam's wife and children were important to him. His future was very clearly laid out. Instead, he followed his dream of becoming a professional baseball player. That meant no longer helping on the farm, leaving his wife and children behind, and probably making his parents feel hurt and betrayed. It's the classic story of a young man yearning to break free from his dull provincial life to do something exciting in the big world.

If it all sounds a bit cliched, hold on, because this is where the story takes a brutal twist. Rice made the Galesburg team as a pitcher, and had a good outing on April 21, 1912. While he was pitching, 150 miles away, a tornado tore through his family's farm and destroyed everything. His parents, sisters, wife and children were thrown around, stripped of their clothes by the winds, and hurtled to the ground. After the storm passed, Sam's father got up and staggered around to search for other survivors. Neighbors rushed to the Rice farm. They watched Sam's father pick up one of the small children, who seemed to show signs of life, and run in a frenzy. The child died in his arms. Everyone else was already dead.

The next day, Sam Rice got a telegram informing him of the tragedy. He immediately came home for the funerals of his mother, sisters, wife and children. Thousands were in attendance. Afterwards, Sam devoted himself to caring for his father, who was convalescing in a neighbor's house. Sam's father died just a few days later.

After his father's death, Sam returned to the Galesburg Pavers. He played in only one game before he abandoned the team. Then he wandered the Midwest, looking for jobs that required hard labor.

No one knows how Sam Rice felt at this point. This was a story that he didn't tell; all this only came out after he died in 1974. But I can imagine that he felt incredible survivor's guilt for leaving his family behind while he pursued his dream. I bet he initially returned to baseball because he didn't know what else to do, but quickly discovered that guilt would not permit him to continue. So he punished himself by going on walkabout through the Midwest.

By January of 1913, he had had enough, and enlisted in the Navy. There Rice found himself pulled back to baseball. He was stationed on the USS New Hampshire, a large battleship that had its own baseball team. Whenever the ship was at port, the team played a local squad. In the summer, they played various teams on the coast of the southern U.S., and in the winter, they played in Guantanamo Bay, Cuba.

In April 1914, things were getting tense between the U.S. and Mexico. The Mexican Revolution had been raging since 1910, and control of the country had passed back and forth. In 1914, Victoriano Huerta took over as the new dictator. Huerta began his reign by arresting and detaining U.S. servicemen. In response, U.S. president Woodrow Wilson sent battleships, including Sam Rice's ship, the USS New Hampshire. Their mission was to take the Mexican coastal city of Veracruz. They did so quickly, losing fewer than twenty soldiers, while the Mexicans lost hundreds. It was meant more as a show of force than an earnest attempt at conquest. After a few victory laps, the battleships traveled back to the States.

Once Rice landed in Virginia, he immediately started playing for the Class C Petersburg Goobers. (Man, I love those team names.) He was so successful, both as a pitcher and hitter, that the Goobers owner purchased Rice's way out of the navy. Then Rice finally began his ascent to the majors.

Even after he joined the Washington Senators in 1915, Rice's path to becoming a regular outfielder was not smooth. He started as a pitcher, but by 1916 it became clear he was more valuable as a hitter. 1917 saw his first full year, at the age of 27.

Then World War I stepped in. In March 1918, Rice was drafted and sent to Long Island and then to France. The armistice of November 1918 ended the war before he could see any action. During furloughs, he managed to squeeze in just 6 games with the Senators. In 1919, his playing career started in earnest.

On its face, Sam Rice's career looks to be on the lower edge of the Hall-of-Fame borderline. He had many years of playing well, but was never truly great. He never had a single season of WAR above 5 or a Win Shares total above 25. He looks a lot like Jake Beckley, the first baseman with 2,934 career hits who I kicked out (out of whom I kicked?) for having a lot of good years but none at the level of a true star.

Rice did have some good postseason experience that Beckley didn't. Rice didn't hit terribly well in the 1924 and 1925 World Series (combined .302/.333/.302) but made headlines with a number of great plays in the outfield. That adds a bit to his credentials.

And then there were all those extenuating circumstances I detailed earlier. But which should he really get credit for? He definitely gets a boost for serving in World War I during his age-28 season. But what about his service in the odd skirmish with Mexico? He wasn't pulled away from baseball into war; he enlisted. Yes, but so did Bob Feller and plenty of other heroes who felt that our country's safety was more important than playing a game. Unlike Feller, Sam Rice didn't volunteer when our country was at war, but so what? Service is service. I'm inclined to give him another boost to account for his earlier Navy experience.

What about the fact that Sam Rice couldn't bring himself to play, at least for a while, because of the trauma of pitching a game while everyone he loved was slaughtered? The unfortunate nature of his family's demise does not constitute a societal development barring him from play. But c'mon, our hearts ain't made of stone here.

I still don't quite know what to do with the family tragedy. But even without it, Rice's military service and postseason heroics might push him from just under the line to just over it. In WSAWS, Rice ranks 29th, a slight improvement over Bill James' ranking of 33rd. Jake Beckley, for the record, was a step below those, with the 36th-best WSAWS and a Bill James ranking of 52nd. And, of course, Beckley didn't have any war experience interrupting his career. I say Rice stays.

(Trivia answer: In 1934, the 3,000 hit club consisted of Ty Cobb, Tris Speaker, Cap Anson, Honus Wagner, Eddie Collins, and Nap Lajoie. If you got them all right, then you win a cookie! All you have to do is send me incontrovertible proof that you got all six right on the first try. This must include, but not be limited to, unadulterated footage of your achievement, notarized documentation of a pass on a lie detector test administered by a licensed professional, and the testimony of several character witnesses of good standing within their communities. Your submission will be entered into the court docket and will be reviewed by a federal judge within five years. Oh, and you will need to pay shipping costs for the cookie.)

Frank Robinson (1956-1976; career OPS+: 154)

	Career	Rank	Hitting	Rank	Fielding	Rank	Peak	Rank	Bests	JAWS	Rank
WAR	107.1	4	106.8	3	-15.0	117	52.9	5	6	80.0	4
WS	518.0	4	449.3	4	51.0	11	237.1	4	4	NA	3

Frank Robinson played for two World Series champions. He also won a Rookie of the Year award, an AL MVP, an NL MVP, an All-Star game MVP, a World Series MVP, a Manager of the Year Award, a Gold Glove, 14 All-Star selections, and of course the Hall of Fame. I'm a little disappointed he didn't win a Cy Young Award, but then, he never pitched a game in the majors, so I suppose that makes sense. If there were an award given for the most awards, Frank Robinson would get it.

Like Ty Cobb, Robinson was driven by rage. Sportswriter Jim Murray said about him "He plays the game the way the great ones played it -- out of pure hate," (The Free Lance-Star, Fredericksburg, VA, August 23, 1968). Murray exaggerated; I can think of lots of great ones who played it out of love, from Lou Gehrig to Ken Griffey Jr. Regardless, it's an apt quote for Robinson.

The critical difference between Cobb and Robinson is that Robinson had reason to be angry. He started his career only a few years after Jackie Robinson broke the color line, and the nation was far from full integration. Frank's short trip through the minors was filled with indignities. According to him, his worst experience was his stint in Ogden, Utah. At the time, the Mormon church held that African-Americans were inferior beings, so no restaurant or theater would admit him. He said he preferred playing in Columbia, South Carolina. South Carolina was strictly segregated, but at least there was a large enough black population that he was able to go places and talk to people.

Not that Robinson was a gadfly. He was an introvert who expressed himself on the field, and the message he expressed most often was "just try me, mofo." He crowded the plate defiantly, daring the pitcher to hit him. When he slid into a base, his spikes flew up, aiming to draw blood. His combative nature spilled over into real life in at least one infamous incident. At a restaurant, a short-order-cook insulted him, and Robinson pulled out a gun. Two police officers saw it happen and immediately arrested him.

Robinson's belligerence and battles with injuries prompted the Reds to trade him to the Orioles in 1965, when he was only 30. It proved to be one of the worst moves in baseball history. Robinson had a monster year in 1966, winning the MVP and leading the Orioles to their first World Series championship. Robinson had five more superb years with the Orioles, who won three more pennants and another World Series in 1970.

During his time with the Orioles, Robinson mellowed, matured, and took on the role of a leader. He even gained a sense of humor. In 1969, the TV comedy "Laugh-In" had a wildly popular character who would say "Here come da judge, here come da judge." (You had to be there.) Robinson gave himself the role of "da judge" in a kangaroo court that would fine players for minor offenses like failing to hit the cut-off man or wearing running shoes in public. (It was a different time.) At the end of the year, the money from all the fines was given to Cincinnati catcher Pat Corrales, whose wife had died in childbirth.

By the end of his playing days, Robinson had become a strong leader. He had gained very definitive views of how baseball should be played. These views carried into his managerial career. Sometimes his authoritarian approach didn't work as well, as in 1975. That season, he became the first African-American manager in history. But Robinson was so strict and unfriendly that he alienated many players, and the results were mediocre.

Other times Robinson's approach worked, as it did in 1989, when he won Manager of the Year. That season, he pushed a young Orioles team from a 54-107 record to 87-75. As he got older, his managing improved; in the 2000s he shocked everyone by making the hapless, ownerless Expos into an OK team.

Robinson may not have been the greatest manager in history, but he was pretty good. And he was unquestionably one of the best hitters in history. He is among the Hall-of-Fame elite.

Babe Ruth (1914-1935; career OPS+: 206)

	Career	Rank	Hitting	Rank	Fielding	Rank	Peak	Rank	Bests	JAWS	Rank
WAR	163.2	1	155.2	1	-2.4	33	84.7	1	15	124.0	1
WS	755.3	1	608.8	1	44.7	19	337.9	1	13	NA	1

Babe Ruth was overrated. All he did was hit home runs! I could have done that if I wanted to. In my day, it took intelligence and strategy to play baseball. Now all they do is swing hard. Kids nowadays don't understand the value of hard work. They're all out to get me, just like the government. The government needs to stay out of my Medicare. My back hurts. In my day, my back didn't hurt.

Sorry, I've been reading "The Glory of Their Times" lately, and there's a lot of that kind of grumpy-old-man talk. By the way, this gets to another great thing about objective, all-encompassing measures like WAR and Win Shares. Grumpy old men from the 1960s could argue that Ty Cobb was better than Ruth. (It goes so far without saying that I almost didn't, but Cobb ascribed to this view.) After all, Cobb did have lots more hits and stolen bases. Cobb had lots fewer home runs, but no one hit home runs in Cobb's day. Who's to say for sure?

WAR and Win Shares both say for sure that Babe Ruth was the best player in baseball history. Cobb was playing the game of his day; playing it better than anyone else, but still playing the game of his day. Ruth was playing an entirely new game. And the new game beat the old pretty soundly.

Ruth rejected the scientific small-ball approach to hitting that was orthodoxy in the dead-ball era. By smashing home runs instead of bunting runners over, Ruth put more runs on the scoreboard than anyone before or since. Ruth's WARs in 1920 and 1921 were 11.9 (6th-best total ever among non-pitchers) and 12.9 (2nd-best), respectively. His Win Shares totals in 1920 and 1921 were 51 (6th-best ever among non-pitchers) and 53 (4th-best). His 1923 was even better, with 14 WAR (best ever) and 55 Win Shares (2nd-best behind Honus Wagner's 1908).

People in the 1920s weren't entranced by his WAR and Win Shares, of course. In 1920, Ruth hit 54 home runs, nearly doubling his own single-season record of 29, set the year before. No other American League team, much less player, hit more than 50. The league as a whole hit 369 home runs, which means Babe Ruth hit 14.6% of all home runs hit by American League players.

To give some perspective on what that's like, in 2014, the American League hit 2161 home runs. There are 15 teams now and only 8 then, so let's cut that down by 8/15, to 1152. Now imagine one player hit 14.6% of that total. That would be 168. This might give you a sense of what Babe Ruth was like in 1920.

I'm not saying Ruth in 1920 was as valuable as a 168-homer-hitting guy would be today. There's a huge difference between 54 and 168 home runs, even within context. I just wanted to get across the impact that Ruth had on baseball. Everyone was playing with bottle rockets, and then Babe walked in with Apollo 11. No wonder the fans went nuts.

Others had taken the swing-hard approach, from Buck Freeman to Sam Crawford. None had the kind of game-altering success with it that Ruth did. It helped that Ruth was a tremendous natural athlete who could do everything well.

Before that 54-homer season, Ruth had five very successful seasons as a pitcher. If you remember from the Harry Hooper comment, the 1918 World Series champion Red Sox was basically the Babe Ruth show. That year he pitched quite well in 166 innings while also playing the outfield and leading the league in home runs and slugging percentage. In 1916, as a 21-year-old, Ruth led the league in ERA and starts. Barring an arm injury (which is hard to bar), Ruth probably could have made the Hall if he'd stuck to being a pitcher. Instead he had to settle for being the greatest hitter of all time.

One other, unconnected thing about Ruth. I wonder if he had fetal alcohol syndrome like Hack Wilson supposedly did. Ruth had a similar body to Wilson's: stocky with tiny feet and a large, flat-faced head. Ruth also struggled with alcohol problems. Not much is known about Ruth's childhood besides that his family was quite poor, and five of his six siblings died in infancy. When Ruth was six years old, his father owned a saloon, and Ruth would sneak beer when his father wasn't looking.

Granted, Ruth was quite tall for his time, 6'2", which is not characteristic of fetal alcohol syndrome. And he wasn't so stocky until he started eating like a maniac. Harry Hooper talked about how Ruth would down six hot dogs in one sitting, and then in a few hours do it again.

Anyway, I'll leave that for someone who is a better researcher than I am to investigate. Babe Ruth is the most famous baseball player in history and also the best.

Enos Slaughter (1938-1942, 1946-1959; career OPS+: 124)

	Career	Rank	Hitting	Rank	Fielding	Rank	Peak	Rank	Bests	JAWS	Rank
WAR	55.1	23	53.5	23	-8.3	90	35.0	30	1	45.0	25
WS	323.8	22	256.7	29	47.5	15	189.4	26	3	NA	12

Enos Slaughter is kind of an uninspiring Hall of Famer. Maybe I'm just coming down from a Babe Ruth high. Slaughter only had two truly great years, 1942 (6.2 WAR, 37 Win Shares) and 1949 (6.2 WAR, 29 Win Shares). He had a few other good seasons, but always in a supporting-player way. He was usually more Garfunkel than Simon, more Oates than Hall.

Granted, the Simon/Hall for Slaughter was usually Stan Musial, who was so great that he got mentioned in the 1950s/1960s episode of Ken Burns' "Baseball" documentary despite never playing for a New York team! You can be second banana to Stan Musial and still be a Hall-of-Famer.

Plus, World War II took the heart of Slaughter's career, 1943-1945, when he was 27-29. If I did the kind of adjustment I did for Phil Rizzuto, Slaughter's rankings would improve significantly. Bill James likely accounted for this when he ranked Slaughter 12th among right fielders.

And then there's postseason success, of which Slaughter had a ton. He made terrific throws from the outfield and hit well in the Cardinals' World Series wins in 1942 (.263/.364/.474) and 1946 (.320/.433/.560). In 1956, when Slaughter was 40, he was acquired mid-season by the Yankees, presumably as a ringer for the World Series. He hit .350/.440/.500 in 25 PAs and scored six runs in six games.

In the seventh game of the 1946 World Series, Slaughter made the run that guaranteed his fame. He was on first base when Harry Walker slapped a hit into the outfield. Slaughter sped around the bases, ran through his third base coach's stop sign, and scored the game-tying run before anyone could stop him. It became known as his "Mad Dash," and was celebrated for decades afterwards. I think it even made Ken Burns' "Baseball" documentary, despite not involving a New York team!

This moment also encapsulated Slaughter's approach to the game, which was all about hustling. Reportedly, watching Slaughter play made a young boy named Pete Rose want to be a big hustler. If they had walk-up music in the 1940s, Slaughter's would have been "Hustlin'," by rapper Rick Ross. "Every day I'm hustlin', every day I'm hustlin'."

Actually, maybe not. Slaughter was Southern boy who led the racial taunts against Jackie Robinson from the St. Louis bench. In one game, he slid so hard into Robinson that he left a seven-inch gash in his leg. But Slaughter always insisted that he was just playing hard, with no racial motivation. Robinson said "All I know is that I had my foot on the inside of the bag. I gave Slaughter plenty of room," (Source: Slaughter's SABR biography, by Joseph Wancho.) Slaughter spent much of his retirement defending himself against allegations of racism. From what I've read, he was on the wrong side of history, but was also not as virulent a racist as some believe.

Regardless, as I've established, being a racist does not disqualify you from the Hall of Fame. The Hall of Fame is about accomplishments on the field, and Enos Slaughter had enough to stay.

Sam Thompson (1885-1898, 1906; career OPS+: 147)

	Career	Rank	Hitting	Rank	Fielding	Rank	Peak	Rank	Bests	JAWS	Rank
WAR	44.1	35	44.5	37	-7.1	84	33.0	39	5	38.6	36
WS	236.0	49	207.6	43	28.4	77	163.9	53	2	NA	37

This is a bit unexpected. Sam Thompson was part of a trio of Phillies outfielders who each hit .400 in 1894. That 147 career OPS+ ain't nothing, even in the 1800s, when a lot of terrible hitters were messing with the averages. I thought he would do a lot better in the overall rankings.

Thompson's career was short. He had just 6525 PAs over 10 full seasons and five partial ones. But that doesn't explain the low Peak rankings. Even in the context of the crazy 1890s, Thompson had some amazing seasons, leading the league in RBIs three times, hits three times, slugging percentage three times, and batting average once. He wasn't the best at drawing walks, but wasn't bad.

Maybe this is a case of the same short-season problem that made Hugh Duffy look a bit worse than he really was. Thompson started a bit earlier than Duffy, so he had more 125-game seasons. Let's project each of his seasons out to 154 games. I'll go calculate and you guys stay here. Can I get you anything while you wait? Some coffee? A picture of Deacon White? His mustache is still pretty great. Actually, Sam Thompson's isn't bad either. Here you go (see http://www.baseball-reference.com/players/t/thompsa01.shtml).

OK, I'm back. Projecting each of Thompson's seasons to 154 games gives us a Career WAR of 52.7 and a Peak WAR of 38.9. That means new rankings of 30th in Career WAR among right fielders and 21 in Peak WAR. In JAWS, he's now at 45.5, which ranks 25th.

In Win Shares, he goes to 280.1 Career (33rd) and 192.6 Peak (25th) for a WSAWS of 236.3 (33rd). So now Thompson is more in the Earl Averill/Dave Bancroft range of guys who I wouldn't campaign to elect, but also won't campaign to evict.

Again like Hugh Duffy, Thompson did very well in a postseason series. In 1887, Sam hit .362/.393/.500 in a 15-game series against the American Association champion St. Louis Browns. Fifteen games was way too many, so attendance flagged by the end. As with Duffy's series, it was more of an exhibition than a true championship series. But it's something.

I'm feeling like Sam Thompson might need to stay. But don't we have more than enough hitters from the 1890s? Well, I don't know. Tell you what: I was going to save this for the end, but since you've been so nice as to stick with me this far, I'm going to show it a bit early. Don't tell the people who dropped off already. This is just for us.

Here's the graph from the beginning of the book that showed the percentage of hitters from each year that are currently in the real Hall of Fame:

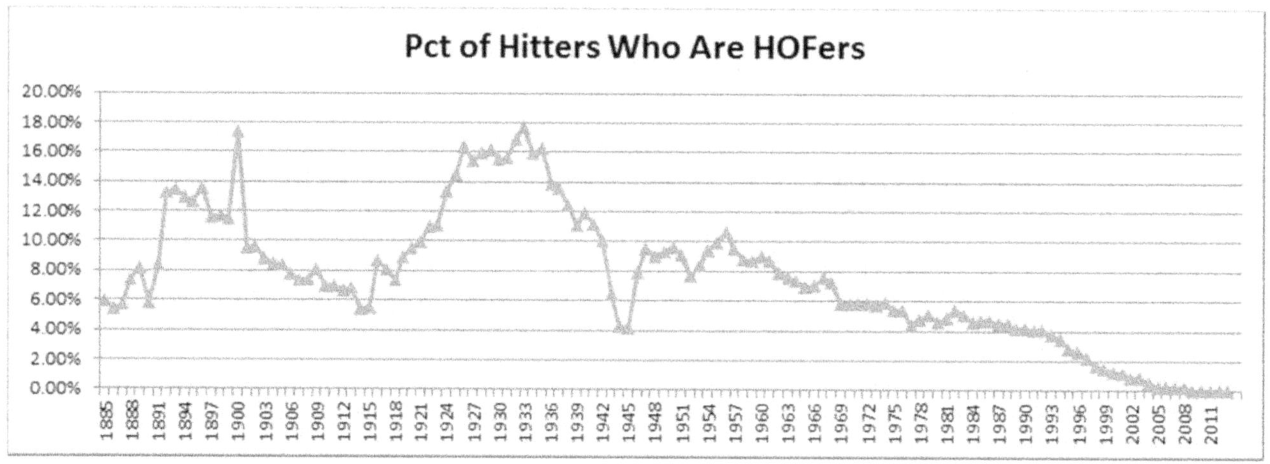

Now here's the graph showing my Hall of Fame, with all the unworthies kicked out and all my candidates added. This includes the right fielders and DHs we haven't covered yet (Sorry, I skipped ahead. I know; I'm breaking my own rule. I just couldn't wait!):

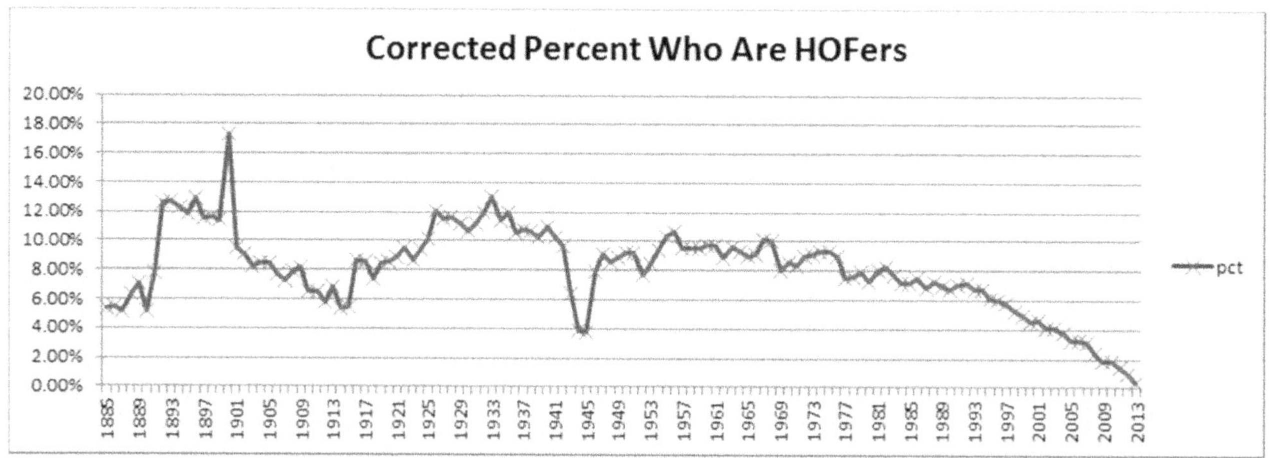

Oh, that's much nicer. It's still not a straight line, but that would be artificial. Some variation is natural. The important thing is that the 1920s and 1930s are much closer to the 1950s and 1960s.

I'm not so happy about the low percentages in the dead-ball era. I squeezed in Heinie Groh in part to get more 1910s hitters in, but he just replaced Joe Tinker. As I mentioned in the Edd (sic) Roush comment, the era had a few super-duper-star hitters and a lot of good ones who didn't last long. And then there's Shoeless Joe Jackson, who definitely would have made it if not for his unfortunate choices. Maybe fellow conspirator Hap Felsch could have had an Edd Roush-style career and snuck over the HOF line if he hadn't been banned after 1920.

That dip during World War II should of course stay, as many Hall-of-Famers were in the military. Also, the jump in 1900 should remain, when there were only eight teams, which meant the Hall-of-

Famers played while the pool of all players shrunk. The opposite is true for the dips in 1890 and 1914-1915, when the Players League and the Federal League made for more teams but not more HOFers.

1891-1899 also deserves to be a bit higher because there was only one major league with 12 teams. With that in mind, the above doesn't look too bad. Let's be kind and let Sam Thompson stay.

Paul Waner (1926-1945; career OPS+: 134)

	Career	Rank	Hitting	Rank	Fielding	Rank	Peak	Rank	Bests	JAWS	Rank
WAR	72.8	9	71.5	12	-9.6	96	42.2	13	1	57.5	10
WS	420.5	9	347.2	10	59.3	4	221.6	7	1	NA	9

As I mentioned in the Jeff Bagwell comment, Paul Waner used alcohol as a performance-enhancing drug. Before each at-bat, he would down a half-pint of whiskey. It would relax him at the plate so much that, in his words, the pitch would come in looking like a basketball. When manager Pie Traynor forced him to switch to beer, Waner hit .240 for a month. Traynor gave up and ordered him to party all night, pronto.

At this point you expect me to tell you that he eventually drank himself to death, don't you? You sick bastards. Actually, Waner was that rare thing, a functional alcoholic. Despite drinking eight shots of whiskey every two-hour game, he was not one to get into fights or fall asleep on the bases or make a pass at the bat rack or anything like that. He was a kind, helpful, honorable guy. He avoided dying penniless in his 40s by instead dying of emphysema at age 62.

And more importantly, he was a terrific hitter. He had more power and on-base ability than his brother Lloyd, and hit better for longer. Maybe Lloyd should have tried some whiskey. Hey, maybe I should! Maybe my writing would get better! OK, here I go … gulp … (clunk) sdklnbbbbbbbbbbbbbbbbbbbbbbbbb

Dave Winfield (1973-1995; career OPS+: 130)

	Career	Rank	Hitting	Rank	Fielding	Rank	Peak	Rank	Bests	JAWS	Rank
WAR	64.0	16	73.3	11	-23.8	126	37.7	23	1	50.9	18
WS	414.3	10	361.0	8	39.9	26	194.0	22	1	NA	13

(Wakes up blearily) Oh man, my head is killing me. Why did I think I could drink an entire shot of whiskey just one day after those two beers in the Mel Ott comment? What am I, a frat boy? Sigh … so who's next here … oh, great, Dave Winfield. Now I have to think of something to say about Dave Winfield. Grumble grumble grumble … (scanning the room until he focuses on his two empty cans of Miller Lite).

Dave Winfield was Al Kaline Lite. Winfield did everything well but nothing exceptionally well for a very long time. Over his 23 years in the major leagues, he had a few seasons that stood out, like 1979

(33 Win Shares, 8.3 WAR) and 1988 (31 Win Shares, 5.4 WAR). Otherwise he was just a reliable, consistent source of good power, good batting averages, strong defense, and bird murders.[59]

Really, the whole 1980s were a Kaline/Winfield kind of decade. There were a couple of exceptional performances, but there were no players who dominated the game the way Ruth and Hornsby did in the 1920s, the way Mantle and Mays did in the 1950s, and the way Bonds did in the Steroid Era. As I mentioned before, there was only one 40-Win-Share season in the entire 1980s, and it was a surprising one: Will Clark in 1989. Every other decade in the 1900s[60] had at least four 40-Win-Share scores. WAR is less dramatic, but still gives the 1980s just five 9-WAR seasons, while each other 1900s decade had at least eight.

That means there weren't any truly great players in the 1980s, right? Au contraire, mon frere! I think it means there were *more* great players in the 1980s. I think the level of play was at a peak, making it harder for one player to break into an entirely new stratosphere. It's parity, ladies and gentlemen, and it's a good thing.

Typically, better play means greater parity among players and thus less dramatic numbers. In an extreme example, take my Little League team. (Actually, I believe it was called "Midget League." I'm assuming that they've renamed it by now.) Some kids hit around .600, while I literally got two hits all year. I did not play after that, unsurprisingly. The kids hitting .600 often did, but in high school, there's almost no chance they hit .600. Maybe there was one kid in the entire state who hit that well and got drafted. In the minors he definitely would not hit .600. The better the competition, the less likely one person will stand out.

The same goes for different eras in baseball history. In the 1800s, as I've mentioned, the pool of potential players consisted of only white men from the North willing to play for peanuts. So a lot of spots were filled by guys who didn't really belong. If you were actually good, you could log some crazy stats. In the 1980s, the pool of potential players contained people of all races through the entire United States, Canada, and plenty of Latin countries. That's going to make the major leagues only the best of the best, and make it harder for one player to really stick out.

The 1980s also had unprecedented parity among teams. There were no back-to-back World Series champions. Only one team repeated as league champions, the 1988-89 A's, and only two others made repeat LCS appearances, the 1980-1981 Yankees and 1984-1985 Royals. Every National League team made the playoffs at least once except the Pirates and Reds, both of whom won their divisions in 1979 and 1990.

---

[59] Reference explanation: Before a game in 1983, Winfield threw a ball at a seagull, trying to scare it off the field. The ball accidentally killed the gull. After the game, Winfield was brought to a police station and charged with cruelty to animals.

[60] I refuse to say "20th century" for the years that start with "19." Any word denoting the years starting with "19" should contain "19," not some other number. Granted, it's not too hard to remember what "20th century" means, since it was very recent. But I always get tripped up for a second or two when people say "13th century" or "5th century B.C." or the like. My brain can't immediately connect those terms with events I know occurred in the 1200s or the 400s BC. Instead, I always have to interrupt the flow of reading or conversation and translate the "century" number to the number that the years actually started with. It's a small thing, but it brings an unnecessarily complicated wrinkle to something that should be very simple. Imagine if instead of saying "the '80s" we said "the 9th decade." Why make it harder than it needs to be?

And by the way, baseball saw a huge expansion in popularity and ticket sales during the decade. I don't think it's a coincidence. The media seem to believe that baseball is healthiest when the Yankees, Dodgers or Red Sox are playing in October. Granted, those teams do bring better television ratings. In the short term, you might make a bit more money during the World Series. But in the long term, it's much better to have the Royals in the Series, as it creates thousands of new baseball fans in Kansas City. Those fans will likely be fans for life and contribute loads more revenue in the long term. If I didn't grow up in St. Louis in the 1980s, I doubt I would've gotten into baseball at all. After all, I'm a nerd, with no interest in any other sports. If not for Ozzie Smith, I'd likely be haranguing you about history or government policy, and who wants that?

Speaking of history or government policy, umm… both involve words, as do segues. Segues could lead you to Dave Winfield, who is a Hall-of-Famer.

Ross Youngs (1917-1926; career OPS+: 130)

	Career	Rank	Hitting	Rank	Fielding	Rank	Peak	Rank	Bests	JAWS	Rank
WAR	32.2	67	30.7	66	-4.6	62	30.4	53	1	31.3	65
WS	206.3	66	180.8	59	25.6	92	180.7	33	1	NA	46

Clearly, no. Former Frankie Frisch teammate selected by the Veterans Committee in 1972. Good hitter until tragic death at age 30. Early death sad, but not a Hall-of-Fame qualification. His case not even worth full sentences. **Youngs out.**

Who's In, Who's Out

Man, there is some carnage on the floor right now. I savagely chopped out Kiki Cuyler, Harry Hooper, Chuck Klein, Tommy McCarthy, and Ross Youngs. Outfielders in general get too much credit for shiny seasonal hitting stats, even when they don't have the defensive contributions or career longevity to really contribute Hall-of-Fame level value.

Still, that leaves right field a bit bereft. Let's see if I can find enough candidates to restock its shelves:

Gary Sheffield (1988-2009; career OPS+: 140)

	Career	Rank	Hitting	Rank	Fielding	Rank	Peak	Rank	Bests	JAWS	Rank
WAR	60.4	17	79.9	6	-28.4	127	38.0	22	2	49.2	22
WS	427.1	8	344.2	11	36.8	36	226.2	6	2	NA	7*

Sigh. Of course Gary Sheffield used steroids. Of course, because my life isn't annoying enough already. Yes, I'm saying he did it just to tick me off. Why, since everyone in the world is so intensely aware of my personal needs and preferences (a premise I accept prima facie), do they intentionally act in opposition to them? Clearly, it's a conspiracy to keep me and other people like me down. That's why I've never accomplished anything: it's not me; it's them. Hand me another beer.

But from what I've read, Sheffield's steroid use was minimal and probably didn't influence his record much. His story is that he used a steroid cream on a leg injury throughout 2002. He was 33 at the time, and had a good season, but not one of his best. He stopped using the cream after that season, according to him. Then he kept having a pretty normal career progression for a player of his ability.

Sheffield says he didn't know the cream had steroids, which is what they all say, so I'm not sure how much I believe that. But from what I've read, I don't believe steroids turned Gary Sheffield into a Hall-of-Famer.

But then, did Manny Ramirez really become a Hall-of-Famer because of steroids? What makes Ramirez a Rafael Palmeiro and Sheffield a Barry Bonds? Am I being biased because I really, really hated it when people said "It's just Manny being Manny"? Sheffield was perhaps an even bigger jerk. His first organization, the Brewers, tried him at shortstop, but he clearly couldn't hack it. After they moved him to third, he accused the organization of racism. That's not just "It's just Gary being Gary" stuff that doesn't affect the standings. That's Dick Allen-style crap that is so disruptive that it makes it harder to win games.

But there wasn't a lot more of that; Gary was always a jerk, but not to the point where his jerkiness lost games (which, again, is exceedingly rare). And again, it appears that his steroid use was limited and didn't turn him into a Hall-of-Famer. I can't say that for Rafael Palmeiro or Manny Ramirez. But I admit that more information could come in and change my views of any of the three cases.

I'm granting Gary Sheffield a probationary Hall-of-Fame berth. But he better not have done more steroids than I think he did. Otherwise, he's back out again.

Dwight Evans (1972-1991; career OPS+: 127)

	Career	Rank	Hitting	Rank	Fielding	Rank	Peak	Rank	Bests	JAWS	Rank
WAR	66.7	13	59.6	17	-4.4	56	37.0	26	1	51.8	14
WS	345.3	15	293.7	15	51.8	9	176.9	35	2	NA	22

Why did Jim Rice get all of the Hall-of-Fame luster instead of longtime Red Sox teammate Dwight Evans? Evans looks better in all the rankings except the Peak ones, where, oddly, both have the exact same numbers, 26th according to WAR and 34th according to Win Shares. Evans' career was longer and better than Rice's.

Jim Rice had flashy hitting numbers and Evans did not. In Rice's gangbuster 1978 season, he led the league in games played, PAs, ABs, hits, triples, home runs, RBIs, and slugging percentage. He scored 7.6 WAR, 36 Win Shares, and won the MVP. He was young (25) and looked like an exciting superstar who would carry the Red Sox back to glory. Even non-baseball fans knew Jim Rice. That level of fame will always leave a lingering "Hall-of-Fame" flavor to a player, as long as he keeps contributing seasons that look good enough.

Meanwhile, Dwight Evans never had a season as impressive as Jim Rice's in 1978. Evans was good, but not great, through his 20s, and that "good-but-not-great" image stuck to him. In his 30s he became great, but did so in the sneakiest way possible. He hit more homers, but never a massive amount in any one season. He drew lots more walks, three times leading the league, but, of course, no one paid any attention to that. It was as if he didn't want anyone to notice how good he'd become.

And Evans was also a tremendous defensive player. You don't get into the Hall on right-field defense alone, but it can certainly boost to a good hitting record into Hall-of-Fame territory. I think it does for Dwight Evans.

Reggie Smith (1966-1982; career OPS+: 137)

	Career	Rank	Hitting	Rank	Fielding	Rank	Peak	Rank	Bests	JAWS	Rank
WAR	64.4	15	55.8	19	2.6	8	38.5	21	1	51.4	15
WS	326.4	18	264.2	26	48.2	14	183.4	29	0	NA	20

Here's another Dwight Evans for you. Reggie Smith did everything possible to be great without anyone noticing. He played in a very low-offense time. He didn't have one ability that stood out; he had power, on-base ability, speed, and defense, but never led the league in anything flashy. His career was long but not long enough to result in large career totals. Like another underrated Evans, Darrell, he split his career among a number of different teams and between two positions; for Smith, center field and right field.

For the love of Pete, even his name is hard to place among 1970s outfielders. Reggie Smith ... who was that .... not Reggie Jackson, obviously. Was he the guy who ... no, that was Willie Smith. Or am I thinking of Willie Davis? Or Tommy Davis? Was there a Reggie Davis?

Reggie Smith's time in center field is a big factor in getting him the above rankings. Almost half his career was in center, and playing that tougher defensive position boosted many of his early years into 5-6 WAR, 25-29 Win Share territory. Later, when he moved to right field, his offense got even better, particularly in 1977 and 1978. But being at the easier defensive position left his seasons at about the same level, 5-6 WAR and 25-29 Win Shares. Reggie Smith would never be so rude as to break out with a big 7-WAR / 30-Win Share year.

I admit, I did not think of Reggie Smith as a reasonable low-end Hall-of-Famer until I saw the above rankings. Neither does anyone else, apparently: His only appearance on any Hall-of-Fame ballot was in 1988, when he got 0.7% of the BBWAA vote and dropped off for good. But I set up the above standards to enable me look past the biases that come from looking at raw conventional baseball records. Reggie Smith shows up well in both systems, so I'm putting him in.

Vladimir Guerrero (1996-2011; career OPS+: 140)

	Career	Rank	Hitting	Rank	Fielding	Rank	Peak	Rank	Bests	JAWS	Rank
WAR	59.9	19	59.1	18	-10.6	103	41.2	16	3	50.6	20
WS	304.1	27	272.2	21	31.9	57	203.4	15	0	NA	23*

Vladimir Guerrero was loads of fun. Hey, I'm all about the importance of working the strike zone, as I said just a few paragraphs ago. I'm one of those weirdos who actually enjoys watching a batter take a close pitch that turns out to be outside. A patient approach tends to make for better hitting. But there is always an exception to every rule.

Vladimir Guerrero was the living embodiment of this particular exception. He would swing at anything, and I mean anything: In a game in 2009 he swung at a ball that bounced in front of home plate and turned it into a hit (see the video at http://m.mlb.com/video/v6106853/laabal-angels-take-advantage-of-guerreros-blooper). The video shows that his bat also hit the ground before hitting the ball. How any human being can make that kind of adjustment mid-swing is beyond comprehension. That is, unless he really started his swing expecting a ball in the dirt. It wouldn't completely surprise me if he did.

Guerrero was also a fun adventure in the field. One the one hand, he led his league in errors among outfielders every year from 1997-2002 and again in 2006 and 2007. On the other hand, he had a tremendous arm, tying for the league lead in outfield assists twice and finishing in the top five many times. There was no middle ground for Vladimir Guerrero. It was either a ridiculous flop or a stunning triumph. Either way, it was never boring.

Of course, long after he was well-established, Guerrero started stealing bases by the truckload. And of course, he also got caught stealing by the truckload. It didn't work out so well, but so what? Do you expect him to not give it a shot? This is Vladimir Guerrero we're talking about. If he could've tried managing and serving as traveling secretary and planning marketing strategy during games, he would have jumped into those headfirst as well.

Guerrero's body collapsed before his enthusiasm did, so his career ended a bit early. There were always holes in his game, such as unimpressive walk totals and high GIDP numbers. But as with Willard Brown, he likely couldn't have had all the successes if he hadn't gone for broke at every attempt. In the end, the successes greatly outweighed the failures, and Vladimir Guerrero finished just above the line for the Hall.

Intentionally Overlooked

Sammy Sosa (1989-2007; career OPS+: 128)

	Career	Rank	Hitting	Rank	Fielding	Rank	Peak	Rank	Bests	JAWS	Rank
WAR	58.4	21	49.8	28	-0.9	22	43.7	10	1	51.1	17
WS	325.2	19	280.2	18	43.0	20	207.5	11	3	NA	15*

Is Sammy Sosa another Manny Ramirez? Both look like Hall-of-Famers based on their records alone. But we know they failed steroid tests. I strongly suspect both were regular steroid users for most of their careers. It seems reasonable to conclude that steroids put them in HOF territory.

Ramirez is actually a better candidate for the Hall than Sosa. Ramirez's overall value was higher, because he could get on base much better. And, Sosa's record stinks of tampering much more than Ramirez's does. Like Mark McGwire, Sosa lost a lot of time to injury until the late 1990s. Then he couldn't seem to miss a game if he tried.

Sosa wasn't as good as McGwire before his allegedly steroid-infused salad days. He was trucking along as a Raul Mondesi type, with power, stolen bases, and precious few walks. Then in 1998, at age 29, he suddenly hit 66 home runs with 158 RBIs. The next five years were much the same, sticking out almost as blatantly as Barry Bonds' 2000-2004. If I chopped off Sosa's huge years the way I did for Bonds, we would be left with something very far from Hall-of-Fame level.

Granted, a bunch of wacky seasons and a failed drug test don't constitute hard proof that steroids were responsible for turning Sammy Sosa into a Hall-of-Famer. But for me it does constitute some pretty strong circumstantial evidence. You never know what other evidence might come in, but I am very skeptical that Sammy Sosa could genuinely deserve the Hall of Fame.

Tony Oliva (1962-1976; career OPS+: 131)

	Career	Rank	Hitting	Rank	Fielding	Rank	Peak	Rank	Bests	JAWS	Rank
WAR	43.1	37	38.3	49	-4.5	61	38.6	20	1	40.8	30
WS	245.7	41	217.4	39	28.2	79	191.6	24	1	NA	21

Oh Tony, Tony, Tony. Tony Toni Tone[61] should do a sad ballad about Tony Oliva's career. He was a great hitter and a delightful fellow who starred for my hometown Twins. But bad knees truncated his career, and he ended with totals below Hall-of-Fame level. He's another Don Mattingly, with good power, good batting averages, and, due to chronic injury, career numbers that are just too low. Bill James graciously ranks Oliva 21st, but WSAWS ranks him 35th. Tony Oliva is inner-circle for the Hall of Very Good, but I can't see him in the Hall of Fame. Let's just leave it at that.

Larry Walker (1989-2005; career OPS+: 141)

	Career	Rank	Hitting	Rank	Fielding	Rank	Peak	Rank	Bests	JAWS	Rank
WAR	72.6	10	62.3	15	1.3	12	44.6	9	3	58.6	9
WS	310.6	25	258.8	28	51.9	8	177.1	34	1	NA	30*

I was expecting to push hard for Larry Walker. I thought he'd be like longtime Rockies teammate Todd Helton, with enough great hitting even when the context of Coors Field is taken into account. WAR is certainly telling me to push Walker hard, all the way to the hoop, and do a backwards slam jimmy jam. Boo-yaa! (R.I.P. Stuart Scott.)

But as soon as I got to that proverbial hoop, Win Shares blocked the shot and screamed, "No go, Flo Jo! Film this on a GoPro and watch it in slo-mo!" I tried to grab the ball and alley-oop it to the lane, but the safety intercepted my pass and slapped it past the left wing and through the wicket for the perfect over. (I don't really understand any sport but baseball.)

Why the big disparity between WAR and Win Shares? There was a similar disparity with Todd Helton. But when I added the estimated value of the years for which I don't have Win Shares data, Helton's WSAWS looked good enough.

I can't do that with Walker. WSAWS covers his entire career and still ranks him 30th. That puts him just below Elmer Flick and Sam Rice, both of whom I barely let stay, and just above Harry Hooper and Kiki Cuyler, both of whom I ejected. At least according to Win Shares, Walker is in the gray area of "I won't campaign to put him in, but I wouldn't campaign to kick him out."

---

[61] Reference explanation: Tony Toni Tone was a 1990s R&B group famous for the very fun "If I Had No Loot" and a bunch of other more tedious songs that sound like every other R&B song ever.

The two systems largely agree on the value of Walker's five full Expos years. From 1990 to 1994, his yearly Win Shares ranged from 20 to 26 and his yearly WARs ranged from 3.4 to 5.4. If anything, Win Shares like him more during that stretch.

But once Walker starts playing a mile high, Win Shares and WAR part company. Walker's 1997 MVP campaign earned him 32 Win Shares, which is terrific, but not even the best among National League right fielders that year (Tony Gwynn got 39 for hitting .372/.409/.549 in 651 PAs). Meanwhile the same performance got Walker 9.8 WAR, a massive number tied for 63rd best all-time. Albert Pujols never had a WAR that high. Neither did Jackie Robinson, Mike Schmidt, Ken Griffey Jr., Joe DiMaggio, Wade Boggs, etc., etc. Color me a bit skeptical.

Besides, at this point in this book, I think Win Shares has thoroughly proven itself more reliable than WAR in evaluating non-pitchers. It's too bad that Win Shares isn't used more widely, but that seems to be Bill James' own fault. If you don't make the numbers widely available, Bill, people aren't going to use your system. Getting the Win Shares data was no easy task. And when I did, I was warned that James has moved on to using both Win Shares and Loss Shares. That approach may have its merits, but largely defeats the purpose. The whole idea is to have everything wrapped up in one number, not two.

Anyway, if I ever get to talk to Bill James, I'll tell him he's fumbling the puck on the three-point line by not devoting a whole website to Win Shares numbers. In the meantime, those same numbers make it hard to believe that Larry Walker completely qualifies for the Hall. If he gets in, I'll let him stay. But I can't advocate for him.

Chapter Ten

~ ~ Designated Hitter ~ ~

The designated hitter was a weird idea from the start. It was instituted in 1973 as a rather clumsy, blatant attempt to infuse more offense in the game. The assumption was that people buy more tickets to see runs being scored than to see pitchers' duels.

I'm not so sure that's true. I remember going to a Twins game once with my roommates, neither of whom were baseball fans. It was a close game that came down to the last plate appearance, in which Jacque Jones struck out and the Twins lost. One of my roommates was so on the edge of her seat during that moment that she said it made her a Twins fan.

Those tense moments are less common when offense is rampant. The more runs are scored, the more likely that one team will blow the other out of the water. That's what makes for truly dull games, when your team is eight runs behind in the sixth inning and you start to think "OK, they could come back, but the odds of that happening are incredibly low, and there are about a thousand million gajillion other entertainment options available to me during these few precious moments I have on earth..."

There are other arguments against the DH that have been rehashed about a thousand million gajillion times in the last 40 years. The game has less strategy when you don't have to pinch hit for the pitcher. No one should pick up a bat if they don't pick up a glove. Etc., etc.

For our purposes, this is all kind of irrelevant. We're basing the Hall of Fame selections on what baseball is, not what should be. Maybe the DH shouldn't exist. But who cares, because it does. It has existed for 40 years, and there have been many DHs who have helped make their teams win. That means they're valuable, which means they're worthy of the Hall of Fame.

Some have suggested that a lifelong DH should never reach the Hall, which is silly. The DH isn't a different beast; it's just on an extreme end of a spectrum. Catchers and shortstops are on one end, where their defense is so important that they can be very valuable without top-notch offense. On the other end of the spectrum is first base, where all the defense you can muster won't really add too many wins to the standings. Just one step beyond that is DH. Because they don't contribute anything on defense, DHs have a higher offensive bar to clear to get into Hall-of-Fame range. Much the same way first basemen have to hit even better than outfielders to be worthy, designated hitters have to hit even better than first basemen.

The trouble with DH is that there have been so few in history, and so few in the Hall, that I can't really do the same ranking system that I've done for the other positions. So the below rankings show where each guy would place if he were a first baseman. In some cases, that's a bit unfair, as with Paul Molitor, who played a lot at second and third base. In some cases, it's a overly generous, as with Frank Thomas, who played first base for a few years as if he were auditioning for a DH job. But it's the best we've got. We'll make adjustments case by case.

Frank Thomas (1990-2008; career OPS+: 156)

	Career	Rank	Hitting	Rank	Fielding	Rank	Peak	Rank	Bests	JAWS	Rank
WAR	73.6	10	79.8	7	-23.4	99	45.3	14	4	59.5	11
WS	406.6	5	400.1	3	6.4	155	227.8	6	7	NA	5*

When Frank Thomas finished his second full season in 1992, I was 16 years old. I had read Bill James' 1988 Baseball Abstract about a dozen times and had sworn a sacred oath to live by its teachings. While other kids were spending their adolescence listening to Nirvana and dating girls, I was alone in my room marveling at Ken Phelps's on-base percentages. (Seriously, check them out sometime. That guy got a raw deal. He deserved better than being a punchline in a "Seinfeld" episode.)

Then Frank Thomas came along, and wow. In the years just before the steroid era, Thomas put up numbers I was not used to seeing. Wade Boggs had batting averages and OBPs, but he was not a power hitter. Mike Schmidt had great power and could take a walk, but he didn't hit for average. Don Mattingly had the triple-crown numbers, but low walk totals. Thomas combined everything a hitter can do (except steals) in a way not seen since Ted Williams.

When Thomas finished eighth in the 1992 AL MVP voting, Joe Carter finished third. I was livid. I was filled with a brand of righteous indignation that only a 16-year-old could muster for something that ultimately doesn't matter. I wrote my own Bill Jamesian article, on blue-lined school notebook paper, arguing that Frank Thomas's ability to draw walks was much more impressive than Joe Carter's ability to pile up RBIs. Frank Thomas had 122 walks that year, while Carter had 36. Meanwhile, Carter beat Thomas by only four RBIs, 119 to 115. Aren't the extra 86 walks worth more than the extra four RBIs?

Of course, any MVP discussion involves more than two pairs of numbers among two players. The point is that baseball at the time really was unprepared for what Frank Thomas brought to the game. It figured it out quickly, and Thomas won MVP awards in 1993 and 1994. Afterwards, many other players cropped up who would hit for average, smash home runs and draw walks, from Manny Ramirez to Todd Helton. But Frank Thomas was the first of the breed and compiled a tremendous record. He is a Hall-of-Famer.

Paul Molitor (1978-1998; career OPS+: 122)

	Career	Rank	Hitting	Rank	Fielding	Rank	Peak	Rank	Bests	JAWS	Rank
WAR	75.5	10	74.8	10	-8.0	57	39.6	21	4	57.6	11
WS	413.5	5	367.5	6	46.3	4	200.1	18	4	NA	6*

Some will say Paul Molitor was a third baseman. Some will say he was a utility player. Others will say he was the second gunman in the Kennedy assassination. (Those people are schizophrenics.) I'm saying he was a DH because he spent the most time there.

It all evens up, somehow: Bill James' overall ranking has him as the eight-best third baseman, and Molitor finishes sixth in WSAWS among first basemen. That similar ranking occurred even though his fielding ranks 61st among third basemen and fourth among first basemen. Molitor will not be denied a top-ten overall spot at whatever position you put him at.

Molitor was integral to the Brewers' only span of greatness, the late 1970s and early 1980s. As I alluded to back in the Robin Yount comment, I kinda like the Brewers. They're supposed to be in this regional rivalry with my hometown Twins, but meh. They play in different leagues, and they're both underdogs from smaller markets in the northern Midwest. Both cities are filled with life and culture but most people on the coasts think they're bland cow towns where farmers sit in dingy diners all day and speak quietly and slowly about guns. Their loss; as the great Minnesota rapper Slug once said, "It sucks that you think where I'm from is wack, but as long as it's enough to keep your ass from coming back."

I'm repeating myself, aren't I. Heck, at this point it's hard not to. I didn't start out thinking this book would be long, but somehow I ended up writing more than 2,000 pages about just the hitters. (Editor's note: We did a lot of editing. If you think this was bloated, you should have seen what we cut.)

Anyway, at any rate, back to the point, Paul Molitor is a clear, no-doubt Hall-of-Famer, obviously, definitely, unquestionably Hall-worthy, well over the line, in the first tier, up the rankings, under the sea, through the wire, beyond the lights, and behind the candelabra;[62] and if he weren't in, I would smash something.

Who's In, Who's Out

Not much change, obviously. Here's one addition:

Edgar Martinez (1990-2008; career OPS+: 156)

	Career	Rank	Hitting	Rank	Fielding	Rank	Peak	Rank	Bests	JAWS	Rank
WAR	68.3	13	66.2	16	-9.7	66	43.5	15	6	56.0	12
WS	304.5	26	291.4	18	13.2	144	182.6	31	4	NA	27*

Neither Paul Molitor or Frank Thomas were controversial Hall-of-Fame candidates. Both played enough at other positions that people could pretend they were something besides DHs. The discussion of whether a DH should ever be in the Hall centers on Edgar Martinez.

As I said at the beginning of this chapter, DH is just another position. But because it has zero defensive value, a career DH really has to be especially exceptional with the bat. Edgar Martinez was. He had all the tools except speed and fielding. For what it's worth, he did play more than 500 games at third base. Note that both his fielding rankings are better than Frank Thomas's.

Like Wade Boggs, Martinez was kept in the minors for a long time to work on his defense at third. With Boggs, maybe it was for the best. But with Martinez, it wasn't. Martinez didn't get his first full season in the majors until he was 27. Someone should have given up much earlier and put him at first base.

---

[62] Reference explanation: I'm tired. Look them up yourself.

Luckily, Edgar still hit so well into his 40s that his career is deserving of the Hall. As an added bonus, he was a lovely man and an exemplary leader of the Mariners' lone period of dominance, 1995-2003. Let's just put him in the Hall already.

Chapter Eleven

~ ~ Pitchers: Introduction ~ ~

OK, pitchers are a whole different ball of wax. Forget everything you read about the hitters. Well, actually, you'll need to remember some of the things you learned about the hitters. Oh crap, I just told you to forget all that. So of course that's all wiped away and you have no idea what I'm talking about. OK, go back and read some of it again. Not all of it; just the good parts. I'd say maybe a third of it is good. So just read every third word and then come back to this.

Got it? Good. Here is the new chart for Negro League pitchers:

Wilbur "Bullet" Rogan (1917, 1920-1938)

	Rank at SP Among Negro Leaguers	Rank Among All Negro Leaguers
SABR	3	11
Monte Irvin	4 among RHP	NA

Bill James has been kicked out! Why? Because he didn't rank Negro League pitchers in the "New Historical Baseball Abstract." It's a bit mysterious: He ranks the top ten at every other position and then just stops after the right fielders. Bill apparently hates pitchers.

Monte Irvin was more conscientious than Bill James was with Negro League pitchers in that he included them at all. But unfortunately, Irvin includes only the five best right-handed pitchers and the five best left-handed pitchers. People do this sometimes, acting like northpaws and southpaws constitute different positions. They don't, of course; they're just different types of the same position. It makes as much sense as having separate lists for righty outfielders and lefty outfielders. Just put all the pitchers together and do a top ten instead of a top five, for Pete's sake. It's not that vital to stick to the exact same number at each position.

This makes for weird rankings because, of course, there are always many more right-handed pitchers than left-handed pitchers. Irvin's top righties are all Hall-of-Famers, while only his top lefty is. He leaves out a bunch of righties that were better than his other four lefties. Sigh. Irvin's pitcher rankings are mostly useless for our purposes. But I'll include them anyway, just for fun.

Now let's look at the "Percent Who Are Hall of Famers" graph for just starting pitchers:

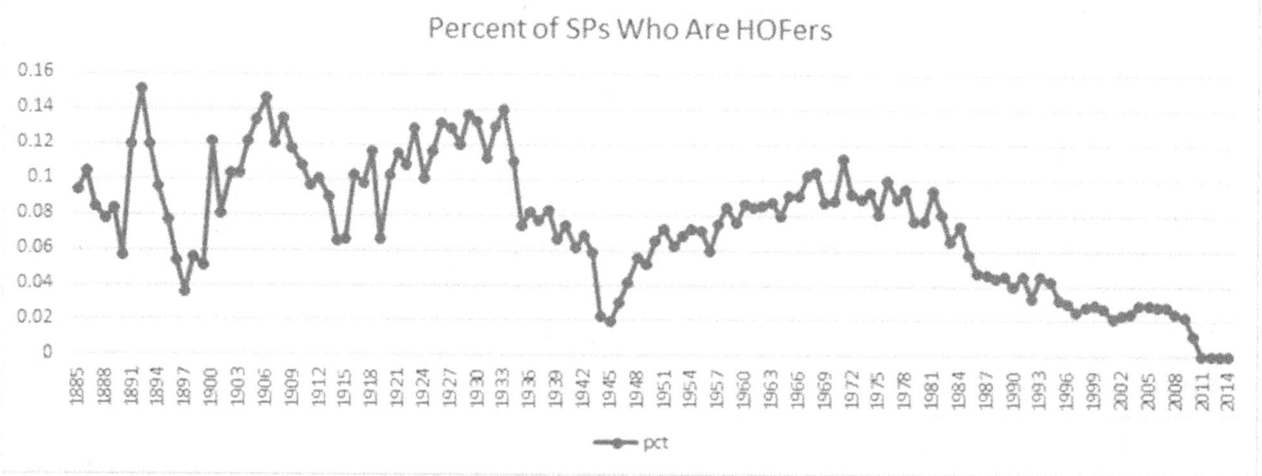

I didn't include relief pitchers because they cause a lot of problems with the denominators in the percentage calculations. If you include every reliever, the total number of pitchers from recent years will shoot up dramatically. Then even if you include the Hall-of-Fame relievers in the numerator, recent percentages look ridiculously small. We'll have to deal with relievers later.

As far as the starters, you can see a big drop-off in the mid-1980s. The dead-ball era through 1933 are overrepresented. The 1800s are chaotic for reasons I'll get into later. The dip during World War II is of course because so many HOFers were fighting. But 1934 through the 1950s are surprisingly low.

I'll try not to base my choices too much on leveling this chart out, but it will be on my mind. More relevant is how the pitcher fares in the overall rankings.

On to the revised chart for MLBers:

Early Wynn (1939, 1941-1944, 1946-1963; career ERA+: 107)

	Career	Rank	Peak	Rank	Bests	Top 5s	JAWS	Rank
WAR	61.3	45	38.6	80	1	3	50.0	53
WS	308.1	26	160.9	58	1	4	NA	40

Bests are the number of seasons the pitcher was the best in baseball, according to WAR or Win Shares. But that's a pretty tall order when it comes to pitchers. There are lots of pitchers each year, many more than at any other position. You can be a legitimate Hall-of-Famer and never be the best pitcher in baseball in any one season. So I also include **top 5s,** which count the number of times the player was among the five best pitchers in baseball in a season. That's a closer analogue to the number of times a third baseman or left fielder was the best at his position.

The bottom right spot is still Bill James's ranking of the player in the "New Historical Baseball Abstract." But Bill only included the top 100 pitchers from the MLB (by which I mean the white major leagues before integration and the integrated leagues after). The Hall of Fame, at this writing, has 71 MLB pitchers (not including people like Al Spalding and Clark Griffith who are in primarily for other accomplishments).

Every hitters' position also got a top 100 in the "New Historical Baseball Abstract," despite the fact that there are always lots more pitchers than third basemen or left fielders. James says he planned to write about more pitchers, but his computer crashed. So that's possible. It's also possible that he despises pitchers, and is engaged in a worldwide conspiracy to denigrate them, by orders of the Illuminati, the Bilderberg Group, Skull 'n' Bones, and, just for fun, let's throw in the Shriners. Just saying, it's possible. I have never heard him deny this assertion.

In defiance of whatever shadowy organizations really pull Bill James's strings, I'm not automatically going to kick out the pitchers Bill James left off. But, well, you wouldn't want to bet on them.

Dividing Up the Pitchers

We're going to have to deal with relief pitchers in a separate chapter. That probably isn't a surprise, since I already left them off my chart. Relievers are a very different animal, especially nowadays.

But even starting pitchers bring complications. Starters' roles have changed dramatically over the decades. I talked about how third base evolved from a defense-first to a power position. That's nothing compared to pitching.

In the 1870s, teams would carry just two pitchers all year, and sometimes just one. These were the days when baseball was seen as a contest between the batter and the fielders, not between the hitter and the pitcher. The pitcher's job was to provide something for the batter to hit.

In the 1880s, teams would carry a few more pitchers, but not many. Starting pitchers would regularly exceed 500 innings per season, and these were seasons that maxed out at around 125 games. Even throughout the dead-ball era, pitching 300 innings in a season was unremarkable, achieved by about 10 pitchers per year. By way of comparison, the most recent pitcher to last 300 innings was Steve Carlton in 1980.

This makes the WAR and Win Shares numbers very high for pitchers from more than 100 years ago. The more you play, the more WAR and Win Shares you're going to compile. Of the top 25 seasonal WAR totals for pitchers, all occurred before 1920, with only three after 1894. Win Shares is even more extreme, with only Walter Johnson's 1913 representing the 1900s or 2000s among the top 25.

Why the difference between WAR and Win Shares? Replacement level, of course. As pitching roles change, replacement level changes. In the 1800s, the replacement level for pitchers was quite high by modern standards. In 1885, Ed Cushman pitched 278 innings with an ERA at league average: 101 ERA+. His WAR is 0.1, just a hair above replacement level. In 1973, Jim Slaton pitched 276 innings with a 101 ERA+ and got 2.7 WAR. That's a big difference. Meanwhile, 1885 Ed Cushman got 10 Win Shares and 1973 Jim Slaton got 13 Win Shares. Not nearly as far apart.

For once, I'm not saying that WAR is out of whack. I'm saying that 275 league-average innings was much more commonplace in 1885. In 1885, John Clarkson pitched 623 innings, while Ed Morris pitched 581 and Hardie Henderson pitched 539. Numbers like that are going to set the replacement level much higher.

As you know, Win Shares doesn't bother with all the replacement level horsehockey. It just takes all the team's wins and divides them among the players in proportion to their contributions. Because they pitched so much, pitchers in 1885 had a huge stake in winning. So they get the most Win Shares.

I prefer the Win Shares approach, but it makes it difficult to compare 1880s and 1970s on the same plane. The top ten in Peak Win Shares totals are Old Hoss Radbourn, John Clarkson, Bob Caruthers, Tim Keefe, Pud Galvin, Kid Nichols, Tony Mullane, Walter Johnson, Cy Young, and Mickey Welch. All were 1800s pitchers except Walter Johnson (1907-1927). Cy Young straddled the two eras (1890-1911).

Because of the replacement-level adjustment, WAR's Peak top ten are a little less 1800s-heavy. But it's still lopsided, with all of them retiring before 1928: Walter Johnson, Cy Young, Kid Nichols, John Clarkson, Pete Alexander, Jim McCormick, Old Hoss Radbourn, Amos Rusie, Christy Mathewson, and Tim Keefe. As a result, 1800s pitchers who were far from legends end up doing well in JAWS: non-HOFer Jim McCormick shows up as the 19th-best pitcher ever, just above Gaylord Perry, Pedro Martinez and Robin Roberts. Other non-HOFers from the 1800s, Tommy Bond, Charlie Buffinton and Tony Mullane, all surround Jay Jaffe's magical Hall of Fame average. They score better than Jim Palmer, Bob Feller, Juan Marichal, Carl Hubbell, and several other no-doubt Hall-of-Famers.

If you read the George Davis comment, you know my position on 1800s ballplayers. Really, my position is to take the Hall of Fame's position. The Hall of Fame, through its selections, has made it clear that 1800s players deserve the same level of recognition as players from any other era. But most fans ignore them because the century feels so distant and the numbers seem so odd. Even when 1800s stars are mentioned, they're segregated to a dusty corner so most fans can easily ignore them.

Unfortunately, that's what we'll have to do. We'll have to have two categories of starting pitchers: Those who played primarily before 1901, and those who played primarily after. Cy Young and a few others straddle the two eras, so we'll have to figure out what to do with them case by case.

We'll start with the 1800s pitchers, just for fun. Then we'll get into the post-1800s pitchers. I'm not going to call them "modern pitchers" or "regular pitchers" or "real pitchers" or anything like that because I want to normalize the 1800s pitchers as much as possible. It's the 1800s pitchers that are the normal ones, I say. They're the ones who play the way you and I play baseball; they're the ones throwing it in there so people can hit it and we can see some action. It's the post-1800s pitchers that are the weird ones, with all their time-consuming trickery and tomfoolery ... feh! In my day, you could take in two games before sundown and then comport oneself to the local publican for a few flagons of ale and a rousing round of bear-baiting! (If I'm going to be a grumpy old man, I'm going to be a grumpy old man from 100 years ago that no living human would recognize.)

Chapter Twelve

~ ~ 1800s Starting Pitchers ~ ~

I'm already changing one thing. Instead of "top 5s," I'm going with "top 3s" for 1800s pitchers. In the 1800s, there often weren't more than about 20 pitchers in baseball in a given year. Being in the top 5 among 20 is really not in the spirit of what we're going for there. Top 3 is a little closer.

John Clarkson (1882, 1884–1894; career ERA+: 133)

	Career	Rank	Peak	Rank	Bests	Top 3s	JAWS	Rank
WAR	84.0	3	74.9	2	2	4	79.4	2
WS	396.3	5	324.8	2	2	4	NA	3

During John Clarkson's first year in the majors, 1882, he was only allowed to pitch underhanded. This was a vestige from the days when the pitchers gave the hitter something to hit so the fielders could provide the real show. No one wanted to see pitching duels; they wanted to see the hitters hit and the fielders field. It was actually a much livelier game then. Those annoying people who say baseball is boring would not have said that about the 1880s game.

This goes back to the 1845 Knickerbockers, widely regarded as the first team to play true baseball (although it's hard to pin down exactly—like most things, baseball was born from an evolutionary process, not a sudden spark of creation). The ninth rule in the Knickerbockers' famous rule book (see http://www.baseball-almanac.com/rule11.shtml) says "The ball must be pitched, not thrown at the bat." "Pitching" was defined as a gentle lob, in opposition to throwing, which was much harder.

By 1882 the rule was deteriorating, as it had proved impossible to enforce. If they really wanted it to work, they should have had a member of the batters' team be the pitcher. If you're going to let the pitcher be a member of the opposing team, of course he's not going to just throw meatballs in there for the opposing team to whack around. He's going to try to help his team by any means necessary. Baseball gave up in 1884 and let pitchers throw overhanded.

John Clarkson proved very good at this. Considering that overhand throwing was newly legal, Clarkson's approach was quite sophisticated. He had unparalleled control of a huge curveball and a good change-up, using a bunch of arm slots to keep hitters guessing. He struck out loads of batters but not with overpowering speed; he was more of a Greg Maddux than a Randy Johnson.

Baseball in the 1800s was characterized by heavy drinking and fights between labor and management. Clarkson was big into both. He was a quiet, sensitive guy who needed plenty of pep talks and didn't take razzing very well. In the evenings he unwound in a big way. He was too hungover to make a start in the 1885 championship series (which, admittedly, was more of an exhibition than anything like a World Series. The previous year's series had ended in a tie, 3-3-1.).

The labor wars may have been more damaging to Clarkson's psyche. In 1889, Clarkson joined the first labor union in the history of sports, the Brotherhood of Professional Ball Players. This was the union organized by our friend John "Monte" Ward, P, SS, Esq. and other disgruntled players. When the Brotherhood formed the Players' League in 1890, Clarkson signed an agreement to sign a contract.

Note that he didn't actually sign a contract; he signed an agreement to sign a contract. When it came time to actually sign a contract, he got nervous about the the new league's stability and stuck with the National League. This was not well-received by his union brothers. After the Players' League folded and its players returned to the NL, they made Clarkson into a pariah. His sensitive nature would be further tested by all the old friends who were now sworn enemies.

They didn't drive Clarkson out of the game, though; 1893 did. That was the year that the distance from the pitcher's mound to home plate was moved from 50 feet to 60 feet, six inches. He was 31 years old and already slowing down a bit, but the new distance proved especially difficult for a pitcher who relied on his curveball breaking at just the right time. He actually pitched pretty well in 1894: A 4.45 ERA is pretty good when your league is at 5.33. But he had had enough.

He went on to run several businesses, but his life was unraveling. In his early 40s, he was put into a sanitarium, which in those days served as a sort of rehab clinic for anyone who suffered a nervous breakdown or addiction. Clarkson had both. His brain was ravaged by anxiety and alcohol, and he couldn't remember anything but stories of his old baseball days. He became paralyzed for a few years and then died of pneumonia at age 47. (Source: Clarkson's SABR biography, by Brian McKenna.)

I asked my wife, a psychoanalyst, what she thought might have afflicted Clarkson. She said "he just went batty," which is a baseball pun that I repeat with some reluctance. She also said he may have had Korsakoff syndrome, a deficiency in vitamin B-1 (thiamin) often associated with alcoholism and/or malnutrition. It's often confused with Alzheimer's syndrome because they have similar symptoms, but they're very different.

Clarkson's election to the Hall no doubt hinged on the fact that he had more than 300 career wins. Pitcher wins is a stat I'm going to try avoid mentioning as much as possible, since they don't get at the heart of performance. But they are at least a vague, second-hand indicator of a pitcher's value. More relevant is the fact that both WAR and Bill James rank Clarkson among the top three 1800s pitchers. He's in.

Pud Galvin (1875, 1879-1892; career ERA+: 107)

	Career	Rank	Peak	Rank	Bests	Top 3s	JAWS	Rank
WAR	73.7	6	62.1	8	1	2	67.9	7
WS	401.0	3	294.9	5	1	2	NA	None

Bill James is not big on Pud Galvin. Though Galvin does reasonably well in Win Shares, James leaves him out of the top 100 pitchers of all time. WAR puts him at 7th, which is on the fringe of 1800s pitchers. His ERA+ is tied for the fourth-lowest among all Hall-of-Fame pitchers, 1800s or otherwise. Why is Galvin in the Hall?

365, that's why. That's how many wins Galvin managed in his long career. It's fifth all time, below the dead-ball-era quartet of Cy Young, Walter Johnson, Christy Mathewson and Pete Alexander, and just above Warren Spahn's 363.

So what? Much the same way the batting averages of Heinie Manush, Chick Hafey, et al., were inflated by the environment of the 1920s and 1930s, Galvin's win totals were inflated by his era. Galvin hit 20 wins in a season ten times, but in those days, anyone who could last a full season would surpass 20 wins. Galvin got exactly 20 wins in 1880, but also lost 35 games and had an ERA+ of 90. Out of only 16 major-league pitchers in 1880, his WAR was 8th and his Win Shares total was 9th. That's not a

"20-win season" as we conceive of it nowadays. That's a Jason Vargas season, not a Justin Verlander season.

But I'm cherry-picking here, or perhaps crabapple-picking, assuming crabapples are disgusting. (They are, right?) As you can see from the above, Galvin also had some legitimately good seasons. He was the best pitcher in baseball once according to each system. He was among the best a few other times, though not many.

Galvin's only really outstanding trait was his longevity. He pitched 6003.1 innings, second only to Cy Young all-time. Galvin was like Jim Kaat or Tommy John: rarely great, but good for long enough to compile some large career totals.

If Jim Kaat or Tommy John were in the Hall, would I kick them out? Honestly, I probably wouldn't. We'll find out when we get to them, but I bet they'd be around the same range as a whole bunch of pitchers, some of which are in and some of which are not. Remember the graph in the Jimmy Wynn comment, the one that charted JAWS vs. WSAWS? It showed that while the first tier of Hall-of-Famers at a position is pretty clear, the second tier gets a little hazier, and then the third and fourth tiers get really hard to distinguish. Let's try that with 1800s pitchers:

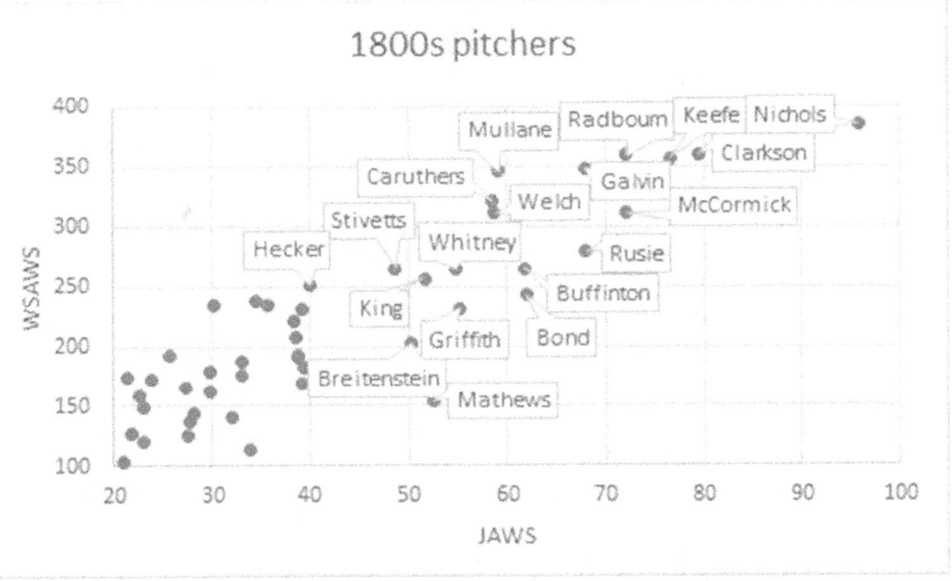

This actually makes Galvin look good. Everyone clearly above him is in the Hall of Fame (Nichols, Keefe, Clarkson, Radbourn) and a few clearly below him are as well (Rusie and Welch).

Many of the pitchers below Galvin didn't last ten years, and thus aren't eligible for the Hall. This brings us to an important point. Yes, Galvin's longevity was largely responsible for his 365 career wins. But in Galvin's days, longevity was no small feat. It didn't come from having a leg ligament transferred to your arm by a groundbreaking physician, a la Tommy John. It came from owning the endurance to withstand the bruising, punishing gauntlet that was pitching in the 1800s. It came from expertly pacing yourself within games and within seasons, while also relying on an inborn ability to withstand incredible stress on your arm. As a great man once said, that kind of thing doesn't grow on trees. (Imagine if it did?)[63]

Pud Galvin may have been a good-but-not-great pitcher who lasted a long time. But "lasting a long time" was by itself an incredible feat in the 1880s. Galvin is a little like Hall-of-Fame second baseman Bid McPhee: By modern standards, his longevity may not be exceptional. But by the standards of his time, it was. Galvin stays.

Tim Keefe (1880-1893; career ERA+: 126)

	Career	Rank	Peak	Rank	Bests	Top 3s	JAWS	Rank
WAR	86.6	2	66.5	6	1	2	76.6	3
WS	413.1	2	298.5	4	1	1	NA	5

Like John Clarkson, Tim Keefe's career was done when the distance from home plate to the pitchers' mound was moved to 60 feet in 1893. But by then he was 36 years old and had pitched 5049 innings (12th-most all-time), so he may not have had much left anyway.

Again like Clarkson, Keefe was a master of deception, using a brilliant changeup and all sorts of arm slots and angles. Honestly, it would have been hard to have much long-term success with any other approach in those days. It's hard to imagine many pure power pitchers surviving 400-600 innings per season for ten or more years.

Unlike Clarkson, Keefe would take multiple steps before releasing the ball, a sort of hop, skip, jump and then throw routine that confused hitters. It must have been lots of fun to watch. A killjoy 1887 rule change put a stop to that silliness, mandating a set position before each pitch, like nowadays. As he did with the many other pre-1893 rule changes, Keefe adapted quickly and kept finding ways to dominate.

Like John Clarkson, Keefe was from Massachusetts. Keefe grew up in Somerset, while Clarkson hailed from neighboring Cambridge. The two towns were quite different: Somerset was working class and Cambridge, home of Harvard University, was a bit upper-crust. Keefe was eager to move into the Cambridge set. As soon as he had stashed a little money from baseballing, he classed up his lifestyle and bought land in Cambridge. He became known as "Sir Timothy," both because of his nice clothes and his naturally gentlemanly demeanor. In his free time he helped coach the Harvard baseball team and started a business that made uniforms and baseballs.

Unlike Clarkson, Tim Keefe was a main character in the real-life incident that inspired "Casey at the Bat." Casey was Dan Casey, and Keefe was the pitcher who (spoiler alert for a 125-year-old poem that everyone has heard) struck him out in the end. It's fun to think about how poems could become huge popular phenomena then, like rap songs nowadays. Maybe modern poets should go back to using rhyme and meter. I get that poems aren't as deep that way, but they end up a lot more fun to recite. Just saying.

[63] Reference explanation: The Lou Brock comment in this book. As I've said before, I've already said so much in this book that I'm left quoting myself. Now I'm quoting myself about quoting myself. We're through the looking-glass here people. (That was also a quote of myself.)

Again unlike Clarkson, Keefe was a stalwart union man. From the beginning of his career he fought against owners' ability to hold down salaries. He and his friend John "Monte" Ward led the Players' League revolt. When the league collapsed, so did Keefe's budding entrepreneurial career. His sporting goods company was heavily invested in the league, and went under in 1891. Because it had been a partnership instead of a corporation, Keefe was personally on the hook for the company's debts. (Word to the wise: Incorporate if you can. The government created corporations for a reason.) He had to sell off most of his property in Cambridge.

Like Clarkson, Keefe struggled after his retirement from baseball. He tried umpiring, but it didn't go well. As a polite, honest paragon of integrity, he was not prepared for the abuse from both players and fans that umpires sustained in the 1890s. Then Harvard dumped him as a coach.

Unlike Clarkson, Keefe did not turn to despair. He gave up on public life and built some homes on the land he had left in Cambridge. For the rest of his long life he quietly supported his family as a landlord. (Source: Another good ol' SABR biography, by Charlie Bevis.)

Like John Clarkson, Tim Keefe definitely belongs in the Hall of Fame.

Kid Nichols (1890-1901, 1904-1906; career ERA+: 140)

	Career	Rank	Peak	Rank	Bests	Top 3s	JAWS	Rank
WAR	116.4	1	75.1	1	3	7	95.8	1
WS	478.9	1	292.2	6	2	6	NA	1

None of that wimping out in 1894 for Kid Nichols. Nichols had a 4.75 ERA in 1894, but that meant a 124 ERA+. Not bad, but it's still tied for the second-worst ERA+ for any full season in his career. Kid Nichols was the best pitcher of the 1800s, bar none.

Several other players at the time were called "Kid," but it wasn't always a term of endearment. In boxing, there was a long tradition of small, feisty fighters being called "Kid." In baseball, "Kid"s were often little guys with chips on their shoulders.

Not so for Kid Nichols. He was a fine, stable teetotaler who just happened to be a tiny little kid when he started playing. He made his major-league debut at age 20, and had a brilliant season with the Boston Beaneaters. Forget Hugh Duffy and Tommy McCarthy (if you haven't already); Kid Nichols was the key to the Beaneaters' great success in the 1890s.

The Beaneaters later became the Braves, so Nichols belongs in the pantheon of Braves pitching superstars, along with Warren Spahn, Phil Niekro, Greg Maddux, Tom Glavine, and John Smoltz. Bill James ranked all pitchers together, and put Kid Nichols 9th among all pitchers from all teams, behind Warren Spahn and ahead of all the rest of the Braves greats. But those rankings were created in 2001, and Maddux still had one good year and a bunch of average years in the tank. Maddux probably overtook Nichols by the end, but it's close.

The point is, Kid Nichols is a Hall-of-Famer.

Old Hoss Radbourn (1880-1891; career ERA+: 119)

	Career	Rank	Peak	Rank	Bests	Top 3s	JAWS	Rank
WAR	76.0	4	68.1	4	0	2	72.1	4
WS	390.7	6	327.3	1	1	3	NA	4

The Win Shares and WAR numbers for 1800s pitchers are a bit ridiculous. I'm trying not to even mention them because they're so out of line with what could ever be accomplished by pitchers who don't throw 500 innings per season. But it's worth noting that in 1884, Old Hoss Radbourn collected 89 Win Shares. That's the largest total in history by a huge margin: Second all-time is pitcher Guy Hecker's 74, also in 1884. WAR puts Radbourn's season third all-time, behind Pud Galvin's 1884 and Tim Keefe's 1883.

Notice a trend? In the early 1880s, pitchers were used like catchers are nowadays. You had one true starting pitcher and one backup, or "change pitcher." The main pitcher started a huge majority of the games and completed almost all of them. The change pitcher would only start a game if the main pitcher was exhausted. Few started every game, but there were no true rotations.

Because teams used so few pitchers, each main starter had an unusually large influence on winning, much the way a quarterback does in football. (So pitchers were both catchers and quarterbacks. I'm going all over the sports world for my analogies. Maybe pitchers were also "silly mid offs," which is a real position in cricket. Cricket is so adorable.)

So why the peak in 1883 and 1884? The National League schedule got longer in those years, going from 82-ish games in 1882 (teams varied in the exact number they actually played) to 96-ish in 1883 to 110-ish in 1884. With a longer schedule come more Win Shares and WAR to go around.

At the same time, longer schedules were making it less feasible to rely so heavily on one starter. By 1884, teams were giving their change pitchers more starts. True two-man rotations were still uncommon, though, and there was lots of variation among teams. Radbourn wasn't the only one pitching a ton in 1884: Pud Galvin started just one fewer game than Radbourn and also exceeded 600 innings.

Radbourn did pitch an unusual amount in a short period of time, starting 41 of 51 games down the stretch. It wasn't supposed to be that way. The Providence Grays started 1884 with a genuine rotation of Old Hoss Radbourn and Charlie Sweeney. Halfway through the season, Sweeney started drinking heavily and behaving erratically. He refused to start an exhibition game, and, in his next league start, he stomped off the field and left the park without permission. The next day he refused to show up.

It was all a stunt to get himself released. Sweeney had secretly been talking to a team in the Union Association, which was luring away good players in an attempt to become a major league. Soon after the Grays released him, Sweeney signed for more money with the Union Association St. Louis Maroons.

There were too many major leagues in 1884. The National League and the American Association were already competing for top talent. The Union Association's pretensions toward major-league status never truly succeeded (though every reference source still lists it as a major league). But it still created a shortage of major-league-ready players.

The Providence Grays' owner contended there were no available replacements for Sweeney. So, in exchange for a substantial raise, Radbourn agreed to serve as the team's only real pitcher.

Radbourn was a stubborn, gruff, hard-drinking barrel of a man. When he decided to start every game, by gum he was going to do it. Most days, his arm was so tired he couldn't lift it over his head. So he relied on his many underhand pitches, including a wide assortment of curveballs. He needed hours to warm up before each game and extensive massages every evening. Somehow he bullied through it, ending with a 59-12 win-loss record that made up the lion's share of the Grays' 84-28 season. In 678.2 innings he sported a 1.38 ERA, good for a 205 ERA+.

Then Radbourn pitched every single inning of a short postseason series against the American Association champion New York Metropolitans, which starred Tim Keefe. Radbourn did not give up a single earned run, and allowed just 11 hits in 22 innings.

When Charlie Sweeney was released mid-season, the Grays were 2.5 games out of first place. After Radbourn took over almost all the pitching, the Grays won the pennant by 10.5 games. So you can see where those 89 Win Shares came from.

Considering the Grays won the pennant by 10.5 games, you'd think they could have found some rookie to make a spot start now and again. But remember that 1884 was only a few years removed from the "starter plus change pitcher" model. I'm sure many viewed Radbourn's workload as relatively reasonable.

Radbourn's arm was not the same after 1884. It was far from useless, but also far from his peak. For six more years, Radbourn was average or above average, apart from one poor season in 1887.

The Grays management was unhappy with his post-1884 performances, and got into several squabbles with him about his effort. It didn't help that Radbourn didn't work very hard at staying in shape or at making friends. He drank an incredible amount, which is not known for accentuating athletic performance.

Regardless, Radbourn's heroic 1884 cemented his popular image as the greatest pitcher of his time. He wasn't the best of his time, but he wasn't far from it. Ironically, he perhaps could have been the best pitcher of the 1880s if his arm hadn't sustained so much stress in 1884. It would make for less of a story, but more wins in the long run.

But don't cry for Radbourn's career. If you're determined to cry, cry for his life after baseball. In 1894, he was shot in the face in a hunting accident. He survived, but his face was horribly disfigured. He lost sight in his left eye and had trouble speaking. For three years he was a recluse, staying all day in his apartment and drinking even more than before. On top of that, he also probably had syphilis, which caused cognitive problems and regular convulsions. A major convulsion left him in a coma, and he died at only 42 years old. (Source: of course, Radbourn's SABR biography, by Brian McKenna)

So yeah, there's another story from the "good old days." Old Hoss Radbourn may not have been the best pitcher of the 1800s, but he's a worthy Hall-of-Famer.

Amos Rusie (1889-1895, 1897-1898, 1901; career ERA+: 129)

	Career	Rank	Peak	Rank	Bests	Top 3s	JAWS	Rank
WAR	69.3	7	66.8	5	1	3	68	6
WS	293.2	10	264.6	10	1	3	NA	2

A few players in baseball history were so good that they changed the way the game was played. Babe Ruth was one, and, to a lesser extent, Amos Rusie was another.

We've already gone through several pitchers who were masters of deception, using large arsenals of curveballs and changeups. Amos Rusie was all about power. He was the Nolan Ryan of the 1890s, racking up incredible numbers of strikeouts and walks by throwing as hard as he could for as long as he could. Rusie, more than anyone else, necessitated the most important rule change of the decade: moving the mound to 60 feet, 6 inches. People were afraid one of his wild, speedy pitches would kill somebody.

It wasn't an unreasonable fear. As I mentioned before, one of Rusie's throws hit Hughie Jennings in the head. Jennings finished the game, but then spent four days in a coma. (And then went on to rack up mind-boggling numbers of HBPs.)

The new distance didn't affect Rusie much. He had his best season in 1894, scoring a 2.74 ERA that was downright incredible for that year: Only three other pitchers managed ERAs below 4, and none were better than 3.70. Curveballs might have been ruined by the new distance from the pitcher to the hitter, but fastballs weren't. After another good year in 1895, Rusie held out the entire season of 1896 for more money.

Time for another story about labor-management fights. Really, we should thank our lucky stars every day that collective bargaining has made baseball stable. Think how weird it would be would be to lose Clayton Kershaw for a year because of a holdout.

Owners never come across well in these stories. Maybe that's my personal bias, as I wasn't born into the plutocrat class. You could argue that when teams lose money, owners have to get creative to find ways to cut costs. Sometimes that means cutting labor costs. That's true of any business that wants to survive.

But I doubt anyone would give New York Giants owner Andrew Freedman any gold stars for his creativity. With a month left in the 1892 season, Freedman released Rusie just to avoid paying a month of his salary. Freedman made some secret agreements with the other club owners to not sign Rusie for 1893 (which we would now call collusion). But the Cubs were all like "fudge that schist"[64] and signed Rusie anyway. Freedman then had to buy him from the Cubs, for much more money than if he had just re-signed Rusie like normal. This did not sit well with Freedman.

Rusie's 1893 Cubs contract contained a bonus of $2,000, and Freedman tried to count the bonus against Rusie's salary. When that didn't work, Freedman fined Rusie for a number of offenses he never committed. There was an uproar across baseball, but Freedman refused to rescind the fines.

Rusie got pitcher/shortstop/attorney/my personal hero John "Monte" Ward on his side and threatened to sue. Now the owners got nervous. If a case went to trial, the whole reserve clause would come under legal review. The reserve clause, remember, bound a player to a team indefinitely, in a sort of indentured servitude. It was in a legal gray area, and owners were not eager to have that gray area replaced with a black-and-white ruling that would probably not go their way.

---

[64] I'm paraphrasing. In eighth-grade earth science class, we had to learn the names of types of rocks, and one of them was "schist." It was one the most high-larious things we'd ever heard, and to this day it's the only one I remember.

Let's talk law. One of the most important laws in the history of this country was enacted just a few years before Freedman's silly pennypinching antics. The Sherman Antitrust Act of 1890 prevented separate companies in the same industry from colluding in any way to decrease competition. Competition is key to capitalism; without it industries tend to become virtual monopolies, companies get crazy rich, innovation gets stifled, and consumers get screwed.

Baseball owners weren't colluding to decrease competition on the field; that wasn't the problem. Through the reserve clause, they decreased competition for talent. As I said in the Luke Appling comment, imagine if your company owned your livelihood. You couldn't quit your job and be hired by another company. But your company could trade you to one of their competitors anytime they felt like it. And they can pay you whatever they want to; your only available negotiating tactic is to stay home and sulk until they give you more money. This is not how capitalism is supposed to work.

The legality of the reserve clause did come up eventually. In 1922, the Supreme Court decided that antitrust law didn't apply to baseball because it was an "amusement." The antitrust law only covers interstate commerce, they said, and amusements aren't commerce because nothing tangible is created. Oh, and it's also not interstate, since each game occurs in only one state. If that makes no sense to you, it's because it's a load of bullschist. Basically, they decided that baseball was a weird, wacky business, and it would just fall apart if owners had to pay players what they were worth.

They may have been right about that last part, actually. Baseball is a weird business. In any other industry, there is room for several winners, and winners keep on winning. Some people will always buy Coke and some will always buy Pepsi (often because they're at a restaurant that only carries Pepsi products). Coke's and Pepsi's respective fortunes might vary a bit when one enters a new market and the other comes up with a hilarious TV ad involving a sassy iguana or whatever. But they're not going to vacillate wildly every year depending on how many games Coke wins against Pepsi.

In baseball, only one team can win the championship; everyone else is basically a loser. If you win, you get lots of money, and, if you don't, revenues can suddenly plummet. This effect was even more extreme in the days when just two teams reached the postseason and the World Series brought a huge payday relative to the regular season. Particularly in the past, teams' revenues were very unstable year to year.

When year-to-year revenue is so unstable and unpredictable, it becomes very easy to make disastrous financial decisions. Say you win the championship one year and then are flush with cash. You sign a big-name pitcher for lots of money. The next year, that pitcher breaks his arm, the team collapses, and you can't pay your bills.

Or you could do everything right and still collapse. Before the reserve clause, star players routinely jumped from team to team in search of better paydays. This was epidemic whenever a new major league like Monte Ward's Players League came along. Successful, wealthy teams could be destroyed within a year.

This kind of thing does not happen to Coke or Pepsi. It might only if Coke or Pepsi had to change their formula every single year. That's essentially what baseball teams are doing: They're offering a slightly different product each year. Many, despite all their efforts, will be offering a worse one. And it will not be a matter of taste; it will be an objectively worse product, measured in wins and losses. Each of these wins and losses will be followed and analyzed on a much larger scale than any normal company's earnings reports.

And Coke and Pepsi don't tend to employ well-known celebrities who have incredible influence on the company's success. As good as Coke's Assistant to the District Manager for Social Media

Logistical Strategy Ideation Solutions might be, if he/she leaves for more money at RC Cola, Coke's earnings report does not hang in the balance.

So it was often very hard to make baseball work as a stable business over the long term. The labor-management turmoil before 1922 wasn't just the fault of lunatics like Andrew Freedman. Often it was a matter of well-meaning owners who didn't want to go broke.

Nowadays the financial instability inherent in running baseball teams is mostly solved thanks to revenue sharing, the carefully restricted number of teams, etc. It took decades of trial and error to figure it all out, and it's still evolving. But everything else is window dressing compared to the antitrust exemption.

The antitrust exemption may have been an injustice, but darned if it didn't make things stable. Monopolies often do. From the Supreme Court decision 1922 to 1960, the same two leagues had the same 16 teams. All those 16 teams survived the Great Depression, which is no small feat for an amusement that depends on people having spare cash. When things finally changed, it was a positive thing, as more teams were added. There were no third leagues like the Players League (1890) or the Union Association (1884) or the Federal League (1914-1915) pulling away players and throwing everything into chaos.

Maybe things were a bit too stable in that period, actually. That was when the Yankees won the pennant every goddamn year (24 out of 39 years, to be exact). With salaries stabilized, the Yankees could afford to find and sign every great prospect, while the Browns could afford to occasionally stumble upon a good player and then sell him to the Yankees. Still, if you read enough about the financial turmoil of the early days of baseball, you understand why the Supreme Court felt it had to adopt a specious justification for letting baseball remain a trust.

I forgot who we were talking about. Oh, Amos Rusie! Yeah, somehow Rusie kept throwing like the dickens until 1898, when something snapped in his arm. He was only 27, and his career was over. It's hard to imagine any other result from throwing monster heat for 500 innings a year. But because he pitched in the 1890s, he compiled enough innings and wins to look like a Hall-of-Famer.

In terms of just his career record, Rusie looks the least impressive of all the 1800s Hall-of-Fame pitchers. And as you know, the Hall of Fame is mostly about career records. But historical importance is a factor too. And Bill James says he was the second-best 1800s pitcher. Rusie belongs in the Hall.

Mickey Welch (1880-1892; career ERA+: 113)

	Career	Rank	Peak	Rank	Bests	Top 3s	JAWS	Rank
WAR	63.1	9	54.5	12	0	1	58.8	12
WS	353.3	7	267.9	9	0	1	NA	None

In all my enthusiasm for yakking about labor issues and tragic deaths, I forgot to talk about why pitcher wins are dumb. Pud Galvin's comment would have been a good spot, but that lovely chart was too enticing. Now is a good time.

I once had a friend who had never learned about baseball. She asked me to give her a few baseball facts that she could whip out to surprise her new boyfriend. We got into pitcher statistics, and I started talking about pitcher wins. She was shocked. "Wait, a single player can get a win? Isn't this a team sport? It's the team's job to win, right?"

Silly woman, let me explain this to you. See, a pitcher gets a win when he pitches most of the game, and his teammates play good enough defense and score enough runs. No, the teammates who fielded well and scored those runs don't get any wins—that would be crazy! And no, pitchers don't necessarily have to pitch well to get wins, as long as their teammates score loads of runs. Usually they pitch well though. Mostly.

Oh, and sometimes, pitchers don't even have to pitch most of the game to get wins. They just have to be lucky enough to be the pitcher of record when their teammates score the run that wins the game. No, they don't have to contribute to that run; in fact they almost never do. Wait, but if you throw your team's first pitch of the game, that doesn't apply. Then you have to pitch 5 innings of the game to get the win. And there might be other caveats too. Let me look this up.

The rules for pitcher wins are convoluted and arbitrary because they're awkwardly propping up a fundamentally flawed idea. As I mentioned in the Al Kaline comment, there are team achievements and there are individual achievements. Team achievements include winning. Individual achievements include pitching scoreless innings and scoring runs, etc. Individuals can contribute to wins, but they can't win games by themselves. So they shouldn't be given wins. Giving one person the win contravenes the whole essence of team sports, that winning is a team effort, with a bunch of people working toward a shared goal.

Win Shares and WAR bridge the gap between team and individual accomplishments by dividing wins among the players in proportion to their contributions. Both would be useless if they just awarded one win to one player per game.

In the mid-1980s, there was a brief period when people were excited about "game-winning RBI." If you drove in the run that won the game, you got a GWRBI. It is sort of like a pitcher win, because it designated one hitter as doing the most to win the game. But it quickly fell into disfavor because people realized that it's meaningless. Getting the GWRBI is only one small part of mounting a successful offense.

Pitcher wins aren't as pointless as GWRBI, but they aren't tons better. They can provide a vague, secondary indication of how well a pitcher did. But because they rely so much on the contributions of teammates' hitting and fielding, they are a step removed from getting at core pitching performance. They have maybe an 80% chance of successfully indicating value. Numbers like ERA are closer to 90%. WAR and Win Shares are closer to 95%. When you've devised better measuring sticks, why keep using the old, worse ones?

It's like if you judged the health of the United States economy by looking at the GDP of all North America. Sure, it'll probably give you a good idea, particularly if the U.S. economy is really gangbusters. But you can do better.

Mickey Welch got a lot of pitcher wins: 307 to be exact. That's why he's in the Hall of Fame. He was a good pitcher, occasionally very good. But he collected 307 wins only because of the time period in which he played. In every other measure, he wasn't a Hall-of-Famer. He wasn't nearly as good as Jim Kaat or Tommy John, both of whom came close but didn't cross that mystical magical phantasmagorical 300-win mark. Welch was more in the range of Dennis Martinez or David Wells or Jamie Moyer. Each of them likely would have won 300 games if they'd pitched in the 1800s. They're very good pitchers, but they're not Hall-of-Famers.

In my reckoning, and both that of WAR and Bill James, neither is Mickey Welch. **Welch is out.**

Who's In, Who's Out

I've kicked Mickey Welch out of the Hall of Fame, and you can tell him I did. If he's got a problem with that, he can take it up with me personally. (But any of his descendants cannot. I don't pick fights with people who are alive.) Do we need a replacement?

Let's see who the systems recommend. When advocating players for the Hall, I try to stick to ones who score in the acceptable range for both WAR and Win Shares. Jim McCormick is in the range according to WAR, with a JAWS that scores 5th among 1800s pitchers, ahead of Amos Rusie and Pud Galvin. WSAWS has him 8th, ahead of Mickey Welch and Amos Rusie but below the rest of the HOFers. He's looking like a solid candidate for the low end.

But Bill James didn't rank him at all. I might know why. For one, McCormick had his best years from 1880 to 1884. Those were the years the schedule was expanding rapidly and teams usually had just one starting pitcher each. That means those pitchers' WAR and Win Shares totals are astronomical compared to every other player. It's a bit apples-and-oranges-ish to compare 1880-1884 pitchers to post-1884 pitchers, not as much as comparing 1800s pitchers to post-1800s pitchers, but similar. WAR and JAWS don't make that distinction, but my ol' buddy Bill James does.

Also, one of McCormick's best performances, that crazy 1884 again, was with the Union Association. This was the league that pulled away Charlie Sweeney, Old Hoss Radbourn's rotation partner. It was trying to become a major league, but didn't get many good players besides Sweeney and McCormick. Bill James has a looooooooong article in the "New Historical Baseball Abstract" about why the Union Association shouldn't be considered a major league, and I'm convinced. McCormick's Union Association season counts in his WAR and WSAWS, but it shouldn't. That knocks him down a notch.

So while I overruled James on Pud Galvin, I don't feel justified doing so with Jim McCormick. Too bad; I had a whole schtick locked and loaded about how McCormick looked like Nick Offerman, who played Ron Swanson in "Parks and Recreation." Look him up on baseball-reference.com and try to disagree.

The other 1800s guys who made Bill James's top 100 overall pitchers are Tony Mullane, Bob Caruthers, and Tommy Bond. He ranked all three lower than HOFers Kid Nichols, Amos Rusie, John Clarkson, Old Hoss Radbourn, and Tim Keefe. In WSAWS, Mullane is about even with Galvin, while Caruthers is bunched in with Welch. In JAWS, Mullane and Caruthers are significantly lower than the six HOFers I'm keeping. Neither look like must-haves.

That leaves Tommy Bond. Bond had a short career, mostly in the 1870s. Maybe he could be in the Jim O'Rourke/Deacon White class of guys who get extra consideration because they played in seasons of around 60 or so games? But O'Rourke and White had lower numbers because no one could compile more than about 375 PAs per year in the 1870s. Pitchers from the 1870s played in the same short seasons but still pitched 400-500 innings per year. It's not quite the same thing. If Tommy Bond makes it some day, good for him, but I don't feel a need to fly his banner.

Will Mickey Welch's ouster make for a shortage of 1800s pitchers? Let's look back at the Percent of SPs Who Are HOFers chart from the introduction. The percentage for the 1800s vacillates wildly, which might seem like a problem. But it is partially due to the constantly changing number of major league teams, which changed the total numbers of major-league pitchers (the denominators in the percentage calculation) but not the number of HOFers (the numerators). The vacillation is also due to how few pitchers there were during the time. Each team had just a handful, if that. That makes for a "small sample size" problem. It means that just one Hall-of-Fame pitcher retiring will make the percentage drop dramatically, and one debuting will make the percentage jump up.

Overall, I don't think there's either a huge shortage or a huge excess of 1800s pitchers. Let's just kick out Welch and move on to the real pitchers.

Chapter Thirteen

~ ~ Post-1800s Starting Pitchers ~ ~

You have to put the cutoff somewhere. I went with 1901, and that's the cutoff everyone uses. It's the first year of the American League, so it makes for a baseball world that's easy for us to understand.

But pitching didn't change overnight on January 1, 1901. Throughout the dead-ball era from 1901-1919, pitchers were still pitching crazy numbers of innings by modern standards. Hundreds topped 300 IPs in a season, and six exceeded 400 (all from 1901 to 1908). The days of "main pitcher and a change pitcher" were long gone, but pitchers still completed every start and often contributed a few relief appearances.

WAR accounts for this by raising the replacement level for dead-ball pitchers. Win Shares does not; it keeps on just taking those team wins and dividing them up by player contributions, regardless of any other considerations. So that means Win Shares shows a bias in favor of older pitchers. Bill James's overall ranking counteracts this effect and rates pitchers of all eras on an equal plane.

We of course want a relatively even number of pitchers from different eras. So when the Win Shares totals seem out of whack with everything else, everything else is probably right.

How Many Should We Aim For?

The benchmark number of Hall-of-Famers at each hitters' position was about 20. If a Hall-of-Famer was well below 20th-best according to both Bill James and JAWS, I was very inclined to kick him out. If a non-HOFer was above or close to 20th according to both systems, I was very inclined to put him in. There were very few instances when I ended up going against that guideline. (Hey, I like my systems!)

But we can't go for the top 20 among post-1800s starting pitchers. Remember that that top-20 number included 1800s hitters. The number of 1800s Hall-of-Famers at each position varied from one (Buck Ewing at catcher, Bid McPhee at second base) to four (first base, right field, left field). There is an average of 2.625 hitters from the 1800s per position. Let's chop three off of that 20 and say we can only have 17 post-1800s starting pitchers in the Hall. So 17 it is. Done and done, and also done.

Just kidding! Did I fool you? Ooh, and now I got your nose! I have ripped your nose off your head with my bare hands and am now taunting you by displaying it between my fingers! I am a homicidal psychopath!

Of course, teams always have more starting pitchers than they do second basemen or right fielders. The sizes of rotations have varied over time, but no one used one- or two-man ones after 1900. In 1901 there were 4.125 starters per major-league team (defining a starter as someone with as many innings as there are league games, which is the current qualification for the ERA title). In 2014 there were only 2.93 pitchers per team who qualified for the ERA title.

I did the same calculation for every year since 1901, and there is a longstanding trend toward fewer ERA qualifiers. Rotations were actually smaller in the old days, so that's not the cause. The reason is that relievers get a lot more innings nowadays, and bad pitchers get replaced mid-season more often.

If we put all the years together, you get an average of 3.45 ERA-title-qualifiers per team. So what if we multiplied 17 by 3.45? That gives us 59. In fact, at this writing the Hall of Fame has exactly 55 post-1800s starting pitchers, not including Negro Leaguers. Negro Leaguers make up another 10, which may be a bit low considering that there are 29 Hall-of-Fame Negro League players in total. I'll try to find another to induct, though Bill James and Monte Irvin make that difficult.

But 59 cannot be as hard a boundary as 20 was for the hitter positions. There are so many pitchers since 1900 that you can't really draw a line that precise. If I did the same sort of JAWS vs. WSAWS graph for post-1800s pitchers as I did for center fielders and 1800s pitchers, first of all, it would be a big mess. If I somehow made it in any way readable, there would be a huge cloud of pitchers around the 59th range, some of whom were immortals and some which were not. The first-tier guys might be pretty clear, but the second tier and third tier would be even harder to nail down than it was for center fielders or 1800s pitchers.

Let's go with a 55-65 range as being the lower boundary for the Hall. Anyone in the 65-75 range will probably qualify for "I wouldn't campaign to put him in, but I won't campaign to kick him out." Anyone well below that range will likely get kicked out. Non-HOFers who are in or above around 65th will get serious consideration.

Sound good? Well, it better, because you have no choice.

Grover Cleveland Alexander (1911-1930; career ERA+: 135)

	Career	Rank	Peak	Rank	Bests	Top 5s	JAWS	Rank
WAR	120.0	4	69.6	3	2	7	94.8	4
WS	476.3	3	253.1	3	5	7	NA	3

Grover Cleveland Alexander is the first in the quartet of dead-ball-era pitchers who dominate many all-time pitcher rankings. Another of the Fab Four closes out this chapter (no spoilers!). That particular unnamed pitcher retired after Alexander's debut year, so they weren't exactly contemporaries. But all four have massive career win totals because they lasted so long during a time when 30 wins per season was not totally uncommon.

But we're not here to talk about pitcher wins, which are dumb, as you know because you read the Mickey Welch comment (right???). We're here to talk about Grover Cleveland Alexander, who was also known as "Pete" because he apparently didn't already have enough names. Pete James Mordecai John Rutherford B. Hayes Alexander was gangbusters throughout the 1910s for the Phillies. In 1915 he led the franchise to their lone pennant before the 1950 "Whiz Kids" team.

In 1917, the Phillies made an odd move. They presumed that Alexander would be drafted into World War I, so they traded him to the Cubs for an underwhelming package featuring Pickles Dillhoeffer, who was as talented as his name would suggest. Alexander was indeed drafted, and did serve. But he came back in 1918 and was still Grover Cleveland Alexander. Were they thinking the war would last 100 years?

Granted, Alexander did come back a different person, not that the Phillies could have predicted that. Alexander served on the front lines of the war and was under constant shelling. He lost all hearing in his left ear and caught some shrapnel in his right ear. His throwing arm was damaged from operating howitzers. The epilepsy he had contracted in his minor-league days got worse.

Alexander was a drinker before the war, and a full-blown alcoholic after it. He mistakenly believed alcohol could calm his epilepsy. Drinking was also his solution to his post-traumatic stress disorder, then known as "shell-shock."

Let's digress. I'm a big fan of the late great comedian George Carlin. He often railed against attempts to neuter language by replacing powerful words with less emotive euphemisms. In one bit, he complained about society moving from "shell-shock" to "post-traumatic stress disorder." Carlin saw it as an injustice to replace such a visceral term with such a dry, clinical one.

In this case, Carlin was wrong. "Shell-shock" was seen as a temporary thing, one that real men tough their way through. "Shock," after all, is something that wears off. It's quite a blow, but you get over it and move on.

Meanwhile, "post-traumatic stress disorder" denotes a serious medical condition that requires intensive therapy and care. You don't just give someone with PTSD a pint of whiskey and a few weeks off and then expect him to come back to the plant. You get some trained specialists and address the problem head-on.

I'm a pragmatist; I support what works. And from what I've read, and from my wife's experience as a psychotherapist, I know it works much better to treat people with post-traumatic stress disorder than it does to pity people with shell-shock. Many more lives are saved when you approach it as a medical condition than when you treat it as a personal struggle. That's much more important than any concern over words losing their punch.

More generally, some people get out of joint when they hear about a new medical or psychological condition. They think there's a terrible danger in "medicalizing" something that they had never thought of in those terms. They scoff at things like "restless leg syndrome" and "chronic fatigue disorder."

The names sound silly; I get that. Doctors might not have the marketing skills to pick good names for disorders. But you should at least have the humility to consider for a moment the fact that you're not a doctor. Your "that name sounds silly" argument might not hold as much weight as that of dozens of studies in peer-reviewed journals and the expert opinions of trained medical professionals. Doctors don't tend to make stuff up just to drum up business. They're not snake oil salesmen. There is an integrity to the profession.

What if there really were people out there whose sleep was constantly interrupted by their restless legs? What if their lives would improve with medication? How is that a bad thing? Maybe some people can barely get through the day because of chronic fatigue, and addressing it will enable them to thrive. Why is that a problem? It's possible that someday we'll find out that these truly aren't real disorders. But let's let the professionals figure that out. Let's not presume we know better if we don't.

I'm belaboring this point for a reason. A lot of people don't get the help they need because they refuse to believe that what they're experiencing might qualify as a medical or psychological condition. Often they refuse to believe the relevant condition even exists, or worse, think medicine or psychology is a load of bunk. I speak from experience: I have a serious anxiety disorder that I left untreated for fifteen years. I thought I could just tough my way through it, but I couldn't. Those fifteen years were filled with pain I didn't need to experience. It's the greatest regret of my life.

The rest of Pete Alexander's life might not have been so painful if PTSD therapy was used instead of booze. He kept performing at basically the same level; his numbers only look less impressive in the 1920s because it was a hitters' era and he was getting old. But his drinking made him infamously unreliable.

After retirement, things got worse. Alexander was in and out of sanitariums and barely scraped by through odd jobs. He couldn't be trusted with money, because it would all go to alcohol. The National

League was worried about how it would all look, so they arranged a pension for him that a friend would carefully dole out.

When Alexander was admitted to the Hall of Fame, he pulled himself together enough to attend the ceremony and look presentable for the cameras. But he was later quoted as saying "I'm in the Hall of Fame … and I'm proud to be there, but I can't eat the Hall of Fame." (Source: Alexander's SABR biography (natch), by Jan Finkel) That captures the state he was in: A living legend who was barely living at all.

Somehow, Alexander survived into his 60s. Though the coroner's report said he died of heart failure, his long-suffering estranged wife believed it was from an epileptic seizure. As with Tony Lazzeri, a seizure is more likely.[65] Grover Cleveland Alexander makes for one of the more tragic members of the Hall of Fame.

Charles "Chief" Bender (1903-1917, 1925; career ERA+: 112)

	Career	Rank	Peak	Rank	Bests	Top 5s	JAWS	Rank
WAR	49.5	92	35.0	128	0	0	42.3	105
WS	231.7	77	142.9	99	1	1	NA	None

Charles Bender did not like being called "Chief." At the time, there were many Native American players, and all of them were nicknamed "Chief." Bender wanted to be known for more than just his racial category. I hesitate to include the "Chief" above, but that is still how he is listed in baseball-reference.com and pretty much every other source.

Bender was a highly intelligent man who had arisen from a very poor upbringing to become a great success in both baseball and real life. He had many talents: trap shooting, fishing, hunting, golfing, billiards, gardening, oil painting, etc. In his retirement he had a successful retail career, and served as a consultant in the diamond and textile trades. Oh, and what have you done this week? Ooh, you binge-watched "House of Cards"? Congratulations! Hold on while I fashion a medal for you that carries the inscription "Charles 'Chief' Bender Memorial Award for Excellence in the Field of Fascinating Achievement." What's your medal size?

Yeah, yeah, yeah, but is Bender a Hall-of-Famer? The above rankings are not so kind. His conventional numbers seem great, but remember that he pitched in the dead-ball era. A career 2.46 ERA might look amazing to modern eyes. But in the dead-ball era, it's merely good, as his 112 ERA+ shows. If he'd pitched at the same level for longer, maybe he'd have a better case. He also didn't pitch that much per season, by the standards of his time.

---

[65] Fans of baseball history may know that Grover Cleveland Alexander and Tony Lazzeri share more than the same (probable) death from the same condition. In the seventh game of the 1926 World Series, the Cardinals led the Yankees 3-2. It was the seventh inning, the bases were loaded, and Tony Lazzeri was coming to bat. Cardinals starter Jesse Haines was looking done. So Alexander, 39 years old and disheveled as hell, ambled to the mound. He epitomized the tough, grizzled old warrior; he had even thrown a complete game the day before. Alexander struck out Lazzeri in dramatic fashion, and a few innings later the Cardinals won their first championship. It became one of the most famous moments in baseball history. After his retirement, Alexander would re-enact the moment on vaudeville stages for a little drinking money.

He did have a great career winning percentage, leading the league three times. This is another problem with wins. On any other team but the terrific 1903-1914 Philadelphia A's, Bender would not have won so much. His winning percentage with the A's was .654, but the team's winning percentage as a whole was .595. Again, Bender's number was good, but not amazing.

Bender didn't have a single truly great year. His top WAR total was 6.3 and his top Win Shares total was 26. The only HOFers with less impressive top seasons are guys who don't belong, relief pitchers, and players like Luis Aparicio and Bobby Wallace who lasted a very long time at very tough positions.

I'm not saying that Bender is a terrible Hall-of-Fame candidate. Who is he comparable to in recent history? Bill James doesn't include Bender in his top 100, so we can't get too many comps from that. WAR has him near Ron Guidry, Vida Blue, and Carlos Zambrano. They were all aces for most or all of their careers. But none quite got to Hall-of-Fame level.

Could you argue that Bender's status as one of the few Native Americans in the Hall should bump him up a few points? It seems a stretch, but let's explore it. You can't compare him to Jackie Robinson or Larry Doby, since there was no color line for Native Americans.

I gave Hank Greenberg some extra points for weathering abuse for his Judaism and for counteracting ethnic stereotypes in a big, public way. From what I've read, Bender weathered many indignities, but less outright abuse than Greenberg did. He did counteract stereotypes, but so did several other Native Americans in the dead-ball era. A terrific catcher named John "Chief" Meyers probably would have deserved the Hall if he'd started his career before age 28. Like Bender, Meyers was known for his sophistication and intelligence, belying the then-dominant image of Native Americans as simple-minded savages. Both Bender and Meyers made important contributions to battling bigotry, but neither had quite the level of cultural impact that Greenberg did.

I don't feel great about trying to quantify such things, as I am neither Jewish nor Native American. But this is the task I've given myself, so I'm going to give it a shot. I could see giving Bender a few extra points for his cultural importance. Unfortunately, I don't think it would be enough points to get him from 100th to the 55th-75th range. With regret, I have to **kick out Charles Bender.** I'm sorry, but the numbers aren't there. There are too many dead-ball pitchers in the Hall, and Bender's numbers are among the least impressive of the bunch.

Bert Blyleven (1970-1990, 1992; career ERA+: 118)

	Career	Rank	Peak	Rank	Bests	Top 5s	JAWS	Rank
WAR	95.3	12	50.7	24	1	6	73.0	13
WS	338.3	14	159.8	59	1	3	NA	34

Grumpy old men never learn. The way it was done when they were young will always be the right way. Any change will always be dismissed as lacking in some essential virtue, usually one intertwined with their conceptions of manliness.

Bert Blyleven is perhaps the most beloved baseball icon in Minnesota, now that Joe Mauer isn't really earning his salary. Blyleven works as a color announcer for most games, and he's lots of fun. He's blessed with an easy friendliness and a goofy sense of humor. He is always counting down to his birthday, and when it comes he wears a silly hat. He is basically Minnesota baseball's fun grandpa.

But in some ways he's still the archetypal grumpy old man. I can't tell you how many times I've listened to him bellyache about how pitchers don't complete games any more. Man, does he ever hate pitch counts. After all, he didn't need them, and he pitched 4970 career innings (which is a heckuva lot, as we say in Minnesota: 14th-most all-time).

Well Bert, most pitchers are not you. You were exceptional. Most people are not exceptional; exceptional people are, by definition, the exception. Here is a partial list of guys who did not have such exceptionally durable arms: David Clyde, Mark Fidrych, and Steve Busby. They all pitched during your heyday. All pitched way too much at very young ages, developed arm troubles, and saw their careers cut short.

And since the 1970s, the game has become even harder on pitchers' arms. There is almost no opportunity to pace yourself. Hitters are better than ever; anything less than 90% effort on every pitch will be punished.

Hitters are also more selective than ever. They're much less likely to get themselves out by throwing their bats at the first or second pitch. There aren't too many Ozzie Guillens nowadays who think "being aggressive" is so important that they'd rather make a very aggressive groundout than risk a strikeout. That means more pitches per hitter, and thus more pitches per game.

Can what I'm saying be backed up with some numbers? Let's test my theory, which I'm calling my "Where have you gone, Ozzie Guillen? A nation turns its lonely eyes to you"[66] theory. (A bit long for a theory name, but it doesn't matter, because I'll never refer to it again.) Baseball-reference.com has data for pitches per plate appearance going back to 1988. That year, there were 3.58 pitches per plate appearance (P/PA). Since then, the number has been steadily increasing, reaching 3.82 in 2014. There is no data for the 1970s, but I wouldn't be surprised if it were around 3.4 pitches per plate appearance.

What does that mean for pitch counts? You can find out by multiplying the P/PA figures by the numbers of plate appearances per team per game (PA/T/G). This number varies depending on how many runs are scored league-wide. When teams score more runs, it takes more batters to get 27 outs, and that means more plate appearances. In 1999 and 2000, when everyone worth his salt hit 50 home runs, there were more than 39 PA/T/G. Meanwhile, 1988 and 2014 happen to be two recent low points for run production. In those years there were basically the same number of PA/T/G: 37.95 in 1988 and 37.85 in 2014.

Multiply the two sets of numbers and you get 136 pitches per team per game in 1988 and 143 in 2014. Back in the Ryne Sandberg comment I blamed long games on players who waste time between pitches. But that's just part of the story. In 2014, games lasted three hours on average, which was a record. Seven extra pitches for each team could easily tack on another 7-15 minutes per game.

Let's just say I'm right about there being 3.4 P/PA in the 1970s. Throughout the decade, there were 38.15 PA/T/G. That would give us 130 pitches per team per game.

It might not seem like a huge jump to go from 130 pitches to 143. But in terms of damage to a pitcher's arm, it's a big difference. Sabermetricians Rany Jazayerli and Keith Woolner created Pitcher Abuse Points to address this issue. (See "Analyzing PAP, Part 1" baseballprospectus.com, May 21,

[66] Reference explanation: Simon and Garfunkel's "Mrs. Robinson," a song I dig because it epitomizes grumpy-old-man-ism: In the 1960s, grumpy old men looked longingly at Joe Dimaggio as the emblem of an idyllic bygone age. In the 1980s they did the same thing for Mickey Mantle. It's the same old story; only the names change.

2002.) They proposed that there isn't much difference between 90 pitches and 100 pitches in terms of strain on a typical starting pitcher. But beyond 100, most pitchers are throwing with fatigued arms. At 120, they're pitching with very fatigued arms. At 140, something is about to snap. The chance of injury rises literally exponentially as the pitch count gets further and further from 100. Only veterans whose arms have been strengthened over a decade or so of professional pitching have a good chance of surviving 130 pitches in a game. Even those guys struggle with 140. Completing a game nowadays is playing with fire.

Blyleven likes to say that pitchers should be trained at younger ages to pitch more innings. Sure, sometimes that works. But sometimes it ends in disaster. Both Kerry Wood and Livan Hernandez were overused when they were young. Wood broke down and spent the rest of his career as an oft-injured reliever. Hernandez kept on chugging forever. You can gamble that your young phenom will turn out to be a Livan Hernandez instead of a Kerry Wood. But it's not a very wise gamble, when you consider the incredible cost of ruining a young star's career. In the long term, the smart money is on treading carefully.

So there's a good chance of incurring huge costs by pushing a starter too much at a young age. What about the benefits? Are they really that great? Is a starter who is trained to pitch complete games really going to bring your team that many more wins? Considering the effectiveness of relief pitchers nowadays, I doubt it. You could leave a starter in and take the chance that he'll get tired and give up some crucial hits. Or you could bring in one of the zillions of modern relievers who throws 95-mph gas. Who has a better chance of getting those last few outs?

Even if you don't have one of those fireballers at the ready, a new pitcher can be more effective just because he's new. Studies have shown that pitchers have the advantage the first time through an order. After that, hitters adjust to what they've seen and gain the edge. In 2015, pitchers allowed a .705 OPS the first time through a batting order and .771 the third time; meanwhile relievers' first time through an order was at .699. (Source: "Game changers: No more 'starter' or 'reliever' labels," ESPN.com, Mike Petriello, November 23, 2015.)

Hitters adjust especially well to relievers, which is why they're relievers in the first place. They have enough to get a hitter out once, but not twice. Mariano Rivera was a terrible starting pitcher in 1995; when hitters got a second look at his cutter, they were able to smash it. In the short term, for the game at hand, it's a better bet to bring in one of your relievers.

So in terms of likely costs and benefits, both long term and short term, it's much wiser to pull a starter too early than too late. But I doubt people who decry pitch counts are really thinking in cost/benefit terms. Often they talk about how complete games reveal great inner strength, true character, the heart of a lion, and all the other macho-bullschist cliches. Completing a start is intertwined with their conceptions of manliness.

I scoff at macho bullschist, but I'm not entirely un-manly. I am also moved when I watch a starter finish a great game. But that doesn't make it smart strategy.

Underneath most macho bullschist you'll find genuinely admirable values. We love watching pitchers complete starts because it demonstrates individual perseverance. In our lives, we all strive to push pain and fatigue aside to get the job done when people are counting on us. That is definitely a good perspective.

But like anything, it can be taken too far. There are limits. There is a point at which you're just sabotaging your potential for future contributions to satisfy your own sense of drama. It brings to mind the old Nietzsche quote "Whatever doesn't kill me can only make me stronger." Per usual,

Nietzsche was wrong. Sometimes, what doesn't kill you can cripple you for life. Work hard, but know when to stop.

You'd think Bert Blyleven would be amenable to sabermetric-inspired advances like adhering to pitch counts. After all, it was the sabermetric community who pushed hard for his inclusion in the Hall of Fame. But then, Bert is a grumpy old man, so you know how that goes. Grumpy-old-mannishness can supersede any other considerations.

The sabermetric community was able to see past the blinders that most people had for Blyleven's true worth. Blyleven played for small-market teams outside the national spotlight. He didn't have terrific win totals each season because most of his teams didn't win much. He didn't reach 300 career wins or get any Cy Young Awards (despite deserving it in 1973, according to both systems, as well as in 1981 according to WAR).

Sneakily, Bert Blyleven dominated, for a long time. If he wasn't hyped as dominant, then it's the fault of the hype machine, not Blyleven. Fun grandpa or grumpy old man, he is a clear Hall-of-Famer.

Mordecai Brown (1903-1916; career ERA+: 139)

	Career	Rank	Peak	Rank	Bests	Top 5s	JAWS	Rank
WAR	56.4	64	41.4	61	0	2	48.9	57
WS	295.6	28	208.6	8	1	5	NA	19

Good ol' Mordecai Brown, better known as "Three-Finger." Jim Abbott was never known as "One-Hand," but that's just how times have changed. Brown's other nickname was "Miner," because he worked in a mine as a teenager. Baseball was a working-class game in those days, but it was still notable for someone to rise from the coal mines to the major leagues.

As you may know, Brown had a disfigured right hand that enabled him to throw some strange pitches. He actually had four fingers, not three. He lost his index finger when, as a child, he got a little too grabby with some mechanized farm equipment. Then he broke his other fingers in a fall. His middle finger was bent and his pinkie was paralyzed.

Brown was the true superstar of the National League's greatest dynasty, the Cubs of 1904-1910. During that time Brown led the team in both WAR and Win Shares by substantial margins. Matchups between him and the Giants' Christy Mathewson were legendary. Brown didn't do a heck of a lot before and after that stretch, which is why his WAR ratings above are low.

Baseball was rowdy in those days, the Cubs especially. This was the team of Frank Chance, who boxed in the offseason, and Johnny "The Crab" Evers, who couldn't sit still for a second. Cubs players often fought each other and landed in the hospital. But no one bothered Brown. He was kind, friendly, and universally respected. Hall-of-Famer fer sure.

Ray Brown (1930-1945, 1947-1948)

	Rank at SP Among Negro Leaguers	Rank Among All Negro Leaguers
SABR	unranked	unranked
Monte Irvin	unranked	NA

Oh dear. This isn't good for Ray Brown. Monte Irvin does include him in a list of right-handed pitchers that just missed his top 5, but Brown is one of 11 pitchers in that list. That means he sees Ray Brown as being among the top 16 right-handed pitchers in Negro League history. Considering that there are 10 Negro League pitchers in the Hall, lefty and righty, that's not exactly an endorsement. At least it suggests that Brown is not a crazy candidate for the Hall.

I kicked out Frank Grant in part because his only ranking was provided by Bill James, who put him 6th among Negro League second basemen. With James abstaining from comment on Negro Leagues pitchers, I have even less for Brown.

Well, I do have a playing record, which I had hardly any of for Grant. Brown is too recent to be in the Seamheads database, and even getting his stats from baseball-reference.com takes some doing. (If you're interested, you'll find them in some weird, hidden, segregated section of the site called the Bullpen.) They say Brown had a 3.20 lifetime ERA in 1284.3 innings. His career record was 105-44, for a .705 career winning percentage, and you know I'm desperate for information when I cite a win-loss record.

But is that Hall-worthy? It looks good, but I can't tell for sure. Should we try his SABR biography, by Chris Rainey? I use the SABR biographies just for stories and biographical information, because they're very good at keeping to verifiable facts. But they still slant toward boosterism; you'll never see one about a Hall-of-Famer that concludes he might be undeserving of the honor. Even the Tommy McCarthy one tries to spin some half-assed rationalization.

Just going by the facts cited in the Ray Brown biography, you get a sense of why he was inducted. It describes Brown as a very successful pitcher and hitter, often batting third or fourth and playing the outfield between starts. There is a long list of impressive accomplishments, in both the Negro National League and in Cuba. Brown was the ace for the Homestead Grays when they dominated through the late 1930s and early 1940s. His best year was 1940 (2.34 ERA in 169 IP according to baseball-reference.com, plus a .311 batting average according to the SABR Negro Leagues Book). Brown also spent two playing years in the service during World War II.

I still wish I had more to go on. But I don't think I have enough reason to kick Ray Brown out. Let's put him in the "I won't campaign to put him in, but I won't campaign to kick him out" category and leave it at that for now.

Jim Bunning (1955-1971; career ERA+: 115)

	Career	Rank	Peak	Rank	Bests	Top 5s	JAWS	Rank
WAR	59.4	49	48.9	32	2	5	54.2	43
WS	256.1	48	169.9	42	2	5	NA	27

Jim Bunning is a very solid mid-range Hall-of-Fame pitcher. His conventional numbers might not blow you away at first glance; he didn't get many of those 20-win seasons that get people all hot and bothered. But he was very good for a long time. That meets established Hall-of-Fame standards.

But we're not here to talk about Jim Bunning's baseball career. We're here to talk about his political career. No, we're not, but just for fun, let's do it anyway.

Bunning definitely was the most successful ballplayer-turned-politician in history. He was a Republican member of the U.S. House of Representatives from 1987 to 1999 and then represented Kentucky in the U.S. Senate from 1999 to 2011.

But he might not make the Congress Hall of Fame. (There is no such thing. But there should be.) In 2006, Time magazine named Bunning among the five worst senators. (Source: Jim Bunning, the Underperformer, April 14, 2006) It said he showed little interest in any policy that didn't involve baseball (of which there is a lot). Toward the end of his tenure he became known for bizarre, offensive statements and for public spats with leaders of his own party. His approval rating plummeted below 40%, which is rare for a Republican in Kentucky.

Someday I might try to write up a Congress Hall of Fame. It would probably generate even less interest than this book, but it would be fun for me. I'm a big fan of history, even that which does not involve baseball (of which there is a lot).

But right now I don't know enough about the history of Congress. Presidents I know; when I was a kid I memorized the list of presidents and read voraciously about all of them. I can tell you more about William Henry Harrison, who was president for a month and then died, than I can about very influential senators like Robert La Follette and Robert A. Taft.

That's my fault, but it reflects a regrettable fact about American political awareness. We put too much focus on presidents and not enough on congresspeople. The founding fathers created the position of president to have few responsibilities beyond foreign policy. This was a time when kings had too much power, and Americans were very averse to making their own version of one.

The word "president" now carries great power and weight, but it was originally a rather bland, clerical term. A president, after all, just presides. He/she doesn't rule, or dictate, or anything as exciting as that. It's a lot more relaxed. The dude presides.[67]

People sometimes say the real first American president was a man named John Hanson, who held the position of president of the Continental Congress from 1781-1782. This was before the U.S. Constitution and our current system; the Continental Congress was a weak initial stab at an American federal government. It was so unwilling to create a single central authority figure that it provided no executive branch at all. All John Hanson did was preside, handling correspondence and signing documents. He found it so tedious that he wanted to quit after a week. The only reason he didn't was because the Congress couldn't reach a quorum, meaning they couldn't get enough representatives together to vote for a replacement. (Source: John Hanson's Wikipedia article.) This is what presidents were in those days.[68]

In 1789, the Constitution we all know and love and misunderstand established an executive branch led by a president with much more significant powers. Still, Congress was meant to be the central authority. Many 1800s presidents deferred to that view and refused to dominate lawmaking. Over the

---

[67] Reference explanation: "The dude abides" is a catchphrase from the Coen Brothers film "The Big Lebowski." There is an army of middle-aged white guys who believe "The Big Lebowski" is the greatest achievement in the history of cinema. Sure, it's a good movie, above average among Coen Brothers fare. But it doesn't compare to "Fargo." Darn tootin'.

[68] And then other sources say Hanson wasn't really the first Continental Congress president, that guys named Samuel Huntington and Thomas McKeon preceded him. Whatever. The point is, they were all American presidents in name only.

1900s, the office of president gained more and more power and stature, and the president is undoubtedly central today.

Still, Robert La Follette and Robert A. Taft should be much more famous than William Henry Harrison. We should know which senators and representatives were instrumental in the legislation that shapes our lives. People talk about things happening during the Reagan administration or the Clinton years as if Reagan and Clinton did them all by themselves. They didn't; this is a democracy, not a monarchy. The prime movers were usually those congresspeople we all profess to hate (except the local one that we vote for every time: "Yeah, Congress is the worst. But my guy/gal is all right.").

Maybe there is something about the office of president that triggers the "monarch" switch in our collective subconscious. Human history made us so accustomed to pinning everything on one ruler that it's hard to think any other way.

Anyway, that was a pretty drastic digression, even for me. Sometimes I just don't have much of interest to say about a guy, but then I think of some tangential point I really want to make. I can't help it! It gets a bit dull to just say "yeah, this guy was good enough" almost every time.

Anyway, anyway, yeah, this guy Jim Bunning was good enough for the Hall of Fame.

Steve Carlton (1965-1988; career ERA+: 115)

	Career	Rank	Peak	Rank	Bests	Top 5s	JAWS	Rank
WAR	90.4	14	54.3	16	2	5	72.4	14
WS	369.5	11	187.4	21	3	5	NA	14

Like Jim Bunning, Steve Carlton was politically conservative. Most ballplayers are. I'm not sure why, and for once I'm not going to conjecture about it.

Bunning was a steady, reasonable enough conservative to get elected to the House and the Senate; he must have been doing something right before he imploded. Meanwhile, Carlton's views were so extreme that he probably couldn't get elected to assistant secretary of the Glenn Beck fan club.

In 1994, Carlton gave a rare interview (see http://thestacks.deadspin.com/thin-air-in-the-mountains-with-steve-carlton-armed-co-478492324, originally published as "Thin Mountain Air" in Philadelpia Magazine, April 1994) to journalist Pat Jordan. "Rare" doesn't really cover it; Carlton refused to speak to the media at all for most of his career. But by 1994, he was retired and low on funds, so he needed to get his name in the papers. He opened up to Jordan, and wow, did it get weird.

They were at Carlton's remote Colorado compound, which Carlton had carefully constructed to protect him from a legion of imaginary threats. The walls of his house were six feet thick to keep out gamma rays. He was also afraid of low-frequency sound waves, which he believed the U.S. and Russian governments were pumping out to control our minds. Of course his giant basement was packed with food and water for when the "revolution" came; did you expect anything less?

To Carlton, pretty much every organization was secretly controlling the world. On separate occasions he cited our true overlords as the British MI-5 and MI-6, then a committee of 300 which meets in Rome, and then the old standby, the Elders of Zion, twelve Jewish bankers meeting in Switzerland. Man, with all those covert organizations trying to rule us at once, the bureaucracy must be ridiculous! No wonder that pothole on my street never gets fixed!

The conspiracy theory that made headlines across the country was Carlton's take on AIDS. He believed the disease was created in a secret lab in Maryland to "to get rid of gays and blacks, and now they have a strain of the virus that can live ten days in the air or on a plate of food, because you know who most of the waiters are." Hoo boy. Wow. I suppose you could give Carlton points for originality.

Throughout the interview with Pat Jordan, Carlton seemed to lack what psychologists call a "theory of mind." That is, he couldn't seem to imagine anything about how other people might think or feel. Other people were a terrifying mystery, and he had no idea what constituted reasonable human behavior. So he believed everything he read, particularly if it focused his bottomless well of anxiety on some distant evil enemy. There was no part of his brain that could butt in and say "You know, that doesn't seem plausible." Lack of theory of mind is a common trait of autism and paranoid schizophrenia, among other disorders. I wouldn't be surprised if Carlton had one or more of those.

The end of his career may have sparked his decline into madness. After four years of pitching terribly in his 40s, teams stopped making offers. He took this as a conspiracy against him instead of what it was, a very reasonable reaction to a player whose career was clearly over.

Before that, Carlton seemed a bit more attuned to reality. He had friends, which was something he apparently couldn't manage after retirement. But the signs of an unusual, fearful mind were there.

While on the mound, he had to push away almost every thought, anxious or otherwise. Before each start Carlton would put himself into a state of meditation, or at least something close to it. He would sit for hours in a soundproof room created especially for him, staring at a picture of ocean waves and listening to a recorded voice saying "I am courageous, calm, confident, and relaxed. I can control my destiny" over and over.

Carlton attributed his success in baseball to his efforts in becoming a martial arts expert. He refused to do normal workouts; instead his training consisted of twisting his fist in a pail of brown rice 49 times, once for each year in the life of a martial arts legend named Kwan Gung. Eastern philosophies calmed him and created a world that made sense to him. In retirement he did yoga for three hours a day.

He kept his approach to pitching very simple. Throughout his career he never had more than three pitches, a rising fastball, a slider, and a curve. He threw what and where his catchers told him to, with little in the way of deception or mind games. Keith Hernandez said that "Steve Carlton threw me (and most batters) 95 percent sliders ... Carlton threw the slider like an automaton: outside corner black, at the knees, every time ..."

All this suggests something that other ballplayers could learn from. Only someone with an extreme level of anxiety would ascribe to so many nefarious conspiracies. People with that much fear usually can't accomplish anything significant, much less a very stressful job like major-league pitching. But with his unorthodox training and preparation, Carlton was able to pitch extremely well, among the best ever.

More players might do well to adopt some of Carlton's techniques for clearing his mind. If it can work for a mind as frantic and disconnected from reality as his, it could work for yours. Just don't listen to the rest of his crazy crap. Except the part about the 300 Romans controlling the world. That's true. I've met them, and they're actually pretty nice guys. They mostly manipulate benchmark interest rates to encourage consumer spending while keeping inflation down. It gets pretty boring when you get into the details.

Jack Chesbro (1899-1909; career ERA+: 111)

	Career	Rank	Peak	Rank	Bests	Top 5s	JAWS	Rank
WAR	41.4	144	40.3	73	1	1	40.9	118
WS	209.6	99	183.1	27	1	1	NA	None

Like Mickey Welch, Jack Chesbro got into the Hall because of one nice-looking win total. In Chesbro's case, it was 41, the number of wins he collected in 1904. That sure is a big number. 41! That's a two-digit number that starts with a different digit than I'm accustomed to! And the year he did it did not start with "18"! Into the Hall he goes!

Chesbro really did put in a great performance, the best of the year according to Win Shares and WAR. But that was the only year that either system has him among the top five pitchers. And he only played nine full seasons, one half-year, and another of 55.2 very poor innings. Among those nine full years, maybe four were quite good (including 1904) and the rest ranged between below-average to above-average.

That 1904 season was so great in part because Chesbro pitched 454.2 innings. Some think that overstrained his arm, but he always denied it. He's probably right; after that year, his numbers look quite similar to those of his earlier years. Plus, he was 30 years old in 1904, so some decline would be expected. His career doesn't follow the pattern of someone who messed up his arm; it looks more like a good pitcher who had one fluke season. He's the pitching version of Roger Maris (or better, Cy Seymour, if you really know your baseball history).

Does it count as a fluke if you know why it happened? In 1904 Chesbro was able to use his spitball a lot more, which was perfectly legal at the time. He also developed what was then called a "slow ball" i.e., a change-up. It made for a great arsenal, but apparently not one that could bring sustained success.

The Hall of Fame's rules for election very explicitly state "No automatic elections based on performances such as batting .400 or more for one (1) year, pitching a perfect game or similar outstanding achievement shall be permitted." Unlike the so-called "Character Clause," this is a rule the Hall has mostly followed. Maris isn't in for those 61 home runs in 1961. Earl Webb isn't in for his record-setting 67 doubles in 1931, and Owen "Chief" Wilson isn't in for his record 36 triples in 1912 (and both impress me more than Chesbro's 41 wins). Jack Chesbro should not be in either. **Chesbro is out.**

Andy Cooper (1920-1939)

	Rank at SP Among Negro Leaguers	Rank Among All Negro Leaguers
SABR	Unranked	Unranked
Monte Irvin	2 Among LHP (kind of)	NA

Sigh … another Negro League pitcher whom my sources are not helping me with. Monte Irvin doesn't actually mention Andy Cooper, but co-writer Phil Pepe sneaks in a comment right after Irvin's bit about Bill Foster. Pepe says "Many would argue that only Willie Foster ranks ahead of Andy Cooper as a left-handed pitcher in Negro Leagues baseball." The implication seems to be that Irvin shouldn't have left Cooper out.

Cooper's career numbers look similar to Ray Brown's: 3.24 ERA in 1592.7 IP, with a 116-57 win-loss record (.671 WP). Cooper played earlier than Brown, with big years from 1923-1930. Bill James says he was the best pitcher in the Negro Leagues in 1923.

After 1931, Cooper's record gets weird, showing only 1-4 games a season, as if he got injured in April every year. Actually, he was playing for a team, the Kansas City Monarchs, that barnstormed full-time instead of playing in a league. He reportedly had some tremendous performances that we have little or no record of. And even if we did, most would be against very inferior competition, like when modern major-league teams play exhibition games against college teams. So we can't go by those stats. But that experience should count in his favor, as barnstorming was a very important part of Negro League ball.

Few Negro Leaguers barnstormed full-time after 1920, but it was a part of life for most, much more than for white players. It was a financial necessity. Even though large Northern cities had booming African-American populations, each city still had only so many potential paying fans with only so much disposable income. No team could fill a park every day throughout a season of more than 100 games.

But when a bunch of famous ballplayers rolled into a small city that didn't have a pro team, it was a big event. You might get to see two teams of professionals or might watch one team of pros play the local semi-pro team. In a city with a small enough African-American population, you might know some of the local players personally. It was as if U2 came to town and sometimes brought Interpol and other times let the local bar band open for them. It sounds pretty fun.

But why were the Kansas City Monarchs barnstorming permanently from 1932-1935? (And were they really the "Kansas City" Monarchs if they never played in Kansas City?) Time for labor-management strife. The Negro Leagues didn't have the stability of being a monopoly legitimized by a very generous Supreme Court. As a result, they were like the white major leagues in the 1800s, and you know how chaotic that was.

In 1927, owners were sick of players jumping from team to team for bigger paychecks. They came up with a new rule that banned contract-jumping players for five years. Andy Cooper, Hall-of-Fame catcher Biz Mackey, and a few others decided to test this rule by joining a barnstorming-only team that played games throughout Hawaii and Japan. When they got back, they were all banned from league play. So they took to barnstorming full-time.

The Monarchs eventually returned to league play and dominated, winning the Negro American League every year from 1937-1940. Cooper wasn't pitching much by then, but he managed the Monarchs each of those years. His string of success was cut short by a stroke and then a heart attack, which killed him at age 43. (Source: Cooper's Wikipedia entry.)

Cooper's case is looking pretty good. His pitching record is impressive, and it doesn't include all his barnstorming. Then for a brief period he was a very successful manager, in a near-Frank-Chance sort of way. He seems like a Hall-of-Famer to me.

Stan Coveleski (1912, 1916-1928; career ERA+: 127)

	Career	Rank	Peak	Rank	Bests	Top 5s	JAWS	Rank
WAR	60.2	47	49.9	27	0	4	55.0	41
WS	244.2	56	185.8	23	0	3	NA	49

I love it when the teams that are historically known as underdogs break out and win a championship. The Cleveland Naps (that's what I'm calling them from now on, whether they like it or not) won it all in 1920, thanks in large part to Tris Speaker and Stan Coveleski.

1920 marked the end of the dead-ball era and the beginning of baseball's true Golden Age. People often think the 1920s' surge in power and offense was due to a new, more tightly wound ball. That was a small factor, but a larger one was the banning of the spitball, scuffball, and any other pitch that involved messing up the ball. Not only did it take a major weapon away from pitchers—imagine if the cutter were suddenly prohibited—but it also meant a cleaner and more intact ball stayed in play. It also helped that umpires were switching to new balls more often during games. No more mushy globs in the late innings that only Babe Ruth could drive.

Only a handful of pitchers, including Stan Coveleski, were grandfathered in and allowed to keep throwing the spitball. Coveleski threw several other pitches, but always used the threat of the spitball to mess with hitters' expectations. He would go to his mouth before every pitch, even for long stretches when he didn't throw a single spitball.

That's according to Coveleski's boasts, anyway. He started life as a shy farmboy, but grew up into kind of a jerk. Here's Coveleski's idea of a hilarious joke. One day he rowed to the middle of a lake with rookie Joe Sewell, the Hall-of-Fame shortstop who eschewed strikeouts. Coveleski asked Sewell if he could swim, and Sewell said no. So Coveleski pushed him into the lake and rowed to shore. (Source: Coveleski's SABR biography, by Daniel R. Levitt.) It was meant as rookie hazing, and Coveleski laughed loud and hard. I might have regarded it a bit differently, as attempted homicide that only a sadist would find funny. But boys will be boys, right? Ha ha ha, it's so great when you almost kill a vulnerable person for no reason.

Back to the great Cleveland Naps triumph of 1920. Coveleski had one of his best years, with 32 Win Shares, 8.5 WAR, and a 2.49 ERA (154 ERA+) in 315 innings. In the World Series, he pitched three complete-game wins, allowing only 2 runs total. He was the Madison Bumgarner of his day.

The 1920 Naps were also notable for an incident in their August 16 game against the Yankees. Cleveland had a star shortstop named Ray Chapman who did everything well, including hitting, fielding, telling stories, singing, and making friends. Everyone loved him. He was the Derek Jeter of his day (except he could field).

Chapman stood in against Carl Mays, a terrific pitcher and grade-A jerk whom everyone hated. Mays had a very deceptive underhand delivery and loved to pitch inside. As Chapman crowded the plate, Mays threw a fastball that smashed into Chapman's head. Blood poured from Chapman's ear and he collapsed. He was able to leave the field, but his skull was fractured, and he died the next day. It remains the only fatality resulting from baseball play.

This terrible tragedy galvanized baseball to adopt batting helmets … no, of course it didn't! It took another tragic beaning, the one that ended Mickey Cochrane's career in 1937, before enough people seriously considered helmets. The 1941 Dodgers were the first team to mandate their use, and in 1953 the Pirates were the last.

A few years after the 1920 Naps triumph, Coveleski was traded to another historical-underdog pennant-winner, the 1925 Washington Senators. This was the team of Walter Johnson, Sam Rice, and Goose Goslin. In the World Series, the Senators faced yet *another* of my beloved historical-underdog pennant-winners, the Pirates of Pie Traynor, Max Carey, and a top-of-his-game, pre-benching Kiki Cuyler. This time, Coveleski didn't pitch particularly well and the Pirates won the World Series in seven games. Oh well. There's always 1920.

Stan Coveleski had a late start to his career and ended with only 11 full seasons. But he was good enough during those years to register as a solid low-end Hall-of-Famer.

Leon Day[69] (1934-1943, 1946-1952)

	Rank at SP Among Negro Leaguers	Rank Among All Negro Leaguers
SABR	5	16
Monte Irvin	3 Among RHP	NA

As with Christy Mathewson and Mordecai Brown, Satchel Paige and Leon Day had matchups that were big events and became legendary. Paige and Day made for an easy contrast: Paige was thin and lanky while Day was short and stocky. Paige had a big, elaborate leg kick while Day threw with a quick, simple delivery. Paige was a natural showman who lived like a king while Day was quiet and businesslike, both on and off the field. I picture the kids loving Paige while the grumpy old codgers who believed they understood the *real* game favored Day. The codgers got bragging rights most often, as Day won three of the duo's four famous battles.

Day's delivery was actually rather remarkable in a way, in that he didn't have a windup at all. He just chucked it in there from his hip. He was known for his explosive fastballs, which meant a lot of stress was put on just a few arm and shoulder muscles. Predictably, he developed arm trouble after a few years. According to him, the straw that broke the camel's back came when he slipped in the shower in 1937.

And in 1937, Day was only 20 years old. 20! At that point he had already been pitching for four years. I talked before about Steve Busby, Mark Fidrych, Kerry Wood, etc. being overused when they were young; imagine the workloads of Negro Leagues pitchers. They had league games and barnstorming, and then many spent winters playing in the Mexican, Puerto Rican, and Dominican leagues. And many, like Day, didn't have true days of rest between starts, because they played in the field.

---

[69] I couldn't even squeeze this in as a pointless digression, so be happy I went with a footnote instead. Apparently Leon Day is also the name of an unofficial holiday on June 25th, a half year before Christmas. It's not in honor of Leon Day or anyone else named Leon. They went with "Leon" because it's Noel backwards, and "Samtsirhc" is unpronounceable. It's mainly observed by crafters, who start planning their Christmas crafts on Leon Day. That is a true fact that I didn't make up. Six months of planning—those must be some kick-ass crafts. The pitcher Leon Day was a mild-mannered guy, but I like to envision him getting caught up in the excitement every June 25 and joining a mob storming Michael's for sales on colorful pipe cleaners and googly eyes.

I wonder if the injury prevented Day from becoming the best pitcher in Negro League history. Bill James says he was the top starter in the Negro Leagues in 1937, when he went 13-0 with a 3.02 ERA (according to his SABR biography). Day was the ace of the Newark Eagles, which also featured an infield of Mule Suttles (Hall-of-Famer), Willie "Devil" Wells (Hall-of-Famer), Ray Dandridge (Hall-of-Famer), and Dick Seay (not a Hall-of-Famer, but quite good), and was owned by the Hall of Fame's only woman, Effa Manley. After the Homestead Grays and the Kansas City Monarchs, the Newark Eagles are probably the best team in Negro Leagues history.

I'm a bit skeptical about how much damage Day's arm really suffered after 1937; by all accounts he still pitched well for many years. Biographies cite plenty of remarkable post-1937 achievements, including great win-loss records and one start with 19 strikeouts. (Source: Day's entry in the Negro Leagues Baseball Emuseum, http://coe.k-state.edu/annex/nlbemuseum/history/players/day.html.) I'd love to cite Day's numbers before and after 1937, but I've found very little in the way of a career record. Baseball-reference.com logs only 427 of his career innings. As always, if you have better information, email my friend Chris E. Keedei at chrisekeedei@yahoo.com.

Regardless, the sources above clearly believe Leon Day had a Hall-of-Fame career.

Dizzy Dean (1930, 1932-1941, 1947; career ERA+: 131)

	Career	Rank	Peak	Rank	Bests	Top 5s	JAWS	Rank
WAR	44.9	117	42.8	56	1	3	43.9	90
WS	182.1	144	171.8	40	1	3	NA	24

Dizzy Dean was another Leon Day. He was also a phenomenal strikeout machine until he hurt his arm in 1937. Unlike Day, Dean wasn't able to do much after the injury. He ended with 1967.1 career innings, the fewest of any starting pitcher in the Hall. There are 29 HOF starters who pitched more than twice as many innings as Dean.

Was Dean so good during his peak that he deserves the Hall? The Peak rankings are good but not as good as I expected, given Dean's reputation. Maybe that's because the Peak covers a player's seven best years, and Dean pitched for only six full years. If you define a Peak as encompassing a player's top five years, as Bill James does, Dean finishes 42nd among post-1800s pitchers in WAR Peak and 20th in Win Shares Peak. His WSAWS goes from 98th to 93rd, while his JAWS goes from 90th to 87th. That's not much of a change. Why didn't that work?

Remember that the JAWS calculation adds the Career and Peak numbers and then divides by two. When you define the peak as top 5 years instead of top 7, it makes the Peak number smaller. That gives it less weight in the calculation. That's a bad thing for Dizzy Dean, because it means more weight for his low Career number. Let's stick with the top seven.

Maybe the calculation always shortchanges players' peaks? After all, it's the great seasons that push teams to championships. A case could certainly be made that Peak is more important than Career. But for the most part, the two go together. Of the players with the 50 best (7-year) Peak WAR numbers, all but seven are among the top 60 in Career WAR.

The seven with high Peaks and low Career totals are Sandy Koufax, Wilbur Wood, Nap Rucker, Noodles Hahn, Dave Stieb, George Uhle, and Johan Santana. Koufax is the only one in the Hall, though Santana has a chance if his arm miraculously heals and he piles up more seasons (and thus gains too much career WAR to remain on this list).

So even if you and I think Peak should matter more than Career, the Hall of Fame apparently does not. As I've said enough times to fill a book (it has), I am following the Hall's lead on what constitutes a Hall-of-Famer. Its selections are slanted toward players with good career totals, so that's what I do too.

Note that Dizzy Dean does not make that list of top-50 WAR Peaks. His Peak was actually not good enough. Like Jack Chesbro, Dizzy was known for one big seasonal win total, 30 in 1934. It was a great performance, the best among all pitchers according to both WAR and Win Shares. But it's not one of the all-time best pitching seasons; it's tied for the 112th-best WAR among starting pitchers since 1901. (Win Shares can't help us with comparisons like that, since it gives more value to pitchers who threw more innings. That gives starters from 100 years ago a huge edge. As I've mentioned, this is more valid, since the more you pitch, the more valuable you are. But it makes it hard to compare pitchers across eras.)

Dean had maybe three other great seasons, two other good ones, and that's about it. Let's compare his seasonal WAR totals to those guys I mentioned above:

Seasons	Dizzy Dean	Sandy Koufax	Wilbur Wood	Noodles Hahn	Nap Rucker	Dave Stieb	George Uhle	Johan Santana
Best	9.0	10.7	11.7	8.9	8.7	7.9	8.8	8.6
2nd best	7.2	10.3	10.7	8.5	8.2	7.7	7.5	7.5
3rd best	7.1	8.6	7.5	7.8	7.8	7.0	7.3	7.2
4th best	6.6	7.4	5.6	7.8	7.2	6.8	6.1	7.1
5th best	5.6	5.7	5.4	6.5	5.8	5.8	5.5	4.8
6th best	4.7	4.4	3.7	6.4	4.8	4.9	4.6	4.2
7th best	2.5	2.1	2.6	0.1	2.1	4.5	3.7	3.7

Why is Dizzy Dean one of the more well-known Hall-of-Famers when his numbers look less impressive than a bunch of pitchers no one really thinks should be in (apart from Koufax)? There must be more to him than just that one 30-win season, right?

There is, and it starts with "p" and ends in "y" and the second letter is "e" and the third letter is "r" and the fourth letter is "s" and the rest of it is "onalit" and it's spelled "PERSONALITY"! Dean consistently led the league in Personality Above Replacement. He was a cocksure hayseed, bursting with boasts and anecdotes that the newspapers loved to recount.

Even his career-ending injury inspired a typical Dizzy Dean story. During the 1937 All-Star Game, Earl Averill hit a liner that struck Dean's foot. After being told that the toe was fractured, Dean allegedly said "Fractured, hell! The damn thing's broken!" (All stories taken from Dean's Wikipedia page.)

One of his more famous quotes is "If ya done it, it ain't braggin'." People still say a modified version, "It's not bragging if it's true." You must remember that Dean didn't have much education, so perhaps he didn't have a good handle on what the word "bragging" means. Cuz see, it is *definitely* bragging if you did it. In fact, that's the only way it could be considered bragging. If you didn't do it, then it's lying. That's quite different.

I wonder, by the way, if the same people who relished Dizzy Dean's braggadocio were the ones who were terribly disturbed by the boasts of Reggie Jackson. To most whites of the time, the boastful white country boy was endearing while the boastful black man was threatening. I bet African-Americans felt the reverse about both.

To be fair, Dizzy's "If ya done it, it ain't braggin'" quote sometimes referred to his reputation for making bold predictions and then fulfilling them. In 1934, the Cardinals rotation featured both Dizzy and his brother Paul, who got the nickname "Daffy." Paul Dean was a quiet, serious person, probably the least daffy person in the nation at the time, but no one let that get in the way of a good mythology. Before the season, Dizzy allegedly said "Me an' Paul are going to win 45 games." When Paul Dean threw a no-hitter to win the 45th game between the two brothers, Dizzy allegedly told him "If I'd a-known you was gonna throw a no-hitter, I'd-a thrown one too!"

I realize that I'm using the word "allegedly" a lot when recounting Dean's quotes. To me they sound like they were written or at least punched up after the fact, by either Dean or a sportswriter. Every Dizzy Dean story seems carefully constructed to be told between pitches of a ballgame. Just take a real incident, tack on a quote that communicates what people wanted to believe about Dean, and voila! You have an anecdote.

As Bill James wrote in his own comment on Dean in "The New Historical Baseball Abstract," the funny, guileless hick was a very popular archetype in the first half of the 1900s. This was a time of urbanization, when people were leaving farms and moving to cities. In 1900, 60% of the American population lived in rural areas. In 1940, it was down to 44%, and it kept dropping. Americans were increasingly attracted to new technology, adopting new urban ways, and becoming educated. But they still missed the simple country life.

People like Dizzy Dean represented what they left behind, in a fun, cartoonish way. Dean defied the Anglo-Saxon ethos of dignity, humility, and self-restraint by seemingly being blissfully unaware of it. City folk could simultaneously laugh at, and with, Dizzy Dean. And it wasn't just Dean; an early strain of what would become stand-up comedy consisted of people like Will Rogers and Andy Griffith telling long, country-fied monologues. This extended into 1950s television, which, as James noted, was filled with funny hicks: "The Beverly Hillbillies," "The Andy Griffith Show," "Green Acres," "Gomer Pyle," etc.

Does anything like this exist nowadays? In my childhood, "Hee Haw" and those "Ernest" movies were in this vein. But that was 30 years ago. Larry the Cable Guy is the only recent example I can think of; I suppose Jeff Foxworthy as well. Now only 19.3% of the country lives in rural areas, and most of us don't have nostalgia for a way of life we never experienced.

Dizzy Dean went on to a very successful broadcasting career, spreading his personality across the nation. His fame was undeniable. Like Rabbit Maranville, his playing career may have been outside the Hall-of-Fame standards, but I have to invoke "It's the Hall of Fame, not the Hall of Stats" and keep him in.

Martin Dihigo (1922-1950)

	Rank at SP Among Negro Leaguers	Rank Among All Negro Leaguers
SABR	2	8
Monte Irvin	5 Among RHP	NA

When I was a teenager, I decided Martin Dihigo was one of my favorite players. I was fascinated by the fact that he had Hall-of-Fame numbers as both a pitcher and a hitter, like if Babe Ruth kept pitching and playing the outfield on his off days. Also, one of Dihigo's barnstorming teams, the Cuban X-Giants,[70] had a super-cool hat. It had a white top, a black bill, and a big bold orange X. I managed to get a reproduction of one and wore it rarely to keep it pristine. I still own it, and it only comes out for weddings and funerals.

This was the early 1990s, when Malcolm X's popularity was experiencing a post-mortem renaissance. People were wearing all sorts of X hats. So no one looked at my cool hat and said "Hey, that's Cuban X-Giants, the team of Martin Dihigo, right?" Not that I minded; I loved Malcolm X too. I used to skip gym class to go read "The Autobiography of Malcolm X" in the library. Even when I rebelled, I managed to make it more nerdy than it would be if I'd followed the rules.

That Malcolm X craze was fun, by the way. When is another historical figure going to become the rage with the kids? Aren't we overdue for Teddy Roosevelt to become hip again? You could call him "T-Rock" and do some of those "rapping" songs about his groundbreaking environmental protections. I'll start you off: "Hey my name is Eddie, and I'm here to say, T-Rock was dope in a progressive way!" (Folds arms over chest in that way that rappers haven't done in 25 years.)

Despite deciding he was one of my favorite players, I didn't learn a lot about Martin Dihigo beyond what was on his Hall-of-Fame plaque. Since then, I've done some reading. Dihigo excelled in every imaginable way, in every league available to him, for a very long time. He played every position except catcher in the Negro Leagues, Mexican League, Venezuela, and the Cuban Winter League from 1922 to 1950.

Dihigo's best year in the U.S. was probably 1935, when he played for the New York Cubans of the Negro National League. According to his baseball-reference.com biography, he hit .335 and hit 9 home runs, the latter of which was third-best in the league, tied with Oscar Charleston and behind only Mule Suttles and Josh Gibson. On the mound he had a 3.54 RA (run average, not ERA), fifth in the league, and a .700 winning percentage, which tied him for fourth. He also stole six bases, tying him for fourth-best. There was no statistical category in either hitting or pitching in which he didn't excel.

Also, he managed his team that year, and for many years after. He was a native Cuban, but spoke English fluently. His intelligence and easygoing nature made him respected and beloved throughout

[70] I've noted this before, but you might have missed it: "Cuban" and "Giants" were both code words meaning it was an all-black team. In the original incarnation of the Cuban X-Giants, none of the players were actually Cuban. Cuba in those days was seen as a place of romance and sophistication, so calling a team "Cuban" gave it a certain je ne sais quoi. They were called the X-Giants because they were made up of players who had defected from a team called the Cuban Giants.

non-white baseball. My teenage whims may have been on to something; I feel like if I could go back in time and watch anyone play, I would choose Martin Dihigo.

Dihigo had another great year in the Negro National League in 1936, but most of his glories were in the Cuban and Mexican leagues. He is the only member of the Baseball Halls of Fame of Cuba, Mexico, and the United States/Canada (that's ours). In Cuba he is known as "El Inmortal" (the Immortal) and his legend survives to this day. If Negro Leaguers could be "first ballot" Hall-of-Famers, Dihigo would be one.

Don Drysdale (1956-1969; career ERA+: 121)

	Career	Rank	Peak	Rank	Bests	Top 5s	JAWS	Rank
WAR	67.1	32	44.7	43	0	4	55.9	36
WS	257.9	47	165.8	47	1	5	NA	29

In "Whatever Happened to the Hall of Fame" (aka "the Politics of Glory"), Bill James went into incredible depth in analyzing Don Drysdale's Hall-of-Fame credentials (p. 388-422). After the exhaustive study, he decided Drysdale doesn't belong. Just a few years later, in "The New Historical Baseball Abstract," he ranked Drysdale 29th among all post-1800s starting pitchers. I think he changed his mind.

James's long analysis of Drysdale in "Whatever Happened to the Hall of Fame" is very good and full of interesting insights. I think it ended up wrong on Drysdale, because, when it was written, James didn't have Win Shares at his disposal. He had created a whole bunch of other numbers to use for Hall-of-Fame standards, but they weren't very good.

You can still see a few of them near the bottom of each baseball-reference.com player page. "Hall of Fame Monitor" and "Hall of Fame Standards" are examples. The main problem with them is that they just award points based on the conventional numbers that players collected. There's no adjustment for different time periods like there is in WAR and Win Shares. They don't cover defense and they don't make allowances for more defense-centric positions. They end up looking reasonable for the best of the best, but that's not of much help. We already knew Willie Mays and Babe Ruth were great. When you get down to the cases that we really need guidance on, they're useless. They'll tell you that Carlos Lee (35 in the Standards number, 78 in Monitor) was better than deserving Hall-of-Famer Elmer Flick (31 and 64), and lots of other weird results.

I'm certainly no Bill James, and "Whatever Happened to the Hall of Fame" is a better book than mine. He's the Darwin, and I'm the assistant biology professor who hopes to publish enough to not perish. Along those lines, I like to think I am building on his work by starting with simpler, better Hall-of-Fame standards. My approach makes for much quicker, and I believe more valid, assessments of Hall-of-Fame worthiness. And it leaves room for lots of hilariously fun asides and digressions! We all love those, right guys? Right? Hello?

Speaking of which ... let's not do that for Don Drysdale. Like Jim Bunning, he is a solid mid-to-low-end Hall-of-Famer. Moving on.

Red Faber (1914-1933; career ERA+: 119)

	Career	Rank	Peak	Rank	Bests	Top 5s	JAWS	Rank
WAR	64.8	35	40.6	68	2	2	52.7	47
WS	291.1	31	163.3	49	2	4	NA	48

Red Faber is a perfectly serviceable Hall-of-Famer. No one would mistake him for Walter Johnson, but he had a few great years, a few more good ones, and a long enough career. His record might not impress most fans, but he's in the range.

Faber's conventional numbers suffer from some bad timing. His two superstar years were for the 1921 and 1922 White Sox, which had just been gutted by the Black Sox scandal. In 1920, Shoeless Joe Jackson, Hap Felsch, Eddie Cicotte, etc., led the White Sox to a 96-58 record. In 1921 they were all banned for life, and the team dropped to 62-92. They would have lost 100 games easily if not for Faber's 11.3 WAR and 37 Win Shares. That WAR is 23rd best among all post-1800s pitching seasons, better than any season by Sandy Koufax, Tom Seaver, Christy Mathewson, Nolan Ryan, and a bunch of other more famous pitchers. Faber's win-loss record that year was 25-15; with something better than the league's second-worst offense behind him, he could have won 30.

But when Faber played badly, his timing may have actually been good. In 1919 he came back from a tour of duty in World War I with a bad case of influenza. That was a serious matter; the 1918 flu pandemic[71] killed 50 to 100 million people worldwide. A weakened Faber played so poorly in 1919 that he sat out of the World Series. Thus he received no overtures to throw games, survived the scandal, and kept pitching for the White Sox through 1933. Granted, Faber was an honest gentleman, and probably would have avoided temptation by sticking with the Eddie Collins/Ray Schalk clan of "Clean Sox." (Source: Faber's SABR biography, by Brian Cooper.)

Much the way all Native American players before World War II were called "Chief," all red-headed players were called "Red." Faber's real first name was Urban, and he was fully of Luxembourgian descent. Luxembourg is one of those tiny countries tucked into the European mainland that make you wonder, "How did they not get conquered?" Luxembourg has around 550,000 people, fewer than the metro area of Toledo, Ohio. But it's a virtual superpower compared to other European countries Andorra (85,000 people), Liechtenstein (37,000), San Marino (32,000), Monaco (30,000), and Vatican City (800).

The Faber family spoke German at home and at church, as did millions of immigrants in the pre-war years. These communities had newspapers entirely in German and many in the first generation never learned English. Immigrants to the U.S. tend to follow the same pattern: The first generation stick to their old language and ways, the second generation try to straddle the old ways and the new, and the

[71] The 1918 flu epidemic is often referred to as the Spanish flu, which is a pretty bad name. People were dying in large numbers across the world, but government censors wouldn't allow American newspapers to print the real death tolls from the warring countries of Germany, Britain, France, and the U.S. They thought that would minimize morale. But Spain stayed neutral in the war, so papers were free to report all the flu deaths there. This made it look like the flu was concentrated mainly in Spain.

third assimilate and become boring ol' Americans.[72] It happened with the Germans, Italians, Chinese, Japanese, etc., etc., and it is already happening with Mexicans and other Latin Americans. Every time a new group arrives, people get scared that the newcomers won't learn English or adopt American ways. Every time, those fears prove unfounded. Everything old is new again.

The Germans may have assimilated a little more quickly than usual, thanks to World War I. Anti-German sentiment was widespread, and everyone with an accent was suspected of being a spy. Overnight a lot of "Schmidt"s became "Smith"s and "Mueller"s became "Miller"s. Sauerkraut was renamed "victory cabbage," and that's not a joke. This was echoed about 100 years later when french fries were renamed "freedom fries" in congressional cafeterias because France objected to the U.S.'s involvement in Iraq. Everything old is new again.

Speaking of old and new, Faber was old enough to get past the new (terrible segue!) restrictions on doctoring baseballs in 1920. Like Stan Coveleski, Red Faber was grandfathered in and got to keep throwing spitballs, though he didn't throw many. In a way, it seems like Faber and Coveleski had an unfair advantage that should affect their Hall-of-Fame cases. But then, those were the rules at the time. Faber and Coveleski played by the rules, put in great performances, and that's that. Red Faber belongs.

Bob Feller (1936-1941, 1945-1956; career ERA+: 122)

	Career	Rank	Peak	Rank	Bests	Top 5s	JAWS	Rank
WAR	63.6	37	51.8	22	3	4	57.7	28
WS	292.4	30	192.2	17	1	5	NA	11

Almost every baseball star of the 1940s served in World War II. Some joined up in 1942, some in 1943, some in 1944. Most waited until they were drafted. Many were assigned to posts far from the action and spent their time playing baseball to entertain the troops.

Not Bob Feller. He was the first American professional athlete to enlist in the military. Because his father was dying, he was offered a military exemption. He refused to take it, and pushed to get into combat. He was assigned to the USS Alabama and fought in the Battle of Tarawa and the Battle of the Philippine Sea. Both were critical in defeating Japan.

This level of self-sacrifice was perhaps not what you might predict if you met Bob Feller in 1936, when he was a 17-year-old kid and cocky as hell. He had good reason to be cocky: He was already a nationwide phenomenon. Plucked out of an Iowa high school by legendary scout Cy Slapnicka, he struck out 15 batters in his first major-league start. He struck out 17 just a few weeks later, tying Dizzy Dean's then-record for a single game. After the season was over, he returned to Iowa to complete his senior year of high school. The governor of Iowa greeted him as he rolled into town. (Source: Feller's Wikipedia page.) I would imagine Bob Feller did not have trouble getting a date for the prom.

---

[72] This idea is based on "Assimilation in American Life," by Milton Gordon. My encapsulation is such a gross oversimplification that it would probably get some academics' heads spinning with rage. But hey, by shoehorning it in, I'm already stretching this book's mandate beyond its breaking point. Be thankful it's getting any mention at all, eggheads.

During his first start in 1937, Feller hurt his arm, and the Cleveland brass immediately shut him down. They knew what a treasure they had, and did not want to jeopardize it under any circumstances. They may not have paid attention to pitch counts in those days, but the perspective was the same: You have to be very careful with young arms.

Still, Feller's arm may have been overtaxed at a young age, as his performance dropped off when he hit his 30s. He may have had an even earlier decline if not for his military service, spanning ages 23-26, preserving his arm somewhat. But judging by his behavior during the war, I'm sure he wasn't concerned about it; he probably would have torn out his own rotator cuff if it meant he could fight. Definite Hall-of-Famer.

Whitey Ford (1950, 1953-1967; career ERA+: 133)

	Career	Rank	Peak	Rank	Bests	Top 5s	JAWS	Rank
WAR	57.3	60	34.7	133	0	1	46.0	76
WS	258.8	45	152.1	71	0	4	NA	21

Like Bob Feller, Whitey Ford served overseas during some of his most crucial ballplaying years: Ford was 22 and 23 when he served in the Korean War. It is known as "The Forgotten War," which is a disgrace. More than 2.5 million people died in the conflict. That deserves remembering.

Ford's years of service bump his JAWS into low-end Hall-of-Fame level. I'm surprised he's that low. He remains quite famous as the ace of the Yankees in the era when they were so good it's irritating. In Ford's first 13 years with the club, the Yankees reached the World Series 11 times. Ford was superb in those World Series, scoring a 2.47 ERA in 146 innings. If I actually thought Ford was on the borderline, that would push him into the Hall.

Why are Ford's WAR totals so low? Through the 1950s he didn't pitch many innings by the standards of the day. Manager Casey Stengel liked to have very large, fluid rotations, often six or more starters. All contributed relief appearances, even Ford. As soon as Ralph Houk took over as manager in 1961, all that went out the window: Ford led the league in innings and got his first 20-win season (25-4, for the 22nd best winning percentage ever). In 1964, he finally had a WAR good enough to rank among the top five of major-league pitchers.

Was Stengel dumb to not use Ford more? It's hard to argue with the results. In the seven years in which Ford was his ace, the Yankees won five pennants and three championships. Under Houk, they were just as good for four years but then collapsed into their first sustained period of losing since 1918.

Casey Stengel wasn't just a goofy, folksy quote machine; he was also a strategic genius. By having large starting staffs, Stengel could keep everyone rested while matching starters with situations. As the best pitcher, Whitey Ford always got the toughest opponents. (Source: "The Bill James Guide to Baseball Managers," Bill James, Scribner, p. 192) That kept Ford's numbers more humble, in terms of both wins and ERA.

It was a pretty bold strategy; I wonder how he got away with it. People tend to get very upset when you go against the grain in pitcher usage, especially if it affects someone's stats. It reminds me of the time in 2003 that the Red Sox tried to do a closer by committee. As soon as one reliever had a bad day, all of New England reacted as if George Steinbrenner had unplugged Ted Williams' cryogenic head and used it as a soccer ball. Never mind that a closer by committee might actually win a team a few more games if done right, but let's leave that discussion for the relievers section.

For now, Whitey Ford is a no-doubt Hall-of-Famer.

Bill Foster (1923-1937)

	Rank at SP Among Negro Leaguers	Rank Among All Negro Leaguers
SABR	6	18
Monte Irvin	1 Among LHP	NA

It's hard to talk about Bill Foster without also talking about his half-brother Rube. People sometimes compare Rube and Bill Foster to Harry and George Wright. Rube was a player, manager, owner, league president, and arguably the most important figure in Negro League history. (SABR's list of important figures puts Satchel Paige, Buck Leonard, Cool Papa Bell, and Oscar Charleston ahead of Rube; yeah, OK, it's hard to argue against those guys.) Rube set up the first truly organized, professional American black league, the Negro National League, in which his half-brother Bill was a terrific player. Similarly, Harry Wright organized the first fully, openly professional baseball team, the 1869 Cincinnati Red Stockings. His brother George was the team's star shortstop.

It's not a perfect comparison: Unlike the Wright brothers, the Fosters never played together. Rube was 25 years older than Bill. They were products of the same father and two different women. Bill didn't even meet Rube until his teenage years, when Rube was already a star. And there was some early friction.

Bill was working in the stockyards of Chicago and tried hard to get on the Chicago American Giants, which Rube owned and managed. Rube refused to even give him a tryout. According to his daughter Doris, Rube wanted Bill to get an education and avoid the life of a Negro League ballplayer. It was a hard life, one of constant travel and little pay.

But Bill wouldn't be stopped, and signed with the Memphis Red Sox in 1923. Rube then demanded that Bill play for both the Giants and the Red Sox. Both teams were in the Negro National League, so Bill had to alternate between the two. The Memphis Red Sox didn't want to do this weird player-sharing arrangement, but Rube was also the league president, so they kinda had to. (Source: Bill Foster's entry in the Negro Leagues Baseball eMuseum, http://coe.k-state.edu/annex/nlbemuseum/history/players/fosterw.html)

I can't begin to figure out how this would work logistically. Negro League teams didn't play league games every day, but still, there would be plenty of times when both teams needed Foster. And where did Bill go when the Red Sox and Giants play each other?

Most likely it worked out however Rube Foster wanted it to. In 1926, Bill was moved permanently to the Giants, against his will. People often accused Rube of rigging the league to the advantage of his own team, and you can see why. It's a clear conflict of interest to be both a league president and an owner/manager of one of the same league's teams.

Around this time, Rube's life was collapsing. In 1926, he was confined to an insane asylum, and he died there in 1930. Rube Foster biographer Larry Lester rather delicately states that "A possible association with La Grange's Chicken Ranch in [Rube's] youth may have subsequently led to his death from syphilis in 1930." ("Rube Foster In His Time," McFarland, p. 231) This was the same "Chicken Ranch" made famous by the Broadway show and movie "The Best Little Whorehouse in Texas."

Sometimes Rube's descent into madness is blamed on exposure to a gas leak that nearly asphyxiated him. It certainly could have contributed to his problems, but syphilis almost always leads to insanity. The gas leak explanation seems like an attempt to cover up an indelicate truth.

Meanwhile, Bill was going gangbusters for his half-brother's team. In 1926, he went 16-6 with a 2.62 ERA in 226 innings. The next four years were much the same. Then he joined the Homestead Grays, which was already a superteam of ridiculous proportions: Oscar Charleston, Josh Gibson, Jud Wilson, Smokey Joe Williams, Ted "Double-Duty" Radcliffe. Wow! That's five Hall-of-Famers plus Radcliffe, who doesn't have a bad case for the Hall.

Rube Foster's unrequited dream was to see the champion of the Negro Leagues play the World Series winner each year. Imagine if those Grays then had to play the 1931 A's of Jimmie Foxx, Mickey Cochrane, Al Simmons, and Lefty Grove. It would have been awesome. Now that would have been a true World Series. Well, actually, no it wouldn't. Maybe if the winner of that then went on the play Cuba's best team, and then Mexico's best, etc.

I guess I'm just describing the World Baseball Classic. I wish that had started a long time ago. I love that thing. I don't care if it interferes with preparations for the MLB season; it's more important to have an international contest. That's how it works in soccer, cricket, and every other truly international sport. It's an old joke that Americans only learn about other countries when we start bombing them. Playing games against them would be a much better method.

At least they had exhibition games in Bill Foster's days that would pit all-stars from white baseball against all-stars of black baseball. These games were very successful, and players on both sides gained tremendous respect for each other. For pretty much every Negro League Hall-of-Famer, there's a quote from Honus Wagner or Charlie Gehringer or someone like that saying he could have been a sensation in the white leagues. Such games planted the idea that African-Americans deserved a shot, and helped lay the groundwork for integration.

After their initial disagreement about Bill's chosen profession, Rube and Bill Foster reconciled. When Rube legally incorporated the Negro National League in 1924, Bill was named as majority stockholder. And when Rube died, Bill had some very kind words, saying "you had to respect the man, and you had to love the man." (Lester, p. 160)

Bill Foster seems like a pretty good dude, and, more importantly, a very good pitcher. Hall-of-Famer.

Bob Gibson (1959-1975; career ERA+: 127)

	Career	Rank	Peak	Rank	Bests	Top 5s	JAWS	Rank
WAR	89.9	16	61.6	9	3	5	75.8	11
WS	319.3	20	201.5	9	2	7	NA	8

Bob Gibson had an incredible 1.12 ERA in 1968. It's one of the more well-known pitching stats. It's not the best ERA since 1900, but does rank third. In 1914, Dutch Leonard had a 0.96 ERA, and in 1906, Mordecai Brown logged a 1.06. Just a tiny notch below Gibson's number are Walter Johnson's 1913 and Christy Mathewson's 1909, both at 1.14.

You might notice that all those seasons besides Gibson's occurred in the dead-ball era. In fact, among the top 30 seasonal ERAs, Gibson's is the only one to occur after 1919. That makes the list of best ERAs a boring one; it doesn't really tell you anything except that pitching was very dominant in the dead-ball era and Bob Gibson was very dominant in 1968.

And even 1968 was kind of a dead-ball-era kind of year. That was the season Carl Yastrzemski led the league with a .301 batting average. The entire National League had a 2.99 ERA. Several pitchers throughout history have led their leagues with ERAs above 2.99. With context taken into account, is even Gibson's 1.12 really as great as it looks?

Yes it is, if baseball-reference.com's ERA+ is to be believed. Gibson's ERA+ in 1968 is sixth-best ever among seasons after 1900. Dutch Leonard's 1906 ERA+ is the second-best, Johnson's 1913 ERA+ is fifth, Brown's 1906 is seventh, and Mathewson's 1914 is tied for fourteenth. Even when you account for the pitching-heavy contexts, these were all amazing seasons.

But wait ... there are some gaps in there. Whose ERA+ was first all-time? Whose was third, and whose was fourth? This gets to the good part about using ERA+ instead of ERA. The all-time best ERA+ after 1900 was Pedro Martinez's in 2000. He had a 1.74 ERA when the American League was at 4.91, more than twice as high as the National League in 1968. Gibson may have pitched more, but inning for inning, Pedro was even better than Bob was in 1968.

Third and fourth best were Greg Maddux in 1994 and 1995, respectively. Maddux had ERAs of 1.56 and 1.63 in leagues with ERAs of 4.21 and 4.18. In terms of regular old ERA, Maddux's and Martinez's numbers score well below a big pile of several dozen dead-ball-era guys. But when you put everything on a level playing field with ERA+, you see how exceptional those two pitchers really were.

Anyway, this comment was supposed to be about Bob Gibson. Namely, Bob Gibson the Brewers pitcher from 1983-1987 who wasn't terribly good. This Bob Gibson was some lame white guy who began his professional baseball career in 1979, four years after the more famous and talented Bob Gibson retired. Why in the name of Bob Gibson (the elder) would Bob Gibson (the younger) go by a name already made famous by Bob Gibson (the elder)? Maybe he had always been called Bob by family and friends. But at some point in his career he could have switched to Bobby, or Rob, or Robert, or Stinky, or Thafunkeehomosapien,[73] or anything—anything would have been better. Did Bob the Lesser want every single fan at the ballpark to hear his name, do a double-take, realize that some lame white guy was coming into the game, and then feel deflated?

Take a look his card at http://www.vintagecardprices.com/pics/1958/120499.jpg. Is it possible to look at that face and *not* feel depressed? Those vacant eyes, staring blankly on nothing but the inexorable futility of existence. That frown, so devoid of effort, as if it were the true resting state of all human experience once the fruitless frenzy of society has dissolved into mist. Even if that guy were named Zapp Funkypants, you would come away from that card knowing within your core that life is a meaningless void. Tack on the fact that that face shares a name with one of the most

---

[73] Reference explanation: Del the Funky Homosapien is a terrific rapper. I tried to go by Thafunkeehomosapien during my college graduation. The administration always asks graduates how they want their names read when they walk across the stage and receive their diplomas. I tried really hard to convince them that my parents originally gave me the middle name "Thafunkeehomosapien." I said I was always embarrassed by it. But my parents would really be touched if they heard it. Only when I heard my name called during the ceremony did I discover that no one in the administration had bought my story. It was a very disappointing graduation.

thrilling, powerful figures in sports history, and it all falls into the realm of parody. Only the most junior and unsophisticated "Saturday Night Live" writer could have invented such a blatant antithesis to the real Bob Gibson.

Speaking as someone writing under a fake name because my real one is a cruel burden on English-speaking society, I can't fathom why anyone would choose to confuse people with his or her name. There's a reason I didn't choose "Bill James" as my nom de plume (though some writer of mystery novels did, which makes it annoying to search for Bill James books on Amazon).

I suppose it gave Bob Gibson (fils) a bit more notoriety than your typical bland mid-'80s middle reliever. And it did secure his spot on my "No, I'm the Other One" team. All of the below were real ballplayers:

C: John Edwards (1961-1974)
1B: George Burns (1914-1929)
2B: Bill Murray (1917)
SS: Mike Tyson (1972-1981)
LF: George Burns (1911-1925: Both George Burnses were quite good. This one came close to a Hall-of-Fame career.)
CF: Ethan Allen (1926-1938)
RF: Eddie Murphy (1912-1926)
SP: Phil Collins (1923-1935)
RP: Bob Gibson (1983-1987)

It's not a great team, but it would make a heck of a party. I'm not sure if Ethan Allen and Mike Tyson would find much to talk about. But maybe if you brought in Jack Daniels (left fielder, 1952) and Johnny Walker (first baseman, 1919-1921) it wouldn't matter.

OK, enough grab-ass. Bob Gibson, the real one, is a central Hall-of-Famer.

Tom Glavine (1987-2008; career ERA+: 118)

	Career	Rank	Peak	Rank	Bests	Top 5s	JAWS	Rank
WAR	81.4	22	44.3	47	1	1	62.9	23
WS	316.2	22	150.4	77	0	5	NA	51

It's well-established nowadays that a pitcher can really only control three things: walks, strikeouts, and home runs. If a pitcher can limit walks and homers and get lots of strikeouts, he can succeed. Once a ball is hit in play, it's out of his hands. Then it's all up to the defense. For the most part, pitchers can't control anything about how a ball in play travels, particularly whether or not it is hit at a fielder. Extreme groundball pitchers can cheat the system a little bit, as can knuckleball pitchers. But for the most part, pitching comes down to BB, HR, and SO, the three so-called "peripherals" (though they are actually more central to pitching than ERA or wins).

Since sabermetrician Voros McCracken figured this out in 1999, it's been proven again and again. If a pitcher has a good ERA one year, but didn't limit walks or homers well or strike out many batters, you can bet the farm on him having a bad follow-up. In that good year he either had lots of luck, an amazing defense behind him, or both. New stats like FIP (fielding-independent pitching) and BABIP (batting average on balls in play) capitalize on this truism and are used by all major league clubs in their decision-making.

Tom Glavine managed a Hall-of-Fame career despite never being terribly remarkable in any of these so-called peripheral numbers. He could strike out a few, but never a ton. He wasn't great at limiting walks. I suppose he had some good years in limiting home runs, allowing fewer than 10 in 1992 and 1995. Still, I have to wonder if he would have ended up as more of a Jamie Moyer if he hadn't pitched for the 1990s Braves. If he had spent his career on the Mariners, would Glavine have had five 20-win seasons, leading the league each time, and ended above 300 for his career?

Not that there's anything wrong with being Jamie Moyer. Both he and Glavine were exceptional in terms of durability and longevity, which can be just as important as lots of strikeouts. Maybe Glavine was more of a Don Sutton, very good for a very long time but seldom dominating. It took Sutton five years to get into the Hall, while Glavine was accepted on his first try with 91.9% of the ballots. All those 20-win seasons will make any baseball fan a bit weak in the knees. Both Glavine and Sutton clearly deserve the Hall.

Lefty Gomez (1930-1943; career ERA+: 125)

	Career	Rank	Peak	Rank	Bests	Top 5s	JAWS	Rank
WAR	38.4	165	35.6	122	0	2	37.0	152
WS	185.3	141	148.5	82	1	2	NA	58

Hmpf. Harumpf, even. Lefty Gomez had a few great years for a few great Yankees teams. In 1934 he had the best WAR and Win Shares totals among American League pitchers. (That was Dizzy Dean's big year in the NL.) In 1937 he had the best Win Shares in all of baseball, while WAR has him second best behind another Lefty G., Mr. Grove. Gomez had a few other good performances, but ended with only ten full SP years. I think we have another Jack Chesbro, or maybe another Dizzy Dean.

Maybe more of a Dean. Gomez was a well-known after-dinner speaker, which was a pretty solid line of work in the 1950s. That was when families were perfect and nuclear, and fathers tried to spend as much time as possible away from them by joining men-only clubs. When there, they needed something to do besides drink beer and shoot pool. So guys like Lefty Gomez were brought in to tell a few funny anecdotes and shake everyone's hands.

Gomez took the opposite tack of Dean, getting humor out of self-deprecation instead of braggadocio. When completing a job application after leaving baseball, he filled in the "Reason for leaving last employment" field with "Couldn't get anybody out." After an unidentified white object was found on the moon in 1969, Gomez said "I knew immediately what it was. It was a home run ball hit off of me in 1937 by Jimmie Foxx." (OK, that one's kinda lame. He was probably desperate for new material at that point.)

I prefer the straight-up goofy stuff that got him his nickname, "Goofy." Once he called South Africa just to talk to anyone from the country. He liked to say that he invented a rotating fishbowl so that fish wouldn't have to circle around so much. He loved planes, and once held up a World Series game to watch one fly overhead. (All stories are from Gomez's SABR biography, by C. Paul Rogers III.)

I gave Dizzy Dean a pass because of his fame, which was largely due to his personality. But Dean was the exception to the rules, not a precedent-setter. The best part of "Whatever Happened to the Hall of Fame" is a chapter called "Arguments," in which Bill James shoots down specious justifications that people often use to push their favorites into Hall-of-Fame consideration. One of them is the "If A then B" argument: If player A is in, and player B is like him in some way, then B should be in too. This is terrible reasoning. If a player is similar to a *majority* of Hall-of-Famers, then he's a legitimate candidate. But if we open the door to everyone who is similar to one guy in the Hall, then its membership will quickly swell into the thousands.

And Gomez doesn't even qualify as a B to Dean's A. Bill James ranked Dizzy Dean 24th among post-1800s starters and Lefty Gomez 58th. Dean is 90th in JAWS, which is not good, but Gomez is 158th. Gomez wasn't as famous as Dean, and definitely wasn't so famous that he can overcome those kinds of rankings. I like Gomez's personality a lot more than Dean's, but that's irrelevant.

OK, enough deliberation. Gomez is blindfolded and in front of the firing squad. I've already said "ready" and "aim" and I'm about to say the third word in that sequence … what was it? Fryer? Yeah! Fryyyer, fryer!!!![74]

Oh my goodness, a letter from the governor just came into my hand. It says "What about the postseason?" A rather abrupt letter, but I take his point. Stand down, men.

Lefty Gomez was quite good in the postseason. In his day, that just meant the World Series. Gomez was in five of them, scoring a 2.86 ERA in 50.1 innings. I've said before that postseason performance can add to a player's case. We might need to get more precise about that if Lefty Gomez is to have a chance.

I have no idea how to factor postseason into a person's WAR and Win Shares. But, for the sake of argument, I'll just pull a method out of my, um, head. Let's say it's three times as important as the regular season. Let's give Lefty Gomez another season of 151 innings and a 2.86 ERA. Across Gomez's career, a 2.86 ERA translates to an ERA+ of 146.

That's good, but it's not enough to save him. During Gomez's time, six pitchers had seasons of between 140 and 160 innings and an ERA+ between 136 and 156. Their WARs range from 2.5 to 5.2. That's not going to bump Gomez from 152nd in WAR into a reasonable range.

OK, men, fire. **Lefty Gomez is out.**

Burleigh Grimes (1916-1934; career ERA+: 102)

	Career	Rank	Peak	Rank	Bests	Top 5s	JAWS	Rank
WAR	53.0	75	40.9	67	0	3	47.0	69
WS	285.8	35	181.7	29	0	4	NA	53

Add Burleigh Grimes to the Stan Coveleski/Red Faber pile. Like them, Grimes got to keep throwing the spitball after 1920. Grimes milked that schtick longer than any of the other 17 grandfathered-in

[74] Reference explanation: Even people who know this reference probably won't get it. "Beavis and Butthead" was a brilliant show, and I don't care if you think you're superior to it. In one episode, Beavis and Butthead played with fire, and in real life that supposedly inspired a kid to play with fire himself. As a result, the episode was banned, and Beavis and Butthead were never allowed to say the word "fire" again. In one episode they got jobs in a fast food restaurant and were taught how to use the fryer. Beavis said "Fryer, fryer!!!" in a maniacal way that was an obvious parody of the whole fire situation.

spitballers, still flickin' the sticky icky one in 1934. I swear, were the early 1920s completely dominated by spitballers?

1920 and 1921 were, but then so was 1919, before the ban. In each of those years, the spitballers were responsible for more than 230 Win Shares. See?

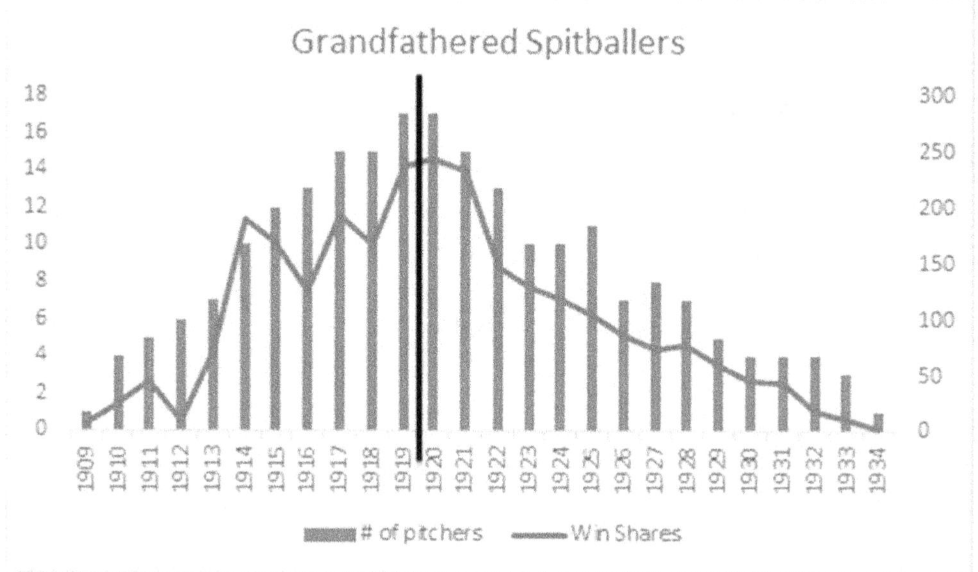

So did throwing the spitball after 1919 give these pitchers a huge advantage? It doesn't really look like it. These guys were grandfathered in specifically because they were at or near their peaks in 1920. And this is the kind of distribution you'd expect from any group of 17 pitchers chosen at their peak, regardless of whether they were throwing a newly banned pitch. If the spitball gave them some large edge, you'd expect a sharp increase in 1920 that lasted several years. Or at least you'd expect the Win Shares totals in 1920 and 1921 (the red line) to peek above the number of pitchers (the blue bars) the way it does in 1914; that would mean more Win Shares per pitcher. A surprising number retired or got injured in the years right after the ban, from 1921-1923.

This quick snapshot at least suggests that the spitball does not confer some huge unfair advantage to pitchers. I wonder if the spitball is really that bad. Ford Frick didn't think so; in 1955, when he was commissioner, he advocated legalizing the spitball. He said there was nothing dangerous about it, which is a good point.

The spitball moves much like a knuckleball, so why is it illegal while the knuckleball is legal? Spit is gross, but that's not a good reason. Is it because the spitball is a lot easier to master than the knuckler? If so, that sounds great to me. I'm a big fan of the knuckleball; I'd like to see more pitchers throw it or something like it.

Granted, in the current pitching-heavy game, few people would advocate a change that could potentially limit offense further. They should have legalized the spitball in 1999 when home runs were so common that the game got silly. That would have been fun. Wouldn't you have enjoyed watching those behemoths try to roid-rage their way through more 70-mph floaters?

One of the best things I ever saw on a baseball field was in a June 28, 1998 game between the Twins and the Cardinals. I was more of a Cardinals fan at the time, so of course I was excited to see Mark McGwire during his record-breaking 70-homer season. The Twins starter was ex-Cardinal Bob

Tewksbury, who kinda looked like your uncle and kinda threw like him too. When McGwire stepped to the plate, to great anticipation, Tewksbury had some very special deliveries for him: three pitches which I swear didn't break 60 on the radar gun. McGwire swung massively and missed wildly on each. I was tickled pink, but most of the crowd didn't notice what Tewksbury had done and were sad that McGwire didn't hit a homer. My point is that everyone except me is an f****** idiot. In the Steroid Era I definitely would have enjoyed more matchups like that.

Anyway, Burleigh Grimes is another pitcher that the average fan would think was below the line for the Hall, but that's only because the average fan is a f******* c********** s************ z********** ø********* moron. Grimes may not have made many headlines or produced many awe-inducing conventional numbers, but he pitched very well for a good long time. He's a low-end Hall-of-Famer.

Lefty Grove (1925-1941; career ERA+: 148)

	Career	Rank	Peak	Rank	Bests	Top 5s	JAWS	Rank
WAR	103.6	7	63.6	6	5	11	83.6	7
WS	391.7	8	224.7	6	4	11	NA	2

Like Earl Averill, Lefty Grove spent some prime years in the minor leagues because his team had no interest in letting him go to the majors. From 1920 to 1924, Grove was the star of the AA Baltimore Orioles, then at the highest level of minor league competition. Grove went 108-36 with a 2.96 ERA at ages 20-24. Major-league teams were desperate to get him, but Baltimore manager Jack Dunn wasn't selling.

These were the days when many minor-league clubs could choose whom to sell to the majors and for what price. The Orioles played in a big city (8th in the U.S. according to the 1920 census) and had lots of fans -- why should they sacrifice their chances for glory just to make some so-called "big-league" club better?

Being an independent minor-league team meant the Orioles could play to win. They didn't have to trudge through games that were basically just exhibitions to provide exercise for the charges of their major-league overlords. Nowadays, everyone playing for Rochester is just auditioning to be in the bigs. It would be nice if at least someone there were trying to playing for the glory of Rochester. It would be nice if someone were happy to be there.

Here in St. Paul, Minnesota, the world's greatest city (OK, that was a bit much, sorry -- it's nicer than you might think, is all I'm saying), we have a very popular independent league team called the Saints. The Saints aren't popular because they play great baseball; they don't. They're popular, in large part, because their fans don't have to watch stars getting yanked away to higher levels as soon as they get good. The Saints get to play for their own pennant race, and their roster decisions are not dictated by a distant major-league master. Major-league baseball may be healthier than ever, but minor-league baseball was much healthier 100 years ago, when teams were more independent and smaller cities got to have their own heroes.

What made the minor leagues so slavish to the majors? As with everything that has ever existed, there is a multitude of reasons, all interacting with each other in a complex morass of causality, and it takes a whole book to give it justice. So let's not do that. One of the reasons I like to yak about goes back to that sweet, sweet anti-trust exemption gifted to the American and National Leagues by the

U.S. Supreme Court in 1922. Being a federally sanctioned monopoly brings lots of money and stability. Minor-league teams didn't have any of that. So minor-league owners were willing to make deals with major-league teams that exchanged an easy, steady stream of players for an easy, steady stream of cash. I can hardly blame them; I have a family to feed, and I probably would have done the same thing.

Point is, Lefty Grove's days with the AA Orioles should be added to his Hall-of-Fame resume. When you do that, you realize he has a good case for being the best pitcher ever. Maybe it's hard to top Walter Johnson, but Grove was better than Cy Young, Christy Mathewson, Grover Cleveland Pete Whatever Else Alexander, Warren Spahn, Bob Gibson, Greg Maddux, Roger Clemens, etc., etc. Grove played during the live-ball era, so he didn't have any Gibsonian ERAs. But he led the league in ERA nine times, the most by far (Roger Clemens is second with six ERA titles).

He should be better known. I have two gauges for the famousness of all-time greats: the 1999 All-Century Team voting and the Sporcle quiz in which you name as many Hall-of-Famers as you can think of.

The All-Century team involved average fans voting for the best players at each position. Grove finished 18th among 26 pitcher candidates, below Nolan Ryan and Whitey Ford and barely above Dizzy Dean, all of whom are piles of week-old dog puke compared to Grove (more about Ryan's incredible overratedness in his comment). Grove had to be added after the fact by a panel of baseball historians. (Source: All-Century Team final voting, ESPN.com, October 23, 1999.)

The Sporcle quiz represents a sample of nerdier baseball fans, who went to the trouble to try to name as many HOFers as they could think of in 20 minutes. Grove got much the same treatment as he did with the All-Century Team. He was named by 59.9% of baseball nerds, which ranked 21st among starting pitchers. Whitey Ford, Nolan Ryan and Dizzy Dean all got more correct guesses than Grove, as did Catfish Hunter, who couldn't hold Grove's jock if it had handles and were slathered with a fungus that adheres to human skin.

Add Lefty Grove to the all-time underrated team along with Eddie Collins and Tris Speaker. And put him in the Hall-of-Fame's secret inner Hall of Fame, which you can only access by inserting a staff in the floor that concentrates sunlight on the left eye of the Babe Ruth plaque.[75]

Jesse Haines (1918, 1920-1937; career ERA+: 109)

	Career	Rank	Peak	Rank	Bests	Top 5s	JAWS	Rank
WAR	32.6	215	21.9	371	0	0	27.3	257
WS	207.1	105	122.8	185	0	1	NA	none

[75] Reference explanation: Something like that happened in one of the "Raiders of the Lost Ark" movies, right? I haven't seen them in ages. They all hinged on prehistoric societies creating booby traps that depended on incredible technical precision surviving flawlessly for centuries in places characterized by rapid erosion and other dramatic environmental changes. I wonder how many people were turned on to archaeology because of those movies, only to be turned off when they took an introductory archaeology course and realized how painstaking and un-swashbuckling it really is.

No, no, no. No and more no. Gratuitous amounts of no. Jesse Haines is Hall of Famer the day my farts win a Grammy. I'm sorry to have to get scatological, but this is what poor Hall-of-Fame choices bring out in me.

Look at those numbers and marvel. In a way, it's sort of beautiful. Here's someone who entered the summit of icons despite being in the JAWS range of Tim Wakefield, Alex Fernandez, Doug Drabek, Mike Hampton, and Jack McDowell. It's almost an inspiration to those of us who spend our lives doing good-but-not-great work. Haines could be a working-class hero: He never had the natural talent of your Hall-of-Fame-type guy, but he came to work every day. He put his head down, worked hard, kept his nose to the grindstone, and went out there to win. Sure, you can say that about every major-league ballplayer who has ever existed. But as long as you put it in those terms, you can make gullible people think he's better than he really is.

Haines lasted a while but had just one great year, in 1927. Even that year wasn't tremendous. I ranked all Hall-of-Fame pitchers by their best single-season WAR total. Haines comes second-to-last, ahead of only Rollie Fingers.

Do I even have to provide the explanation of how Haines got in the Hall? I'll give you a first letter: "F." Yes, Frankie freakin' Frisch freely flung friends forth from fair-ishness for Fame (Hall thereof). Jesse Haines and Frisch were teammates from 1927-1937, on Cardinals teams that won four pennants and two World Series. Haines was on the BBWAA ballot from 1939 to 1969 and never got above 8.3%. In 1970, Frisch and co. threw him in along with Earle Combs.

I think this represents the last of the players I have to review from the Frisch/Terry reign of frischin' terror. Let's take stock of the players from Frisch's teams, the 1919-1926 Giants and the 1927-1934 Cardinals, who are in the Hall and note whether they deserve it:

<u>1919-1926 Giants (at least 200 games):</u>

1083 games: Ross Youngs: NO
1060 games: George Kelly: NO, NO, NO!!!
1000 games: Frankie Frisch: deserving
524 games: Dave Bancroft: yeah, I guess
473 games: Travis Jackson: NO (but not overwhelmingly so)
311 games: Bill Terry: deserving but overrated
297 games: Freddie Lindstrom: NAY

<u>1927-1937 Cardinals (at least 200 games):</u>

1311 games: Frankie Frisch: deserving
788 games: Joe Medwick: deserving
777 games: Jim Bottomley: NEIN
617 games: Chick Hafey: NYET
308 games: Jesse Haines: HAKUNA (no in Swahili)
281 games: Dizzy Dean: too famous to be undeserving
271 games: Johnny Mize: deserving

Yeah, that's pretty bad. I only kick out about 10-15% of HOFers, and for the above teams I've kicked out half. And Frisch gets counted twice among the deserving.

I realize that sometimes I'm too hard on grumpy old men. Maybe I'm a little disrespectful to my elders. Maybe Bert Blyleven didn't deserve to be the exemplar of the "real men complete games" faction. But I firmly believe that grumpy old men and their self-serving biases have much too much power in all aspects of society. Frankie Frisch's poor Hall-of-Fame choices, based on his very grumpy-old-man ethos of "They don't make 'em like they did in my day", make for an admittedly superficial example. I could get into more important examples, but I'll restrain myself for once. For now, **Jesse Haines is out**.

Waite Hoyt (1918-1938; career ERA+: 112)

	Career	Rank	Peak	Rank	Bests	Top 5s	JAWS	Rank
WAR	51.8	79	34.0	142	1	1	42.9	99
WS	263.2	43	145.7	90	1	3	NA	67

A big reason the Hall of Fame has too many hitters from Golden Age of the 1920s and 1930s is because it was a hitters' era. The inflated numbers of the time fooled voters, and they still fool even the most sophisticated fans. When people complain about poor Hall-of-Fame selections, they tend to focus on Roger Bresnahan or Johnny Evers instead of Chick Hafey or Lloyd Waner.

But there are also too many Hall-of-Fame pitchers from the 1920s and 1930s. And, being from hitters' era, their pitching numbers look worse than they really are. Frankie Frisch and others just loved their buddies too much. I feel as though I may have mentioned this before.

And maybe, to try to be a bit more fair, their definition of what constituted Hall-of-Fame numbers was a bit more liberal than ours. Maybe they were thinking that the top 2.5% of players deserved the Hall instead of the top 1.5% that is the current rough standard. Waite Hoyt would certainly qualify under the 2.5% standard. Too bad it's not the current one.

Hoyt is in the JAWS neighborhood of Kenny Rogers and David Wells. All three pitchers had long careers but no truly great seasons. Hoyt was never among the top five starters in any season.

Then what are all of Hoyt's WAR and Wins Shares "bests" and "top 5"s in the above? They're actually on the relief pitcher side of the equation. From 1933-1937, Hoyt was a great reliever for the Pirates. What is that really worth?

Relief pitching was a very different thing in those days; nowadays we'd call it being a swingman. In 1934, Hoyt relieved in 31 games, started 17, and totaled 190.2 innings with 15 wins and 5 saves. That's certainly valuable, good for 4.8 WAR and 18 Win Shares. But he wasn't like a modern relief ace; he wasn't coming in the ninth with the game on the line. He took over when a game was looking bad and got the occasional vulture win or 3-inning save. There weren't many other pitchers in this role, so those "bests" and "top 5"s don't mean a lot.

If not for those years in relief extending his career, Hoyt would be another Chief Bender. He would have just some good-but-not-great starter seasons in a too-short career. Thanks to those swingman years, Hoyt's career is long enough to get acceptable Win Shares totals. Bill James puts him on the borderline. But WAR says "no."

What about the postseason? Hoyt was superb in World Series play, with a 1.83 ERA in 80.3 innings. Let's use the same method I used for Lefty Gomez to give Hoyt credit for his performance. Multiplying by three gives Hoyt an extra season of 241 innings and a 1.83 ERA.

That's one heck of a season. If you go by the league ERA over Hoyt's career, that would be a 220 ERA+. That happens very rarely; the closest analogue would be Pedro Martinez in 1997, when he had a 219 ERA+ in 241 innings. He got a 9.0 WAR that year. The only pitcher within Hoyt's career span to have a season like that was Lefty Grove in 1931: 217 ERA+, 288.2 innings, 10.1 WAR.

So let's give Waite Hoyt a 9.5 WAR season and see if that has an effect. Let's not bother with Win Shares, since it already gives Hoyt a pass. Bill James probably included post-season performance in ranking Hoyt 67th among post-1800s starters.

	Career	Rank	Peak	Rank	Bests	Top 5s	JAWS	Rank
WAR	61.3	46	39.5	76	1	1	50.4	53
WS	263.2	43	145.7	90	1	3	NA	67

Wow, that does change things. That gets Hoyt into low-end HOFer territory.

Incisive readers might realize that I didn't make the same adjustment for all other pitchers, and it's a bit unfair to rank a post-season-juiced Hoyt among pitchers who did not get the same boost. To add postseason performance similarly for all pitchers throughout history, we'd have to account for the fact that there are a lot more postseason games nowadays. But then there are also more teams, which makes it harder to get into the World Series. Then again, the whole thing is unfair to pitchers like Fergie Jenkins whose teammates were never good enough to get into the postseason … factoring all this into a calculation would take a thousand years, and by then human civilization will have collapsed into desert biker gangs killing each other for oil,[76] which would mean lower book sales for me. And this book is nothing if not a desperate cash grab to fill my oil reserves.

My point was just to discover whether the WAR total would be boosted significantly if you added postseason performance. Even if by some statistical magic I were able to do it for everyone, I'm thinking Hoyt could end up around 70th or so in JAWS. With that, and Bill James' endorsement, Waite Hoyt qualifies for the "I wouldn't campaign to include him, but I won't campaign to kick him out" division of the Hall.

Carl Hubbell (1928-1943; career ERA+: 130)

	Career	Rank	Peak	Rank	Bests	Top 5s	JAWS	Rank
WAR	67.5	30	47.3	35	1	4	57.4	31
WS	303.9	27	196.1	13	2	4	NA	12

Here's a nice easy case. While Lefty Grove was the best pitcher of the Golden Age, by a huge margin, Hubbell was the second-best. In the years from 1920-1941, Hubbell leads all non-Grove pitchers in WAR, edging Dazzy Vance by a score of 67.2 to 63.0. (Grove, by the way, was at 109.9.) In Win Shares during that period, Hubbell is second again, his 295 barely topping Red Ruffing's 293. (Grove? 392.)

Grove only played in the American League, while Hubbell played in the National, so they were each kings of their leagues. In those days, the leagues were very separate; teams in different leagues almost never even made trades with each other. It was some pride or precedent thing, but it makes

[76] Reference explanation: "Mad Max".

no sense to me. Leagues were each just one division each, so giving your leaguemate a player it needs means strengthening your competition. I'd want to do the opposite, only making trades with the teams I never play. But then, that's why they don't pay me the big bucks.

Not that Carl Hubbell was ever in danger of being traded. He played for the Giants for 16 years, leading them to three pennants and one championship. The Hubbell-era Giants came after Frankie Frisch departed for the Cardinals, but they still had Bill Terry. So the team had a mix of worthy and unworthy HOFers: Hubbell, Mel Ott and Terry, but also Travis Jackson and Freddie Lindstrom.

Hubbell got a bit of a late start for a no-doubt Hall-of-Famer, debuting mid-season in 1928, when he was 25. In 1926 Hubbell had established himself in the minors and was invited to the Tigers training camp. But Ty Cobb, then managing the Tigers, wouldn't let Hubbell throw his signature pitch, the fadeaway, a.k.a. screwball. Cobb believed it wrecked pitchers' arms.

But then, not throwing the screwball wrecked Hubbell's chances of making the team. He pitched terribly and was sent down. After two years of failing in the minors, Hubbell was released. Then he was picked up by the Giants, who let him pitch his screwball, thus letting him dominate. (Source: Hubbell's SABR biography, by Fred Stein.)

Once again, being a great ballplayer does not make you a good manager. Maybe Cobb could have relented after Hubbell's second year of flailing sans screwball?

But who knows; maybe Cobb saved Hubbell's career. Cobb was right in thinking that screwballs ruin young arms. Christy Mathewson threw one, but he was the exception. As Rob Neyer discusses in "The Neyer/James Guide to Pitchers," (Fireside, P. 52-55) you don't hear much about screwballs any more because they're not worth the risk. Newer pitches like the split-finger fastball fulfill a similar function without as much arm strain. Screwballs involve a very unnatural motion that most human arms can just not sustain. A normal curveball involves twisting your wrist clockwise for a right-hander (counterclockwise for a lefty), while a screwball involves twisting your wrist the other way. Go ahead and try that. See what I mean? You quickly slam into the limit of what your arm can accomplish. (My apologies if your arm just broke. Rub some dirt on it and get back to reading.)

Hubbell lasted until age 40 throwing his famous screwball, so he was obviously able to handle it. But the ages when he wasn't throwing it, 23 and 24, are years in which pitchers often sustain career-shortening injuries. Even when pitchers come back after such injuries, they tend to remain injury-prone, as with Bret Saberhagen and Dwight Gooden. There's something about how arms develop in their early 20s that makes them fragile, as if the tendons are not quite at full strength. In "Baseball Prospectus" they call this the "injury nexus," and if a young phenom can get through it unscathed, he can have a long career.

It's very speculative that Hubbell may have been better off laying off the screwball for a few years, but it's worth a thought. Regardless, Hubbell is a lock for the Hall.

Catfish Hunter (1965-1979; career ERA+: 104)

	Career	Rank	Peak	Rank	Bests	Top 5s	JAWS	Rank
WAR	41.4	145	35.1	126	0	1	38.2	140
WS	205.1	108	148.0	84	0	2	NA	55

Here's another Lefty Gomez. Like Gomez, Catfish Hunter had a few good seasons in a short career playing for many great teams. Hunter also pitched a bunch in the postseason, with a 3.26 ERA in 132.1 innings. Should we try to tack on those innings like we did with Gomez and Waite Hoyt?

Now we see another limitation of my clumsy attempt to add postseason performance to JAWS. Multiplying Hunter's postseason total by three would make for a 367-inning season. Only two pitchers achieved more than 360 innings in a season during Hunter's career: Wilbur Wood in 1972 and Mickey Lolich in 1971. It doesn't seem valid to give Hunter an extra year like that. Why should postseason performance all count as one season, anyway? With this method, what would we do with Andy Pettitte, who pitched 267 innings in the postseason? Give him an extra 801-inning year? Whoever created this system is an idiot.

More to the point, with Hunter's JAWS at 140th, we'd have to add around 10 WAR to get Hunter anywhere close to the HOF borderline. And Hunter was not spectacular in the postseason like Waite Hoyt was. Hunter's career postseason ERA, 3.26, was exactly the same as his career regular-season ERA, which got him a 104 ERA+. That means that in the postseason, Hunter was average.

He was known as a big-game pitcher, but that's largely because he was on teams that played lots of big games. Hunter was a good-not-great starter thrust into extraordinary circumstances. There were two clear A.L. dynasties in the 1970s: The 1971-1975 A's, who won the division each year and the World Series three times, and the 1976-1978 Yankees, who reached the Series three times and won it twice. Hunter was on both teams.

Doesn't that mean Hunter was a "natural-born winner" who "just knew how to win" and "brought a culture of winning to the clubhouse" and "would win when winds went winny-win-wa-win" and so forth? Maybe, but he didn't win those games by himself. Those teams were stacked. The A's had Reggie Jackson, Sal Bando, Gene Tenace, Rollie Fingers, Vida Blue, Bert Campaneris, Joe Rudi, and Hall-of-Fame manager Dick Williams. When he left the A's, Hunter chose to sign with the Yankees because they were already great. They had Reggie Jackson, Willie Randolph, Graig Nettles, Thurman Munson, Ron Guidry, Sparky Lyle, non-Hall-of-Fame manager Billy Martin, and "true Yankee spirit" (groan).

Hunter was the ace of the A's clubs (except in 1971 when Vida Blue was a world-beater), but was not very good for the 1976-1978 Yankees. It was a pitchers' era, so he got a few good-looking ERAs. Because he pitched a lot of innings on very good teams, he collected lots of 20-win seasons, five straight from 1971 to 1975. He picked a perfect time to do it; in the early 1970s the four-man rotation was popular and starters still completed games, which made for large seasonal win totals. From 1971 to 1975, there were 55 seasons of more than 20 wins, 10.5 per year. From 2010 to 2014, there were only 14, about 3 per year.

By the way, was Reggie Jackson ever called a "natural-born winner" who "just knew how to win," etc.? Cuz he was also on both of these teams, and he was pretty amazing. Compared to Jackson, Hunter was hardly the straw that stirred the drink.[77]

---

[77] Reference explanation: Soon after joining the Yankees, Reggie Jackson called himself the "straw that stirs the drink," also specifying that catcher Thurman Munson was not similarly stirring-straw-esque. Munson was the "true Yankee" hero du jour, and he didn't take this criticism well. In general, he was not the most expansive of fellows. When asked if Munson was "moody", Sparky Lyle said "Munson's not moody; he's just mean. When you're moody, you're nice sometimes." ("Baseball's Greatest Insults," Kevin Nelson, Fireside, p. 41) The larger point is that the late 1970s Yankees

Speaking of Reggie, Hunter was not as loaded with personality as you might expect from a Southern fella called "Catfish." It was not a genuine nickname; A's owner Charlie Finley just assigned it to him to make him seem more colorful. Finley had a lot of odd ideas like that; some brilliant, some less so. Hunter was a likable, easygoing fellow, so when someone gave him a nickname for no good reason, he went with it.

Because he wasn't colorful, **I'm kicking out Catfish Hunter**. Also, a 104 ERA+ over a relatively short career is not very impressive. Bill James puts him in the HOF range, but I don't care. If Bill James wants to challenge me on this, I dare him to tell it to my face in the alley behind Fenway Park. Oh, yeah. It's on. After I get his autograph, give him a hug, and pat his big, round belly to see if it will make him giggle, you motherflippers best beLIEVE I'm gonna rip him a new one by carefully, politely laying out my case. If, after all that, he still isn't convinced, I'll stare him straight in the eyes and tell him that he's probably right and that I'm really sorry I brought it up. Awww yeah!

Ferguson Jenkins (1965-1983; career ERA+: 115)

	Career	Rank	Peak	Rank	Bests	Top 5s	JAWS	Rank
WAR	84.9	18	51.8	21	1	4	68.3	19
WS	321.2	18	181.0	31	1	5	NA	22

Fergie Jenkins was a sort of Bizarro Catfish Hunter. Catfish got to play for the 1970s A's and Yankees, while Jenkins was stuck with the Cubs and Rangers. Catfish pitched a bunch in the postseason, while Jenkins never reached it once. Hunter's career was short, while Jenkins' was long. Hunter is not a legitimate Hall-of-Famer, while Jenkins certainly is.

Jenkins' Cubs teams had the potential to make the playoffs. From 1967 to 1972, the Baby Bears were above .500 each year, finishing third three times and second three times. They had Ron Santo, Billy Williams, Jenkins, and, as I mentioned earlier, the desiccated remains of Ernie Banks at first base. Replacing Banks wouldn't have won them anything alone, but it and a few other moves might have.

Jenkins is the only Canadian-born Hall-of-Famer, and is likely to remain so unless they elect Larry Walker (who, as you know, I wouldn't campaign against, but can't campaign for). Maybe Joey Votto has a shot someday.

Looking through the list of other successful Canadian major-leaguers, I notice that almost all were adorable in some distinctly Canadian way. Matt Stairs was a big ol' beer-drinkin' hoser of the Zap Rowsdower[78] variety. Justin Morneau and Corey Koskie are cute because they were Twins, and I challenge you to say "Corey Koskie" with a Minnesota accent and not sound adorable. Ryan Dempster, in the great Canadian comedy tradition, has a legitimately good Harry Caray impression, and does it with charming aplomb. I don't know if there's anything about Russell Martin or Jason Bay that's particularly cute, but they're not un-cute. I'd estimate about 75% of Canadian ballplayers have some distinct brand of Canadorability.

---

represent the best counterexample to the idea that you need "team chemistry" to win. Those Yankees had the chemistry of a nuclear bomb, and they won like crazy.

[78] Reference explanation: Zap Rowsdower was the hero of "Final Sacrifice," a Canadian film that you would have only seen if you saw the "Mystery Science Theater 3000" version of it.

Anyway anyway, I'm just shootin' the breeze at this point. Fergie Jenkins is obviously a Hall-of-Famer.

Randy Johnson (1988-2009; career ERA+: 135)

	Career	Rank	Peak	Rank	Bests	Top 5s	JAWS	Rank
WAR	102.1	8	62.0	7	2	8	82.0	8
WS	327.4	17	176.8	34	2	8	NA	42

After being elected to the Hall of Fame, Randy Johnson talked about how hard it is for a man of his height, 6'10", to repeat his delivery. Tall pitchers are always seen as having an advantage in part because their long arms can swing the ball around faster. But swinging it around faster means less room for error. In Johnson's words, "for someone who is 6'1", 6'2", he has less body to keep under control, so it's a lot easier." (Source: "Randy Johnson went from "Wild Thing" to "Big Unit" before the Hall of Fame," Los Angeles Times, Mike DiGiovanna, January 6, 2015) It was an obvious slam on the much shorter Pedro Martinez, who was elected the same year. Pedro was furious! The next time they meet, sparks will fly! (Nothing after the quote is true, but that's how I would edit this if it were a reality show.)

Like Carl Hubbell, Johnson got a late start to his career, but made up for it big-time. His first full season was at age 25 with the Expos. They traded him and some other pitchers mid-season to the Mariners for Mark Langston. Langston pitched very well but then left as a free agent the next year. It's one of those trades that looks terrible with the benefit of hindsight. But who knew Johnson would eventually master those tricky tall-man mechanics?

It certainly took him a while to do so. He led the league in walks in each of his first three full years with the Mariners, once giving up 152 walks in just 201.1 innings. That makes for 6.8 walks per nine innings, the sixth-highest ratio of any starter who pitched at least 162 innings. The top five were Tommy Byrne in 1949, Hal Newhouser in 1941, Tommy Byrne again in 1950, Adonis Terry in 1894, and Sam Jones in 1955. Byrne in particular was something special: He walked 8.22 per inning in 1949 (179 batters in 196 innings), one more per inning than anyone else has ever.

None of those seasons were especially bad overall, despite so many free passes. After all, if these guys allowed lots of hits and homers along with all the walks, their managers would not have allowed them to complete 162 innings. Johnson had league-average ERAs during his three formative wild years. In 1993, at age 29, he finally managed a reasonable walk rate, which put the final piece in place. From then on, he got better and better, culminating in four straight Cy Young awards from 1999-2002, at ages 35-38. He didn't hang it up until he was 45.

Let's stop for a moment and admire the fortitude that Randy Johnson needed to become great. Despite what your grandpa says, almost all ballplayers nowadays work very hard. How many, though, face the same problem for years and years and just keep chipping away at it until they find the answer? Have you, in your professional life, ever been stymied by one thing you just couldn't do well, and then spent four years working and working and working until you got it? I know I haven't. I've been working on this book for a year and a half and I'm already phoning it in.

During his seasons in the minors, which covered his early-20s injury nexus, Johnson never pitched more than 140 innings. It's possible that not being terribly good in those years saved him from being overworked, which enabled him to become a workhorse in his old age.

Despite being a superstar of unique ability, and loads of fun to watch, Johnson never seemed to capture the national imagination. I doubt many non-baseball fans know anything about him the way they do about Derek Jeter, Alex Rodriguez, Roger Clemens, etc. The only TV ad I remember seeing him in was one for GEICO, and everyone in human history has been in a GEICO ad. They only make about seven billion each year.

That might be because Johnson didn't star in a big media market. But I have a sneaking suspicion that it might be, at least partially, because Johnson was not exactly ... how can I say this as politely as possible ... hmmmm. Hm. OK, let's put it this way: if Randy Johnson wanted to break into showbiz, he would have trouble passing as a convincing romantic lead. With the right makeup he could carve a Richard Kiel[79] or Michael Berryman[80] career, but that would be about it. I'm not saying you have to be Lou Boudreau to cross over from baseball fame into widespread fame. But perhaps Johnson could have drawn a few more fans on Ladies' Night if he'd cut off that nasty mullet. C'mon, Randy. Who outside of Canada was not making fun of mullets in 2001?

Maybe that's a good thing about sports; it's one of the few professions in the modern world in which looks don't matter at all. Results count, not smile wattage. You can be ugly and proud, letting your greasy mullet fly high, figuratively and literally. Johnson's greasy mullet took him all the way to the upper reaches of the Hall.

Walter Johnson (1907-1927; career ERA+: 147)

	Career	Rank	Peak	Rank	Bests	Top 5s	JAWS	Rank
WAR	165.6	2	89.5	1	6	10	127.5	1
WS	560.2	2	290.5	1	4	11	NA	1

Randy Johnson became great. Walter Johnson was born great. He was great with his first major-league pitch at age 19. He was better than great through his 20s, when he would pitch 320-370 innings per year, complete 29-38 starts, and have ERA+s ranging from 164 to 259. After one god-awful year in 1917 when he had an ERA+ of only 120 (his ERA was over 2, for Christ's sake!), he produced two more incredible seasons to close out the dead-ball era. Then he was merely great through the 1920s. Finally in 1924 and 1925, the Senators collected more than one good player, and Johnson got to experience two pennants and one championship.

As I write this, fans are voting for the "Franchise Four", the best four players in each team's history. The winners will be unveiled during the 2015 All-Star Game. Because no Yankee is retiring after 2015, MLB had to invent some gimmick to occupy their staff of bad poets and slow-motion film editors. I know I should stop caring about such things, but I'm already pre-cringing over the selections fans

---

[79] Reference explanation: Richard Kiel was a 7'2" actor best known as Jaws from the James Bond series. "Mystery Science Theater 3000" fans know him as the star of "Human Duplicators" and "Eegah". "Mystery Science Theater 3000" fans might also like to know that I worked as an intern for six episodes of the show. No joke. The stories I could tell about Crow T. Robot ... that bastard.

[80] Reference explanation: Michael Berryman is a staple of horror films, best known as "Pluto" from "The Hills Have Eyes." Maybe it's a bit unfair to compare Randy Johnson to a man who has a rare medical condition that left his features distorted. But there aren't a lot of tall, unpretty people in Hollywood to choose from. They're mostly tiny and gorgeous.

will make. I'm betting Omar Vizquel will get more votes than Tris Speaker, for example. My fellow Twins fans sure as hell better select the greatest pitcher in history to be one of their four, or I swear, I will staple a cheesehead hat to Mary Tyler Moore's head. (Edit after the All-Star Game: It happened. If you know Mary Tyler Moore's home address, please contact my friend Chris E. Keedei at chrisekeedei@yahoo.com.)

Walter Johnson would not approve of such talk. He was a pure gentleman: soft-spoken, modest, and dignified. In the era of rowdyists Ty Cobb and Johnny Evers, Johnson never got into brawls, fought with umpires, or even threw at batters.

You know how some people get hyperventilatingly cynical when their heroes turn out to be jerks? As if one bad egg means the entire world has avian flu? If Kirby Puckett disappoints you, well, just switch to someone like Walter Johnson. There are plenty of good ones to choose from.

Like Babe Ruth, Walter Johnson was playing a different game than the rest of the league. If you plopped Johnson into today's game, he probably wouldn't look like a hard thrower. But by the standards of his time, he was mind-blowingly fast. His strikeout totals are like Babe Ruth's home run totals, in that he'd lead the league by huge margins. From 1901 to World War II, only two pitchers had 300 strikeouts in a single season: Walter Johnson and Rube Waddell, who each did it twice. In Johnson's best overall year, 1913, he struck out 243 batters while no one else in the A.L. struck out more than 166.

Johnson's 1913, by the way, is the best season by any pitcher since 1901. His WAR that year, 14.6, also beats any season ever by any hitter, including Babe Ruth. The second-best pitching season ever is Walter Johnson the year before: 13.5 WAR in 1912. You have to go down almost another point of WAR, 12.6, to get to the third-best, Cy Young in 1901. (Number four, interestingly, is Dwight Gooden in 1985. Man, what could have been, eh? He was only 20 years old in 1985 and pitched 16 complete games. There were many factors dooming Dwight Gooden from a Hall-of-Fame career, but overwork must have been one of them.)

If the Franchise Fours could have a big NCAA-style bracket and fight it out amongst each other, Walter Johnson better end up in the Final Four. Babe Ruth, Honus Wagner and Willie Mays would be my other three. Though it's hard to leave out Ted Williams. And Oscar Charleston. And Omar Vizquel, of course.

Addie Joss (1902-1910; career ERA+: 142)

	Career	Rank	Peak	Rank	Bests	Top 5s	JAWS	Rank
WAR	43.7	128	38.4	89	0	1	41.1	114
WS	191.1	129	168.2	43	0	1	NA	69

There's no crying in baseball. It's one of those movie quotes that is used way too often by well-meaning uncles (see also anything from "Caddyshack"). But it's also true.

Lots of crying was involved in electing Addie Joss in the Hall of Fame. The guy died in 1911, when he was only 31 years old. The Hall broke their own rules to elect Joss: he appeared in only 9 seasons, and 10 seasons are required. This selection happened in 1978, when, you would think, most tears had dried.

At the risk of sounding like a monster, boo-freakin'-hoo. Sure, Joss had some nice numbers in the deadest of dead-ball days. Sure, he was a hale fellow well-met. Sure, he used his engineering background to invent an electric scoreboard in 1908.[81] We all know these things. But as with Ross Youngs, tragic death is not a Hall-of-Fame qualification, any more than a career-ending injury is. Without further ado, **Addie Joss is out.**

Sandy Koufax (1955-1966; career ERA+: 131)

	Career	Rank	Peak	Rank	Bests	Top 5s	JAWS	Rank
WAR	49.0	95	46.1	36	2	5	47.5	67
WS	193.4	126	167.3	45	3	5	NA	9

Continuing on a theme ... Koufax retired at age 30, because the act of lifting his arm to comb his hair caused him extreme pain. Like Old Hoss Radbourn, Koufax bullied his way through a dead arm to pitch an incredible amount. Radbourn kept trying, with less success, after his huge 1884 season. Koufax kept having huge seasons until it just wasn't worth it any more.

Koufax's problems didn't come from pitching too much during the "injury nexus" like, presumably, Dwight Gooden. Koufax made his debut at age 19, but was mediocre until age 25. During that span he was never trusted with more than 175 innings a year. Then in 1962 he started kicking ash and taking names, and he was all out of beer.

After the 1964 season Koufax developed a circulatory ailment. If he had been handled carefully from then on, maybe he could have lasted until he was 40. Instead, the Dodgers saw it as a make-or-break moment: they would make him into a workhorse or break him. They successfully made him into a workhorse for two years of 320-plus innings each, more than he'd ever thrown before. Then he broke.

JAWS has Koufax on the borderline of the Hall of Fame. The brevity of his career is obviously the main problem, which I understand; as I've said many times, it's about what you did, not what you hypothetically could have done if not for a bad break. But also, Koufax's Peak numbers are also not as high as you might expect. His run of dominance lasted just six years, so that seven-year Peak figure doesn't do him justice.

And then there's the fact that JAWS doesn't consider the postseason. Koufax dominated the 1963 and 1965 World Series, winning the World Series MVP each year. The 1965 series is especially remarkable. He refused to pitch in Game 1 because it fell on Yom Kippur. In Game 2, he allowed one run in six innings and took the loss (once again, win-loss records are dumb). Then he pitched shutouts in games 5 and 7 to clinch it.

In 57 career World Series innings, Koufax finished with a 0.95 ERA. Multiply the innings by three and translate the result to WAR and you get an extra season of ten gazillion WAR, which launches Koufax into the Intergalactic Hall of Fame.

---

[81] In case it wasn't clear, that's true. Between the 1908 and 1909 seasons Addie Joss devised a scoreboard that kept track of balls and strikes. The Cleveland Naps (who were actually called that then) installed it in the outfield, and it became known as the Joss Indicator. It didn't work very well, but it was improved upon. (Source: Joss's SABR biography, by Alex Semchuck.)

Sandy Koufax was unquestionably great. I would never dispute that. But he remains a bit overrated. In the All-Century Team voting, he finished second among starting pitchers, after only Nolan Ryan. That's too high. Remember that Koufax had those great numbers in the 1960s, when pitching was dominant. In terms of WAR, he had two years that were truly sensational, two others at MVP-level, and two more that were just plain-ol' good. After that, it drops off a cliff. You can see the numbers in the Dizzy Dean comment. They're terrific, but nothing compared to those of Walter Johnson, Cy Young, Lefty Grove, Roger Clemens, Tom Seaver, Greg Maddux, etc.

Koufax got all those All-Century Team votes because he was cloaked in a mythology that made people think he was the greatest thing since hot cakes and ice skates. A lot of things from the 1960s have a similar glow, because they occurred when baby boomers were young. During the 1970s and '80s baby boomers became proficient at mythologizing anything and everything that had dazzled their prepubescent hearts.

I've already tirade-ed plenty about baby boomers' enviable capacity for propagating their nostalgia as fact. And admittedly, my flock, Generation X, is also no great shakes; we spent our youths ignoring politics and feeling sorry for ourselves.

But here's something you may not have heard: Did you know that the so-called "Millennials" (nee Generation Y) is actually the greatest generation since the Greatest Generation? You probably heard that they're self-obsessed smartphone freaks who play scary video games and wear dumb-looking beards and don't appreciate the true value of Sandy Koufax, etc. Maybe, but Millennials also have historically low levels of violence, binge drinking, cigarette smoking, drug use, teenage pregnancy, and pretty much every other quantifiable measure of generational wherewithal. They are less sexist or bigoted than any group of young people in human history. And I'm getting this from an article in the Economist, ("Oh! You pretty things!" July 12, 2014) so that pretty much makes it true. Provided us oldsters haven't destroyed the planet beyond repair, we're in good hands.

At any rate, Sandy Koufax may be just a baby-boomer hero; he may not compare with Jaden Braden Hopslam, the 15-year-old with a handlebar mustache who will break all pitching records while wearing a uniform made of organic hemp that converts greenhouse gases into artisanal Mallomars. But Koufax is a certain Hall-of-Famer.

Bob Lemon (1946-1958; career ERA+: 119)

	Career	Rank	Peak	Rank	Bests	Top 5s	JAWS	Rank
WAR	**48.8**	**96**	**39.0**	**77**	**0**	**3**	**43.9**	**91**
WS	**232.4**	**74**	**176.5**	**36**	**1**	**6**	**NA**	**41**

Early death doesn't move me. Military service does. From 1943-1945 Bob Lemon spent his early 20s in the Navy fighting Hitler (not directly). He actually played a handful of major-league games in 1941 and 1942, but as a third baseman. Throughout his entire minor-league career he was a hitter, pitching only two innings.

While in the service Lemon pitched a few games on a lark and impressed veterans Birdie Tebbetts and Johnny Pesky. Lemon started the 1946 season as an outfielder, but Tebbetts and Pesky convinced the Cleveland ownership to give him a try as a pitcher. (Tebbetts played for the Tigers and Pesky for the Red Sox; why they were helping the opposition is beyond me.) Lemon was skeptical, but agreed to the switch when he learned that he would make more money as a pitcher. It worked almost immediately, and by 1948 he was one of the best starters in baseball. (Source: Lemon's Wikipedia page.)

Hm, should I become a Hall-of-Fame pitcher or remain a terrific major-league outfielder? I don't know; what kind of salary are we talking about here? Also, after I retire, should I become President of the United States or Batman?[82] Tough choice; which job has a better dental plan?

This kind of quick transition from the field to the mound happened every so often in the 1880s, when competition was at such a low level that an exceptional athlete could step into either role. But by the 1940s, the game had advanced past the point where you could pitch in the majors without years and years of nurturing and training.

Lemon stepped right into it. Cleveland great Mel Harder taught him a slider in 1946, and it worked so well that Lemon ended up with the eighth-best slider of all time according to "The Neyer/James Guide to Pitchers."

Who knows; maybe Lemon could have become a Hall-of-Fame outfielder. He certainly hit well, at least early in his career. In 1948, Lemon hit .286/.331/.487 (119 OPS+) in 129 PAs. In 1949, he had an MVP-candidate slash line: .269/.331/.556 (134 OPS+). His 7 home runs that year project to 34 in a full 600-PA season. If only he could have played the outfield when he wasn't pitching … but I know, you gotta preserve those precious arms.

A big chunk of Lemon's WAR and Win Shares totals are from his hitting, which is of course rare for pitchers. And that's totally valid for our purposes here; everything you do on a ballfield to help your team win should count. If Jamie Moyer hit like 1949 Bob Lemon on a consistent basis, he'd be a deserving HOFer.

I don't know why JAWS hates Bob Lemon, but I don't care. Giving him three extra years for his military service bumps him comfortably into HOF territory.

Ted Lyons (1923-1942, 1946; career ERA+: 118)

	Career	Rank	Peak	Rank	Bests	Top 5s	JAWS	Rank
WAR	71.5	24	40.9	66	0	2	56.2	35
WS	311.0	24	163.1	50	1	4	NA	37

Ted Lyons didn't play a single game in the minors, going straight from Baylor University to the White Sox. After a few years, he became an ace and stayed one until 1931.

Then, like Sandy Koufax, his arm broke. His best pitch, a cut fastball, was gone for good. Lyons didn't have the option of just playing through the pain; he couldn't really compete without his fastball.

[82] Reference explanation: Batman is a man dressed like a bat who punches people because he thinks they committed crimes. It works better than you might think. He is the main character in the wildly successful movies "Batman," "Batman Begins," "Batman Returns," "Batman Remains," "Batman Leaves For a Spell," "Batman Was Here a Minute Ago … " etc.

Did he give up? Did he just shrug his shoulders, say "well, it's been fun" and slink away like a quitter? Yes! I mean, no! Lyons reinvented himself as a junkball pitcher, relying much more on a knuckleball.

Many pitchers get crafty when their fastballs don't zip any more. But how many rely much more on a knuckleball? Heck, the only knucklers I hear about are from pitchers who throw almost nothing else. How often have you heard of someone who featured a knuckler among a large assortment of other pitches?

Actually, quite a few did in the 1930s. The knuckleball became a bit of a fad at the time, according to Rob Neyer in the "Neyer/James Guide to Pitchers." (p. 42) Only a few, most notably Eddie Rommel, were knuckleball pitchers as we think of them today, throwing the floaty one almost exclusively. Most had lots of other pitches. In the fad's peak, in the late 1930s and 1940s, Neyer estimates that about half of all major-league pitchers threw a knuckleball occasionally.

The trend may have been motivated by desperation; even by the standards of baseball's true Golden Age of 1920-1941, the early 1930s were a high-water mark for offense. So why didn't the knuckleball make a similar comeback during the Steroid Era? It's not like anything else was working very well. According to Neyer, only John Smoltz even gave it a shot.

For decades the knuckleball has had an entrenched stigma of being a freak pitch that only a few lovable oddballs attempt. This seems strange, when you think about it. What makes the knuckleball so darn special? Is it really so hard to throw it that you can't develop any other good complementary pitches?

Yes, according to Hoyt Wilhelm, the Hall-of-Fame knuckleballer from the 1950s and 1960s. Wilhelm often said that you can't throw a great knuckleball unless you throw it almost exclusively.

But then, couldn't an OK one prove useful? Isn't an amazing endorsement of the knuckleball to say you can succeed in the majors by throwing it and almost nothing else? What other pitch, besides Mariano Rivera's cutter, can you say that for? When a pitch has that much potential, you'd think even a mediocre one could fool a few batters each game in the right spots. It worked in the 1930s, after all.

And heck, learning a knuckler is proven to extend your career beyond a reasonable length. Even when every other pitch is lost, that one tends to stay. Despite the fact knuckleballers comprise less than 1% of pitchers in the past 50 years, they make up three of the six pitchers who threw more than 100 innings at age 45 or older. Those three, Hoyt Wilhelm, Charlie Hough and Phil Niekro, pitched 1401.2 combined innings in extreme baseball-old-age, while the non-knuckleballers, Jamie Moyer, Nolan Ryan and Tommy John, threw 987.1.

It worked for Ted Lyons too. He was 45 in his last season, 1946, when he had a 148 ERA+ in 42.2 innings. He only stopped pitching because he was chosen to become the White Sox manager, which led him to take himself off the roster. Later he said he never wanted to manage, but felt obligated to do so. He had been with the White Sox for 25 years, was universally beloved, and didn't want to let anyone down. (Source: Lyons's SABR biography, by Warren Corbett.)

That 1946 season represents a small sample size, but Lyons was great before it. In 1942, he led the league in ERA and completed all 20 of his starts. If not for the war, he could have easily had three more good years of about 12-14 wins each, which would have put him at or near 300 for his career. He was too old to be drafted, so no one would have blamed him for continuing to play. Instead he enlisted and served in the Marines from 1943-1945.

Another secret to Lyons' late success was that, after his arm injury in 1931, he only started 20-27 games each year. He was called "Sunday Pitcher" because he handled and almost always completed one game of the Sunday doubleheaders that were de rigueur at the time. Most pitchers might not need so much rest, but it worked for Lyons. As we saw with Whitey Ford, a creative approach to a pitching rotation can bring great dividends.

Nowadays franchises are adopting all sorts of new strategies, from defensive shifts to infinitely increasing specialization of relievers. But they seem to have blinders on when it comes to a few things, like knuckleballs and more varied rotation setups. Both were good enough to give Ted Lyons a legitimate Hall-of-Fame record. They might be worth exploring.

Greg Maddux (1986-2008; career ERA+: 132)

	Career	Rank	Peak	Rank	Bests	Top 5s	JAWS	Rank
WAR	106.9	6	56.3	12	3	6	81.6	9
WS	394.4	7	183.5	26	3	10	NA	13

Sometimes a minor kerfuffle arises over which team's hat will be depicted on the plaque of a new Hall-of-Famer. Dave Winfield caused a controversy by choosing the Padres instead of the Yankees, with some accusing him of being paid to do so. Gary Carter chose the Mets and Andre Dawson chose the Cubs, but the Hall of Fame forced both to go in as Expos. (Rightly so, if you ask me. C'mon guys. You both had your best years with the Expos, and that poor dead team deserves some kind of legacy.) Wade Boggs chose the Devil Rays, the team for which he had played two mediocre seasons to close out his career. Thankfully the Hall ignored him and gave his image a Red Sox cap.

It's all silly, I suppose. I'm sure the Hall's founders never anticipated that such hullabaloos would be made over which logo could be found on which plaque. But everything that touches the Hall of Fame gains great import and great press.

Greg Maddux displayed tremendous sensitivity by requesting that his plaque go hatless, I repeat, hatless.[83] I don't think anyone outside the north side of Chicago could have blamed him for choosing the cap of the Braves, the team for which he earned three Cy Young awards, won four ERA titles, starred for 11 years, and reached the postseason ten times, the exception being 1994 when there was no postseason. But Maddux was a classy guy.

Classiness fit into his public image, that of "The Professor" who wore glasses, did crossword puzzles to relax, and outsmarted batters left and right. But he showed a different side within those millionaire frat houses known as major-league locker rooms.

In one of his favorite pranks, he would go up to a rookie who was showering and engage him in a serious dialogue about baseball strategy. This served to distract the poor sap while Maddux peed on his foot. (Source: "Rookies Had Good Reason to Fear Showering with Greg Maddux," Deadspin.com, Barry Petchesky, July 11, 2014) When Chipper Jones got his first major-league hit, they saved the ball in the dugout, and Maddux picked his nose and spread his booger all over it. There are other stories which ex-teammates dare only allude to that involve Maddux putting some undisclosed bodily

[83] "Simpsons" reference. It'll just sound lame if I try to explain it.

substances on sanitary socks and in chili. (Source: "Is Greg Maddux the Most Disgusting Person to Be Voted In Baseball's Hall of Fame?" Sportsgrid.com, Eric Goldschein, January 9, 2014.)

I'm not much of a man, but I'm man enough to enjoy a bit of gross-out guy humor. I think it humanizes Professor Maddux to hear about him acting like a scuzzy roommate. If you like your Hall-of-Famers amusingly multifaceted, Greg Maddux is your guy.

Juan Marichal (1960-1975; career ERA+: 123)

	Career	Rank	Peak	Rank	Bests	Top 5s	JAWS	Rank
WAR	63.1	39	51.9	20	1	5	57.5	30
WS	261.1	44	186.2	22	0	5	NA	20

Juan Marichal was always the second banana, first to Sandy Koufax and then to Bob Gibson. Throughout his career, Marichal garnered just one Cy Young Award vote, for third place in 1971. He scored a massive 10.3 WAR in 1965, leading all of the majors by a large margin. But Koufax won the Cy Young because he went 26-8 while Marichal was at 22-13. That's how it goes: You lose some, and you lose some.

Instead of Cy Young Award votes, Marichal won the important stuff, the games. While Koufax and Gibson worked like hell to overpower hitters, Marichal smoothly outsmarted his opponents with a whole host of pitches thrown from several angles. All of his pitches came with a giant leg kick and an easy motion. Since Marichal smiled a lot and never broke a sweat, some people thought he wasn't trying very much. Those people weren't looking hard enough.

Considering Marichal's easygoing demeanor, it's odd that for many years he was best known for a fight. On August 22, 1965, the Giants faced the Dodgers. The franchises' historic rivalry was at a high pitch, as both were in the pennant race. Both of the games' starters, Sandy Koufax and Juan Marichal, pitched inside a ton during the first few innings. When Marichal came to the plate the first time, Dodgers catcher Johnny Roseboro called for a few pitches that came uncomfortably close to Marichal's body. Marichal didn't flinch at any of them. But when Roseboro threw the ball back to the mound a little too close to his ear, Marichal spun around and smashed Roseboro's head with the bat. A huge brawl ensued. Roseboro sustained a big gash on his forehead and Marichal got a large fine and nine-day suspension. (Source: Marichal's SABR biography, by Jan Finkel.)

That's it? That's all Marichal gets for cold-cocking someone in the head with a bat? It was a different time, I know. As I discussed in the Jud Wilson comment, it was once deemed acceptable and even proper for men to resolve disputes by hitting each other to the point of exhaustion. Because, you see, if one party puts forth an argument, and another party asserts a contravening view, then whoever punches the hardest must be correct. Also, if a man is accused of a crime, you just make him pull a stone from a pot of boiling water. If the resulting burns on his hand heal within three days, he's innocent. If his burns fester and grow infected, he's guilty and must be executed.[84]

---

[84] This was one of the "trials by ordeal" used to determine guilt or innocence in England during the Dark Ages (which some people call the Early Middle Ages, but funk that -- in England especially, those ages were pretty darn dark). Other trials by ordeal involved walking over red-hot plough blades or holding onto a red-hot iron for a few minutes. The accused would assuredly sustain serious injury,

If something like the Marichal-Roseboro brawl happened nowadays, I would hope the modern Marichal would face some criminal charges. Hitting someone in the head with a bat is assault, case closed. I don't care if it happens on a baseball field or in the pine barrens of New Jersey; it's assault, and it's against the law for a very good reason.

Moreover, isn't it odd that baseball players are allowed to hit each other at all? Occasionally we still see silly brawls in which millionaires beat each other up over alleged violations of subjective interpretations of obscure unwritten rules. As spectators, we outwardly cluck our tongues in disapproval while we inwardly thrill at the bloodsport. Oh my goodness, it's terrible. Let me see that replay one more time. Yes, it really is awful. OK, just one more time. So I can keep analyzing how awful it is, you know. Let's get some more opinions about it. Terrible, right guys?

When not on the grand stage of major-league sports, punching another person is serious business, no? A major-league-style brawl between two gangs on the streets of Minneapolis would get the perpetrators thrown into the paddywagon and sent to the hoosegow, yes? Especially if the whole thing were caught on several cameras from multiple angles. Why is it that you can only get away with pummeling another human by being a famous millionaire in a tight-fitting outfit?

At this point, I have to plead ignorance. I'm not a lawyer. I turn instead to my friend Joe, who is a legalized lawyer, who knows legality as it pertains to law and writes on legal pads and everything:

> Assault and the Batter
>
> By Joseph A. Pettigrew, Esq, J.D., etc.
>
> Hey folks. I understand a legal opinion was requested? Happy to help. That'll be $575. From each of you. Just kidding – it's free! How come? Well, because while I am a lawyer, I'm not *your* lawyer. So this is not legal advice. Don't go around bashing people with bats and then say, "Well, but Joe said I could," because I didn't, and you can't.
>
> Ed's absolutely right. Assault (and battery) are crimes – which means that you can be arrested, charged, and punished by the state. They're also torts – which means that they come with berries and whipped cream. No, not that kind of tort – chocolate icing is much more common. No, for reals – a tort means that someone has done you wrong, and you can sue them in civil court for damages. Broadly, battery is an intentional action that results in a harmful or offensive contact of another person. Assault is an intentional action that makes someone aware an immediate threat of a battery on that person. So, if you're, say, a batter who just got plunked on purpose, and your dander's up,[85] and you run at the pitcher with your fist cocked, and launch a punch at his face, the moment before you hit him, it's an assault, and the moment after you hit him it's a battery.[86] Same goes for the pitcher, assuming it was an intentional beanball – when the batter realizes the pitch is heading for his head, it's assault. When it plunks him – battery.[87]

---

which was the whole point. If God saw fit to heal your injuries within a few days, you were deemed innocent of whatever crime you were accused of. If not, you were guilty, and were exiled or executed. Or you just died from your injuries and saved everyone the trouble. This is the origin of the phrase "trial by fire." My larger point is that life sucked in those days. Be happy you live when and where you do.

[85] Please, lower your dander, for heaven's sake.

[86] Again, this all could have been prevented if only you had kept your dander down.

[87] You can have an assault without a battery, and vice versa, but I'd rather not go into the details here. If you're interested, give me a call. Or ask Ed. I explained it to him at some point.

These things happen all the time, of course. So why isn't every professional ballplayer in the history of the game currently sitting in jail? Well, because most of them have died, and keeping them in jail would just be unsanitary. Also, because there are defenses for this kind of thing. You can get away with assault and battery in baseball as long as it's within the bounds of what's considered "usual" behavior within the game for retribution and brawling. Not that it isn't assault and battery; but the assaulter has a defense that the assaultee gave his implied consent and/or assumed the risk that "normal" baseball fighting might take place. The California Supreme Court has actually held that *intentional* beanballs are part of the game, and that you can't successfully sue if someone successfully tries to hit you – *in the head* – with a 100 mph fastball. Just part of the game, you know. You signed up for it. Even though it's explicitly against the official rules of the game.[88]

It's only when you go outside the realm of acceptable violence that you can get in trouble.

Jose Offerman was a two-time MLB All-Star, playing across 15 big-league seasons with seven teams.[89] In 2007, after his MLB career was over, Offerman was playing for the independent league Long Island Ducks against the Bridgeport Bluefish. After being hit by a pitch, Offerman charged the mound – with his bat – and in the ensuing melee,[90] the Bridgeport catcher, John Nathans, suffered a severe concussion and essentially never played professional baseball again. Just part of the game, though, right? Well, not in this case. Offerman was actually arrested by Bridgeport police, and charged with second-degree assault. And Nathans, the concussed catcher, later sued him in a civil suit. Offerman got probation on the criminal count, and the charges were dropped at the end of probation. In the civil suit, a jury found him guilty of assault on Nathans (but not battery, somehow), and awarded damages of around $1,000,000. So there were some real-life consequences for in-game behavior.

Julio Castillo was a minor-league pitcher in the Cubs organization in 2008. During an otherwise run-of-the-mill brawl, Castillo fired a ball at full speed toward the opposing dugout - and missed high, hitting a fan in the head, giving him a concussion, among other head injuries. Castillo was arrested for felony assault, and wound up being sentenced to 30 days in jail and three years of probation.

The lesson? If you bring a bat to a fistfight, or knock out a fan, you could get in trouble. (Although people have asked whether it was only because these were minor leaguers - would Jose Offerman the Dodger have been charged for the same actions? Good question.) Follow the Rules, though, and you're probably okay. If you've lost your copy of the Rules, Earl Weaver can lend you his. And then have Mike Boddicker hit you in the ribs with a fastball because you looked at him funny. Part of the game.

By the way – while Marichal was never criminally charged with anything for the head-smashing incident, John Roseboro did sue him in civil court for $110,000, which goes to show that even for the free-wheeling 60's, Marichal had violated baseball etiquette, and possibly the law. They wound up settling the case for $7,500, without Marichal admitting wrongdoing. Marichal and Roseboro ended up as good friends, with Roseboro advocating for Marichal's Hall of Fame election. When he finally made it into the Hall, Marichal thanked Roseboro in his speech.

---

[88] Congress has actually tried on a couple of occasions to pass legislation explicitly making sports fights illegal, but it's never gotten anywhere. Lots of other commentators have argued that if it's not squarely within the rulebook, (the actual rulebook, not the "Unwritten Rules") then fighting should be punished more severely within the sport, and the justice system should play a bigger role as well. They've done this a little in baseball, with increased warnings for brushback pitches, and have really done so in basketball, where you are now automatically suspended if you leave the bench for a fight.

[89] Ed can analyze whether Offerman should be in the Hall of Fame. Not for me to judge.

[90] French for "big ol' fight." Things sounds more genteel in French.

Right on, thanks Joe! Interesting stuff. So as with most things, there is a legal gray area. It's all about whether someone really wants to raise a stink and challenge an assault in the courts, which most ballplayers will not want to do. Anyway, Juan Marichal, assault or no, is a no-doubt Hall-of-Famer.

Rube Marquard (1908-1924; career ERA+: 103)

	Career	Rank	Peak	Rank	Bests	Top 5s	JAWS	Rank
WAR	32.0	221	29.0	210	0	0	30.5	221
WS	206.7	106	145.6	90	0	0	NA	none

Jesse Haines has some competition for worst Hall-of-Fame pitcher. In JAWS, Rube Marquard is just a bit above Haines, whose comparables, if you remember (and there's no reason you should), are Jack McDowell, Tim Wakefield, Alex Fernandez, Mike Hampton, and Doug Drabek. Recent pitchers close to Marquard in JAWS are Derek Lowe, Brandon Webb, John Denny and Mike Boddicker. All these gentlemen were good pitchers and fine citizens who helped their teams win. But none should be allowed to sniff the ass of a dog who took a dump two blocks away from the Hall of Fame.

We know why the Frisch/Terry Veterans' Committee junta selected Jesse Haines, who played with Frisch on some good Cardinals teams. But why did they choose Rube Marquard, who was of a generation before Frisch and Terry? (And it goes without saying that they were the ones who did. I'll just go ahead and say it: They did, in 1971.)

Like outfielder Harry Hooper, Rube Marquard was a breakout star of the Lawrence Ritter book "The Glory of Their Times." Instead of doing actual research about old-timers, the Frischans read that one book. Perhaps they looked up the career stats of the book's better storytellers just to make sure they could justify a selection. Marquard pitched in the dead-ball era, so he had an OK career ERA and squeaked past 200 career wins. He had three 20-win seasons with the very good Giants teams of the 1910s. That's good enough boys, he's in. Meeting adjourned. Let's go get a beer.

If only someone in those meetings could have taken the Henry Fonda part in "12 Angry Men" and forced everyone to consider the facts more carefully. As you can see from the above rankings, Marquard was good, but not great. But on top of that, his inspiring stories in "The Glory of Their Times" have turned out to be a big ol' pile of bullschist. They were skillfully taken apart by Larry Mansch in a 1996 edition of the SABR journal "The National Pastime" (p. 16).

Marquard's origin story paints him as the archetypical young boy with big dreams who was held back by a stern, authoritarian father. According to Rube's account, his father told him that if he left home to play baseball, there would be no going back; his father would never speak to Rube again. But young Rube dar'st not contravene his God-given destiny, so off he sojourned to the tryouts, only 16 years old, hopping trains like a hobo, his dewy eyes glistening with hope over tear-stained cheeks. (I'm embellishing here; Lawrence Ritter isn't the only one who can invent details to make a story feel more cinematic. Ritter might not be responsible for Marquard's lies, but he did much more than just transcribe stories; see Rob Neyer's "Big Book of Baseball Legends," Fireside, page 146.)

Fifteen years later, Rube was a well-established celebrity. One day, out of the blue, his father showed up outside the clubhouse, aged and humbled, desperate to speak with him. Magnanimously, the prodigal Rube deigned to reconnect with his cowed patriarch. The full story is longer and more melodramatic; I'm shortening it out of disrespect.

It's all a load of crap. Larry Mansch found plenty of newspaper articles from early in Marquard's career that prove his entire family, including his father, regularly came to his games and expressed full support for Rube. Marquard also fabricated his year of birth so that he could be 16 when he left home; he was actually 19.

So maybe Marquard just exaggerated a bit! That's what all great storytellers do, right? Maybe there's a kernel of truth; maybe his father really was unhappy when he left, but came around only a few years later instead of 15! Look, I understand the desire to spin a good yarn. But Marquard slandered his own father and faked his birth year just to make himself look slightly more heroic. What kind of person does that?

And that wasn't Rube's only fabrication. He also lied to Ritter about being a lifetime teetotaler, saying "I never drank a drop." He painted himself as a paragon of clean living, saying that no ballplayer should "carouse and chase around." In reality, he was well-known in the 1910s for both carousing and chasing around. He even married a vaudeville/burlesque performer after stealing her from her husband.

It's the bald-facedness of it that gets to me; Marquard was a star and his escapades were famous at the time. To check up, all you have to do is read a few old papers, like Mansch did. If only Ritter had spent a little more time fact-checking and a little less time mythologizing, we could have been spared Rube Marquard polluting the Hall of Fame with his presence.

Besides being unworthy of the Hall of Fame, Marquard is unworthy of any further mention. **Rube Marquard is out.**

Pedro Martinez (1992-2009; career ERA+: 154)

	Career	Rank	Peak	Rank	Bests	Top 5s	JAWS	Rank
WAR	84.0	19	58.2	11	2	6	71.1	16
WS	249.8	53	161.7	54	2	3	NA	26

I've already mentioned Pedro Martinez enough to give a solid impression of what I think of him. Martinez was the new Sandy Koufax, except that he was even better. Neither pitcher came close to that magical moogical mysticaboogical[91] win number 300, and both had relatively brief runs of dominance: six years for Koufax, six and a half for Martinez. But while Koufax quit after his peak, Martinez tacked on a few more good seasons.

Martinez's peak was better too. Pedro's 2000 was the best season from either of them, 11.7 WAR. That's the fourth-best season by any pitcher since World War II, behind only Dwight Gooden in 1985, Steve Carlton in 1972, and Roger Clemens in 1997. Koufax had two WARs above 10, but nothing like that. Here are their peak years side by side, with the best one in bold:

---

[91] I thought this was from the Disney song "Bippity Boppity Boo," but I looked up the lyrics and there's nothing like it in there. Did I try to think of something else that would have worked better? No! Couldn't be bothered. At this point in this massive tome, I'm running with "good enough."

rank	Martinez	Koufax
best WAR	**11.7**	10.7
2nd best	9.7	**10.3**
3rd best	**9.0**	8.6
4th best	**8.0**	7.4
5th best	**7.2**	5.7
6th best	**6.9**	4.4
7th best	**6.5**	2.1

Martinez's 2000 was clearly one of the best seasons ever, with a WHIP (walks plus hits divided by innings pitched) that stands as the greatest in history, even better than all those dead-ball-era and 1800s guys. His win-loss record was 18-6 that year, so he didn't have a chance at the MVP award that he may have deserved.

In 1999 he did have a chance at an MVP, because he went 23-4. That year there was a controversy when Martinez narrowly finished second in the MVP voting to Ivan Rodriguez. Both had hecks of years (I believe that's the proper pluralization for "heckuva year"), but Martinez was better according to WAR, with a 9.7 easily beating Rodriguez's 6.4. (The top hitter in WAR was not Rodriguez but Derek Jeter, who finished sixth in the MVP voting. Was there actually a time in human history when Jeter was underrated?)

Their WARs were not the source of the controversy, of course. As you may know, MVP ballots require voters to select the top ten players in order. Martinez had the most first-place votes, but was left off entirely by two writers, LaVelle Neal III of Minneapolis and George King of New York. They asserted that pitchers are not "all-around players" and thus should not be considered for the MVP.

Wow, that's a dumb argument. What does it matter whether or not a player is "all-around"? All that matters is whether the player helps bring lots of wins. Who cares how he does it? If he caused your team to win an extra 20 games by sticking the pitcher's mound up his nose, then he should be MVP. Only winning is important, not the aesthetics of how you make it happen.

Win Shares provides a more sensible justification for depriving Pedro Martinez of the MVP. Because starters pitch relatively little nowadays, they are involved in fewer plays and thus can have less value. In 1999, Roberto Alomar, Manny Ramirez and Jeter tied for first in the AL with 35 Win Shares. Rodriguez had 28, and Martinez had 27. Pedro's Win Shares total was extremely good for a pitcher, tied for 15th-best of any pitcher since 1977. Win Shares isn't saying it's impossible for a pitcher to win the MVP; just very unlikely. You'd have to be as good as Martinez for something like 260 innings instead of his 213.

Beyond that, Neal and King could have had a larger point. Maybe pitchers shouldn't be considered for the MVP; after all, they have a Cy Young Award, and there isn't a hitter-only award of similar prestige. I might support a campaign to change the rules of eligibility. That would be the right way to go about it.

Neal and King went about it the wrong way. They didn't have any right to fill out their ballots based on their personal opinions of who should and shouldn't be eligible. Determining eligibility was not their job. Their only job was to look through all the eligible candidates and rank them. Rules and precedent dictate that pitchers are available for the MVP. Writers are supposed to recuse themselves if they feel they can't follow the rules and consider pitchers.

In every presidential election, a few people vote for Mickey Mouse in a childishly cynical protest. (None of the candidates is practically perfect in every way![92] Boo to all government!) I suppose those folks aren't expected to recuse themselves. But in the MVP race, there are only a precious few dozen voters (which is itself a problem, but that's another topic). Each vote can make or break the outcome. Neal and King should have been stripped of their voting rights for a few years. If you break the rules, then you don't get to play.

I might be arguing with no one here. This appears to be a settled issue: both Justin Verlander and Clayton Kershaw recently won MVP awards. But the sort of arrogance and weird logic that those writers displayed will always exist. And besides, I probably didn't have to waste time convincing you that Pedro Martinez is a deserving Hall-of-Famer.

Christy Mathewson (1900-1916; career ERA+: 135)

	Career	Rank	Peak	Rank	Bests	Top 5s	JAWS	Rank
WAR	101.7	9	66.5	4	3	8	84.1	6
WS	425.6	5	246.3	4	1	10	NA	7

Like Walter Johnson, Christy Mathewson was a grand gentleman in a rough-hewn era. Mathewson had an even classier public image than Johnson, that of a handsome, college-educated family man who respected everyone and was beloved in return. Mathewson was a Derek Jeter from 100 years ago, spending almost his entire career with a very successful New York team and bringing more plaudits per pitch than anyone of his time.

I mentioned this in the Roger Bresnahan comment, but it bears repeating: In the 1905 World Series, Mathewson pitched three shutouts, allowing only 14 hits and one walk in 27 innings. The Giants had a series ERA of 0.00 in six games, permitting only three unearned runs. Those were the days of hockey-type scores, but this was beyond anything anyone had ever seen. The series marked the beginning of Mathewson's superstardom; soon his face was hawking everything from leg garters to shirt collars. (That's not much of a range, admittedly, but those were the most old-timey ones, so I went with them.) Look at pictures of him (see http://baseballhall.org/sites/default/files/styles/fullscreen_image_popup/public/externals/3f5c8990df59fdfbecc4e2d1853753ed?itok=OpT4yL0I) and you can see why he crossed over into mainstream American hero worship. He just exudes modesty, warmth, and class.

But this being the early 1900s, Mathewson's life couldn't be all wine and roses. In 1906, Mathewson contracted and nearly died from diphtheria, one of the many horrible diseases that we've had the luxury of forgetting about, thanks to vaccines. (Anti-vaxxers should be thrown in jail for child

[92] Reference explanation: "Mary Poppins" again. Have you seen it lately? My daughter got into it, and holy cow, it is good. That Dick Van Dyke couldn't do a convincing cockney accent if his bleedin' life depended on it, but man, he was an amazing physical comedian.

endangerment, by the way. For Christ's sake, have the basic human level of humility to realize that reading a few Web sites does not make you more knowledgeable about a medical issue than 99% of all doctors.) Then in 1908, four spectators fell and died during the makeup game for the famous "Merkle's Boner" contest; Mathewson felt personally responsible because, if he had given the word, the Giants would have refused to play the game.

Two of Christy's brothers were ballplayers. His brother Nicholas was scouted by major-league clubs, but privately, Christy told them not to sign him. He knew his brother wouldn't be able to take the pressure. In 1909, Christy discovered the body of Nicholas, dead from a self-inflicted gunshot wound. Christy probably felt guilty over his brother's suicide, regardless of whether he was really at fault in any way.

Mathewson pushed through all his private pain and kept dominating the National League until around 1914, when his body couldn't take it any more. Despite all the innings he had pitched, it wasn't an arm problem; it was a mysterious pain in his left side. It was probably tuberculosis, though no one knew it at the time. His other ballplaying brother, Henry, died of the disease in 1917, and Christy would finally succumb to it in 1925. Oh, and also, in 1918, Christy caught the same influenza that afflicted Red Faber, the epidemic that killed 50 to 100 million people worldwide. Mathewson got it in France while serving in World War I, where he also was exposed to mustard gas.

I don't mean to portray Mathewson as some sort of sickly sad sack. He endured all of the above without complaint, always maintaining his impeccable integrity. He epitomized strength, both physical and moral.

In the 1910s, players were betting on games in epidemic proportions, threatening the health of the game. As with steroids in the late 1990s, few inside the game had the courage to stand up to it. Mathewson did. In 1918, Mathewson was managing the Reds, and he suspended his star first baseman, Hal Chase,[93] for throwing a game. Later he suspected the 1919 World Series would be fixed, and watched the series carefully, taking notes about each obvious misplay. He gave the league his notes, and they proved instrumental in prosecuting the Black Sox. (Source of all of the above: Mathewson's SABR biography, by Eddie Frierson.)

The Hall of Fame was invented for people like Christy Mathewson.

---

[93] I'm sparing you a digression about Hal Chase; look him up. He was a magnetic personality, and everyone who saw him play came away thinking he was a superstar (even though, in the final numbers, he wasn't that great). Meanwhile, he was throwing games left and right and drawing dozens of other players into his schemes, for little reason but the thrill of it. In my amateur diagnosis, he had anti-social personality disorder, a.k.a. sociopathy or psychopathy. Sociopaths are often the most charming people in the world, but underneath they have no conscience, no empathy, and nothing to live for but cheap thrills. Few are killers, but all are dangerous. If you're interested, I strongly recommend "The Sociopath Next Door," by Martha Stout. It's a fascinating book, and it accomplishes the very important task of teaching the rest of us how to spot sociopaths so we can avoid them at all costs.

Joe McGinnity (1899-1908; career ERA+: 120)

	Career	Rank	Peak	Rank	Bests	Top 5s	JAWS	Rank
WAR	57.7	58	52.4	19	1	5	55.1	40
WS	269.6	39	221.4	7	2	4	NA	36

Joe McGinnity insisted that he got his nickname, "Iron Man," because he worked in an iron foundry during the off-seasons. Maybe, but the name stuck for a lot of other reasons. If he had worked as a florist, no one would be calling him "Flower Man" McGinnity today.

McGinnity pitched an incredible amount during the 19-Aughts.[94] He was famous for starting and usually completing both games of doubleheaders. In 1903, he pitched 434 innings and in 1904 he pitched 408. Even in those days, not many could match those totals. Ed Walsh might have a slight edge in the Iron Man competition, since he also had two 400-plus inning seasons during the decade: one at 464, and another at 422. Either way, those two were the endurance champs; only Jack Chesbro and Vic Willis also topped 400 in a season in the entire 1900s (not just the 19-Aughts, but every year starting with "19" -- argh, see what I meant in that last footnote?)

Plus, McGinnity just looked like he was made of iron. Big, stocky, and with a glare that could cut glass, Joe McGinnity was not someone with whom one would necessarily be well-advised to f***. He and his longtime rotation-mate Christy Mathewson made for a fun odd couple, personality-wise. You could get lost in Mathewson's eyes; if you got lost in McGinnity's, you better call for a police escort out.

Before hitting it big in baseball, McGinnity owned a saloon, and often served as his own bouncer. On the field he instigated several controversial brawls, one in which he spit in the face of an umpire, and another in which he chased after an opposing player, tackled him, and punched the daylights out of him.

McGinnity was with the Giants during in the famous "Merkle's Boner" game of 1908, but he couldn't pitch that day. So he tried to start a fight with the Cubs first baseman and fellow ruffian Frank Chance, in the hope that both would get thrown out of the game. He spit on Chance, stepped on his toes, called him names, and everything else he could think of, but Chance was too smart to fall for it. At the end of the game, McGinnity threw the ball away in the scuffle so that Johnny Evers couldn't tag Merkle out. (Source: McGinnity's SCHMABR biography -- ha ha, no, it's another SABR biography, this one by Michael Wells.)

For a man of such brute strength, you might think McGinnity made his living from a fastball. But you'd be wrong. Even in the 19-Aughts, you couldn't pitch 400 innings throwing gas. He was a pretty crappy pitcher in the minors until he devised an underhand curve that he called "Old Sal." That pitch launched him into the majors at age 28. He threw it and an assortment of other pitches from wildly different angles for ten years in the majors, and then kept throwing them in the minors until age 54.

---

[94] That is, 1900-1909. There really should be a better way to say that. I can't say "1900s" because that sounds like the whole century, and I'm trying to refer to just that one decade. And I refuse to say something pretentious like "the first decade of the 20th century," for reasons I discussed in another footnote back in the comment for … oh Lord, who even remembers at this point.

With such a short major-league career, Joe McGinnity could hardly be thought of as a top-flight HOFer. But like Stan Coveleski, he was good enough during his short tenure to deserve the honor.

Jose Mendez (1907-1926)

	Rank at SP Among Negro Leaguers	Rank Among All Negro Leaguers
SABR	10	34
Monte Irvin	unranked	NA

Jose Mendez is a bit of an odd fit among Negro League Hall-of-Famers. He played in the Negro Leagues from 1917-1926, but his record there, for what it's worth, is not Hall-of-Fame worthy. By 1917 he was already 32 years old and hobbled by arm injuries. He pitched occasionally, managed the Kansas City Monarchs, and served as utility infielder. Unlike Martin Dihigo, Mendez played the field more out of necessity; rosters were so small that everyone needed to contribute every day. Mendez was a versatile fielding whiz but a bad hitter, a Nick Punto who could also contribute an occasional pitching gem.

Mendez did his real Hall-of-Fame work in his native Cuba from 1907-1916. There, in the limited league play we have numbers for, he went 63-34 with a 2.87 ERA in 919 innings. His team, the Almendares, won loads of pennants with Mendez leading the league in many categories. Mendez clearly belongs in the Cuban Baseball Hall of Fame. But does he need to be in the American/Canadian one?

In saying that, I'm pretending it's possible to extricate the Cuban leagues from the American Negro Leagues. Especially before Rube Foster established the Negro National League in 1920, there was so much crossover between the countries that it's artificial to think of them as existing in separate environments. The country of your birth determined where you got your start, but if you were good enough, you played anywhere and everywhere a person of color could play, from Cuba to Japan.[95] If you really want to review the credentials of Cool Papa Bell, Ray Dandridge, Willie "Devil" Wells, etc., you have to include their time in Cuba, Mexico, the Dominican Republic, etc.

Same deal in reverse for the likes of Martin Dihigo and Jose Mendez. I suppose if neither of them had made any significant contributions to any American team, we could ignore them. Mendez's American play may not have been close to Dihigo's, but it's enough to earn him consideration.

It's a telling indictment of white American racism, by the way, that dark-skinned people from very different cultures, countries, and languages could mix together and play ball while white players couldn't even play with English-speaking people who lived in the same cities. But telling indictments of white American racism before the Civil Rights Era are not exactly hard to come by.

At least white major-league teams would often play dark-skinned opponents after the regular season was over. The Cincinnati Reds or Pittsburgh Pirates would show up in Havana during the winter to play exhibition games against the best Cuba had to offer. But when I use the word "exhibition", I

---

[95] See http://www.npr.org/sections/codeswitch/2015/07/14/412880758/the-secret-history-of-black-baseball-players-in-japan?utm_source=facebook.com&utm_medium=social&utm_campaign=npr&utm_term=nprnews&utm_content=20150714

don't intend to give it the connotation that it has now, that of "meaningless screwing around" or "let's give some rookies some work and see how they do." These were serious contests in which each side played to win. It was "real" baseball, even though there was no pre-set schedule of the Almendares playing the Pirates a dozen times each summer.

And in those exhibitions, Jose Mendez shone. Against the Cincinnati Reds in 1908, he threw 25 innings, allowed only 8 hits and no runs, struck out 24 and walked 3. He wasn't always that dominating, but he always displayed Hall-of-Fame talent against the best white major league teams.

As I mentioned in the Andy Cooper comment, many teams in those days were often more like rock bands on tour, with each matchup being a big event that would garner a lot of excitement and a lot of top-flight competition. Mendez excelled in exhibitions; why shouldn't that count? You wouldn't throw the Beatles out of the Rock and Roll Hall of Fame just because they didn't have a set schedule of 162 gigs in England each year, would you? (I like to extend my metaphors to the point at which they break and destroy my argument.)

As much as I love the sound of the barnstorming model, it probably wouldn't work nowadays. That's not what baseball is any more, for better and for worse. The thrill of barnstorming was based on hearing superhuman legends about players who you never got to see with your own eyes until they came to town. Now if you want to see what a pitcher looks like, you can just watch him on TV or look him up on YouTube. Watching him in person is more fun, but not *that* much more. It's not quite like seeing your favorite band; it doesn't have quite the same visceral impact.

Now the fun of baseball is largely derived from rooting for your team to add to the long history of legendary champions. It's less about the particular game on the field and more about what that game could mean for future glories. The game itself doesn't mean much outside its context.

Context! That's an important word for this book. If you're playing a drinking game while reading this, you should drink two shots of Jagermeister when you hit the word "context." It doesn't come up a lot, but when it does, it's a big deal. Context is king.

When you take context into account, Jose Mendez looks much more like a Hall-of-Famer. He may not have played many of those league games that we value so much in modern times. But that was not the context of his time. Within the context he was given, he proved himself to be one of the best pitchers in the world. I think he's a Hall-of-Famer.

Hal Newhouser (1939-1955; career ERA+: 130)

	Career	Rank	Peak	Rank	Bests	Top 5s	JAWS	Rank
WAR	63.0	40	52.5	18	1	5	57.8	27
WS	263.3	42	199.1	11	2	6	NA	32

The greatest tragedy of World War II was that it made the 1940s a kind of wonky decade for baseball history. (Joke.) The biggest stars of the entire decade were probably Ted Williams, Joe Dimaggio, and Bob Feller. But each has a three-year bite out of their record because they were off doing more important things.

With so many stars gone, baseball from 1942-1945 is easily ignored and often dismissed as weirdo amateur hour. People often cite the Browns' one-armed outfielder in 1945, Pete Gray, as evidence that the level of play was low. Rubber had to be devoted to war materials, so in 1943 balls were instead made with balata, which made them hard to drive. Home run totals plummeted, which of course makes people think that the hitters stunk.

The Cardinals had a legitimate dynasty from 1942-1944, winning three pennants and two championships. They won 105 or more games each year, earning a three-year winning percentage that was the fourth best of any team of the 1900s. (Top three: 1906-1908 Cubs, 1905-1907 Cubs, 1929-1931 A's.) But they're seldom listed among the greatest teams in history because they did it during the war and got to keep most of their stars, including Stan Musial, Marty Marion, and Mort Cooper.

Only a couple of Hall-of-Famers played through the entire decade. Lou Boudreau's arthritic ankles kept him stateside, and Hal Newhouser had a leaky heart valve. Newhouser tried several times to join the fight but was turned down each time.

Stuck at home, he became arguably the best pitcher of the 1940s. Arguably, but the argument gets complicated. His WAR during the decade, 54.6, easily beats second-best Feller's 38.2. But that's hardly fair. Feller spent nearly four years in the service that Newhouser did not. Cut out 1942-1945 for both of them and you get Feller beating Newhouser, 36.2 to 29.6. But that's hardly fair either; Newhouser played major-league baseball in those years and played well. Those performances still count for something. This argument is starting to seem pointless.

The more important argument concerns whether Newhouser has Hall-of-Fame stats just because he fattened up on weak competition during the war years. Let's look at his record a little more carefully. He wasn't great at first, but give the kid a break; in his 1939 debut he was only 18 years old. Pearl Harbor brought the U.S. into the war on December 7, 1941, so major-league rosters were first stripped in 1942. Newhouser had a great ERA that year, at age 21, but pitched only 183.2 innings and had an 8-14 record. He probably got a boost from a lower level of competition. But it's not like it launched him into the stratosphere.

Newhouser's 1943 was a bit of a step back. It wasn't until 1944, when he was 23, that he broke out. He won MVP awards in both 1944 and 1945, with years that were crazy good -- I'm talking, uh ... sigh ... "amazeballs." (Ugh, that didn't feel good. But to promote this book, I'll need to train myself to write like they do in social media. The key seems to be turning all language up to 11. Everything you come across has to be the Greatest. Thing. Ever. Here are the headlines I have so far for Facebook posts: "Best. Book. Ever. You Will Not BELIEVE What It Says." "You've Been Analyzing Hall of Famers the Wrong Way This Whole Time. Number 134 Will Blow You Away." "You'll Never Think About Rabbit Maranville The Same Way Again." Here's the smug subhead for all of the above: "Because baseball.")

In 1946, all the best ballplayers were back, but Newhouser did not miss a beat. He led the league in wins and ERA again, and had his second-best seasonal WAR, even better than his 1944. From 1947-1949 he kept pitching very well, if not at his peak. (Sorry, I mean, he was still AMAZEBALLS! As is EVERYTHING EVER!) So it's not as if 1942-1945 sticks out like a sore thumb in his career. His numbers got a boost, but when baseball came back to normal he was still very good.

After an OK year in 1950, Newhouser hurt his arm, at only 30 years old. He hobbled through a few more years and then ended it. (Overwork again, a la Bret Saberhagen and Dwight Gooden? I'm telling you, the more you study the pitchers who didn't win 300 games, the more careers you see get cut short by arm injuries. They've always been epidemic; the difference is that now teams are trying harder to avoid them.) Newhouser's grand total of 2993.3 career innings isn't much, topping only ten other Hall-of-Fame starters.

You could argue that Newhouser's years during the war should be knocked down a peg. But a peg or two down from the above rankings would still keep Newhouser in Hall-of-Fame range. The two systems put him at 27th and 32nd, which scores about average among Hall-of-Famers. Put Newhouser a bit below average and he's still a Hall-of-Famer, regardless of what Jay Jaffe says. (OMG! Epic Takedown of Sabermetric Hero! Because baseball.)

Phil Niekro (1964-1987; career ERA+: 115)

	Career	Rank	Peak	Rank	Bests	Top 5s	JAWS	Rank
WAR	96.6	11	54.5	15	2	5	75.6	12
WS	375.7	10	175.2	37	1	5	NA	25

There are lots of advantages to mastering the knuckleball. You can extend your career into an age where getting carded makes for a high-larious story to bore all your friends with. ("So I told him, 'No offense taken -- I consider it a compliment!'") And you can pitch an incredible amount.

From 1977-1979, at ages 38 to 40, Phil Niekro pitched more than 330 innings each year, leading the league each time. He also led in starts and complete games each year. He provided both quantity and quality, with ERA+s of 111, 142, and 119.

But because he was playing for poor Braves teams, he lost a lot of games. When Mike Maroth lost 21 games for the Tigers in 2003, people made a big deal of the fact that Brian Kingman was the last to lose 20, in 1980. Technically, yes, Kingman was the last. But Phil Niekro was the true master of the big-loss season during the "Star Wars"/"Muppets" years. He lost 20 in 1977, 18 in 1978, 20 in 1979, and 18 in 1980. Each total led the league. In 1979, he led the league in both wins and losses, going 21-20.

His 1978 was the best of the bunch, scoring 10.0 WAR. Since 1967, when they started awarding Cy Young awards to each league, there have been 22 seasons in which pitchers led all of baseball with 9.5 WAR or better. For seasons that are that good, it's usually hard for Cy Young Award voters to screw up. All of those 22 seasons won the Cy except six: Niekro in 1978, Roger Clemens in 1990, Mark Fidrych in 1976, Bert Blyleven in 1973, Wilbur Wood in 1971, and Bob Gibson in 1969.

Clemens and Fidrych each finished second and Wood finished third in Cy Young voting, all losing to pitchers who had more wins. Gibson didn't get any votes, but they only had first-place votes in 1969, no seconds or thirds. Niekro finished sixth, and Blyleven seventh.

I covered how underrated Bert Blyleven was in his comment, but obviously Niekro got short shrift too. Niekro wasn't entirely one of a kind; Wilbur Wood was similar, at least for a while. He was also a knuckleballer who pitched very well an incredible amount each year. Wood came up earlier in the Dizzy Dean comment: He had a few great seasons but too short of a career for the Hall.

Did the game change so much within the past 40 years that the 300-inning knuckleballer has become impossible? The closest thing we've had to a Niekro or Wood lately is Tim Wakefield, who was a ton of fun but not as effective or prolific as those guys. He usually scored a league-average ERA and rarely exceeded 200 innings. In 2012, R.A. Dickey gave me hope for a new knucklin' nonagenarian, but since he's settled into league-average performances over solid, but not huge workloads.

Granted, pitchers like Niekro and Wood were never exactly commonplace. And maybe no manager will ever again have the chutzpah to deviate enough from typical pitching staff usage to make a 300-

inning knuckleballer possible; after all, his team's closer might wilt, collapse, and die if he can't pitch the ninth for every single three-run lead. For now we can just revel in the memories of the likes of Wilbur Wood and clear Hall-of-Famer Phil Niekro.

Satchel Paige (1927-1936, 1940-1949, 1951-1953, 1965)

	Rank at SP Among Negro Leaguers	Rank Among All Negro Leaguers
SABR	1	1
Monte Irvin	2 among RHP	NA

Early in his career, Satchel Paige liked to say that he threw nothing but a fastball. It was so fast, aimed with pinpoint control, that he didn't need anything else. He actually had two different fastballs: One he called a "bee ball," which was mostly straight, and one he called a "jump ball," which sounds a bit like a slider from how he describes it. Very occasionally he threw a curve, and it always fooled batters, since they were always looking for fastballs. His was similar to Steve Carlton's limited but effective arsenal.

But Paige hurt his arm in 1938, lost his killer fastball, and had to get creative. Unlike the near-robotic Carlton, Paige was very good at getting creative. His most famous creation was his hesitation pitch. I'll let him tell the story:

"The idea came to me in a game, when the guy at bat was all tighted up waiting for my fast ball. I knew he'd swing as soon as I just barely moved. So when I stretched, I paused just a little longer with my arms above my head. Then I threw my arm forward but I didn't come around with my arm right away. I put that foot of mine down, stopping for a second, before the ball left my hand.

"When my foot hit the ground that boy started swinging, so by the time I came around with the whip he was way off stride and couldn't get anywhere near the ball. I had me a strikeout." ("The Neyer/James Guide to Pitchers," Bill James and Rob Neyer, Fireside, page 333.)

I'm sure Paige was not disturbed by the fact that the hesitation pitch was fun to watch. Along with being the Negro Leagues' best pitcher, he was its best entertainer. One of his favorite things to do was to order all his infielders to sit down, and then strike out the batter. Once again, the Negro Leagues sound a lot more fun than the self-serious major leagues of today.

Paige joined those white major leagues in 1948, just 42 years young. The first time he tried his hesitation pitch, American League president Will Harridge banned it. What a killjoy. Maybe Harridge was scared it would spread and enable pitchers to dominate. But he could have at least given it some time to find out of it was really that effective.

Harridge seems like one of those people who get terrified when someone tries something new and interesting. This was the same guy who angrily cancelled the contract of Eddie Gaedel, the 3'7" little person who got one plate appearance, a four-ball walk, with the Browns in 1951.

As always, Paige adapted. By 1950 he was throwing just about every pitch known to man from every possible angle. He had great names for each of them: His changeup was his "nothing ball," his knuckleball was his "bat-dodger," and his forkball was his "whipsy-dipsy-do." In more than 25 years of professional pitching, he had gone from the most limited arsenal of any Hall-of-Famer to the most diverse.

Like Dizzy Dean and Reggie Jackson, Paige had braggadocio and style. He was a natural showman who could back up his swagger with incredible play. But to me, Paige always seemed to have a bit more dignity than your average hot dog. There is some melancholy in the way he looks in pictures and in his quotes like "Don't look back. Something might be gaining on you."

I could be projecting that onto him; it's very easy to imagine victims of racial segregation to be more saintly than they actually were. If so, I'm not the only one: Paige's popular image remains that of a man of considerable depth and intelligence who also relished putting on a great show. He was deservedly the first Negro Leaguer elected to the Hall of Fame.

Jim Palmer (1965-1967, 1969-1984; career ERA+: 125)

	Career	Rank	Peak	Rank	Bests	Top 5s	JAWS	Rank
WAR	**69.4**	**28**	**48.0**	**34**	**1**	**2**	**58.7**	**25**
WS	**310.8**	**25**	**191.4**	**19**	**3**	**6**	**NA**	**16**

Man, the 1970s were a Golden Age for pitchers. You can find lots of great pitchers in every era, of course, as long as you look past the biases of conventional numbers. WAR does this, and it makes the 1970s pack look unusually impressive. The below compares the top pitchers from the 1960s, 1970s, and 1980s. The HOFers are in bold.

1960s Pitchers	1960s WAR	1970s Pitchers	1970s WAR	1980s Pitchers	1980s WAR
Juan Marichal	**55.3**	**Tom Seaver**	**67.3**	Dave Stieb	48.6
Bob Gibson	**54.4**	**Phil Niekro**	**64.9**	**Bert Blyleven**	**38.2**
Sandy Koufax	**48.0**	**Gaylord Perry**	**59.4**	Roger Clemens	35.7
Jim Bunning	**46.2**	**Bert Blyleven**	**58.2**	Bob Welch	35.2
Don Drysdale	**44.6**	**Jim Palmer**	**54.6**	Fernando Valenzuela	33.2
Larry Jackson	35.9	**Fergie Jenkins**	**53.1**	Orel Hershiser	32.9
Jim Maloney	35.4	**Steve Carlton**	**44.6**	Bret Saberhagen	32.2
Dean Chance	33.5	Wilbur Wood	43.3	John Tudor	31.3
Sam McDowell	30.1	**Nolan Ryan**	**41.6**	Dwight Gooden	30.7
Chris Short	28.9	Rick Reuschel	40.9	Charlie Hough	30.7

Perhaps the real story here is how sad the pack of 1980s pitchers looks. (Dave Stieb?!?!?) More about that later.

The 1970s pitchers clearly outclass those of the other two decades. The 1960s are supposed to be the era of the pitcher, but the best four from the 1970s beat every one of the 1960s pitchers. And after the top five 1960s Hall-of-Famers, the quality drops off dramatically.

Note that none of the HOFers from the 1970s are borderline guys. I suppose a lot of people felt Bert Blyleven was at the borderline, since it took him 14 years on the ballot to get the nod. But if his teams had managed to score enough runs to get him 13 more of those pitcher wins that everyone likes so much, he'd have hit 300, and his selection wouldn't have taken so darn long.

And, by the way, the only reason people started thinking you needed 300 wins to get into the Hall was because of the 1970s pack of superstars. Before the 1970s, you definitely did not need 300 wins to get in. Everyone with more than 250 is in the Hall except a few pitchers from the 1970s or later (plus a couple of those 1800s guys who ruin every argument). Guys like Eppa Rixey and Red Faber probably wouldn't have had a chance if not for their 250-plus win totals. Thankfully, no one seems to think 300 wins are a prerequisite any more, since John Smoltz and Pedro Martinez both got in without controversy.

Unlike Blyleven, Jim Palmer did not suffer from underratedness. Playing for some great Orioles teams, he collected lots of wins and lots of Cy Young Awards. Dock Ellis[96] liked to call Palmer "Cy" or "Cry." When asked why, Ellis said "Because if he doesn't win the Cy Young every year, he cries about it." ("Baseball's Greatest Insults," Kevin Nelson, Fireside, p. 59.)

Palmer rubbed a lot of people the wrong way, including his longtime manager, Earl Weaver. Weaver was never pleased with Palmer's frequent maladies. Here's one of Weaver's quotes about Palmer:

"Jimmy is the guy who introduced me to the ulnar nerve, for example, which I thought he'd invented. He's had so many physical problems - back, shoulder, elbow, forearm - that I thought he'd just run out of ailments and had just made one up when he said his ulnar nerve was bothering him. Then I had to see a doctor about swelling in my right hand, and he said, 'You've got an ulnar nerve problem.' 'I must have caught it from Jim Palmer,' I told him." ("Baseball's Greatest Insults," Kevin Nelson, Fireside, p. 60.)

Weaver was a genius, perhaps the best manager in history after John McGraw. And he was a lot like McGraw: tough, pugnacious, brilliant, and never afraid to try something different. I'm usually inclined to believe him.

But it's also possible that Jim Palmer was ahead of the curve. He was a smart guy too. Weaver plays the situation for laughs, but in so doing he admits that Palmer knew about the importance of the ulnar nerve when he did not. That's a telling little fact.

Who knows; maybe Palmer's precautions enabled him to pitch as much and as well as he did. He still pitched a good amount from 1969-1974, leading the league in innings once and exceeding 270 four times. Then he seemed to give in to Weaver's demands from 1975-1978, leading the league in innings three times and throwing 323 in the other. After that stretch he was never quite the same. He was 33

---

[96] Dock Ellis, some of you may know, was the pitcher who threw a no-hitter while high on acid. At one point in the game, he thought Richard Nixon was the umpire and Jimi Hendrix was the hitter. It was the '70s, man. I was born in 1976, so I saw it all. One time my buddy ate so much Count Chocula that he stripped down to his Underoos and started biting off the heads of my Star Wars figures. It was crazy, man.

years old in 1979, so some regression is to be expected. But plenty of pitchers of Palmer's ability have accomplished more than he did from 33 onward.

It's not hard to imagine that Palmer could have avoided a few of his mid-30s injuries if his manager had taken his arm's health more seriously. I say that with major benefit of hindsight, of course. And it didn't prevent Jim Palmer from having a hands-down Hall-of-Fame career.

Herb Pennock (1912-1917, 1919-1934; career ERA+: 106)

	Career	Rank	Peak	Rank	Bests	Top 5s	JAWS	Rank
WAR	44.9	116	35.9	116	1	2	40.4	123
WS	239.6	66	147.5	85	0	1	NA	none

Yankees. Herb Pennock was another one of those damn Yankees. Damn Yankeeeeees! Yankees, Yankees, Yankees, I'd like to say no thankees, but you can bet the bankees that the Yankees give us spankees to our aaaaasses … (I've never seen "Damn Yankees," but I assume one of the songs goes something like that.)

Actually, being a Yankee doesn't tend to get you more awards than you deserve. For example, Yankee players don't win a disproportionate number of MVPs. Derek Jeter never won one, despite possibly deserving it a few times and being the Most Valuable Dreamboat in America's crush journal for what felt like a thousand years. In my lifetime (since 1976), the Yankees have won 11 pennants but their players have won only four MVPs.

And there aren't an inordinate number of Hall-of-Famers who got in just because they were on good Yankees teams. So far, I've only had to kick out Earle Combs and Lefty Gomez, and their selections weren't nearly as egregious as those of George Kelly, Tommy McCarthy, Lloyd Waner, Jesse Haines, Rube Marquard, etc.

Like Combs and Gomez, Herb Pennock wasn't a terrible choice. He spent 1918 serving in World War I, and he was great in the postseason, with a 1.95 ERA in 55 innings. But even taking those factors into account only bumps him from Javier Vazquez/Brad Radke territory to Kenny Rogers/Jimmy Key territory in terms of JAWS. Again, not bad, but below the line. I might give him a pass if Bill James had ranked him in his top 100, but he didn't.

Herb Pennock is hardly a disgrace to the Hall of Fame. But we can do better. Let's **kick Pennock out** and replace him with some more deserving players.

Gaylord Perry (1962-1983; career ERA+: 117)

	Career	Rank	Peak	Rank	Bests	Top 5s	JAWS	Rank
WAR	91.0	13	52.8	17	0	4	71.9	15
WS	369.2	12	184.3	25	1	4	NA	17

Let's play word association. I'll say a word or phrase and you give me the first thing that comes to your mind. So if I say "water" you might say "dentist," since dentists use water. I will then diagnose you with a dentist fetish, and introduce you to some friends of mine who have fetishes for dentist fetishists. There's no psychological validity to any of this, but now that I think about it, word association could be the basis for a good online dating site. It's just "science"-y enough to fool people who don't know much about science.

Anyway, here's your phrase: Gaylord Perry. Did you think "spitball"? I know I did, and I knew it was coming. I tried to think "dentist," but I couldn't, because Gaylord Perry was not a dentist, to my knowledge. I admit, I haven't kept up with him since his retirement. I should give him a call and ask him if he's a dentist.

The point is that the rumors of Perry using of the spitball were so prevalent that the pitch came to define him. It was the lead story every time he started a game: Is he throwing it? After 1967, it became illegal to touch your mouth before a pitch. So then the question became: How does he throw it? Does he hide Vaseline or slippery elm or an affectionate puppy in his glove or in his hair or his eyeball or what?

Perry always denied throwing the spitball, but that was just part of the ruse. Late in his career, he wrote a book called "Me and the Spitter: An Autobiographical Confession" (Saturday Review Press, 1974). In it he methodically details all his past chicanery, and then sums it up by saying "Of course, I'm reformed now. I'm a pure law-abiding citizen." I picture him saying those words with a sly smile and fingers crossed behind his back. Gaylord Perry was like a character in an "Ocean's Eleven"-style heist movie. You know what he's doing is wrong, but it's just so fun to watch him outsmart those rich jerks and get away with it.

His opponents did not find his actions so charming. In a desperate campaign to find evidence against him, they put Perry through a series of indignities, including but not limited to:

- Searching his ears during a game
- Ruffling through his hair and cap during a game
- An umpire sneaking up behind him and ripping his cap off his head
- Making him pull his pant legs up to his knees
- An umpire wiping his face and neck with a towel and then examining the towel's contents
- An opposing manager charging him on the mound, grabbing his cap, throwing it to the ground and kicking it
- Chemically analyzing balls he had thrown
- Ruling a pitch illegal because it moved like the umpire assumed a spitball would

No one ever found anything. I suppose that last one sort of found something, in that Perry threw a pitch that dropped suddenly at the plate, and the umpire called it a spitball. It wasn't just the umpire being a jerk; it was in accordance with a new league rule that allowed umpires to judge pitches to be spitballs just by how they looked. This was tantamount to saying "You look nervous, as if you just robbed a bank. I don't care if there is no evidence attaching you to a bank robbery, or even any report of a bank having been robbed. You're under arrest." Perry's team, the Cleveland Americans,[97] set up a

---

[97] They were not actually called that then, but that's my new idea for a replacement name for the Team Which Must Not Be Named. In the early days, there was no tradition of each team having a set-in-stone name apart from its city of origin. American League teams were often referred to as the Americans just to distinguish them from teams from other leagues. The names that are now de rigueur started out as nicknames, sort of like how the Yankees are occasionally called "The Bronx Bombers." More to the point, who could object to a team being called the Americans? We have the Nationals, so why not Americans? What's the matter, do you hate America?

private demonstration of his new forkball for the umpires. They agreed it did move like a spitball, and the stupid new rule quietly went away. (Source: Perry's SABR biography, by Mark Armour.)

This represented the apex of the pathetic, flailing crusade to catch Perry violating a prohibition that was basically unenforceable. In even attempting to police his spitball, his opponents and the baseball establishment always looked like Roscoe P. Coltrane to Gaylord Perry's Duke boys.[98] Perry was always one step ahead of the law: By the time of the ludicrous "if it looks like a spitball, it's a spitball" rule, Perry could gather enough moisture from his own sweat to throw all the wet ones he wanted.

Again, besides the ick factor, there is nothing wrong with the spitball. In the 1910s, it was so effective that it threw off the balance of the game. But hitters have advanced tremendously in the past 100 years. New pitches like the forkball/split-fingered fastball have much the same movement. It's silly that the spitball is still illegal.

What with all the spitter hoo-ha, it's easy to overlook how great Gaylord Perry was. His spitball was only part of his repertoire: His slider, fastball and curve could have been enough for a Hall-of-Fame career. Some said he used the spitball sparingly, but the threat of it had a great psychological effect on the batter.

Perry lasted into his mid-40s, largely because he never stopped tinkering. Late in his career he made up a new pitch, a "puff ball," which released with a cloud of resin dust that would distract the hitter. It was almost immediately outlawed.

Along with being one of the more entertaining and unique pitchers in baseball history, Gaylord Perry was one of the best. Clear Hall-of-Famer.

Eddie Plank (1901-1917; career ERA+: 122)

	Career	Rank	Peak	Rank	Bests	Top 5s	JAWS	Rank
WAR	89.9	15	50.5	26	0	1	70.2	18
WS	359.8	13	195.6	14	0	4	NA	30

Eddie Plank was the Jim Kaat or Tommy John of his time. That's a slight exaggeration, as Plank was better than either of them, even when you adjust for context. But like them, Plank was never considered a big star, just a good pitcher who lasted a long time. His conventional numbers look remarkable now, but were less so in the dead-ball era. He was overshadowed on his own team, the Philadelphia A's, by Rube Waddell, Chief Bender and Jack Coombs. In the 1910 World Series, Plank rode the bench while Bender and Coombs pitched every inning.

---

[98] Reference explanation: There was a brief window in my childhood in which neither "Star Wars" nor baseball dominated my thoughts, hopes and dreams. For about a year I was fascinated with "The Dukes of Hazzard," a TV show that brought the "rednecks in car chases" formula of "Smokey and the Bandit" to the small screen. Somehow, whenever I played "Dukes of Hazzard" with my friends, I always ended up being Roscoe P. Coltrane, the comically inept police officer whose catchphrase was "Gue, gue, gue." In those days we only had about five TV channels and no Internet. We scavenged pleasure out of the few morsels of entertainment we were given.

Quietly, Plank kept piling on good season after good season until he'd completed a Hall-of-Fame career. He also had a quiet personality: smart, stable and taciturn. He provided a stark contrast to teammate Rube Waddell, but then, so did everybody. Just wait until we get to Waddell's comment.

Also, Waddell was a thrilling, dominant strikeout machine, while Plank was boring to watch. He was a dawdler on the mound, tugging his hat, asking for a new sign, adjusting his shirt, staring at the runner, etc. It would be par for the course in the current game, but it was was unusual in those days. Before baseball parks had lights, you had to get the game in before sundown. If a game lasted too late into the evening, the umpire would call it on account of darkness. Some games were replayed, but some weren't. As a result, every team had a handful of tie games each year. Baseball may be the only major sport that doesn't have a clock, but before lights, there was a feeling of being on the sun's clock.

Hey, I just had a thought. You know the shot clock in basketball? Before it was instituted, the team with the lead near the end of the game would just dribble endlessly until the game was over. I wonder if a pitcher ever tried doing something similar in the days before lights. If a game had a 3:00 start time, and he got an early lead, he could waste enough time on the mound to get the game called early on account of darkness. I've never heard of it happening, but I wouldn't be surprised. Everything else imaginable was attempted to gain an edge. As always, if you know of any incidents like this, contact my friend Chris E. Keedei at chrisekeedei@yahoo.com.

Eddie Plank may not make for the most thrilling Hall-of-Famer, but he's in for sure.

Eppa Rixey (1912-1917, 1919-1933; career ERA+: 115)

	Career	Rank	Peak	Rank	Bests	Top 5s	JAWS	Rank
WAR	55.4	66	33.4	148	0	1	44.4	87
WS	311.2	23	163.0	51	0	2	NA	64

Speaking of Jim Kaat/Tommy John types, Eppa Rixey is in the Hall of Fame because he had 266 career wins. He also lost a lot of games, 251, ninth-most of any pitcher ever. But that's largely because he played for a lot of poor-hitting Phillies and Reds teams.

He is the only Hall-of-Fame pitcher whom the Cincinnati Reds could reasonably claim as their own. Tom Seaver played for the Reds for a few years, but he's a Met for sure. He had 76.1 career WAR as a Met and just 18.6 as a Red. Ditto for Christy Mathewson, Old Hoss Radbourn, Amos Rusie, Dazzy Vance, and Mordecai Brown (plus Rube Marquard and Jesse Haines, though I hesitate to refer to them as Hall-of-Famers): All played for the Reds at some point but had more WAR elsewhere.

Considering the Reds have been around since 1882, that's surprising. The Braves haven't had a ton more success over the years than the Reds: 17 pennants for the Braves and three World Series titles to the Reds' 10 pennants and five championships. But according to my team-with-the-most-WAR standard, the Braves can claim Kid Nichols, John Clarkson, Warren Spahn, Phil Niekro, Greg Maddux, Tom Glavine, and John Smoltz. Cleveland has just five pennants and two championships, but they get Cy Young, Addie Joss, Stan Coveleski, Bob Feller, Bob Lemon and Early Wynn. The Reds just get Eppa Rixey. "I got five pieces of candy!" "I got a chocolate bar!" "I got a quarter!" "I got a rock."[99]

Then again, the Pittsburgh Pirates would be happy to have Rixey. No Hall-of-Fame pitcher could be considered a Pirate. Their all-time pitching WAR champs are Babe Adams, Bob Friend, Wilbur Cooper, and Sam Leever. None are realistic Hall-of-Famers, and no one, to my knowledge, is stumping for any of them.

And Eppa Rixey isn't really too bad. He had a long career with a couple of great seasons. Plus, he spent his 27-year-old season fighting in World War I. The Hall of Fame has established that that's good enough.

Personally, I like him because he was a college boy. Rixey was pursuing a bachelor's degree in chemistry at the University of Virginia when he was discovered by National League umpire Cy Rigler. Rigler tried to talk him into trying out for the Phillies, but Rixey refused, seeing a better future as a chemist. (Those were the nutty days when a chemist made more money than a major-league baseball player.) Then Rigler promised to split his finder's fee with Rixey. Since his family was struggling financially, Rixey gave in. (If you're wondering why an active umpire was scouting players, the National League was too. They outlawed the practice as a result of Rigler's actions.) (Source: Rixey's SABR biography, by Jan Finkel.)

In the off-seasons, Rixey got his master's degree in chemistry and also studied math and Latin. Then he taught high school Latin and wrote poetry in his spare time. These were not the kinds of things in which Babe Ruth or Joe McGinnity involved themselves.

That reminds me: Have you heard about this football player, John Urschel, who also does mathematical research and has had several of his papers published in major journals? (See "NFL player John Urschel just published a paper in the Journal of Computational Mathematics," Vox.com, Joseph Stromberg, March 23, 2015.) I love stuff like that. It seems so rare. Nowadays you have to devote all your energy to just one thing to be a success. You have to be a boring obsessive toiling in one small field for 80 hours a week to get anywhere. Being a Renaissance Man means being a failure. I may seem obsessive about baseball history, but there are actually so many interesting things in the world I want to explore. I find people like Urschel much more inspiring than the Bill Gateses of the world who limited their lives to one thing and slept under their desks throughout their 20s and so forth.

Regardless, Eppa Rixey is on the low end of Hall-of-Famers. The above rankings suggest he clears the bar, and that's good enough for me.

Robin Roberts (1948-1966; career ERA+: 113)

	Career	Rank	Peak	Rank	Bests	Top 5s	JAWS	Rank
WAR	86.0	17	54.8	14	3	7	70.4	17
WS	337.8	15	198.6	12	5	6	NA	15

[99] Reference explanation: "It's the Great Pumpkin, Charlie Brown." I admit, I stole this joke from an old "Baseball Prospectus" annual.

The factoid you may have heard about Robin Roberts was that he gave up a lot of home runs. That he did: 505, the second-most ever, behind Jamie Moyer. (Man, Moyer comes up a lot in this book. I think I secretly love him. I might just recommend him for the Hall ...) But the 1950s were a homer-heavy time; if Cy Young pitched then he would have the all-time homers-allowed record, no diggity.[100]

Offenses in the 1950s were basically just walks and homers, with almost no stolen bases. If the essence of 1950s baseball could be captured in one Sportsflics card, it would depict Eddie Yost slowly trotting to first base.[101] That might be a small part of why attendance plummeted during the decade, only to be turned around when franchises started moving to new cities. Once again, baby boomers, if that's baseball's "Golden Age," I'm a dentist. (I am not a dentist.)

File Robin Roberts in with Lefty Grove. Both are all-time great pitchers who remain underappreciated. Grove dominated the 1930s, and Robin Roberts was the best pitcher of the 1950s. Let's do another of those fun top-ten charts by decade. Here are the best pitcher WARs from the 1930s, 1940s and 1950s. The Hall-of-Famers are in bold:

1930s Pitchers	1930s WAR	1940s Pitchers	1940s WAR	1950s Pitchers	1950s WAR
Lefty Grove	**78.3**	**Hal Newhouser**	**54.6**	**Robin Roberts**	**60.4**
Carl Hubbell	**55.5**	**Bob Feller**	**38.2**	**Warren Spahn**	**57.3**
Mel Harder	45.0	Dizzy Trout	37.4	Billy Pierce	43.7
Lefty Gomez	**43.4**	Harry Brecheen	32.4	**Early Wynn**	**37.1**
Dizzy Dean	**43.0**	Dutch Leonard	31.7	Bob Rush	32.9
Wes Ferrell	42.6	Mort Cooper	28.7	Sal Maglie	31.6
Red Ruffing	**38.2**	Bucky Walters	28.5	Johnny Antonelli	31.0
Tommy Bridges	35.8	Claude Passeau	27.4	Ned Garver	28.1
Larry French	35.1	Tex Hughson	25.7	**Whitey Ford**	**26.6**
Ted Lyons	**32.1**	Rip Sewell	25.0	Mike Garcia	26.2

[100] Am I misusing "no diggity"? I'm pretty sure it means "no doubt." It's from a song that came out when I was in college, but even then I wasn't cool enough to understand what it meant.

[101] Lots to unpack here. Sportsflics were baseball cards from the late 1980s that, when you turned them a bit to the side, would flash to a different image, thus creating the world's shortest and most unsatisfying movies. If you laid up nights fantasizing of seeing Candy Maldonado move from one pose to another and back again, then Sportsflics cards were for you. Also Eddie Yost was a Washington Senators third baseman during the 1950s who figured out that if you just sat there and watched a lot of pitches go by, you could draw 130 walks a year. He wasn't the only one: Ferris Fain and Eddie Joost also drew incredible numbers of walks in the post-war era by refusing to bite on anything but the ideal pitch.

Granted, there is always some arbitrariness inherent in grouping anything by decade. You won't see Bob Lemon in the above because his greatness spanned 1948 to 1956. He foolishly didn't time his period of dominance to fall within years that have the same third digit according to the Gregorian calendar that most of us use in the West. If we were still using the Julian calendar like we SHOULD be,[102] Lemon might get his due (or might not -- I can't do the translation).

Ooh, better, we should all switch to the calendar I invented, in which every month has exactly 28 days except for a brand-new month called Rocktober, which has 29. (Do the math -- 12 months of 28 days each plus one month of 29 days equals 365.) Rocktober would be at the end of the year, and all you're allowed to do during Rocktober is rock.

This would mean that every month, the same day of the month would fall on the same day of the week. If it's the 6th, you know it's Friday. Then next year, Rocktober's extra day would push Friday to the 7th. Wouldn't that be easier?

My calendar wouldn't change the numbering of the years, so it's irrelevant to Bob Lemon and Robin Roberts and everything I was just talking about. But think about it: You'd always know how long each month is. They're all exactly 28 days, except for Rocktober. You'd never again have to try to conjure up that stupid rhyme-ish thing that was apparently written in Elizabethan England because it goes "Thirty days hath September, April, June and November. All the rest hath 31, save February, which hath 28, except when it's 29 … man, this really doth not need to be so complicated. Pope Gregory XIII really screwth the pooch on this one."

I recognize that my plan would separate Christmas and New Year's by inserting Rocktober between them. People like to have those in one long break, I know. No problem: Rocktober will be made entirely of federal holidays. It could be like August is in France, except with more rockin'. (To be fair, almost everything is more rockin' than France. Can you think of a single French rock band? I can't. That country has to have the lowest ratio of electric guitars to white people[103] in the world.) Each day

---

[102] Again, I only use "grumpy old man" arguments when I want to look through rose-colored glasses at times decades or centuries before my birth. In 1584, Pope Gregory XIII introduced the Gregorian calendar to replace the Julian calendar. It added .002% more time to each year, which actually makes a difference. Under the Julian calendar, the date of Easter kept getting farther and farther from the spring solstice, where it was originally. The date of Easter, see, is determined by the lunar calendar, which makes sense because … um … Jesus is living on the moon now? I might have to call up a theologian on this one, and ask him if he's a dentist.

[103] Most white people have this weird obsession with electric guitars. I don't think I'm telling tales out of school here. Electric guitars are great, no doubt -- probably the best instrument ever. But white people, as is their wont, turned them into objects of worship. At heart, white people are Puritans. They like to create arbitrary, picayune rules about everything imaginable and then judge people based on how well they can conform to the maddeningly complex panoply of spoken and unspoken rules. This rule-making compulsion, believe it or not, even extends to the instrumentation of their music: Many of them insist a band should have nothing but electric guitars and drums. They call this unnecessarily limited form of music "rock," and are always concerned about whether it's dying. It isn't dead and never will be, but it's accomplished everything it possibly can several times over. It's become like jazz, reserved for a small population of nerds. Rock was put into a nursing home for its own safety and security. Radiohead accomplished the unenviable task of convincing rock that it needed to retire; by progressing from "The Bends" to "OK Computer" to "Kid A", they slowly eased

of Rocktober will commemorate a different rocker, each chosen with an online poll. C'mon, baby boomers, tell me you wouldn't love a holiday devoted to the Beatles or Elvis.

Anyway, back to Robin Roberts. He was obviously not as good as Lefty Grove, but who was? Roberts was good enough to beat Warren Spahn for the best of the 1950s. That surprised me, I admit. Roberts didn't get into national headlines very often, since he played for the Phillies. His lone postseason appearance was with the 1950 "Whiz Kids" Phillies, a team that is still remembered because they had success during the 1950s and were not the Yankees. (Other teams in this category include the 1959 "Go-Go" White Sox, the 1955 "Boys of Summer" Dodgers, and the 1954 Cleveland Americans, who went 111-43.)

And Roberts became the best pitcher of the 1950s despite dropping off significantly in 1956. That year he was only 29, and overwork probably contributed to his early decline. But those young years of being overworked were pretty darn sweet. Go to baseball-reference and check out Robin Roberts' numbers from 1950-1955. He pitched more than 300 innings per year, always with an ERA+ of 121 or better. He led the league in starts six years in a row. From 1952-1955, he led the league in wins and complete games every year. If the Cy Young Award had existed then, Roberts would have collected a string of trophies that rivaled those of Randy Johnson or Greg Maddux.

Another of Roberts' claims to fame is that he helped get Marvin Miller into baseball. In 1954, Roberts became the National League representative for the Players Association. In those days, the players did all the negotiations by themselves. They were wildly overmatched. Their opponents in these negotiations, mind you, were a pack of wildly successful millionaires armed with all the lawyers that millions can buy. The players may as well have been your uncle Bill serving as his own counsel against Johnny Cochran. Once again, throwing or hitting a ball well does not make you expert in everything that touches the sport of baseball.

Roberts was elected to the position by his peers, so he felt obligated to take it. But he had the wisdom and humility to recognize that he was ill-suited for the job. He knew that he was a guy who threw balls, not someone sufficiently versed in labor negotiations to represent the legal and financial interests of hundreds of workers. When he resigned from the post in 1959, Roberts urged the association to hire an executive director who could fight for them as hard as they deserved.

In 1964, the players were locked in another in a series of battles with owners over how much TV revenue should go into the pension fund that kept many retired players alive. Roberts asked the National League representative, Bob Friend, for the chance to speak to the Player's Association. In his speech, Roberts again implored the group to hire an executive director from outside the baseball world. The Association was convinced, and let Roberts and Jim Bunning (ironically, perhaps, considering his later career) offer the job to Marvin Miller, a brilliant veteran of steel unions. (Source: Roberts' SABr biography, by Ralph Berger.)

Roberts later begged off responsibility for unleashing Marvin Miller on baseball, which is disappointing but not surprising. In the macho world of baseball, it's seen as insufficiently manly to take credit for any pinko commie union stuff, even if that pinko commie union stuff enriched both your brethren and the game as a whole beyond anyone's wildest dreams.

Marvin Miller is one of the most important non-players in baseball history, up there with Ban Johnson, Judge Kenesaw Mountain Landis, Rube Foster, Branch Rickey, and precious few others.

---

hipster white people into the realization that sounds not created by electric guitars might not be horrible to hear.

Miller almost single-handedly brought free agency, arbitration, and everything else that took baseball into a new age, one of unheard-of revenue for both players and owners. Baseball was the first sport to undergo this transition; Miller changed not just baseball, but all of sports.

The fact that Marvin Miller is not in the Hall of Fame is beyond preposterous. Maybe he was kind of a jerk sometimes. So what? So was Ted Williams. Maybe you don't agree with his politics. So what? Do you agree with Ty Cobb's? Do any of the negative feelings you may have about Miller change the impact he had on the game? I would happily see a hundred more Rube Marquards and Jesse Haineses elected if it meant Marvin Miller could get his rightful place.

Anyway, Robin Roberts is in the Hall of Fame, and few people deserve it more.

Wilbur "Bullet" Rogan (1917, 1920-1938)

	Rank at SP Among Negro Leaguers	Rank Among All Negro Leaguers
SABR	3	11
Monte Irvin	4 among RHP	NA

I'm going to see how many connections I can make between Wilbur "Bullet" Rogan and other Hall-of-Fame Negro League pitchers. He threw in a quick, no-windup delivery, just like Leon Day. He was known as "Bullet Joe" even though his full name was Charles Wilber Rogan; the nickname came because he had a fastball that rivaled that of "Smokey Joe" Williams. Rogan wasn't just a speed guy though; like a latter-day Satchel Paige, he had tons of different pitches thrown from different angles. That's three connections!

Martin Dihigo is the best parallel, as Rogan was brilliant on the mound and with the bat. In 1922, Rogan hit .369/.453/.660 as a pitcher/outfielder. He hit 13 home runs, second in the league after Oscar Charleston. He was also second in pitcher wins and had the third-best ERA+ over 193.7 innings. Seamheads.com gives Rogan 32.6 Win Shares in 1922, for a team that played only 85 games. That would be more than 60 Win Shares in a 162-game season, better than any season in the white majors since the days of Old Hoss Radbourn. Rogan was Lefty Grove and Jimmie Foxx combined into one person.

And 1922 was not a fluke for Rogan. In 1921 he got 34.6 Win Shares in 95 games. That year Seamheads lists Rogan as the best hitter in Negro League baseball, but they could have also named him best pitcher, as he led the league with a 235 ERA+ and pitched 204 innings. In 1923 he earned 30.1 Seamheads Win Shares in 86 games, as the Monarchs finally beat Rube Foster's Chicago American Giants (for whom Bill Foster threw 8 innings -- that's five connections) for the pennant.

Rogan became manager of the Monarchs in 1926, taking over for Jose Mendez. (That's six!) Unlike Andy Cooper, (seven) Rogan was not a good manager, at least not at first. He had an army background, serving from 1914-1920, which perhaps explains why he managed as if he were a drill sergeant. He barraged players with orders and screamed at people who made mistakes. He tended not to trust young players and often gave too much playing time to the veterans who were his friends. (Source: Rogan's Wikipedia page.)

In those days, before teams had legions of coaches supporting each limb of each player, a big part of managing was teaching players how to improve. Rogan was a bad teacher in the way that many great players are: They are accustomed to performing so well that they can't understand why you can't do the same. It comes so naturally to them that they have never had to break it down and put it into words. Even if they can put it into words, they often don't have patience for mere mortals who can't do exactly what they did; Ted Williams was like that during his four mostly unsuccessful years as a manager. Jim Bouton illustrated this tendency of great players to be bad instructors in "Interview with Former New York Yankees Pitcher Jim Bouton" (Newyorkbaseballfans.com, Shawn Collins, August 7, 2013):

"[Great players] can't relate and a lot of them don't know how they do it. You know when Yogi Berra was named batting coach for the Yankees, I saw his first clinic that he conducted in the batting cage during spring training. He couldn't explain what he did. He started saying, 'Well, your hands have to be ... ah, forget your hands. Your feet, make sure that your feet are. um ... because when the ball comes, you turn and have your hips ... ahh, just watch me!'"

To his credit, Bullet Rogan eventually learned how to manage and teach. He certainly was never bad enough to sink the Monarchs, who kept winning under his watch. But he probably shouldn't have been given the job of leading one of the best teams in the Negro Leagues without first demonstrating some managerial ability. I've been over this before: Ty Cobb and Rogers Hornsby both became managers because they were good at hitting balls, not because they were good leaders of men. The Negro Leagues took this approach too.

Anyway, Bullet Rogan doesn't need managing added to his resume; he was one of the best players in Negro League history, and is a no-doubter for the Hall (unlike Ray Brown -- did I get everybody?).

Red Ruffing (1924-1942, 1945-1947; career ERA+: 109)

	Career	Rank	Peak	Rank	Bests	Top 5s	JAWS	Rank
WAR	70.4	25	41.3	63	0	3	55.8	37
WS	320.6	19	162.1	53	0	3	NA	44

Red Ruffing is the fourth of the Golden Age HOF Yankee pitchers to slide under our lens. It's not an impressive bunch, by Hall-of-Fame standards; I kicked out Lefty Gomez and Herb Pennock and only let Waite Hoyt stay with some reservations. Ruffing, though, is the real deal.

Ruffing got his start as an average or slightly-worse-than-average starter for the much-worse-than-average 1920s Red Sox. Then as soon as he joined the Yankees, zing zam zoom, Ruffing's ... well, his win-loss percentages sure turned around in a hurry. It still took him a few years to log a good ERA: 1932 saw his first ERA+ above 104, with a healthy 132. From then on, it was all gravy and no gas, as they say (nobody says that).

Ruffing might look unimpressive at first, what with his 109 career ERA+ and suchlike. But he probably has the most "but also"s of any pitcher in the Hall. Let's go through them:

Military: Ruffing was still pitching very well when he joined the war effort in 1943. Then he was 37 years old and had four dependents and four missing toes. Each time he had a new child, he cut off one toe and gave it to him or her as a symbolic gesture of parental sacrifice, in accordance with an old Luxembourgian tradition. (Not true! He lost his toes in a coal mining accident when he was 15. But did I fool you for a second at least?)

Despite all these marks against him, he got drafted and was accepted for noncombat duty. Mostly he gave P.E. lessons and played baseball to entertain the troops. When he got back to major-league ball in 1945 he was still effective, but injuries quickly knocked him down. Maybe if Hitler hadn't been such a smelly fart machine,[104] Red Ruffing would have had a few more good seasons and stretched his 273 career wins to 300.

Postseason: Playing for the Yankees meant plenty of World Series appearances, and Ruffing excelled in them. In 85.2 career World Series innings he had a 2.63 ERA, which was really, really good in the 1930s. If there had been a World Series MVP in 1938, Red Ruffing could have won it, as he allowed only three earned runs in two complete games, both of them Yankee wins.

Hitting: Ruffing rivals Bob Lemon for the title of best-hitting pitcher in history. Since 1901, Ruffing has the most career hitting WAR by a pitcher, 15.0. Few pitchers outside the Negro Leagues have been worth batting anywhere but ninth, but Ruffing was. In 1930 he was good even by 1930 standards, hitting .364/.402/.584 (150 OPS+) in 117 PAs. He was used as a pinch hitter 257 times in his career, and didn't fare terribly by the standards of that very tough job: .258/.300/.316. At the height of his hitting prowess, he was often walked to get to the Yankees' leadoff hitter, Frankie Crosetti.

That's not only a tribute to Ruffing's hitting; it's also a condemnation of Crosetti's. Crosetti was a great-fielding shortstop but a mediocre-to-bad hitter. The 1930s Yankees were overflowing with great hitters. Why did they bat Crosetti leadoff?

The main reason, as far as I can tell, was that Crosetti stole bases. Among managers, there is a longstanding irrational need to bat base-stealers first. Speed can certainly be helpful, but not when it supersedes the much more important need of having a leadoff hitter who can get on base. If you don't get on base, that basestealing ability is rendered moot. As they say, you can't steal first base.

Very few players in the 1930s stole bases. But Crosetti was one of them, leading the league with 27 SBs in 1938. That, apparently, earned him the top spot in the batting order, which, I remind you, always gets the most plate appearances each year: Crosetti had 757 PAs in 1938, which led all of baseball. Both Crosetti and Lou Gehrig played in every game in 1938, but Gehrig batted fifth and thus totaled 689 PAs. Imagine how many more runs the Yankees could have created if Lou Gehrig had had an extra 60 plate appearances instead of Frankie Crosetti.

I know, I know, speed at the top of the order is about more than just stolen bases. It's about ability to take an extra base, break up the double play, distract the pitcher, etc. But how important is all that small-ball stuff when the rest of your order is comprised of Lou Gehrig, Joe Dimaggio, Joe Gordon,

---

[104] That might seem like an insufficiently damning appellation for the worst human being in history, but trust me, it really would have burned Hitler where it counts. See, his whole life he had stomach problems that, in times of stress, resulted in "meteorism," which is defined as "violent bouts of farting, along with alternate bouts of diarrhea and constipation." I'm not making any of this up; read Der Fartenfuhrer: The Story of Hitler's Illnesses (Neatorama.com, Miss Cellania, March 24, 2014) for the full, great story. Meteorism is often caused by eating undercooked pork, so Hitler became a vegetarian to try to keep his farting under control. That didn't work, so he enlisted a quack doctor who fed him dozens of pills a day. One pill contained strychnine, the active ingredient in rat poison, and atropine, which causes hallucinations, confusion, and excitement. Another contained live bacteria harvested from the feces of a "Bulgarian peasant of the most vigorous stock." When Hitler was in the bunker near the end of the war, this quack doctor was shooting him up with strong amphetamines several times a day, which turned him into a speed freak. Throughout it all, nothing stopped Hitler's meteorism, and he (and those around him) kept suffering from his chronic farting as he slipped farther and farther into the depths of madness.

Bill Dickey, Tommy Henrich, Red Rolfe and George Selkirk? It doesn't matter if you're on first base or second when Gehrig smashes a homer. The important thing is to just get on base.

I'm not saying that small ball is useless. I'm just saying that it's a lot more important when you're batting in front of singles hitters. Then, being on second base can mean the difference between scoring on a single or being stranded at third. Really, base stealers should be hitting sixth on most teams.

Managers and broadcasters love small ball because it involves plenty of strategy to think and talk about. It gives them lots of opportunities to look smart and prove themselves to be among the group of true baseball experts. But big ball scores more runs than small ball does. Therefore, it's better.

In making this criticism, I'm disparaging Yankee manager Joe McCarthy (no relation to Tommy), who is one of the five greatest managers in history. He obviously did a lot of things right; in 1938 the Yankees were in the midst of four straight World Series wins. In their book "Baseball Dynasties," Rob Neyer and Eddie Epstein agree that the 1936-1939 Yankees were the greatest dynasty in the history of baseball.

So I'm picking a nit here. But I'm especially interested in this nit because it exhibits a specific brand of myopia that afflicts experts in many fields. They get so caught up in the "little things," such as the value of speed at the top of the batting order, that they forget about the "big things," like getting a good hitter in position to get the most PAs.

There is certainly some value in the little things that only experts can appreciate. But they pale in comparison to the big things that everyone knows well. When your identity is wrapped up in being among the Most Noble Order of baseball experts, you get sucked into the groupthink[105] that overemphasizes the small things. If you tried batting Lou Gehrig first, people would question whether you belong in the elevated class.

Anyway, this is yet another bit of conventional wisdom that is changing lately. The Rays gained some publicity a few years ago for batting on-base machine and slow-as-molasses catcher John Jaso leadoff. The leadoff hitter with the most runs scored in 2013 and 2014 was the Cardinals' Matt Carpenter, who had no speed but got on base a lot.

So the point is, or at least was, that even if you're unimpressed by Red Ruffing's pitching record, add on the war service, the postseason, and the hitting, and I don't see how you can question his Hall-of-Fame berth.

Nolan Ryan (1966, 1968-1993; career ERA+: 112)

	Career	Rank	Peak	Rank	Bests	Top 5s	JAWS	Rank
WAR	81.8	21	43.3	52	0	2	62.6	24
WS	332.2	16	145.0	93	0	1	NA	23

105 "Groupthink" is another of my favorite psychological concepts that is often misunderstood. It occurs when everyone in a group starts thinking the same way in order to conform and keep everything harmonious. The Bay of Pigs invasion is often cited as a tragedy that came from groupthink among John F. Kennedy's cabinet. It's a very bad trap to fall into, especially when the group is made of a bunch of rivals, like baseball managers are.

Nolan Ryan was the Derek Jeter of the early 1990s. Ryan was very good, a no-doubt Hall-of-Famer. But he did a few things so well that people thought he was the greatest human being on the planet. They ignored the things he didn't do so well, which he did really, really badly.

Ryan got a freaky number of strikeouts by throwing freakishly hard, all the freakin' time. Sometimes that worked like gangbusters, as during his record seven no-hitters. Other times it didn't go so great: He led the league in wild pitches six times and in walks eight times, twice allowing more than 200. Randy Johnson figured out how to limit his walks to a reasonable level when he was 29; Ryan didn't get there until he was 33. And even then, he was still leading the league in walks. His 2795 career walks is of course the most ever, and is 52% more than the second-highest total, Steve Carlton's. That's a much bigger margin than exists with Ryan's career strikeout record, where he leads Randy Johnson by 17%.

Ryan's style of pitching was about as flashy as can be. Meanwhile, his personality was the opposite of flashy. He was a tough, taciturn Texan, the kind of man in Ford truck commercials and sentimental modern country tunes[106] in which they talk about their hard-workin' daddies. He never stopped working hard: The main reason he could throw heat well into his mid-40s was that he always stuck with a tough training regimen.

I told you already that fans voted Nolan Ryan as the top pitcher of the 1900s in the All-Century Team. That would have been a perfect choice if it were the All-Strikeout-and-No-Hitter Team. But there is more to pitching than just the fun stuff. Ryan-mania has calmed down by now, but I'm sure many people still think he's one of the top ten pitchers ever. He ended up on three Franchise Fours despite deserving only one (the Angels).

Like Derek Jeter, Nolan Ryan is a solid mid-range Hall-of-Famer. Both had things they did exceptionally well (hitting and strikeouts, respectively) and both had major holes in their game (defense and walks, respectively). Both clearly deserve the Hall. But they should be remembered in the Eddie Plank/Luke Appling range of greats, not the Walter Johnson/Honus Wagner range.

Tom Seaver (1967-1986; career ERA+: 127)

	Career	Rank	Peak	Rank	Bests	Top 5s	JAWS	Rank
WAR	110.5	5	59.5	10	1	6	85.0	5
WS	388.8	9	192.6	16	1	8	NA	6

Meanwhile, Tom Seaver was great at everything. He struck out tons of batters, limited walks and homers, and pitched a ton. We already saw him leading the very impressive group of 1970s pitchers in WAR. He belongs among Walter Johnson, Lefty Grove, Cy Young, and Grover Alexander as one of the very best of the best of the best.

[106] As opposed to old-style country songs, which were always about tragedy. Someone pointed this out to me recently, and it struck me as very true: Nowadays, country songs tend to be happy tunes that celebrate being a country boy, with trucks and beer and sweet ladies and American flags, etc. These were not the kinds of things that Johnny Cash or Loretta Lynn sang about, to say the least.

Continuing on the Eppa Rixey theme ... Tom Seaver is the only Met pitcher in the Hall, but that's not a criticism. The Mets are one of 14 major-league expansion teams since 1961. The only expansion teams that can claim their own Hall-of-Fame pitcher are the Mets, the Diamondbacks (Randy Johnson), and the Angels (Nolan Ryan). And both Johnson and Ryan spent a lot of time on other teams.

Tom Seaver is obviously the best player in Mets history. Does anyone else dominate his franchise's history as much Seaver dominates the Mets'? Maybe Tony Gwynn and the Padres? Time to bring out the WAR ratings.

Let's compare each franchise's top player, according to career WAR, to its second-best. There are other ways you could do this, but this is just for Shasta and giggles, so who cares.

Team	Top WAR	Top Player	2nd Best WAR	2nd Best Player	Pct Better
ARI	51	Randy Johnson	31	Brandon Webb	65%
ATL/MLN/BSN	142	Hank Aaron	108	Kid Nichols	31%
BAL/SLB	95	Cal Ripken	78	Brooks Robinson	22%
BOS	123	Ted Williams	96	Carl Yastrzemski	28%
CHC	84	Cap Anson	72	Ron Santo	17%
CHW	74	Luke Appling	71	Ted Lyons	4%
CIN	77	Pete Rose	74	Johnny Bench	4%
CLE	79	Nap Lajoie	74	Tris Speaker	7%
COL	61	Todd Helton	48	Larry Walker	27%
DET	144	Ty Cobb	92	Al Kaline	57%
HOU	79	Jeff Bagwell	65	Craig Biggio	22%
KAN	88	George Brett	47	Kevin Appier	87%
LAA	52	Chuck Finley	45	Jim Fregosi	16%
LAD/BKN	67	Don Drysdale	66	Pee Wee Reese	2%
MIA	26	Hanley Ramirez	25	Josh Johnson	4%
MIL/SEP	76	Robin Yount	59	Paul Molitor	29%
MIN/WAS	165	Walter Johnson	63	Rod Carew	162%
NYM	79	Tom Seaver	49	David Wright	61%
NYY	142	Babe Ruth	112	Lou Gehrig	27%
OAK/KCA/PHA	76	Eddie Plank	72	Rickey Henderson	6%
PHI	106	Mike Schmidt	71	Robin Roberts	49%
PIT	120	Honus Wagner	94	Roberto Clemente	28%
SDP	68	Tony Gwynn	31	Dave Winfield	119%
SFG/NYG	154	Willie Mays	112	Barry Bonds	38%

SEA	70	Ken Griffey Jr.	68	Edgar Martinez	3%
STL	128	Stan Musial	91	Rogers Hornsby	41%
TAM	41	Evan Longoria	36	Ben Zobrist	14%
TEX/WAS	49	Ivan Rodriguez	44	Rafael Palmeiro	11%
TOR	57	Dave Stieb	48	Roy Halladay	19%
WAS/MON	55	Gary Carter	48	Tim Raines	15%

I nailed Tony Gwynn's dominance of Padres history. I should have predicted George Brett would lap the field of Royals. Who knew Kevin Appier would be number two for them, by the way? Man, that guy was underrated.

I definitely didn't think Randy Johnson would be the best Diamondback ever by such a huge margin. I expected Luis Gonzalez to be either first or second. But he may have been a bit overrated, with numbers that were a product of a wacky time for hitters.

How about Don Drysdale charting as the best Dodger ever? Didn't see that coming. But there are a whole bunch of other players just below his 67 WAR and Pee Wee Reese's 66: Duke Snider is at 65 WAR, Jackie Robinson is at 61, Zach Wheat at 59, Dazzy Vance at 58, etc. Robinson only got ten years with the Dodgers because of segregation; I'm sure if we used JAWS instead of just career WAR, Robinson would be first.

The big story is how overwhelmingly Walter Johnson is the best Washington Senator/Minnesota Twin in history. Once again, if he doesn't make the Franchise Four, I swear, Minnesota, I will force Garrison Keillor and Prince to switch bodies a la "Freaky Friday." Sure, "Prairie Home Companion" would be a lot better, at first anyway. But pretty soon you'd have Garrison Keillor's voice singing and body writhing to "Sexy M.F." Is that what you want? (Edit after the All-Star Game: I'm still waiting for Mary Tyler Moore's address. Now I also need Garrison Keillor's address and some way to get into Paisley Park. And then I need a "Freaky Friday" potion. This is looking like lots of work. Ah, forget it.)

Also, Dave Stieb?!?!?

So anyway, I'm tired now. Tom Seaver is great.

Hilton Smith (1932, 1937-1948)

	Rank at SP Among Negro Leaguers	Rank Among All Negro Leaguers
SABR	8	28
Monte Irvin	unranked	NA

Dang it! I left Hilton Smith out of my comment for Bullet Rogan. Well, I wouldn't be the first to overlook Hilton Smith.

In the late 1930s and 1940s, Hilton Smith played for some great Kansas City Monarchs teams alongside Satchel Paige. The SABR biography of Smith, by Ralph Berger, makes this fact abundantly clear, usually pairing it with the phrase "in his shadow." Apparently, Smith was always in Paige's shadow, couldn't get out from under Paige's shadow, and was not very happy about being under said shadow. The SABR author must have taken a cue from Smith himself, who comes across like a whiny fifteen-year-old boy whose older brother is captain of the football team. Here's a quote from Smith so you can see what I mean:

"I won 161 games and lost only 32 but most people do not even know of me. I took my baseball seriously. Doing the job and being the best pitcher I could be was my aim. I'm taking nothing away from Satch, he produced and could clown around and get away with it. Being in the shadow of Paige really hurt me but there was nothing I could do about it. My personality was opposite of that of Satch. I never did crawl out from under his shadow."

There's a lot to sink your teeth into in Smith's quote. I personally enjoy chewing on the meaty morsels of passive-aggression that Smith packs into "I'm taking nothing away from Satch, he produced and could clown around and get away with it." Really, Hilton? You're taking nothing away from Satch by saying he was a clown who got away with it? Well, I'm not taking anything away from you by saying that you sound like a bitter old man consumed by jealousy of a teammate who was a better performer.

Granted, it probably wasn't easy to be on the same pitching staff as Satchel Paige. Paige was such a drawing card that he started almost every game, but then left after three innings. Smith would relieve and pitch about as well. Sometimes Satchel failed to show up, and Smith had to go to the mound wearing Paige's jersey and pretend to be him for a while. Paige was a rock star and acted like it. Contemporaries always get jealous of those guys, sometimes with good reason.

Moreover, Paige was a legend of the type that could only exist in the days before TV and good record-keeping. Now, players are grounded in reality by their footage and their numbers. In those days, fans had little to go on besides stories. Satchel Paige was the greatest in Negro Leagues history at generating stories. Stories made Satchel Paige truly mythological, in a way that no player has been for decades. Going to see him pitch was immersing yourself in the magic of the myth.

Meanwhile, there was no mythology surrounding Hilton Smith. No one told stories about quiet, businesslike old Smith going up there and getting some outs. Maybe if Smith and Paige had lived in a modern era, Smith would have gotten more of the due he clearly felt he deserved. People would have looked at his numbers and thought, "Wow, Hilton Smith was pretty darn good too." Maybe he could have been seen as the John Smoltz to Paige's Greg Maddux.

Along those lines, Smith looks like a solid low-end Hall-of-Famer. SABR seems to think so, even if Monte Irvin does not. And the numbers we have for him do indeed look impressive. Hopefully a Hall-of-Fame berth is enough to get him out from under that nasty ol' shadow.

John Smoltz (1988-1999, 2001-2009; career ERA+: 125)

	Career	Rank	Peak	Rank	Bests	Top 5s	JAWS	Rank
WAR	69.5	27	38.8	79	0	1	54.2	44
WS	288.1	33	136.2	122	1	1	NA	75

Was John Smoltz ever known as John "Sluggo" Smoltz? That always comes into my brain when hear his name, but I may have made it up. The only nicknames I can find for Smoltz are "Smoltzie" (yawn) and "Marmaduke." (huh?[107]) Well, he'll always be Sluggo to me.

That's not the fact that usually leads off a comment about John Smoltz. Usually it's that he was a member of perhaps the greatest rotation trio in history: The 1990s Braves' Smoltz, Tom Glavine and Greg Maddux. Other times people bring up that Smoltz was a great starter and a great closer, the only pitcher ever to have more than 200 wins and more than 150 saves.

But is that really that special? Couldn't any great starter become a great closer? Kinda, yeah. John Smoltz made people realize this, I think. He made people rethink the pedestal they had put closers on.

There was a period of 25 years there from the late 1970s to the early 2000s when closers were tremendously overrated. They were seen as this special breed of pitcher with a unique ability to throw balls when the inning number turned to "nine." This perspective resulted in a lot of relievers winning MVPs and Cy Young Awards. The reasoning went: They pitch in more games, and in more crucial innings, so they are more valuable, right?

Well, no. There is the rather significant problem of relievers pitching so few innings. Nowadays closers throw 60 innings and starters throw 180. That means closers would have to be three times as valuable per inning to have a comparable value to starters. Closers might be a bit more valuable per inning, but not three times more. It's like comparing the careers of Addie Joss and Eddie Plank. Joss may have been better per inning, but had about half as many innings. Plank was clearly more valuable.

Don't take my word for it. Let's look at all the MVP and Cy Young Award winning relievers, and compare their WAR and Win Shares totals to those of their leagues' best:

MVPs

Year	MVP	MVP's WAR	Best WAR	Player with Best WAR	MVP's WS	Best WS	Player with Best WS
1950	Jim Konstanty	4.7	8.1	Eddie Stanky	23	32	Stan Musial
1981	Rollie Fingers	4.2	6.7	Dwight Evans	17	27	Rickey Henderson
1984	Willie Hernandez	4.8	10.0	Cal Ripken	24	37	Cal Ripken
1992	Dennis Eckersley	2.9	8.9	Roger Clemens	18	34	Roberto Alomar

[107] Smoltz got the nickname from Dale Murphy because he was gangly and friendly. Onetime teammate Joe Boever explained the nickname by saying, "He's just like a big dog. You tell him 'no, no, no' and he goes ahead and does something anyway. But you have to laugh." (see http://baseball.playerprofiles.com/sampleplayerprofile.asp?playerid=552)

Cy Young Awards

Year	Cy Young Winner	Cy's WAR	Best P WAR	Pitcher with Best WAR	Cy's WS	Best P WS	Pitcher with Most WS
1974	Mike Marshall	3.1	9.1	Jon Matlack	21	28	Phil Niekro
1977	Sparky Lyle	3.7	8.3	Frank Tanana	20	29	Jim Palmer
1979	Bruce Sutter	4.9	7.6	Phil Niekro	22	24	Phil Niekro
1981	Rollie Fingers	4.2	5.6	Bert Blyleven	17	18	Steve McCatty
1984	Willie Hernandez	4.8	7.9	Dave Stieb?!?!?	24	25	Dave Stieb?!?!?
1987	Steve Bedrosian	2.3	7.1	Bob Welch	16	21	Orel Hershiser
1989	Mark Davis	4.5	7.0	Orel Hershiser	19	21	Orel Hershiser
1992	Dennis Eckersley	2.9	8.9	Roger Clemens	18	26	Roger Clemens
2003	Eric Gagne	3.7	7.4	Mark Prior	25	25	Eric Gagne

Win Shares gives a lot more value to closers than WAR does, but still agrees with only one of the above awards, Eric Gagne in 2003. According to WAR, most of these awards are wildly undeserved.

Before the days of one-inning saves, relievers showed up a bit better in WAR. Bruce Sutter had 101.1 innings in 1979, and Willie Hernandez had 140.1 innings in 1984. Rollie Fingers got 78 innings in 1981, a season that was shortened to 110 games. (Blyleven had 159.1 innings that year). Then relievers had to be just twice as effective per inning to compare to starters instead of three times as effective. WAR says they didn't get there, but at least they came closer than Dennis Eckersley did.

In his comment for Dennis Eckersley in the "New Historical Baseball Abstract," Bill James had a good analogy for the folly of giving Eckersley an MVP in 1992. In 1961, Jerry Lynch had an amazing season as a pinch-hitter: .404 with power in 47 ABs. He got lots of key hits that led to wins, and his Reds won a surprise pennant. Overall, he hit .315/.407/.624 in 210 PAs, with an OPS that would have led the league had he had enough PAs to qualify. As a pinch-hitter, he hit in crucial spots late in games, the same way Eckersley pitched in crucial spots late in games. Both did very well in those crucial spots. Would Lynch deserve an MVP? I doubt many people would go for that. Then why did they go for Eckersley? What's the difference?

Anyway, we can get into this more in the relievers section. The point is that John Smoltz's success as a reliever and starter doesn't make him some sort of crazy two-way player, like Martin Dihigo or Bullet Rogan. He just had a few years where he couldn't start, so unfortunately, he had to close. Thankfully, he got back to starting, and doing it well, from 2005-2007.

Let's talk about some fun stuff about Smoltz; I feel bad that I used most of his comment to rant about relief pitchers. He was drafted by the Tigers, but never played for the big-league club. When he was just 20 years old, the Tigers traded him for 36-year-old veteran Doyle Alexander. It was one of those Mark Langston-for-Randy Johnson deals that only look lopsided with the benefit of hindsight. Nine out of ten times, the prospects in those deals break their arms or can't develop another pitch or whatever. And at the time, it looked like a great success for the Tigers: Alexander was terrific down the stretch and propelled Detroit into the playoffs.

It's a shame Smoltz never got to play for the Tigers, since he grew up in a Tiger-mad family. His grandfather, also named John Smoltz, was a groundskeeper for the Tigers for many years. His father, again named John Smoltz, was, naturally, a professional accordion player. (Not a joke.) This John did get to play accordion for the Tigers at a party celebrating their 1968 World Series. (Source: Smoltz's SABR biography, by Warren Corbett.)

At any rate, with that bite out of his starting career, John Smoltz hardly ranks among the Hall's elite. But he's good enough.

Warren Spahn (1942, 1946-1965; career ERA+: 119)

	Career	Rank	Peak	Rank	Bests	Top 5s	JAWS	Rank
WAR	100.1	10	51.7	23	1	8	75.9	10
WS	409.8	6	188.2	20	3	10	NA	5

Did you know that Warren Spahn's personal integrity helped limit the abilities of National Enquirer and TMZ? I'll explain.

Spahn served with distinction in World War II. He was drafted into the Army and saw action in the Battle of the Bulge. He earned a Purple Heart because a bit of shrapnel hit him in the neck, an injury he later shrugged off as "only a scratch."

But to hear a cheapie "biography" tell it, Spahn virtually won the war all by himself. In 1958, Milton Shapiro wrote "The Warren Spahn Story," which was aimed at children. He invented most of it out of whole cloth, including that Spahn earned a Bronze Star and that after being hit by shrapnel he was carried out on a stretcher.

When he heard about the book, Spahn was horrified. This was anathema to the "band of brothers" ethos of World War II veterans: Many didn't even like to discuss the war, much less permit people to spread false rumors of their achievements. Spahn was worried that people might think he planted the stories.

Later Shapiro admitted that he never interviewed or even approached Spahn, any of his family, any of his teammates or opponents, or the Braves. He just found some newspaper clippings and filled in the rest. He even contrived a whole subplot involving Spahn and his father, complete with lots of melodramatic made-up dialogue.

But because none of the lies about Spahn were negative, they didn't qualify as libel. Libel is defined as a published false statement that damages a person's reputation. Shapiro's lies didn't damage Spahn's reputation; they artificially inflated it.

Spahn sued anyway, seeking an injunction to prevent the book's further publication. It was the first time anyone had sued over false praise. The defendant in the case was the book's publisher, which insisted it was within its constitutional rights of free speech and free press. Spahn won, the publisher appealed, and Spahn won again.

That wasn't the end. The case went through eleven different court decisions, even crossing the desk of the U.S. Supreme Court. Finally, five years after the original case, Spahn won for good, ending the book's publication and earning $10,000 in damages.

It was never an issue of money for Spahn; he actually lost a lot of money in the extended legal battle. It was a matter of principle. He strongly believed no one should endure blatant lies being published about them, positive or negative. It proved to be a landmark case, and helped shape all later publications that report on public figures. If not for Spahn, the National Enquirer and TMZ might be even more horrible than they already are. (Source for all the above: "Warren Spahn's Legal Legacy: The Right to be Free from False Praise," Ray Yasser, University of Tulsa Digital Commons, 2008.)

When not in court, Spahn also pitched. He did so a lot: He is eighth all time in career innings despite (or perhaps because of -- remember the injury nexus) spending ages 22-24 in the service. When Spahn made the All-Century Team in 1999, fellow winner Sandy Koufax called him the greatest pitcher ever. Koufax said he deserved the All-Century Team "not only for what he did on the field -- he'll kill me for doing this -- he pitched the whole damn century." (Source: "Cheers and tears for the All-Century Team," Deseret News, Associated Press, October 25, 1999.)

And Spahn pitched extremely well. For you charming old-timers who still think pitcher wins are the ultimate measure of ability, you'll be happy to hear that Spahn hit 20 wins in 13 seasons, leading the league eight times. It helped that his Braves teams scored lots of runs, what with Hank Aaron and Eddie Mathews. Still, Spahn pitched at least 250 innings every year from 1947-1963 and had his first subpar ERA in 1964, at age 43. With any team, he would have been great.

Warren Spahn was a man of great ability, achievement, and integrity. He is an inner-circle Hall-of-Famer.

Don Sutton (1966-1988; career ERA+: 108)

	Career	Rank	Peak	Rank	Bests	Top 5s	JAWS	Rank
WAR	67.4	31	34.0	141	0	1	50.7	52
WS	289.7	30	140.7	103	0	0	NA	28

Quantity vs. quality comes up a fair amount in these Hall-of-Fame arguments. There are a handful of cases among hitters: Elmer Flick was more on the quality side and Max Carey on the quantity side. But it's more relevant to pitchers. Pitchers are more likely to sustain career-shortening injuries, which makes for more "quality" pitchers who were great for precious few years. It also makes the "quantity" pitchers more rare and thus more valuable.

While Dizzy Dean and Sandy Koufax are the ultimate quality guys, Don Sutton was definitely a quantity guy. He was good, if never terrific, for a long time. BBWAA voters were hesitant to put him in the Hall despite his 324 wins. In "Whatever Happened to the Hall of Fame," Bill James demonstrated very clearly that, at that writing, Sutton was by far the most-qualified pitcher on any ballot who wasn't in. Then on his fifth try, Sutton got the nod.

For some reason, people seem more hesitant to elect "quantity" pitchers than "quantity" hitters. Of the top 30 hitters in career plate appearances, all are in the Hall except steroid cases (Barry Bonds and Rafael Palmeiro) and the ones who aren't eligible yet (Pete Rose, Derek Jeter, Omar Vizquel, Alex Rodriguez). Of the top 30 post-1800s pitchers in career innings, several who have been eligible for a long time aren't in, namely Tommy John, Jim Kaat, Jack Powell, and Frank Tanana.

Don Sutton may have been of a class with those guys, but he was at the head of it. He's a HOFer.

Dazzy Vance (1915, 1918, 1922-1935; career ERA+: 125)

	Career	Rank	Peak	Rank	Bests	Top 5s	JAWS	Rank
WAR	59.9	48	49.2	30	2	5	54.6	42
WS	241.9	59	176.5	35	2	4	NA	31

Dazzy Vance has one of the odder career paths of any Hall-of-Famer. His first full year in the majors was in 1922, when he was 31 years old. From then on he dominated, leading the National League in strikeouts seven straight times, often by huge margins. In his best overall year, 1924, he had 262 strikeouts, beating out his teammate Burleigh Grimes, who had 135. No one else in the league had more than 86. Like Bob Feller, Vance was playing a different game than everyone else.

But Vance wasn't just some sort of Nolan-Ryan-esque one-dimensional fireballer: He also allowed a reasonable number of walks and homers. He led the league in ERA three times, but it should have been more. Baseball-reference has a stat called Fielding-Independent Pitching (FIP), which is basically what a pitcher's ERA should have been, if he had had an average defense behind him. It's based on the Voros McCracken theory I mentioned back in the Tom Glavine comment, that holds that pitchers can only control home runs, walks and strikeouts. Vance led the NL in FIP seven out of eight years from 1924-1931.

Vance has half of Randy Johnson's career. Why didn't he get to have a whole Randy Johnson career? He got his start in professional baseball at age 21, but was plagued by arm trouble throughout his many years in the minors. He'd pitch well and then his arm would hurt, and then he'd pitch badly. It went like that for ten years before he hit on a solution.

It was probably the only time in history that playing poker in New Orleans turned someone's life around in a positive way. At one point during the poker game, Vance hit his arm at the edge of a table, causing him tremendous pain. The next day he went to a doctor. Vance had seen dozens of doctors, but this one did something different -- mysteriously, no one knows what. My theory is that Dr. Facilier[108] gave him a talisman filled with Walter Johnson's blood. So-called "experts" with their so-called "knowledge" and so-called "rational thought" believe it was just some doctor who knew how to take bone chips out of an elbow. (Source: Vance's SABR biography, by Charles F. Faber.)

That kind of thing is routine nowadays. I'm sure bone chip removal is done in between innings of a pitcher's start, as a preventative measure. But in the 1910s, sports medicine not only didn't exist;

[108] Reference explanation: The Disney film "The Princess and the Frog." The good thing about having kids nowadays is that you get to see kids' movies and shows, most of which are about ten zillion times better than the ones I grew up with in the 1980s. As a kid I begged my parents for the opportunity to watch "He-Man." Recently I watched a He-Man Christmas special and was gobsmacked at how awful it was. It may have been the worst thing I've ever seen. And I've seen almost every movie that "Mystery Science Theater 3000" has ever ridiculed.

medicine barely existed. If Vance had been born in the 1990s, he might have been among the five best pitchers ever. Because of his delayed start, he isn't. But he's a Hall-of-Famer no diggity.

Rube Waddell (1897, 1899-1910; career ERA+: 135)

	Career	Rank	Peak	Rank	Bests	Top 5s	JAWS	Rank
WAR	58.6	52	49.6	29	1	4	54.1	45
WS	238.3	67	184.6	24	0	3	NA	46

Rube Waddell. Oh boy. Learning about Rube Waddell gives you a great insight into what a weird, wonderful world baseball was 100 years ago. Not that Rube was in any way typical of his time or of any time in history. But the mere fact that such a bizarre human being could exist and thrive at the highest level of competition indicates that sports in the dead-ball era were much less professionalized, and thus much more loose, more unpredictable, and more likely to display the weird underbelly of human society.

Back in the Hughie Jennings comment, I described Waddell as "developmentally disabled," which is the currently proper term for what was once called "retarded."[109] But Waddell's lifetime predated such thoughtful designations. At the time he was just considered an oddball: sometimes lovable, sometimes frustrating.

He was guileless and full of joy, but would drive his managers crazy with his unreliability. He would fail to show up for his starts, and then be discovered fishing or playing marbles with street kids. One time he disappeared for days during spring training, and then was spotted leading a parade through Jacksonville, Florida. Another time he went missing and was found wrestling alligators. (Source for this and the below: Waddell's SABR biography, by Dan O'Brien.)

Rube loved fires and fire engines, and would often jump in and help firefighters with a blaze. The rumor spread that once he heard a fire engine during a start and then ran into the street to chase it. That never happened, but it definitely fit with his public image.

Like most baseball stars of the time, Waddell was recruited to join the vaudeville circuit. Despite playing the role of himself, he was supposedly one of the worst actors to ever grace the stage. He was only allowed out for about two minutes each scene, but according to the reviews, it was enough to ruin the show. (Man, I would have loved to see it.) His showbiz career ended badly: A dispute over advance pay led the company to dump him and his bags in an alley in Philadelphia.

---

[109] Apologies if my use of the "r" word is offensive, but I don't think many people know what "developmentally disabled" means yet. It's odd to think that "retarded" was once the proper, non-derogatory substitute term for "idiot" or "moron" or "imbecile." But it's true, and if you think about it, you can realize why. After all, "retard" as a verb just means "to slow down"; it was intended just to convey that the person had been slowed down cognitively. It only gained a negative connotation after it was misused by mean kids and dumb frat boys. And before that, "idiot," "moron," etc. were proper, non-derogatory terms that turned evil from misuse. Hopefully, "developmentally disabled" is such a mouthful that it will never turn into a playground taunt, so we'll never have to replace it with something else.

While it lasted, the show was a hit. People loved to watch Waddell, the way you might love to watch The Who drummer Keith Moon. Like Moon, Waddell had a sweet side underneath all the wild-man antics.[110] In one game, a pitch hit A's outfielder Danny Hoffman in the temple and knocked him unconscious. Waddell swung to the rescue, throwing Hoffman over his shoulder, carrying him off the field, flagging down a carriage, and getting him to the hospital. The whole night, Waddell sat beside Hoffman and held ice on his head. Many felt Waddell's quick intervention saved Hoffman's life.

It wasn't all funny and sweet stuff. During one game Waddell jumped into the stands and beat up a fan. He went through three tumultuous marriages, and each ended in divorce on grounds of "lack of support" or "gross neglect of duty." After his second wife sued for divorce, he was accused of assault and battery of both his father- and mother-in-law.

Somehow, A's manager Connie Mack was able to extract the best out of Waddell. It's hard to think of two people who were more different. Mack was dignified, sober, quiet, and brilliant. Waddell was the opposite of all those things. But this was typical of Mack; a big part of his genius was in his ability to get the most out of players with difficult personalities. He was just so genuinely, impeccably honorable that he could inspire anyone's loyalty. He was baseball's Mr. Rogers.

Everyone knew about Rube's talent, but few other managers were willing to deal with him. He was first signed by the Pirates in 1897, without pitching a game in the minors. Manager Patsy Donovan was introduced to him at a team meal. After the meal, Donovan released him. Reportedly all it took was listening to Waddell speak for a few minutes.

Connie Mack was never happy when Waddell missed games, got wildly drunk, and engaged in off-the-field controversies. He suspended Waddell many times. But he was still able to squeeze out of Rube some amazing performances, without which the A's likely would not have won pennants in 1902 and 1905.

Like Dazzy Vance and Amos Rusie, Waddell was a strikeout artist like no one else of his time. He led the league in strikeouts every year from 1902 to 1907, usually by ridiculous margins. In 1904, he struck out 349 hitters; second was Jack Chesbro with 239. Those 349 strikeouts set a post-1901 record that went unchallenged until 1946, when Bob Feller came painfully close with 348. It went unbroken until Sandy Koufax struck out 382 in 1965. Out of the five best seasonal strikeout totals from 1901-1945, Waddell had three of them in three straight years, 1903-1905. (Walter Johnson has the other two.)

During a play fight with a teammate in 1906, Waddell injured his shoulder. Afterwards he was never quite as great, but still had enough good years to collect respectable career totals.

Of course, things didn't end well for Rube. In 1911, he was pitching for a small-town team and living with its manager. When the town was threatened by flooding, Waddell stood for hours in cold water stacking sandbags. He caught pneumonia and then tuberculosis.

His descent came quickly. Connie Mack and his business partner, Ben Shibe, paid for Waddell's stay at a sanitarium. Mack, who always held great affection for Rube despite all the problems he caused, insisted that no expense should be spared. Waddell died in 1914, only 37 years old.

---

[110] You may have heard stories about Keith Moon's debauchery and destruction, but my favorite involves him visiting the Monty Python troupe while they wrote "Life of Brian." Moon played Scrabble with John Cleese, and Moon would put down words like "the" and "but" while Cleese put down the likes of "jeremiad" and "querulous." Far from getting annoyed, Moon loved every second of it, and kept bugging Cleese to play more. He was like a kid getting to play with his dad.

After Waddell's death, Connie Mack said "He may have failed us at times but to him, I and the other owners of the Athletics ball club, owe much." And Waddell owed Mack the opportunity to have a genuine Hall-of-Fame career.

Ed Walsh (1904-1917; career ERA+: 145)

	Career	Rank	Peak	Rank	Bests	Top 5s	JAWS	Rank
WAR	65.5	34	61.9	8	0	5	63.7	22
WS	265.2	41	235.9	5	3	6	NA	18

Another pitcher with a brief period of brilliance! I miss Don Sutton. At my age, you're not looking for excitement as much as stability. I want a pitcher I can rely on year-in and year-out; I don't care if he's a bit boring sometimes.

Not that I'd kick Ed Walsh out of bed for eating crackers. Look at those Peaks! (OK, yuck, joke is now over.) Like Rube Waddell, Ed Walsh spent a few dead-ball years being mind-bogglingly good. A big reason for his huge seasonal WAR and Win Shares totals were his massive numbers of innings, even more than Joe "Iron Man" McGinnity. Walsh would start 35-45 games, completing 30-40 of them, and then relieve in another 10-20. In his last big year, 1912, he led the league in games pitched, games started, games finished, saves, and of course innings.

And Walsh was not some Phil-Niekro-esque soft tosser. He started out with a fastball and curve, but really hit the big time when perfected a spitball. He said the key to his success was never easing up, throwing as hard in the beginning of the game as he did in the end. Walsh was a fiercely competitive tough guy who wanted nothing more than to work as much as he did.

But arm tendons don't care about the content of your guts. When they've had enough, they go. At 32, Walsh's arm broke down. He went to a favorite doctor among ballplayers named "Bonesetter" Reese. (All doctors should have cool nicknames, in my book. Cancerkiller, Hemorrhoidharmer, you fill in the rest.) After three minutes of manipulations, Bonesetter said Walsh was fixed. He wasn't. (Source: Walsh's SABR biography, by Stuart Schimler.)

Walsh wasn't the type to blame anyone but himself: He acknowledged that he should have rested his arm after 1912. The injury did enable him to avoid the typical late-career numbers, which steadily get worse until you're out of the league. Thus he ends up looking very good in rate stats: He has the best career ERA and best career FIP of all time. And beyond that, there's the fact that he only pitched in the dead-ball era: His ERA+ overcomes that bias, and he ranks tenth all-time in that stat. (At this writing, Clayton Kershaw is ahead of him in career ERA+, but he probably won't stay there. Because he is still active, he has also not gone through the later phase of his career. Any time you rank active players with retired ones in rate stats you have to take that into account. If Miguel Cabrera were ahead of Ty Cobb's lifetime batting average right now, you can bet bitcoins to cronuts that he won't be when he retires.)

So Ed Walsh isn't the best pitcher in history, but I don't think anyone ever accused him of that. He is certainly a deserving Hall-of-Famer.

"Smokey" Joe Williams (1907-1932)

	Rank at SP Among Negro Leaguers	Rank Among All Negro Leaguers
SABR	4	13
Monte Irvin	1 among RHP	NA

Monte Irvin says Smokey Joe Williams was better than Satchel Paige. That's crazy talk, but a lot of people felt the need to give someone besides Paige the title of best ever. Otherwise, it gets boring. You don't look like an expert when you declare that most famous Negro League pitcher in history is also the best. You look like an ordinary fan.

I don't think Irvin was consciously thinking "I gotta think of someone besides Paige so I look like an expert." Few people set out to deceive, especially not a fine fellow like Monte Irvin. This is actually an example of a subconscious trap that all people tend to fall into. When you identify yourself with a group of people, you adopt the ideas and thought patterns of that group. Usually, that's a good thing, but sometimes, the group has subconscious biases that lead it astray. I'm sure Irvin and others genuinely felt that Smokey Joe Williams was the best Negro Leagues pitcher ever. But if they approached it more rationally, they'd realize that there's no choice but Paige.

This is a phenomenon that I've covered before; MVP voters liked to give the award to the guy with the exciting new stat line rather than to Willie Mays and Mickey Mantle every year. Writers don't get paid to tell you what you already know; they have to come up with new stuff to stay employed. Sometimes this mission turns into a bias that clouds their judgment.

You see this turned up to 11 in the world of political punditry. Even more than with baseball, presidential elections create a ravenous demand for drama and analysis. This demand can never be satisfied by the naturally occurring supply of genuinely interesting events. So pundits fill the gap by overanalyzing every inflection of every speech of every candidate in terms of how it will affect the votes of lower-middle-class Asian-American mothers of three from Ohio who enjoy playing Stratego. Inevitably, pundits predict that every new story will tip the election one way or another. You don't get paid to say "Yeah, that won't affect anything; Obama still has a huge chance of winning." You get paid to say "OMG! You see where Obama said 'uh' there? That means Romney has it in the bag." That's the kind of stuff that gets your name in the headlines and gets you talking-head gigs on CNN.

This sort of nonsense created the need for a rational, statistically valid method for predicting the results of elections. Enter Nate Silver and fivethirtyeight.com. Rather than the BBWAA-type approach taken by most political pundits, he took a SABR-type approach, using sophisticated statistical techniques to make more objective, valid predictions. The key is basing them on what proved accurate in the past, not what you find reasonable. You also have to be willing to evaluate your own past predictions with the same objective eye, and then continually improve your methods to fix past failures. I guarantee most political pundits don't even remember their past predictions, much less try to learn from the ones that went wrong.

And by the way, Nate Silver came from baseball: He wrote for Baseball Prospectus and created a system for predicting ballplayer performance called PECOTA (an acronym jerry-rigged so that it matched the name of 1980s Royals infielder Bill Pecota). Silver is the most famous example of someone who went from baseball stats to more important things, but he's not the only one. I, for example, owe my career as a data analyst to Bill James and sabermetrics. If not for the interest they sparked in me, I'd probably be another English-major barista desperate for a publishing job that will never come. Baseball statistics and sabermetrics can turn people on to analytical, statistically valid thinking the way "The Nutcracker" can turn kids on to ballet. It might be a frivolous entry point, but you need a fun one if you're going to have any converts.

Anyway, Smokey Joe Williams. He may not have been Satchel Paige, but he wasn't far off. As his nickname suggests, he threw very hard. He was also known as "Cyclone Joe" for the same reason. Anyone with a good fastball in the dead-ball era was nicknamed either "Rube" after Rube Waddell or "Cy" after Cyclone "Cy" Young. Even the name "Smokey Joe" may have been a reference to Red Sox pitcher "Smokey Joe" Wood. They did love referential nicknames in those days.

Man, I wish John McGraw had discovered Williams and tried to pass him off as full-blooded Native American instead of Charlie Grant. Williams actually was half Native American, and probably could have "passed," as they say.

And he would have dominated the white major leagues. His peak came before 1920, when the formal Negro Leagues began, so his numbers are debatable and often garnered against far inferior barnstorming competition. But the evidence we have is so overwhelming that there's no question as to his greatness.

In his day, numbers didn't create fame as much as stories of great performances. There is no shortage of those for Williams. He struck out 27 in a 12-inning game against the Kansas City Monarchs, who of course were no slouches at the plate. In 1917 he no-hit the New York (white) Giants, striking out 20. Put him with Rube Waddell, Dazzy Vance and Bob Feller as a rare strikeout talent in an era with few of them.

Like Satchel Paige, Williams started with a fastball and brilliant control, but lasted for more than 20 years by adapting when the heater waned. He was still pitching well in his mid-40s. From 1928-1932 he played for the legendary Homestead Grays teams of Oscar Charleston, Josh Gibson, and Judy Johnson. Willie Wells, Jud Wilson, and Ray Brown also played for some of those teams. I've talked a lot about the Kansas City Monarchs, but those Homestead Grays are typically considered the best team the Negro Leagues ever had to offer.

Smokey Joe Williams may be the second-best pitcher in Negro Leagues history, but that's hardly faint praise. Certain Hall-of-Famer.

Vic Willis (1898-1910; career ERA+: 117)

	Career	Rank	Peak	Rank	Bests	Top 5s	JAWS	Rank
WAR	63.5	38	49.6	28	1	3	56.5	34
WS	292.7	29	199.3	10	1	3	NA	72

Vic Willis gives me hope that Wally Schang, Sherry Magee, Bill Dahlen, and Heinie Groh could one day be enshrined. Willis was selected in 1995, 85 years after his last pitch and 48 years after his death. Few fans were clamoring for Vic Willis' induction, but the Veterans Committee uncovered his record and realized it was worthy.

This wasn't yo' grandpa's Veterans Committee (assuming your grandfather was Frankie Frisch). In the 1990s the Veterans Committee was at peak effectiveness. They skillfully filled in gaps by inducting underrated MLB stars (George Davis, Richie Ashburn, Jim Bunning, Hal Newhouser, Nellie Fox), great Negro Leaguers (Leon Day, Bullet Rogan, Willie Wells, Smokey Joe Williams) and qualified non-players

(Frank Selee, Lee MacPhail, William Hulbert, Bill Veeck). After one misfire in 2001 (Bill Mazeroski), the rules were radically altered and the committee stopped producing anything for years. Looks like someone overreacted.

It might not have just been because of Mazeroski. Many baseball fans greeted these selections, especially the guys from the 1800s, with something to the effect of "Why bother? He and all his fans are dead." Even Bill James could fall into this way of thinking. A few years before shortstop George Davis was selected by this peak-form Veteran's Committee in 1998, James devoted a chapter to him in "Whatever Happened to the Hall of Fame?" After a long demonstration that Davis should be in the Hall instead of Joe Tinker, James frustratingly concludes "George Davis is dead. He is forgotten. I can't see that it would accomplish a hell of a lot to vote him a plaque now." (p. 216)

I think it would accomplish a hell of a lot, Bill. For starters, it would accomplish the Hall of Fame's central reason for being. It is there to honor the best players and most important figures in history. This gives it an educational function: When a player is in the Hall, people want to learn about him. Then, you see, he'll no longer be so forgotten. The Hall of Fame doesn't exist just to make nostalgic fortysomethings dewy-eyed upon watching their childhood heroes get plaques on ESPN. That's a pleasant side effect, but not the central mission.

I'm not sure why Willis didn't get noticed before the 1990s, while the likes of Chief Bender and Addie Joss did. Willis had 249 wins, so he didn't hit the magic 250 that used to guarantee a spot. He wasn't known for contributing to a famous team, because he was stuck for most of his career with mediocre Braves squads. But he did play for the great 1898 Braves, which went 102-41 and also starred Kid Nichols, Jimmy Collins, Hugh Duffy, and Billy Hamilton. And he did end up on the great 1909 Pirates, which went 110-42 and also starred Honus Wagner and Fred Clarke. Granted, Willis could hardly be said to be the central figure of either team.

Likely, it was just a matter of stories. Vic Willis didn't star in many stories about the old days. Even his SABR biography is a bit dull. Usually I strip-mine those for material for these comments, but Willis' doesn't give me much besides salary disputes. I'm left without any idea of what Willis was like as a person.

Oh well. I know what he was like as a ballplayer, and that qualifies him for the Hall.

Early Wynn (1939, 1941-1944, 1946-1963; career ERA+: 107)

	Career	Rank	Peak	Rank	Bests	Top 5s	JAWS	Rank
WAR	61.3	45	38.6	80	1	3	50.0	53
WS	308.1	26	160.9	58	1	4	NA	40

Early Wynn was good for a long time, at times superb, and also spent some time in the military. It seems like he was a bit of a jerk. He was big on throwing at hitters, which I understand is sometimes necessary, but when you throw at a guy's head you're taking it too far. (Source: SABR, probably.)

OK, that gets all that crap out of the way. I gave an assessment of Wynn's career, a vague impression of his personality, and I brought up an issue I could spout off about. (Sorry grammar nerds -- an issue off about which I could spout.) Let's move on to a name game.

Early Wynn has a great baseball name. It's tailor-made for the the lame puns that characterize newspaper headlines. "Early Wins Again." "Cleveland Seeks an Early Win Today." And so forth. Who else had names that included baseball terms?

There are plenty of other "Wynn"s of various spellings: Randy Winn, Marvell Wynne, Jim Wynn, a few others. Win Ballou's full name was "Noble Winifred Ballou," so it counts. (I'm ignoring nicknames, since that would be too easy.) Plus you get "ball" in his name, which makes him a double-threat. Al and Ivey Wingo have last names that sound like chants at Japanese ballgames.[111] Dave Winfield has a good one, when you think about it: It has both "win" and "field."

That segues to the "Field" variants: Cecil and Prince Fielder are the most famous. Fielder Jones' first name really was "Fielder." Perhaps you assumed that, since "Fielder" would be the most boring, anonymous baseball nickname ever. It would be like being called "Person."

There was a second baseman in the 1920s named Johnny Rawlings, if you can believe it. It sounds like the main character of a cheesy series of children's books from the 1950s. No doubt he had a girlfriend named Bess who lived in Smalltown and made apple pies for bald eagles.

Then there are the unflattering names. Grant Balfour, for example, has a terrible name for a pitcher. Granting ball four is typically a bad idea. Kyle Lohse pronounces his name "Loshe," but that's like Dr. Frankenstein pronouncing his name "Fronkensteen" in "Young Frankenstein." Kyle, if it were supposed to be pronounced "Loshe" your family should have spelled it "Loshe." People who speak English expect the "sh" sound to spelled "s" and then "h," not "h" and then "s." If we could all just transpose letters willy-nilly for our pronunciations, then "Early Wynn" could be spelled "Aelrw Ynyn." And good luck pronouncing that if you're not Welsh.[112]

And though it's not necessarily a baseball-specific name, I have to squeeze Tony Suck in here. He was a real player who played briefly and badly in 1884, that crazy year when Old Hoss Radbourn pitched almost every day and got 59 wins. I am the proud sponsor of Tony Suck's page in baseball-reference.com. When I was a teenager, I discovered his name in the Baseball Encyclopedia and was tickled and amused to no end. He was born Charles Anthony Zuck, but in the 1880s being called "Tony Suck" was apparently preferable.

---

[111] I've never been to a game in Japan, but apparently, it's a gas. There's never a moment when the crowd isn't chanting something in unison, often something in English that's only semi-sensical like "Run! Go! Get!" I got a hint of that atmosphere when I attended the first-ever World Baseball Classic. Korean fans chanted the name of their country over and over and over the whole game. You might think it would be annoying, but it was pretty awesome. I never thought Americans would be the ones to look staid and overly quiet, but our baseball fans are positively Scandinavian by world standards.

[112] I went to Wales once, and the best part was trying to pronounce Welsh street signs. In Welsh, "W"s and "y"s are strictly vowels: "w" is pronounced "oo" and a "y" sounds like "eh." So you get places like Cwmystwyth, a real town in eastern Wales. Two "l"s in a row like "ll" mean that you have to make an "l" sound while clearing your throat at the same time. So saying Doug Llewelyn's name properly really took some practice. (Reference explanation: Doug Llewelyn was a guy who would interview people who had just come out of Judge Wapner's court in "The People's Court," a 1980s daytime show that was the godfather of "Judge Judy" and all the rest of them. By the way, did you know that Judge Judy makes $45 million per year? She is the highest-paid person in all of television. It goes to show you that being a tiny old white lady angrily telling young people to shape up can sell big-time if you put it on TV.)

And there are lots more baseball-specific names: Joe Start, John Strike, Matt Batts, etc., etc. And Early Wynn is a Hall-of-Famer.

Cy Young (1890-1911; career ERA+: 138)

	Career	Rank	Peak	Rank	Bests	Top 5s	JAWS	Rank
WAR	168.5	1	79.3	2	5	13	123.9	2
WS	633.9	1	279.2	2	3	9	NA	4

As I alluded to before, Cy Young's real first name was not Cyrus or anything of the sort. His name was Denton True Young, but he was known as "Cyclone," or "Cy" for short, because of his fastball. Would the Denny Young Award carry the same je ne sais quoi? Maybe, maybe not.

But enough stuff about names. Young is in some ways an awkward fit for this post-1800s section. He had most of his best years in the 1890s, pitching 400-plus innings a year and regularly registering more than 10 WAR. But when the clock turned to 1901 he was pretty darn amazing too: four years of 9+ WAR, including 12.6 in 1901. No one else came close to dominating two different centuries.

You may know that Young holds the all-time record for wins, with 511. He also holds the record for losses, games started, complete games, innings, hits allowed, earned runs allowed, and batters faced. He came from an era in which pitchers maxed out around 10-13 seasons because of heavy workloads. Fastball pitchers like Cy survived even fewer. But he stretched into the new era and made it through 22.

Maybe it's a bit unfair to pit the rest of the post-1800s pitchers against Cy Young. Maybe they should only have to compete with his post-1901 numbers. Rickey Henderson didn't turn out to be a Hall-of-Famer if cut in half. But if anyone could, it would have to be Cy Young. Let's try it:

Cy Young (1901-1911; career ERA+: 130)

	Career	Rank	Peak	Rank	Bests	Top 5s	JAWS	Rank
WAR	72.5	24	64.0	6	1	6	68.2	20
WS	280.8	32	233.8	6	0	4	NA	NA

Yup, still a HOFer. This spans Young's career from when he was 34 to when he was 44, which should be his twilight years. And he still looks better than Nolan Ryan and lots of other no-doubt HOFers. The man was simply incredible. Only Walter Johnson and Lefty Grove can compete with him as the best pitcher in history.

Who's In, Who's Out

Whew, that chapter sure was a marathon, for both of us. It took us both a long time, we're now exhausted, and we puked several times. And now we get little oval bumper stickers that enable us to shamelessly brag to complete strangers about something that thousands of people achieve each week![113] And we got to puke on the shoes of the following innocent bystanders:

- Charley "Chief" Bender
- Jack Chesbro
- Lefty Gomez
- Jesse Haines
- Catfish Hunter
- Addie Joss
- Rube Marquard
- Herb Pennock

Not that many, really. That's only 8 out of 65, making for a lower ratio than any other position. Let's try to find some better candidates:

Roger Clemens (1984-2007; career ERA+: 143)

	Career	Rank	Peak	Rank	Bests	Top 5s	JAWS	Rank
WAR	140.3	3	66.3	5	3	11	103.3	3
WS	438.0	4	193.0	15	5	11	NA	10

Remember Barry Bonds? Big fella, steroid accusations, etc? In the comment for him I savagely chopped off the part of his career that could in any way be construed as juiced. He no longer looked like the greatest player since Babe Ruth, but he was still among the top five left fielders ever.

Let's try the same with Roger Clemens. Barry Bonds' record saw a sudden shift around 1999 from super-duperstar numbers to broken-video-game numbers. The shift isn't as dramatic with Clemens, but the allegations start around the same time. In 1998 he hired Brain MacNamee, who is quoted in the Mitchell Report saying he first injected Clemens with steroids that year. 1998 happened to be an incredible year for Clemens. His 1997 was even better, and a bit out of context compared to his previous seasons, especially considering he was 34 years old. Let's be extra safe and cut it off before 1997. That covers only his Red Sox years.

Doing so drops Clemens from 4916 career innings to just 2776, about the same as Pedro Martinez. His win-loss record is now 192-111 instead of 354-184. It's a big cut, probably too big. Let's see what it leaves us with:

---

[113] Reference explanation: Those "26.2" stickers you see on the back of cars. Look, running a marathon is indeed an achievement to be proud of. But so are a thousand other achievements that would be gauche to advertise on your car. I wrote a book of around 875 pages, but I can't imagine slapping "I wrote an excessively long book!" on my bumper. Remember when "My child is an honor student at Blah Blah High" bumper stickers were rampant? Then came the backlash: "My dog is smarter than your honor student," etc. Now you don't see those honor student stickers much. It's not just me; most people tend to dislike boasts in bumper sticker form. Stick to oversimplified political bromides.

Roger Clemens (1984-1996; career ERA+: 144)

	Career	Rank	Peak	Rank	Bests	Top 5s	JAWS	Rank
WAR	81.3	23	60.5	10	2	8	70.9	17
WS	248.0	47	177.4	34	4	5	NA	NA

That's definitely still a Hall-of-Famer. He's still the best pitcher not in the Hall of Fame. The only reason to keep him out is the moral absolutism I've already discussed. And it's worth noting that Clemens was found not guilty for lying to Congress about his steroid use. Let's get Clemens in.

Mike Mussina (1991-2008; career ERA+: 123)

	Career	Rank	Peak	Rank	Bests	Top 5s	JAWS	Rank
WAR	83.0	20	44.5	46	0	3	63.8	21
WS	274.1	37	138.5	112	0	4	NA	54(ish)

That (ish) next to Bill James' overall rank denotes that he ranked Mussina 54th in 2001, before Mussina had plenty more good seasons. I unfortunately can't provide the WSAWS ranking like I did with hitters, because, as you know, recent pitchers have a big disadvantage in Win Shares.

But 54th still qualifies, which gives you an idea of how good Mike Mussina was. He was never the best pitcher in all of baseball, but that's a pretty tall order for pitchers. He was among the top five 3 or 4 times according to the two systems. That's pretty darn good.

He's in the same JAWS range as Eddie Plank, which is an apt comparison. Plank and Mussina were both the type to be clear aces on a mediocre team or a number-two or -three starter on an awesome team. And both did it for a long time. Plank had more wins and a lower ERA, but that's just because he pitched in the dead-ball era and Mussina pitched in the Steroid Era.

After two years of balloting at this writing, Mussina hasn't cracked 25% of the BBWAA vote. Just when I thought BBWAA voters had gotten smarter when it came to pitchers, here they are dissing Mussina. Mussina is clearly better than John Smoltz, who got in on the first try. What's going on?

I wish I knew. In every stat, conventional or otherwise, Mussina looks better. Smoltz was with great Braves teams, but Mussina was with great Yankees teams. Smoltz won a Cy Young Award, but Mussina should have won the 2001 one (he had the AL-best WAR), which went to Roger Clemens because he had 20 wins. Are people still impressed that Smoltz had those few years as a closer? As I said, that was a regrettable interlude in his starting career, not evidence that he was some sort of wild two-way player.

I suppose I shouldn't be reading into the John Smoltz selection too much. Maybe that was just a fluke, the one time the BBWAA selected a mid-range pitcher without years of deliberation. Let's hope Mussina doesn't have to wait too much longer.

P.S.: Mike Mussina is also cool because he's a crossword enthusiast (I'm using a rather liberal definition of the word "cool" here). Mussina showed up in "Wordplay," a fun documentary about New York Times puzzlemaster Will Shortz and other crossword mavens. Another of my completely unmarketable and unremunerative skills is making crosswords, which I did to great acclaim for my college newspaper. By the way, if you ever want to make a college career counselor flustered and confused, tell him/her you want to become a professional crossword maker after graduation.

In the real (cruel) world, I discovered that getting your puzzle into the New York Times, the peak achievement for a crossword maker, will get you about $150. I was good by the standards of a small college's puzzle master, but definitely not ready for the New York Times. So if I had worked really hard, day after day, year in and year out, at some point I might have been good and lucky enough to earn a check for $150. Even as a dumb kid I was practical enough to realize that that was a waste of time.

People say you should do what you love, and you will never work a day in your life. "Follow your passion," they say. Successful people love to say things like that, because it worked for them. These people were lucky enough to love doing things that people wanted to pay them to do, like starting tech companies or trading derivatives or whatever. But what if you only enjoy doing things that no one wants to pay you to do? I'm expecting my hourly rate in writing this book will be around $0.01. And that's the best-case scenario.

Even more annoying are the people who succeeded in things that a lot of people love to do, like playing baseball. Major-league players will often spout the myth that with hard work, anyone can do anything. I swear to you, no amount of hard work would make the body I was born with, one I inherited from a long line of geeky indoorsy types, into a major-league-caliber ballplayer. Hard work is vital, but so is genetics. I had to cut my losses early and accept the fact that my passion for playing baseball was not going to lead to anything but pain. Thank God I did.

Imagine if everyone followed their passions indefinitely: The world would be half poets and half professional video game players. Millions of insurance adjuster and factory worker jobs would go unfilled. If you want to have buses, you need people driving them. Those who end up doing so often feel like failures because they aren't passionate about it. They should feel like the solid, responsible family breadwinners they are. Some of us don't get to just follow our passions into riches. Maybe life is a little more complicated than just "follow your passion"; maybe practical realities come into play too. Anyway, let's move on.

Curt Schilling (1988-2007; career ERA+: 127)

	Career	Rank	Peak	Rank	Bests	Top 5s	JAWS	Rank
WAR	79.9	23	49.0	31	0	3	64.5	20
WS	252.7	52	147.0	88	0	4	NA	61(ish)

As with Mike Mussina, Schilling got that 61st Bill James ranking before he had a few more great seasons, including his entire tenure with the Red Sox. Add on Schilling's bloody sock and otherwise stellar postseason play (2.23 ERA in 133.1 innings) and he might just deserve to be above Mussina. Whatever; both are clearly qualified.

I'm a little worried, though. Both have been stuck at around the same percentages the last few years. As I mentioned before, the ballot is so overstuffed with valid candidates that many writers are finding it impossible to get them all under the arbitrary 10-player limit. Every year is going to add a few more worthy players, and the problem is just going to get worse and worse.

Usually, the Hall of Fame doesn't reform its procedures until a terrible pick is made or no one gets in at all. The latter is often seen as more disastrous, as it means no grand, publicity-inducing induction ceremony in July. In 2013, not too many people crowded into Cooperstown's hotels to celebrate Veterans Committee selections Deacon White, Hank O'Day, and Jacob Ruppert.[114]

If a new super-duper-star comes on the ballot each year, he will get elected while Mike Mussina, Curt Schilling, Tim Raines, Jeff Bagwell, Barry Bonds, Roger Clemens, Edgar Martinez, Lee Smith, Jeff Kent, etc., etc. split the ballot of holdovers and all stay stuck below 75%. Let's check on that by looking at the ballots of the next few years:

2017: Ivan Rodriguez, Manny Ramirez, and Vladimir Guerrero all make their debuts on the ballot. Rodriguez and Ramirez will be punished for their alleged and blatant (respectively) steroid use. They will likely get stuck at around the same level for a long time, a la Barry Bonds and Roger Clemens. Guerrero is qualified, but not clearly enough to get in on the first try. Maybe this will create an opening for Tim Raines (55.0% in 2015) or Jeff Bagwell (55.7%). This will be Raines' last eligible year, thanks to the stupid new "10 years and you're out" rule. So there could be an eleventh-hour groundswell of support for him, like there was for Bert Blyleven. Or more likely, the ballot will be split 20 ways and no one will get in. This could be the crisis we're looking for, the one that will motivate change.

2018: Hopefully, last year's debacle will compel the Hall to alter its election procedures. If not, President Rand Paul will cry "socialism" and deregulate the Hall of Fame, leaving all future selections to the free market. The players whose campaigns get the most donations from millionaires will fill the airwaves with ads. New-to-the-ballot Chipper Jones should receive enough money from Ted Turner to ensure the spot he clearly deserves. Jim Thome has a chance, but also might suffer the Jeff Bagwell stigma, in which he is punished for hitting home runs during the same years in which people took steroids. Scott Rolen will also be newly eligible, but will have to pray that George Soros or Sheldon Adelson is secretly a Cardinals fan. I'm not seeing much room here for Schilling, Mussina, et al.

2019: Mariano Rivera will get in without a struggle. You can assume that anyone to whom MLB devoted a whole All-Star Game will get in on his first attempt. I'm in favor of Roy Halladay and Todd Helton, but they won't have a chance unless writers get a lot smarter in the next few years and give up the dumb notion that only inner-circle Hall-of-Famers deserve to get in on their first tries. Maybe there will be an opening here for Mussina, Schilling, or Bagwell. Edgar Martinez will be in his last year of eligibility, and hopefully will have garnered enough support to get in.

2020: Derek Jeter. Derek Jeter, Derek Jeter, Derek Jeter, Derek Jeter? Derek Jeter. It would be a grave dishonor to Derek Jeter's unbounded benevolence to allow any mere mortal to enter the Hall alongside the Greatest Human Being Ever to Walk the Earth. In fact, the second his plaque is mounted, the Hall of Fame will spontaneously ignite, all that idolatrous Babe Ruth and Ted Williams

---

[114] All these guys had been dead for more than 70 years when they got the call. Deacon White you should know about; he was the third baseman/catcher from the 1870s who believed the Earth was flat. Hank O'Day was an umpire, and I don't know if I'll ever have enough spare time to devise a JAWS-style set of standards for umpires, so I'll just assume he deserves the Hall. Jacob Ruppert was the co-owner of the Yankees from 1915-1922 and sole owner from 1923-1939, during which time they went from mediocre to the greatest team in history. So he seems to deserve it. I'm only sad that he was the one to keep the Yankees rather than his original co-owner, the extremely cool-named Tillinghast L'Hommedieu Huston.

memorabilia will burn, and up from the ashes like a phoenix will arise the Derek Jeter Center for Derek Jeter Worship, In Honor of Derek Jeter. Baseball will also cease to exist, because without Derek Jeter playing it, it is naught but a desecration of His name.

Throughout all these years, the steroid cases are wild cards. No one can predict if enough voters will ever give up on their moral absolutism and let Bonds and Clemens in. Ivan Rodriguez might get an earlier pass, as Mike Piazza did. I don't foresee a road out for Manny Ramirez.

Overall, I'm seeing some opportunities in there for Mussina and Schilling. I certainly hope they don't have to wait for the Veterans Committee (not its real name any more, but it doesn't have a single name any more, so we are left with no choice but to keep calling it that), because no one seems good enough for them lately.

Wes Ferrell (1927-1941; career ERA+: 116)

	Career	Rank	Peak	Rank	Bests	Top 5s	JAWS	Rank
WAR	61.6	44	55.0	13	1	6	58.3	26
WS	233.1	72	191.7	18	1	6	NA	35

Wes Ferrell's career ERA was 4.04. He had 193 wins. He fell apart at age 29, so his career was short. It's not surprising that he never got more than 5% of the BBWAA vote.

But from 1929-1936, Wes Ferrell was a dominant player. The greatness of his pitching is masked by the big-hitting 1930s; his 4.19 ERA in 1936 earned a 126 ERA+. And he pitched a lot, leading the league in starts twice, complete games four times, and innings three times.

Still, Ferrell would be in the Kenny Rogers/Jimmy Key/Ron Guidry range of non-HOFers if not for his hitting. Ferrell was possibly the best-hitting pitcher of all time. In his career, he hit .280/.351/.446, for an even 100 OPS+. A shortstop or catcher who hit that well and fielded well over a long career would deserve the Hall. In 1935 Ferrell hit .347/.427/.533 (141 OPS+), earning 2.6 WAR just for his hitting, a record for pitchers post-1901. His career hitting WAR ranks fourth all-time for pitchers, behind only Red Ruffing, Walter Johnson (is there anything that guy couldn't do?), and George Mullin. But those three had lots more PAs; per PA, no one beat Ferrell.

Has hitting ever been a factor in the Cy Young Award? I don't think it has, but it should be. If the award had existed in 1935, it may have come up. That year Ferrell's 8.5 Pitching WAR was second to Lefty Grove's 9.5. But when you add in hitting, Ferrell beats Grove convincingly, 11.0 to 8.8. In Win Shares, Ferrell edges Grove barely in pitching alone, 30 to 29. But when you add in hitting, Ferrell is on top 35-29. Of course, in the real world, Ferrell's league-leading 25 wins would have ensured him the award. In the MVP voting he finished second to Hank Greenberg, while Grove finished 14th.

That year, Ferrell and Grove were first and second in WAR among all American Leaguers. (In Win Shares, Ferrell was still tops, but Grove was seventh.) They both played for the Red Sox, both having been purchased by owner Tom Yawkey in his effort to turn the then-perpetual doormats into contenders. I mentioned this in the comment for Joe Cronin, who joined the team in 1935 as its shortstop/manager. These moves didn't bring immediate championships; the Red Sox were stuck around .500 each year. But these moves, more than anything else, made Boston into a Red Sox town. If the Sox had continued to stink, they might have moved to Milwaukee instead of the Braves.

Ferrell's brother Rick is in the Hall, but doesn't deserve to be. What if I just snuck into the Hall of Fame late at night and wrote "Wes" over all the "Rick"s in the displays? I could leave the same picture on the plaque, as they looked pretty similar. Would anyone even notice? I suppose there's only one way to find out ...

Luis Tiant (1964-1982; career ERA+: 114)

	Career	Rank	Peak	Rank	Bests	Top 5s	JAWS	Rank
WAR	66.7	33	44.6	44	0	2	55.6	38
WS	253.5	51	151.7	73	0	5	NA	45

Hey, I'm back from trying to change all the "Rick"s to "Wes"es in the Hall of Fame. It turns out that some people did notice, most notably the SWAT team that immediately surrounded me and brought me to jail. I should mention that I'm writing this from death row. They do NOT mess around with the Hall of Fame in Cooperstown.

On to Luis Tiant. You'd think that pitchers from the late 1960s and early 1970s would be overrepresented in the Hall of Fame, since they had great conventional numbers. But the only one I had to kick out was Catfish Hunter, and he wasn't that terrible.

Luis Tiant has gotten some, but not a ton of support for the Hall. His first year on the ballot, he got a solid 30.9%. Usually anyone who starts that strong will eventually get in. But the next year he dropped to 10.5% and languished in that range until he timed out.

The BBWAA voting is weird that way. For anyone new to the ballot, the BBWAA always starts by taking the same perspective as the average fan: They know about around 50 guys, the inner-circle Hall-of-Famers, and think any new candidate has to match up with those. (That gave rise to the silly "first-ballot Hall-of-Famer" thing that makes some voters postpone voting for a clearly qualified player because he's not deemed first-ballot material. Who cares whether he's "first-ballot" or not? If he deserves it, he deserves it.) Then, over the years, vote totals tend to build as more and more people get convinced that a player belongs. Eventually logic reigns and a player like Bert Blyleven gets in.

But it doesn't always work out that way. Many players languish at around the same level of support all 15 years (now stupidly limited to 10). Dave Parker stayed on the ballot for the full 15 years, always stuck between 10-25%. He's not quite qualified for the Hall, so it's good that his candidacy never made any headway.

As you can see from the above rankings, Tiant deserved to be in the Blyleven situation, instead of the Parker one he got. He didn't quite have the longevity of Blyleven, but was otherwise similar. Tiant was always good, and sometimes great. His best year was in 1968, when he had a 1.60 ERA and led the AL in WAR among pitchers. But he was overshadowed by all the eye-popping pitcher numbers that year, including the 31 wins of Denny McLain's that won him the Cy Young Award unanimously. (Win Shares preferred McLain, who pitched loads of innings, but put Tiant second.)

Tiant didn't get crazy win totals like McLain did because he didn't play for many great teams. But he definitely pitched well enough for long enough to deserve a spot.

Roy Halladay (1998-2013; career ERA+: 131)

	Career	Rank	Peak	Rank	Bests	Top 5s	JAWS	Rank
WAR	64.7	36	50.6	25	2	5	57.7	29
WS	152.8	206	132.6	143	1	3	NA	NA

Ignore not only the lack of a Bill James ranking, but also the Wins Shares numbers above. They only go through 2008, and Halladay had some of his best years from 2009-2011. We can only go by WAR on this one, and they make Roy Halladay look pretty darn qualified.

I got into an argument online a while back about Halladay's worthiness for the Hall of Fame. I try to avoid online arguments as much as possible, because the Internet turns ordinary people into rage-aholic sociopaths. There's something about typing alone under a fake name that unleashes the inner Viking in every meek dingus with an Internet connection.

It can be a dangerous phenomenon. Some people, particularly women, get harassed with virulent hate speech and fear for their lives. That is fundamentally wrong. I would like to see a law passed that says you have to use your real name for anything you post online. I'm serious. If you're going to say something, you need to have the basic courage to make your identity known.

In all online arguments, this is where someone says "Whatever happened to free speech?" The answer to that question is always "You apparently don't understand what 'free speech' means." Free speech does not mean anonymous speech. Speech is the act of saying "I believe this." The "I" is just as important as the "this." For the statement to be valid, you have to at the very least identify yourself, thus attaching the message to your conception of yourself and others' conception of you. If you don't have the courage to do that, it's not a real opinion. It's just a brain fart, with no relevance or worth.

When you identify yourself, you accept the consequences of your speech. This is the part most often misunderstood: Even when people post under their own names, they often experience a backlash for something they said and scream "Whatever happened to free speech?" This again reveals a wild misunderstanding of the concept. Free speech does not mean consequence-free speech. It only means you can't be thrown in jail for what you say. But you can definitively be fired for what you say. Your organization can be boycotted for what you say. And you can at the very least experience people despising you and arguing vehemently against what you say. It's part of the rest of the world's free speech rights to freely speak about how horrible your speech was.

Man, that just turned into an online-style rant! At this point, your job is to ignore everything I just said and launch into your own rant. We'll both continue in that vein for a while until we devolve into curses and name-calling. Then everything will be solved!

Anyway, the point was that I got into it online with some average fans over Roy Halladay's worthiness for the Hall. They were looking at Halladay's record, comparing it to the likes of Greg Maddux, and saying Halladay didn't measure up. I referenced this in the introductory chapter. It's like saying no movie should win an Oscar unless it's as good as "Citizen Kane." The bar is not actually that high.

Roy Halladay was the best pitcher in baseball a few times, and among the best several other times. He won two Cy Young Awards and deserved each, leading the league in pitching WAR both times. He also led the league in pitching WAR on two other occasions. Win Shares gives him just one league-leading performance, but again, Win Shares only goes through 2008.

He didn't have a long career, but he pitched for 16 years. During several of those years he was a workhorse, leading the league in innings four times.

Check out that ERA+ number. It ranks tied for 21st among all pitchers with at least 2000 career innings, tying him with Sandy Koufax. All the pitchers above Halladay are in the Hall except those who are still on the BBWAA ballot, plus Noodles Hahn, who pitched only eight years and 2029.1 innings (Halladay had 2749.1). And the ten pitchers below Halladay in career ERA+ are either in the Hall, on the ballot, or still playing. (The unfortunately named Nig Cuppy breaks the streak thanks to his 2283 innings from 1892-1901).

Roy Halladay is not Greg Maddux. But he is maybe 80% of Maddux. That's enough for a Hall-of-Famer.

Kevin Brown (1986, 1988-2005; career ERA+: 127)

	Career	Rank	Peak	Rank	Bests	Top 5s	JAWS	Rank
WAR	68.3	29	45.4	39	1	3	56.9	32
WS	241.9	60	151.3	76	1	5	NA	62

Kevin Brown was on the BBWAA ballot just once. He got only 2.6% of the vote, which made him drop off for good. He didn't even get the chance to build up a case over time. Sigh.

By the way, that's another dumb rule in the BBWAA selection procedures: If you don't make 5% of the ballot, you're off for good. Before they instituted this rule, plenty of deserving HOFers got their starts below 5%: Al Simmons, Goose Goslin, Home Run Baker, Red Faber, Stan Coveleski, Joe Medwick, Gabby Hartnett, etc., etc.

As I've mentioned, the Hall of Fame comes up with a rule like this every so often to try to engineer the number of Hall-of-Famers that come in each year. There's no rhyme or reason to what they try; they behave like they're operating the rabbit ears on old TV sets. Move it this way. OK, that didn't work, so move it the other way. OK, try holding the antenna and standing on one foot. OK, try the other foot. There! I can see Ed Sullivan now. Don't move a muscle. Wait, he's gone! What did you do?

There are better ways. For example, they could do a ranked choice ballot with an automatic runoff, as many propose for political elections. Or don't listen to me: Consult with someone who is an expert on voting systems. Bill James is not an expert on voting systems, but he devised a much better one from scratch in "Whatever Happened to the Hall of Fame?" I won't go into it further so that you have to buy that book. Plus, if you read the whole thing, the last page has candy! (Candy not guaranteed.)

Al Simmons, Goose Goslin, et al. got under 5% because people had a different conception of Hall-of-Famer at the time. Those conceptions change often, usually for the better, but sometimes for the worse. The BBWAA's conception of what makes for a Hall-of-Fame pitcher has been really terrible with the last 20 years or so. They have no interest in the middle class of pitchers, the Jim Bunning types. You have to be Tom freakin' Seaver to get in. Again, the John Smoltz selection could be a sign of things turning more reasonable. Or it could be a fluke. We'll see I suppose.

It's not just that most BBWAA voters missed the boat on Kevin Brown and other recent mid-HOF-range pitchers. It's that practically all of them did. A full 97.4% of BBWAA voters did not think Kevin Brown deserved the Hall. The disparity is alarming: You're either in on the first ballot or you're off on the first ballot. Shouldn't at least a handful of writers understand that the Hall of Fame is more than 50 guys?

Or maybe career win totals are the only thing that BBWAA voters look at? Like Roy Halladay, Kevin Brown had several years of dominance (twice leading the league in pitcher WAR, once in pitcher Win Shares) and a career of good length. But because he pitched in the 1990s, he didn't come close to 300 wins. In any other era he surely would have hit 250 at least.

You know the drill by now. Pitcher wins are stupid, so ignore them. Bill James rated Brown relatively low because he did the ratings in 2001, before Brown had a few more good years. JAWS says he's in the range. He deserves a spot.

"Cannonball" Dick Redding (1911-1932; 120 ERA+)

	Rank at SP Among Negro Leaguers	Rank Among All Negro Leaguers
SABR	7	21
Monte Irvin	6 among RHP (basically)	NA

At the end of his chapter on right-handed Negro League pitchers, Monte Irvin essentially acknowledges that picking only five was dumb. He can't help but include Dick Redding in his top five but also can't see any way to kick out Smokey Joe Williams, Satchel Paige, Leon Day, Bullet Rogan or Martin Dihigo. He ends up saying "let's just say that my list of the 'top five' right handed pitchers in Negro League history has six names on it." Give in, Monte. Just go for the top six. You won't be breaking any laws, I swear.

My other source, SABR, agrees on "Cannonball" Dick Redding. He has their highest overall ranking of anyone not in the Hall of Fame. Just among the pitchers, he beats out HOFers Hilton Smith and Jose Mendez, and of course Ray Brown and Andy Cooper, whom SABR left out entirely.

So who is this "Cannonball" Dick Redding fellow? As you can guess from his nickname, he threw very fast. He was very intimidating in the mound, and loved to pitch inside. Off the field he was a kind, quiet man; Buck Leonard said that Redding didn't smoke, drink, curse, or even argue.

Redding did most of his best work in the dead-ball era, which limits his stats. Remember that the Negro National League started in 1920; that year serves as a dividing line much like 1876 does for white major leagues. Redding did pitch after 1920, and well, but by then he was more of old workhorse.

Thank goodness for Seamheads.com. They're the only online source I've seen that is able to compile a sizeable statistical record for Redding. It shows 2077.7 innings with a 120 ERA+. Larry Lester, biographer of Rube Foster and go-to guy on all things Negro Leagues, combed through box scores and found a lifetime record of 2947 innings and a career 2.51 ERA. (Source: "Cannonball Dick Redding: Iron Man IV," Thenationalpastimemuseum.com, Larry Lester.) Both records compare favorably to other HOF Negro League pitchers.

This being the old days, Dick Redding found a tragic end. In 1948 he suffered from some sort of mental illness, often referred to as a "strange malady", and died in a mental hospital.

You know I'm not satisfied with that. I want to know exactly what the malady was and why it led to such a quick death. Mental illnesses don't tend to do that, unless they compel someone to commit suicide. I'm not saying that Dick Redding committed suicide; unfortunately I'm not saying anything, because I don't know anything. There appears to be no real information out there about Redding's death.

Maybe Redding's family would prefer this information to remain confidential. Maybe they have a right to privacy about what must have been a very tragic event. Why do I need to know?

Well, I suppose I need to know because I firmly believe in "warts-and-all" history. Like most kids in high school, I was bored by history class. It was just a recitation of accomplishments by people who seemed very alien to me. The ambiguities that make life interesting never came through: Everyone was a hero, except a handful who were villains. No one seemed to own the complexities and rough edges that make real people interesting.

I didn't fall in love with history until college, when I started to hear about the crazy stuff. Benjamin Franklin always seemed like a pedantic, bizarre science nerd until I learned about his randy side. The monarchs of England were just a long list of people sharing a short list of first names until I learned how colossally inadequate some of them were for any sort of leadership position. A good story needs three-dimensional characters. My high-school history books were giving me one dimension each, at most.

This isn't the fault of the history teachers. It isn't even the fault of the textbook makers. It's the fault of the American public, or at least parts of it. As Diane Ravitch details in her book "The Language Police: How Pressure Groups Restrict What Students Learn," (Vintage, 2004) both extremists on the right and on the left ensure that history is as dull as possible by sanitizing history books. Right-wingers make sure any founding father or other establishment figure is depicted as a flawless saint. Left-wingers make sure that any victim of oppression is depicted as a flawless saint. This turns all historical figures into a dull, grey mishmash, distinguished only by factoids that must be regurgitated onto a test paper and then forgotten.

So I'd like to give some flesh to this skeleton of a personality called "Dick Redding" by learning about his struggles off the field. Otherwise, he exists in my mind only as another in a long list of people who could throw balls well.

And moreover, the nature of his psychological troubles should not tarnish his greatness in the least. There is still a stigma attached to mental disorders, as if they are the result of some kind of moral weakness. Nothing could be further from the truth. Psychological disorders are no different from other medical disorders. You wouldn't cover up someone's struggles with cancer for fear that it might reflect poorly on his character. Maybe people thought that way in Dark Ages, but not now. Similarly, we must move past the notion that mental disorders are anything to be ashamed of. People don't get major depressive disorder because they're dummies who don't know how to "look on the bright side." They get it from a combination of genetics and environmental stimuli, just like any other disease. They deserve to be understood and respected for the struggles they've endured.

Sometimes people protectively shield the public from the unpleasant truths about victims of brutal institutional racism, like Dick Redding. Such people have their hearts in the right place. But I think the whole, warts-and-all truth is especially important in these cases. Yes, it's important to show how such victims could overcome the odds and excel despite the societal oppression that hung on their shoulders with every step. But it's equally as important to reveal if such victims were pushed beyond their capacity to cope and were destroyed by that oppression. Then those of us who have never experienced such conditions can gain a fuller empathy for them. That will further motivate us to ensure nothing similar happens to anyone in the future. I have no idea if Redding's mental condition was sparked or exacerbated by endemic racism. I wish I did. If I knew it was, I could feel sorrow, regret for the actions of my ancestors, and a deeper emotional connection with a man I never knew.

So as always, contact chrisekeedei@yahoo.com with any information about what killed Dick Redding. And regardless of whether his mental struggles stay forever confidential, his ratings and stats make him look like a strange omission from the Hall of Fame.

Urban Shocker (1916-1928; career ERA+: 124)

	Career	Rank	Peak	Rank	Bests	Top 5s	JAWS	Rank
WAR	58.7	51	45.0	40	0	4	51.9	48
WS	225.6	81	165.8	46	0	2	NA	60

As I've alluded to already, I'm hoping this book launches my career as a hip-hop artist named Urban Shocker. My searing, incisive lyrics will give voice to the frustrations of contemporary middle-aged white guys who care too much about the Baseball Hall of Fame. A lot of words rhyme with "Groh," so watch out, Kanye.

The man born Urbain Shockor to father William Shockor and mother Anna Shockor (nee Spies -- even his mom had a cool maiden name) changed his name to Urban Shocker because writers constantly misspelled his real name. (A smart policy I heartily endorse.) While in the minors, he broke the ring finger on his pitching hand. The top knuckle on the finger was permanently bent, which gave him a "slow ball" (i.e., change-up) that dropped suddenly like a spitball. The pitch enabled him to have terrific control; in a time when most pitchers struck out fewer than they walked, Shocker's career SO/BB rate was 1.5. That was fourth-best amongst all pitchers with at least 2000 innings during Urban Shocker's career span (top three: Grover Cleveland Alexander, Walter Johnson, and Wilbur Cooper).

But I'm not arguing in favor of Shocker because of his BB/SO rates. Over a nine-year period, Shocker was a consistently great pitcher, at times superb. In 1921, he earned 7.8 WAR and 30 Win Shares with a 127 ERA+ in 326.2 innings. The next year, he got 7.3 WAR and 29 Win Shares for a 140 ERA+ in 348 innings. In the A.L. of those years, no one was going to best the other Urban, Red Faber, but Shocker was right behind him. The rest of his full seasons were about at the same level of performance, but with a little less WAR and fewer Win Shares because he pitched fewer innings.

He didn't have many full seasons, though. He broke into the majors at age 25 and pitched well, but got few opportunities on a Yankees team that was loaded with pitching. It wasn't until he was traded to the Browns in 1918 that he was given a regular rotation slot.

Then Shocker got drafted into World War I. He sacrificed a little less than a season to the service; it's not a huge factor, but it still adds to his credentials. Once he returned, in 1919, he finally got the chance to become a star.

For the next six years, Shocker was a legitimate ace. Those years cemented him as the best pitcher in the history of the St. Louis Browns, which is damning with faint praise, I realize. But as I said way back in the George Sisler comment, the Browns were actually not bad at the time. In 1922, when Shocker had 7.3 WAR and 29 Win Shares, the Browns went 93-61 and finished just a single game behind the Yankees. George Sisler hit .420/.467/.594 (170 OPS+), and outfielder Ken Williams was almost as good (.332/.413/.627, 164 OPS+, 39 HR and 37 SBs, becoming the only 30 HR - 30 SB player ever until Willie Mays in 1956). But the next year Sisler's eyes broke, and the Browns slowly descended into becoming the St. Louis Browns we all know and pity.

Shocker sacrificed some playing time in 1923, but I don't know whether he should be given extra credit for it or not. The Browns had a bizarre rule prohibiting players' wives from accompanying the team on road trips. (Wouldn't you want the wives there to keep the boys in line? You really want your fellas out bein' cake-eaters at the drum, blowin' their kale on giggle water and tomatoes?[115]) Shocker took a stand against this rule by refusing to go on a road trip in September without his wife. He was suspended for the rest of the season.

Shocker was a bit of a loner, baby, a rebel. He would squirrel himself away with a bunch of newspapers from various cities, scouring them for some small edge against the competition. In the days before the Internet, ESPN, KFAN, etc., newspapers were all you had for information about other teams' hitters. You often didn't even have stats do go on. He'd notice that Joe Batter struck out three times yesterday against Joe Pitcher, who had a great curveball. Then he'd know to throw Joe Batter plenty of curveballs. Shocker was the Brian Bannister[116] type who nowadays would be poring over Baseball Prospectus and Fangraphs for any information that could give him an advantage.

In 1925, the same Yankees who had chucked Urban Shocker aside like a fat man throwing a lobster in the garbage got him back for a basket of puppies who then all got the mange. He pitched well for them through the 1927 season, when the Yankees ran roughshod over baseball.

But Shocker's heart was failing, literally. He had to sit up nights because if he lay down, he would choke uncontrollably. By 1928, he had dropped from 190 pounds to 115. He tried to retire, but after spring training, a large salary offer coaxed him into returning to the Yankees.

Shocker got into only one game that year. One day while pitching batting practice, he collapsed on the field and was quickly released. Yankees manager Miller Huggins proved heart-warmingly understanding about Shocker's life-threatening condition, declaring, "Shocker has gone because he could not get into shape to pitch. He ignored his chance when we were down in Florida." (Yeah, Miller. People often collapse on baseball fields and then become incapacitated because they skipped spring training. Hold on while I get you an honorary medical degree from Johns Hopkins.) In September, Shocker died of heart failure and pneumonia. (Source for all the above: Shocker's SABR biography, by Joseph Wancho.)

Shocker had fewer than 200 career wins (gasp! Oh Lawdy, I'm gettin' the vapors ...). So the inevitable comparisons are with Dizzy Dean, Sandy Koufax, Rube Waddell, and Ed Walsh, the legitimate HOF starters who also didn't crack 200. (Lefty Gomez and Addie Joss also didn't make 200, but I kicked them out.) Shocker doesn't compare to Waddell or Walsh, who each had several dominant seasons. He didn't have one gangbuster season like Dean's 1934 or Koufax's 1963 or 1966. But in his short career, he had more good seasons than either of them. Shocker had eight seasons at 4.0 or more WAR; Koufax and Dean each had six such seasons. Shocker's Peak WAR of 45.0 (40th-best ever) beats Dean's (42.8, 56th), and comes close to Koufax's (46.7, 36th).

I'm not saying Urban Shocker was as good as Sandy Koufax; he didn't have Koufax's mega-seasons or excellence in the postseason. But I do believe Shocker was significantly better than Dean and a bunch of other Hall-of-Famers that I let stay (Waite Hoyt and Eppa Rixey come to mind).

---

[115] That is all legitimate 1920s slang, in case you're some kind of pipe-trotter who couldn't slip-ee-dip his own grumble juice up Sweet Street! (That is all illegitimate 1920s slang that I made up.)
[116] You know about Brian Bannister? He's the coolest. He had modest skills, at best, but managed at least one good year for the Royals by becoming an early adopter of sabermetric perspectives.

If only he had waited just a few years to die of heart failure ... maybe Miller Huggins was right. If he'd just gone to spring training like he was supposed to, he could have pitched ten more seasons and won the Tour de France in each offseason.

As always, the conditions surrounding Urban Shocker's late start and early demise do not qualify his Hall-of-Fame case one bit. The above numbers still show him to be a Stan Coveleski type who was good enough during his brief tenure to earn a spot as a mid-range HOFer.

Rick Reuschel (1972-1981, 1983-1991; career ERA+: 114)

	Career	Rank	Peak	Rank	Bests	Top 5s	JAWS	Rank
WAR	70.0	26	43.8	49	1	1	56.9	33
WS	239.9	65	136.7	118	0	1	NA	70

Now we get into some candidates that will make you say "What? Him?" Just keep in mind that the Hall has established itself as a bigger place than you might think it is. If there's room for Ted Lyons and Burleigh Grimes (and there is), there's room for Rick Reuschel.

Bet you didn't know Reuschel was the best pitcher in all of baseball in 1977, at least according to WAR. That year, he had a 2.79 ERA (158 ERA+) in 252 innings. He even had a win-loss record that could pass muster with Cy Young Award voters: 20-10 for a Cubs team that went 81-81. Steve Carlton won the Cy with similar conventional numbers: 23-10, 2.64 ERA (153 ERA+) in 283 innings. It's not hard to see why Carlton won the award, since he had more wins, a lower ERA, and more innings. But Carlton had a much lower WAR: 5.9 to Reuschel's 9.4.

What made Reuschel 3.5 WAR better than Carlton? Reuschel pitched in much tougher home park, which is is reflected his better ERA+. Per inning, Reuschel was a bit more effective. But Carlton pitched more. Shouldn't those two effects wash out?

There's another factor not reflected in ERA+: team defense. ERA, and by extension ERA+, tries to eliminate the effects of defense by taking unearned runs out of the calculation (hence, earned runs average). But that is clumsy at best and useless at worst. Unearned runs are based on errors, and errors are probably the dumbest stat in baseball.

Dumbest, Daniels? Really? Dumber than pitcher wins? Yes. Dumber than RBIs? Oh, you betcha. Those might be indirect second-hand measures of value, but least they are determined by rules. Errors are determined by the judgments of one dude watching each game.

I don't mean to diss official scorers, who are doing the best they can. But they're not given enough to work with. Errors are so ridiculously vague and nebulous that they don't deserve to even be considered a statistic. If you score the games you attend, you'll find that maybe once per game something that you thought was a hit turns out to be an error or vice versa. That's not a sign of bad scorers, official or amateur; it's a sign of a bad system.

In assessing an error, the poor official scorer has to determine whether a play could have been made, if not for some flub by the fielder. Usually the flub is clear: maybe the fielder bobbles a ball or drops it or throws it into the stands or accidentally eats it or whatever. But as to whether a play should have been made? How often can you really determine that with a high degree of certainty? If you really think you can determine for sure whether every play should have been made, wouldn't that make baseball very boring? Every time the ball was hit you'd immediately know the outcome. Errors would be the only thing keeping it interesting.

So that's two determining factors for errors that require varying degrees of subjectivity. That's not good. Any statistic in any field of endeavor is meaningful only if it entails very few subjective assessments. Pure objectivity might be impossible, but you should aim to get as close to it as you can. Errors don't even try; they are almost entirely based on subjective assessments. They may be expert subjective assessments, but they're still subjective.

There are a few clear rules in determining errors. But even those don't make much sense. For instance, you have to make physical contact with the ball to earn an error. How many times have you seen Delmon Young or Manny Ramirez take a terrible route on an easy fly ball and let it go for a double? They didn't touch the balls, so those are not errors. And how many times have you seen shortstops dive to knock down sure hits but then rush their throws and miss the first basemen? They touched the balls, so those are often errors.

Errors attempt to measure how good your catches and throws are. That's important, for sure. But it's not even all there is to defense. Even more important is range: how well you can get to the ball in the first place. Only recently, with range factor stats, have we been able to measure that vital part of defense. It's always something that you could notice if you watched a player a ton, and people like Brooks Robinson and Ozzie Smith got well-deserved reputations for their range. But beyond the obviously stellar performers, it's really hard to sort out the rest without some objective stats.

Imagine if batting average did not exist. You would surely notice that Wade Boggs got a lot of hits. He would be considered the Ozzie Smith of hitting. But even if you watched every TBS Braves game in the 1980s, would you have a good sense of whether Dale Murphy or Bob Horner got more hits per at-bat? (Did you think it was Murphy? Actually, both hit exactly .273 for the 1980s Braves.)

Errors may be hopeless, but other fielding stats are getting better all the time. And they show a big difference between the defense of Reuschel's 1977 Cubs and the defense of Carlton's 1977 Phillies. Baseball Reference has a stat called Rtot, which measures the total runs either saved or given up by a team's defense compared to the average. The Phillies were the league best in this number, saving 62 runs above average throughout the year. The Cubs were second-worst, saving 42 runs fewer than average. That's a difference of 104 runs over a season. And those are not all unearned runs; many of those runs show up in ERA.

The best way to see how those different defenses affected Reuschel and Carlton is to look to FIP. Fielding Independent Pitching (FIP) takes defense out of the calculation much more effectively than ERA, with its reliance on clumsy old errors and unearned runs. Only FIP can account for the very different defenses that Reuschel and Carlton had behind them. It shows Reuschel with a FIP of 3.03 and Carlton at 3.47 in 1977. This is a significant factor in Reuschel beating Carlton in WAR.

But I don't see it being enough to make for the large WAR difference between them. There are other factors in the WAR calculation, but I'm getting a bit bored with this. (Apologies if you have an adequate attention span.) I suspect Reuschel's 1977 WAR may be too high; his Win Shares that year were 26, the same as Carlton's.

Sorry, I got a little bogged down in that 1977 season because WAR made such a fuss about it. The larger point is that Rick Reuschel lasted a long time with occasional moments of brilliance. That's far from inner-circle Hall-of-Fame stuff. But he has good company among the Ted Lyonses and Burleigh Grimeses in the low-to-middle range of valid Hall-of-Famers.

David Cone (1986-2001, 2003; career ERA+: 121)

	Career	Rank	Peak	Rank	Bests	Top 5s	JAWS	Rank
WAR	62.5	41	43.5	50	0	3	53.0	46
WS	206.3	107	130.2	149	0	2	NA	84

I'm only including David Cone below Rick Reuschel because Bill James ranked Cone lower. Both JAWS and I think Cone was significantly better.

Maybe James didn't like the fact that Cone didn't get 200 wins. In both "Whatever Happened to the Hall of Fame" and "The New Historical Baseball Abstract" he brings up win-loss records a lot. He clearly dug them, at least then. That was 15-20 years ago, so maybe by now he's moved on along with the rest of us.

Besides, David Cone probably would have hit 200 wins if not for the 1994-1995 strike. It's not quite as honorable as missing baseball to defeat Hitler, but players should be given credit for time lost during the strike. It was a societal change that made a whole group of players unable to play. It wasn't some individual twist of fate that shortened someone's career.

Cone was at top form then, winning the Cy Young Award in 1994 and finishing fourth in 1995. The strike ate up about 65 games through the two seasons, which deprived Cone of about 13 starts. If he'd been credited with wins in just six of those he'd have hit that fancy 200-win level. More importantly, his rankings above would have been given a bit of a boost.

For me, David Cone occupies the same brain space as Kevin Brown. Both were aces who deserved Cy Young Awards several times. Both were a step or two down from the Randy Johnson/Pedro Martinez class, but compare favorably to the Joe McGinnity/Stan Coveleski type of HOFers. Both were irascible fellows who perhaps made some enemies among writers. Both received less than 5% on the first BBWAA ballots and dropped off for good.

Cone actually has an edge on Brown in one category: postseason play. Cone had a 3.80 ERA over 111.1 innings, which is pretty darn good in the Steroid Era. In the World Series alone, he had a 2.12 ERA over 29.2 innings. Brown was good in championship series but bad in the World Series.

Plus, Cone is cooler. He works as a color commentator and often makes reference to Fangraphs and other baseball-nerd talismans (talismen?). During the 1994-1995 Cone strike served as a player representative and gained great respect for then-district court judge Sonia Sotomayor, who forced the MLBPA and owners back into negotiations. Cone testified on Sotomayor's behalf during her nomination hearings in Congress. (Source: Cone's Wikipedia page.)

Maybe I should have put Cone above Brown and Reuschel. Oh well, it hardly matters. All three should go in someday.

Bucky Walters (1934-1948, 1950; career ERA+: 116)

	Career	Rank	Peak	Rank	Bests	Top 5s	JAWS	Rank
WAR	54.2	69	43.0	55	0	4	48.6	58
WS	258.2	46	180.5	32	1	4	NA	59

Put Bucky Walters in with the "fewer than 200 wins, but who cares" camp. He had 198 and would have had more if he hadn't started his major-league career as a third baseman.

He was a great fielder at third base but not the best of hitters. Occasionally he would pitch, and people told him he should stick to the mound. He refused, saying he liked to play every day. Eventually he relented.

His first few years of pitching might not look great, but he was playing half his games in the pitchers' graveyard of Philadelphia's Baker Bowl. The distance from home plate to the right-field foul pole was only 280 feet, and the right-field power alley was only 300 feet away. They tried to ameliorate the situation by erecting a 60-foot fence in right field, but that just made almost every hard hit by a left-hander into a double. It was more extreme even than the Green Monster, which is 37 feet high and 310 feet from home. The Baker Bowl was the stadium that fooled people into thinking Chuck Klein was a Hall-of-Famer.

As an aside, isn't it weird that baseball stadia are allowed to have different dimensions? In every other sport, the field of play is exactly the same. Imagine if the Packers decided they wanted to help their defense by extending their field ten yards. There is a strong possibility that some individuals outside Wisconsin might raise objections to such a plan, in the gentle, tentative, tactful manner that football fans are famous for. But a baseball team can help its defense by moving fences out. I don't understand why that's allowed.

Anyway, halfway through the 1938 season Bucky Walters thankfully got traded to the Reds, who played in a grown-up-sized baseball stadium. Then he went apeschist, leading the league in wins, ERA, ERA+, complete games, and WHIP in both 1939 and 1940. He also hit and fielded well, as you would expect from someone who switched from third base. He was an earlier Bob Lemon, excelling in everything.

The Reds won the pennant both years and the Series in 1940. This was the club of HOFer Ernie "Schnozz" Lombardi and the "Jungle Club" infield of Frank "Wildcat" McCormick, Lonnie "Leopard" Frey," Billy "Jaguar" Myers, and Billy "Tiger" Werber. Walters won a well-deserved MVP in 1939 and McCormick won it in 1940. Hall-of-Fame manager Bill McKechnie deserves the credit for this fun mini-dynasty, as he took over the Reds in 1938 and acquired Walters and other key players. It's a team that should be better known, and would be if it had happened in a larger city.

Walters had several more good years, if none quite as great as those two world-beaters. He kept pitching through World War II, despite being 1-A, the highest level of eligibility for the draft. He just happened to be one of the few whose number didn't come up.

Should we knock Walters' performance during the war down a peg? If we did, we'd probably take him out of legitimate Hall-of-Fame consideration. So we should address it.

It's true that Walters was pitching against inferior competition from 1943-1945. But so were Old Hoss Radbourn and John Clarkson in the 1800s, as compared to now. Heck, so was Walter Johnson, when compared to the bigger, stronger, better-prepared hitters Roger Clemens had to face. We could knock points off of every white player who played before integration, since his competition was watered down by not having to play against Josh Gibson and Satchel Paige.

My position is that the level of competition is irrelevant to Hall-of-Fame cases. The Hall-of-Fame is about honoring the best who played, regardless of the quirks of their times. When someone is prevented from playing, by being drafted into the military, he should get a boost. But if he didn't get drafted, he should not get points taken off.

I compared Bucky Walters to Bob Lemon, and in the advanced stats Walters actually looks a bit better. Plus, the 1940s are a bit thin on Hall-of-Fame pitchers. I say Bucky should be in.

Bret Saberhagen (1984-1995, 1997-1999, 2001; career ERA+: 126)

	Career	Rank	Peak	Rank	Bests	Top 5s	JAWS	Rank
WAR	59.2	50	43.3	53	1	4	51.3	49
WS	194.0	124	134.1	132	1	4	NA	68

This may be another "Really, him?!?" candidate for you. But try to keep an open mind.

Bret Saberhagen was a dominant pitcher when healthy. He unfortunately wasn't healthy much. I can't be 100% positive that his career was shortened by overuse during his 20-24-year-old injury nexus. But it really looks like it. He had 1066.2 innings before his age-25 season, and only 1496 after.

As with Bucky Walters and Urban Shocker, Saberhagen's career numbers might not look Hall-of-Fame-y. But at his peak, he was among the best in baseball. And his career was long enough to pass the bar.

Hey, I have a fun idea. Let's look at all the pitchers who had 900 or more innings before their age-25 season and see how they did. Let's restrict it to post-World-War-II players, since the injury nexus was apparently less deadly in the olden days when pitchers didn't throw quite as hard.

OK, that gives us a list of 42 guys. How many crapped out early? That is, how many had low innings at 25 and older?

We have to ignore Clayton Kershaw, C.C. Sabathia, and Felix Hernandez because they're still pitching. That brings us to 39. Of those, 11 didn't last another 900 innings after their age-24 season: Jeremy Bonderman, Steve Avery, Denny McLain, Don Gullett, Gary Nolan, Dave Boswell, Clay Kirby, Art Houtteman, Billy Hoeft, Bob Moose, and Wally Bunker. That seems like a lot.

And then there are the members of the injury-nexus club who did almost nothing after their 30th birthdays. Larry Dierker, Dick Ellsworth, Dean Chance, and Mike Witt had 2000 innings before their age-30 seasons but fewer than 100 after. Dan Petry, Joe Coleman, Chuck Stobbs, Pedro Ramos, Sam McDowell and Mike McCormick survived only a bit better: All had at least 1700 innings before 30 and fewer than 350 after. That gets us to 22 pitchers, over half of our sample of 39.

There are a few success stories in this group of 39: Don Sutton, Bert Blyleven, Greg Maddux, Frank Tanana and Robin Roberts kept pitching forever. But as I mentioned, Roberts' effectiveness dropped off big-time after age 28. Almost all of the rest of the "injury-nexus survivors" struggled to stay healthy, including Dwight Gooden, Fernando Valenzuela, and Bret Saberhagen. Don Drysdale pitched 200-300 innings every year from age 20 to 31 and then managed just 62.2 more innings. And so on.

I wish I had a good control group to compare this bunch to, but I don't. All pitchers are brittle, even those who don't pitch a lot during the injury nexus. But this certainly seems like a higher-than-usual rate of collapse. With the corpses of young pitching phenoms littering baseball history, maybe you can understand why the Nationals were super-protective of Stephen Strasburg. Having pitching all figured out at 21 years of age can be both a blessing and a curse. You almost pray for your team's pitching prospects to be like Randy Johnson and have lots of improvements to make in their early 20s.

Unlike Valenzuela, Gooden, and many others, Saberhagen managed to be healthy often enough, and just great enough when healthy, to get HOF-range numbers in the above grid. Once again, his career win total is low, so he doesn't have a prayer to actually make the Hall. But it would be great if he did.

Dave Stieb (1979-1993, 1998; career ERA+: 122)

	Career	Rank	Peak	Rank	Bests	Top 5s	JAWS	Rank
WAR	57.2	61	44.8	41	1	4	51.0	50
WS	211.3	95	149.5	79	2	4	NA	63

Dave Stieb, we have learned, was one of the most underrated pitchers ever. He's the best Blue Jay in history by far. He had the best WAR among 1980s pitchers by a pretty huge margin. As I mentioned, it's a bit arbitrary to give that particular ten-year span such importance. But Stieb also tops the field from 1979-1988 and from 1981-1990. And his 1980s total, 48.6, was quite good: It would have put him third if he had pitched in the 1960s, ahead of Sandy Koufax, Jim Bunning, and Don Drysdale.

I didn't do those charts with Win Shares because it (validly) gives lots more value to pitchers from the distant past who threw many more innings. I didn't want you knuckleheads thinking all the pitchers in the 1930s were better than all the pitchers of the 1950s or what have you. But within a single decade that effect is minimized; pitchers didn't throw that much more in 1980 than in 1989. Let's see who has the most Win Shares in the 1980s:

Pitcher in the 1980s	Win Shares
Dave Stieb	176.8
Jack Morris	152.7
Dan Quisenberry	152.5
Bert Blyleven	137.8
Bob Welch	135.0
Fernando Valenzuela	134.7
Charlie Hough	133.8
Lee Smith	124.8

Nolan Ryan	123.8
Frank Viola	120.9

Again, pretty dominating. Stieb beats Morris and Quisenberry by the equivalent of one Cy-Young-Award-level season. But Dave Stieb never won 20 games in a season and had only 176 in his career! Ask me if I care. I'll wait.

Ring ring! Hello, phone? Someone's calling me! Hello! Yes, this is he. Thank you for asking. I don't care, in fact! OK. Yes, thanks, I know. Yes. Yes, I'm working on that. Huh. Wow. That's ... well ... the next one will be better![117] OK. Yes. Well, now you're just trying to hurt my feelings. OK. OK. I really have to hang up now and get back to work.

Euch. Remind me not to ask people things again. The 1980s might have been a historical low point for great starting pitching, but Dave Stieb was still great. WAR says he was the best pitcher in all of baseball in 1984, and best in the American League in 1982 and 1983. Win Shares says he was baseball's best in 1982 and 1984, and puts him below only Dan Quisenberry in 1983. He didn't win tons of games any of those years, but he pitched a lot, and very well.

He obviously deserved a few AL Cy Young Awards, but they always went to someone else. The most baffling non-Stieb to win was Pete Vuckovich in 1982. It's not like Vuckovich won 20 games, which is the typical reason for a bad Cy Young selection. Vuckovich was 18-6 with a 3.34 ERA (114 ERA+) in 223.2 innings, collecting 2.8 WAR and 13 Win Shares. I suppose Stieb didn't look tons better on the surface: 17-14 with a 3.25 ERA in 288.1 innings. But it earned him 7.7 WAR and 25 Win Shares. No one had 20 wins that year, so the writers apparently panicked and randomly stabbed at the guy from the winning team; Vuckovich was on the pennant-winning Brewers while Stieb pitched for the last-place Blue Jays. Vuckovich had the league's best winning percentage (thanks to the hard-hitting "Harvey's Wallbangers" Brewers offense), so I guess that was good enough.

Vuckovich was a symptom of a dark time for starting pitchers. As we saw from the chart showing Hall-of-Famers by year, things really drop off in the 1980s. I'm not consciously trying to straighten the line in the below; I'm going by those overall ranks in the above. But doing so has the effect of straightening that line. Let's check out that chart again:

[117] Reference explanation: "Plan 9 From Outer Space" director Ed Wood sent his first film, "Glen or Glenda," to some producers, and then called them to see what they thought. They laughed in his face and told him it was the worst film they had ever seen. His response was "Well, the next one will be better!"

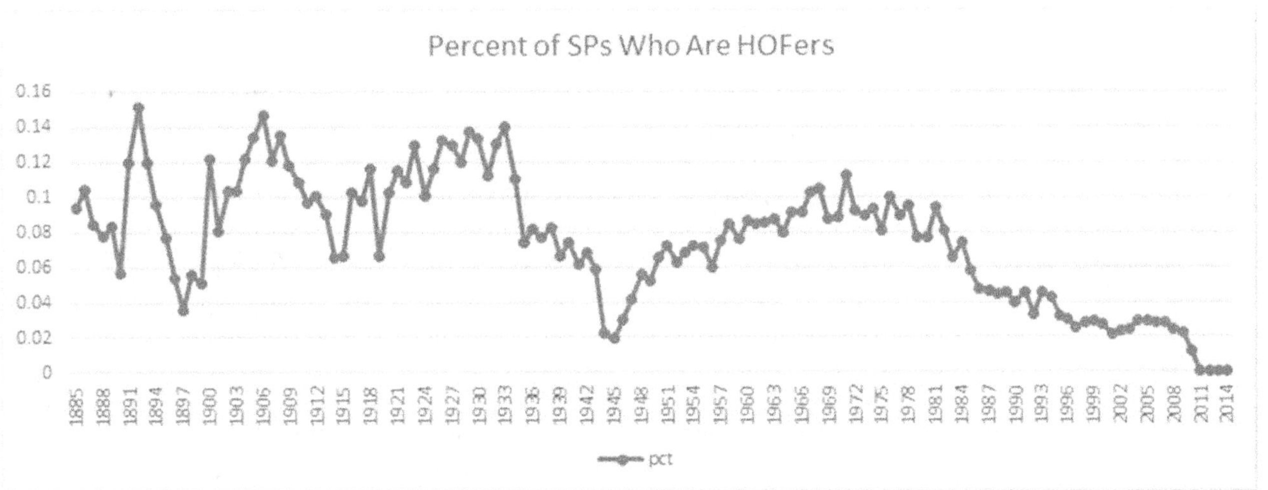

The drop-off really occurs in 1984 when all those 1970s pitchers start retiring. Keep in mind that this chart does not show the raw number of Hall-of-Famers each year; it shows the percentage of pitchers who were Hall-of-Famers. Each time that expansion creates more major-league teams, more total pitchers end up in the denominator of that equation. To keep around the same percentage throughout history, we would need more Hall-of-Famers from recent years than there were in the distant past.

I can foresee people objecting to this idea. They might say that we should aim for a roughly similar raw number of Hall-of-Famers throughout history, instead of for a similar percentage. There are always maybe seven or so truly HOF-worthy pitchers in the majors at once, they might say, regardless of whether the MLB has 16 teams or 30.

"A-ha!" I will say to those people. "You're forgetting the Negro Leagues. Obviously, you're a racist." That always ends every argument even better than bringing up the Nazis.[118]

There were in fact more than 16 major-league teams in the old days: There were also Negro League teams. I was sadly unable to include the Negro Leagues in the above, but maybe someone who is better at that sort of thing than I am could figure out how. If someone did, it probably wouldn't change the pre-World-War-II percentages much, because you'd add both Negro League HOFers to the numerators and all Negro-League pitchers to the denominators. We would also have a higher raw number of Hall-of-Fame pitchers from the first half of the 1900s than we do from the 1980s. Adding Stieb, Saberhagen, etc. would even that out.

[118] In the early days of the Internet discussion forums, there was an informal rule that the first person to compare something to the Nazis automatically lost the argument. That should be a rule that applies to every aspect of life. Unless you're talking about genocide, it's not valid to compare anything to the Nazis. In fact, it's grossly offensive. You defang and trivialize the true, brutal horror of the Nazis by equating them with whatever petty qualm you have about Social Security or parking violations or some other minor inconvenience that makes you feel icky in your pampered little life. Moreover, it reveals how paper-thin your argument is. If you can't make a case without linking the thing you dislike to the worst thing in the history of the world, you don't really have a case at all.

So anyway, Dave Stieb is another Urban Shocker. He was great for about ten years without ever having a single season that blew anyone away. His career was a little short, but it was long enough to get good numbers in the above. I'd be happy (and very surprised) to see him join the Hall.

Tommy John (1963-1974, 1976-1989; career ERA+: 111)

	Career	Rank	Peak	Rank	Bests	Top 5s	JAWS	Rank
WAR	62.0	42	34.7	132	0	0	48.4	60
WS	275.6	35	125.4	175	0	1	NA	54

I think that every good pitching prospect should have mandatory preventative Tommy John surgery, regardless of how strong his arm ligaments are. And don't take out one of his leg ligaments for it, like usual. He might need a backup. Take one of mine, or one from some other big baseball fan. It's not like we're using them for anything much. We sit at computers all day and then come home and sit in front of TVs. How many ligaments do you need to walk from your car to your couch and back again?

Imagine the pride you'd feel if one of your ligaments helped throw a shutout in the World Series. It would be a true team effort, far beyond just being a regular fan. You could finally be justified in referring to your favorite team as "we."

That's all silliness, of course. But should the famous surgery named after Tommy John add to his Hall-of-Fame credentials? I'm thinking no, since it's not like he used his skill and ability in that achievement. Dr. Frank Jobe, the surgeon who performed and perfected the surgery, might have a legitimate claim to the Hall. But Tommy John was just the subject of the change. It would be like giving a plaque to the ball that Hank Aaron hit for his 715th home run.

Luckily for Tommy John, his career was good enough to rank among low-end Hall-of-Famers. He was a poor man's Don Sutton, with loads of good years without ever having a really great one. He had four seasons above 5 WAR but none above 6.

To be honest, I don't think I would advocate for John if not for the above overall rankings. It does feel like a player should have some truly great seasons to qualify as a Hall-of-Famer. But then, "does feel like"s and "should have"s are irrelevant for the approach of this book. The above standards are based on what the Hall of Fame has established is worthy of a plaque.

And this doesn't mean everyone who had a long career without a big season qualifies; Jack Powell and Frank Tanana didn't pass muster. Tommy John is more an exception than a rule.

Then again, I did ignore Ron Cey and Buddy Bell despite their low-end-HOF overall rankings. They also had long, good careers but few if any great seasons. I just couldn't go for them because I was already pushing for so many 1970s third basemen (Graig Nettles, Darrell Evans, Sal Bando) to add the existing ones (Mike Schmidt, George Brett, Brooks Robinson, Ron Santo). Is there also a glut of 1970s pitchers?

Let's take a look at that big beautiful year-by-year chart again. Here's what the the real Hall of Fame has:

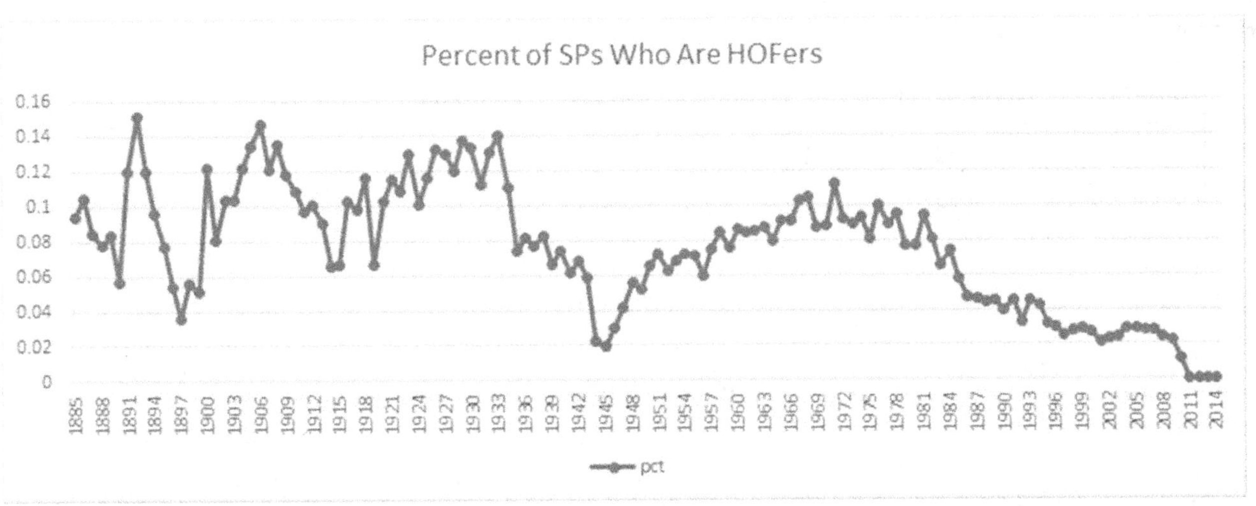

And let's look at what you get when you make all of my changes, including the ones I haven't gotten to yet (again, I read ahead, sorry):

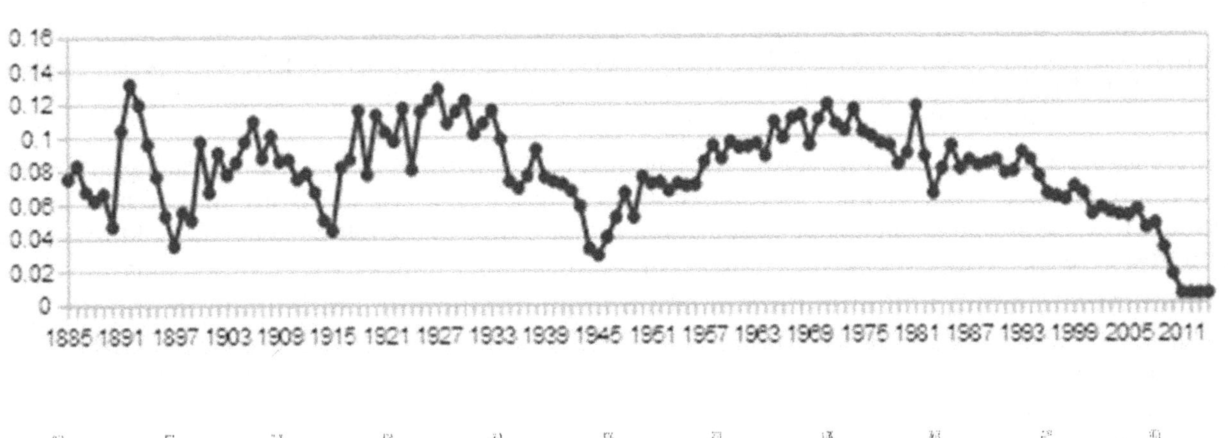

Sorry it doesn't look as pretty -- let's just say that computers and me sometimes don't get along. Hopefully you can see that things evened out a bit. The 1940s and 1950s still look a bit low, but I managed to add enough from the 1960s through the present and subtract enough from the dead-ball and Golden Age to put them all on roughly the same plane.

So the 1970s don't look totally out of whack, even with the addition of Tommy John and others. I'm satisfied.

Orel Hershiser (1983-2000; career ERA+: 112)

	Career	Rank	Peak	Rank	Bests	Top 5s	JAWS	Rank
WAR	56.8	63	40.4	71	0	2	48.6	59
WS	209.3	100	133.7	136	1	4	NA	71

Why not Orel? Having lived through the 1980s, I can see why people wouldn't think Dave Stieb was a Hall-of-Famer. He might deserve it, but he was never a household name. Orel Hershiser, meanwhile, was a superstar, for a few years at least. In 1988 he was the most celebrated player in all of baseball, with competition only from Jose Canseco.[119] (Weird to think of Canseco being a beloved hero, isn't it? It happened. I was there.)

In 1988 Hershiser went 23-8 with a 2.26 ERA in 267 innings, winning the Cy Young Award unanimously. He ended the year with 59 straight scoreless innings, breaking the record of 58 held by Don Drysdale. (Hershiser's streak was broken in the first inning of his first start of 1989.) Then he dominated the postseason, earning MVP Awards in both the NLCS and the World Series. For Pete's sake, Hershiser won the Sports Illustrated Sportsman of the Year Award. How many non-HOFers have done that?[120]

And it was more than just that one year. Hershiser was great before and great for at least one year after. Then injuries hit. After three straight years of leading the National League in innings, by pure coincidence I'm sure, he tore his rotator cuff. Dr. Frank Jobe, creator of Tommy John surgery, made Hershiser the first major-leaguer to get a reconstructed shoulder. Hershiser was not such a world-beater afterwards, but he was pretty good for many years.

Personally, I've always had a lot of affection for Hershiser. He's a smart, funny, self-effacing guy who once described his chest as "concave." Nerdier than Greg Maddux by far, he always looked and sounded like the nicest math teacher in high school, the one who made lame jokes with a knowing wink, and you couldn't help but laugh.

Hershiser was known early in his career for being too timid and getting rattled easily. His manager, Tommy Lasorda, would yell at him for being too respectful to batters, a trait that may be kinda adorable, but is perhaps not ideal for a major-league pitcher. Lasorda gave him the nickname

---

[119] Remember that? Canseco was the first to achieve 40 home runs and 40 stolen bases in a season, which was a big deal in 1988. Everyone was already abuzz about the 30 HR - 30 SB club, which had added four members the year before (Eric Davis, Howard Johnson, Darryl Strawberry, and Joe Carter). Then Jose Canseco heightened it by inventing a brand-new 40-40 club. A few years later, steroids took over and the herd was much more besotted with big homer totals. I bet you don't even know who else is in the 40-40 club besides Canseco. I didn't until I looked it up: Barry Bonds, Alfonso Soriano and Alex Rodriguez.

[120] Actually, there have been a few. Johnny Podres won it in 1955 despite a mediocre regular season. He got the award because he pitched well in Brooklyn's first World Series championship; as I've mentioned, people in the 1950s got really excited when someone besides the Yankees won. Other non-HOFer Sportsmen of the Year have been Pete Rose, Dale Murphy (partially for his philanthropy), Mark McGwire, Sammy Sosa, and Curt Schilling, plus not-yet-eligibles Derek Jeter and Madison Bumgarner.

"Bulldog" and did not mean it ironically. (I can't envision Lasorda ever doing anything ironically.) The idea was to give Hershiser a tougher persona. Surprisingly, it worked. For all of Tommy Lasorda's faults as a manager (overusing Hershiser, for example), he knew how to motivate people.

Perhaps thanks to Lasorda, Hershiser had a David Cone-ish start to his career. Perhaps also thanks to Lasorda, he had a more of a Tommy-John-ish end. Taken altogether, it looks like good low-end HOFer stuff to me.

Billy Pierce (1945, 1948-1964; career ERA+: 119)

	Career	Rank	Peak	Rank	Bests	Top 5s	JAWS	Rank
WAR	53.2	73	37.8	95	1	3	45.5	79
WS	245.2	55	148.5	83	0	4	NA	50

We're into the "Bill James Recommends" section now. Bill James has never explicitly recommended Pierce for the Hall, to my knowledge. But he did rank him amongst a lot of HOFers. In JAWS, though, Billy Pierce is borderline. I don't understand why.

Does it hurt Pierce's case to say he was the Dave Stieb of the 1950s? Probably, but it's true. Pierce may not have dominated the 1950s WAR standings the way Stieb dominated the 1980s, but he finished a solid third behind Robin Roberts and Warren Spahn. Pierce pitched enough innings for the ERA title every year from 1949 to 1962 and had an ERA+ above 100 each year. In 1955 he led all of baseball with a 1.97 ERA and 200 ERA+, also leading in WHIP, FIP, and any other acronym ending with "IP" that you could come up with. It was the best ERA and ERA+ of the decade, and it only got him 6.9 WAR.

Maybe WAR doesn't like Pierce much because he didn't pitch loads of innings a year the way Roberts, Spahn and Bob Lemon did. But Pierce was hardly a weakling, finishing above 250 innings four times and leading the league in complete games three years in a row. Perhaps, as happened to Edd Roush, this is a case of a few outliers, Roberts and Spahn, messing up the replacement level for everyone else.

Whatever. The 1950s is surprisingly low on HOF pitchers, and Billy Pierce looks like a solid choice to even that out.

Carl Mays (1915-1929, career ERA+: 119)

	Career	Rank	Peak	Rank	Bests	Top 5s	JAWS	Rank
WAR	50.2	87	38.3	90	0	1	44.2	88
WS	255.7	49	183.2	27	0	4	NA	33

Bill James is vouching for Carl Mays here. Everyone else in the world hates Carl Mays. To this day, most babies' first words are "Carl Mays was a jerk." Remember, this is the guy who killed Ray Chapman with a pitch in 1920. Mays didn't intentionally kill Chapman, but he didn't learn much from the incident. For the rest of his life he preached the importance of throwing high and inside.

He was the Ty Cobb of pitching, and of course, the two hated each other. Mays may not have gotten into as many fights as Cobb did, but controversies still followed him wherever he went. After sustaining some razzing from a crowd in Philadelphia, he threw a ball into the stands and hit someone in the head. One time his farm house burned to the ground, and he was convinced it was arson committed by one of his many enemies.

At one point in 1919, Mays got so frustrated with the play of his Red Sox teammates that he walked off the field and refused to play with them again. So the Sox traded him to the Yankees.

This caused a major legal battle. American League president Ban Johnson tried to invalidate the trade, because he was worried this would set a precedent that any player could demand a trade any time he wanted. Johnson lost the battle and the trade went through. (Source: Mays' SABR biography, by Allan Wood.)

But Johnson's nightmare scenario did not come to pass: This did not set off a deluge of players pulling Mays' stunt. That's because most players are not a-holes willing to abandon their teams over a few bad plays.

Carl Mays probably wasn't a deeply disturbed menace to society. He reminds me more of A.J. Pierzynski. Pierzynski, as I understand it, has no filter, none of the normal social restraints that most people rely on to navigate the world. He just says what he thinks all the time, and doesn't care how it might affect anyone else. Carl Mays was like that.

So Carl Mays was a pretty unpleasant guy. If he came onto the BBWAA ballot this year, he wouldn't get a vote. But that's the good thing about revisiting Hall-of-Fame cases for players from decades ago. The biases created by a player's personality recede, and it becomes just about how well he helped the team win. As I discussed in the Pete Rose comment, we love sports in part because they represent a reduced reality: All that matters is winning. Everything else is trivia. You can be violent, like Cobb, and still win. You can be unpretty, like Randy Johnson, and still win. Unlike almost every other profession in existence, in which kissing butt and taking (down) names are vital skills, sports are about performance and nothing else.

Carl Mays made his team win. He was a submariner whose knuckles would come close to scraping the ground when he pitched, a style that resulted in lots of ground balls. Because his career straddled the dead-ball era and the Golden Age, his conventional numbers are modest compared to that of Chief Bender and the like. But in real terms, Mays was always great.

Also, he was terrific in World Series play, with a 2.35 ERA over 57.1 innings. Most of those innings were in 1921 and 1922, but his best performance was in 1918. Mays allowed only two runs in 18 innings to push the Red Sox to their last championship of the 1900s.

With the harshness of Carl Mays' persona reduced over the decades into anecdotes, he looks like a Hall-of-Famer.

Jim Kaat (1959-1983; career ERA+: 108)

	Career	Rank	Peak	Rank	Bests	Top 5s	JAWS	Rank
WAR	51.4	80	38.4	87	0	1	44.9	83
WS	271.4	38	141.9	103	0	2	NA	56

Personally, I feel more comfortable saying Jim Kaat is a Hall-of-Famer than saying Tommy John is. The overall rankings favor Tommy John, but Kaat had more exceptional years. While John never exceeded 6 WAR in a season, Kaat had 7.1 in 1974 and 7.8 in 1975. Amazingly, he was 35 and 36 in those two peak years.

For both John and Kaat, longevity is the main selling point. John is 15th all-time in career innings, and Kaat is 18th (excluding 1800s guys). They pitched well for a long time, just like Eppa Rixey, Early Wynn, Ted Lyons, Red Ruffing, etc. For the millionth time, that's a Hall-of-Famer, as defined by the membership of the actual Hall. If you don't think it's a Hall-of-Famer, you're inventing your own definition for your own personal Hall. You're welcome to do that all day, but don't delude yourself into thinking it has anything to do with the real-life Hall.

Plus, Bert Blyleven's election to the Hall already threw open the door for Dutchmen who played primarily for the Twins. Blyleven was one of only 12 major-leaguers in history born in the Netherlands. (Don't call it "Holland" -- that's a state within the Netherlands, not the whole country. It's like calling the United States "New York.") Kaat doesn't match Blyleven's level of Dutch street cred, but he was born in Zeeland, Michigan and attended Hope College in Holland, Michigan. Both towns were settled and dominated by Dutchies.

I am half Dutch, and proud of it. I think the Netherlands is one of the best countries in the world, and not for the reasons you're thinking, Mr. Dirty Mind. The Dutch have the best approach to life, which is basically "You go do what you want. I'm going to bed early." They are a hardworking, businesslike people who legalized a bunch of vices but don't indulge in them much. The Dutch smoke less marijuana per capita than the people of the United States, Canada, Australia, and about a dozen other countries where it's illegal. (Source: World Drug Report 2011, United Nations Office on Drugs and Crime, p. 177,) The Netherlands is a country of responsible grown-ups who already got past their crazy youths but aren't going to begrudge others theirs.

Anyway, back to Jim Kaat. He won 16 Gold Glove awards, but that's almost meaningless. I have mentioned postseason awards very little, and even then just to ridicule them. I have mentioned All-Star selections even less (zero, I believe). Both have been so flawed over the years that none are valid Hall-of-Fame credentials, especially when compared with WAR and Win Shares.

Even by the standards of postseason awards, Gold Gloves for pitchers are at the bottom of the barrel. Once a pitcher gets a good reputation with the glove, he tends to win the award every single year. It's very rare for a new pitcher to come along and wow people so much with his defense that he can overtake some entrenched Gold Glove winner. Pitcher defense just gets too little attention for people to know who was the best each year.

And for good reason. Pitchers handle so few fielding opportunities each year that their defense can never make much difference. Throughout his long career full of Gold Gloves, Kaat handled only 1062 chances. Mario Mendoza, the light-hitting shortstop of the famous Mendoza line, had more than twice as many chances, 2182, in around three full seasons' worth of innings in the field (3807 innings). Edgar Martinez played only 592 games in the field but still had more chances than Kaat, 1440.

In each of Kaat's 25 big-league seasons, he made a ridiculously small number of plays to go by for any sort of award-giving. Within a single year, the difference between the best-fielding pitcher and the second-best is razor-thin, if it exists at all. There is an element of chance in everything, and that element of chance is especially prominent in things with small sample sizes. A season of pitcher's fielding represents a sample size so small as to be meaningless. You may as well award the Silver Sluggers according to which hitters have the best Aprils.

Maybe it's for the best that the same pitcher gets the Gold Glove each year. If we did actually award Gold Gloves by who has the best stats, we'd be favoring the guy with .01 Fielding Win Shares over the guy with 0.009999. That doesn't really mean anything. Almost any selection would necessitate splitting the finest of hairs.

It's actually worse than that: The Win Shares spreadsheet I have doesn't even bother calculating Fielding Win Shares for pitchers. Every pitcher season just gets a big fat 0 in the Fielding Win Shares column. Their hitting does count toward their grand totals, but their fielding is ignored.

And besides, a pitcher's defense shows up in his ERA, just like the defense of his teammates. It's just another element of his efforts to prevent runs. (By the way, if a pitcher made an error that resulted in a run, should it be counted as unearned run? I don't think so. He made the error, so he earned it.)

So Jim Kaat should melt down all his Gold Gloves and make them into a necklace. Let's assume each Gold Glove award is about 20 pounds, to just pull a number out of thin air that doesn't sound crazy. And let's assume each is made of solid gold, because I always assume anything called "gold" is solid gold. Gold is currently trading at $1170.53 an ounce, according to a Web site I just found that promises me "MONEY! MONEY! MONEY!," which I believe at face value because those are three things I need. So that means all of Kaat's 16 Gold Gloves are worth a combined $5,993,114. That would definitely make a necklace that would turn some heads on Old-Timers Day.

So that's Jim Kaat: a hardworking, businesslike Dutchman wearing a $6 million 320-pound gold rope who should be in the Hall of Fame.

Intentionally Overlooked

Per usual, these are the candidates who draw lots of support, but I can't see a way to recommend based on the standards I'm using.

Jack Morris (1977-1994, career ERA+: 105)

	Career	Rank	Peak	Rank	Bests	Top 5s	JAWS	Rank
WAR	44.1	125	32.8	154	0	1	38.4	139
WS	222.9	85	130.3	148	0	2	NA	none

After Nolan Ryan, Jack Morris is probably the most overrated pitcher of my lifetime. Morris's greatest skill was pitching a lot of innings for teams that scored lots of runs. He was another Catfish Hunter, who is quite close to him in JAWS; others in their vicinity include Bob Welch and Fernando Valenzuela.

There is a lot of value in being above average for a lot of innings per year, no doubt. But it doesn't make you a Hall-of-Famer. Morris got most of his wins for the 1980s Tigers, the team of Lou Whitaker, Alan Trammell, and Darrell Evans, all of whom deserve the Hall but haven't made it yet. Plus, they had Lance Parrish at catcher, Kirk Gibson and Chet Lemon in the outfield -- man, you could plop Tony Suck at third (which they often did, employing a lot of Tom Brookens) and still have a world-beating offense.

Maybe Jack Morris "pitched to the score"? That's a dumb idea that has been debunked by many studies, including this one by Joe Sheehan ("The Jack Morris Project," Baseballprospectus.com, April

24, 2003). Any pitcher who lets up because he's ahead is a pitcher who turns wins into losses. If he's tired, he'll help the team a lot more by giving way to the relievers.

Yes, Morris had that one great game in the 1991 World Series. That certainly helps his case. But it's not enough to get his above numbers into the right territory. His other postseason experience is not stellar: Including that game, he was at 3.80 over 92.1 innings.

People can sometimes blow a single game out of proportion. Don Larsen, as you may know, pitched a perfect game in the World Series. He remained on the BBWAA ballot for the full 15 years, even though his career record was 81-91 with a 3.78 ERA (99 ERA+) in 1548 innings. JAWS lists him as a relief pitcher, and puts him 66th all time, near Armando Benitez and John Wetteland. He didn't deserve to stay on the ballot for more than a year.

Morris also lost some time to the 1981 strike, and should get credit for that. Again, it's not enough to get him over the hump. He also lost some time to the 1994-1995 strike, but he should thank his lucky stars for that, as he was pitching terribly by then.

Jack Morris doesn't have the worst Hall-of-Fame credentials I've ever seen. He's more Herb Pennock than Jesse Haines. But neither of those guys should be in, and Morris shouldn't either.

Jamie Moyer (1986-1991, 1993-2012, career ERA+: 103)

	Career	Rank	Peak	Rank	Bests	Top 5s	JAWS	Rank
WAR	50.4	86	33.2	151	0	1	41.8	109
WS	217.0	91	112.3	248	0	0	NA	NA

Nah, I'm just kidding. No one is really pushing for Jamie Moyer to be in the Hall of Fame. But I teased it in the text and brought him up a lot (and I think I love him), so I thought I'd see where he ranks. And there's also this: If you send Chris E. Keedei at chrisekeedei@yahoo.com the exact number of times the words "Jamie Moyer" appears in the text of this book, you will be entered into a drawing for a very special prize. This is a real contest, honest. I reserve the right to end the contest whenever I feel like and send a crappy, worthless prize to the winner. But see, many people will want that prize, which will give it loads of value. Ditch that 529 plan for your child's college expenses; win this prize and you are guaranteed to get your child into Harvard and launch him/her into a career as a famous Hall-of-Fame pitcher / swashbuckling archaeologist / avuncular astrophysicist.

Chapter Fourteen

~ ~ Relief Pitchers ~ ~

Baseball has always had relievers. But throughout the first half of baseball history they were almost always the worst pitchers on the staff. They were brought in only when the starter had collapsed and the game looked lost. All relievers were mop-up men -- the full-time ones, at least.

When the manager wanted a good pitcher to relieve a game, he used one of the other starters. For several years, Mordecai "Three Finger" Brown held the all-time record for career saves, not that anyone knew it at the time. Brown was never a "reliever" in the modern sense of the term, but he would come in when his fellow starters got too tired. Only within the last 40 or so years have relief pitchers become a glamor position deemed worthy of the Hall of Fame.

In my formative years, the 1980s, relief pitchers had been elevated to the status of gods. It was lots of fun to see a relief ace come in during the late innings and blow everyone away. It was a new thing, and baseball writers have never met a new story that they couldn't get overly excited about. They gave relievers loads of post-season awards. Rollie Fingers, Willie Hernandez and Dennis Eckersley won MVPs. In the John Smoltz comment I covered how silly that was.

By now the hype has died down, cooler heads have prevailed, and relief aces are seen as very nice but not legitimate MVP candidates. They may be more valuable per inning than the average starter, because they pitch in more crucial innings. But they pitch so many fewer innings that it's no contest. In the final tally, they are much less valuable than starters. Quality is very important, but quantity is too.

Unfortunately, there are several relief pitchers in the Hall now, so that means relievers in general are Hall-worthy. Specifically, five relievers are in, which means we probably shouldn't go outside the top seven or so.

JAWS Gets TMJ

The JAWS relief pitcher list on baseball-reference.com includes anyone who pitched in relief in at least 50% of their games. A few Hall-of-Famers get lots of love: Goose Gossage, Dennis Eckersley, and Hoyt Wilhelm all do great. Rollie Fingers and Bruce Sutter do not.

Normally I would just conclude that Fingers and Sutter were overrated and don't deserve the Hall. But when I looked closer at the JAWS list I found some strange things. A surprising number of old guys beat out Fingers and Sutter, and I'm talking pretty darn old. Bobby Shantz, John Hiller, Firpo Marberry, Ellis Kinder, Turk Farrell, Lindy McDaniel, Stu Miller, and Syl Johnson all retired before Ronald Reagan became president, and a few of them predated Truman. This was well before relief pitching was considered a Hall-worthy job.

Most of these pitchers spent a lot of time as starters. Each of them had at least 120 career starts except Hiller (43), Miller (93), and McDaniel (74). Most spent a few years starting but did more relieving. Few are really legends.

Firpo Marberry was the most fun of the bunch, working as a great starter and reliever at the same time. In 1929, he led the league in games pitched and saves, and also threw 250.1 innings. He finished 21 games and started 26. He doesn't really belong in the same category as Bruce Sutter, who never started a single game in the majors.

As you know, WAR rewards starting pitching a heck of a lot more than relief pitching. This JAWS list is supposed to be a list of greatest relief pitchers, and most of them are gaining their rankings from their starting. That hardly seems fair. Imagine if the JAWS list of first basemen were mostly players like Ernie Banks who gained most of their value at shortstop, but squeaked in because they played a majority of their games at first. That would not be a valid list of first basemen.

Maybe Firpo Marberry really did contribute more to his teams than Rollie Fingers or Bruce Sutter did. But the Hall of Fame has not proven very interested in this type. The short list of relief pitchers in the Hall of Fame is made up of true-blue full-or-near-full-time relievers, not Marberry-ian swingmen or players who switched back and forth. Only Dennis Eckersley had a lot of starts, and he is in the Hall mainly for becoming the early exemplar of the one-inning closer. When the Hall of Fame says "relief pitcher," it means "closer."

The JAWS lists are supposed to be based on the standards set by the Hall of Fame, not just in terms of performance, but also in terms of roles. The starting pitchers are split off from the relievers for this reason. The swingmen should be split off for the same reason.

A few modern relievers rank above Fingers and Sutter, but they serve to illustrate the problem. They are Tom Gordon (203 career starts), Greg Swindell (269) and Kerry Wood (178). They may have all had more valuable careers than Sutter, because they each spent many years being good starters. But were they better relievers? Gordon got 13.2 of his career 34.9 WAR when he was a reliever. For Swindell, it's 7.5 of 30.3. For Kerry Wood, it's only 3.4 of 26.7. Their experience starting is giving them an unfair boost. I don't think anyone would really say that Kerry Wood was a better relief pitcher than Bruce Sutter.

The problem is that the JAWS list includes anyone who had 50% or more games in relief. Let's change that to 80%. Doing so kicks out the Firpo Marberry and Kerry Wood types but retains Lindy McDaniel, Stu Miller and a few others who came close to being modern-style relievers. It limits the total pool to just 64 relievers. But that shouldn't be a problem, since we only need 5-7.

Win Shares gives us less of a problem here. It rewards relief pitching much more than WAR does, so modern-style relievers dominate even when you define relievers at 50% of appearances in relief. But for the sake of consistency, let's also restrict the Win Shares charts to pitchers who threw in relief 80% of the time.

Unfortunately, that leaves Marberry and the few other early swingmen in limbo, with no chance to make it as either a reliever or starter. The Hall of Fame has them in the same limbo: No swingman has ever come close to the Hall. Firpo Marberry was the best of the bunch, and he never got more than 1.9% support by the BBWAA. If I were bolder, maybe I'd make up a whole new position of swingman with its own Hall-of-Fame standards. But I'm not. The Hall of Fame is in charge here; I'm just the nerdy accountant trying to keep its balance sheet consistent.

On that note, let's get to the the genuine relievers:

Dennis Eckersley (1975-1998, career ERA+: 116)

	Career	Rank	Peak	Rank	Bests	Top 5s	JAWS	Rank
WAR	63.0	NA	38.1	NA	0	2	50.5	NA
WS	282.7	NA	135.1	NA	2	4	NA	NA

This is what I was just talking about. Eckersley's many "NA"s above came because I changed the JAWS and Win Shares lists from pitchers who relieved 50% of the time pitchers who relieved 80% of the time. This removed Eckersley from the relief pitcher lists, and rightly so.

He is best known as a relief pitcher, but most of his value comes from his years as a starting pitcher. He spent an equal number of years in each role: 12 as a starter (1975-1986) and 12 as a reliever (1987-1998). His years of starting earned him 45.7 Career WAR and his years of relieving earned him 16.8 WAR. I'm leaving him in the relief pitcher section just because that's what he is best known for, and that's how the Hall of Fame classifies him. But I'd secretly rather have him among the starters.

Even by the low standards of relief pitchers, Eckersley wasn't that great, at least according to WAR. Both of his WAR "top 5s" came when he was a starter; he was never one of the five best relievers. He came closest in his MVP year of 1992, when his WAR was sixth-best among major-league relief pitchers. At least he was fifth among American League relievers.

Win Shares likes relief pitchers better, so it sings a different tune. SP Dennis Eckersley still beats RP Dennis Eckersley, but by a smaller margin, 169 Win Shares to 132. And it says that Eckersley was indeed the best reliever in baseball in 1992, and among the top five relief pitchers in 1988 and 1990. And I suppose I am on record saying that I trust Win Shares more ... grumble grumble ... OK, maybe Eckersley was pretty valuable as a reliever. Still, he wasn't as valuable as people thought. He got in the A's "Franchise Four" instead of Lefty Grove, which is like saying mules are bigger than elephants.[121]

Eckersley also provides further evidence for what I said in the John Smoltz comment: Any good starter could become a great reliever. It's not as if Eckersley suddenly learned to throw like Aroldis Chapman once he hit the bullpen. He was just a good pitcher who could fool batters once, but no longer had the stamina or stuff to do it twice. This phenomenon occurs even in the current age when pitchers are groomed to be closers: In 2014, the best reliever according to WAR, by a huge margin, was failed starter Wade Davis.

Even if classifying Eckersley as a reliever is problematic, he looks good among all pitchers. Bill James has him as the 32nd-best pitcher ever, including 1800s guys and relievers. If we put him among starters, his JAWS would be at 54th, between Don Sutton and Early Wynn. He may be overrated, but he's a HOFer.

---

[121] Anyone get that? The current mascot of the A's is an elephant, in part because it's really hard to dress up as an "athletic," whatever that is exactly. (Maybe all players are "athletics"? That would be an odd mascot: some guy in a baseball uniform doing silly dances. Fans would think the bullpen catcher went crazy.) The team has been associated with elephants since 1905, when Giants manager John McGraw said that A's owner Ben Shibe had a white elephant on his hands. Much the same way the song "Yankee Doodle Dandy" turned an insult into a rallying cry, the A's took on the white elephant as a mascot. It remained an elephant-centric team until the 1960s, when the A's were in Kansas City and Charlie O. Finley was their owner. Finley switched the mascot to a live mule that he would parade around the field. Reportedly, the switch from a Republican icon to a Democratic one was an attempt to pander to the many Democrats in the Kansas City area. (Source: The Oakland A's' Wikipedia page.)

Rollie Fingers (1968-1982, 1984-1985, career ERA+: 120)

	Career	Rank	Peak	Rank	Bests	Top 5s	JAWS	Rank
WAR	26.1	12	19.2	22	1	2	22.7	15
WS	188.4	4	109.7	12	1	4	NA	none

Bill James anticipated that people would be shocked he left Rollie Fingers out of his top 100 pitchers ever. He says that Fingers had very good taste in teammates; being on the 1970s A's and then the early-1980s Brewers made Fingers a household name. (The crazy mustache didn't hurt.) In terms of ERA, he finds Fingers to be in a class with Jeff Reardon, Ron Perranoski, and Gene Garber, well below the Hall-of-Fame or near-Hall-of-Fame class of Goose Gossage, Dan Quisenberry, Bruce Sutter, Hoyt Wilhelm, Kent Tekulve, Lee Smith, and Sparky Lyle.

Indeed, for a career reliever, a 120 ERA+ is not tremendous. Among the 89 relievers with more than 1000 career innings, Fingers' ERA+ ranks 22nd. His actual ERA, 2.90, sure looks nice, but it was attained under some very good conditions for pitchers.

When he was elected to the Hall, Fingers was the all-time record-holder in career saves. That at least means he pitched longer than the likes of Dan Quisenberry and Sparky Lyle. Otherwise, it means nothing. Saves are the second-dumbest statistic in baseball, after errors. They're a lot like pitcher wins, except their weird, arbitrary rules make even less sense. You can get the save if you pitch the ninth and don't blow a three-run lead. What kind of crazily low standard is that for an achievement? Any pitcher with an ERA below 9.00 can do that almost every time. That's a spot for your mop-up man, not an opportunity to waste your best reliever.

Instead, your best reliever should be coming in when the game is tied. That's when you need scoreless innings the most. But many managers still use the second- or third-best bullpen arm in those situations until they get a lead. Then they bring in the closer for the easier task of maintaining that lead. Instead of having to pitch an unknown number of scoreless innings, the closer has to pitch just one inning and allow either no runs or one or two, depending on the score.

I sympathize with managers in this situation; often their hands are tied. The save stat puts pressure on managers to conform to its prescribed bullpen usage pattern. If you don't allow your closer to get that save, his stats will suffer, as will his future earnings. And fans will go ballistic.

This is a case of the tail wagging the dog. A statistic is supposed to measure performance, not dictate strategy. Baseball writer Jerome Holtzman invented the save stat in 1960 to reward achievement within a very specific role that had been carved out for a few pitchers at the time. But there's no guarantee that that specific role is or always will be optimal for every team.

Saves demonstrate the problems with codifying a strategy into a metric. Imagine if the country's economic performance statistics were based on how many people and businesses had land lines. In the 1960s, that may have made sense, as access to that form of communication meant more rapid and efficient trade. To boost economic numbers, the government might incentivize more land lines. For a while this might actually improve the performance of the economy. But that incentive would then stifle innovation in cell phones, which have boosted productivity beyond the capability of land lines. Things improve over time, and statistics must reflect those improvements. If they don't, they should be discarded and replaced.

The only valid statistics in baseball involve scoring runs or preventing them, not the particular pitcher usage patterns that some people at one point thought might optimally accomplish those tasks. This goes for pitcher wins: Why can't you get a win if you start a game but pitch fewer than five innings? What if a team had a better chance of winning if it let two starters pitch four innings each? And this goes double for saves: Shouldn't you use your best relief pitcher only in the most crucial moments: tie games, one-run leads, or one-run deficits? Doing so would mean fewer saves for your best reliever. But it might mean more wins for your team. The latter is obviously more important.

So yeah, I don't care that Rollie Fingers had the most saves for a while. There are five relievers in the Hall, and Fingers wasn't among the top ten ever. Even if you give him a little extra credit for missing time due to the 1981 strike, he's not there.

But then, there is the old "It's the Hall of Fame, Not the Hall of Stats" rule ... and man, it would really apply to Fingers. He is quite famous. I've given the "ITHOF, NTHOS" exemption only to Rabbit Maranville and Dizzy Dean. Both of them were below the HOF borderline. But they were not as far below it as Rollie Fingers is. A JAWS of 15th, when 7th is the rough cutoff ... that's just not acceptable.

I'm kicking out Rollie Fingers. He was a lot of fun, and we all thought he was more valuable than he really was. Now we know better.

Goose Gossage (1972-1989, 1991-1994, career ERA+: 126)

	Career	Rank	Peak	Rank	Bests	Top 5s	JAWS	Rank
WAR	42.0	3	32.0	1	1	7	37.0	3
WS	217.5	1	135.5	1	1	5	NA	2

Meanwhile, we were all right about Goose Gossage. He was always great. He started his career when relief pitchers were Real Men who threw 130+ innings a year. Most such Real Men blew out their Real Arms and Really Sucked after a few seasons. But Gossage was the rare survivor.

I don't even want to call Gossage a "closer," because he was so different from a modern closer. In 1975, 1977, and 1978 (interrupted by one unsuccessful year as a starter), Gossage appeared in more than 60 games and pitched around 2 innings per. He finished most games he appeared in, but not as many as modern closers do. He would come in when the game was on the line and the starter was gassed, regardless of whether it was the seventh inning or the ninth. It makes a lot more sense to me. Too bad only Gossage and few others could hold up under the workload.

Many of Gossage's appearances were not save situations, because starters would not automatically come out of the game if they had a lead. That kept Gossage's save totals modest by modern standards. In the more relevant numbers, WAR and Win Shares, Gossage was exceptional. His 1975 holds the all-time record for WAR in a season by a reliever, 8.2. Only Jim Palmer's 8.5 prevented him from becoming the only relief pitcher to ever lead a league in Pitching WAR. Gossage's 1977 total, 6.0, ranks 8th all-time among relievers.

Win Shares gives more credit to relievers generally, and less credit to Gossage specifically. Still, Gossage's career and peak both rank as the all-time best. Bill James ranks him second after Hoyt Wilhelm, but Win Shares suggest he should be first. He's one of the greats, and deserves the Hall.

Bruce Sutter (1976-1986, 1988, career ERA+: 136)

	Career	Rank	Peak	Rank	Bests	Top 5s	JAWS	Rank
WAR	24.6	14	24.6	5	1	3	24.6	8
WS	167.6	8	133.4	3	1	4	NA	4

Bruce Sutter ranks just a bit better than Rollie Fingers. It's not a huge difference, but it is a significant one. Sutter had more truly great seasons, including a 1977 that got him 6.5 WAR and 27 WAR. He had two more seasons with more than 4.5 WAR and more than 20 Win Shares; Fingers never exceeded either number (though he was on pace to do so in 1981).

Sutter pitched ten straight years of 80-120 innings and then collapsed. It's not a lot of endurance, but it's better than most of the guys who pitched 130 per for a few years. Sutter represented a transitional point between the 130+-inning guys of the 1960s and1970s to the one-inning pitchers of today. From 1976-1983, Sutter never pitched fewer than 82.1 innings and never more than 107.1. In 1984, he pitched 122.2, which may have been too many. The next year he was terrible and the year after he was injured. A few years later the 120+ inning reliever was extinct; the last one to throw 120 without starting at least five games was Duane Ward in 1990.

Can bringing a new pitch to the majors be counted as a Hall-of-Fame credential? Not really, at least by my performance-based system. If it could, Sutter would get a boost by popularizing the split-fingered fastball. He didn't invent it, but he learned it in the minors and probably wouldn't have made the majors without it. Soon after Sutter's early years, coach Roger Craig started teaching it to anyone who would listen, and it spread like wildfire.

The splitter was often mislabeled a forkball, a much older pitch. In the "Neyer/James Guide to Pitchers," (p. 45-51) Rob Neyer has a devil of a time pinning down what exactly the difference is between the two, along with other confusing issues. We sometimes think of pitches as distinct, but they aren't. Sometimes the same pitch gets called different things by different people, and other times different pitches get called the same thing. Pitches exist more on a spectrum than as a set of clearly different things with distinctly defined dividing lines.

Anyway, Sutter can stay in as a low-end HOF reliever.

Hoyt Wilhelm (1952-1972, career ERA+: 147)

	Career	Rank	Peak	Rank	Bests	Top 5s	JAWS	Rank
WAR	47.3	2	26.9	3	0	7	37.1	2
WS	212.5	2	127.7	4	0	7	NA	1

What a weird pitcher. Wilhelm was a knuckleballer, which is weird enough. He was 29 in his rookie season, and didn't quit until he was 49. That's weird.

Plus, he was possibly the best relief pitcher in history, the first one in the Hall of Fame, and he pitched in the 1950s and 1960s? There were relievers then? I mean, good ones, not just mop-up guys and swingmen?

There were a few, but not many. Lindy McDaniel and Stu Miller were terrific pitchers who qualify as relievers under my 80% rule (although Miller is right at 80%). Wilhelm had only 52 starts in 1070 career games (4.9%). And half of those were in one season, 1959. That year he started 26 games, pitched 226 innings, and led the league in ERA with a 2.16 mark.

Wait, what? Wilhelm was a good starter? Aren't you supposed to be a bad starter to fall into relief pitching? Why didn't that great season lead to Hoyt Wilhelm becoming another Phil Niekro?

That knuckler can mess with people's minds in more ways than one. I've already discussed how the knuckleball should be used more in an ideal world. Wilhelm's example shows why it isn't in the real world.

When Wilhelm was young, the knuckleball was seen as a pitch that a major-league veteran would pick up so he could hang on for a few more years. That put it outside the comfort zone of amateur and minor-league coaches.

When developing prospects, coaches look for things they can coach. They know how to mentor wild young kids who throw killer fastballs and snapping curves but don't know what to do with them. Coaches mold throwers into pitchers by teaching location. But there's no locating a knuckleball. You throw it down the middle and it locates itself.

What do you tell a guy throwing a knuckleball? You don't even know how he does it. Sure, he's getting them out here in Dubuque, but will that gimmicky crap fool major-leaguers? Probably not, because it doesn't fit into my preconceived notions of how things work. I am an expert in this field, after all. Anything within this field that I don't understand makes me feel insecure in my expert-ness. So therefore it must be garbage.

Leo Durocher deserves credit for realizing that Wilhelm could help a major-league club. Durocher brought him up to the Giants but consigned him the bullpen, saying, "the knuckler can fool 'em for four or five innings, even if Wilhelm doesn't have the hard stuff to go nine." (Source for this and the other stories: Wilhelm's SABR biography.) Wilhelm had successfully been going nine for for seven seasons in the minors, but hey, at least Durocher understood that Wilhelm could get major-leaguers out. In his rookie year, Wilhelm led the league in ERA with a 2.43 mark in 159 innings, all in relief.

The other ERA title of Wilhelm's that I mentioned earlier was achieved seven years later, when Wilhelm was 36 and starting games for the Orioles. Paul Richards, the manager of the Orioles, said he never understood why Wilhelm was used in relief: Wilhelm could come in with a man on base and then allow a passed ball. Clearly, there was no consensus on what to do with a problem like Hoyt Wilhelm. With no prevailing wisdom to guide them, different managers had to go on different hunches.

After witnessing Wilhelm's success in the rotation, Durocher admitted he may have made a big mistake in keeping him in the bullpen. By the way, I'm gaining a lot of respect for Leo Durocher from this story. I always thought he was an arrogant egotist, which he was. But here he is trying something new with a unique situation, seeing it work well, and later admitting he still may have done it wrong. These are not things arrogant egotists usually do. These are the things geniuses usually do.

In 1960, the Orioles were loaded with starting pitchers, a so-called "Kiddie Corps" of under-25 phenoms. Despite leading the league in ERA as a starter the year before, Wilhelm became the one to go to the bullpen. Better to let the old knuckleballer with the rubber arm pitch half as many innings so that the young guys can overtax their arms and flame out in a few years (as almost all of the Kiddie Corps did).

Wilhelm was so weird that people didn't know what to do with him, even when he got great results. Several times he was released despite pitching well. He would have a few bad outings, and teams would decide he was worth less than than their third backup infielder and let him loose. Any other player with a track record like Wilhelm's would get a chance to turn things around. Not the old weirdo. Wilhelm wouldn't complain, though; he would just sign somewhere else and pitch brilliantly again.

One time he was released because his catchers hated catching him. Wilhelm never once led the league in wild pitches, but his teams led the league in passed balls every year from 1954-1967. The Cardinals traded a good first baseman, Whitey Lockman, to get him, but then dumped him by the end of the year because of all the passed balls.

Hoyt Wilhelm kept weirding everyone out, kept being underused and underrated, and kept getting hitters out at a historic rate. Among all pitchers of all types and stripes with at least 1000 career innings, Wilhelm's ERA+ is sixth, tied with Walter Johnson and Smokey Joe Wood. (Top five: Mariano Rivera, Pedro Martinez, some 1800s guy named Jim Devlin, Clayton Kershaw (who probably will fall lower by the time he's done), and Lefty Grove.)

I think Hoyt Wilhelm became the first relief pitcher in the Hall because managers didn't have the knowledge or sense to let him become a Phil-Niekro-esque Hall-of-Fame starting pitcher. But those sorts of hindsight hypotheticals are always dangerous. Maybe if Wilhelm had remained a starter, he would become another Wilbur Wood: great for a few years, but not long enough for the Hall. Regardless of what could have been, Wilhelm was one of the best relief pitchers ever.

Who's In, Who's Out

I didn't enjoy kicking Rollie Fingers out of the Hall of Fame. He is a fun character and a likeable guy. But hey, it wasn't me doing the out-kicking; it was the rankings. Just doing my job. I don't make the rules. If you have a complaint, you'll have to talk to my manager. He's out right now. Just leave a message on his voicemail and I'm sure he'll get back to you within 40,000 business days.

Who can replace Fingers? Have there been any relief pitchers since the 1980s? I can't think of any. Oh, there was this one guy who played for a team you may not have heard much about ... The New York Something-Or-Others ... let me ask my manager and get back to you ...

Mariano Rivera (1995-2013, career ERA+: 205)

	Career	Rank	Peak	Rank	Bests	Top 5s	JAWS	Rank
WAR	57.1	1	28.9	2	7	11	43.0	1
WS	202.8	3	122.6	5	3	9	NA	3*

Rivera was too recent to be rated by Bill James, so that asterisk denotes that he is third in WSAWS (Win Shares Career averaged with Win Shares Peak, as with JAWS). With starting pitchers, I mostly ignored Win Shares and didn't bring up WSAWS. Win Shares gives us apples-and-oranges problems of comparing 400-inning starters from 100 years ago with 200-inning starters from today. But with relievers we're only comparing relatively recent players, especially since we're limiting it to players with 80% relief appearances. There have been different types of those, as I've mentioned: the 130-inning relievers vs. the 70-inning closers. But the WSAWS list for relievers isn't dominated by one or the other. I think it's OK to use.

Back to Mariano Rivera. He was a failed starter, but it's not like Dennis Eckersley. Eckersley was a terrific starter until he burnt out. Rivera never had any success starting, because he had one great pitch and nothing else. That happens to be a perfect profile for a great closer, and he became the best ever.

A good thing about the current climate of relief-pitcher-mania is that it extracts more value out of Rivera types. Throughout baseball history there have been plenty of one- and two-pitch pitchers who could fool batters once a game, but not twice. Until relief pitching became a legitimate profession, those guys were essentially worthless. Now they can be valuable. They're still not as valuable as the pitchers who throw three times as many innings, but it's an improvement.

I should make it clear that I'm in full support of relief pitching in general. I think individual relief pitchers are overrated, but it clearly works better to bring in relievers than to wait until a starter falls apart, as I mentioned in the Bert Blyleven comment. Because it enables teams to win more games, both in the short term and long term, relief-pitching-mania gradually overcame the "pain don't hurt" "whatever doesn't kill me makes me stronger" macho bullschist of complete-game purists.

Well, hold on. I make it sound like rational cost-benefit analyses caused relief-pitching-mania to surpass the emotion-based pseudo-reasoning of complete-game-mania. That probably wasn't quite it. As with everything, emotions change minds, not reasoning. Reasoning tends to be selected or manufactured to support the decisions emotions have made.

Emotions may be satisfied when a tired pitcher battles through a complete game. But emotions are even more satisfied when a fireballing closer runs in to great applause and kick-ass theme music, and then strikes out the side. I think the fun of that superseded the fun of complete games, and thus closers became popular (and a bit overrated). I suppose few people enjoy things because they satisfy rational cost-benefit analyses. Maybe that's just me and a few other robots like me ... sigh ... beep boop beeeeeep (in descending tones, like a sad Artoo Detoo).

Anyway, Mariano Rivera was the best closer of all time. I'm not willing to say he was the best reliever of all time, since Goose Gossage and Hoyt Wilhelm also have good cases there. But among his 70-innings-per-year peers, Rivera was the hands-down best.

Rivera's 205 career ERA+ is silly good. Second place among pitchers with at least 1000 innings is Pedro Martinez, at 154. Martinez pitched more than twice as many innings, so maybe that's an unfair comparison.

And relievers always have lower ERAs than starters, in part because of the dumb rule involving inherited runners. Does it make any sense to you that if a relief pitcher comes in with runners on, and then lets them score, the runs are completely credited to the starter? As if the reliever had nothing to do with it? The rule seems to presume that the pitcher had a 100% chance of allowing those runners to score. And when relievers don't do their jobs, they get off scot-free, in terms of ERA. Those allowed runs should be split evenly between the starter and reliever. One pitcher put the runners on, and the other allowed them to score. Give 50% to each. They're both responsible, and ERA should reflect that.

So let's take out the starters and limit the ERA+ rankings to modern-style career relievers (80% of games relieving, at least 500 career innings). Rivera is still the champ, but by a lesser margin, with Billy Wagner grabbing second place at a 187 ERA+. What if we go with JAWS' version of a reliever (more than 50% of games relieving)? Same result, and there's not much difference. In fact the first player with more than 10% of games starting is Kris Medlen, tied for 42nd place. Those modern closers sure are effective.

Point is, Mariano Rivera will get into the Hall in his first try, and deserves it.

Dan Quisenberry (1979-1990, career ERA+: 146)

	Career	Rank	Peak	Rank	Bests	Top 5s	JAWS	Rank
WAR	25.4	13	23.1	8	2	3	24.2	10
WS	154.9	12	135.3	2	4	5	NA	4

Quisenberry's 10th in JAWS for genuine relievers is a bit low. It's just outside of that top 5-7 range I talked about. But man, there is such a thin hair dividing these pitchers. Bruce Sutter is 8th with 24.6 JAWS, Joe Nathan is 9th with 24.4, and Quisenberry is 10th with 24.2. That's so close as to be basically meaningless.

In terms of overall rankings, Quisenberry is basically the Carl Mays of relievers. James ranked Carl Mays quite high, but WAR had him below the dividing line. If WAR had said "NO!!!!" I would have ignored Mays. But since it was more like "Eh, I'm not so sure," I put Mays in. Ditto for Quisenberry.

In terms of personality, Quisenberry was basically the opposite of Carl Mays. Quisenberry was a charming, erudite delight. He could be counted on for funny, self-deprecating quotes like "I found a delivery in my flaw." (Source: "Dan Quisenberry Quotes," Baseball-almanac.com.) Like Eppa Rixey, he enjoyed writing poetry, publishing several poems in 1995 and later a whole book of the stuff. While doing post-game interviews for the Royals, he would play a game with his fellow broadcasters in which they had to seamlessly work words like "homily" and "prevaricate" into their on-air descriptions.

That last story came from Bill James' comment on Quisenberry in "The New Baseball Historical Abstract." It's an especially affectionate tribute to what sounds like a wonderful man. James ranked Quisenberry 68th among all pitchers ever, including 1800s guys and other starters. It's far from slam-dunk HOFer territory: Quisenberry is below Jim Kaat, Ron Guidry, and Lefty Gomez and above Bucky Walters, Clark Griffith (who is in the Hall as an executive) and Urban Shocker. It's the range where, in my system, you could be in or out depending on what WAR thinks. And with WAR, you may remember, Quisenberry barely qualifies.

So I don't feel 100% sure that Quisenberry crosses the line. He had five tremendous seasons in which he pitched more than 125 innings and led the league in saves each time. Most of the rest is good, but there isn't much of it. Among all the relievers who threw 130 innings a year in the pre-Eckersley days, Goose Gossage is by far the best, and then you have Quisenberry barely edging out everyone else.

Still, Quisenberry could be the best relief pitcher not in the Hall besides Mariano Rivera. Maybe that's good enough. Tragically, he died of brain cancer at only 45 years old. He could have given one of the best acceptance speeches ever.

Lee Smith (1980-1997, career ERA+: 132)

	Career	Rank	Peak	Rank	Bests	Top 5s	JAWS	Rank
WAR	29.6	5	21.1	12	0	2	25.4	6
WS	168.1	7	115.2	7	0	5	NA	none

Lee Smith was a survivor. He was closing games in 1982, when he pitched 117 innings in 72 games. He was still closing games in 1995, pitching 49.1 innings in 52 games. He survived the days of overworked (but very valuable) relievers and kept chugging away in the Dennis Eckersley era of one-inning (but less valuable) closers.

In the process, he collected lots of saves, holding the career record until first Trevor Hoffman and then Mariano Rivera demolished it. Smith had endurance. But was he ever excellent?

Not often. He certainly had some good years, but few that either WAR or Win Shares get too excited about. His career length got him an acceptable JAWS ranking. But Bill James didn't rank Smith among the 100 best pitchers ever. That's a bad sign.

I was going to pass on Smith until I saw his WSAWS. He ends up 8th, on the borderline, but just a few points below Dan Quisenberry. Apart from Bill James' opinion, there's not good enough reason to select Quisenberry and not Smith. The two had very different careers, with Quisenberry having a great peak and Smith lasting a long time. But on balance, very little separates one from the other. I could reject them both or accept them both. I've decided to be a nice guy and accept 'em both. C'mon in fellas. Enjoy.

Intentionally Overlooked

Trevor Hoffman (1993-2010, career ERA+: 141)

	Career	Rank	Peak	Rank	Bests	Top 5s	JAWS	Rank
WAR	28.4	6	19.6	20	1	4	24	11
WS	158.7	10	100.7	23	2	3	NA	15*

Euch. I thought Trevor Hoffman was just a step below Mariano Rivera. Both WAR and Win Shares tell me that he is several steps below, and those steps lead outside of the Hall's doors and into the Hall of the Very Good. His JAWS number is tied with Billy Wagner and just an inch below Dan Quisenberry. So that's basically borderline.

Hoffman was too recent to be ranked by Bill James, but his WSAWS is 15th. Because Win Shares aren't calculated after 2008, his 2009 and 2010 are left out of the equation. I tried to guess at what they would be, but even my most generous assessments don't raise his WSAWS high enough. He still ends up significantly below Dan Quisenberry/Lee Smith territory.

Trevor Hoffman was something special. But with only five relievers in the Hall now (four of which were true relievers), you have to be something beyond special to get in the Hall. Quisenberry and Smith are already a stretch; anyone less qualified than them can't pass. That might be too high of a standard, but right now that's how it is.

And I don't have the right to make a much more generous standard for Hall-of-Fame relief pitchers. As with all the other positions, I want to stay within the bounds of the current Hall. For relievers, that means the top 5-7 ever. Even with all his saves, Trevor Hoffman doesn't look like one of the 5-7 best relievers ever. My condolences to Padres fans everywhere. I sadly can't recommend him.

Chapter Fifteen

~ ~ Goodbyeee!!!!![122] ~ ~

And that would appear to be that.[123] I suppose I could go through the HOF credentials of the umpires, pioneers, executives, and managers in the Hall. (We hear a record scratch in the distance. Crickets chirp. Awkward cough from the audience. Sad trombone slide. A "boi-oi-oing!" sound just for fun.) But I have no WAR and Win Shares for those, so I would be going by nothing but my personal judgements. As a completely unknown writer to everyone but my friends and family, I don't exactly have the reputation or standing to do that. Though my judgements came out a lot in this book (perhaps too much), the basis was always in objective numbers. If this book is such an overwhelming international success that people actually want to know what Noted Hall of Fame Expert Eddie Daniels thinks of the HOF credentials of Morgan Bulkeley and Nestor Chylak, I will be both very surprised and very willing to write those up.

For now, it's time to cut myself off. No more taking records into context for their time period. No more judging the effects of steroids on players' careers. No more recounting tragic early deaths. No more decrying the underrated-ness of batters' walks and the overrated-ness of relief pitchers. No more Frankie Frisch, and no more Ty Cobb (thank goodness). And no more Bill James. Yeah, I said it. Bill can go use sophisticated sabermetric techniques to analyze the win potential of my foot up his ass. (Just a weird joke. I of course have nothing but respect and admiration for one of my biggest heroes. Thank you Bill, for everything.)

I'm outtie 5000. I'm Swayze. See ya, wouldn't wanna be ya. (Actually, I probably would.) I hate to see you go, but I love to watch you leave. (Don't take that the wrong way. I respect you as a person.) Love, peace and hair grease. Thank you, Minnesota, you've been great! There will be no encore (unless you want one)! See you next time (if you're willing)! I love you all!

---

[122] Penultimate reference explanation: "Goodbyeee" was the title of the final episode of "Blackadder Goes Fourth," by far the best (in my view) of the Blackadder series. The episode provided a surprisingly touching and serious finale to an otherwise unsentimental and funny show.

[123] Final reference explanation: One of the "Hitchhiker's Guide to the Galaxy" novels, I forget which. I always felt "that would appear to be that" was a wonderfully English way to qualify something that really doesn't need to be qualified. As a Midwesterner, I can kinda sorta understand that a bit, you know?

Appendix

Really? You really want to wade through the ugly muck of counter-arguments and counter-counter-arguments for changing the name of the Cleveland Indians and other race-based teams? OK, but I warn you, I'm not going to be nice any more. All the stuff I said before about being understanding so as to not provoke a defensive response is out the window. This kind of thing can wallow in the depths of pointless, destructive human combat. It's the intellectual equivalent of professional wrestling. But if you want to, here we go:

Justification 1: "It's not so bad. They're just being too sensitive." Wait, who are you to tell people what they should be sensitive about? How is that your decision? You have never been part of that ethnic group, so you don't know what those words feel like to them. Oh, by the way, you're a fat loser. Oh, did that offend you? Well, you shouldn't be so sensitive!

Justification 2: "Some people aren't offended!" Teams with offensive names are smart enough not to try the "They're just being too sensitive" argument. Football's Washington R****** get their media people to say things like "We have met with several Native American people who don't mind the name." Huh? So what? There are many thousands of Native American people who definitely do mind the name. Are you saying that for their feelings to be valid, they must have 100% universal agreement among all Native Americans in existence? That is a preposterously high standard.

If universality were required, no civil rights struggle in history would have ever occurred. In the 1960s, you could find African-Americans who did not want to end Jim Crow. In the 1970s, you could find women who were against women's rights. It doesn't have to be unanimous. Many, many people are offended by these team names, and that's enough.

Justification 3: The old slippery slope. When they have nothing else to stand on, rationalizers trot out the "slippery slope" argument. They say, well, if we change this, what next? Will we have to rename the Pirates because the name offends actual pirates? Do we need to rename the Cardinals because some guys in the Vatican get offended? It's a slippery slope!

Leaving aside that neither of those are in any way valid comparisons to an offense felt by an entire ethnic group, the slippery slope argument is always a load of crap. It's a load of crap in any argument about any subject. It's a last-ditch attempt used by someone who intensely dislikes something but has no legitimate reasons for disliking it. It's a scare tactic that conjures up invalid, ridiculous "logical" extensions that no one has ever or will ever seriously consider.

Former senator Rick Santorum once argued that allowing gay people to get married will create a slippery slope in which people will be free to marry dogs. Only in a perverted mind would those two things in any way constitute two dominoes, in which you tip one and the other would inevitably fall. One is a union between two consenting adult human beings. The other is a sick farce involving two very different species, one of which has no conception of toilets, much less the eternal bond of matrimony.

Moreover, only in a very ignorant view of humanity would anyone think that life is some sort of domino game, in which accepting one thing forces us to accept something else. As human beings, we are in charge of what we decide to do in the future. We can accept and reject any idea that comes along, regardless of what happened before. Why would anyone say "OK, well, I suppose if consenting adults who are in love can marry each other, now we have no choice but to allow some lunatic to marry an animal. Both involve marriages that have previously been banned, after all. Hey, my hands are tied!"

Maybe the "slippery slope" argument comes from the legal system, in which one case can set a precedent that influences other future cases, in ways no one intended. But this is not a court of law, where changing one team's name would set some sort of precedent that a savvy lawyer could use to get the Yankees renamed the "Northern-Americans." This is a single incident, in which people could for once, at almost zero cost to themselves, make a kind gesture to a long-oppressed minority.

We're not talking about marrying dogs, and we're not talking about changing the name of the Pirates. We're just talking about the Indians. Even if changing the Indians' name actually did set some sort of precedent, it would not be "change team names if anyone, anywhere gets offended." It would be "change team names if they're pointlessly offensive to entire ethnic groups." We don't have the New York Jews or the San Francisco Chinese. We shouldn't have the Cleveland Indians.

Do you have any other counter-arguments you'd like to try? By no means do I presume that I could possibly address every justification that can sprout from humanity's boundless compulsion to suppress self-awareness of any possible mistake, however small. If you have comments, please send them to chrisekeedei@yahoo.com. But as always, be polite. I may not have been terribly polite in the above, but I'm trying to set up a double standard here. If you're not polite, your email will be deleted and I will never see it.

Acknowledgements

Thanks to Erin Dykhuizen, Joe Pettigrew, Sean Shore, Stephanie Wilson, Larry Lester, Leslie Heaphy, Stew Thornley, and the people at BillJamesOnline.com and SABR for their assistance.

Thanks to Bill James and Rob Neyer for creating a style for me to shamelessly copy.

www.ingramcontent.com/pod-product-compliance
Lightning Source LLC
Chambersburg PA
CBHW080605090426
42735CB00017B/3337

9780997073942